Advances in Applied Sport Psychology

Advances in Applied Sport Psychology aims to bridge the gap between research and practice in contemporary sport psychology. The book draws together reviews of cutting-edge research in key areas of applied sport psychology, assesses the implications of this research for current practice, and explores future avenues of research within each thematic area.

The book surveys the scientific literature underpinning the most important skills and techniques employed in contemporary sport psychology, examining key topics such as:

- imagery
- goal setting
- self-talk
- stress management
- team building
- efficacy management
- attention control
- emotion regulation
- mental toughness.

Representing the most up-to-date review of current scientific research, theory and practice in sport psychology, this book is a vital resource for all advanced students, researchers and practitioners working with athletes and sports performers.

Stephen D. Mellalieu is a Senior Lecturer in Applied Sport Psychology and Director of Postgraduate Studies in the Department of Sports Science, Swansea University, UK. **Sheldon Hanton** is a Professor in the Cardiff School of Sport at the University of Wales Institute, Cardiff, UK.

Advances in Applied Sport Psychology

A review

Edited by Stephen D. Mellalieu
and Sheldon Hanton

Routledge
Taylor & Francis Group

LONDON AND NEW YORK

First published 2009
by Routledge
2 Park Square, Milton Park, Abingdon, Oxon OX14 4RN

Simultaneously published in the USA and Canada
by Routledge
711 Third Avenue, New York, NY 10017

Routledge is an imprint of the Taylor & Francis group, an informa business

© 2009 Selection and editorial material, Stephen D. Mellalieu and
Sheldon Hanton; individual chapters, the contributors.

This edition first published in paperback 2010

Typeset in Goudy by Wearset Ltd, Boldon, Tyne and Wear
Printed and bound in Great Britain by TJ International Ltd, Padstow, Cornwall

British Library Cataloguing in Publication Data
A catalogue record for this book is available from the British Library

Library of Congress Cataloging in Publication Data
Advances in applied sport psychology : a review / [edited by]
Stephen Mellalieu and Sheldon Hanton.
p. cm.
Includes bibliographical references and index.
1. Sports–Psychological aspects. 2. Sports literature. I. Mellalieu, Stephen
D. (Stephen David) II. Hanton, Sheldon.
GV706.4.A355 2009
796.01–dc22

2008025829

ISBN10: 0-203-88707-3 (ebk)
ISBN10: 0-415-44763-1 (hbk)

ISBN13: 978-0-203-88707-3 (ebk)
ISBN13: 978-0-415-44763-8 (hbk)
ISBN13: 978-0-415-57702-1 (pbk)

Contents

Contributors

Declan Connaughton is a Senior Lecturer in Sport Psychology at the University of Wales Institute, Cardiff, UK. He has published in and reviewed for a number of international peer-reviewed journals, including the *Journal of Applied Sport Psychology*, the *Sport Psychologist*, *Research Quarterly for Exercise and Sport*, the *Journal of Sports Sciences* and the *International Journal of Sport Psychology*.

Jennifer Cumming is a Lecturer in Sport and Exercise Psychology in the School of Sport and Exercise Sciences at the University of Birmingham, UK. Her research mainly focuses on the effective use of imagery by athletes, exercisers and dancers. She has published this work in several leading journals in the field.

David W. Eccles is the Lead Research Scientist for the Centre for Expert Performance Research and Assistant Professor at the Learning Systems Institute and Department of Educational Psychology at the Florida State University, USA. His research has been published in a wide range of sport and human factors journals.

James Hardy is a Lecturer within the School of Sport, Health and Exercise Sciences at Bangor University, UK. He has published numerous peer-reviewed articles predominantly focusing on self-talk and group dynamics in both the sport and exercise domains. James is currently on the editorial board for *Athletic Insight*.

Michael B. Johnson is currently an Assistant Professor of Educational Psychology at the University of Texas-Pan American. He was also recently honoured with the 2007 UTPA College of Education Outstanding New Faculty Researcher Award. Dr Johnson has also taught classes in educational psychology, assessment, counselling techniques and career counselling.

Marc V. Jones is a Reader in Sport and Exercise Psychology at Staffordshire University, UK. In addition, Marc also works as a consultant and is accredited by the British Association of Sport and Exercise Sciences and a Chartered Sport and Exercise Psychologist with the British Psychological Society.

Kieran M. Kingston is a Senior Lecturer and Discipline Director of Sport Psychology at the University of Wales Institute, Cardiff, UK. Kieran has been a British Association of Sport and Exercise Sciences Accredited Sport Psychologist since 1997, and has acted as a consultant in a variety of individual and team sports. Most recently he has worked with athletes in professional golf, rugby, and track and field.

Paul J. McCarthy is a Senior Lecturer in Sport and Exercise Psychology at Staffordshire University, UK. Paul has published in international peer-reviewed journals, including *Journal of Sports Sciences, Psychology of Sport and Exercise* and *The Sport Psychologist*. He is a British Association of Sport and Exercise Sciences Accredited Sport and Exercise Psychologist and is currently consulting at a professional football club academy.

Aidan Moran is a Professor of Cognitive Psychology and Director of the Psychology Research Laboratory in University College, Dublin, Ireland. A Fulbright Scholar, he is the inaugural Editor-in-Chief of the *International Review of Sport and Exercise Psychology* (published in 2008 by Routledge/ Taylor and Francis, Oxford). He is a psychology consultant to many of Ireland's leading professional sports performers and teams.

Emily Oliver is currently undertaking a Ph.D., focusing on self-talk and self-determination theory, within the School of Sport, Health and Exercise Sciences at Bangor University, UK. In addition to her research, Emily teaches undergraduate courses covering physical activity and health, and motivation.

Richard Ramsey is a Post-doctoral Research Fellow in the School of Psychology at the University of Nottingham, UK. His current research, funded by the Economic and Social Research Council (ESRC), uses functional magnetic resonance imaging (fMRI) to investigate how individuals understand the goals and intentions of other people's actions.

Lindsay Ross-Stewart is a Doctoral student in the Psychology department at the University of North Dakota. Her research focuses on Bandura's self-efficacy theory, with a particular interest in imagery as a source of self-efficacy and as a tool for performance enhancement. Lindsay is also engaged in consulting with university-level athletes.

Sandra Short, Ph.D., is a Professor in the Department of Physical Education, Exercise Science and Wellness at the University of North Dakota in Grand Forks, where she also holds an adjunct appointment in the Psychology department. Dr Short is also an associate editor for *The Sport Psychologist*, and the founding co-editor for the *Journal of Imagery Research in Sport and Physical Activity*.

Owen Thomas is a Senior Lecturer in Sport Psychology within the Cardiff School of Sport at the University of Wales Institute, Cardiff, UK. He has been a British Association of Sport and Exercise Sciences Accredited Sport Psychologist since 2002, and is at present one of the lead national sport psychologists within the English Golf Union support programme.

David Tod currently lectures in the Department of Sport and Exercise Science, Aberystwyth University, UK. In addition, he has published research on applied sport psychologist training and development, and is on the editorial board of the journal *Qualitative Research in Sport and Exercise*.

Mark A. Uphill is a Senior Lecturer in Sport and Exercise Psychology at Canterbury Christ Church University, UK. A British Association of Sport and Exercise Sciences Accredited Sport Psychologist, Mark has experience of consulting with a range of individual and team athletes. Mark has published in international peer-reviewed journals and has made contributions to scholarly textbooks.

Kylie M. Wilson holds a research and teaching position in the School of Sport within the University of Wales Institute Cardiff, UK, is an accredited sport psychologist with the British Association of Sport and Exercise Sciences, and a contracted psychology provider to the British Gymnastics Association and Welsh Rugby Union.

Acknowledgements

We would first like to thank all the authors for their contributions to this book. We hope that it brings as much satisfaction to them as it has to us. We are also greatly indebted to all the reviewers who gave up their time to provide comprehensive and insightful feedback on each of the respective chapters. Our gratitude is also extended to Routledge for commissioning the book, and to all the staff at the Sport and Leisure Section of Routledge Publishing who have been extremely professional in their correspondence guiding us throughout the publication process.

Lastly, we would like to give a special mention to thank our respective families for their ongoing love and support throughout the production of this book and our professional careers.

Introduction

The past two decades have seen considerable expansion and development in sport psychology research. The wealth of literature that has emerged has not only examined a broad range of topics with both academic and practical significance within the field, but has also incorporated other areas of sport and exercise science and various branches of the psychology discipline itself. In such an industrious environment, a critical element of the advancement of knowledge necessitates that regular summarisation, reflection and feedback is undertaken in any given research area – a task often fulfilled by a literature review. A review of literature functions as an initial vehicle for a topic's organisation, further reorganisation and defined structure. It serves to direct future investigation, establishing reference points and foundations for continued progress. Indeed, due to their comprehensive nature, reviews frequently require considerably greater page allocation in scientific outlets in comparison to original research articles.

While literature reviews typically conducted in sport psychology tend to focus on the conceptual and theoretical aspects of a topic, they sometimes neglect the synthesis of knowledge areas surrounding the applied aspects of our field. This is, after all, at the forefront of where research informs practice application. In addition, while many excellent chapters and/or texts exist that address how to use psychological techniques in practical 'how-to' contexts, few have presented detailed and contemporary critical appraisals of the conceptual grounding behind applied sport psychology practice. Our intention with *Advances in Applied Sport Psychology* is to provide a library for professional members of the sport psychology community who adhere to the 'theory-to-practice' philosophy. This collection offers up-to-date reviews of key areas in applied sport psychology research from leading academics in the field with a distinctive conceptual, theoretical and practical focus. Specifically, this edited collection seeks to provide the reader with recent peer-reviewed works of the scientific literature underpinning the value and utility of psychological techniques and associated skills taught to, and used, by sports performers.

We hope that the reviews contained within this edited collection will appeal as a comprehensive, thought-provoking resource for graduates, doctoral students, academics and professionals working within the field of sport psychology. We also hope the book promotes a more systematic approach to advancing knowledge in the discipline, and catalyses and facilitates the development of theoretical frameworks for future research in applied sport psychology. Although all the topics in this text come under the rubric of applied sport psychology, our intention, through a policy of allowing independence to the contributors of this book, was that every chapter was envisaged to be a discrete contribution, each with its own implications and recommendations for future study. Subsequently, as editors, it was not our goal to try to organise a synthesis of the topics of each chapter into one absolute theory of sport psychology. Instead, we intended to provide researchers and practitioners with the opportunity to explore a range of topics to guide their respective activities. While this text is intended primarily for researchers in applied sport psychology, we hope the empirical evidence presented in each chapter regarding the efficacy of various psychological skills and strategies, together with the dissemination of this body of research work into practical implications for applied practice, will enable consultants to derive enhanced value for their own respective professional practice.

The format of each chapter has been standardised as much as possible to resemble works published in academic journals. For example, the narrative is generally divided into several parts: an introduction to the chapter and the applied area; a subsection clarifying and defining the key terms adopted; an up-to-date and comprehensive exposition, discussion and critical analysis of both qualitative and quantitative research undertaken; the implications of this work for professional practice and the future directions for research in the area.

This book contains nine chapters. Chapter 1, by Jennifer Cumming and Richard Ramsey, begins with a review of literature on imagery interventions designed to achieve varying psychological outcomes related to sporting performance. Specific emphasis is placed on the contemporary theoretical frameworks guiding such work, together with discussion of how recent advancements in the cognitive neurosciences inform intervention design and measurement. Finally, different intervention approaches are compared together with suggestions for future research.

In Chapter 2, James Hardy, Emily Oliver and David Tod critically review the literature examining the antecedents, nature and effects of self-talk in sport. Within their discussion, the authors consider the potential theoretical frameworks associated with self-talk, with a particular focus on self-efficacy theory and self-determination theory. The review then proceeds to consider the literature examining the effectiveness of self-talk interventions, and the implications for professional practice and future research in this under-investigated area.

In Chapter 3, Kieran Kingston and Kylie Wilson provide an overview of the theory and research that supports the reported benefits of setting goals. In describing and illustrating the diverse approaches to studying goals in sport, the authors consider the application of that knowledge base across a variety of sporting contexts. The chapter then seeks to move the debate regarding the application of goal setting forward by providing guidance on the application of goal setting in sport settings and impetus for future research concerning this application.

Chapter 4, written by Owen Thomas, Stephen Mellalieu and Sheldon Hanton, reviews the stress-management literature in applied sport psychology. After defining and discussing relevant terminologies and conceptual distinctions, the chapter considers research in relation to the traditional reduction and contemporary restructuring approaches to the management of the responses associated with competitive stress, together with the need to examine the competitive-stress process within a temporal context. The commentary then summarises relevant contemporary research to guide recommendations for practitioners conducting stress-management interventions before concluding with a discussion of future research possibilities within the area.

Chapter 5, written by Mark Uphill, Paul McCarthy and Marc Jones, reviews the conceptual, theoretical and empirical basis for the regulation of emotion in sport. The authors illustrate theoretical models explaining how emotions may be generated and sustained, and in so doing highlight a range of strategies (e.g. reappraisal) that may be theorised to assist athletes in emotion regulation. A contemporary review of the evidence-base for sport psychology practitioners to base their emotion-regulation interventions upon is also discussed. The chapter concludes with consideration of the implications for professional practice and the future of research on emotion-regulation in sport.

Chapter 6 is entitled 'Attention in sport'. Here, Aidan Moran discusses that, despite a century of empirical research on attentional processes in humans, great confusion still exists regarding what concentration is and how it can be measured and improved in sport performers. In an effort to resolve such confusion, the chapter provides a comprehensive critical review of research in this field. Following an explanation of the nature and characteristics of concentration, the main theories and issues arising from research in this field are evaluated. The chapter concludes by outlining some promising new directions for further research on attentional processes in performers.

Sandra Short and Lindsay Ross-Stewart, in Chapter 7, then proceed to review the research on the techniques that have been used to build, maintain and regain self-efficacy/confidence in sport. This chapter uses self-efficacy theory as the conceptual framework and focuses on the sources of self-efficacy beliefs (including performance accomplishments, vicarious experiences, verbal persuasion, physiological states, emotional states and imagery). The review then highlights how these sources can be used as a general guide for interventions with attention on the mechanisms and procedures for change.

In Chapter 8, David Eccles and Michael Johnson discuss the limited consideration of a social-cognitive perspective to research into team sports. The chapter highlights how team sports involve complex inter-individual thought processes and communication schemes that can be impacted by and influence the team's performance. It then proceeds to explore the existing literature in industrial/organisational human factors, and social-cognitive psychologies, and relates this research to feasible sport psychology strategies and techniques that could be implemented in group and team situations with the goal of positively impacting sport team performance.

In the ninth and final chapter, Declan Connaughton and Sheldon Hanton discuss the literature on mental toughness to highlight pertinent conceptual and methodological issues. The authors consider how positive psychological characteristics and the use of mental skills have been associated with, and linked to, a multitude of mental toughness definitions. Studies that have attempted to address mental toughness in a more empirical manner are then examined, with the aim of providing a clear perspective of the most recent empirical research. The chapter concludes with the provision of practical implications and future directions to stimulate research activity in this emerging area.

Stephen D. Mellalieu
Sheldon Hanton

1 Imagery interventions in sport

Jennifer Cumming and Richard Ramsey

Introduction

Imagery is described as an experience that mimics real experience, and involves using a combination of different sensory modalities in the absence of actual perception. White and Hardy explained that "we can be aware of 'seeing' an image, feeling movements as an image, or experiencing an image of smell, taste or sounds without experiencing the real thing" (1998: 389), whereas Moran defined imagery as "perception without sensation" (2004: 133). Another commonality among definitions is the notion that individuals are self-aware and conscious during the imagery experience (Richardson, 1969). For example, White and Hardy distinguished imagery from dreaming because the individual is awake and conscious when imaging.

Among sport performers and coaches, imagery is a popular and well-accepted strategy for enhancing various aspects of performance. The importance of this strategy is reflected in anecdotal reports of successful athletes. For example, Ronaldinho, a midfielder for FC Barcelona and one of the world's best footballers, eloquently described his use of imagery before the World Cup in 2006 in an article appearing in the *New York Times Sports Magazine*:

> When I train, one of the things I concentrate on is creating a mental picture of how best to deliver that ball to a team-mate, preferably leaving him alone in front of the rival goalkeeper. So what I do, always before a game, always, every night and every day, is try and think up things, imagine plays, which no one else will have thought of, and to do so always bearing in mind the particular strengths of each team-mate to whom I am passing the ball. When I construct those plays in my mind I take into account whether one team-mate likes to receive the ball at his feet, or ahead of him; if he is good with his head, and how he prefers to head the ball; if he is stronger on his right or his left foot. That is my job. That is what I do. I imagine the game.
>
> (4 June 2006)

Descriptive research also suggests that imagery is frequently used by the best athletes. In their study of the elements of success, Orlick and Partington (1988) found that 99 per cent of Canadian Olympic athletes surveyed reported using imagery as a preparation strategy. Furthermore, higher-level athletes or those with more experience typically report greater use of the strategy than their lower-level or less-experienced counterparts (e.g. Barr and Hall, 1992; Cumming and Hall, 2002a, 2002b; Hall et al., 1998; Salmon et al., 1994).

Not surprisingly, imagery has become a widely researched topic within the field of sport psychology as evidenced by numerous published studies, recent book chapters (e.g. Callow and Hardy, 2005; Moran, 2004; Murphy et al., 2008), an entire book (Morris et al., 2005), and the introduction of a journal devoted to publishing imagery research in the physical domain (*Journal of Imagery Research in Sport and Physical Activity*). The aim of our chapter is to complement this body of literature with a review focusing specifically on imagery interventions. The emphasis will be on contemporary frameworks guiding such work with particular reference to the applied model of imagery use (Martin et al., 1999) and the PETTLEP model (Holmes and Collins, 2001). We will also discuss how recent advancements in the cognitive neurosciences may inform intervention design and measurement with recommendations made for best practice.

Key terms

A useful starting point in any review is to clarify the meaning of key terms frequently used in the literature. Indeed, there has been confusion resulting from the interchangeable use of "visualisation" and "mental practice" with imagery. Several authors have argued that these terms are referring to related but distinctly different constructs (e.g. Morris et al., 2005; Murphy and Martin, 2002). While visualisation denotes a particular sensory modality (i.e. vision), imagery encompasses all different "quasi-sensory or quasi-perceptual experiences" (Richardson, 1969: 2). In research, imagery is the preferred and most commonly used term since athletes' images are not limited to just those experienced in the mind's eye (e.g. Munroe et al., 2000). Murphy and Martin (2002) have explained that imagery should also be carefully distinguished from mental practice; that is, imagery is a specific mental process that can be mentally practised. However, mental practice does not necessarily involve imagery but can also refer to other types of mental processes including self-talk and modelling.

The most recent debate addresses the conceptual difference between imagery type, function and outcome (for a more detailed discussion, see Murphy et al., 2008; Short et al., 2006). The term "imagery type" has been used to describe both the content of an athlete's imagery (e.g. imaging oneself perfectly executing a skill) and the function or purpose that imagery is serving (e.g. skill refinement) leading to uncertainty among authors. As an illustration, items on the Sport Imagery Questionnaire (SIQ; Hall et al., 1998) were originally described as measuring imagery content (Moritz et al., 1996), then later referred to as functions (Hall et al., 1998, 2005). Short et al. (2006) noted that this shift in meaning of the SIQ items has led to the synonymous use of "type" and "function". For example, Martin *et al.* referred to these as interchangeable terms in their review of literature and development of an applied model. Imagery type is mostly referred to as "the function or purpose that imagery is serving" (1999: 249); but content is alluded to when the authors predict that cognitive imagery types might serve a motivational function by enabling athletes to focus in competitive settings. Hall (2001) has also explained that knowing something about the content of an athlete's imagery does not necessarily indicate what function this imagery is serving. To continue with the above example, an athlete might describe imaging the perfect execution of a skill in a competitive situation. Three possible functions of this image are skill refinement, motivation and self-efficacy enhancement. The athlete might be using the imagery for one, two or all three of these functions. Adding to the confusion is that other authors have used "type" to refer specifically to the sensory modality employed (Driediger *et al.*, 2006; Munroe *et al.*, 2000; Munroe-Chandler *et al.*, 2007). To resolve the conundrum, Murphy *et al.* (2008) proposed that *imagery type* should be reserved for describing the content of an image (i.e. "what"), whereas *imagery function* should denote the purpose or reason for employing the image (i.e. "why"). Finally, *imagery outcome* should describe the result of the imagery (e.g. improved skill performance, increased motivation, higher levels of self-efficacy).

With these definitions in mind, the items of the SIQ would probably be more appropriately referred to as imagery types that can be used for different cognitive and motivational functions by athletes (Murphy *et al.*, 2008; Short *et al.*, 2006). We will return to this particular concept later in the chapter when reviewing literature surrounding the applied model of imagery use. It is important to point out, however, that researchers should be careful in their employment of the term "use" when describing athletes' imagery, because "use" implies that athletes are deliberately engaging in the strategy when this is not necessarily the case. Indeed, there is evidence to suggest that performers will experience some amount of imagery in a spontaneous manner (Evans *et al.*, 2004; Nordin and Cumming, 2005b; Nordin *et al.*, 2006). For this reason, Nordin and Cumming (2006) favoured terminology such as "imaging" rather than "use of imagery" when describing dancers' imagery in the development of the Dance Imagery Questionnaire (DIQ).

Review of the literature

The early imagery research was dominated by experimental designs comparing the effectiveness of imagery alone to physical practice, no practice, or varying combinations of imagery and physical practice, for the acquisition and performance of motor skills (for reviews, see Driskell *et al.*, 1994; Feltz and Landers, 1983; Hall, 2001; Jones and Stuth, 1997). Effect sizes reported in the three different meta analyses carried out on this literature have ranged from small (0.26; Driskell *et al.*, 1994) to large (0.66; Hinshaw, 1991) in magnitude. These findings suggest that imagery is an effective means of improving performance, but is less effective than physical practice. Several moderators were also identified as influencing imagery effectiveness to help shed light on previous discrepant findings. Variables considered as moderators included the type of task being imaged, the experience level of the performer, the duration and timing of the imagery practice, and the individual's ability to generate and control vivid images. Less commonly reported were field-based imagery interventions specifically designed to enhance athletic performance. The results of these studies were equivocal, with some reporting significant improvements compared to a control group (e.g. Grouios, 1992; Study 1 of Hardy and Callow, 1999; Isaac, 1985), while others reported no significant differences (e.g. Mumford and Hall, 1985; Rodgers et al., 1991), or mixed findings across performance variables (e.g. Blair et al., 1993; Burhans et al., 1998). Unfortunately, these studies varied greatly in their design, from the duration of the intervention to the level of athlete involved, making it difficult to draw comparisons and pinpoint the reasons underlying the equivocal findings. However, several authors have raised consistent concerns with the methodology of imagery intervention studies that may help to understand these results (e.g. Goginsky and Collins, 1996; Jones and Stuth, 1997; Murphy and Jowdy, 1992). Callow and Hardy (2005) summarised these concerns as being a failure to take confounding variables into account (e.g. imagery ability), employing flawed research designs (e.g. lack of manipulation checks to verify if the participants are imaging as instructed), the lack of empirically tested theories underpinning the intervention, and not clearly differentiating the functions of imagery.

Over the last decade, there has been a surge in the number of published cross-sectional studies, along with a growing number of field-based interventions. Researchers have examined imagery as part of a mental-skills training package, and generally found significant improvements to performance and psychological factors such as the interpretations of the symptoms associated with competition anxiety (e.g. Hanton and Jones, 1999; Mamassis and Doganis, 2004; Sheard and Golby, 2006). Performance has been less frequently measured when imagery is the only mental skill delivered in an intervention. The majority of these studies have instead focused on the improvements found to self-confidence (e.g. Callow and Waters, 2005), or related constructs of self-efficacy (e.g. Jones et al., 2002) and collective efficacy (e.g. Munroe-Chandler and Hall, 2004). When performance is measured, however, the results have consistently shown the benefits of using imagery (e.g. Smith et al., 2007). Most promising is the trend for recent research to carry out methodologically sound and theoretically based interventions. This task has been made much easier thanks to the introduction of two models to the imagery literature that can be used separately or in conjunction with each other to guide interventions. Each of these models will now be discussed in turn.

The applied model of imagery use

The applied model of imagery use (Martin et al., 1999) describes the manner in which athletes can use imagery to achieve a variety of cognitive, affective and behavioural outcomes. The sport situation, the types of imagery used and imagery ability are considered as three factors that contribute to the effectiveness of an imagery intervention. At the heart of the model is the notion that "what you see is what you get"; in other words, imagery content should correspond with the intended outcomes. For instance, Moritz *et al.* (1996) have suggested that an athlete who wishes to develop, maintain or regain sport confidence (i.e. function) should image being confident (i.e. content). Furthermore, the nature of the sport situation (e.g. training, competition and rehabilitation) should be considered for imagery to have positive effects. To continue with the above example, an athlete might image being confident during a period of rehabilitation to regain the confidence lost due to being injured. Finally, imagery ability will likely influence the impact of an imagery intervention such that better imagers will benefit more. Altogether, the model proposes that athletes should use the appropriate type of imagery in the given sport situation to help them to achieve their goals.

Imagery types

There are five types of imagery mentioned in the model. However, Martin *et al.* (1999) recognised that these do not constitute an exhaustive list and further imagery types may be added as they are identified in the literature. These types stem from Paivio's (1985) analytical framework and were conceptualised further by Hall *et al.* (1998) while developing the SIQ. Paivio initially proposed that imagery serves both cognitive and motivational functional roles, with each operating at specific and general levels. Hall *et al.* later suggested that motivational general (MG) imagery was best understood when divided into arousal and mastery subtypes resulting in the following:

*   cognitive specific (CS): imagery of sport skills or rehabilitation exercises (e.g. running style, penalty flick in field hockey).
*   cognitive general (CG): imagery of strategies, game plans and routines (e.g. man-to-man defence, give-and-go offence, pre-shot routine).
*   motivational specific (MS): imagery of specific goals and goal-oriented behaviour (e.g. achieving a personal best, winning a medal).
*   motivational general arousal (MGA): imagery of somatic and emotional experiences (e.g. stress, arousal, anxiety and excitement).
*   motivational general mastery (MGM): imagery of coping and mastering challenging situation (e.g. staying focused and positive after making an error, being confident in an important competition).

Employing the SIQ, it has been consistently found that athletes image all five types, but tend to report a higher frequency of motivational as compared to cognitive images (e.g. Cumming and Hall, 2002a; Hall *et al.*, 1998; Moritz *et al.*, 1996; Munroe *et al.*, 1998; Vadocz *et al.*, 1997). Martin *et al.* (1999) consider the imagery types to be functionally orthogonal. That is, athletes might use these imagery types alone or in combination with each other. It is important to point out that, although these labels are intended to reflect imagery functions, they have been historically explained in terms of what athletes are imaging (e.g. Hall et al., 1998, 2005; Martin et al., 1999; Munroe et al., 2000). Content and function were therefore considered as one and the same in the development of the model, although many authors have now argued that this is not necessarily the case (e.g. Abma et al., 2002; Callow and Hardy, 2001; Hall, 2001; Hall et al., 1998; Murphy et al., 2008; Nordin and Cumming, 2005a, Short et al., 2002, 2004a, 2006; Vadocz et al., 1997). We will return to this point later in the chapter when discussing the mixed findings of the applied model to date. For clarity, we have therefore chosen to separate type and function in our description of the model.

Recent qualitative enquiries in dance (Hanrahan and Vergeer, 2000; Nordin and Cumming, 2005b), exercise (Giacobbi et al., 2003; Short et al., 2004b), sport (Calmels et al., 2003) and injury rehabilitation settings (Driediger et al., 2006; Evans et al., 2006; Vergeer, 2006) suggest that other types of imagery exist. Body-related images, in addition to those considered to be MGA imagery, are one such example. These include anatomical images related to posture and alignment (Hanrahan and Vergeer, 2000; Nordin and Cumming, 2005b), health- and appearance-related images (Gammage et al., 2000; Giacobbi et al., 2003; Nordin and Cumming, 2005b), and images of the internal physiological processes of healing (Driediger et al., 2006; Evans et al., 2006; Hanrahan and Vergeer, 2000). To illustrate the latter, an injured badminton player interviewed by Driediger et al. said:

> I would try to imagine what the tear looked like and I think about how it feels and how it's going to heal and try to think about how it's coming together while it's healing, or during the rehabilitation process.
>
> (2006: 266)

Such healing images are captured on a sub-scale of the Athletic Injury Imagery Questionnaire-2 (AIIQ-2; Sordoni et al., 2002), and are positively associated with self-efficacy (Sordoni et al., 2002) and satisfaction with the rehabilitation experience (Law et al., 2006). Both exercisers and dancers have reported appearance-related images. For example, female aerobic exercisers interviewed by Giacobbi et al. said "I imagine myself being toned" and "I see myself losing weight" (2003: 168). Interestingly, this is the most frequently reported imagery type by exercisers, and positively associated with self-reported exercise behaviour (Gammage et al., 2000; Hausenblas et al., 1999) and behavioural intention (Rodgers et al., 2001).

There is also growing interest in kinaesthetic imagery, which Callow and Waters have defined as "imagery involving the sensations of how it feels to perform an action, including the force and effort involved in movement and balance, and spatial location (either of a body part or piece of sports equipment)" (2005: 444–445). Munroe et al. (2000) previously noted that the varsity athletes interviewed in their study frequently mentioned kinaesthetic images. Further-more, an athlete's ability to kinaesthetically image has been positively associated with state confidence (Hardy and Callow, 1999; Moritz *et al.*, 1996; Monsma and Overby, 2004) and negatively associated with the intensity of cognitive anxiety symptoms (Monsma and Overby, 2004). Finally, Hardy and Callow (1999) found the combination of visual and kinaesthetic imagery led to greater skill acquisition and performance benefits than visual imagery alone for expert rock climbers learning four ten-move boulder problems (Experiment 3). Altogether, these studies suggest that kinaesthetic imagery is a particularly important type of imagery for athletes. Interestingly, Martin *et al.* (1999) suggested that kinaes-thetic images (and other sensory modalities) might eventually be considered in the model, but felt that there was insufficient evidence at that time to warrant inclusion. Since the model has been published, Callow and Waters have carried out a single-subject multiple baseline study with three male professional flat-race horse jockeys to examine whether kinaesthetic imagery could improve state sport confidence. In line with their rationale that kinaesthetic imagery could serve as a form of performance accomplishment, a significant increase in state sport confi-dence was found for two of the three participants following a kinaesthetic imagery intervention. The authors consequently concluded that images, which match the actual sensations of successful performance, could be a useful tool for enhancing confidence.

Other images worth mentioning are those of an artistic nature, which are relevant to aesthetic sport athletes whose artistic ability is judged in competition. Professional dancers interviewed by Nordin and Cumming (2005b) reported images of characters and roles including behaviours, emotions and qualities that they might want to emphasise in a piece. The role and movement quality imagery sub-scale of the DIQ measures these images along with expression, movement quality (e.g. harmony between movements and music) and metaphors (i.e. images depicting actions and sensations that are not necessarily objectively possible). In a follow-up study, Nordin and Cumming (in press) found that aes-thetic sport athletes (e.g. artistic gymnasts, equestrian vaulters) reported using role and movement imagery, but not to the same extent as dancers sampled in the same study. Nevertheless, the findings suggest that imagery related to aesthetic expression could provide the basis of an imagery intervention aimed at enhancing the artistry of aesthetic sport athletes. Metaphorical images may also be helpful in communication, to identify and express thoughts and emotions, assist focus and concentration, maintain confidence and aid relaxation (Murphy *et al.*, 2008). Furthermore, direct effects on performance have been found follow-ing the use of metaphorical imagery with dancers. Sawada *et al.* (2002) carried out an intervention with 60 children, and showed that children who received metaphorical instructions performed a short dance sequence more accurately than children who had received either verbal descriptions of the movements or no instruction. Improvements to the performance of certain dance moves have also been reported following a metaphorical imagery intervention with adult dancers (Hanrahan and Salmela, 1990; Hanrahan *et al.*, 1995).

Imagery functions

There are a multitude of reasons why athletes engage in imagery (e.g. Munroe *et al.*, 2000; Nordin and Cumming 2005a; for reviews, see Murphy and Martin, 2002; Murphy *et al.*, 2008). The majority of these fall broadly into the cognitive and functional roles proposed by Paivio (1985). *Cognitive reasons* include learning and improving performance, memorising, planning and strategising, and improving understanding. When examined at the specific and general levels, the CS function pertains specifically to skill development (i.e. to work on technique and to make changes) and performance (i.e. to perform as well as possible in any given situation), whereas the CG function similarly describes strategy development and execution (Munroe *et al.*, 2000). *Motivational reasons* include enhancing motivation, changing thoughts and emotions, and regulating physiological responses. Munroe *et al.* described the MS function as being used by athletes to understand what it takes to achieve process and outcome goals. The MGA function pertains to the regulation of emotions and activation levels (e.g. to psych up, maintain composure, or relax). Finally, the MGM function is used to stay focused, confident, positive and mentally tough (i.e. work through difficult situations and deal with adversity). *Healing reasons* have also emerged as a function in the injury-rehabilitation literature (Calmels *et al.*, 2003; Driediger *et al.*, 2006; Nordin and Cumming, 2005b). For example, the athletes interviewed by Driediger *et al.* reported using imagery to aid in the healing process, for pain management and the prevention of injury. In addition, dancers interviewed by Nordin and Cumming (2005b) used imagery to rejuvenate and revitalise as well as for spiritual healing. Finally, *artistic reasons* for using imagery may be to communicate with one's audience, to add meaning, to enhance the quality of one's movements and to choreograph a sequence or routine (Murphy *et al.*, 2008).

Imagery outcomes

The model suggests three categories of outcomes that can be achieved through imagery: (a) facilitating the learning and performance of skills and strategies; (b) modifying cognitions; and (c) regulating arousal and competitive anxiety. Moreover, the content of an athlete's images will systematically determine what result has been achieved (Short *et al.*, 2006). Recall that the applied model is based on the premise that imagery type will lead to a harmonious outcome. For example, a figure skater trying to improve their technique of a salchow jump (CS imagery function) may image the successful take-off and landing of the jump (CS imagery content). If effective, the result of such imagery would then be qualitative improvements in performance and increased jump consistency (CS outcome). Research has generally supported this idea by demonstrating that skill-based images will lead to improved skill performance (e.g. Durand *et al.*, 1997; Hall *et al.*, 1994; Nordin and Cumming, 2005a; for a review, see Driskell *et al.*, 1994; Hall, 2001), and are more effective than goal-based imagery for performance improvements of beginner runners (MS content;

Burhans *et al.*, 1988), arousal-based imagery for a strength task (MGA content; Murphy *et al.*, 1988), or confidence-based imagery for a sit-up task (MGM content; Lee, 1990).

Skill-based images have also resulted in outcomes beyond those predicted by the "what you see is what you get" principle (e.g. Anshel and Wrisberg, 1993; Calmels *et al.*, 2004b; McKenzie and Howe, 1997; Martin and Hall, 1995; Nordin and Cumming, 2005a). Imaging the "perfect stroke" led to significantly greater voluntary practice time of a golf-putting task (inferring greater motivation) than either the performance + outcome imagery group or the no-imagery control group (Martin and Hall, 1995). Anshel and Wrisberg (1993) found that tennis players' imagery of performing mechanically correct serves resulted in increased somatic (i.e. heart rate) and cognitive arousal. Both McKenzie and Howe (1997) and Nordin and Cumming (2005a) reported increased self-efficacy following imagery of dart throws. Finally, the CS sub-scale of the SIQ has been positively associated with increased trait confidence (Abma *et al.*, 2002) and facilitative interpretations of the symptoms associated with cognitive and somatic anxiety (Fish *et al.*, 2004).

Less research attention has been given to images of strategies, routines and game plans. Indeed, when the applied model was initially published, evidence in support of CG imagery was mainly anecdotal in nature or case study reports (e.g. Fenker and Lambiotte, 1987; White and Hardy, 1998). There have been a few studies to show that imagery of skills sequenced together led to improvements in the performance of that sequence when compared to a control group (Blair *et al.*, 1993; Hardy and Callow, 1999). Only recently have interventions been undertaken to examine strategy-based images, and this research has led to mixed findings. Jordet (2005) used a single-case intervention design to show the effects of an intervention consisting of skill and strategy images with elite football players. He found improved exploratory visual activity for two out of the three players involved. By comparison, imaging the execution of football strategies did not lead to significantly improved implementation of these strategies in game situations for players on an Under-13 team (Munroe-Chandler *et al.*, 2005). The CG sub-scale of the SIQ has also been positively associated with state and trait sport confidence (Abma *et al.*, 2002; Callow and Hardy, 2001).

With respect to goal-based images, Martin and Hall (1995) found that imaging "a perfect stroke" combined with "the golf ball rolling across the green and into the hole" (performance + outcome imagery) led to significantly greater number of balls holed compared to imaging the perfect stroke only or control group. Moreover, participants in this condition also set higher goals for themselves and adhered more to their training regime, but did not demonstrate greater voluntary practice behaviour. MS imagery has also been positively associated with achievement goals (Cumming *et al.*, 2002), state and trait sport confidence (Abma *et al.*, 2002; Callow and Hardy, 2001; Evans *et al.*, 2004), and self-efficacy (Mills *et al.*, 2000).

Images of somatic and emotional experiences such as oneself competing in a race have resulted in measurable physiological changes in heart rate and respiration (Gallego *et al.*, 1996; Hecker and Kaczor, 1988). Martin *et al.* (1999) explained that MGA images contain necessary information about the physiological and emotional response of the performer (termed "response propositions"; Lang, 1977, 1979) to bring about these measurable increases in activation. Furthermore, Murphy *et al.* (1988) found that images of anger and fear prior to a strength task led to increased reports of feeling anxious, whereas images of being relaxed were associated with decreased levels of state anxiety intensity in another study (Murphy and Woolfolk, 1987). The MGA sub-scale of the SIQ, which describes images of being excited, stressed, psyched-up and anxious, has been associated with a greater intensity of symptoms associated with cognitive and somatic anxiety (Monsma and Overby, 2004; Vadocz *et al.*, 1997). Finally, Cumming *et al.* (2007) carried out a comparison of different forms of MGA imagery content (i.e. relaxation images, psyching-up images and competitive anxiety images), MGM imagery, and a combination of MGA and MGM imagery (termed "coping imagery" in this study) on heart rate response and self-reported psychological states. A total of 40 competitive individual sport athletes imaged five different imagery scripts, delivered in a counter-balanced order, and describing the immediate moments before performing in a hypothetical competition. As expected, only imagery scripts that contained somatic response information (MGA psyching up imagery, MGA anxiety imagery and coping imagery) led to significant increases in heart rate and anxiety intensity.

Similar to the above imagery types, associations have been found between MGA images and mastery cognitions. Certain SIQ studies report MGA imagery to be positively associated with state sport confidence (Moritz *et al.*, 1996), trait sport confidence (Abma *et al.*, 2002) and self-efficacy (Mills *et al.*, 2000). Other studies, however, have found a negative relationship to exist (Callow and Hardy, 2001; Monsma and Overby, 2004). On the surface, these contradictory findings may seem a little puzzling. However, they do make sense from the point of view of Bandura's (1997) self-efficacy theory. More specifically, MGA imagery may fulfil a source of self-efficacy called "physiological and affective states" by enabling individuals to experience optimal activation levels. If the content of imagery does not match the desired activation level, self-efficacy may lower. In support, Cumming *et al.* (2007) found that MGA anxiety imagery resulted in less self-confidence and more debilitative interpretations of symptoms associated with pre-competition anxiety than MGA psyching up imagery, MGM imagery and coping imagery. Lower levels of confidence were also reported after MGM relaxing imagery. These findings led the authors to suggest that athletes should be careful to use the aspect of MGA imagery that will lead to their desired activation level, and images of being anxious in competition without corresponding feelings of mastery may be problematic for certain athletes. By comparison, combining MGA and MGM content allows the athlete to simultaneously experience high levels of anxiety and self-confidence. Termed "confident coping", Jones and Hanton (2001) have suggested that this psychological state will enable athletes to view the symptoms associated with competitive anxiety in a more facilitative manner. Along similar lines, an intervention combining both MGA and MGM imagery led to lower levels of per-ceived stress and increased self-efficacy before and during a rock-climbing task (Jones *et al.*, 2002).

Finally, numerous SIQ studies have shown the MGM sub-scale to be positively associated with state sport confidence (Callow and Hardy, 2001; Fish *et al.*, 2004; Monsma and Overby, 2004; Mortiz *et al.*, 1996; Vadocz *et al.*, 1997), trait sport confidence (Abma *et al.*, 2002), self-efficacy (Beauchamp *et al.*, 2002; Mills *et al.*, 2000) and collective efficacy (Shearer *et al.*, 2007). Experimentally designed research has also found that mastery images lead to increased self-efficacy (Feltz and Riessinger, 1990) and state confidence (Cumming *et al.*, 2007), whereas intervention studies have reported improvements to state confidence (Callow *et al.*, 2001) and collective efficacy (Munroe-Chandler and Hall, 2004). More recently, Nicholls *et al.* (2005) carried out an MGM imagery intervention to enhance the flow experiences of high-performance golfers. Employing a single-subject replication reversal design, three of the four participants reported increased intensity of flow states, and all four reported increased frequency of flow states and percentage of successful golf shots, albeit these changes were relatively small in nature. Other studies have also shown a direct association between MGM imagery and better performance (Beauchamp *et al.*, 2002; Nordin and Cumming, 2005a; Short *et al.*, 2002), lower levels of cognitive and somatic anxiety intensity (Cumming *et al.*, 2007; Monsma *et al.*, 2004), and more facilitative anxiety interpretations (Cumming *et al.*, 2007).

Altogether, there seems to be some amount of congruence between the content of athletes' images and the outcome of their imagery that is consistent with the applied model's "what you see is what you get" principle. There is growing evidence, however, which shows that imagery will offer more results beyond what meets the eye (Nordin and Cumming, 2005a). More specifically, a number of investigations have found that one imagery type can be related to several outcomes (Callow and Waters, 2005; Calmels *et al.*, 2003; Evans *et al.*, 2004; Nicholls *et al.*, 2005; Nordin and Cumming, 2005a, 2008; Short *et al.*, 2002, 2004a). The relationships between different imagery types and outcomes therefore appear more complex than initially considered by the applied model. If imagery type were replaced by function, however, the predictions would likely hold more consistently. Instead of content systematically determining the out-comes, it would instead be the function of that imagery. To explain their find-ings, for example, Callow and Hardy (2001) stated that it might not be what is being imaged that influences confidence, but rather the function that imagery is serving. As long as the imagery is effective, there would then likely be a match between the athlete's reason for imaging and the outcome achieved. The chal-lenge then becomes to select the appropriate content that will serve the intended function, which is an issue that we will address in the next section.

In addition to the three categories of outcomes outlined, the model could be expanded to include outcomes related to the imagery process, injury rehabilita-tion and, unexplored as of yet, artistry and other more aesthetic aspects of performance. Several studies have already found significant increases in the frequency of athletes' imagery following involvement in an imagery inter-vention (Callow *et al.*, 2001; Cumming *et al.*, 2004; Cumming and Ste-Marie, 2001; Evans *et al.*, 2004; Munroe-Chandler *et al.*, 2005; Rodgers *et al.*, 1991). Imagery ability has also been found to improve (Calmels *et al.*, 2004b; Cumming and Ste-Marie, 2001; Rodgers *et al.*, 1991) and imagery sessions found to be more systematic and detailed (Evans *et al.*, 2004; Rodgers *et al.*, 1991). With respect to the rehabilitation process, Cupal and Brewer (2001) found significant improvements in knee strength, rehab anxiety and pain following a relaxation and guided imagery intervention with patients recovering from anterior cruciate ligament (ACL) reconstruction surgery. The imagery content included the physiological processes at work during each stage of recov-ery (e.g. visualise scar tissue releasing during wall slide), positive emotional coping responses (e.g. reinterpreting pain as pressure) and different sensory modalities (e.g. visual and kinaesthetic).

Personal meaning

It is now well acknowledged that a particular image can serve one or multiple functions depending on the meaning the image holds for the athlete (e.g. Callow and Hardy, 2001; Hall *et al.*, 1998; Nordin and Cumming, 2008; Short *et al.*, 2002, 2004a, 2006; Vadocz *et al.*, 1997). Indeed, Martin *et al.* (1999) borrowed the concept of meaning from Ahsen's (1984) triple-code model to explain that the same image can be interpreted differently across athletes and elicit different individual reactions. As we will see later in the chapter, the concept of personal meaning also plays a similar role in Lang's bioinformational theory (1979) as one of three types of propositional informa-tion (i.e. meaning propositions). Martin *et al.* illustrated the point with the findings of Hale and Whitehouse (1998) who asked football players to imagine taking a potentially game-winning penalty kick with either a "pressure" or "challenge" appraisal emphasis. Those participants in the challenge situation reported their anxiety symptoms to be more facilitative than participants in the pressure situation. Responses made by participants in interviews or open-ended questionnaires at the completion of intervention studies also reinforce the idea that the imagery experience is a highly personal one. For example, a golfer participating in an MGM imagery study (Nicholls *et al.*, 2005) described his images as serving an MGA function (e.g. ease worries, decrease tension) in addition to the intended MGM (e.g. feel more confident and focused). For similar reasons, Short *et al.* (2004a) suggested that researchers should verify with their participants that the perceived image function is consistent with the research or intervention goals. Furthermore, when designing interventions, the imagery function should first be considered (Short and Short, 2005). Imagery content could then be decided upon in conjunction with the athlete to ensure that the images are serving the desired function. Moreover, Short and Short advised that the images selected are viewed as facilitative in manner. For instance, an elite rugby union player described certain MGA and MGM as debilitative and intrusive to his performance by creating inappropriate activa-tion levels (Evans *et al.*, 2004). He instead preferred to use technical and tacti-cal images to achieve motivational outcomes, including increased motivation and self-confidence.

Sport situation

Of all the components included in the applied model, the least researched is the sport situation. Martin *et al.* (1999) reviewed preliminary evidence demon-strating that the use of imagery as a pre-competition strategy led to greater performance compared to a control group. They also pointed out that these studies did not include a manipulation check so it is unknown how much or what types of imagery were used by the participants. In the experiment subse-quently carried out by Cumming *et al.* (2007), types of pre-competition imagery were compared, but actual performance was not assessed in case certain types had a debilitative effect on the performer. They found that images resulting in appropriate activation levels and psychological states for the athlete (MGA psyching up imagery, MGM imagery and coping imagery) led to greater predic-tions of performance compared to those that did not (MGA anxiety imagery, MGA relaxing imagery). The next step would be to carry out intervention research that is particular to pre-competition as well as the other timeframes outlined in the applied model (i.e. training and rehabilitation). Further con-texts have also been suggested, including exercise situations (Hall, 2001) and phases of the competitive season (Cumming and Hall, 2002a), which can also be considered when planning an intervention study.

Imagery ability

According to the applied model, the effectiveness of an imagery intervention will be dependent on the athletes' ability to image. Research supports this asser-tion by demonstrating that individuals higher in imagery ability show greater performance improvements following a skill-based imagery intervention (e.g. Goss *et al.*, 1986; Rodgers *et al.*, 1991). McKenzie and Howe (1997) found that imaging ten dart throws across 15 treatment days led to enhanced self-efficacy only for participants with superior imagery ability. Furthermore, Vergeer and Roberts (2006) found that flexibility gains were positively associated with reports of imagery vividness. As a more complete test of the model, Gregg *et al.* (2005) examined whether ease of imaging influenced the relationship between different types of imagery and track-and-field performance over an indoor season. Visual and kinaesthetic imagery ability significantly predicted greater CS imagery use, but the interaction between CS imagery and imagery ability failed to predict an athlete's best performance of the season.

Evidence in support of imagery ability as a moderating variable has recently been found in a study with exercisers (Cumming, 2008). Concerns have been raised by Gregg *et al.* (2005) and others (e.g. Martin *et al.*, 1999) that typically employed imagery ability questionnaires, such as the revised version of the Movement Imagery Questionnaire (MIQ-R; Hall and Martin, 1997), are not designed to assess the motivational aspects of imagery. Cumming therefore added companion scales assessing ease of imaging to the Exercise Imagery Inventory (EII; Giacobbi *et al.*, 2005). Similar to the SIQ and DIQ, the EII normally assesses the frequency with which individuals use different imagery types (i.e. appearance-health imagery, exercise technique imagery, exercise self-efficacy imagery and exercise feelings imagery). Of these types, it was found that exercisers' abilities to create appearance-health images moderated the relationship between imagery frequency and leisure-time exercise, coping efficacy and scheduling efficacy. This interaction revealed that exercisers who imaged their appearance and health more frequently and found it easier to see and feel these images, also tended to exercise more. Moreover, these individuals also had stronger beliefs about their ability to cope with challenges and difficulties related to exercising, and scheduling exercise sessions. Consequently, there is now some existing evidence to suggest that imagery ability is a moderating variable for imagery types beyond that of skill-based ones and outcomes in addition to performance. Although more testing is needed, particularly with valid and reliable measures of imagery ability, the findings do reinforce recommendations made to include strategies for improving imagery ability when planning imagery interventions.

Summary

The introduction of the applied model to the sport imagery literature has sparked an abundance of studies, both cross-sectional and experimental in nature, to test the various predictions made. In addition to building a literature surrounding the model, other positive consequences can be noted in terms of the methodological concerns previously outlined. Not only are the studies guided by a theoretically and empirically based model, but they have also tended to include measures to screen for possible confounding variables and manipulation checks to verify that the intervention is being received and carried out as intended. The model has therefore achieved its main aim of being a useful guide for both research and applied work. Our review of this literature has led us to suggest that the predictions made by the model are also generally supported. However, there is a need to clearly distinguish imagery type from function, with image-meaning bridging the gap between concepts. Researchers should therefore consider different ways of establishing the perceived imagery function and to monitor whether these perceptions change throughout the intervention. This recommendation is particularly important to consider when there is not an obvious congruence between what the athlete is imaging and why. There is also enough evidence to now include additional imagery types and outcomes in the model. Others (Murphy *et al.*, 2008) have further commented on individual difference variables (e.g. age, gender, participation level, motivational orientations, etc.) and other moderators (e.g. duration and amount, deliberateness, direction, perspective) that may also be considered.

Finally, the applied model has been generally examined in injury rehabilitation, exercise, sport and dance. However, there has been limited work done so far in specific situations (e.g. during training, prior to competition) and more research is encouraged in this respect.

The PETTLEP model of motor imagery

The PETTLEP model of motor imagery (Holmes and Collins, 2001, 2002) is founded on the notion that a functional equivalence exists between imagery and motor performance. That is, similar brain structures to those that coordinate overt actions (i.e. motor structures) are also activated during imagery of actions (e.g. Ehrsson *et al.*, 2003; Fadiga *et al.*, 1999). Moreover, it is this similarity in neural activity when one performs imagery practice that provides the mechanism through which imagery functions to modulate subsequent motor and sports performance. Importantly, it has been argued that the effectiveness of an imagery intervention is determined by how well these same brain areas are activated through imagery (Holmes and Collins, 2002). In light of this proposed mechanism, the PETTLEP model of motor imagery was designed as a tool that sport scientists could use to heighten the equivalence between imagery and actual performance and thus improve the effectiveness of imagery interventions.

The acronym "PETTLEP" represents the seven elements of the model: Physical, Environment, Task, Timing, Learning, Emotion and Perspective. The fundamental premise behind each element is the same: in order to maximise functional equivalence and therefore optimise the impact of an imagery intervention, the imagery performed should match actual performance as closely as possible. The "physical" element is concerned with the extent to which the physical nature of imagery reflects that of actual performance. For example, a batsman in cricket who is mentally practising a shot should assume a characteristic posture, wear typical sportswear, hold appropriate equipment and image the physical responses that would occur in real performance of the skill. The "environment" element refers to the physical environment that the imagery is performed in being identical (if possible) to the actual performance environment. Moreover, the imagery environment should mimic a personalised and multisensory experience akin to the real-life performance of any given individual. In continuing with the above example, imagery of a cricket shot should ideally be performed on an individual's actual cricket pitch – or, if this is not possible, photographs or DVDs could be used as an alternative. The "task" element suggests that the imaged task should correspond as closely as possible to the real task. That is, the specific content of imagery performed should specifically mimic actual performance. For example, a cricket player should mentally practise the type of shots they would typically play in a match, thus reflecting their current level of performance or stage of learning. The "timing" element conveys that imagined performance should be temporally matched to the same speed as actual performance (i.e. real-time). The "learning" element suggests that an individual's imagery practice should be analogous to their current stage of learning and subsequently acclimatise as skill level develops. The "emotion" element suggests that imagery should incorporate all emotions and arousal typically experienced during actual performance. However, it has been since noted that any negative thoughts that could be detrimental should be replaced with positive ones (Smith et al., 2007). The "perspective" feature suggests that imagery should be performed from a visual perspective that represents the view taken by the athlete when actually performing the task (i.e. internal or external). While there has been debate in the literature on the benefits of one perspective over another (e.g. Cumming and Ste-Marie, 2001; Hardy and Callow, 1999), within the PETTLEP model both perspectives are considered to access appropriate motor representations and potentially strengthen the neural network. Moreover, sports performers may find that the perspective taken during imagery practice may be contingent on the demand of the task being imaged. It has previously been demonstrated that taking an external perspective can be more beneficial when form or body coordination is an important feature of the to-be-learned movement. Conversely, it is more advantageous to use an internal perspective for open skills that depend heavily on perception for their successful execution (Hardy and Callow, 1999). Therefore, Holmes and Collins (2001) suggested that the imagery perspective employed should be appropriate for both the individual and the task.

In accordance with bioinformational theory (Lang, 1977, 1979, 1985), the PETTLEP model also advocates that, for imagery to be optimally effective, each element should include stimulus (i.e. information concerning the stimuli in the environment), response (i.e. the cognitive, behavioural and affective responses of an individual to given stimulus in an environment) and meaning propositions (i.e. the perceived importance of the behaviour). By including these propositions into imagery practice, the correspondence (or functional equivalence) to physical practice should increase which, in turn, should raise the effectiveness of an imagery intervention at facilitating performance.

Evidence

Following the publication of the PETTLEP model, there has been a growing endeavour to empirically test the assumptions made. To this end, experimental studies have proved valuable for affirming the viability of the model as an effective tool to raise the functional equivalence that imagery has with performance and, in doing so, increase the effectiveness of imagery interventions delivered in sporting settings. More specifically, consistent evidence has been provided which highlights that imagery more functionally equivalent to actual performance will have more pronounced effects on subsequent sports performance compared to less functionally equivalent imagery (Callow et al., 2006; Smith and Collins, 2004; Smith and Holmes, 2004; Smith et al., 2001, 2007).

Clear and consistent evidence has demonstrated that manipulating the "physical" and "environment" elements of the model has beneficial effects on sports performance (Smith and Collins, 2004; Smith et al., 2001, 2007). For example, one experiment from Smith *et al.* (2007) involved implementing a six-week imagery intervention with university-level hockey players where the physical and environment components of the PETTLEP model were manipulated. Three different intervention groups used imagery to practise ten hockey penalty flicks every day for six weeks. Each group either: (a) wore hockey clothes while standing on a hockey pitch (i.e. physical + environment); (b) wore hockey clothes while standing at home (i.e. physical only); or (c) wore normal clothes while sitting down at home (i.e. no PETTLEP elements). The control group did not perform imagery but instead read hockey literature. The post-test results showed that the most functionally equivalent form of imagery practice (i.e. wearing hockey clothes while standing on a hockey pitch) scored significantly higher compared to a less functionally equivalent forms of imagery practice (i.e. wearing hockey clothes while standing at home or wearing normal clothes at home). All forms of imagery practice resulted in significantly higher performance scores compared to control. These data support the assumption that to maximise performance facilitation from imagery interventions, the physical and environment aspects of the model should be delivered in a functionally equivalent manner.

Ramsey *et al.* (2007) manipulated the "emotion" element of the model using a sample of university football players. In their study, participants took ten penalties prior to and following a six-week intervention period. Two imagery interventions, which differed only in their emotional content, were compared to a control group who performed a stretching routine. Each group performed their intervention four times per week with approximately half the sessions performed on their football pitch and the other half at home. At post-test, both imagery groups scored significantly higher points than the control group, but no significant differences were observed between the two imagery groups. These particular findings again support the contention that using PETTLEP-based imagery practices is an effective way to design performance-facilitating imagery interventions in sport. However, the data do not support the model's proposal that increasing functional equivalence through the inclusion of emotions felt during real-life performance has any beneficial effect on sports performance. However, it should be noted that the authors recognised that the testing environment for the experiment was not a competitive live-match atmosphere. Consequently, the inclusion of competitive emotions in one of the imagery interventions may not have resulted in additional benefits to performance due to the lack of actual competitive emotions felt during the post-test session. A tentative proposal is offered by Ramsey *et al.* that elements of the model may function differently in training and competition. However, this needs to be empirically tested and is an interesting area for future research.

The studies outlined above measured the effect on sports performance of individual elements of the PETTLEP model or, in some cases, combinations of different elements. Investigating all seven elements together, Smith *et al.* (2007; Experiment 2) compared two imagery groups to a physical practice group and a no-imagery control on the performance of a Full Turning Straight jump on a gymnastics beam. The imagery groups either performed: (a) imagery consisting of all seven elements of the model; or (b) imagery using a written script that included descriptive information about the environment and task (i.e. stimulus propositions). Each group performed their task three times per week for six weeks. The results demonstrated that the physical practice group and the PETTLEP imagery group performed better than the other two groups in the post-test. Additionally, no differences were found between the physical practice group and PETTLEP imagery group.

Summary

Altogether, there is growing evidence confirming the predictions made by the PETTLEP model. The central focus of these findings has suggested that the PETTLEP model of motor imagery is an effective tool for designing performance-facilitating imagery interventions in sport. Furthermore, the majority of evidence is consistent with the model's proposal that more functionally equivalent imagery interventions provide more compelling performance-facilitation effects compared to imagery interventions less functionally equivalent with performance. A main strength of the model is that it is underpinned by robust neuroscientific evidence and a clearly articulated mechanism for the observed performance effects from imagery practices. However, the model is still relatively new and has not yet been widely tested. We encourage researchers to continue testing each element of the model, in isolation and in combination with other elements. In this way, individual element characteristics could be discerned as well as the interactive effects with other elements of the model. Such findings may reveal that certain elements are more important to manipulate than others to achieve the specific desired outcome (e.g. improved performance, increased self-efficacy and modified interpretations of anxiety).

A further important future development for the PETTLEP model would be for testing to take place in a variety of settings with a mixture of populations. Not only is the model relevant for a variety of sporting environments with athletes of differing levels of ability, but also clinical and rehabilitative populations. The latter setting may include patients who have lost function in limbs and need recovery or clinicians who aim to develop motor expertise. In addition to these future developments, some limitations of the model should be recognised. Even though evidence has been presented showing performance benefits following the inclusion of all seven PETTLEP elements (Smith *et al.*, 2007; Experiment 2), it may not always be feasible to do so. For instance, sick or injured athletes who use imagery as a substitute for training sessions they cannot complete may find it difficult to satisfy the "physical" and "environment" elements of the model. As a compromise, these athletes could hold relevant sporting equipment during their imagery practices and incorporate kinaesthetic feelings but be unable to adopt the physical position. In addition, athletes may use imagery to supplement training when they cannot make it to the sports facilities. In this instance, when the "environment" cannot be manipulated, the athletes might make use of pictures/

video clips of the venue as well as to focus more so on the other PETTLEP elements to optimise functional equivalence.

Implications for professional practice

Our review of the literature has revealed that researchers are taking heed of previous recommendations to improve the methodology of imagery studies and adopt testable frameworks to guide their work. While this is now becoming the norm for studies published over the past five years or so, there are still exceptions slipping through the net. Rather than highlight the weak studies, we will instead emphasise elements of good practice evident in the literature with the hopes that these become standard among imagery researchers. Goginsky and Collins (1996) have also made a detailed list of recommendations for the interested reader to consider when planning their own research design.

Screening measures

Measures are often given prior to the commencement of an imagery intervention to provide researchers with information about their participants' previous experience with and knowledge of imagery as an intervention technique. Athletes' perceptions of imagery are important to consider because they are less likely to image when they do not perceive it as being relevant to improving their performance or competing effectively (Cumming and Hall, 2002a). Information can therefore be given to participants about the nature of imagery and the typical benefits received. Moreover, athletes with low imagery abilities are also less likely to benefit from an intervention. Assessing their general ability to image may reveal that training exercises are necessary before the intervention is given. The majority of researchers have shown a preference for using the MIQ-R, and applied the criteria of scoring at least a 16 (i.e. images are neither easy or difficult; Callow *et al.*, 2001, 2006; Smith and Collins, 2004) on both the visual and kinaesthetic sub-scales to indicate adequate imagery ability. Others have used more stringent criteria of scoring at least 20 (i.e. images are somewhat easy to see or feel; Short and Short, 2005; Short *et al.*, 2002). An alternative measure is the Vividness of Movement Imagery Questionnaire (VMIQ; Isaac *et al.*, 1986), with researchers using the criteria of scoring under 72 (Hardy and Callow, 1999; Smith and Holmes, 2004). Researchers have also administered the SIQ to examine athletes' frequency of imaging (Cumming *et al.*, 2004; Evans *et al.*, 2004). However, it is important to point out that the original version of this questionnaire does not assess ability unless certain dimensions are added (e.g. ease of imaging, vividness, controllability; see Cumming, 2008; Nordin and Cumming, 2008).

As far as we know, research has yet to establish whether a particular score on the MIQ-R and VMIQ does indeed indicate that a participant will benefit from the intervention, and would suggest this to be valuable line of enquiry for future research. Moreover, we would like to encourage researchers to carefully consider whether the information gained from these measures will be appropriate for the nature of the intervention given. Goginsky and Collins (1996) raised a similar point by asking researchers to consider whether the imagery questionnaires are appropriate to the task. If the intended intervention will focus on motivational images, for example, it might be more enlightening to use the Motivational Imagery Ability Measure for Sport (MIAMS; Gregg and Hall, 2006) or the SIQ with added imagery ability dimensions. Goginsky and Collins also suggested that the task being imaged might demand a particular type of imagery ability that cannot be appropriately measured with currently established question-naires. Researchers have consequently developed study-specific measures to use alongside questionnaires that have previously been validated (e.g. Cumming and Ste-Marie, 2001). Finally, these screening measures can also be re-administered at the end of the intervention to examine changes in the imagery process. No study has yet examined, for example, whether an athlete's ability to create motivational or emotional images improves with experience.

Manipulation checks

Because imagery is not an observable behaviour, it is important to have docu-mented evidence that participants are engaging in the intervention (Goginsky and Collins, 1996). Manipulation checks are now more commonly employed during and at the completion of an intervention to verify that the imagery is being used as intended. In certain interventions, athletes have also been encour-aged to modify the imagery content to suit their individual needs and note the changes made (e.g. Munroe-Chandler et al., 2005). These manipulation checks are normally designed specifically for the needs of a particular study, but some researchers have also administered validated questionnaires such as the full SIQ (Callow et al., 2001; Evans et al., 2004) or a shortened version (Munroe-Chandler et al., 2005). Field-based interventions will often ask participants to report on their imagery perspective, ease of imaging, use of imagery as outlined in script, number of imagery sessions completed, and perceived effectiveness of the imagery (Callow and Waters, 2005; Callow et al., 2006; Cumming and Ste-Marie, 2001; Munroe-Chandler et al., 2004, 2005; Ramsey et al., 2007). Imagery diaries monitor participants' use of imagery throughout an intervention (Callow and Waters, 2005; Cumming et al., 2004; Ramsey et al., 2007; Shambrook and Bull, 1996; Smith et al., 2001). Participants may be asked to note difficulties that they encounter during imagery or use the diary as a self-monitoring strategy to promote adherence to the intervention. Social validation checks are also employed to verify whether procedures were acceptable to the participant and if they were satisfied with the results (Hanton and Jones, 1999; Jordet, 2005). Similarly, post-intervention interviews are used to gain a more in-depth account of the participants' view of the intervention (Callow et al., 2001; Jordet, 2005; Smith et al., 2001). Finally, experimentally designed research will employ manipulation checks to establish understanding of and adherence to instructions given, the use of other psychological strategies and demand characteristics (e.g. whether participants guessed the true nature of the experiment and acted in accordance with this purpose; Feltz and Riessinger, 1990; Goginsky and Collins, 1996; Martin and Hall, 1995; Nordin and Cumming, 2005a; Ramsey *et al.*, 2008; Taylor and Shaw, 2002).

Training exercises

Researchers have employed training exercises prior to the commencement of an intervention to develop the imagery abilities of participants (e.g. Callow *et al.*, 2001; McKenzie and Howe, 1997), to clarify the difference between internal and external imagery perspectives (e.g. Blair *et al.*, 1993), or to introduce the participants more generally to the concept of imagery (e.g. Callow and Waters, 2005). Callow and Waters (2005) have used Hardy and Fazey's (1990) Mental Rehearsal Programme to first introduce participants to general imagery training, which was then followed by standardised training in the targeted imagery type (i.e. kinaesthetic imagery). Others have followed recommendations made by Lang *et al.* (1980) to carry out exercises that make participants more aware of the stimulus and response information in their imagery (Cumming *et al.*, 2007; Smith and Collins, 2004; Smith and Holmes, 2004). This procedure is based in bioinformational theory and involves drawing the participants' attention towards specific stimulus details of the scene as well as encouraging them to experience relevant physiological and emotional responses during their imagery. A similar method to improving imagery ability is to introduce images in layers, starting with simple images and then adding details or different sensory modalities in sequence. For example, Calmels *et al.* (2004a) carried out an imagery intervention to improve the selective attention of three national softball players while at bat. The intervention involved 28 imagery sessions organised in five stages describing the successful performance of different batting scenarios (e.g. balls delivered as curve balls or fast balls). With each stage, the amount of detail and complexity of the scenario being imaged increased by including the position of potential runners on different bases and possible distracters (e.g. weather, noise, unfair umpire). The participants demonstrated improvements in at least two of the three dimensions of selective attention measured (i.e. effectively integrate many external stimuli at one time, narrow attention when needed, and make fewer mistakes due to being overloaded by external stimuli). In another paper, Calmels *et al.* (2004b) also described significant improvements in vividness ratings (ranging from 15.8 per cent to 32.3 per cent) for these players.

Rather than excluding individuals from studies due to their low imagery ability, imagery exercises may instead provide an opportunity to develop these abilities to a level where the intervention would be successful. Not only would participation be maximised, but employing these exercises would also reinforce to athletes that imagery is a skill that can be developed and refined through practice. We consequently encourage researchers to incorporate training exercises when appropriate into their intervention, using theory as a guide. Moreover, the nature of these exercises should be reported in papers to make replication possible in future work. The extent to which exercises enable participants to create more vivid images has not yet been extensively evaluated. Nor, as mentioned above, have criteria been established for the necessary level of imagery ability to be achieved before imagery interventions become successful. Both issues would be useful lines of future research enquiry for the continued improvement of imagery interventions.

Individualising the intervention

The possible benefits of individualising the imagery intervention include the athletes finding the intervention more meaningful, enjoyable and easier to perform, increased adherence, and continued use of imagery following termination of the study. Single-subject multiple-baseline designs are a feasible means to individualising the intervention because: (a) large samples are not necessary; and (b) design complexity can be reduced (Callow and Hardy, 2005; Callow et al., 2001). In this design, the intervention is introduced to the different participants at staggered points of time. If the baselines of all participants change when the intervention is introduced, then the effects can be attributed to the intervention. In their study with three professional flat-race horse jockeys, for example, Callow and Waters (2005) developed five different imagery scripts in conjunction with each participant.

Action research was recently introduced to the imagery literature by Evans et al. (2004), and is another means to individualising an intervention with a small number of participants. They describe the aim of action research as being to solve day-to-day problems and/or intervene in real-life situations to improve practice (also see Castle, 1994). It involves a cyclical process of planning, acting, observing and reflecting with collaboration and feedback occurring between the researcher and client. The intervention is not predetermined in advance, but evolves in response to individual needs. Evans et al. highlighted several advantages of using this design to improve the imagery effectiveness of an elite rugby union player. They were able to gain detailed insights into the participant's use of imagery, particularly certain debilitative aspects of motivational images and a preference for using cognitive images. Moreover, they were able to conduct the intervention over 14 weeks of the competitive season, lending high ecological validity to the study. Finally, feedback was derived from multiple sources including semi-structured interviews, daily diaries and the SIQ.

It is also possible to individualise group-based research designs. In experiments examining the effect of response propositions on certain outcomes, for example, participants can be asked to provide stimulus information based on their own experiences (e.g. Cumming et al., 2007). An alternative approach is to apply multiple baseline designs to the group level (e.g. Munroe-Chandler and Hall, 2004; Munroe-Chandler et al., 2005).

In addition to personalising the content of an imagery script, researchers may also consider the participants' preferred mode of delivery. For instance, Callow and Waters (2005) gave participants the choice of what format they would like their imagery scripts to be presented in – as either collated in a written booklet or recorded on audiotape. In our work, we have found that athletes also voice a preference for who reads out the scripts, the perspective the script is written from (i.e. first person vs third person), and the tempo, pitch and rhythm of how the script is read. When video clips are supporting the imagery intervention, it also likely that participants may favour viewing the clips from a certain perspective (e.g. sideways, front on) or for the clips to depict a particular person (e.g. themselves, more accomplished athlete). Finally, it is also worth considering whether a script is even necessary. It might be the athlete's preference, for example, to receive general instructions and advice on the types of response propositions to base their imagery upon, rather than having a structured script to follow. For these reasons, we involve the athlete not only in the development of the imagery content but also in the finer details of how that imagery is delivered.

Objective measures of the imagery experience

Because imagery is an internal experience that cannot be directly measured, researchers tend to rely on the subjective reports of their participants. Although questionnaires and in-depth interviews are certainly informative and do have an important place in the research area, they are also limited to images experienced at a conscious level and are subject to some degree of retrospective bias. Objective measures can add further insights into the imagery experience while it is occurring and provide useful feedback to the participants. For instance, Olympic medallist Alex Bauman described timing his imagery of swimming races:

> The best way I have learned to prepare mentally for competitions is to visualize the race in my mind and to put down a split time. The splits I use in my imagery are determined by my coach and myself, for each part of the race. For example, in the 200 individual medley, splits are made up for each 50 metres because after 50 metres the stroke changes. These splits are based on training times and what we feel I'm capable of doing. In my imagery I concentrate on attaining the splits I have set out to do.
>
> (As quoted in Orlick, 2000: 116)

Within the research context, objective measures will indicate that images are actually occurring and provide evidence in support of certain theoretical frameworks. Heart rate, respiration rate and skin conductance are often obtained to demonstrate a basic tenet of bioinformational theory that vivid images containing response propositions will result in an actual physiological response (Cumming *et al.*, 2007; Gallego *et al.*, 1996; Hecker and Kaczor, 1988). Electromyographic (EMG) and electroencephalographic (EEG) recordings have similarly been used to test this hypothesis (Smith and Collins, 2004; Smith *et al.*, 2003).

As the PETTLEP model and the theory of functional equivalence grow in popularity, imagery researchers would also benefit from using techniques that are more common to the neurosciences. Indeed, advances in cognitive neuroscience may aid sport-imagery research to progress from a descriptive stage, where underlying mechanisms are speculated upon, to an explanatory stage, where underlying mechanisms can be more clearly discerned. One technique used to measure brain activity is functional magnetic resonance imaging (fMRI). Within the context of fMRI, a typical measure is the Blood Oxygen Level Dependent, or BOLD, response. The BOLD response is based on a physiological response to brain activation where red blood cells move from a state of oxygenation to deoxygenation during functional activity. At differing levels of oxygenation, the MR signal of blood is different and this difference can be detected by an MR pulse sequence. Thus, fMRI is not a direct or invasive measure of neuronal activity within the brain, but instead infers brain activity based on levels of blood oxygenation. An advantage of this technique is that it will indicate the degree of functional equivalence between imagery and actual movement by demonstrating common areas of brain activation. Unfortunately, due to the confined space with a scanner and the importance of maintaining a still head position, only a limited amount of movement can be performed during testing. As a result, the majority of fMRI studies investigating imagery to date have answered fundamental questions in terms of imagery and execution equivalence. For example, Ehrsson et al. (2003) used fMRI to measure brain activity during finger, toe and tongue actions. When compared to rest, the same motor areas were activated during imagined and executed movements. Furthermore, the imagery activity was organised in a samatotopic fashion consistent with the motor homunculus. That is, brain activation during imagined finger, toe and tongue actions corresponded with the location of activation during actual finger, toe and tongue actions respectively. Hence, not only were similar motor structures active during imagery, but the activity was also organised in a similar manner.

The future for imagery research

Our review of the literature suggests a growing evidence base in support of both the applied model of imagery use and the PETTLEP model. Intertwined in our review are suggested avenues of future research with respect to predictions made by both models, and possible elaborations to the applied model. Investigating the interaction of both models is an obvious next step. The applied model enables investigators to consider the "why", "what", "where" and "when" of the intervention, whereas the PETTLEP model can specify the "how". Take, for example, an intervention to be carried out with novice tennis players to improve service reception (CS imagery function) during training (sport situation). The physical and environment elements of PETTLEP can be included by having participants dressed in their kit, standing on the court and holding their racket. Furthermore, skill-based images (imagery type) that are performed in real-time (timing element) and match the individuals' current level of performance (task element) can evolve as further learning (learning element) takes place. Combining both models in a single intervention should enable functionally equivalent imagery to be performed that is personally meaningful to the individual in achieving their goals.

Another logical next step for imagery research is to move beyond healthy populations into clinical ones. Testament to this idea, a recent study has offered encouraging findings using imagery training as a restorative tool to assist patients with chronic spinal cord injury (Cramer *et al.*, 2007). They found that in participants devoid of voluntary motor control and peripheral feedback, imagery training improved motor performance and altered brain function. With this in mind, the applied model has already been proposed for use in rehabilitation and exercise settings (Hall, 2001). Also, as mentioned above, it would be useful to examine the PETTLEP with a mixture of populations. Consequently, sport scientists armed with theoretically based models would likely have a great deal to offer intervention work that is already becoming popular with clinical populations.

Finally, we have suggested that neuroscientific techniques, such as fMRI, can help to explain why imagery interventions function to improve sporting performance. A further important use of fMRI in imagery research is to take steps towards validating imagery questionnaires. Pen and paper imagery assessments are commonly used – results from which make valuable contributions to our understanding of imagery-behaviour relations. However, if a more objective measure, such as brain activity, correlated with questionnaire forms of imagery indices then this would affirm the viability of questionnaire-based imagery assessments that are typically used in the field. For example, Amedi *et al.* (2005; see also Cui *et al.*, 2007) found a positive correlation between the BOLD response activity during visual imagery of objects with scores on the Vividness of Visual Imagery Questionnaire (VVIQ; Marks, 1973). This study highlights the potential capability for brain activity to function as a more objective measure of one's imagery abilities in comparison to questionnaire-based assessments.

References

Abma, C. L., Fry, M. D., Li, Y. and Relyea, G. (2002). Differences in imagery content and imagery ability between high and low confident track and field athletes. *Journal of Applied Sport Psychology*, 14, 67–75.

Ahsen, A. (1984). ISM: the triple code model for imagery and psychophysiology. *Journal of Mental Imagery*, 8, 15–42.

Amedi, A., Malach, R. and Pascual-Leone, A. (2005). Negative BOLD differentiates visual imagery and perception. *Neuron*, 48, 859–872.

Anshel, M. H. and Wrisberg, C. A. (1993). Reducing warm-up decrement in the performance of the tennis serve. *Journal of Sport and Exercise Psychology*, 15, 290–303.

Bandura, A. (1997). *Self-efficacy: the exercise of control*. New York: W. H. Freeman.

Barr, K. and Hall, C. (1992). The use of imagery by rowers. *International Journal of Sport Psychology*, 23, 243–261.

Beauchamp, M. R., Bray, S. R. and Albinson, J. G. (2002). Pre-competition imagery, self-efficacy and performance in collegiate golfers. *Journal of Sports Sciences*, 20, 697–705.

Blair, A., Hall, C. and Leyshon, G. (1993). Imagery effects on the performance of skilled and novice soccer players. *Journal of Sports Sciences*, 11, 95–101.

Burhans, R. S., Richman, C. L. and Bergey, D. B. (1988). Mental imagery training: effects on running speed performance. *International Journal of Sport Psychology*, 19, 26–37.

Callow, N. and Hardy, L. (2001). Types of imagery associated with sport confidence in netball players of varying skill levels. *Journal of Applied Sport Psychology*, 13, 1–17.

Callow, N. and Hardy, L. (2005). A critical analysis of applied imagery research. In D. Hackfort, J. L. Duda and R. Lidor (eds), *Handbook of research in applied sport and exercise psychology: international perspectives* (pp. 21–42). Morgantown, WV: Fitness Information Technology.

Callow, N. and Waters, A. (2005). The effect of kinaesthetic imagery on the sport confidence of flat-race horse jockeys. *Psychology of Sport and Exercise*, 6, 443–459.

Callow, N., Hardy, L. and Hall, C. (2001). The effects of a motivational general-mastery imagery intervention on the sport confidence of high-level badminton players. *Research Quarterly for Exercise and Sport*, 72, 389–400.

Callow, N., Roberts, R. and Fawkes, J. Z. (2006). Effects of dynamic and static imagery on vividness of imagery, skiing performance, and confidence. *Journal of Imagery Research in Sport and Physical Activity*, 1. Retrieved 12 April 2007, from www.bepress.com/jirspa/vol1/iss1/art2.

Calmels, C., Berthoumieux, C. and d'Arripe-Longueville, F. (2004a). Effects of an imagery-training programme on selective attention of national softball players. *The Sport Psychologist*, 18, 272–296.

Calmels, C., D'Arripe-Longueville, F., Fournier, J. F. and Soulard, A. (2003). Competitive strategies among elite female gymnasts: an exploration of the relative influence of psychological skills training and natural learning experiences. *International Journal of Sport and Exercise Psychology*, 1, 327–352.

Calmels, C., Holmes, P., Berthoumieux, C. and Singer, R. N. (2004b). The development of movement imagery vividness through a structured intervention in softball. *Journal of Sport Behaviour*, 27, 307–322.

Castle, A. (1994). Action research for developing professional practice. *British Journal of Therapy and Rehabilitation*, 1, 155–157.

Cramer, S. C., Orr, E. L. R., Cohen, M. J. and Lacourse, M. G. (2007). Effects of motor imagery after chronic, complete spinal cord injury. *Experimental Brain Research*, 177, 233–242.

Cui, X., Jeter, C. B., Yang, D., Montague, P. R. and Eagleman, D. M. (2007). Vividness of mental imagery: individual variability can be measured objectively. *Vision Research*, 47, 474–478.

Cumming, J. (2008). Investigating the relationship between exercise imagery, leisure time exercise behaviour, and exercise self-efficacy. *Journal of Applied Sport Psychology*, 20, 184–193.

Cumming, J. and Hall, C. (2002a). Athletes' use of imagery in the off-season. *The Sport Psychologist*, 16, 160–172.

Cumming, J. and Hall, C. (2002b). Deliberate imagery practice: the development of imagery skills in competitive athletes. *Journal of Sports Sciences*, 20, 137–145.

Cumming, J. and Ste-Marie, D. M. (2001). The cognitive and motivational effects of imagery training: a matter of perspective. *The Sport Psychologist*, 15, 276–287.

Cumming, J., Hall, C., Harwood, C. and Gammage, K. (2002). Motivational orientations and imagery use: a goal profiling analysis. *Journal of Sports Sciences*, 20, 127–136.

Cumming, J., Hall, C. and Shambrook, C. (2004). The influence of an imagery workshop on athletes' use of imagery. *Athletic Insight: the Online Journal of Sport Psychology*, 6(1). Retrieved 6 August 2007, from www.athleticinsight.com/Vol6Iss1/InfluenceofImageryWorkshop.htm.

Cumming, J., Olphin, T. and Law, M. (2007). Physiological and self-reported responses to different motivational general imagery scripts. *Journal of Sport and Exercise Psychology*, 29, 629–644.

Cupal, D. D. and Brewer, B. W. (2001). Effects of relaxation and guided imagery on knee strength, reinjury anxiety, and pain following anterior cruciate ligament reconstruction. *Rehabilitation Psychology*, 46, 28–43.

Driediger, M., Hall, C. and Callow, N. (2006). Imagery use by injured athletes: a qualitative analysis. *Journal of Sports Sciences*, 24, 261–271.

Driskell, J. E., Copper, C. and Moran, A. (1994). Does mental practice enhance performance? *Journal of Applied Psychology*, 79, 481–491.

Durand, M., Hall, C. and Haslam, I. R. (1997). The effects of combining mental practice and physical practice on motor skills acquisition: a review of the literature and some practical implications. *The Hong Kong Journal of Sports Medicine and Sports Science*, 4, 36–41.

Ehrsson, H. H., Geyer, S. and Naito, E. (2003). Imagery of voluntary movement of fingers, toes, and tongue activates corresponding body-part-specific motor representations. *Journal of Neurophysiology*, 90, 3304–3316.

Evans, L., Hare, R. and Mullen, R. (2006). Imagery use during rehabilitation from injury. *Journal of Imagery Research in Sport and Physical Activity*, 1. Retrieved 1 October 2006, from www.bepress.com/jirspa/vol1/iss1/art1.

Evans, L., Jones, L. and Mullen, R. (2004). An imagery intervention during the competitive season with an elite rugby union player. *The Sport Psychologist*, 18, 252–271.

Fadiga, L., Buccino, G., Craighero, L., Fogassi, L., Gallese, V. and Pavesi, G. (1999). Corticospinal excitability is specifically modulated by motor imagery: a magnetic stimulation study. *Neuropsychologia*, 37, 147–158.

Feltz, D. and Landers, D. M. (1983). The effects of mental practice on motor skill learning and performance: a meta-analysis. *Journal of Sport Psychology*, 5, 25–57.

Feltz, D. and Riessinger, C. A. (1990). Effects of in vivo imagery and performance feedback on self-efficacy and muscular endurance. *Journal of Sport and Exercise Psychology*, 12, 132–143.

Fenker, R. M. and Lambiotte, J. G. (1987). A performance enhancement programme for a college football team: one incredible season. *The Sport Psychologist*, 1, 224–236.

Fish, L., Hall, C. and Cumming, J. (2004). Investigating the use of imagery by elite ballet dancers. *Avante*, 10, 26–39.

Gallego, J., Denot-Ledunois, S., Vardon, G. and Perruchet, P. (1996). Ventilatory responses to imagined exercise. *Psychophysiology*, 33, 711–719.

Gammage, K., Hall, C. and Rodgers, W. (2000). More about exercise imagery. *The Sport Psychologist*, 14, 348–359.

Giacobbi, P. R., Hausenblas, H. A., Fallon, E. A. and Hall, C. (2003). Even more about exercise imagery: a grounded theory of exercise imagery. *Journal of Applied Sport Psychology*, 15, 160–175.

Giacobbi, P. R., Jr., Hausenblas, H. A. and Penfield, R. D. (2005). Further refinements in the measurement of exercise imagery: the Exercise Imagery Inventory. *Measurement in Physical Education and Exercise Sciences*, 9, 251–266.

Goginsky, A. M. and Collins, D. (1996). Research design and mental practice. *Journal of Sports Sciences*, 14, 381–392.

Goss, S., Hall, C., Buckolz, E. and Fishburne, G. (1986). Imagery ability and the acquisition and retention of movements. *Memory and Cognition*, 14, 469–477.

Gregg, M. and Hall, C. (2006). Measurement of motivational imagery abilities in sport. *Journal of Sports Sciences*, 24, 961–971.

Gregg, M., Hall, C. and Nederhof, E. (2005). The imagery ability, imagery use, and performance relationship. *The Sport Psychologist*, 19, 93–99.

Grouios, G. (1992). The effect of mental practice on diving performance. *International Journal of Sport Psychology*, 23, 60–69.

Hale, B. D. and Whitehouse, A. (1998). The effects of imagery-manipulated appraisal on intensity and direction of competition anxiety. *The Sport Psychologist*, 12, 40–51.

Hall, C. (2001). Imagery in sport and exercise. In R. N. Singer, H. Hausenblas and C. M. Janelle (eds), *Handbook of sport psychology* (2nd edn, pp. 529–549). New York: John Wiley and Sons.

Hall, C. and Martin, K. A. (1997). Measuring movement imagery abilities: a revision of the Movement Imagery Questionnaire. *Journal of Mental Imagery*, 21, 143–154.

Hall, C., Schmidt, D., Divand, M. and Buckolz, E. (1994). Imagery and motor skills acquisition. In Sheikh, Anees A. and Korn, Errol R. (eds), *Imagery in sports and physical performance* (pp. 121–134). Amityville, NY: Baywood Publishing Company

Hall, C., Mack, D., Paivio, A. and Hausenblas, H. (1998). Imagery use by athletes: development of the sport imagery questionnaire. *International Journal of Sport Psychology*, 29, 73–89.

Hall, C., Stevens, D. and Paivio, A. (2005). *The Sport Imagery Questionnaire: test manual*. Morgantown, WV: Fitness Information Technology.

Hanrahan, C. and Salmela, J. H. (1990). Dance images – do they really work or are we just imagining things? *Journal of Physical Education, Recreation and Dance*, 61, 18–21.

Hanrahan, C. and Vergeer, I. (2000). Multiple uses of mental imagery by professional modern dancers. *Imagination, Cognition, and Personality*, 20, 231–255.

Hanrahan, C., Tétreau, B. and Sarrazin, C. (1995). Use of imagery while performing dance movement. *International Journal of Sport Psychology*, 26, 413–430.

Hanton, S. and Jones, G. (1999). The effects of a multimodal intervention programme on performers: II. Training the butterflies to fly in formation. *The Sport Psychologist*, 13, 22–41.

Hardy, L. and Callow, N. (1999). Efficacy of external and internal visual imagery perspectives for the enhancement of performance of tasks in which form is important. *Journal of Sport and Exercise Psychology*, 21, 95–112.

Hardy, L. and Fazey, J. (1990). *Mental rehearsal*. Leeds: National Coaching Foundation.

Hausenblas, H., Hall, C., Rodgers, W. and Munroe, K. (1999). Exercise imagery: its nature and measurement. *Journal of Applied Sport Psychology*, 11, 171–180.

Hecker, J. E. and Kaczor, L. M. (1988). Application of imagery theory to sport psychology: some preliminary findings. *Journal of Sport and Exercise Psychology*, 10, 363–373.

Hinshaw, K. E. (1991). The effects of mental practice on motor skill performance: critical evaluation and meta-analysis. *Imagination, Cognition, and Personality*, 11, 3–35.

Holmes, P. S. and Collins, D. J. (2001). The PETTLEP approach to motor imagery: a functional equivalence model for sport psychologists. *Journal of Applied Sport Psychology*, 13, 60–83.

Holmes, P. S. and Collins, D. (2002). Functional equivalence solutions for problems with motor imagery. In I. Cockerill (ed.), *Solutions in sport psychology* (pp. 120–140). London: Thomson.

Isaac, A. R. (1985). Imagery differences and mental practice. In D. F. Marks and D. G. Russell (eds), *Imagery* (pp. 14–18). Dunedin, NZ: Human Performance Associates.

Isaac, A., Marks, D. and Russel, E. (1986). An instrument for assessing imagery of movements: the Vividness of Movement Imagery Questionnaire (VMIQ). *Journal of Mental Imagery*, 10, 23–30.

Jones, G. and Hanton, S. (2001). Pre-competitive feeling states and directional anxiety interpretations. *Journal of Sports Sciences*, 19, 385–395.

Jones, L. and Stuth, G. (1997). The uses of mental imagery in athletics: an overview. *Applied and Preventive Psychology*, 6, 101–115.

Jones, M. V., Mace, R. D., Bray, S. R., MacRae, A. W. and Stockbridge, C. (2002). The impact of motivational imagery on the emotional state and self-efficacy levels of novice climbers. *Journal of Sport Behaviour*, 25, 57–73.

Jordet, G. (2005). Perceptual training in soccer: an imagery intervention study with elite players. *Journal of Applied Sport Psychology*, 17, 140–156.

Lang, P. J. (1977). Imagery in therapy: an information-processing analysis of fear. *Behaviour Therapy*, 8, 862–886.

Lang, P. J. (1979). A bio-informational theory of emotional imagery. *Psychophysiology*, 16, 495–512.

Lang, P. J. (1985). Cognition in emotion: concept and action. In C. Izard, J. Kagan and R. Zajonc (eds), *Emotion, cognitions, and behaviour* (pp. 192–226). New York: Cambridge University Press.

Lang, P. J., Kozak, M. J., Miller, G. A., Levin, D. N. and McLean, A. Jr. (1980). Emotional imagery: conceptual structure and pattern of somato-visceral response. *Psychophysiology*, 17, 179–192.

Law, B., Driediger, M., Hall, C. and Forwell, L. (2006). Imagery use, perceived pain, limb functioning and satisfaction in athletic injury rehabilitation. *New Zealand Journal of Physiotherapy*, 34, 10–16.

Lee, C. (1990). Psyching up for a muscular endurance task: effects of image content on performance and mood state. *Journal of Sport and Exercise Psychology*, 12, 66–73.

McKenzie, A. D. and Howe, B. L. (1997). The effect of imagery on self-efficacy for a motor skill. *International Journal of Sport Psychology*, 28, 196–210.

Mamassis, G. and Doganis, G. (2004). The effects of mental training programme on juniors' pre-competitive anxiety, self-confidence, and tennis performance. *Journal of Applied Sport Psychology*, 16, 118–137.

Marks, D. F. (1973). Visual imagery differences in the recall of pictures. *British Journal of Psychology*, 64, 17–24.

Martin, K. A. and Hall, C. (1995). Using mental imagery to enhance intrinsic motivation. *Journal of Sport and Exercise Psychology*, 17, 54–69.

Martin, K. A., Moritz, S. E. and Hall, C. (1999). Imagery use in sport: a literature review and applied model. *The Sport Psychologist*, 13, 245–268.

Mills, K. D., Munroe, K. and Hall, C. (2000). The relationship between imagery and self-efficacy in competitive athletes. *Imagination, Cognition, and Personality*, 20, 33–39.

Monsma, E. V. and Overby, L. Y. (2004). The relationship between imagery and competitive anxiety in ballet auditions. *Journal of Dance Medicine and Science*, 8, 11–18.

Moran, A. P. (2004). *Sport and exercise psychology: a critical introduction*. London: Routledge.

Moritz, S. E., Hall, C., Martin, K. A. and Vadocz, E. (1996). What are confident athletes imaging? An examination of image content. *The Sport Psychologist*, 10, 171–179.

Morris, T., Spittle, M. and Watt, A. P. (2005). *Imagery in sport*. Champaign, IL: Human Kinetics.

Mumford, B. and Hall, C. (1985). The effects of internal and external imagery on performing figures in figure skating. *Canadian Journal of Applied Sport Psychology*, 10, 171–177.

Munroe, K., Giacobbi, P. R., Hall, C. and Weinberg, R. (2000). The four ws of imagery use: where, when, why, and what? *The Sport Psychologist*, 14, 119–137.

Munroe, K., Hall, C., Simms, S. and Weinberg, R. (1998). The influence of type of sport and time of season on athletes' use of imagery. *The Sport Psychologist*, 12, 440–449.

Munroe-Chandler, K. J. and Hall, C. R. (2004). Enhancing the collective efficacy of a soccer team through motivational general-mastery imagery. *Imagination, Cognition, and Personality*, 21, 51–67.

Munroe-Chandler, K. J., Hall, C. R., Fishburne, G. O. J. and Hall, N. (2007). The content of imagery use in youth sport. *International Journal of Sport and Exercise Psychology*, 5, 158–175.

Munroe-Chandler, K. J., Hall, C. R., Fishburne, G. J. and Shannon, V. (2005). Using cognitive general imagery to improve soccer strategies. *European Journal of Sport Science*, 5, 41–49.

Murphy, S. M. (1994). Imagery interventions in sport. *Medicine and Science in Sports and Exercise*, 26, 486–494.

Murphy, S. M. and Jowdy, D. P. (1992). Imagery and mental practice. In T. S. Horn (ed.), *Advances in sport psychology* (1st edn, pp. 221–250). Champaign, IL: Human Kinetics.

Murphy, S. M. and Martin, K. A. (2002). The use of imagery in sport. In T. S. Horn (ed.), *Advances in sport psychology* (2nd edn, pp. 405–439). Champaign, IL: Human Kinetics.

Murphy, S. M. and Woolfolk, R. L. (1987). The effects of cognitive interventions on competitive anxiety and performance on a fine motor skill accuracy task. *International Journal of Sport Psychology*, 18, 152–166.

Murphy, S. M., Nordin, S. M. and Cumming, J. (2008). Imagery in sport, exercise and dance. In T. S. Horn (ed.), *Advances in sport psychology* (3rd edn). Champaign, IL: Human Kinetics, pp. 297–324.

Murphy, S. M., Woolfolk, R. L. and Budney, A. J. (1988). The effects of emotive imagery on strength performance. *International Journal of Sport Psychology*, 10, 334–345.

Nicholls, A. R., Polman, R. C. J. and Holt, N. L. (2005). The effects of individualized imagery interventions on golf performance and flow states. *Athletic Insight: the Online Journal of Sport Psychology*, 7(1). Retrieved 6 January 2006, from www.athleticinsight.com/Vol7Iss1/ImageryGolfFlow.htm.

Nordin, S. M. and Cumming, J. (2005a). More than meets the eye: investigating imagery type, direction, and outcome. *The Sport Psychologist*, 19, 1–17.

Nordin, S. M. and Cumming, J. (2005b). Professional dancers describe their imagery: where, when, what, why, and how? *The Sport Psychologist*, 19, 295–416.

Nordin, S. M. and Cumming, J. (2006). Measuring the content of dancers' images: development of the Dance Imagery Questionnaire (DIQ). *Journal of Dance Medicine and Science*, 10, 85–98.

Nordin, S. M. and Cumming, J. (in press). Comparison of dancers and aesthetic sport athletes' imagery use. *Journal of Applied Sport Psychology*.

Nordin, S. M. and Cumming, J. (2008). Type and function of athletes' imagery: testing prediction from the applied model of imagery use by examining effectiveness. *International Journal of Sport and Exercise Psychology*, 6, 189–206.

Nordin, S. M., Cumming, J., Vincent, J. and McGrory, S. (2006). Mental practice or spontaneous play? Examining which types of imagery constitute deliberate practice in sport. *Journal of Applied Sport Psychology*, 18, 345–362.

Orlick, T. (2000). *In pursuit of excellence: how to win in sport and life through mental training*. Champaign, IL: Human Kinetics.

Orlick, T. and Partington, J. (1988). Mental links to excellence. *The Sport Psychologist*, 2, 105–130.

Paivio, A. (1985). Cognitive and motivational functions of imagery in human performance. *Canadian Journal of Applied Sport Science*, 10, 22S–28S.

Ramsey, R., Cumming, J. and Edwards, M. G. (2007). Examining the emotion aspect of PETTLEP based imagery and penalty taking performance in football. *Journal of Sport and Exercise Psychology*, 29, S196–S197.

Ramsey, R., Cumming, J. and Edwards, M. G. (2008). Exploring a modified conceptualisation of imagery direction and golf putting performance. *International Journal of Sport and Exercise Psychology*, 6, 207–223.

Richardson, A. (1969). *Mental imagery*. New York: Springer.

Rodgers, W., Hall, C. and Buckolz, E. (1991). The effect of an imagery-training programme on imagery ability, imagery use, and figure skating performance. *Journal of Applied Sport Psychology*, 3, 109–125.

Rodgers, W. M., Munroe, K. J. and Hall, C. R. (2001). Relations among exercise imagery, self-efficacy, exercise behavior, and intentions. *Imagination, Cognition and Personality*, 21, 55–65.

Salmon, J., Hall, C. and Haslam, I. R. (1994). The use of imagery by soccer players. *Journal of Applied Sport Psychology*, 6, 116–133.

Sawada, M., Mori, S. and Ishii, M. (2002). Effect of metaphorical verbal instruction on modelling of sequential dance skills by young children. *Perceptual and Motor Skills*, 95, 1097–1105.

Shambrook, C. J. and Bull, S. J. (1996). The use of a single-case research design to investigate the efficacy of imagery training. *Journal of Applied Sport Psychology*, 8, 27–43.

Sheard, M. and Golby, J. (2006). Effect of a psychological skills training programme on swimming performance and positive psychological development. *International Journal of Sport and Exercise Psychology*, 4, 149–169.

Shearer, D. A., Thomson, R., Mellalieu, S. D. and Shearer, C. R. (2007). The relationship between imagery type and collective efficacy in elite and non-elite athletes. *Journal of Sports Science and Medicine*, 6, 180–187.

Short, S. E. and Short, M. W. (2005). Differences between high- and low-confident football players on imagery functions: a consideration of the athletes' perceptions. *Journal of Applied Sport Psychology*, 17, 197–208.

Short, S. E., Bruggeman, J. M., Engel, S. G., Marback, T. L., Wang, L. J., Willadsen, A. and Short, M. W. (2002). The effect of imagery function and imagery direction on self-efficacy and performance on a golf-putting task. *The Sport Psychologist*, 16, 48–67.

Short, S. E., Hall, C. R., Engel, S. R. and Nigg, C. R. (2004b). Exercise imagery and the stages of change. *Journal of Mental Imagery*, 28, 61–78.

Short, S. E., Monsma, E. V. and Short, M. (2004a). Is what you see really what you get? Athletes' perceptions of imagery functions. *The Sport Psychologist*, 18, 341–349.

Short, S. E., Ross-Stewart, L. and Monsma, E. V. (2006). Onwards with the evolution of imagery research in sport psychology. *Athletic Insight: the Online Journal of Sport Psychology*, 8(3). Retrieved 26 March 2007, from www.athleticinsight.com/Vol8Iss3/ImageryResearch.htm.

Smith, D. and Collins, D. (2004). Mental practice, motor performance, and the late CNV. *Journal of Sport and Exercise Psychology*, 26, 412–426.

Smith, D. and Holmes, P. (2004). The effect of imagery modality on golf putting performance. *Journal of Sport and Exercise Psychology*, 26, 385–395.

Smith, D., Collins, D. and Holmes, P. (2003). Impact and mechanism of mental practice effects on strength. *International Journal of Sport and Exercise Psychology*, 1, 293–306.

Smith, D., Holmes, P., Whitemore, L., Collins, D. and Devonport, T. (2001). The effect of theoretically based imagery scripts on field hockey performance. *Journal of Sport Behaviour*, 24, 408–419.

Smith, D., Wright, C., Allsopp, A. and Westhead, H. (2007). It's all in the mind: PETTLEP-based imagery and sports performance. *Journal of Applied Sport Psychology*, 19, 80–92.

Sordoni, C., Hall, C. and Forwell, L. (2002). The use of imagery in athletic injury rehabilitation and its relationship to self-efficacy. *Physiotherapy Canada*, Summer, 177–185.

Taylor, J. and Shaw, D. F. (2002). The effects of outcome imagery on golf-putting performance. *Journal of Sports Sciences*, 20, 607–613.

Vadocz, E., Hall, C. and Moritz, S. E. (1997). The relationship between competitive anxiety and imagery use. *Journal of Applied Sport Psychology*, 9, 241–253.

Vergeer, I. (2005). The role of mental images throughout injury recovery: an exploratory study. *Journal of Sports Sciences*, 23, 180–181.

Vergeer, I. (2006). Exploring the mental representation of athletic injury: a longitudinal case study. *Psychology of Sport and Exercise*, 7, 99–114.

Vergeer, I. and Roberts, J. (2006). Movement and stretching imagery during flexibility training. *Journal of Sports Sciences*, 24, 197–208.

White, A. and Hardy, L. (1998). An in-depth analysis of the uses of imagery by high-level slalom canoeists and artistic gymnasts. *The Sport Psychologist*, 12, 387–403.

Woolfolk, R. L., Parrish, W. and Murphy, S. M. (1985). The effects of positive and negative imagery on motor skill performance. *Cognitive Therapy and Research*, 9, 335–341.

2 A framework for the study and application of self-talk within sport

James Hardy, Emily Oliver and David Tod

Introduction

A glance through applied sport psychology textbooks reveals that self-talk is one technique commonly included in mental-skills training programmes and is proposed by sport psychologists to regulate cognitions, emotions, behaviour and performance (e.g. Zinsser *et al.*, 2006). In addition, research suggests self-talk is one of the common psychological strategies used by athletes, and that coaches believe it helps build performers' confidence (e.g. Wang *et al.*, 2003; Weinberg *et al.*, 1992). However, some investigators have suggested there is limited, if any, support that self-talk enhances competitive performance (Gardner and Moore, 2006; Martin *et al.*, 2005). One reason for the lack of evidence may be because, traditionally, self-talk has not received as much attention from researchers as compared with other psychological techniques (e.g. imagery, goal setting). In recent years, however, self-talk has been examined more frequently and there now exists a number of empirical attempts to evaluate its usefulness for athletes.

Athletes may use self-talk for reasons other than performance enhancement, such as to build self-efficacy, learn new techniques, or with non-performance-related issues (e.g. coping with media demands). A review of self-talk literature that adopts a broader perspective than only examining the strategy's influence on performance will likely provide various benefits. For example, summarising the current knowledge may provide practitioners with guidance for using self-talk and help researchers to identify areas for future investigations. The purpose of the current chapter is to: (a) summarise existing literature within a sequential framework highlighting self-talk's antecedents and consequences, with an emphasis on how self-talk might be beneficial for athletic performance; (b) identify areas for future research; and (c) present applied implications for practitioners, athletes and coaches. A useful starting point, however, is to define self-talk.

What are we talking about? Defining self-talk

Defining constructs within the social sciences has important implications, not least for the measurement of the phenomenon under investigation (cf. Carron et al., 1997). Without socially agreed definitions, it is difficult to identify and synthesise research relevant to a topic, and investigators are unable to determine suitable ways to measure variables. Over a decade ago, Hardy et al. (1996) argued that reaching a consensus regarding a self-talk definition was a fundamental issue needing to be addressed before other lines of inquiry could be pursued profitably. It was not until relatively recently, however, that an in-depth discussion of what constituted self-talk was published (see Hardy, 2006).

Via his review of existing definitions used in the literature, Hardy (2006) identified self-talk as separate from other cognitive processes (e.g. imagery, day dreaming). An emphasis was placed on the sport-oriented statements that athletes say to themselves as opposed to their general (non-sport-related) thoughts. Given the overlap between self-talk and automatic thoughts, it is possible that such self-statements occur automatically or in a more deliberate manner (e.g. intervention cues). As a result, self-talk refers to those automatic statements reflective of, and deliberate techniques (e.g. thought-stopping) athletes use to direct, sports-related thinking. In addition, Hardy identified a number of overlapping dimensions which were representative of the nature of self-talk. These included a frequency dimension, which refers to how often athletes use self-talk as well as an overtness dimension, which considers if self-talk is said either overtly, and is potentially audible to others, or covertly, and is inaudible to others. The third dimension, valence, refers to the content of self-talk. Self-talk's content can range from being positive, and offering praise (e.g. "good stuff") to negative, and reflecting a form of criticism (e.g. "pathetic"; cf. Moran, 1996). The fourth dimension, motivational interpretation, overlaps with the content of self-talk but differs in that it refers to whether athletes view the content of their self-talk as either motivating or de-motivating. The final dimension refers to the reasons why athletes might use self-talk, with the two broad functions being self-instruction and motivation. Both of these general functions have been further refined into more specific functions (Hardy et al., 2001a). Consequently, the instructional function can be subdivided into two functions. First, cognitive-specific self-talk assists the athlete to learn or execute individual skills (e.g. a back somersault). Second, cognitive general self-talk helps the athlete to focus on overall performance (e.g. intensify workouts) and execute strategies (e.g. backward tumble run). Conversely, the motivational function can be divided into three specific functions. First, the motivational-mastery function is associated with mental toughness, focus, confidence and mental preparation – all required if the athlete is to master successfully his/her circumstances. Second, the motivational-arousal function helps athletes to relax, "psych" themselves up and otherwise control their arousal levels. Third, the motivational-drive function is more global than the other two motivational functions, and is related to keeping the athlete on track to achieving his/her goals. As a result, this function is associated with maintaining or increasing drive and effort levels.

Based on the aforementioned dimensions, it is suggested that self-talk is multidimensional in nature (e.g. frequency, valance), referring to verbalisations or

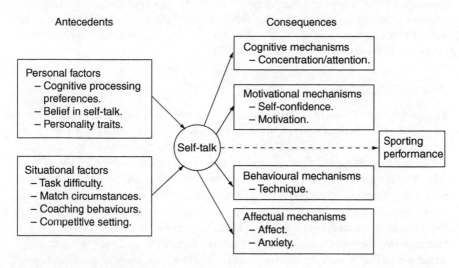

Figure 2.1 A framework for the study of self-talk.

statements that are addressed to the self, and not others (i.e. social speech), has interpretative elements associated with the content of the words employed and can serve at least two functions, including motivation and self-instruction (Hardy, 2006).

Within this chapter, we propose a framework to help more fully understand self-talk (see Figure 2.1). The framework presents potential antecedents of self-talk in the form of two general categories, namely situational and personal-level factors. Self-talk is proposed to affect a number of performance-oriented consequences (e.g. enhanced skill execution, strength), and this key element of the model is the focus of the present review. Additionally, the throughput model highlights a number of possible underpinning mechanisms that explain the self-talk/performance relationship, specifically categorised as cognitive, motivational, behavioural and affective variables. Literature, which examines the relationships presented by the throughput model, is then reviewed sequentially in this chapter.

Antecedents of self-talk

Despite an ever-increasing body of literature examining the effects and nature of self-talk, research investigating the antecedents of self-talk is relatively sparse (Hardy, 2006; Van Raalte *et al.*, 2000). This is perhaps not surprising given the absence of an established theoretical grounding for self-talk literature (Hardy, 2006), combined with a tendency for researchers to focus on the effects of self-talk on performance. Given the wide-reaching behavioural, motivational, affectual and cognitive consequences of self-talk presented in the current chapter, it is suggested that a greater understanding of the factors that shape and influence athletes' self-talk is required (Zourbanos *et al.*, 2006). The model presented within this chapter proposes two types of antecedents, personal and situational factors, which may influence athletes' self-talk.

Personal antecedents

The present subsection covers a number of personal-level antecedents to athletes' use of self-talk. The first individual-level antecedent is drawn from Paivio's (1971) dual coding theory. Individuals' cognitive processing preferences for encoding information is an aspect of this theory that has relevance to athletes' use of self-talk. Paivio proposed that each person prefers encoding and processing information either verbally or non-verbally. This can be equated to favouring information in the form of text and verbal instructions or visual demonstrations and imagery. Relative to mainstream psychology, processing preference has received limited attention in the sports domain (e.g. Thomas and Fogarty, 1997). For example, while a number of instruments have been developed to assess this preference in parental discipline (e.g. Ways of Thinking Questionnaire, Paivio; Individual Differences Questionnaire, Paivio and Harshman, 1983), an established measure of cognitive processing preference within the sporting context is absent. One of the few sports oriented studies is Thomas and Fogarty's field-based experiment that assessed whether golfers with a verbal or non-verbal preference would respond best to a self-talk or imagery intervention, respectively. Utilising a golf-specific measure of processing preference purposefully designed for their investigation (and as such "was not a valid measure of the verbaliser–visualizer tendency"; 1997: 101), the results did not offer support for their preference–intervention hypothesis. However, of relevance to self-talk in the present context is the hypothesis that athletes with a strong verbal cognitive processing preference would be likely to use self-talk more frequently than athletes with a strong non-verbal processing preference. Although this hypothesis may have intuitive appeal, research has yet to confirm it.

There is perhaps some overlap between the aforementioned antecedent (information-processing preference) and a second possible antecedent of self-talk, belief in self-talk. Studies of interventions in non-sporting contexts have suggested that a belief or expectancy about intervention effectiveness may be a precondition for it to be effective (e.g. Oikawa, 2004). From the limited literature focusing on belief in self-talk, it can be gleaned that athletes and participants in laboratory-based studies perceive that belief in self-talk is a relevant issue. For example, participants in a dynamic balancing study reported holding a reasonably strong belief (32.46 out of a maximum of 40) that their use of positive and negative self-talk impacted on performance (Araki *et al.*, 2006). Also, 70 per cent of those tennis players responding to a questionnaire item about the influence of their self-talk believed that self-talk influenced the outcome of their matches (Van Raalte *et al.*, 1994). That believers won more points than non-believers offers support for the tennis players' self-report responses. While it is possible that belief in self-talk may be a moderator of the effectiveness of self-talk interventions (Thomas and Fogarty, 1997), we are aware of only one study that has examined whether belief in self-talk is related to athletes' use of the mental skill. Van Raalte *et al.* (1994) found that believers and non-believers did not differ in the amount of observable self-talk they employed during their competitive tennis matches. Amongst other issues (e.g. relatively incomplete measurement of self-talk), it is possible that a small sample size ($N = 23$) may have contributed to this lack of support for belief in self-talk as an antecedent of the use of self-talk.

The possible individual antecedents addressed so far are quite specific to self-talk. However, there are some emerging data to support the notion that more global personality traits might be related to the use of self-talk by athletes. For example, Perry and Marsh (2000) discussed a situation concerning extremely negative self-talk displayed by an elite swimmer. They surmise that it was the swimmer's negative self-concept that helped to explain the self-talk exhibited. Another example of a personality-oriented antecedent of self-talk is trait anxiety. Conroy and Metzler (2004) applied Benjamin's (1996) Structural Analysis of Social Behaviour (SASB) tiered circumplex model of self-concept to assess recreational athletes' use of self-talk. However, these researchers also measured three forms of trait anxiety, and demonstrated a relationship between anxiety and state use of self-talk. Specifically, self-talk was most strongly associated with fear of failure and sport anxiety, and mildly correlated with fear of success. For example, SASB specific negative self-talk categories (e.g. self-blame, self-attack) were positively related to fear of failure, whereas positive self-talk categories (e.g. self-affirm, self-protect) were negatively correlated to fear of failure. While both self-concept and forms of anxiety may be antecedents of self-talk, preliminary evidence suggests that a motivation-based personality disposition, achievement goal orientation, might be another. This is because Harwood *et al.* (2004) found that elite junior athletes with a higher-task/moderate-ego goal profile used significantly more positive self-talk in practice and competition compared to athletes with lower-task/higher-ego and moderate-task/lower-ego goal orientation dispositions. Given that many of the findings reviewed in the present subsection were generated from investigations that were unable to establish causal relationships (e.g. cross-sectional questionnaire designs), additional research is needed to test the above conceptualising. Furthermore, drawing from the personality research, it would also seem prudent to understand the role of situational factors contributing to athletes' use of self-talk.

Situational antecedents

Research that examines the effects of situational factors on the use and content of self-talk has focused specifically on issues such as task difficulty (e.g. Behrend *et al.*, 1989), match circumstances (e.g. Van Raalte *et al.*, 2000) and the influence of significant others (e.g. Zourbanos *et al.*, 2006). A consistent finding in mainstream psychological research is of a quadratic relationship between task difficulty and private speech (i.e. overt self-talk), in that the greatest use of private speech is observed on moderately difficult tasks (Behrend *et al.*, 1989; Ferneyhough and Fradley, 2005). Furthermore, Ferneyhough and Fradley found some support for their proposal that, in line with Vygotsky's (1962) theoretical propositions, self-talk primarily serves a self-regulatory function. As such, self-talk is used to cope with more difficult tasks but is less likely to be employed for tasks that are perceived as too hard or for which no strategies have been learned or developed. In addition to examining if these results apply to sporting tasks, researchers could also examine if task difficulty influences athletes' self-talk valence (i.e. do difficult tasks stimulate negative self-talk?).

Evidence from a sporting context provides some support for an effect of match circumstances on the use of self-talk. Van Raalte *et al.* (2000) investigated antecedents of tennis players' positive and negative self-talk and found that match circumstances, such as point outcome or serving status, were related to the likelihood of subsequent self-talk. Specifically, logistic regressions identified that negative self-talk was predicted by match circumstance for all participants, and that 78 per cent of participants used more negative self-talk following a lost point. Additionally, Van Raalte *et al.* reported that match circumstances predicted use of positive and instructional self-talk for 61 per cent and 28 per cent of participants, respectively. Although Van Raalte *et al.*'s findings should be interpreted with caution (due to the aforementioned reasons, e.g. only observable self-talk assessed), it seems reasonable to propose that in a sport setting match circumstances and progress within a game can have an effect on self-talk. This hypothesis is further supported by findings from a study carried out with recreational physical activity participants. Conroy and Metzler (2004) found that participants used more positive and fewer negative types of self-talk while succeeding compared to when they were failing. Specifically, while succeeding, participants reported that they used more self-emancipating, self-affirming, self-protecting and self-controlling self-talk, and less self-blaming, self-attacking and self-neglecting self-talk. At least one other research finding has relevance to match circumstances impacting on the use of self-talk. Hardy *et al.* (2004) found that athletes reported an increase in the frequency of self-talk use from pre-season through the competitive season. In explaining this result, they suggested that such increases coincided with an increase in the importance of matches. In addition, the increased usage of self-talk was reflective of an enhanced allocation of mental resources when the situation was deemed important or the task is more difficult (i.e. at critical stages of the season).

An additional situational factor that may influence the use and content of self-talk is the presence and behaviour of those around the athlete, especially significant others. Research with pre-school children has shown that they produce a greater frequency of private speech in the presence of significant others, such as mothers (Behrend *et al.*, 1989). Additionally, in educational environments, teachers' negative statements have been associated with an increased frequency of negative self-talk in male students, and teachers' positive statements with an increase in positive self-talk in both male and female students (Burnett, 1999).

Interestingly, it was also found that students' self-talk mediated the relationship between the feedback received from teachers and changes in students' self-concept, highlighting the importance of understanding the relationships between the causes and effects of self-talk. More recently, Lantolf (2006) proposed a model in which a fundamental aspect of language acquisition involves modelling or imitation, suggesting that language used in private speech is modelled from the social speech of others. This echoes Bandura's (1977, 1982) social learning theory wherein behaviours are modelled and learnt from those around the individual. Taken together, the studies described above would seem to imply that the behaviour and use of language by significant others may be an important precursor of athletes' self-talk.

Within sport, coaches are frequently considered an influential "significant other", therefore it seems important to consider their effect on athletes' self-talk. Cross-cultural findings suggest that coaches promote the use of positive self-talk by their athletes and perceive it to be an effective confidence-enhancing intervention (e.g. Weinberg *et al.*, 1992). However, there appears to be conflicting evidence regarding the potential influence of a coach on athletes' reported use of self-talk. For example, Hardy and Hall (2006) identified that the majority of athletes (61 per cent) report that their coaches have previously promoted self-talk, and that the reasons why self-talk was encouraged (e.g. to increase confidence, to improve concentration) were similar to the reasons why the athletes themselves used self-talk. Nonetheless, Hardy and Hall found that perceived coaches' promotion of self-talk was unrelated to the frequency of athletes' self-talk. In contrast, in a study with Greek athletes, Zourbanos *et al.* (2006) found that coaches' negative activation behaviours, including distracting athletes or acting inappropriately, were directly related to athletes' thoughts of failure and negative self-talk. A related study by the same authors (Zourbanos *et al.*, 2007) found evidence that coaches' statements to their athletes mediated the coach behaviour/self-talk association. In particular, whereas supportive behaviour predicted positive coach statements, which in turn predicted athletes' positive self-talk, negative behaviour was positively associated with negative coaching statements that were subsequently correlated with negative self-talk (Zourbanos *et al.*, 2007). Taken together, these findings may suggest that it is the actual behaviour of coaches, rather than their endorsement of particular strategies, which is most strongly related to athletes' self-talk. That coaching behaviours impact on athletes' use of self-talk concurs with Lawrence and Valsiner's (2003) model of self-talk, in which self-talk is proposed to be a mechanism through which social influences and social messages are evaluated and internalised by the individual.

Although currently under-researched, it is worth considering that the presence and behaviour of team-mates and opponents may also influence athletes' use of self-talk. It seems plausible that social learning may take place between team members, and if, for example, a respected team captain is observed using self-talk, this may increase the likelihood of other athletes adopting this strategy. We are currently unaware of any research that directly supports this proposition; however, some findings hint that this (i.e. the presence or absence of others) may be an area of interest to explore. Hardy *et al.* (2005b) identified that individual sport athletes make greater use of the functions of self-talk than team sport athletes, possibly due to an increased reliance on oneself for feedback or encouragement during a game. Additionally, Gould and Weiss (1981) found that subjects who observed a model using positive self-talk had enhanced performances relative to those who observed the use of negative or irrelevant self-talk, and that self-efficacy did not mediate this relationship. It is possible that subjects could have adopted the observed positive self-talk strategy, which in turn could have resulted in enhanced performance, although this was not measured.

A final situational factor impacting on self-talk is the competitive setting. Athletes have reported using more self-talk in competition than during practice (Hardy *et al.*, 2005b), and there is some emerging self-presentation-related evidence to suggest that this could be explained by the presence of an opponent. Van Raalte *et al.* (2006) conducted an experimental study that involved dubbing positive, negative or neutral self-talk over video footage of tennis players. They found that players shown with dubbed positive self-talk were perceived as being better players than when negative or neutral self-talk was used, and proposed that athletes may use self-talk to enhance their self-presentation. Given that self-presentation strategies (e.g. portraying a fresh and upbeat image towards the end of a long tennis match) may be most relevant to the competition setting, the findings of Hardy *et al.* (2005b) may lend some support to Van Raalte *et al.*'s suggestion. However, it could be argued that overt speech is not truly self-talk if it is purposely directed or addressed to someone else. It may be that self-presentational aspects represent a secondary function of some kinds of self-talk, rather than their primary purpose.

From the situational-based research discussed above, it is apparent that, regardless of whether the content of self-talk explicitly relates to the environment, situational factors can influence the frequency and nature of self-talk, and therefore potentially its effect on performance. However, given the limited investigation of the antecedents of self-talk within the sporting domain, more in-depth examination of the aforementioned (individual and situational) antecedents is warranted, as well as the identification of alternative candidates (e.g. perceived competence). In addition, although individual and situational antecedents were presented separately, it is likely that both groupings of preceding factors interact to influence athletes' use of self-talk. One such potential interaction worthy of future examination is between perceived competence and success/failure situations on the production and response to negative self-talk. As stated previously, one of the contributing factors for the lack of research focusing on self-talk's antecedents is that the relationship between self-talk and performance has traditionally received far greater attention by researchers.

Self-talk and performance

Central to our framework is the self-talk/performance relationship. Given that applied sport psychologists have long advocated the use of self-talk as a performance-enhancement strategy (e.g. Harris and Harris, 1984), it should not come as a surprise that a common emphasis in the self-talk literature has been its association with sporting performance. As a result, a diverse set of methodo-logical approaches have been employed, and both variables have been opera-tionalised in a number of different ways. Somewhat in line with Kerlinger's (1986) view of science in the behavioural sciences, the present review of the self-talk/performance literature has been organised into two categories repre-senting the findings of descriptive and experimental designed studies.

Descriptive research

In qualitative interviews, athletes have indicated a belief that self-talk influences their competitive performance (e.g. Gould *et al.*, 1992a, b). Although such study designs cannot generate evidence that self-talk is related to performance, this finding offers insight into the likelihood that athletes will be receptive to learn-ing about the technique. Nonetheless there is evidence to suggest that belief in self-talk is related to enhanced performance (e.g. Hardy *et al.*, 2004; Van Raalte *et al.*, 1994). Alternatively, there is also evidence to suggest that belief in self-talk is not as strongly linked with performance as the type of self-talk employed (e.g. Araki *et al.*, 2006). Researchers adopting quantitative descriptive designs have found relationships between various types of self-reported self-talk and measures of performance (e.g. Mahoney and Avener, 1977; Rotella *et al.*, 1980). In an early study, for example, divers chosen to compete in the Pan American Games reported using more self-instruction during competition than non-qualifiers (Highlen and Bennett, 1983). Non-qualifiers reported praising themselves more than qualifiers. Perhaps these results indicate that during competition athletes benefit from having task-relevant thoughts (that might be provided via instruc-tional self-talk) rather than non-task-relevant thoughts (even if in the form of self-praise). Qualifiers also reported engaging in more self-talk during training and competition than non-qualifiers, and engaging in more positive self-talk prior to competition.

The above-cited studies involved the use of paper and pencil questionnaires to measure self-talk. Some investigators have adopted observational or think-aloud techniques (e.g. Baker *et al.*, 2005). Using observational techniques with junior tennis players, Van Raalte *et al.* (1994) found that, although negative self-talk was positively associated with losing, positive self-talk was not signific-antly related to winning. It was suggested that positive self-talk was more likely to be internalised and, as such, not measured by the observational technique employed. In a subsequent study with adult players, Van Raalte *et al.* (2000) found that at an individual-participant level self-talk predicted the outcome of the following point for just a small proportion of the sample. From their sample of 18 individuals, positive self-talk predicted performance significantly for two players and approached significance for one person. The authors concluded that positive self-talk appeared to increase the likelihood of losing the next point for two players and winning the next rally for one person. For one individual, negative self-talk approached significance for increasing the likelihood of winning the next point. Finally, instructional self-talk increased the likelihood for one player of losing the following rally. Perhaps it is understandable that self-talk did not frequently predict competitive performance outcome, given the number of other variables that may potentially determine the outcome of a tennis rally.

Generally, the findings of descriptive research have hinted at a relationship between reported self-talk use and performance. A number of factors have clouded a more concrete understanding of this possible relationship, including equivocal findings and inconsistent conceptualisation and measurement of self-talk. One way to enhance the quality of descriptive research is to develop valid and reliable self-talk measures that are supported by substantial psychometric evidence. Such questionnaires have only recently been developed and are still undergoing validation, such as the Self-Talk Questionnaire (S-TQ; Zervas et al., 2007) or the positive self-talk sub-scale of the Test of Psychological Strategies (Thomas et al., 1999). Both of these instruments have the advantage of focusing on specific aspects of self-talk as well as being multi-item measures of self-talk, unlike the Self-Talk Use Questionnaire (Hardy et al., 2005b). One aspect of the psychometric testing process could include calibration against behaviour and events in people's lives (Andersen et al., 2007; Sechrest et al., 1996). Calibration involves representing research measures in metrics that are understandable and meaningful, and helps with the interpretation of research findings. For example, how large does the difference between scores on a self-talk questionnaire need to be before a demonstrable difference in self-confidence can be expected? As another example, how much do athletes need to increase their amount of self-talk before a change in skill execution will occur?

The successful development of inventories such as the S-TQ holds great promise for the area of self-talk; however, as descriptive investigations generate co-relational data, it is difficult to infer that self-talk actually influences performance. Experimental evidence is needed for such conclusions. This, along with the conceptualisation of applied self-talk interventions as independent variables, might explain why much of the research focused on the self-talk and performance relationship has employed experimental designs. The next section reviews these studies.

Experimental research

In many experimental investigations, self-talk has been included as part of a multi-intervention package, with results indicating that such approaches are associated with enhanced skill execution and improved psychological states (e.g. Cumming et al., 2006; Hanton and Jones, 1999; Thelwell et al., 2006). However, studies employing mental-skill packages provide limited evidence that a particular mental skill, such as self-talk, is helpful on its own, even if it was the primary intervention (e.g. Elko and Ostrow, 1991). The investigations relevant to this section are those that have generated data about self-talk in its exclusivity.

A number of researchers have conducted experimental studies and the majority have provided some evidence that self-talk leads to improved skill execution (e.g. Dagrou and Gauvin, 1992; Perkos *et al.*, 2002; Ziegler, 1987). Many of the supporting studies have used sound research-design principles such as the inclusion of control groups, manipulation checks, random allocation of participants and counterbalanced interventions (e.g. Hatzigeorgiadis *et al.*, 2004; Johnson *et al.*, 2004; Weinberg *et al.*, 1984). However, a relatively narrow range of tasks have been utilised, as approximately two-thirds of studies have involved coordination or precision-based skills such as darts throwing (e.g. Masciana *et al.*, 2001), soccer shooting (e.g. Papaioannou *et al.*, 2004), basketball shooting (e.g. Theodorakis *et al.*, 2001) or swimming (e.g. Rushall, and Shewchuk, 1989). The remaining studies have largely examined endurance or strength-based tasks (e.g. Theodorakis *et al.*, 2000, Studies 3 and 4; Weinberg *et al.*, 1984). Future investigations might also consider examining the influence of self-talk on (a) contact power-based skills, such as tackling in rugby league; (b) artistic skills, such as floor routines in gymnastics; and (c) skills that involve interaction with teammates, such as scrummaging in rugby union.

Researchers have explored the effects of different types of self-talk on performance, with the most common being instructional, motivational, positive and negative self-talk. Instructional self-talk includes those statements designed to enhance performance by stimulating correct actions via proper attentional focus and movement patterns (Theodorakis *et al.*, 2000). Instructional self-talk has been the type of self-talk most frequently investigated experimentally. When compared to control conditions, instructional self-talk seems to enhance the performance of a number of tasks including those associated with badminton (e.g. Theodorakis *et al.*, 2000, Study 2), basketball (e.g. Perkos *et al.*, 2002), soccer (e.g. Theodorakis *et al.*, 2000, Study 1) and tennis (e.g. Cutton and Landin, 2007; Ziegler, 1987). For example, Ziegler found that instructional self-talk led to increased rates of forehand and backhand returns for tennis beginners. Additionally, Landin and Hebert (1999) found that skilled varsity-standard tennis players improved their execution of volleying at the net following the use of the cue words "split" and "turn". However, Harvey *et al.* (2002) found that golf pitching accuracy did not differ between instructional self-talk and control conditions, although pitching consistency was enhanced via instructional self-talk compared to both negative self-talk and control conditions.

In an attempt to more closely examine the effects of instructional self-talk, Theodorakis *et al.* (2000) proposed a task-demand-oriented matching hypothesis. They postulated that instructional self-talk would be better suited to skill, timing or precision-based tasks than motivational self-talk, whereas motivational self-talk would be optimal for strength or endurance-based movements. Motivational self-talk refers to statements designed to help performance via building confidence, enhancing effort, increasing energy expenditure and creating a positive mood (Theodorakis *et al.*, 2000). An increasing number of studies have tested this task-demand matching hypothesis. With regard to skill, timing or precision-based tasks, instructional self-talk has been found to improve soccer passing and badminton French short serve execution as compared with motivational self-talk and control conditions (Theodorakis *et al.*, 2000, Studies 1 and 2). Both instructional and motivational self-talk have led to improved water polo throw accuracy, although the effect of instructional self-talk was stronger than motivational self-talk (Cohen's *d* effect sizes 1.39 vs 0.99, respectively; Hatzigeorgiadis *et al.*, 2004, Study 1). However, with regard to endurance or strength-based tasks, motivational self-talk has improved water polo throwing distance in comparison to instructional self-talk and control conditions (Hatzigeorgiadis *et al.*, 2004, Study 2). Both instructional and motivational self-talk, as compared against control conditions, improved vertical jump height (Tod *et al.*, 2007) and knee-extension strength (Theodorakis *et al.*, 2000, Study 4). Finally, no differences on a three-minute endurance sit-up task were reported between instructional self-talk, motivational self-talk and control conditions, although all three groups improved across the three trials (Theodorakis *et al.*, 2000, Study 3). If one accepts Theodorakis *et al.*'s (2000) proposition that positive self-talk can be equated with motivational self-talk, then there are some equivocal findings from additional studies that contribute to the evaluation of the task-demands matching hypothesis (e.g. Harvey *et al.*, 2002; Rushall and Shewchuk, 1989). In summary, the supportive results for the use of instructional self-talk have been obtained across a variety of tasks, and using participants from novice (e.g. Anderson *et al.*, 1999) to skilled (e.g. Landin and Hebert, 1999; Mallet and Hanrahan, 1997) performers. Concerning the task-demands matching hypothesis, at the moment there appears to be greater support for the use of instructional self-talk for relatively fine motor-skill tasks than for the use of motivational self-talk for more gross motor-skill tasks. Given the important applied implications of this hypothesis, additional research is warranted.

Similar trends have emerged from the experimental study of positive self-talk as those from the assessment of instructional self-talk. There is experimental evidence that suggests that, when compared against a control condition, positive self-talk enhances skill performance across a variety of tasks and skill levels (Masciana *et al.*, 2001; Rushall and Shewchuk, 1989; Tynes and McFatter, 1987), although there are also non-supporting results (Harvey *et al.*, 2002; Tenenbaum *et al.*, 1995; Weinberg *et al.*, 1984). Masciana *et al.* (2001), for example, found that positive self-talk led to better dart-throwing performance compared with physical instruction-drilling and a Zen-based approach. In the Zen-based approach, participants were asked to not use any particular strategy but remain in an everyday frame of mind and allow performance to emerge without anticipation, expectation or rehearsal. As another example, national-standard skiers utilising positive self-talk significantly improved cross-country skiing performance compared with the control condition (Rushall *et al.*, 1988). In contrast to these supportive findings, Weinberg *et al.* (1984, Study 1) found no differences between positive self-talk and a no-intervention control for distance running. Also, Harvey *et al.* (2002) did not find differences between positive self-talk and a control condition for golf-pitching accuracy or consistency. Researchers have also compared the effects of positive and negative self-talk with some equivocal results emerging. Van Raalte *et al.* (1995) replicated Dagrou *et al.*'s (1992) supportive findings for the benefits of positive self-talk for a darts-throwing task; however, Harvey *et al.* did not find differences between positive and negative self-talk for pitching accuracy and consistency with experienced golfers.

One possible explanation for the mixed results from the examination of positive versus negative self-talk could be related to athletes' individual differences with regard to how they motivationally interpret the content of their self-talk. Hardy *et al.* (2001b) found that a number of high-school athletes reported the use of very negative self-talk prior to practice and competition settings that was in fact very motivating for themselves. This supports the suggestion by Goodhart (1986) that negative self-statements can be encouraging and Van Raalte *et al.*'s (1995) finding that participants assigned to a negative self-talk group held higher expectations concerning future performance. Although what constitutes positive/negative self-talk should be governed by the content of the statements used, whether those statements are detrimental or beneficial for performance probably varies across individuals. To accommodate such a possibility, initial attempts have been made to allow performers to generate their own self-talk, but again results have been mixed (Hamilton *et al.*, 2007; Harvey *et al.*, 2002; Rushall *et al.*, 1988; Rushall and Shewchuk, 1989). While Hamilton *et al.* reported greater improvement of stationary cycle endurance performance for self-selected positive as compared to self-selected negative self-talk, Harvey *et al.* reported findings supportive of a null hypothesis.

The relationship between positive self-talk and performance may not be understood fully until researchers have explored further the interactions between self-talk content and athletes' interpretations of that content. In the studies that assessed the effects of self-selected self-talk, participants have received guidance in the selection of self-talk cues, along with examples, and this may not represent truly self-selected self-talk. In addition, if participants are given self-talk examples by an investigator during their performance of tasks (e.g. Hamilton *et al.*, 2007), then the study may actually be examining the influence of verbal encouragement in combination with self-talk on performance rather than self-talk exclusively. It may be difficult to examine truly self-selected self-talk experimentally, however, because researchers lose some control over their intervention groups.

There are a number of design issues to consider when evaluating the results from experimental research. The first, as mentioned previously, is that the relatively narrow range of tasks employed may limit the generalisability of previous findings. The second factor (also related to generalisability) refers to the types of individuals used as participants. While over half the studies have employed students or novices as participants, the remaining studies have used individuals ranging from those with some experience (junior-level athletes) to highly skilled, experienced competitors (national-level athletes). Findings from such a diverse sample of research participants provides support for the use of self-talk to improve motor-skill execution for a range of athletes.

The third issue has relevance to ecological validity and refers to the setting within which data has been collected. The overwhelming majority of research has taken place in non-competitive situations. Some attempts have been made to assess competitive performance, but generally limited evidence has emerged that performance has improved within this setting (e.g. Johnson *et al.*, 2004; Landin and Hebert, 1999; Maynard *et al.*, 1995). For example, Johnson *et al.* focused on football goal-shooting but concluded they were unable to collect enough data to assess the effects of self-talk in competition. As another example, Landin and Hebert's tennis volleying study obtained supplementary data indicating that post-intervention female tennis players approached the net more often in competition. The physical and psychological demands placed on athletes most likely vary between practice and competition. Consequently, it cannot be assumed that the results from the current research transfer to the competitive environment, and this is an area for future investigation.

Athletes, however, do not report employing self-talk solely to enhance competitive performance. As reflected by the functions of self-talk (cf. Hardy *et al.*, 2001a, b), self-talk may be used for a variety of reasons such as to build self-confidence, reduce anxiety and enhance skill learning – highly pertinent to the practice setting. Examination of the self-talk and performance literature provides evidence that it leads to enhanced skill execution and there are two possible competitive performance oriented implications for athletes. First, self-talk seems to assist individuals to acquire and master technical skills quicker, and such accelerated learning may enhance aspects that contribute to overall competitive performance, such as line-out jumping in rugby union. Second, as self-talk (especially motivational self-talk) helps individuals to produce higher levels of strength or endurance, if this were achieved in the practice setting, then over time such training may help athletes become better conditioned for their sports. In many situations, it may be somewhat naive to ask if self-talk enhances overall competitive performance given the various factors that may influence athletic outcome. Instead, researchers may be able to offer practitioners and athletes more useful guidelines if they focus on specific components that contribute to overall competitive performance (e.g. can self-talk help a weightlifter train at a higher intensity?).

A fourth design issue concerns the use of control groups and manipulation checks. In Hardy *et al.* (2005a), manipulation checks revealed that a priori groups were not obtained. Participants in the experimental groups used both instructional and motivational self-talk strategies they had been assigned as well as other types of inner dialogue. Also, most control participants used self-talk spontaneously. In a more recent study, participants were asked to say their self-talk cues out loud (in Hardy *et al.*, 2005a, participants used self-talk covertly) and manipulation checks indicated that the majority, although still not all, participants had used just their assigned self-talk cues (Tod *et al.*, 2007). These studies highlight the difficulty in forming distinct experimental groups. Potentially, in previous research, where no differences between self-talk conditions have been observed, the results might reflect that separate groups were not

formed. As Hardy *et al.* (2005a) noted, researchers have typically asked participants how frequently they employed their assigned verbal cue. Such manipulation checks do not assess if participants also made use of additional self-talk
cues. At a minimum, investigators should employ manipulation checks allowing
participants to report all their self-talk cues and use of other strategies, such as
imagery. Researchers might then be in a position to discard participants from
their sample in order to form distinct groups. Alternatively, investigators could
form groups based on ratios, such as those individuals who report 75 per cent of
their self-talk as instructional in nature (Hardy *et al.*, 2005a).

Overall, the research to date would indicate that self-talk can influence
performance. As highlighted, there are some limitations to the existing literature that has examined the self-talk/performance relationship; research in this
area has not been exhausted. However, it may be of greater importance for
researchers to now also consider second-phase research questions addressing
potential moderators and mediators of this relationship. Not only might this
allow a better understanding of the self-talk/performance relationship but also
provide much needed research-based guidance for practitioners.

Underpinning mechanisms

A number of researchers have made reference to possible mediating mechanisms
that might help to explain the self-talk/performance relationship (e.g. Hardy
et al., 1996). As can be seen in Figure 2.1, we have clustered the potential underpinning mechanisms into four groups reflecting cognitive, motivational, behavioural and affective processes. Although pertinent literature is reviewed for each
mechanism separately, it is likely that the underpinning explanations work in
tandem. Of those mechanisms discussed, it is the cognitively oriented explanations of the self-talk/performance relationship that have received most attention
from self-talk researchers.

Cognitive mechanisms

While the term "cognitive mechanisms" is rather vague, we have employed it here
to specifically reflect processes such as information processing, concentration,
attention control and attentional style; all of which athletes, coaches, consultants
and researchers value highly for effective performance. For example, the prominent attention-oriented sports-psychology researcher, Bruce Abernethy, stated
that "it is difficult to imagine that there can be anything more important to the
learning and performance of sport skills than paying attention" (2001: 53). Over
the years, a number of self-talk researchers have proposed self-talk to be an effective technique for enhancing athletes' concentration levels and that attention
might be a mechanism to help explain how self-talk can influence performance
(e.g. Hatzigeorgiadis *et al.*, 2004; Landin, 1994; Landin and Herbert, 1999). For
example, Landin proposed that verbal cues could be used to increase focus as well
as to direct and redirect performers' attention.

In support for the above proposition, junior tennis players reported that their use of self-talk positively influenced their concentration (Van Raalte et al., 1994). Descriptive qualitative findings from Hardy et al. indicated that by far the most commonly cited reason why athletes who represented their universities employed self-talk was to aid their concentration (e.g. "to clear my mind and focus on the task at hand"; 2001a: 315). A quantitative follow-up study found that a diverse set of athletes made use of self-talk to assist their focus very frequently, although significantly more frequently in conjunction with competition as compared to practice settings (Hardy et al., 2005b). Moreover, a number of experimental studies have assessed participants' perceptions with regard to concentration following self-talk interventions (e.g. Perkos et al., 2002). For example, through the use of post-experimental check questionnaires, participants have consistently endorsed the use of self-talk cues to improve concentration for the learning of basketball skills (Chroni et al., 2007; Perkos et al., 2002) as well as throwing and jumping track and field events (Goudas et al., 2006).

Taken together, while the aforementioned findings offer preliminary support that self-talk and concentration are positively related to one another, it is only through the inclusion of pre-/post-intervention measures that studies can illustrate improvements in concentration. Although not the main focus of their study, Hatzigeorgiadis et al. (2007) reported a significant decline in the number of interfering thoughts (or inappropriate attention) following a self-talk intervention. This finding replicates the results of an earlier study by Hatzigeorgiadis et al. (2004) which, importantly, included a control group. Again, a significant reduction in the number of interfering thoughts was reported for both instructional and motivational self-talk groups compared to the control group. The investigators equated this to an improvement in concentration during task execution. These findings offer insights into cognitively oriented mechanisms of the self-talk/performance relationship, especially as performance was enhanced by the self-talk intervention, and that interfering thoughts were correlated to performance of the precision-throwing task. However, it is worthwhile to make note of two issues: first, it is possible that a reduction in the occurrence of a negative event, interfering thoughts, is an indirect measure of concentration and does not automatically equate to an improvement in the occurrence of a positive event, increased concentration. Second, neither the aforementioned post-experimental endorsement nor the interfering-thoughts approach assess an especially pertinent aspect of concentration – the focus of attention on task-relevant stimuli (Hardy et al., 1996). For example, it is possible for a defender in football to concentrate intensely on the ball during a high long-ball pass made by the opposition, instead of paying attention to the run being made by the attacker s/he should be marking. This example illustrates the importance of an appropriate focus of attention and, in particular, how an athlete can fully attend to the task at hand but not necessarily to the most relevant task stimuli.

A number of researchers have theorised that self-talk can assist athletes to focus on task-relevant stimuli (e.g. Landin, 1994) and have forwarded Nideffer's (1976) conceptualisation of attentional style as a framework to better understand attention. Nideffer conceptualised attentional style along two dimensions: (a) width, ranging from narrow (a few stimuli) to broad (many stimuli); and (b) direction, ranging from internal (thoughts and feelings) to external (events occurring around the athlete). These two dimensions form four attentional styles or foci; narrow-internal, narrow-external, broad-internal and broad-external. Given that with different situations the use of different attentional styles are required, and that most sporting environments are fairly dynamic, there is a need to be able to maintain, intensify and change attentional focus optimally. Ziegler (1987) stated that knowing how to pay attention is as equally important as knowing what to attend to for task execution. It is possible that self-talk may be one tool to help athletes achieve these aims (Hardy, 2006; Landin, 1994). Although, to date, we are unaware of a published self-talk study that has explicitly measured the concept of different foci of attention, Ziegler (1987) designed a verbal self-directed stimulus cueing technique (self-talk intervention) around the dynamic attentional phases of successful tennis groundstroke execution. The verbal cues reflected the source of the stimulus ("ball"), direction of the ball ("bounce"), contact with the ball ("hit") and preparation for the next ball ("ready"). As Perkos et al. (2002) stated, the four phases reflect a changing of attentional focus from broad-external to narrow-external and back to broad-external again. Ziegler reported an accelerated rate of learning for both shot technique and execution. Researchers have also demonstrated that participants quite strongly endorse the utilisation of self-talk as a technique to enhance appropriate attention during football (Johnson et al., 2004), tennis (Landin and Hebert, 1999) and water-polo (e.g. Hatzigeorgiadis et al., 2004) tasks. In fact, at least two studies have highlighted that self-talk might work through an attention mechanism, regardless of the type of self-talk employed (i.e. instructional or motivational; Hatzigeorgiadis, 2006; Hatzigeorgiadis et al., 2004). This is an interesting finding as Hardy (2006) hypothesised that instructional self-talk would have greatest relevance to attentional focus. Why a motivational cue such as "I can" should decrease the number of interfering thoughts to the same extent as instructional cues offering specific task execution information is currently unclear. One possible explanation might be linked to the general and somewhat vague manner in which concentration has been operationalised thus far. For example, the above studies have been quite vague about what exactly their participants have focused on (e.g. "It got me more mentally into what I was doing" (Landin and Hebert, 1999: 277): "concentrate on what I had to do" (Hatzigeorgiadis et al., 2007: 243)).

Borrowing from the more recent focus-of-attention literature might offer guidance for future self-talk/attention-oriented research. Inspection of this literature indicates two broad foci: an internal focus of attention involves concentration on movements of the body, whereas an external focus refers to the performer attending to the *effects* of the body's action (Wulf and Prinz, 2001). Research on attentional focus (e.g. Wulf et al., 2000) suggests that the adoption of an external focus of attention is associated with superior learning of motor skills over an internal focus of attention. Using skilled golfers (handicap < 9),

Bell (2006) examined whether or not attentional focus during a chipping task could be manipulated via an instructional cue-word intervention. The lack of support for his self-talk/attentional focus hypotheses (e.g. internally oriented self-talk would lead to the adaptation of an internal focus of attention) was explained by the nature of his participants. The golfers recruited were skilled and experienced; consequently, due to a habitual use of a particular attentional focus, they may have been desensitised to the effects of focus cues different to the focus of attention they typically employed.

The aforementioned study highlights a relevant issue to the study of self-talk and attention: much of the research so far has employed relative novices as participants. Although not in itself a concern, it does limit the generalisability of the research findings. Nonetheless, it has been suggested that the use of self-talk as a tool to attend to relevant task cues may have greatest pertinence for those at earlier stages of learning (Hatzigeorgiadis *et al.*, 2007). The following quotation from Ziegler's tennis study supports this sentiment as well as hinting at a possible explanation: "The strength of the cueing [self-talk] technique may be in accelerating initial skill acquisition and not in reacting to the more complex demands in the actual competitive tennis environment" (1987: 410). Landin (1994) applied the work of Wrisberg (1993) to further expand upon why the self-talk/attention association may be particularly relevant for beginners. Wrisberg noted three functions/stages of information processing that could positively influence performance. The first stage involves the processing of perceptual information, whereby skilled athletes automatically search through the array of information facing them; self-talk was proposed to assist novice performers in the search and identification of relevant stimuli. Decisions about how best to respond relates to the second stage of processing. While skilled athletes are able to quickly select the most appropriate response, self-talk might assist beginners' decision-making by reducing the number of options they have to choose from. The final information-processing stage involves the *initiation* of correct movement patterns following decision-making. Self-talk was proposed to assist the athlete to best ready the body for action (e.g. a sprinter saying "set") as well as help "chunk" complex information sequences which then require less attention to perform. The self-talk/attention research conducted to date offers some, albeit preliminary, support for the contention that self-talk might be particularly relevant for beginners, as much of the research carried out, which has happened to employ novice participants, supports the proposition of a causal relationship between self-talk and attention/concentration.

In summary, the present subsection reviewed research and theory relevant to possible cognitive mechanisms underpinning the self-talk/performance relationship. In particular, it illustrates how the increasing body of literature has progressed and preliminarily substantiates the hypothesis (at least at a general level) that concentration-oriented processes might help to explain how self-talk can assist skill execution. It is recommended that further in-depth examination of the aforementioned cognitive process is warranted. Future research should incorporate various measures of attention (e.g. eye gaze, psycho-physiological variables) which will allow more in-depth assessment of athletes' focus of attention. This, in turn, should afford a better understanding of the self-talk/performance relationship.

Motivational mechanisms

The model presented within the current chapter proposes that motivational mechanisms may also mediate the self-talk/performance relationship. Coaches, physical educators and sport psychologists have long recognised the importance of maximising motivation (Likang, 2004), and the link between motivational factors and performance has previously been established in multiple domains, including sport (Scully and Lowry, 2002), education (Shui-Fong and Yin-Kum, 2007) and business (Day and Allen, 2004). Additionally, athletes have reported using self-talk for motivational functions (e.g. Hardy *et al.*, 2001a), and have shown a preference for using motivational types of self-talk (Goudas *et al.*, 2006). This subsection of the chapter will focus on the influence of self-talk on two specific motivational factors, namely self-efficacy and persistence.

Self-efficacy theory (Bandura, 1997) provides a possible framework to underpin the effects of self-talk on motivational and performance outcomes (Hardy, 2006). Self-efficacy can be viewed as a situational-specific form of self-confidence, and has attracted a wealth of attention in sport-psychology literature over the past four decades. Self-efficacy has a moderate positive association with performance (Moritz *et al.*, 2003) and has also been associated with enhanced effort (Weinberg, 1986), positive affect (Brown *et al.*, 2005) and long-term behavioural persistence (McAuley *et al.*, 2007). Self-efficacy is conceptualised as a motivational variable as it has been proposed to influence the initiation of behaviour, effort and persistence following failure (Lane *et al.*, 2002). Bandura's (1997) theory proposes four antecedents to self-efficacy, namely mastery experience, vicarious experience, emotional arousal and verbal persuasion. It is suggested that self-talk may influence self-efficacy by acting as a form of self-delivered verbal persuasion, and that positive self-talk, for example, might increase self-efficacy, and subsequent effort, persistence and performance (Hardy, 2006).

Cross-cultural research has shown that positive self-talk is widely perceived and promoted as an effective strategy to enhance athletes' self-efficacy (Weinberg *et al.*, 1992). However, thus far only limited research has explored this relationship, and although initial findings appear promising, there are some contradictory results. For example, Hardy *et al.* (2005a) found that participants' valence of self-talk was positively correlated with their self-efficacy to carry out a sit-up task. Furthermore, intervention package studies involving self-talk have resulted in increases in athletes' self-confidence (e.g. Mamassis and Doganis, 2004; Thelwell and Greenlees, 2003). For example, Thelwell and Greenlees found that tri-athletes reported that the use of motivational self-talk increased their self-confidence and motivation during their events. Furthermore, qualitative research has identified that athletes report using cognitive-based confidence-management strategies such as thought-stopping and positive self-talk to avoid debilitating interpretations of anxiety (Hanton *et al.*, 2004). However, in an experimental study, Cumming *et al.* (2006) reported that performance but not self-efficacy changed over time as a result of assigned experimental condition (debilitative versus facilitative imagery and self-talk), and that although facilitative self-talk was associated with enhanced performance this was not accompanied by increases in self-efficacy. Cumming *et al.* suggested that novice dart throwers' inaccurate and inflated perceptions of self-efficacy at the start of the investigation may help to explain the lack of self-talk (or imagery) effects observed.

Statements about the independent role of self-talk in influencing self-efficacy can also be made. For example, although not the main purpose of their study, Landin and Hebert (1999) reported increases in skilled tennis players' efficacy to win points at the net following a self-talk intervention designed to improve volleying at the net. However, Gould and Weiss (1981) found that even though observing positive self-talk resulted in enhanced performance relative to observing negative or irrelevant self-talk, participants' self-efficacy was not the major mediating variable in this relationship.

Despite some contradictory findings within the sport literature, research from clinical psychology does provide additional support for the notion that self-talk can be used to impact upon self-efficacy or self-confidence, as would be predicted by cognitive-behavioural theories. An in-depth naturalistic study by Patzel (2001) found that women leaving abusive relationships reported using and reframing self-talk as a strategy to increase their self-efficacy for action. Cognitive restructuring (reframing or reconstructing cognitions: Zinsser *et al.*, 2006) has also been shown to reduce clinical symptoms and enhance self-efficacy in headache patients (Scopp, 2003). Finally, Klein (1996) found significant correlations between the self-talk and self-efficacy of therapeutic counsellors, although the causal effect in this situation is unclear. Given the consistent findings of a relationship between self-efficacy and sporting performance, and some promising initial findings relating to self-talk and self-efficacy (e.g. Landin and Hebert, 1999), this would seem an important area for sport psychologists to explore further.

Moving from a cognitive to a behavioural motivational variable, the second possible mediator that will be discussed in this subsection is persistence, or long-term goal commitment. The hierarchical framework presented by Hardy *et al.* (2001a) proposes that athletes' self-talk can serve three motivational functions: arousal regulation, mastery and drive. Hardy *et al.* recognised that drive is a somewhat imprecise concept, stating that it was concerned with "assisting the athlete to keep on course to achieve their goals" and is "associated with maintaining or increasing drive and effort levels" (2001a: 88). The use of "persistence" in the current article is considered analogous to Hardy *et al.*'s "drive" function.

Self-talk's possible relationship to motivation, especially behavioural aspects of motivation, has received very little investigation within the sports domain. However, research within an educational environment provides strong evidence linking self-talk and both long- and short-term persistence. Chiu and Alexander (2000) found that children who engaged in a higher proportion of metacognitive private speech (i.e. overt self-talk reflecting awareness and regulation of one's own thinking; Manning *et al.*, 1994) were more likely to persist and strive to complete a challenging task, as well as more likely to work without an adult's assistance. Deficiencies in the use of private speech (i.e. less task-relevant private speech) have been associated with significantly shorter task persistence and poorer task performance in children with learning disabilities, relative to typically developing children (Harris, 1986). Additionally, Callicott and Park (2003) examined the functional role of self-directed speech as a verbal antecedent to subsequent academic responding and academic engagement. They reported moderate to strong effect sizes for self-talk, when paired with reinforcement, as an antecedent to corresponding academic behaviour, which was maintained across withdrawal and delayed conditions. In students (10–14 years), Wolters (1999) found that use of motivational strategies, including performance-focused and mastery self-talk, predicted students' use of learning strategies, effort and classroom performance.

Given that motivational self-talk appears to be a widely promoted perform-ance-enhancing strategy within sport psychology, the limited investigation into its effects on motivational variables is somewhat surprising. As it has been argued that "self-referent thought plays a paramount role in most contemporary theories of human behaviour" (Bandura, 1997: 8), it is important for future research to advance our knowledge of the effects of self-talk on athletes' moti-vation. Given that a number of theories applicable to motivation have been successfully embraced by sport-psychology researchers, helpful frameworks such as self-efficacy theory (Bandura, 1997) and goal-orientation theory (Nicholls, 1984) should also be adopted by self-talk researchers.

Behavioural mechanisms

Given the amount of time coaches spend fine-tuning their athletes' technique, and the biomechanical literature examining how skilled performers execute actions, both coaches and sport scientists value the role good technique plays in underpin-ning skilled performance. Based on the emerging literature reviewed in this subsec-tion, it is reasonable to hypothesise that changes in movement patterns are likely to contribute to the influence that self-talk has on performance. To date, however, researchers have not explicitly examined the mediating role that movement patterns may have on the self-talk and performance relationship; this represents an avenue of research worthy of attention. There have been, however, some initial attempts to examine the ways that movement patterns might change with self-talk. In an intervention study lasting three weeks with grade-three stu-dents (8/9 years old), instructional self-talk led to greater improvements in over-hand throw technique compared with a traditional teaching strategy (including demonstration, skill instruction and feedback) and a demonstration-only strategy (Anderson *et al.*, 1999). Utilising a performance measure of tennis groundstroke returns that combined strict behavioural criteria (e.g. racquet head above wrist, stepped forward on opposite leg, ball contacted on racquet side of body, etc.) as well as the outcome of the shot landing in the designated backcourt area, Ziegler

(1987) reported that her instructional self-talk cues enhanced the learning of both backhand and forehand groundstrokes. Following on from this, and using a single-subject multiple-baseline design with five female NCAA Division I tennis players, the use of instructional self-talk was associated with improved volleying technique (Landin and Hebert, 1999). In fact, self-talk was more strongly related to the tennis players' movement patterns than volleying outcome (i.e. accuracy in landing the ball into a backcourt corner target). There is also evidence that self-talk helps to improve novice tennis players' forehand technique when compared with control conditions and other learning strategies (e.g. Cutton and Landin, 2007). Perhaps it is understandable that self-talk interventions might help with skill learning. During the beginning phase of skill learning, novices "talk" themselves through movements (Coker *et al.*, 2006; Fitts and Posner, 1967). Self-talk interventions, particularly of the instructional type, may ensure that novices' inner dialogue is suitable for their learning. Although the tennis players in the Landin and Hebert study were skilled, the volleying movement examined was considered a team weakness by the coaches, and was not performed in an expert manner.

In the studies cited above, movement patterns were evaluated subjectively by trained assessors according to a checklist. Such investigations are likely to be complemented by those that use objective measures of movement parameters. Such studies, however, are only just beginning to be reported at conference level. For example, the muscles around the hip and knee joint contribute to vertical jump height (Lees *et al.*, 2004) and preliminary investigations have examined if self-talk influences knee and hip kinematics. Tod *et al.* (2007) investigated the effects of instructional ("bend and drive") and motivational ("I can jump high") self-talk on the vertical-jump performance of 24 healthy male and female college students. Using a within participant design and counterbalanced interventions, both instructional and motivational self-talk led to greater centre of mass displacement (i.e. participants jumped higher) compared with a neutral self-talk cue (counting down from 1,000 in groups of seven). There were no differences among the self-talk conditions. Both self-talk types were also associated with increased angular velocity around the knee joint (i.e. participants drove up quicker prior to leaving the ground). In a similar study using male rugby union players, motivational self-talk, but not instructional self-talk, was associated with greater centre of mass displacement compared with a no-instruction control. Motivational and instructional self-talk also lead to increased angular hip displacement and velocity (Edwards, 2007). These two investigations provide preliminary evidence that self-talk may influence movement kinematics. However, more research is needed, particularly in the form of studies adopting designs that allow for the assessment of mediating variables (see Baron and Kenny, 1986).

Affective mechanisms

Although there has been much debate in the sport and exercise psychology literature concerning the definition and conceptual distinction of the terms "affect", "mood" and "emotion" (see Ekkekakis and Petruzzello, 2000, for a brief review), we have used the phrase "affective mechanisms", as an umbrella term overseeing this family of concepts. Findings from meta-analytic reviews confirm both the wealth of research attention the affective states/performance relationship has received and the existence of the association (e.g. mood, Beedie *et al.*, 2000; anxiety, Woodman and Hardy, 2003). Furthermore, widespread theorising within mainstream psychology has linked cognition and affective states together (e.g. Lazarus, 1991; Mischel and Shoda, 1995; Newell, 1990). Partially supporting the results from meta-analyses as well as the previous statement, Meichenbaum and Butler argued "that one should consider cognition and emotion as two very closely related, ongoing, changing streams of experience that interact with one another and affect overt behaviour" (1979: 141). Other authors have conceptualised cognition as underpinning affective states; for example, cognitive-behavioural models emphasise the importance of inner speech in the development of affective disorders (e.g. Beck, 1976).

Findings from mainstream psychological research offer support for the link between self-talk and affective states – in particular, anxiety. For example, data from Spanish undergraduate students revealed a moderately strong negative relation between positive self-talk and symptoms of depression, anxiety and anger, as well as a positive correlation of similar magnitude for negative self-talk (Calvete *et al.*, 2005). In another investigation examining the role of self-statements in the experience of anxiety, Kendall and Treadwell (2007) reported that regardless of whether children (9–13 years old) were classified as having an anxiety disorder or not, anxious oriented self-talk (e.g. "I am very nervous") more consistently predicted anxiety than did depressed and positive self-talk. Moreover for those children with an anxiety disorder, changes in anxious self-talk mediated the effects of cognitive-behavioural therapy.

It was, perhaps, based on similar findings to those described above, as well as their abundance of practical experience of working with athletes, that sport psychologists Hardy *et al.* (1996) suggested that one of the underpinning mechanisms of the self-talk/performance relationship was concerned with effectively controlling anxiety. Some support for such a proposition can be found within the sports-psychology research literature. For example, the motivational-arousal function reported by Hardy *et al.* (2001a) is comprised of three more specific athlete-elicited reasons for their use of self-talk; to relax, to psych up and to control nerves. Some slightly stronger evidence originates from a study which found relationships between high-school athletes' use of self-talk and affect prior to practice and competition (Hardy *et al.*, 2001b). More specifically, affect was operationalised in line with Russell's (1980) circumplex model of affect consisting of two independent dimensions: valance (i.e. unpleasant–pleasant) and intensity (i.e. sleepiness–aroused). The valance dimension of self-talk was positively related to the valance dimension of affect, and motivational interpretation was positively associated with the intensity dimension of affect. However, as the data were collected in a cross-sectional manner, the study was unable to reveal information about the causal direction of the self-talk/affect relationship.

Nevertheless, findings from intervention studies might offer some support for such causal claims. A number of packaged mental-skills intervention studies hold limited relevance to the present affective mechanisms section. Although most have focused on performance, some investigators (e.g. Hanton and Jones, 1999; Prapavessis *et al.*, 1992) have also examined state anxiety as a dependent variable, with interventions creating more desirable affective states (e.g. lower state anxiety). Furthermore, evidence from cognitive restructuring intervention studies supports the cognition/affect causal relationship. For example, in a study grounded in Suinn's (1987) Positive Thought Control technique, Maynard *et al.* (1995) conducted a 12-week intervention with semi-professional football players. Those receiving the cognitive restructuring intervention reported lower levels of cognitive anxiety and interpreted symptoms of cognitive anxiety as being more facilitative for performance compared to control group members.

However, given that most cognitive-restructuring techniques incorporate imagery, these findings do not offer support for the presence of a self-talk/affective states association. That said, a finding within the self-talk literature does offer some preliminary support to the idea that self-talk can enhance affective states. Focusing exclusively on self-talk, Hatzigeorgiadis *et al.* (2007) reported that both cognitive and somatic anxiety were significantly lower when their water polo shooting task participants employed a form of anxiety-control self-talk ("calmly") as compared to instructional self-talk ("ball–target"). Although the size of this effect accounted for approximately 20 per cent of anxiety variance, it is possible that the potency of anxiety-controlling self-talk was underestimated as the laboratory setting was not particularly anxiety provoking (Hatzigeorgiadis *et al.*, 2007). Furthermore, given that a control condition was not established (or necessary for the primary purpose of the study), statements that the self-talk cue caused a decrease in anxiety cannot be made.

It is hoped that the preceding discussion on affect-related mediators of the self-talk/performance relationship has highlighted that, although some preliminary support for this premise may be present, substantial gaps in the literature exist. Given that sports anxiety is very closely linked to competition, and that anxiety and other affective states (e.g. depression; Lane and Terry, 2000) can be detrimental to athletes' competitive performance, researchers are encouraged to more closely examine the self-talk/affective states relationship, the effects of self-talk on anxiety and the effect of self-talk within anxiety-provoking situations. It is likely that investigations into these types of areas would develop valuable findings for practitioners.

Implications for professional practice

Given the importance of theory and research-based practice, the aforementioned sequential model hints at a number of applied implications pertinent to consultants wishing to employ self-talk with their athlete-clients. However, as there are a number of limitations to the existing self-talk knowledge base (e.g. the causal direction of self-talk's many associations has not been fully established), some caution is needed in interpreting the findings within the self-talk literature. For example, there has been a relative lack of research emphasis on the use of self-talk in the competition setting, a setting of primary importance for most consultants. Consequently, it is unclear whether many research findings (e.g. Hatzigeorgiadis *et al.*, 2004) can be generalised to this critical setting.

Given that the perceived issue or desired outcome should drive the mental skill employed (Vealey, 1988), when considering the employment of self-talk, the consultant should first address whether or not self-talk is (a) a symptom of an underlying issue; (b) a potentially useful intervention strategy to resolve an issue (e.g. lack of confidence); or (c) itself the issue, or the cause of the issue, at hand (e.g. excessive negative self-talk). In their in-depth discussion of their experiences of consulting with elite athletes from a number of different sports, Perry and Marsh (2000) illustrate how self-talk offers insight into the effects that self-concept can have on cognitions and behaviours. As a result, they conclude by stating that addressing self-talk issues in such situations "would be like patching the crack in the roof when it is the foundation of the house that needs attention" (Perry and Marsh, 2000: 74). Clearly, if self-talk is most appropriately conceptualised as a symptom of an underlying issue, then the most effective form of intervention should address the cause of the issue (e.g. negative self-concept) rather than merely a symptom (e.g. self-talk).

On the other hand, should the consultant view the use of the basic mental skill of self-talk to be an effective intervention to enhance an advanced mental skill, such as self-confidence, then a number of issues should be considered. Of utmost importance is whether or not the employment of self-talk is likely to be the *most* beneficial intervention. Remaining with the self-confidence example, there may be alternative and more potent sources of efficacy beliefs, other than verbal persuasion, of relevance to the client (e.g. vicarious experiences). Although the self-talk research literature is relatively underdeveloped, it highlights the possibility of at least two general-level moderators of the effectiveness of self-talk interventions. The first moderator is cognitive-processing preference (Paivio, 1971). Although research support from within the sports domain is mixed (e.g. O'Halloran and Gauvin, 1994; Thomas and Fogarty, 1997), findings from educational psychology offer support that this is an important issue to incorporate into self-talk interventions (e.g. Riding and Ashmore, 1980; Riding and Buckle, 1990). The practical implication from this potential moderator is that if a client has a non-verbal cognitive-processing preference then it is possible that a non-verbal (perhaps imagery) based intervention approach would be of greater benefit to him/her. The second general-level moderator is belief in self-talk. Again, although somewhat equivocal, researchers have reported that belief in the effects of self-talk is positively related to performance (Hardy *et al.*, 2004; Van Raalte *et al.*, 1994). Consequently, it is possible that an athlete's belief in their self-talk might moderate the effectiveness of self-talk interventions and as such, consultants working with clients with a strong lack of belief should pursue alternative intervention options.

From the consultant effectiveness literature, two additional factors may influence the effectiveness of self-talk interventions. First, the working alliance or collaborative relationship an applied sport psychologist and athlete share may well influence the athlete's belief in, and willingness to use, self-talk (see Tod and Andersen, 2005). Underpinning the working alliance is the practitioner's ability to develop a rapport and communicate with the athlete. Second, effective practitioners are able to help athletes adapt interventions, such as self-talk, to their specific needs (see Anderson et al., 2004). These additional factors provide a context within which athletes may learn to use self-talk to address their issues.

However, once it has been established that a self-talk strategy is the most suitable intervention, then the coach, consultant and, most importantly, athlete should work collaboratively to develop the tailored self-talk cues to be employed (Hardy, 2006). The fostering of ownership over the self-talk intervention should increase the likelihood that the client will adhere to the intervention and, as such, maximally benefit from it (cf. self-determination theory; Deci and Ryan, 1985). When the self-talk cues have been decided upon, the issue of whether the cues should be said overtly or covertly needs to be addressed. This is most probably dependent on matching the client's preference so as to not cause excessive disruption to task performance. However, one advantage to the use of overt self-talk, particularly in the initial phase of the self-talk intervention, is that coach and consultant are able to observe if the cues are being utilised appropriately. If not, modifying the cues or the timing of when the cues are employed can take place.

When devising the content of the self-talk intervention, the consultant should bear in mind the matching hypothesis forwarded by Martin et al.'s (1999) applied model of imagery use. Thus, it is critical that the content of the self-talk is congruent with the desired outcome of the intervention and contains the most appropriate information within the cue. For example, employment of motivational arousal types of self-talk should be most beneficial for psyching up and relaxation outcomes, whereas instructional (skill-specific) self-talk should most strongly assist skill development and refinement. However, it is possible that a self-talk phrase may serve more than one function (e.g. a gymnast learning a standing tucked backward somersault who repeats the self-instruction phrase "strong block" may feel this assists the rotation of the somersault as well as enhance his/her arousal levels prior to task execution). Hatzigeorgiadis et al. (2007) offer some preliminary support for this desired-outcome matching hypothesis. They found that novice participants reported significantly less cognitive and somatic anxiety prior to a water-polo task when they used a relaxation-oriented motivational arousal cue ("calmly") as compared to an instructional (skill-specific) self-talk cue ("ball–target"). Should the desired outcome revolve around enhanced motor-learning and execution, then the task-demands matching hypothesis advanced within the self-talk literature (e.g. Theodorakis et al., 2000) also offers practical guidance. As such, when successful task execution requires timing, accuracy and coordination, research findings suggest that instructional types of self-talk would be most beneficial. Given that recent researchers (Zervas *et al.*, 2007) have suggested that more frequent use of instructional (and motivational) self-talk is positively associated with more successful performance, consultants might encourage their clients to employ instructional self-talk on a frequent basis. However, findings from Conscious Processing Hypothesis (CPH; Masters, 1992) studies would suggest otherwise. CPH offers an explanation for the phenomenon commonly known as "paralysis by analysis" experienced by skilled athletes under anxious conditions. It suggests that this debilitating phenomenon is caused by the reinvestment of explicit rules about how to execute the task. Explicit rules are not dissimilar to instructional self-talk – thus, the (frequent) use of process-oriented instructional self-talk might have extremely undesirable effects for the skilled athlete (especially when they are anxious). Researchers have proposed that the creation of more holistic attentional states, via holistic process goals (Kingston and Hardy, 1997), offers the performer task-relevant information without the priming of the reinvestment of explicit rules. Consequently, there may be situations when consultants should create holistic (e.g. "smooth") rather than detailed process-instructional (e.g. "head still", "wrists firm", "full turn") cues.

Landin (1994) has also offered practical advice concerning the development of verbal instructional cues for task execution. He proposed that five factors need to be considered during the development of effective verbal cues: (a) brevity; (b) accuracy; (c) the information to be cued; (d) the nature of the task; and (e) the ability level of the performer. In particular, verbal cues should be brief, phonetically uncomplicated, logically associated with the particular elements of the respective task, as well as being compatible with the rhythm and timing of the task. Moreover, tasks with distinctive phases lend themselves more easily than their counterparts to use of cue words. Landin, somewhat in line with CPH, warns that "excessive detail in the verbal cues can overload the learner and disrupt the motor activity" (Landin, 1994: 305).

Within the existing self-talk literature there appears to be a greater amount of applied advice for enhancing performance than psychological states (and this may reflect that more research has focused on the influence self-talk has on performance than on psychological states). This is unfortunate as this chapter has identified a number of psychological states that may help to explain the performance-enhancing effects of self-talk. Nevertheless, should the identified desired outcome be motivationally related, then it might be worthwhile for consultants to also consider their clients' motivational interpretation of the content of potential cues. With this in mind, more effective cues should be viewed by the client as motivating as opposed to de-motivating (Hardy *et al.*, 2001b). Furthermore, given that Peters and Williams (2006) found that individuals from East Asian cultures responded more positively to negative types of self-talk than those from Western cultures, cultural differences should be considered where applicable.

Following the completion of a needs analysis, a situation may arise whereby the consultant identifies that self-talk itself is the issue at hand (e.g. excessive negative self-talk) or is the cause of the issue at hand (e.g. excessive negative self-talk undermining self-confidence). In such cases, Zinsser *et al.* (2006) recommend that before the client can gain control over his/her self-talk, he/she must first become aware of it. This then allows the client and consultant to identify types of self-talk that are beneficial or a hindrance to performance. Zinsser *et al.* state the importance of understanding when and how to talk to oneself. As a result, they offered a number of interesting methods a consultant can employ with a client in order to obtain an enhanced awareness and foster an in-depth understanding of the athlete's use of self-talk (see Zinsser *et al.*, 2006, for a thorough review of awareness-enhancing techniques). These include retrospection via the viewing of video footage, the use of imagery, self-talk logbooks and a paper clip activity (involving the transferring of clips from one pocket to another when a targeted statement has been identified). To date, research has not investigated which awareness-enhancing protocols are effective (or most effective). It is the authors' experience, however, that the combined use of a self-talk logbook with a frequency-counting activity offers both breadth and depth to the narrow information gained from the sole reliance on a counting activity. In addition, although there are concerns regarding the accuracy of retrospective techniques, they may well help consultants to identify the typical ways that athletes respond to specific situations.

Once awareness has been achieved, Zinsser and colleagues (2006) offer a range of techniques designed to improve the client's control over his/her self-talk. It is not the intention of the authors to cover the techniques forwarded by Zinsser *et al.*, as they offer an excellent review including good detail as to how they might be best utilised. However, we would like to echo their comments concerning the first technique they describe, thought-stopping. Thought-stopping is referred to in many sport-psychology textbooks (e.g. Weinberg and Gould, 2007); however, when used on its own (i.e. without supplementary techniques), it is likely to exacerbate the problem of inappropriate self-talk. As a result, we would encourage consultants to abandon its use. This recommendation is grounded in Wegner's (1994) Ironic Effects Theory that has relevance to conditions of high cognitive load, such as competitive settings where athletes can be cognitively anxious. The theory predicts that when an athlete experiences anxiety, a change of cognitive control systems takes place which actually increases the likelihood of the occurrence of the very event (e.g. reducing the occurrence of a negative statement) he/she is trying to avoid. The supportive evidence for the theory's predictions imply that, rather than reducing the frequency of a negative statement, an increased frequency occurs. Rather than focusing on helping athletes deal with thoughts they wish to avoid (e.g. thought-stoppage), a more proactive strategy may be to assist them in identifying thoughts they want to have at specific points of time. In a powerlifting context, for example, instead of using thought-stoppage to deal with thoughts such as "don't be so weak" prior to a lift, consultants might help athletes to develop cues such as "I am strong" or "This bar is easy". Indeed, findings by Dugdale and Eklund (2002, Study 2) offer some support for this suggestion.

Future directions for self-talk research

Given the rather underdeveloped nature of the self-talk literature compared to other mental skills (e.g. imagery), there are a number of possible avenues for self-talk researchers to pursue. It is our hope that the framework presented in this chapter acts as a stimulus for future research. Additional research is needed, focusing on many of the issues reviewed. This is especially relevant to the proposed underpinning mechanisms of the self-talk/performance relationship. Furthermore, potentially applicable theories to the study of self-talk (e.g. self-efficacy theory) have been previously presented. As we believe that little would be achieved by replicating this previous work, the interested reader is referred to Hardy (2006). Instead, we would encourage researchers to test the predictions gleaned from the previously mentioned framework. Although the concepts within the framework have been presented in a sequential manner (e.g. antecedents–self-talk–mediator–performance), it likely that circular relationships exist. This is not only relevant to the reviewed relationship between self-talk and anxiety (e.g. trait anxiety to self-talk to state anxiety) but may also be pertinent to other associations (e.g. self-confidence to self-talk to self-confidence). Given that the present framework presents a number of possible underpinning mechanisms of the self-talk/performance relationship, the lack of previously reported mediation-based investigation is somewhat surprising. Although not directly relevant to our framework, Conroy and Coatsworth (2007) have incorporated self-talk into mediation-oriented models. They found that changes in self-talk played a mediatory role in youth swimmers' relationship between coaching behaviour and the situational form of anxiety, fear of failure. As already highlighted, there is a need for additional moderation and/or mediation-based investigations involving self-talk, as these afford greater understanding of relationships.

Additionally, as mentioned previously, one reason why sport psychologists use and promote self-talk is the belief that it enhances competitive performance. A number of research directions were suggested throughout the section examining the self-talk–performance relationship (e.g. a wider range of tasks) and generally these will not be revisited here. It is sobering, however, to conclude that, although self-talk enhances skill execution, there is limited data that competitive performance is improved. Nevertheless, the lack of evidence that self-talk enhances competitive performance does not imply that self-talk does not, or cannot, help competitive performance. There is still much scope for researchers to explore the possibility. In some sports, it may be possible to examine if self-talk influences overall performance, such as weightlifting or golf. As mentioned above, however, it is unlikely in many instances that self-talk influences overall competitive performance given the number of other factors that play a role. Researchers might extend knowledge by examining the ways that the strategy influences the skills and attributes that contribute to overall competitive performance.

In recent years, there has been a movement within mainstream psychology towards empirically supported interventions. One result of this movement has been the identification of criteria for determining if there is evidence to support the use of interventions for particular issues (Gardner and Moore, 2006). For example, according to the three levels of criteria published by Chambless and colleagues (e.g. Chambless and Ollendick, 2001; Chambless *et al.*, 1998), self-talk would be considered an experimental treatment with respect to competitive sports performance. By drawing on these criteria, however, to guide research design, sport-psychology researchers might produce evidence for self-talk to be considered a well-established intervention for competitive performance in a range of sports. One criteria, for example, suggests there needs be at least two good between-group experiments showing that self-talk is superior to a placebo or other interventions, or is equivalent to an already-established treatment with adequate sample sizes. A full description of Chambless and colleagues' criteria is beyond the scope of this chapter, and interested researchers are referred to Chambless and Ollendick (2001).

Additional important issues for future research to consider are the need for improvements in standardising the conceptualisation and measurement of self-talk, as well as enhanced awareness of the limitations of different research designs (e.g. self-report questionnaires versus observation). On the one hand, findings by Hardy *et al.* (2005b) suggest that observational measures of self-talk may only afford assessment of less than 25 per cent of the total amount of self-talk used by athletes – leaving a relatively incomplete picture. On the other hand, however, an issue pertinent to the employment of self-report questionnaires is that of retrospective recall. More particularly, athletes vary in their recall abilities, and the knowledge of competitive results may influence retrospection (Brewer *et al.*, 1991). Previous researchers interested in cognitive processes have recommended that, whenever appropriate, both concurrent and retrospective techniques are utilised (Ericsson and Simon, 1993).

In the current chapter, the mechanisms for how self-talk might influence skill execution or performance have been advanced, with a consistent conclusion being the need for more empirical research. Although research along these lines will advance knowledge, multidisciplinary research may also be needed to establish a complete understanding. For example, as a psychological intervention, self-talk may well influence cerebral cortex functioning, and hence higher psychological states such as self-efficacy and concentration. Changes in higher psychological states and cerebral cortex may result in changes to movement patterns via alterations in motor unit recruitment, synchronisation or firing rate. Research along any one line of inquiry (e.g. affective mechanisms) may only provide a partial picture of how self-talk helps athletes. Investigators might consider examining a range of variables and using a range of measurement techniques. Researchers could examine, for example, changes in (a) attention or self-efficacy via self-report measures; (b) mood and affect via questionnaires; (c) movement patterns via kinematic analysis; and (d) electrical muscular activity via electromyography.

Conclusion

The present chapter included a comprehensive review of the literature pertaining to self-talk in the sports setting. Particular emphasis was placed on a throughput framework that helped to guide the review. An important aspect of the current framework is the discussion of research and theory relevant to the possible underpinning mechanisms of the self-talk/performance relationship. A number of mediatory mechanisms were advanced although a paucity of research testing such relationships currently exists. Despite the relative lack of self-talk research compared to other mental skills, there is adequate theory and research to support the implications offered for professional practice.

References

Abernethy, B. (2001). Attention. In R. N. Singer, H. A. Hausenblas and C. M. Janelle (eds), *Handbook of sport psychology* (2nd edn, pp. 53–85), New York: John Wiley.

Andersen, M. B., McCullagh, P. and Wilson, G. J. (2007). But what do the numbers really tell us? Arbitrary metrics and effect size reporting in sport psychology research. *Journal of Sport and Exercise Psychology*, 29, 664–672.

Anderson, A., Miles, A., Robinson, P. and Mahoney, C. (2004). Evaluating the athlete's perception of the sport psychologist's effectiveness: what should we be assessing? *Psychology of Sport and Exercise*, 5, 255–277.

Anderson, A., Vogel, P. and Albrecht, R. (1999). The effect of instructional self-talk on the overhand throw. *Physical Educator*, 56, 215–221.

Araki, K., Mintah, J. K., Mack, M. G., Huddleston, S., Larson, L. and Jacobs, K. (2006). Belief in self-talk and dynamic balance performance. *Athletic Insight: the Online Journal of Sport Psychology*, 8(4). Retrieved 26 January 2007, from www.athleticinsight.com/Vol8Iss4/selftalkandperformance.htm.

Baker, J., Côté, J. and Deakin, J. (2005). Cognitive characteristics of expert, middle of the pack, and back of the pack ultra-endurance triathletes. *Psychology of Sport and Exercise*, 6, 551–558.

Bandura, A. (1977). Self-efficacy: toward a unified theory of behavioural change. *Psychological Reviews*, 84, 191–215.

Bandura, A. (1982). Self-efficacy mechanisms in human agency. *American Psychologist*, 37, 122–147.

Bandura, A. (1997). *Self-efficacy: the exercise of control*. New York: Freeman.

Baron, R. M. and Kenny, D. A. (1986). The moderator–mediator variable distinction in social psychological research: conceptual, strategic, and statistical considerations. *Journal of Personality and Social Psychology*, 51, 1173–1182.

Beck, A. T. (1976). *Cognitive therapy and emotional disorders*. Madison, WI: International Universities Press.

Beedie, C. J., Lane, A. M. and Terry, P. C. (2000). The profile of mood states and athletic performance: two meta-analyses. *Journal of Applied Sports Psychology*, 12, 49–68.

Behrend, D., Rosengren, K. and Perlmutter, M. (1989). A new look at the effects of age, task difficulty, and parents' presence on children's private speech. *International Journal of Behavioural Development*, 12, 305–320.

Bell, J. (2006). Self-talk and attentional focus on performance in golf. Unpublished M.Sc. thesis, University of Wales, Bangor, UK.

Benjamin, L. S. (1996). *Interpersonal diagnosis and treatment of personality disorders*. New York: Guildford.

Brewer, B. W., Van Raalte, J. L., Linder, D. E. and Van Raalte, N. S. (1991). Peak performance and the perils of retrospective introspection. *Journal of Sport and Exercise Psychology*, 8, 227–238.

Brown, L. J., Malouff, J. M. and Schutte, N. S. (2005). The effectiveness of a self-efficacy intervention for helping adolescents cope with sport-competition loss. *Journal of Sport Behaviour*, 28, 136–150.

Burnett, P. C. (1999). Children's self-talk and academic self-concepts: the impact of teachers' statements. *Educational Psychology in Practice*, 15, 195–200.

Callicott, K. J. and Park, H. (2003). Effects of self-talk on academic engagement and academic responding. *Behavioural Disorders*, 29, 48–64.

Calvete, E., Estevez, A., Landin, C., Martinez, Y., Cardenoso, O., Villardon, L. and Villa, A. (2005). Self-talk and affective problems in college students: valence of thinking and cognitive content specificity. *The Spanish Journal of Psychology*, 8, 56–67.

Carron, A. V., Brawley, L. R. and Widmeyer, W. N. (1997). The measurement of cohesiveness in sport teams. In J. L. Duda (ed.), *Advances in sport and exercise psychology measurement* (pp. 213–226), Morgantown, WV: Fitness Information Technology Inc.

Chambless, D. L. and Ollendick, T. H. (2001). Empirically supported psychological interventions: controversies and evidence. *Annual Reviews of Psychology*, 52, 685–716.

Chambless, D. L., Baker, M. J., Baucom, D. H., Beutler, L. E., Calhoun, K. S., Crits-Christoph, P. *et al.* (1998). Update on empirically validated therapies II. *The Clinical Psychologist*, 51, 3–16.

Chiu, S. and Alexander, P. A. (2000). The motivational function of preschoolers' private speech. *Discourse Processes*, 30, 133–152.

Chroni, S., Perkos, S. and Theodorakis, Y. (2007). Function and preferences of motivational and instructional self-talk for adolescent basketball players. *Athletic Insight: the Online Journal of Sport Psychology*, 9(1). Retrieved 20 August 2007, from www.athleticinsight.com/Vol9Iss1/BasketballSelfTalk.htm.

Coker, C. A., Fischman, M. G. and Oxendine, J. B. (2006). Motor skill learning for effective coaching and performance. In J. M. Williams (ed.), *Applied sport psychology: personal growth to peak performance* (5th edn, pp. 17–39), Boston: McGraw-Hill.

Conroy, D. E. and Coatsworth, J. D. (2007). Coaching behaviours associated with changes in fear of failure: changes in self-talk and need satisfaction as potential mechanisms. *Journal of Personality*, 75, 383–419.

Conroy, D. E. and Metzler, J. N. (2004). Patterns of self-talk associated with different forms of competitive anxiety. *Journal of Sport and Exercise Psychology*, 26, 69–89.

Cumming, J., Nordin, S. M., Horton, R. and Reynolds, S. (2006). Examining the direction of imagery and self-talk on dart-throwing performance and self-efficacy. *The Sport Psychologist*, 20, 257–274.

Cutton, D. M. and Landin, D. (2007). The effects of self-talk and augmented feedback on learning the tennis forehand. *Journal of Applied Sport Psychology*, 19, 288–303.

Dagrou, E. and Gauvin, L. (1992). Self-talk: a mediator of performance. *Science and Sports*, 7, 101–106.

Dagrou, E., Gauvin, L. and Halliwell, W. (1992). Effects of positive, negative, and neutral language on performance motivation. *Canadian Journal of Sport Sciences*, 17, 145–147.

Day, R. and Allen, T. D. (2004). The relationship between career motivation and self-efficacy with protégé career success. *Journal of Vocational Behaviour*, 64, 72–91.

Deci, E. L. and Ryan, R. M. (1985). Intrinsic motivation and self-determination in human behaviour. New York: Plenum Publishing Co.

Dugdale, J. R. and Eklund, R. C. (2002). Do not pay any attention to the umpires: thought suppression and task-relevant focusing strategies. *Journal of Sport and Exercise Psychology*, 24, 306–319.

Edwards, C. (2007). Effects of motivational and instructional self-talk on power production during the vertical jump test in university rugby union players. Unpublished B.Sc. dissertation, University of Wales, Aberystwyth, UK.

Ekkekakis, P. and Petruzzello, S. J. (2000). Analysis of the affect measurement conundrum in exercise psychology. *Psychology of Sport and Exercise*, 1, 71–88.

Elko, P. K. and Ostrow, A. C. (1991). Effects of a rational-emotive education programme on heightened anxiety levels of female collegiate gymnasts. *The Sport Psychologist*, 5, 235–255.

Ericsson, K. A. and Simon, H. A. (1993). *Protocol analysis: verbal reports as data*, Revised Edition. Cambridge, MA: MIT Press.

Ferneyhough, C. and Fradley, E. (2005). Private speech on an executive task: relations with task difficulty and task performance. *Cognitive Development*, 20, 103–120.

Fitts, P. M. and Posner, M. I. (1967). *Human performance*. Belmont, CA: Brooks/Cole.

Gardner, F. and Moore, Z. (2006). *Clinical sport psychology*. Champaign, IL: Human Kinetics.

Goodhart, D. E. (1986). The effects of positive and negative thinking on performance in an achievement situation. *Journal of Personality and Social Psychology*, 51, 117–124.

Goudas, M., Hatzidimitriou, V. and Kikidi, M. (2006). The effects of self-talk on throwing and jumping events performance. *Hellenic Journal of Psychology. Special Issue: Self-talk in sport psychology*, 3, 105–116.

Gould, D. R. and Weiss, M. R. (1981). The effects of model similarity and model talk on self-efficacy and muscular endurance. *Journal of Sport Psychology*, 3, 17–29.

Gould, D., Eklund, R. C. and Jackson, S. A. (1992a). 1988 U.S. Olympic wrestling excellence: I. Mental preparation, precompetitive cognition, and affect. *The Sport Psychologist*, 6, 358–382.

Gould, D., Eklund, R. C. and Jackson, S. A. (1992b). 1988 U.S. Olympic wrestling excellence: II. Thoughts and affect occurring during competition. *The Sport Psychologist*, 6, 383–402.

Hamilton, R. A., Scott, D. and MacDougall, M. P. (2007). Assessing the effectiveness of self-talk interventions on endurance performance. *Journal of Applied Sport Psychology*, 19, 226–239.

Hanton, S. and Jones, G. (1999). The effects of a multimodal intervention programme on performers: II. Training the butterflies to fly in formation. *The Sports Psychologist*, 13, 22–41.

Hanton, S., Mellalieu, S. D. and Hall, R. (2004). Self-confidence and anxiety interpretation: a qualitative investigation. *Psychology of Sport and Exercise*, 5, 477–495.

Hardy, J. (2006). Speaking clearly: a critical review of the self-talk literature. *Psychology of Sport and Exercise*, 7, 81–97.

Hardy, J. and Hall, C. R. (2006). Exploring coaches' promotion of athlete self-talk. *Hellenic Journal of Psychology*, 3, 134–149.

Hardy, J., Gammage, K. and Hall, C. (2001a). A descriptive study of athlete self-talk. *The Sport Psychologist*, 15, 306–318.

Hardy, J., Hall, C. R. and Alexander, M. R. (2001b). Exploring self-talk and affective states in sport. *Journal of Sports Sciences*, 19, 469–475.

Hardy, J., Hall, C. R. and Hardy, L. (2004). A note on athletes' use of self-talk. *Journal of Applied Sport Psychology*, 16, 251–257.

Hardy, J., Hall, C. R., Gibbs, C. and Greenslade, C. (2005a). Self-talk and gross motor skill performance: an experimental approach? *Athletic Insight: the Online Journal of Sport Psychology*, 7(2). Retrieved 26 August 2005, from www.athleticinsight.com/Vol7Iss2/SelfTalkPerformance.htm.

Hardy, J., Hall, C. R. and Hardy, L. (2005b). Quantifying athlete self-talk. *Journal of Sports Sciences*, 23, 905–917.

Hardy, L., Jones, G. and Gould, D. (1996). *Understanding psychological preparation for sport: theory and practice of elite performers*. Chichester: Wiley.

Harris, D. V. and Harris, B. L. (1984). *The athlete's guide to sports psychology: mental skills for physical people*. New York: Leisure Press.

Harris, K. R. (1986). Effects of cognitive-behaviour modification on private speech and task performance during problem solving among learning-disabled and normally-achieving children. *Journal of Abnormal Child Psychology*, 14, 63–76.

Harvey, D. T., Van Raalte, J. L. and Brewer, B. W. (2002). Relationship between self-talk and golf performance. *International Sports Journal*, 6, 84–91.

Harwood, C., Cumming, J. and Fletcher, D. (2004). Motivational profiles and psychological skills use within elite youth sport. *Journal of Applied Sport Psychology*, 16, 318–332.

Hatzigeorgiadis, A. (2006). Instructional and motivational self-talk: an investigation on perceived functions. *Hellenic Journal of Psychology*, 3, 164–175.

Hatzigeorgiadis, A., Theodorakis, Y. and Zourbanos, N. (2004). Self-talk in the swimming pool: the effects of self-talk on thought content and performance on water-polo tasks. *Journal of Applied Sport Psychology*, 16, 138–150.

Hatzigeorgiadis, A., Zourbanos, N. and Theodorakis, Y. (2007). The moderating effects of self-talk content on self-talk functions. *Journal of Applied Sport Psychology*, 19, 240–251.

Highlen, P. S. and Bennett, B. B. (1983). Elite divers and wrestlers: a comparison between open- and closed-skill athletes. *Journal of Sport Psychology*, 5, 390–409.

Johnson, J. J. M., Hrycaiko, D. W., Johnson, G. V. and Halas, J. M. (2004). Self-talk and female youth soccer performance. *The Sport Psychologist*, 18, 44–59.

Kendall, P. C. and Treadwell, K. R. H. (2007). The role of self-statements as a mediator in treatment for youth anxiety disorders. *Journal of Consulting and Clinical Psychology*, 75, 380–389.

Kerlinger, F. N. (1986). *Foundations of behavioural research* (3rd edn). New York: Holt, Rinehart, and Winston.

Kingston, K. and Hardy, L. (1997). Effects of different types of goals on processes that support performance. *The Sport Psychologist*, 11, 277–293.

Klein, D. L. (1996). Relationship of counsellor trainee internal dialogue, self-efficacy and hypothesis formation to therapeutic performance. *Dissertation Abstracts International Section A: Humanities and Social Sciences*, 56, 4281.

Landin, D. (1994). The role of verbal cues in skill learning. *Quest*, 46, 299–313.

Landin, D. and Hebert, E. P. (1999). The influence of self-talk on the performance of skilled female tennis players. *Journal of Applied Sport Psychology*, 11, 263–282.

Lane, A. M. and Terry, P. C. (2000). The nature of mood: development of a conceptual model with a focus on depression. *Journal of Applied Sport Psychology*, 12, 16–33.

Lane, A. M., Jones, L. and Stevens, M. (2002). Coping with failure: the effects of self-esteem and coping on changes in self-efficacy. *Journal of Sport Behaviour*, 25, 331–345.

Lantolf, J. P. (ed.). (2006). *Sociocultural theory and second language learning: recent advances*. Oxford: Oxford University Press.

Lawrence, J. A. and Valsiner, J. (2003). Making personal sense: an account of basic internalization and externalization processes. *Theory and Psychology*, 13, 723–752.

Lazarus, R. S. (1991). Cognition and motivation in emotion. *American Psychologist*, 46, 352–367.

Lees, A., Varenterghem, J. and De Clercq, D. (2004). The maximal and submaximal vertical jump: implications for strength and conditioning. *Journal of Strength and Conditioning Research*, 18, 787–791.

Likang, C. (2004). Achievement goal theory. In T. Morris and J. Summers (eds), *Sport psychology: theory, applications and issues* (2nd edn, pp. 152–174), Milton, QLD, Australia: Wiley.

McAuley, E., Morris, K. S., Motl, R. W., Hu, L., Konopack, J. F. and Elavsky, E. (2007). Long-term follow-up of physical activity behaviour in older adults. *Health Psychology*, 28, 375–380.

Mahoney, M. J. and Avener, M. (1977). Psychology of the elite athlete: an exploratory study. *Cognitive Therapy and Research*, 1, 135–141.

Mallett, C. J. and Hanrahan, S. J. (1997). Race modelling: an effective cognitive strategy for the 100 m sprinter? *The Sport Psychologist*, 11, 72–85.

Mamassis, G. and Doganis, G. (2004). The effects of a mental training programme on juniors' pre-competitive anxiety, self-confidence, and tennis performance. *Journal of Applied Sport Psychology*, 16, 118–137.

Manning, B. H., White, C. S. and Daugherty, M. (1994). Young children's private speech as a precursor to metacognitive strategy use during task engagement. *Discourse Processes*, 17, 191–211.

Martin, G. L., Vause, T. and Schwartzman, L. (2005). Experimental studies of psychological interventions with athletes in competition: why so few? *Behaviour Modification*, 29, 616–641.

Martin, K. A., Moritz, S. E. and Hall, C. R. (1999). Imagery use in sport: a literature review and applied model. *The Sport Psychologist*, 13, 245–268.

Masciana, R. C., Van Raalte, J. L., Brewer, B. W., Branton, M. G. and Coughlin, M. A. (2001). Effects of cognitive strategies on dart throwing performance. *International Sports Journal*, 5, 31–39.

Masters, R. S. W. (1992). Knowledge, knerves and know-how: the role of explicit versus implicit knowledge in the breakdown of a complex motor skill under pressure. *British Journal of Psychology*, 83, 343–358.

Maynard, I. W., Smith, M. J. and Warwick-Evans, L. (1995). The effects of a cognitive intervention strategy on competitive state anxiety and performance in semiprofessional soccer players. *Journal of Sport and Exercise Psychology*, 17, 428–446.

Meichenbaum, D. and Butler, L. (1979). Cognitive ethology: assessing the streams of cognition and emotion. In K. R. Blankstein, P. Plinker and J. Polivy (eds), *Advances in the study of communication and affect. Volume 6: Assessment* and *modification of emotional behaviour*. New York: Plenum Press.

Mischel, W. and Shoda, Y. (1995). A cognitive-affective theory of personality: reconceptualising situations, dispositions, dynamics and invariance in personality structure. *Psychological Review*, 102, 246–268.

Moran, P. A. (1996). *The psychology of concentration in sport performance*. East Sussex: Psychology Press Publishers.

Moritz, S. E., Feltz, D. L., Fahrbach, K. R. and Mack, D. E. (2003). The relation of self-efficacy measures to sport performance: a meta-analytic review. *Research Quarterly for Exercise and Sport*, 71, 280–294.

Newell, A. (1990). *Unified theories of cognition*. Cambridge, MA: Harvard University Press.

Nicholls, J. G. (1984). Conceptions of ability and achievement motivation. In R. Ames and C. Ames (eds), *Research on motivation in education: Vol. 1* (pp. 39–73), New York: Academic Press.

Nideffer, R. M. (1976). Test of attentional and interpersonal style. *Journal of Personality and Social Psychology*, 34, 394–404.

O'Halloran, A. and Gauvin, L. (1994). The role of preferred cognitive style in the effectiveness of imagery training. *International Journal of Sport Psychology*, 25, 19–31.

Oikawa, M. (2004). Does addictive distraction affect the relationship between the cognition of distraction effectiveness and depression? *Japanese Journal of Educational Psychology*, 52, 287–297.

Paivio, A. (1971). *Imagery and verbal processes*. New York: Holt, Rhinehart, and Winston.

Paivio, A. and Harshman, R. (1983). Factor analysis of a questionnaire on imagery and verbal habits and skills. *Canadian Journal of Psychology*, 37, 461–483.

Papaioannou, A., Ballon, F., Theodorakis, Y. and Auwelle, Y. V. (2004). Combined effect of goal setting and self-talk in performance of a soccer-shooting task. *Perceptual and Motor Skills*, 98, 89–99.

Patzel, B. (2001). Women's use of resources in leaving abusive relationships: a naturalistic inquiry. *Issues in Mental Health Nursing*, 22, 729–747.

Perkos, S., Theodorakis, Y. and Chroni, S. (2002). Enhancing performance and skill acquisition in novice basketball players with instructional self-talk. *The Sport Psychologist*, 16, 368–383.

Perry, C., Jr. and Marsh, H. (2000). Listening to self-talk, hearing self-concept. In M. B. Andersen (ed.), *Doing sport psychology* (pp. 61–76). Champaign, IL: Human Kinetics.

Peters, H. J. and Williams, J. M. (2006). Moving cultural background to the foreground: an investigation of self-talk, performance, and persistence following feedback. *Journal of Applied Sport Psychology*, 18, 240–253.

Prapavessis, H., Grove, J. R., McNair, P. J. and Cable, N. T. (1992). Self-regulation training, state anxiety, and sport performance. *The Sport Psychologist*, 6, 213–229.

Riding, R. J. and Ashmore, J. (1980). Verbaliser–imager learning style and children's recall of information presented in pictorial versus written form. *Educational Studies*, 6, 141–145.

Riding, R. J. and Buckle, G. (1990). The effects of cognitive style and mode of presentation on learning performance. *British Journal of Educational Psychology*, 63, 297–307.

Rotella, R. J., Gansneder, B., Ojala, D. and Billing, J. (1980). Cognitions and coping strategies of elite skiers: an exploratory study of young developing athletes. *Journal of Sport Psychology*, 2, 350–354.

Rushall, B. S. and Shewchuk, M. L. (1989). Effects of thought content instructions on swimming performance. *The Journal of Sports Medicine and Physical Fitness*, 29, 326–334.

Rushall, B. S., Hall, M., Roux, L., Sasseville, J. and Rushall, A. C. (1988). Effects of three types of thought content instructions on skiing performance. *The Sport Psychologist*, 2, 283–297.

Russell, J. A. (1980). A circumplex model of affect. *Journal of Personality and Social Psychology*, 39, 1161–1178.

Scopp, A. L. (2003). An effective tool in headache treatment. *Headache and Pain: Diagnostic Challenges, Current Therapy*, 14, 115–127.

Scully, D. and Lowry, R. (2002). Why we do – and why we don't! *The Psychologist*, 15, 418–429.

Sechrest, L., McKnight, P. and McKnight, K. (1996). Calibration of measures for psychotherapy outcome studies. *American Psychologist*, 51, 1065–1071.

Shui-Fong, L. and Yin-Kum, L. (2007). The roles of instructional practices and motivation in writing performance. *Journal of Experimental Education*, 75, 145–164.

Suinn, R. M. (1987). Behavioural approaches to stress management in sport. In J. R. May and M. J. Asken (eds), *Sport psychology* (pp. 59–75). New York: PMA.

Tenenbaum, G., Bar-Eli, M., Hoffman, J. R., Jablonovski, R., Sade, S. and Shitrit, D. (1995). The effect of cognitive and somatic psyching-up techniques on isokinetic leg strength performance. *Journal of Strength and Conditioning Research*, 9, 3–7.

Thelwell, R. C. and Greenlees, I. A. (2003). Developing competitive endurance performance using mental skills training. *The Sport Psychologist*, 17, 318–337.

Thelwell, R. C., Greenlees, I. A. and Weston, N. J. V. (2006). Using psychological skills training to develop soccer performance. *Journal of Applied Sport Psychology*, 18, 254–270.

Theodorakis, Y., Chroni, S., Laparidis, K., Bebetsos, V. and Douma, I. (2001). Self-talk in a basketball-shooting task. *Perceptual and Motor Skills*, 92, 309–315.

Theodorakis, Y., Weinberg, R., Natsis, P., Douma, I. and Kazakas, P. (2000). The effects of motivational versus instructional self-talk on improving motor performance. *The Sport Psychologist*, 14, 253–272.

Thomas, P. R. and Fogarty, G. J. (1997). Psychological skills training in golf: the role of individual differences in cognitive preferences. *The Sport Psychologist*, 11, 86–106.

Thomas, P. R., Murphy, S. M. and Hardy, L. (1999). Test of performance strategies: development and preliminary validation of a comprehensive measure of athletes' psychological skills. *Journal of Sports Sciences*, 17, 697–711.

Tod, D. and Andersen, M. (2005). Success in sport psych: effective sport psychologists. In S. Murphy (ed.), *The sport psych handbook* (pp. 305–314), Champaign, IL: Human Kinetics.

Tod, D., Thatcher, R., McGuigan, M. R. and Thatcher, J. (2007). *The effect of instructional and motivational self-talk on performance and the kinematics of the vertical jump.* Paper presented at the 12th European Congress of Sport Psychology, Halkidiki, Greece.

Tynes, L. L. and McFatter, R. M. (1987). The efficacy of "psyching" strategies on a weight-lifting task. *Cognitive Therapy and Research*, 11, 327–336.

Van Raalte, J. L., Brewer, B. W., Lewis, B. P., Linder, D. E., Wildman, G. and Kozimor, J. (1995). Cork! The effects of positive and negative self-talk on dart throwing performance. *Journal of Sport Behaviour*, 18, 50–57.

Van Raalte, J. L., Brewer, B. W., Rivera, P. M. and Petitpas, A. J. (1994). The relationship between observable self-talk and competitive junior tennis players' match performances. *Journal of Sport and Exercise Psychology*, 16, 400–415.

Van Raalte, J. L., Cornelius, A. E., Brewer, B. W. and Petitpas, A. J. (2006). Self-presentational effects of self-talk on perceptions of tennis players. *Hellenic Journal of Psychology*, 3, 164–179.

Van Raalte, J. L., Cornelius, A. E., Hatten, S. J. and Brewer, B. W. (2000). The antecedents and consequences of self-talk in competitive tennis. *Journal of Sport and Exercise Psychology*, 22, 345–356.

Vealey, R. (1988). Future directions in psychological skills training. *The Sport Psychologist*, 2, 318–336.

Vygotsky, L. S. (1962). *Thought and language*. Cambridge, MA: MIT Press.

Wang, L., Huddleston, S. and Peng, L. (2003). Psychological skill use by Chinese swimmers. *International Sports Journal*, 7, 48–55.

Wegner, D. M. (1994). Ironic processes of mental control. *Psychological Review*, 101, 34–52.

Weinberg, R. (1986). Relationship between self-efficacy and cognitive strategies in enhancing endurance performance. *International Journal of Sport Psychology*, 17, 280–293.

Weinberg, R. S. and Gould, D. (2007). *Foundations of sport and exercise psychology* (4th edn). Champaign, IL: Human Kinetics.

Weinberg, R. S., Grove, R. and Jackson, A. (1992). Strategies for building self-efficacy in tennis players: a comparative analysis of Australian and American coaches. *The Sport Psychologist*, 6, 3–13.

Weinberg, R. S., Smith, J., Jackson, A. and Gould, D. (1984). Effect of association, dissociation and positive self-talk strategies on endurance performance. *Canadian Journal of Applied Sport Sciences*, 12, 25–32.

Wolters, C. A. (1999). The relation between high school students' motivational regulation and their use of learning strategies, effort and classroom performance. *Learning and Individual Differences*, 11, 281–299.

Woodman, T. and Hardy, L. (2003). The relative impact of cognitive anxiety and self-confidence upon sports performance: a meta-analysis. *Journal of Sports Sciences*, 21, 443–457.

Wrisberg, C. A. (1993). Levels of performance skill. In R. N. Singer, M. Murphey and L. K. Tennant (eds), *Handbook of research on sport psychology* (pp. 61–71), New York: Macmillan.

Wulf, G. and Prinz, W. (2001). Directing attention to movement effects enhances learning: a review. *Psychnomic Bulletin and Review*, 8, 648–660.

Wulf, G., McNevin, N., Fuchs, T., Ritter, F. and Toole, T. (2000). Attentional focus in complex motor skill learning. *Research Quarterly for Exercise and Sport*, 71, 2229–2239.

Zervas, Y., Stavrou, N. A. and Psychountaki, M. (2007). Development and validation of the self-talk questionnaire (ST-Q) for sports. *Journal of Applied Sport Psychology*, 19, 142–159.

Ziegler, S. G. (1987). Effects of stimulus cueing on the acquisition of groundstrokes by beginning tennis players. *Journal of Applied Behaviour Analysis*, 20, 405–411.

Zinsser, N., Bunker, L. and Williams, J. M. (2006). Cognitive techniques for building confidence and enhancing performance. In J. M. Williams (ed.), *Applied sport psychology: personal growth to peak performance* (5th edn, pp. 349–381). Boston: McGraw-Hill.

Zourbanos, N., Hatzigeorgiadis, A. and Theodorakis, Y. (2007). A preliminary investigation of the relationship between athletes' self-talk and coaches' behaviour and statements. *International Journal of Sports Science and Coaching*, 2, 57–66.

Zourbanos, N., Theodorakis, Y. and Hatzigeoriadis, A. (2006). Coaches' behaviour, social support and athletes' self-talk. *Hellenic Journal of Psychology, Special Issue: Self-Talk in Sport Psychology*, 3, 150–163.

3 The application of goal setting in sport

Kieran M. Kingston and Kylie M. Wilson

Introduction

The scientific or theoretical rationale for promoting goal setting as an effective motivational tool was based on work in industrial and organisational psychology. Consequently, Locke's 1968 'theory' of goal setting led to a broader interest in the utilisation of goals, primarily in the industrial and organisational sector, but more recently in the context of sport. Here it has prompted theory testing, the objective of which has been to establish a reliable basis for the promotion of the technique within sports settings and with sports performers (Hall and Kerr, 2001).

Edwin Locke defined a goal simply as 'what an individual is trying to accomplish; it is the object or aim of an action' (Locke *et al.*, 1981: 126). However, it is important to note that, while goals are portrayed as the drive behind goal-directed behaviour (Locke and Latham, 1985), they do not necessarily always function at a conscious level – they may go in and out of conscious awareness (Hardy *et al.*, 1996a). According to Locke and Latham (1990), while goals may help initiate action, their active pursuit does not always require them to be elevated to consciousness. Based on this premise, Locke's (1968) goal-setting theory was developed to explain enhanced productivity in the workplace. Locke, however, considered his initial propositions as simply providing the foundations for a theory of task performance, recognising that in its current form, it only considered the strength of a functional relationship between goals and performance on some specific task (cf. Hall and Kerr, 2001). In their later text, Locke and Latham (1990) integrated up-to-date research findings on the topic of goal setting to provide a more thoroughly grounded conceptual base for their 'theory' of goal setting in sport.

According to the theory, goals have two functional characteristics that dictate the extent to which task performance is influenced: the content of the goal and the requisite intensity with which it is to be pursued. The content refers to the nature of the goals (implicitly this describes what is to be accomplished if goal-attainment occurs), and the intensity reflects the perceived resource requirement to attain the level of performance demanded by the content (Hall and Kerr, 2001). These characteristics are reflected in the two fundamental premises of goal-setting theory. First, difficult goals lead to higher levels of performance than easy goals, and second, that specific goals lead to higher levels of performance than vague, do-your-best goals, or no goals. This second premise reflects a reduction in the ambiguity of evaluating success (Locke and Latham, 1990). The widespread support for both premises, verifying Locke's (1968) predictions regarding difficulty and specificity, led some (e.g. Mento et al., 1987) to suggest that these effects warranted the elevation of goal theory to the status of a scientific law. Despite this, Locke and Latham (1990) pre-empted possible criticisms of their proposals by suggesting that more comprehensive explanations of the relationship between goal setting and performance may be achieved if human action is considered in the context of motives, values and sources thereof, while arguing that such a perspective may actually offer less specific explanatory power with respect to task performance (cf. Hall and Kerr, 2001).

In their seminal text, Locke and Latham (1985) argued that goal-setting effects in industrial/organisational settings should be transferable to sports because of the common concern with achieving some end-results, contextual similarities, and the commonality in the cognitive processes and physical actions utilised across sport and occupational settings. Indeed, they went still further and suggested that, since performance was 'easier' to measure in sport than in industrial and organisational contexts, the benefits of goal setting would be more pronounced (Locke and Latham, 1985). The primary purpose of the present chapter is to explore the efficacy of Locke and Latham's assertions.

Goal setting in sport

Early reviews examining goal-setting 'theory' in the domain of sport suggested that, while there is some evidence supporting the contentions implicit in the theory, many studies examining the goal setting–performance relationship in sport and physical activity have failed to find similarly strong support to those portrayed from within industrial and organisational settings (e.g. Burton, 1992, 1993; Hall and Byrne, 1988; Weinberg and Weigand, 1993). Nevertheless, reflecting on the meta-analytical procedures of Kyllo and Landers (1995),[1] and their reviews of 1992 (Burton, 1992) and 2002, Burton and Naylor (2002) suggested that, as the number of goal-setting studies in sport increase, results in the sport domain look more like general goal-setting findings. In summarising their review findings, they highlighted two inescapable conclusions: first, goals work, and second, the process of effective goal setting is more complex than it appears, or is often portrayed. It might be reasonable to (at least partly) attribute the first conclusion to two factors: (1) the utility of more appropriate methodologies arising as a consequence of healthy academic debate (e.g. between Locke and Weinberg and Weigand in the early 1990s), and (2) a broadening of conceptual approaches which go beyond examining simple performance effects. This second issue, however, begs the question: how can we illuminate the 'complex' process of goal setting in such a way as to shift goals from something that athletes and coaches intuitively know can help, to a situation where the effectiveness of goals can be maximised for individual performers across a variety of sporting situations?

According to Burton and Naylor (2002), the notion of goals can be studied in two fundamental ways. First, goals can be considered as a direct motivational strategy (borne of Locke's original conceptualisation), where they function as specific standards of performance that regulate behaviour in terms of attention and effort. In this case, they have the capacity to engender motivation, or to promote stress when they are in doubt (Burton and Naylor, 2002). While this populist conception of goals and the research that has adopted that view within sport settings will form the basis of this critique, it is our view that it is limiting not to consider the potential underlying factors that may well influence (a) the discrete moment to moment goals that individual's set; and (b) the cognitive, affective and behavioural responses to setting and striving towards those goals. Consideration for these individual and contextual factors will, we feel, help to narrow the gap between the research process surrounding goals and the messages that it conveys, and the day-to-day grind of applied practice utilising goal setting. Therefore, while it is not our intention to review the vast research examining goal perspectives in sport (interested readers should refer to a number of extensive reviews, e.g. Duda, 2001; Harwood *et al.*, 2000; Roberts, 2001), we will adopt the standpoint that, in addition to contextual variations, both inter- and intra-individual differences should be considered within the process of goal setting in sport.

The second fundamental way in which goals can be studied is where goals act, or are considered as the cognitive drivers for involvement in activities. In this case, goal perspectives (Nicholls, 1984, 1989) reflect the personal meaning of ability and success, which in turn dictate cognitions, behaviours and affect. Nicholls' (1984, 1989) achievement–goal theory provides the theoretical framework for the study of goal perspectives in sport. The principle behind the achievement–goal approach is that individuals engage in achievement contexts to demonstrate competence, and, further, they adopt goals that most closely reflect their cognitive beliefs about what is required to maximise achievement in that particular context (Harwood *et al.*, 2000). As Harwood *et al.* articulate, individuals have a personal theory of what achievement means to them, and they set goals that both meet their needs and reflect and satisfy their personal theory. Nicholls suggested that two types of achievement goals existed. Individuals who feels successful/competent when they experience gains in mastery (i.e. improve their own performance, regardless of others) are said to be task involved. Individuals who feel successful/competent when they outperform others (i.e. norm referenced) are said to be ego involved (see Harwood *et al.*, 2000, and Kingston *et al.*, 2006, for a review). Nicholls further proposed the existence of two independent goal orientations that reflected a proneness to different types of involvement in any particular achievement settings: labelled task and ego orientations. There has been much debate over the orthogonality of achievement goals, and while Nicholls' (1989) work has often been interpreted as supporting the orthogonality of (dispositional) goal orientations, there is a strong suggestion that 'one cannot be both task and ego involved at the same moment in time' (1989: 240; Harwood et al., 2000). This moment-to-moment fluctuation in goal states is entirely plausible, and at an applied level, there is considerable anecdotal evidence supporting the view that athletes switch from one goal state to another during performance. Although we will not review the extensive literature on goal perspectives, it has been argued that achievement goals not only play a significant role in an athlete's decision to invest in an activity, but they give 'meaning' to the pursuit of personal goals (cf. Hall and Kerr, 2001). Consequently, although their conceptual underpinnings are different, any review of individual goal-setting practices could be further illuminated by considering the achievement goals that an individual holds.

Our purpose within this overview of goal-setting research is to provide a broad overview of the current 'state of play' with regards to the application of goal setting in sport. Initially, we will consider the research that has adopted Locke's (1968) conceptualisation of goals (as conscious regulators of actions) at an individual level; however, rather than repeating material provided in recent extensive reviews (e.g. Burton and Naylor, 2002; Hall and Kerr, 2001), we will attempt to provide a succinct summary of the research, Specifically, in this first section, we will focus on work that has considered those factors variously described as: moderators, attributes or parameters of goals (for example, goal difficulty, goal specificity, goal proximity, goal focus, goal commitment and feedback). Having examined goals and considered to a degree their cognitive drivers at an individual level, we will examine the application of goal setting in the team environment. The more fine-grained discussion of goal setting in team environments reflects the evolving nature of work in this area, and the application of principles from industrial/organisational settings to sport teams.

Throughout our review, we will consider the application of this work to performers, and our intention is to adopt a critical perspective. Having reviewed the various literatures, we will identify some 'issues' associated with the application of goals in sport and our view on their potential solutions, before concluding with some additional proposed directions for future research. The equivocal nature of research that has taken goal setting from the realm of business to sports settings has often challenged practitioners to decipher what research 'messages' mean to them as they apply goal-setting principles. Our objective within this 'issues' section is to try to give some clarity to these muddied waters, and while doing so, provide an impetus for more effective research into goal setting.

Goal setting at an individual level

According to Locke's original operationalisation, goals are considered as 'discrete' end states that regulate human action by specifying an aim or an objective standard for a specific task (Hall and Kerr, 2001). Consequently, this notion of goals has formed the basis of research examining goals utilising goal-setting theory as the framework. There have been a number of comprehensive reviews examining goal-setting research in the context of sport; interested readers are directed towards the works of Hall and Kerr (2001), and Burton and Naylor

(2002), from which we have drawn widely in this first section. To summarise, while early reviews (e.g. Burton, 1993; Weinberg, 1992) provided very limited support for the major premises of goal-setting theory that specific, difficult goals have a positive effect on performance when compared to vague, do-your-best goals, or no goals, the more recent meta-analysis of Kyllo and Landers (1995) has given some scope for optimism (cf. Burton and Naylor, 2002). Specifically, in examining some 36 sport studies, they found an overall mean effect size of 0.34 in support of goal setting. Although providing clear evidence of a statistical effect, the level of conclusive support it generated remained modest, and significantly lower than the effect sizes obtained when examining goal setting in other contexts (Hall and Kerr, 2001). Burton and Naylor's (2002) review of 56 published works on goal setting in sport, however, indicated that 79 per cent of the studies demonstrated moderate to strong goal-setting effects. While Burton and Naylor's work does paint an increasingly positive picture, the mixed effects described suggest that sport research consistently fails to provide convincing support for the central theoretical premises of Locke's theory (Hall and Kerr, 2001). The focus of this section is to consider those critical variables that have been argued to moderate the goal setting–performance relationship. To clarify, a moderating variable in this context is one that affects the direction and/or strength of the predictive relationship between goal setting per se and subsequent cognitions, behaviours and affect (Baron and Kenny, 1986). The moderating aspects we will consider here are associated with goal difficulty, goal specificity, goal proximity, goal focus, goal commitment and feedback. Critical examination of these and the research surrounding them will, it is hoped, provide some explanation for the mixed findings of goal setting studies in sport, and help to close the research–applied practice gap.

Goal difficulty

One of the most tested aspects of Locke's (1968) theory revolves around the relationship between goal difficulty (often examined in association with goal specificity) and performance. This reflects one of the central tenets of Locke and Latham's (1990) goal setting theory that, assuming the individual has the capacity to reach them, a positive linear relationship exists between goal difficulty and performance. Further, while difficult goals were postulated to lead to greater effort and persistence, performance has been shown to plateau once upper ability levels are reached (Weinberg, 1994). While general goal-setting reviews supported the goal-difficulty hypothesis (reporting mean effect sizes of between 0.52 and 0.82), research has shown that, rather than leading to a withdrawal of effort, goals that exceeded individual performance capacity resulted in individuals self-setting more realistic goals (cf. Burton and Naylor, 2002). Perhaps as a consequence of this fact, in sport there is no clear evidence that the predictions of Locke and associates stand up. While excessively difficult goals may not be achieved, any assumption that low-ability performers are incapable of performing well in response to the challenges of extremely difficult goals is somewhat off the mark (Hall and Kerr, 2001). A meta-analysis carried out by Kyllo and Landers (1995) investigating easy, difficult and improbable goals reported that only moderate goals produced a large effect size (0.53) on performance, and that athletes prefer a combination of moderately difficult goals rather than exclusively difficult goals. Further, in their recent review of goal-difficulty literature, Burton and Naylor (2002) reported that, out of 19 studies, only ten had supportive evidence for the goal-difficulty hypothesis.

Several reasons have been posited to account for these contradictory findings. First, the operational definition of 'difficult' is unclear (Weinberg, 1994). Locke (1991) did suggest that, to ensure specific goals were difficult, they should be set at a level at which no more than 10 per cent of the subjects can reach them; however, this fails to account for the potential mediating effects of both competition and perceptions of ability. Moreover, if one takes a broader view of goals than simply considering them in terms of numeric objectives, it is impossible to quantify levels of difficulty in terms of, for example, goals that pertain to individual behaviours or performance processes.

Although there is obvious potential for unrealistic goals to elicit negative performance effects, this has not been substantiated (Burton and Naylor, 2002). Indeed, there is some research evidence that suggests that improbable or difficult goals do not cause reductions in effort or persistence (Weinberg et al., 1986), and in fact, Hall and Kerr (2001) suggest that such (difficult) goals may cause these individuals to redefine their goals in line with what they perceive attainable. This might lead one to speculate that perhaps absolute difficulty is not really the central issue, but rather it is the individual motivational consequences of realising an inability to achieve their initial goals that is important. Clearly, the mechanisms by which goals of varying difficulties influence performance warrants further investigation is sport settings.

Goal specificity

The notion that goal specificity, or the precision of goals, promotes better performance than general do-your-best goals was widely supported in the early goal-setting literature (see Locke et al., 1981, for an extensive review). In their revision of goal-setting theory, Locke and Latham (1985), however, predicted that precision was a less important moderator than difficulty; rather that specificity interacts with difficulty to enhance performance, i.e. it has an indirect influence. Furthermore, Locke and Latham hypothesised that, when difficulty is controlled, the effect of specificity is to reduce the ambiguity in evaluating success, and thus lowers performance variance, i.e. specificity contributes primarily to enhance performance consistency (Burton and Naylor, 2002). However, there has been no conclusive support for this proposal.

Although, goal difficulty and goal specificity have not been studied independently in sport, a significant body of work has identified specific goals as leading to enhanced performance over vague, general, or no goals (cf. Hall and Kerr, 2001). However, despite this apparent support, it has been suggested that as many as one-third of all studies in sport fail to substantiate that goal specificity has stronger effects than simply doing one's best (Burton *et al.*, 1998). This inconsistency suggests that one of the central predictions of goal-setting theory is again not fully supported. In those studies that failed to distinguish between the effects of experimental and control manipulations, however, trial main effects were consistently found – this suggests that all groups (i.e. regardless of whether they were setting specific, general, vague or do-your-best goals) improved over time. This might be attributed to subjects in the less-specific groups setting personal goals (Hall and Kerr, 2001).

Methodological weaknesses, failure to assess personal goals, the motivation and spontaneous goal setting of control subjects, and task characteristics have all been posited as explanations for the lack of support for Locke and Latham's (1985) propositions (Locke, 1991). Hall and Kerr (2001), however, argued that certain contextual characteristics unique to sport encourage participants to make do-your-best goals specific. Detailed knowledge of the activity and associated performance standards, and the fact that many people engage in sport of their own volition, naturally results in participants placing a higher value on effort and specifying what their best performance will be. Boyce (1994) validated this suggestion when finding that two-thirds of control subjects set specific numeric goals, and that the purpose of setting these was to create intra-individual competition. Clearly one of the limiting factors of Locke's (1991) arguments to explain anomalous results in sport is the failure to consider individual motivation and sport knowledge that influence behaviours and cognitions (Hall and Kerr, 2001), a point that will be raised again later in this section.

Goal proximity

Although not explicit in Locke's (1968) original paper, Locke and Latham (1985) hypothesised that long-term goals in conjunction with short-term goals would lead to better performance than long-term goals alone. According to Weinberg (1994), this was because long-term goals were viewed as too vague to have a significant motivational impact in the present. The area of 'goal proximity' has however received scant attention in sport.

The meta-analysis of Kyllo and Landers (1995) provided only limited support for Locke and Latham's hypothesis. Specifically, from the studies reviewed, a combination of short- and long-term goals generated an overall effect size of 0.48, compared to short-term goals alone (0.38) and long-term goals alone (0.19). Two of the principle studies in sport (Hall and Byrne, 1988; Weinberg *et al.*, 1988) reported similar results in that no performance differences were found between the long-term goal group, short-term goal group and the combined goal group. However, they did find that subjects assigned a combination of short-term and long-term goals did perform better than the 'do-your-best' subjects. In the only study to explicitly support Locke and Latham's (1985) hypothesis, Tenenbaum *et al.* (1991) used a ten-week muscular-endurance sit-up test to investigate goal proximity. They reported that groups assigned long- and short-term goals improved in their performance, but the group given a combination of short- and long-term goals demonstrated the greatest performance improvement. In their recent review, Burton and Naylor (2002) reported that three of eight studies had shown that combinations of long- and short-term goals were superior in their effects to either alone. What these results appear to indicate is that goals per se are better than no goals, yet the ideal 'recipe' of more proximal or more distal goals is unclear. Consequently, proximity recommendations to practitioners are potentially confused (Burton and Naylor, 2002).

In terms of the mechanisms of potential beneficial effects, Hall and Byrne (1988) suggested that short-term goals provided a useful feedback device, enabling participants to feel a sense of achievement and consequential increases in self-efficacy in pursuit of long-term goals. This proposal sits comfortably couched within Bandura's (1986) theory of self-efficacy, since performance accomplishment (goal achievement) is the strongest predictor of efficacy expectations. Similarly, depending on the nature and focus of such goals, comparisons of current levels of performance with aspirational levels (i.e. a long-term goal) has the potential to undermine self-efficacy, motivation and performance if those current levels indicate failure or a lack of progress (Hall and Kerr, 2001). A number of other explanations have been proposed for the benefits of short-term as opposed to long-term goals. Burton (1989) argued that the increased controllability (and thus flexibility) of short-term goals enabled them to be readily raised or lowered in order to ensure they remained optimally challenging. A number of researchers (e.g. Hall and Byrne, 1988; Kirschenbaum, 1985; Locke and Latham, 1990) have suggested that, while long-term goals provide individuals with direction for achievement strivings, their motivational impact depends on short-term goals serving as effective markers in the achievement process (cf. Hall and Kerr 2001).

Goal focus

Unlike the other potential moderators of the goal setting–performance relationship, goal focus (a phrase coined by Burton and Naylor in their 2002 review) has not been studied directly except in the context of goal-setting intervention programmes, or observation and evaluation of goal-setting practices. Nevertheless, the evidence to date (e.g. Burton, 1989; Filby et al., 1999; Kingston and Hardy, 1994, 1997; Kingston et al., 1992; Zimmerman and Kitsantas, 1996) suggests that the specific nature of the goal in terms of its primary focus has significant implications in terms of its effect on behaviours and cognitions.

The first study to consider goal focus was Burton's (1989) goal-setting training study. Burton found that an educational programme focusing on the setting of personal numeric performance standards (performance goals) with collegiate swimmers led to greater performance, more adaptive perceptions of success, satisfaction and higher levels of perceived competence than a control condition. Burton surmised that control participants (and thus the non-trained population) would base perceptions of competence mainly on social comparison and objective outcomes (e.g. a finishing place in a race, or winning and losing), although this was not checked explicitly. Further, he argued that outcome goals (the attainment of which were largely reliant on the performance of others) lacked the flexibility and control necessary to ensure consistent success and to allow individuals to fully internalise credit for that success (Burton, 1989).

Developing this line of research into goal focus, a number of researchers (Hardy and Nelson, 1988; Kingston and Hardy, 1994, 1997; Kingston *et al.*, 1992; Zimmerman and Kitsantas, 1996) clarified and broadened the goal-focus distinction in sport by separating what Burton defined as goals that view success in terms of 'surpassing personal performance standards' (1989: 107), i.e. performance-based self-referenced goals, into two categories termed 'performance' and 'process' goals. It should be noted, however, that Zimmerman and Kitsantas labelled what Burton (1989) regarded as 'performance goals' as 'product' goals. Consequently, three 'types' of goal focus were recognised within goal-setting research (e.g. Hardy and Nelson, 1988). First, outcome goals are based on the outcome of a specified event and may involve interpersonal comparison of some kind (e.g. a finishing place in a race or winning and losing; Kingston and Hardy, 1997). Performance goals are self-referenced, and refer to a specific end product of performance; they normally involve a numeric value (Duda, 2001), and can be achieved by the performer relatively independently of others (e.g. the total number of putts taken in the duration of a round of golf; Kingston and Hardy, 1997; Kingston *et al.*, 2006). Finally, process goals centre on the execution of behaviours, skills and strategies (e.g. technique, form, thought processes to regulate behaviour) that are integral to effective task execution. Examples of a process goal would include a high follow-through phase in a basketball free throw or perhaps a full-court press in a team situation (Kingston *et al.*, 2006).

Research into process goals supported the validity of the tripartite distinction of goal focus. Zimmerman and Kitsantas (1996), using a learning paradigm, found process goals to be more effective than product (performance) goals in the development of a dart-throwing skill, but also facilitating of self-efficacy, appropriate attributions and intrinsic interest. In their season-long intervention with amateur golfers, Kingston and Hardy (1997) similarly supported the use of such a goal focus. Both subjects trained in the use of performance and process goals improved their skill levels over the course of the season compared to a no-training control group. Furthermore, those subjects utilising process goals also improved at a faster rate, and experienced positive changes in self-efficacy, cognitive anxiety control and concentration. More recent research has shown that goal focus can be predicted by contextual motivational factors (e.g. intrinsic motivation; Wilson and Brookfield, in press), and process goals relative to outcome and performance goals have been shown to be the strongest positive predictor of the positive psychological state of Flow and its constituent components (Kingston and Goldea, 2007).

While the mechanisms through which process goals influence performance have not been directly examined, the specific nature of these goals has led to some tentatively supported suggestions. There is a general consensus in the literature examining goal focus that one of the key distinguishing factors between the different goal 'types' relates to their controllability and flexibility (e.g. Burton, 1989; Burton and Naylor, 2002; Filby et al., 1999; Kingston and Hardy, 1997). Process goals, which can focus on technique, movement form, self-regulation and strategy at an individual level, are completely under the control of the performer, in that providing the necessary regulatory skills are present, there is no reason why any external factors should disrupt such a focus. Although focusing on absolute standards that are end-products of performance, the self-referenced nature of performance goals ensures that they are mainly under the control of the individual (Jones and Hanton, 1996). According to Burton (1989), their more flexible and controllable nature enables them to be raised or lowered to ensure optimal challenge. Nevertheless, contextual factors such as the performance of the opposition, the specific environmental conditions and during-event personal performance levels all have the potential to disrupt achievement of these numeric 'products' of performance. Finally, outcome goals, which are based on social comparison (for example, winning or placing in a race), are, by their nature, largely reliant on external factors (e.g. an opponent's performance) for their achievement, and are therefore largely uncontrollable. It might be logical therefore to think of goal focus as existing on a continuum based on the degree of control over which the performer exerts on the goal, or more accurately to consider control as a key mediator of the goal-focus behaviour and cognition relationship.

In addition to control, a number of other potential mechanisms have been identified through which process goals in particular influence performance. These have received some, albeit limited, empirical support. Facilitating attentional focus (Hardy and Nelson, 1988; Kingston and Hardy, 1997), reducing task complexity (Kingston and Swain, 1999; Zimmerman and Kitsantas, 1996), increasing self-efficacy (Kingston and Hardy, 1997; Zimmerman and Kitsantas, 1996), intrinsic interest (Zimmerman and Kitsantas, 1996), reducing the tendency to worry about social evaluation (Kingston and Hardy, 1997) and providing building blocks to ensure desired performance levels are achieved (Burton and Naylor, 2002) have all been proposed as reasons why process goals support performance. Conversely, it has also been suggested that, in accordance with Master's (1992) investment hypothesis, encouraging athletes to use process goals that focus their attention to specific aspects of a movement might actually inhibit performance (Hardy et al., 1996b; Masters, 1992; Kingston and Hardy, 1997). Clearly, research examining the nature of process goals, their potential differential effects on learners and skilled athletes, and the specific mechanisms through which the different goal types influence task performance is required to illuminate this area still further.

Although researchers (e.g. Burton, 1989; Kingston and Hardy, 1997; Zimmerman and Kitsantas, 1996) have generally compared one goal focus to another in a specific sport context, the overriding message that comes from such studies is that performers should use a variety of goal types to optimise their immediate and long-term effects.

Support for this proposal has been increasing. For example, Jones and Hanton (1996) reported that the majority of the 91 swimmers in their sample set at least two types of goal, with nearly half of the sample using a combination of perform-ance, process and outcome goals. It was also reported that not one of the sample set outcome goals exclusively. Filby *et al.* (1999), in the first sport-based study to directly compare goal types in isolation and in combination, investigated the effect of a multiple goal setting style on performance outcome in training and competition. Although their control group was found to have engaged in spon-taneous goal setting, the results suggested that multiple-goal strategies led to significantly greater performance compared to any goal type in isolation. In addi-tion to confirming the potential for outcome and performance goals to be dysfunctional if used inappropriately, they contended that adopting a 'process' focus prior to and during performance would be beneficial when combined with the motivational benefits of outcome and performance goals. This finding was consistent in both practice and competition conditions. In their recent review, Burton and Naylor (2002) found that six out of seven studies examining goal focus supported the efficacy of using a combination of process, performance and outcome goals rather than using any individually. Most recently, in a study of mixed-ability athletes, Munroe-Chandler *et al.* (2004) reported that participants utilised a variety of goal types for both training and competition, and specifically, goals were more outcome-focused in competition, whereas in training they were more based on self-referenced criteria (i.e. performance or process focused).

The body of research relating to the benefits of process goals, the widespread use of rewards in sport and the extensive use of all goal types by athletes reinforces the argument that it is not so much the specific types of goals that athletes use in the context of their sport, but more the framework in which these goals are organised and prioritised (Kingston and Hardy, 1994, 1997). Filby *et al.* (1999) in supporting these views argued that process goals are most beneficial when used within a hierarchy of goals that include performance and outcome goals. Such a strategy, they argued, is likely to have significant advan-tages when compared to simply dichotomising process and outcome goals because they are respectively 'good' or 'bad'.

While recognising the incongruence of theoretical frameworks and the moti-vational functions of the contrasting conceptualisations of goals renders a 'merging' of the literatures problematic, we would like to highlight some research that illustrates the potential relationships between achievement goals (i.e. wider views of what achievement represents) and the specific discrete goals that per-formers utilise. As we discussed briefly in the introduction, we hold the view that, in addition to considering goals as direct regulators of behaviour, it is also important to consider the cognitive drivers behind the setting of specific types of goal, and the oft-reported moment-to-moment shifts in goal focus that occur during engagement in sport-based activities. Adding weight to this suggestion, Hall and Kerr (2001) argue that goals should be studied with the view that per-sonal meaning acts as a critical mediator underpinning the goal-setting process, and this 'meaning' is reflected in the goals that athletes set.

Burton (1992) attempted to illustrate the potential link between achieve-ment goals and discrete goal 'states' in his competitive-goal setting model. Within it, he described how dispositional orientations would interact with perceived ability to dictate the specific goals athletes set. While a number of problems existed with the model which limits its use (for example, a number of critical relationships are either unclear, or cannot be accommodated by the model, key constructs are not adequately defined, and it fails to account for the use of multiple goal types, or the orthogonality of achievement goals, cf. Hall and Kerr, 2001), it has at least provided an impetus for adoption of an achievement-goal framework for examining personal goals.

The relationship between achievement goal orientations (an individual's tendency to be task and/or ego involved) and the actual goal performers set was fuelled by a debate between Hardy (1997, 1998) and Duda (1997). Duda (1992) argued that ego-oriented athletes were more likely to set outcome goals, while Duda et al. (1991) suggested that task-oriented individuals were more con-cerned with the intrinsic facets or processes of performance; however, no empir-ical evidence was provided to support this later suggestion. In questioning this view, Hardy (1997) argued that there was no a priori reason why athletes with high levels of ego orientation would not set process goals if it served to satisfy their achievement orientation (i.e. to outperform others).

In an attempt to clarify this debate, Wilson et al. (2006) examined the rela-tionship between process goals and goal orientations in a sample of 150 rugby union players. In line with Duda et al.'s (1991) assertions, correlation and regres-sion analysis results confirmed that a task orientation (i.e. 'I have a personal desire to improve my performance', similar to task orientation as defined by Nicholls, 1984, 1989) had a strong relationship with process goals. However, correlation results also showed that an ego orientation (i.e. 'I have a personal desire to out-perform my opponent') had a positive relationship with process goals, which lends support to Hardy's (1997) argument. Wilson et al. (2006) concluded that those who influence the achievement context (i.e. coaches) should not discourage high levels of self-directed ego orientation as these athletes may also set process goals if it serves to satisfy their achievement orientation (Hardy, 1997, 1998; Hardy et al., 1996a).

If we consider the results of these studies in the context that achievement goals not only play a significant role in an athlete's decision to invest in an activity, but that they give 'meaning' to the pursuit of personal goals (cf. Hall and Kerr, 2001), it may not be the discrete goal per se that is important, but more the achievement-based meaning attached to them. Future research needs to clarify the relation-ship between goal perspectives (in particular task and ego-involvement) and the discrete type of goals performers set (i.e. outcome, performance, process).

Other potential moderating variables

Hall and Kerr (2001) also identified goal commitment and the availability of feedback as important moderators in the goal setting–performance relationship.

There exists, however, limited research in sport that has explicitly examined these aspects – consequently, they will be dealt with only in passing.

Locke and Latham (1985) hypothesised that goal setting will only be effective when feedback regarding progress towards an individual's goal is present. The difficulty of testing such a hypothesis in sport is that it is almost impossible to prevent participants from receiving feedback in some mode or another while the retaining ecological validity of any manipulation that is carried out. In physical activity settings, however, feedback plus goals has been found to be better at facilitating aerobic endurance performance, than either feedback or goals in isolation (Bandura and Cervone, 1983). Focusing on feedback 'type' (cf. Hall and Kerr, 2001), Hall *et al.* (1987) found concurrent or terminal feedback to have no effects on the goal-performance relationship.

Although there is no clear support for Locke and Latham's hypothesis in sport settings with generally goal-directed participants, it makes sense that any moderating effects of feedback may be attributable to increases in effort (when goal achievement is in doubt). However, the caveat to this proposal is that when feedback indicates a wide discrepancy between current levels of performance and goals, diminishing self-efficacy might lead to negative motivational and performance effects. Clearly, these predictions have yet to be validated in ecologically valid sport-based studies.

In their seminal text, Locke and Latham (1985) hypothesised that higher levels of commitment should lead to higher levels of performance. Further, in 1990, the same authors (Locke and Latham, 1990) argued that a great level of choice in the process of setting goals would lead to greater commitment. Nevertheless, few performance differences have been identified between subjects being assigned goals and those engaging in participatory goal setting (Hall and Kerr, 2001). In anticipating potential confounds, Locke and Latham (1990) argued that, when goals are assigned, the level at which such goals are set influences the performers' perception of their anticipated capability (or certainly the assigner's view of their capabilities), which in turn affects self-efficacy. Conversely, they propose that giving goal choice may lead to choices of non-optimal challenge. Despite tentative support that assigned goals within a weight-training programme facilitated performance compared to self-set goals (Boyce and Wada, 1994), researchers have remained cautious with regards to Locke and Latham's (1990) explanations which imply that simply assigning goals to sport participants is as effective as involving them in the process (cf. Hall and Kerr, 2001). Certainly, given that choice and autonomy (along with relatedness) have been identified as fundamental psychological needs which specifically facilitate intrinsic motivation and psychological well-being (Deci and Ryan, 1985), it seems logical that autonomy in the process of goal setting will facilitate its effectiveness and have positive motivational consequences. Research to date (e.g. Boyce, 1992; Hall and Byrne, 1988), however, has failed to produce conclusive evidence to support this view.

In reflecting on Kyllo and Landers' (1995) meta-analysis, which identified that cooperative and participatively set goals had greater effects than assigned goals,

Hall and Kerr (2001) indicated that the degree to which the performer has ownership of the goals may be critical, with a lack of ownership reflecting in a lack of personal commitment, investment and performance. Although little research has considered specific strategies to enhance commitment, publicly as opposed to privately setting goals has been found to lead to greater levels of performance (Kyllo and Landers, 1995). It is also unclear as to whether such goals were participatively set, or what processes were involved in making them public.

One potential strategy to facilitate commitment is to encourage athletes to engage in strategic planning (Hall and Kerr, 2001), and indeed Locke and Latham (1990) identified such planning as a necessary precursor to the positive effects of goal setting on performance. Certainly, a number of researchers have explored the strategic use of different types of goals either through observation of goal-setting practices, or through experimental manipulations as part of a goal-setting training programme. Although goal commitment was not examined explicitly in such studies, it is reasonable to suggest that involvement in the process of setting and organising goals might facilitate commitment. Clearly, this proposal needs to be confirmed empirically.

Drawing primarily on the reviews of Hall and Kerr (2001), and Burton and Naylor (2002), this review of individual goal-setting research that had adopted a state conceptualisation of goals started from the position that the robust support for goal setting in industrial and organisational (I/O) settings had not transferred to sport settings. Although Locke (1991, 1994) has argued that methodological confounds can largely explain these disparate findings, examination of the literature implies that the very nature of sport and those engaged within it are equally accountable. If we take each of the potential moderators in turn, we are left with the following broad conclusions:

1   Moderate levels of goal difficulty appear most effective in facilitating performance, and responses to extremely difficult goals are not as predicted in Locke and Latham's (1985) theory of goal setting – low-ability individuals faced with such goals redefine personal goals to ensure they are salient and achievable.

2   While specific goals have been found to be better than no goals or vague goals, subjects instructed to 'do their best' do not perform any worse. This can be attributed to personal goal setting, which, it is argued, reflects fundamental differences of sport participants and within sport settings.

3   In terms of proximity, combinations of long-term and short-term goals have more positive effects on performance than any single level of proximity alone. However, this research tends to simply illustrate that goals per se are better than no-goals. Further, short-term goals appear to act as flexible and controllable stepping-stones that help to provide feedback and a sense of achievement.

4   Goal-focus research suggests that process goals have some specific benefits; however, it is also apparent that all goal types have the potential to facilitate performance and cognitions. It is clear that athletes utilise multiple

goal types, and that this has wider benefits – the challenge is to confirm the ideal recipe of goals, the mechanisms behind their effects and their organisation within a framework of applied goal setting. Finally, given the role of achievement goals as cognitive drivers, it is important to consider their role within the process of goal setting in sport.

5   There is a dearth of research examining feedback (with respect to goal setting) in sport settings. This may be because it is almost impossible to effectively constrain feedback and retain a reasonable degree of ecological validity in such work.

6   In terms of goal commitment, although Locke and Latham (1990) argued that 'choice' should facilitate goal commitment, there is little evidence to support this. Rather, it is suggested that it is the degree of 'ownership' with regards the goal-setting process and the goals themselves that may be critical.

It is apparent from this overview that the varied research examining these potential moderators of the goal setting–performance relationship has raised as many questions as it has answered. A great deal of quality research needs to done, and a number of critical issues need to be addressed to effectively illuminate the area of individual goal-setting practices in sport. We hope to begin to address these later in this chapter.

Goal setting in a team environment

Many sports are played in teams, yet the focus of sport-psychology research has been principally on individuals (Woodman and Hardy, 2001). As teams are a prevalent and salient part of sport (Widmeyer *et al.*, 1992), it is imperative to explore the application of goal setting with teams.

Locke and Latham (1985) briefly discussed the application of goal setting within team sports in their review. They stated that setting goals for individual and team sports are 'basically the same in the sense that in team sports, each individual has a specific job to do that requires particular skills' (1985: 212). However, they also highlighted that a key difference between individual and team sport is that teams require cooperation and coordination to facilitate effective performance. It is the concepts of coordination and cooperation, and the impact these concepts may have on the application of goal setting within teams, that will be the focus of this section.

Burton and Naylor (2002) described team/group goals as objectives established for the collective performance of two or more individuals, and group goal setting as the actual processes that underpin such actions. According to O'Leary-Kelly *et al.* (1994), goal setting with teams, as opposed to individuals, is unique due to the fact that (a) several goals (team, unit, individual) may be operating simultaneously; (b) difficult goals may not lead to increased effort and persistence due to the coordination requirements of team sport; and (c) the actual goal-setting process with teams is more challenging due to increased numbers and coordination demands. Nevertheless, the lack of research focused on team goal setting in comparison to research focused on individual goal setting and other team processes (i.e. cohesion) in sport might, in part, be attributable to the lack of a specific conceptual framework.

Carron's (1982) Conceptual Model of Cohesiveness in Sport Teams has been employed by early researchers to aid them in making predictions regarding the role goal setting may play in teams (see Carron and Hausenblas, 1998, for a review). For example, research examining the group structure component of Carron's (1982) model has found goal setting contributed to role clarity and role acceptance (Locke et al., 1981).

Zander (1971) hypothesised that goals within teams are generated by both individuals and the team. Individuals set personal goals and goals for the team, while goals generated by the team focus on goals for members and/or collective team goals. Bray et al. (2002) supported Zander's hypotheses in a sample of 155 male and 80 female intercollegiate athletes from various teams. Specifically they found that athletes set both group and individual goals and reported setting team goals for members and members' goals for the team. Ducharme et al. (1996) interviewed varsity athletes from 17 teams and found that individuals set goals for themselves and for the team, and the team set collective goals, yet the team did not set goals for its members. The equivocal findings of Bray et al. (2002) and Ducharme et al. (1996) raises questions over the predictive ability of Zanders' hypothesised relationships and highlights that further research testing these relationships is required. It is apparent from the research to date that both Carron's (1982) conceptual model and Zander's (1971) proposed relationships between individual- and team-generated goals lack predictive ability and specificity regarding the actual role goals play within teams.

Researchers have suggested several ways that goals impact on performance within teams. For example, goals affect team performance by influencing team focus (Widmeyer and Ducharme, 1997), inter-group communication and overall team commitment and satisfaction (Widmeyer et al., 1985). However, the influence of team goals on team performance has been hypothesised to be through the mediating effect of cohesion (Brawley et al., 1993; Carron et al., 1997, 2002, 2003; Widmeyer and Ducharme, 1997; Widmeyer et al., 1992). The following section details research that has focused on cohesion as a mediator of the team goal setting–performance relationship.

Research in team goal setting

In contrast to research examining goal setting with individual athletes, there is a comparative lack of empirical research focused on examining the influence of team goal-setting processes. It has been suggested that group goal setting directly influences performance via cohesion by providing a team 'focus' which promotes inter-group communication and facilitates overall commitment and satisfaction (Widmeyer and Ducharme, 1997). Widmeyer et al. (1992), in their study of 145 team athletes, found that having a clearly stated team goal was viewed as the most important contributor to task cohesion, and second most important for social cohesion. Acceptance of a team goal was rated as the top contributor to social cohesion. Limitations of both Widmeyer and Ducharme (1997) and Widmeyer *et al.* (1992) are (a) the cross-sectional nature of the research design limits the authors' ability to draw cause-and-effect conclusions; and (b) the 'snap-shot' look at the nature of goals within team sports. A number of intervention/longitudinal studies have attempted to address these issues.

More recently, in an attempt to establish a framework for a team goal-setting intervention, Kingston *et al.* (in preparation) investigated the impact of a team goal-setting intervention on cohesion and self-rated performance. The experimental group ($n = 10$) participated in two workshops designed to establish team goals, unit goals and individual goals for the season. Results indicated that the experimental group had significant increases in cohesion (group integration task, group integration social, attraction to the group social) scores compared to the control participants. The intervention group also had significant increases in the perception of team performance compared to the control group.

Outside of research that has examined goals in the context of cohesion effects, Brawley *et al.* (1992) investigated the nature of team goals using 154 athletes from college and community teams across one competitive season. Participants were asked to list up to five team goals for both practice and competition. Results showed that 70 per cent of team goals set by athletes throughout the season were non-specific (e.g. work hard in practice) and lacked description. Athletes focused primarily on team process goals (e.g. to run the team offence correctly 85 per cent of the time) for training (92 per cent) and team outcome goals (e.g. to win) for competition (51 per cent) throughout the course of the season. Brawley *et al.* (1992) also suggested that goals set with teams lack the specificity and behavioural dimensions recommended by previous individual goal-setting research (e.g. Albinson and Bull, 1988).

Using a method of performance-posting, Anderson *et al.* (1988) manipulated goal setting and goal sharing by setting goals (player-and-captain-agreed hit-rate per minute) and displaying goal achievement (graph displaying each team member's actual hit-rate per minute) with a male ice hockey team over two seasons. As a result of the goal setting and sharing manipulation, team performance improved significantly for the two years of the study. Anderson *et al.* (1988) found that goal sharing had a greater effect on performance than did goal setting or praise, but acknowledged that goal sharing is crucial for goal setting and vice versa (Bandura and Simon, 1977). Although there are some questions regarding the reliability of the goal-setting measures employed (Locke and Latham, 1984), Lee (1988) examining the relationship between self-efficacy, goal setting and performance (win/loss record) using nine female field hockey teams, found that team performance was positively related to setting team performance goals. Mediation analysis revealed that group goal setting had a stronger predictive relationship with winning percentage than self-efficacy. Using a qualitative research design with 14 elite (NCAA Division I) coaches, Weinberg *et al.* (2001) showed that the goal-setting process for teams was distinct to individual goal setting with regards to context (practice versus competition) and focus (physical versus psychological). Key outcomes of the research indicated that team goals tended to be coach-dictated for competition yet player-derived for practice, and goals for practice tended to be focused on physical aspects whereas goals for competition were more psychologically focused. Nevertheless, the results also highlighted many similarities between goal-setting processes for team and individual athletes (i.e. player involvement, setting of process, performance and outcome goals).

In a comparison of individual versus group goal setting, Johnson et al. (1997) examined ten-pin bowling performance in 12 three-man novice bowling teams. Participants in the group goal-setting condition ($n=4$ teams) attempted to achieve, for each game, an overall team score which was the average of individual team members' score from the previous game. The group goal-setting condition significantly improved their bowling performance compared to the individual goal-setting condition and 'do your best' control. Those in the group goal-setting condition also set more difficult personal goals (when initial ability was controlled for). Johnson et al. concluded that group goal setting may have facilitated bowling performance due to the nature of the task (i.e. skill execution involving cognitive decision-making components). Supporting this contention, Jackson and Williams (1985) found that participants performed better individually on simple cognitive tasks, but on difficult tasks, being in groups facilitated performance. Johnson and colleagues also suggested that social support, the task demanding cooperation and task planning developed through having a common focus, all lead to increased quality, accuracy and speed of performance (Johnson and Johnson, 1985).

Critique of team goal-setting research

Locke (1991), in his critical review of early research into goal setting in sport, highlighted a number of issues directed primarily at studies examining goal setting with individuals. Many of the issues raised, however, can be equally applied to the team goal-setting literature. The first methodological flaw identified by Locke (1991) was the manipulation failure of the 'do your best' goal condition. Participants in control or 'do your best' groups in the team goal-setting intervention studies outlined above (Brawley et al., 1993; Johnson et al., 1997; Kingston et al., in preparation) may have engaged in personal and/or team goal setting, unless they were specifically prevented from doing so. Of the few strategies identified by Locke (1991), the most pertinent and easily manageable without undermining the ecological validity of field-based studies would be to conduct post-intervention interviews to assess whether control group participants did actually engage in personal/team goal setting. Perhaps one of the key issues when researching goal setting within teams might not be the type of goal set. A more critical moderator of the goal setting–team performance relationship may in fact be teams engaging in the process of systematically developing goals and the strategic planning involved when team members work towards goal attainment.

Another research issue that may impact upon the effectiveness of team goal-setting research is whether assigned goals are sufficiently challenging. This is more critical for research conducted in laboratory settings or for research involving concocted groups/teams (i.e. Johnson *et al.*, 1997) when participants are performing unfamiliar tasks. When participants have no pre-conceived idea about what their performance standards are, any goal set for them is fairly arbitrary until they record a baseline score. Johnson *et al.* (1997) attempted to minimise the impact of this issue by assigning teams a goal that was 30 per cent more difficult than the performance standard the team achieved at baseline. However, clearly this limits the nature of team goals to those based on numeric targets (i.e. performance goals). For team goal-setting research conducted in the field (Brawley *et al.*, 1993; Kingston *et al.*, in preparation), goals were primarily generated by participants, with guidance from a sport psychologist or coach, and were developed to be both challenging yet realistic.

A further potential moderator or confound identified by Locke (1991) was the issue of competition between participants during individual goal-setting research – clearly, this may impact upon results and should be controlled for. When considered in the context of team goal-setting research, this issue is rather more complex. Team goals are normally assigned by the practitioner, or developed and agreed upon by the coach and/or team. This should result in team members attempting to cooperate with other team members in their attempt to achieve the team goal. However, when a team goal is set, individual team members may also set personal goals that they believe will contribute to the team goal. If each team member has personal goals, this may result in conflict between team members when they are trying to achieve their personal goals. To minimise competition between team members, personal goals should be shared, developed and agreed upon by all team members. Future research should investigate the impact of these processes (personal goal sharing, personal goal inter-team-member agreement) upon team performance and other cognitive/motivation variables in team goal-setting intervention studies.

As discussed earlier, Locke and Latham (1985) suggested key differences between individual and team sports were the concepts of coordination and cooperation. The next sub-section will consider these aspects and the research surrounding them. As Fiore *et al.* (2001) state, it is through the examination of these two concepts within team goal setting that our conceptual understanding will advance.

Goal setting to influence coordination in teams

Steiner (1972) argued that a team's actual productivity is the result of its potential productivity minus its faulty processes (i.e. poor coordination). The concept of coordination within team-sport research has received scarce attention despite Steiner's suggestion that effective coordination may lead to increased team productivity (Germain, 2005; Wilson and Mellalieu, 2007). Eccles and Tenenbaum (2004) proposed a social–cognitive conceptualisation of team coordination and communication in sport. For the purposes of this chapter, we will focus solely on the coordination aspect as it relates specifically to goal-setting applications within teams. Eccles and Tenenbaum defined coordination as 'integrating the operations of the team in a timely way to form a composition of operations that achieves satisfactory performance' (2004: 543). Before the model is outlined in relation to goal setting, some background information and definitions are salient to facilitate understanding.

Industrial and organisational (I/O) psychologists utilised the terms 'task work' (i.e. elements of a team member's tasks that are not related to other team members' tasks) and 'teamwork' (i.e. elements of a team member's tasks that are related to other team members' tasks) when describing team processes. It is the concept of teamwork that introduces the need for coordination (Bowers et al., 1997; McIntyre and Salas, 1995; Smith-Jentsch et al., 1998). Cannon-Bowers et al. (1993) suggested that each team member's knowledge of task work and teamwork must be at least similar to other team members' knowledge (i.e. shared by all team members) for coordination to be effective. The sharing of task work and teamwork knowledge by team members is coined 'shared knowledge' or 'shared mental models' (Stout et al., 1999) and is a critical element of coordinated behaviour within teams. Ward and Eccles (2006) go further and propose that goals and strategies of each team member must, at the very least, be similar or complementary to those of others on the team for coordination and successful performance to ensue.

With these concepts in mind, Eccles and Tenenbaum (2004) hypothesised that teams require coordination (which relies on shared knowledge) to perform effectively. Their model (see Figure 3.1) predicts that shared knowledge is acquired through coordination that is developed prior to performance, within performance and after performance. Eccles and Tenenbaum identified 'setting goals and objectives' as a pre-performance coordination process. Pre-performance coordination comprises of preparatory behaviours that enable a team to achieve shared knowledge prior to performance. A limitation of Eccles and Tenenbaum's (2004) original conceptualisation is the lack of detail regarding the actual processes (i.e. setting goals and objectives) that impact upon shared knowledge and coordination.

Within I/O psychology settings, researchers examining the influence of shared knowledge to enhance team coordination have focused on the role of goal setting. For example, Larson and Schaumann (1993) found that specific, difficult team goals were beneficial (i.e. increased motivation, improved performance) when task-coordination requirements were low or when teams were allowed to develop task action plans prior to task execution. When task-coordination requirements were high (like in many interdependent team sports, e.g. basketball, hockey, football), specific, difficult team goals resulted in reduced performance levels. Because individuals have multiple goals (i.e. personal, unit and team), coordination losses may occur if there is a conflict between the team member's individual goals and team goals. For example, a full-back in rugby union may want to counter-attack with ball in hand, while the team goal is to play a territory game plan that requires him or her to kick. The result of this conflict between the full-back's personal goal and the team goal may result in

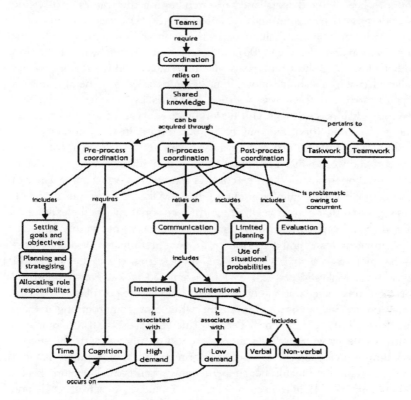

Figure 3.1 Conceptual framework of coordination in teams (source: reprinted, with permission, from D. W. Eccles and G. Tenenbaum, 2004).

coordination losses between the full-back and his/her unit who, anticipating that the full-back will kick, get into a position to chase the kick. However, the full-back runs at the opposition to satisfy his or her personal goal, becomes isolated and eventually loses possession.

In order to avoid team-performance decrements, Gully *et al.* (2002) suggested that (a) highly interdependent tasks and sports (e.g. rugby union, football, hockey, basketball) are likely to lead to the adoption of goals that facilitate cooperative strategies and coordination; (b) motivation to coordinate should increase when personal goals match team goals; (c) group members should have an adequate representation of their team members' individual goals; and (d) knowledge about the team and individual goals of one's team members are central features of shared knowledge and team functioning. These suggestions have not been empirically tested within a sporting context and would provide valuable information for coaches regarding the impact of team goal setting on performance and coordination.

There has been limited sport-based research testing the role of goal setting that is underpinned by Eccles and Tenenbaum's (2004) conceptual model of coordination in team sports. Preliminary evidence from a qualitative study conducted by Wilson and Mellalieu (2007) indicated that elite rugby union coaches utilised both long- and short-term goals with individuals and the team. Coaches also believed that goals should move from being detailed to general as match time approached, and there was a strong emphasis by coaches on the link between individual process goals, unit performance goals and team performance/outcome goals. In addition, outcome goals (e.g. 'Finish in the top four of the premiership') were only utilised with regards to long-term goals set at the outset of the season and were avoided in preparation for individual games. An interesting point raised by the majority of the coaches interviewed was the avoidance of performance goals with a numerical quality (e.g. 'Make 12 tackles in a game'). Coaches suggested that players might chase their personal goal at the expense of a team goal (e.g. 'Keep our defensive alignment 90 per cent of the time'), resulting in coordination losses and deterioration in team performance. Coaches highlighted that performance goals which focused on percentages were more effective for players (e.g. 'Make 80 per cent of your attempted tackles') and speculated that this focus on a percentage, as opposed to a number, helped players to maintain focus on individual goal achievement while not compromising a focus on team goals during performance. Perhaps this is because goal attainment is sufficiently vague to warrant fine-grained attention. Aligned with the suggestion regarding individual athletes, teams performing in a sport context may not give up when goals are difficult, but simply readjust their goal. Therefore, Eccles and Tenenbaum (2004) may need to consider including re-setting goals and objectives in the within-performance part of their model.

Cooperation and competition effects of goal setting within teams

According to Deutsch (1949, 1973), there are two types of goals that are applicable in team settings – independent and interdependent goals. Individuals who set independent goals in teams give priority to their personal goals over group goals. Individuals who set interdependent goals subordinate their personal goals to the goals of the group. Deutsch (1980) also distinguished between two types of interdependent goals, namely cooperative (i.e. one's movement towards their goal facilitates others achieving their goals) and competitive (i.e. one's movement towards their goal makes it less likely others will achieve their goals). Tjosvold (2001b) suggested that individuals who set cooperative interdependent goals (a) want to encourage team members to perform effectively; (b) are optimistic about their interactions with team members and feel confident they can rely on others; (c) are able to exchange information and resources, coordinate actions and manage conflict constructively; and (d) result in teams that are high in friendliness, attraction and team spirit (i.e. cohesion). In contrast, team members that set competitive interdependent goals (a) suspect others will not help them and may work against them; (b) fail to exchange resources fully, coordinate with difficulty, resort to threats and insults that embarrass and arouse fears of losing face and escalate their conflict; and (c) result in teams that are characterised by self-reliance, disinterest in coordination and distance from others (Tjosvold, 2001a). Research in I/O settings testing Deutsch's (1980) argument (that teams who set cooperative interdependent goals engage in adaptive team processes, functioning and performance), showed that cooperative interdependent goals were found to be associated with, but not sufficient for, successful interactions, suggesting a limitation to the argument. Tjosvold (2001a) concluded that cooperative goal interdependence needs to be supplemented with interpersonal skills (i.e. open communication, emotional intelligence and problem-solving coping skills) to facilitate coordination and productivity.

In applying Deutsch's (1980) argument to sport, team members should be encouraged to set and work towards individual goals (interdependent cooperative) that facilitate other team members' goal achievement. For example, a football player may want 'to get the ball into the penalty box 20 per cent more times per game', which is congruent with his/her team members' goal 'to get 20 per cent more attempts on goal per game'. However, as Tjosvold (2001) suggested, these two players would also need interpersonal skills (i.e. evaluate their goal progress together) to ensure they were both working together to achieve their goals.

In general, research findings from industrial and organisational settings have indicated that cooperative interdependent goals led to increased shared vision (Wong *et al.*, 2005) and were positively associated with a problem-solving approach and learning from mistakes (Tjosvold *et al.*, 2004). Managers who were described as 'cooperative interdependent goal setters' were thought to influence their employees effectively (Tjosvold *et al.*, 2001). In a sporting context, the findings of Wong *et al.* (2005) suggest that if performers were encouraged to set cooperative interdependent goals this may lead to the empowerment of team members (Kidman, 2001) and unity amongst the team. In contrast, setting competitive interdependent goals (i.e. 'Ensure I, as opposed to my striking partner, get 80 per cent of goal shooting opportunities in this game') and independent goals (i.e. 'Ensure I mark my opponent effectively 90 per cent of the time during this game') may lead to athletes neglecting the interests of their team members.

In sport, getting team members to set interdependent cooperative goals may promote problem-solving interactions that may lead to less repetition of mistakes. For example, the use of 'blaming' interactions (i.e. 'Player A did not kick accurately from the corner and that is why I could not get my shots on target'), if done in an open, honest and constructive manner, may promote accountability for players' actions (Tjosvold *et al.*, 2004). This accountability may promote effective decision-making, coordination and performance. However, this suggestion has not been empirically tested in a sport setting and is an avenue for future research.

In order to be perceived as an effective leader by their athletes, coaches should try to set cooperative interdependent goals for/with their athletes (and avoid setting competitive interdependent and independent goals; Tjosvold *et al.*, 2001). Due to the nature of cooperative interdependent goals, cooperative strategies (i.e. communicating plans, problem-solving, coping with setbacks) are required between team members and between coach and team members to facilitate goal achievement. Consequently, it may be the utilisation of these strategies that moderates the relationship between goals and performance – this area would be a challenging focus for future research.

Goal sharing

Team performance is generally influenced by the degree to which team goals are shared (Swezey and Salas, 1992). In order to increase coordination, promote cooperative interdependent goal strategies and enhance team members' shared mental models, each individual team member's goals should be shared. Goal sharing represents knowledge of a goal rather than having a common goal (Lee *et al.*, 1991). Earley and Northcraft (1989) suggested that sharing goals facilitates member cooperation, and the discussion of performance strategies may minimise conflict/coordination losses arising from task interdependence. Hollenbeck and Klein (1987) argued that sharing goals increases commitment to one's goal. Anderson *et al.*'s (1988) findings indicated that goal sharing should increase coordination, decrease the potential for conflict and improve task performance in highly interdependent teams (e.g. field hockey).

Earley and Northcraft (1989) suggested that the advantages of sharing goals will only be realised if team members work together to develop their individual goals so there is agreement and approval among team members of each person's individual goals. For example, future research should extend the protocols outlined by Munroe *et al.* (2002) and Kingston *et al.* (in preparation) to include an additional stage whereby individual athletes would develop and share their personal goals with relevant team members. This process would involve: (a) a discussion between team members about how each individual would contribute to the achievement of unit/team goals; (b) how each individual would support team members in their movement towards personal goal achievement; and (c) development of unit-/team-based strategies to minimise difficulties in the achievement of personal goals. Future research should examine the impact of goal sharing on performance and other coordination-related behaviours (i.e. communication, problem-solving) in teams that are highly interdependent (i.e. hockey, football, basketball, rugby union) to test Earley and Northcraft's (1989) suggestion.

Within a team context, it is also important to ensure that goals are cooperative, especially within highly interdependent teams (Tjosvold *et al.*, 2001, 2004; Wong *et al.*, 2005). For example, an individual team member's process goals should lead to the attainment of a unit's (sub-group of team members normally with specific common roles) performance goal, which should also lead to the attainment of the team's outcome goal. The link between the three goals should be transparent to all team members (Wilson and Mellalieu, 2007). Any goal within the team that is competitive (i.e. the achievement of the goal will lead to failure to achieve another goal) may be detrimental to performance.

In the preceding paragraphs, we have attempted to highlight how goal-setting research mainly conducted in I/O settings has implications and application to sport. However, Cannon-Bowers and Bowers (2006) suggested that lessons learned in the workplace may not generalise to sports teams for several reasons. For example, sports teams may require more interdependence compared to working groups due to the nature of the tasks and time pressures involved in sport (for a full review of the differences between work groups and sports teams, see Cannon-Bowers and Bowers, 2006). In addition, O'Leary-Kelly *et al.* (1994) highlighted that I/O psychology research frequently utilises concocted groups (i.e. formed for the purpose of the research; McGrath, 1984) in laboratory settings to examine the impact of goal setting on performance and other cognitive/behavioural variables. The results of studies that involve concocted groups/teams, as opposed to intact or natural groups/teams, should therefore, be interpreted with caution.

Overarching implications from team goal-setting research (sport and I/O settings) are that: (a) cohesion appears to mediate the goal setting–performance relationship; (b) the sharing of personal goals that contribute to team goals may influence coordination, performance and reduce conflict; (c) team goals should be difficult (to enhance collective motivation) but teams should be allowed to develop action plans prior to performance when performance coordination demands are high; (d) coaches should encourage athletes to set cooperative interdependent goals to enhance motivation, shared vision, effective problem-solving, effective superior–subordinate relationships and performance and finally; (e) coaches should discourage their athletes from setting competitive interdependent and independent goals to avoid team members engaging in exploitation, blaming and developing ineffective superior–subordinate relationships. The challenge for researchers in sport settings is to design field-based research studies with high ecological validity in order to explore the propositions outlined here.

Conceptual and practical issues

Throughout this critique a number of issues have arisen that have potentially undermined the transfer of the findings of goal-setting research from industrial/ organisational settings to the context of sports. Many of these issues have been considered briefly already, as part of the reviews; however, the purpose of this section is to highlight those that we think are most pertinent in terms of moving the study and use of goal setting in sport forwards. In highlighting these issues, we will also attempt to provide some potential solutions in terms of how work in these areas may be developed to facilitate the use and application of goal setting in sport.

One of principal factors undermining the transferability of goal-setting findings from industrial and organisational settings to the sport domain is the operationalisation of goals. As discussed in the introduction, Locke and associates (Locke, 1968; Locke and Latham, 1985, 1990) recognised that their view of goals as the object or aim of an action – that is, 'what an individual is consciously trying to do' (Locke, 1968: 159), was limited in so far that it provided only a first-level explanation of human behaviour (Hall and Kerr, 2001). It can be described as such because it only deals with the immediate precursors of human action, and makes no attempt to specify broader roots of human action. According to Beggs (1990), what is apparent from the early descriptions of goals and the research regarding their effects, is that they were focused solely on maximising output, rather than considering other cognitions (e.g. needs, values, attitudes) which are regarded as the backdrop to action (Locke and Henne, 1986; cf. Beggs, 1990). This limited view of goals has been acknowledged previously; for example, Hall and Kerr (2001) suggested that Locke and Latham's (1990) operational definition excludes aims focusing on the behavioural processes or the antecedents of performing some action.

In the sport domain, activities often take place in an overtly competitive context, motives are often intense as well as being varied and changeable, arousal and anxiety can be rife, and coaches interact in a manner that both supports and at times undermines facilitative cognitions and performance. Given these factors and the limitations of Locke and Latham's conceptualisation of goals outlined in the previous paragraph, it is unsurprising perhaps that research into goal setting in the dynamic world of sport has often produced results incongruent with those found in business-type settings. Adopting an approach based on Locke's (1968) and Locke and Latham's (1990) operationalisation of goals does not account for multi-level views of goals, for example in terms of their antecedents and affective consequences, and fails to accommodate many of the factors and relationships that go on within sport and its participants. One might argue therefore that, in order to fully report on the potential benefits of goals to coaches and athletes (as Locke and associates were able to do with respect to employee motivation) there is a need to consider: (a) the motivational aspects of goals; (b) their antecedents; and (c) their regulatory effects. Burton's (1992) competitive goal-setting model was argued to provide a more comprehensive explanation of goal-setting processes in sport; however it has been criticised at a number of levels which limits its usefulness as a heuristic tool. The criticisms have taken a number of forms: (a) the failure to substantiate a number of assumptions it makes at a conceptual or empirical level (e.g. the relationship between goal orientations and goal-setting styles); (b) the lack of precision in the description of relationships between key constructs; (c) it fails to accommodate the notion of orthogonality within achievement goals; and (d) it does not account for the potential overriding effects of situational factors (e.g. motivational climate) on goal orientations (cf. Hall and Kerr, 2001). Burton and Naylor (2002) have since proposed a revised model, which holds some promise, however, some limitations appear to remain – exhaustive testing will, nevertheless have the potential to illuminate understanding of the underpinnings, functions and effects of goals.

Goal parameters

In sport, there is limited evidence to support Locke and Latham's (1990) theory in relation to the notion of goal difficulty; in fact, athlete responses to extremely difficult goals, rather than leading to a withdrawal of resources, often lead individuals to redefine their goals in line with what they view as being achievable. Perhaps this indicates that absolute goal difficulty is not really the key issue; rather, as practitioners we should concern ourselves with the potential motivational consequences of athlete realisation that they are unlikely to achieve their performance or outcome goal. If, however, athletes hold multiple goals (as has been supported by the work of, for example, Filby *et al.*, 1999; Jones and Hanton, 1996), or have multiple criteria for success, then the potential negative effects of failing to achieve a target level of performance could be buffered by achievement of other goals. For example, focusing on behaviours associated with technique or employing specific self-regulation strategies can still be carried out successfully. Consequently, the potential negative motivational and cognitive effects of quantifiable 'failure' can be softened by executing specific processes, or by the learning opportunities associated with refining these processes.

In terms of goal specificity, the lack of direct support for Locke's prediction – that subjects simply instructed to do their best will perform worse than those with specific objectives – raises one of the central issues potentially undermining the transferability of research in this area to sports. The failure of experimental conditions to discriminate between goal effects suggests that, personal, perhaps even spontaneous, goal setting occurs irrespective of the manipulation or lack thereof (in the case of control group participants), and attempts to control it. One could argue that, in spite of experimental control, the process of internalising, processing and problem solving, and then strategising, is an integral part of engagement in achievement activities such as sport. Consequently, even a relative beginner who has actively pursued other such sports, when met with a new task/challenge, is likely to engage in, or revert to, evaluation and performance strategies adopted in similar evaluative (self or other) situations. The issue of how and why this 'learned response' has been acquired and socialised is of course open to conjecture, and should continue to be explored and debated.

The issues associated with proximity and the focus of goals could be argued to be two sides of the same coin – research in both areas reinforces the need for goal setting to be a systematic process. This process should exist within a framework where immediate goals facilitate the achievement of wider objectives, and where the organisation and prioritisation of such goals reflects a variety of personal and situational factors. Short-term goals which are controllable and flexible, and which maximise opportunities for ongoing feedback and achievement (e.g. process-based goals), should be used as stepping stones, or an immediate focus in pursuit of specific performance outcomes (e.g. hitting a target or achieving a predetermined numeric product of performance). Furthermore, these intermediate targets might reasonably represent the route by which longer-term or broader/

wider objectives, such as winning a tournament (i.e. an outcome goal), might be realised. Such a framework may enable: (a) the positive motivational and affective qualities of the different goals to be maximised, while buffering against the potential negative effects associated with, for example, a lack of control over social comparison based targets; and (b) athletes' use of multiple goals to be harnessed in a more structured and strategic manner. To summarise, longer-term outcome-based goals give an overall direction to which performers allocate personal resources, while short-term process goals can act as more immediate objectives – the pursuit of which will facilitate intensity.

When formulating their theory, Locke and Latham (1990) identified a number of factors that they argued would determine the strength of the goal setting–performance relationship: ability, feedback, commitment, task complexity and barriers to goals. Consideration of these factors was clearly a driver for the hypotheses described by Locke and Latham (1985), and which underpinned their proposed systematic examination of goal-setting theory in the context of sport. It is apparent from reviewing the literature on goal setting in the context of sports that these factors can be affected by the nature of the goals themselves. For example, increased levels of goal commitment have been linked to strategic planning by the athletes in pursuit of their goals, and to the degree to which the performer has ownership of the goal (Hall and Kerr, 2001). Both of these are more likely to be supported by controllable personalised self-referenced goals that act as meaningful 'stepping-stones' in pursuit of wider longer-term objectives (i.e. process goals). If we take this line of logic, and apply it to all those factors outlined by Locke and Latham (1990), examination of the literature suggests that goals set should ideally satisfy the following criteria: (a) support perceptions of ability; (b) facilitate commitment; (c) ensure ongoing feedback regarding immediate performance and progression towards wider objectives; and (d) have strategy development and ongoing planning as integral parts of the goal-setting process.

In addition to considering those variables that might alter the nature of the relationship between goals and performance, one also needs to consider the mechanisms through which goals influence performance (i.e. the mediating variables). According to Locke and Latham (1990), the direct mediators might include: focusing the individual on task-relevant cues, optimisation of effort and persistence over a protracted period. They further suggested that once goal commitment is achieved, these direct mediators operate automatically. At an indirect level, problem-solving and strategic planning facilitate goal attainment. The challenge for researchers aiming to provide a more parsimonious theory of the relationship between goal setting and performance is to develop a clearer picture of the variables that determine the strength of the relationship between goals per se and performance, as well as identifying the mechanisms through which different types of goals facilitate performance and its associated cognitions, behaviours and affective responses.

In association with this need to more effectively examine those variables that are 'hypothesised' to moderate or mediate the relationship between goals and performance, it is important to consider the use of acronyms as an applied tool when promoting goal setting in sport. One of the original acronyms used was SCRAM (Fuoss and Troppman, 1981), which described the properties of goals that should lead to effective performance as being specific, challenging, realistic, achievable and measurable. Similarly, the acronyms of SMART, SMARTER and MASTER (representing: measurable, adjustable, specific, time-based, exciting and realistic) have also been used, though their origins do not appear to be documented to our knowledge. While on one hand the use of such acronyms can potentially facilitate goal choices, adherence and act as useful educational tools, they do perpetuate a relatively narrow conceptualisation of goals, and so may not always be as useful as they first appear. For example, in the context of setting goals associated with numeric 'products' of performance (e.g. a time to achieve in a race, or a score to achieve in, for example, a round of golf), the appropriateness of such goals can be broadly evaluated against the acronym. However, sometimes such numeric targets might actually become a hindrance (Beggs, 1990; Kingston and Hardy, 1997). For example, Wilson and Mellalieu (2007) conducted a qualitative investigation with elite rugby union coaches and found that when setting goals for individuals performing in team sports, numbers attached to performance/process goals should be avoided (e.g. 'Make 12 tackles in the next game'), because this may result in athletes focusing on achieving their individual goal at the expense of a team goal (e.g. 'Keep our defensive organisation intact 90 per cent of the time'). They suggested that more appropriate measurable goals should focus on percentages (e.g. 'Make 90 per cent of my tackles in the next game') to avoid such issues. Furthermore, given that many of the goals that athletes set do not fall into this 'type' (see Burton and Naylor, 2002; Jones and Hanton, 1996; Munroe-Chandler *et al.*, 2004), i.e. they are equally likely to be associated with processes of performance in the immediate sense, the use of such acronyms might actually create confusion and/or undermine educational efforts. Clearly such educational approaches should ensure that all goal types are considered when promoting effective goal setting in sport.

Personal and situational factors

According to Hall and Kerr (2001), the critical process that influences goal effects is not so much the goal itself, but rather the athletes' interpretation of information concerning progress towards those goals. Specifically, athletes' goal perspectives give meaning to the investment of personal resources directed at accomplishing some discrete goal. Thus, achievement goals provide a framework within which an individual can interpret performance-related information, i.e. judging competence and defining success or failure. This lends further support for the view that, in order to fully understand goal effects, goal setting should be examined from a multi-level perspective where antecedents, cognitions and affect are considered.

Another social-cognitive approach to motivation that might aid understanding of inter-individual differences in the setting of goals is Deci and Ryan's (1985) self-determination theory. Self-determination theory considers the regulatory processes through which goals are pursued. Deci and Ryan (2000) argue that the impact of goals reflects the extent to which attainment of, and the process of, goal pursuit satisfies the fundamental human needs of competence, autonomy and relatedness. They go further to suggest that the fulfilling of these needs is what gives goals their psychological potency, and thus if goals were not related to these needs, their impact on achievement would be negligible. Research should therefore consider the potential mediating role that individual psychological needs and other such variables have on the goal setting–performance relationship.

Motivational climate

According to achievement-goal theory (Nicholls, 1984, 1989), goal orientations (individual tendencies to be task and/or ego involved) interact with individual perceptions of the achievement environment to determine moment-to-moment states of involvement (task or ego involvement). An important socio-environmental factor assumed to predict cognitive and affective responses is the motivational climate created by the coach or leaders (Ntoumanis, 2001), and the motivational attributes of these are presumed to play a critical role psychologically, emotionally and behaviourally (Duda, 2001). Based on work in education settings (Epstein, 1989), and grounded in the achievement-goal framework, Ames (1992) proposed that two motivation climates existed which could be applied to a sport context; namely, mastery and performance climates. A mastery climate was in operation if individuals were given time to master a task, effort was rewarded, groups were not based on ability, mistakes were emphasised as being part of learning and success was evaluated with regards to personal improvement (Ames, 1992). A performance climate was in operation if there was a set time to master a task, superior performance over others was rewarded, groupings were based on ability, mistakes were punished and success was evaluated with regards to outperforming others (Ames, 1992). Recent studies have suggested that the motivational climate is more important than goal orientations in determining individual levels of motivation (e.g. Cury et al., 1996).

To date, no research has empirically tested the relationship between motivational climate and the actual goals performers set. There is evidence to support the link between a mastery climate and task orientation and a performance climate and ego orientation (e.g. Brunel, 1999; Creswell et al., 2003; Newton and Duda, 1999; Standage et al., 2003). Accepting the limitations of incongruent theoretical underpinnings, one might still predict that a similar relationship exists between climate and the nature of goals, as that which has been proposed to exist between goal orientations and discrete goals (i.e. task orientation and process goals, ego orientation and process/outcome goals). For example, individual athletes exposed to a strong mastery climate might set more process goals compared to athletes in a strong performance climate, who may set more outcome goals (but not predispose them against setting process goals; see Wilson et al., 2006).

In support of the essence of these propositions, recent research by Reinboth and Duda (2006) suggests that a mastery climate may be supported by (amongst other things) encouraging athletes to develop internalised performance stand-ards through self-monitoring and ongoing performance evaluation, both of which reflect a process-based focus for goals. At a practical level, creating a more task-involving 'mastery' motivational climate by applying Epstein's (1989) TARGET dimensions has the potential to facilitate the use of goals based on learning, development of skills and evaluation of performance relative to per-sonal (as opposed to normative) standards. Ames (1992) identified several struc-tural features of the achievement context that influence motivational climate. To foster a mastery climate, Ames contends that (a) tasks should be inclusive, self-referenced and based on an individual's ability level; (b) learners should be involved in decision-making regarding the tasks and they should be recog-nised and evaluated in terms of individual effort, knowledge and skill develop-ment; (c) they should work in small, mixed-ability, cooperative groups; and (d) should be given flexible (and maximal) time for improvement (cf. Morgan and Kingston, 2008).

Preliminary research suggests that manipulation of the TARGET structures can facilitate a more mastery-involved motivational climate and enhance moti-vational responses (Morgan and Carpenter, 2002; Morgan and Kingston, 2008; Theeboom *et al.*, 1995). The obvious extension of this work is to identify and clarify whether these effects are attributable to a change in the goals and/or the meaning attached to goals in this type of achievement context.

Reconceptualisation of goal focus

We have previously argued that employing Locke's original view of goals in sport was perhaps overly narrow. Additionally, exploration of the literature into the specific primary focus of goals and anecdotal accounts of goal setting in applied situations leads us to propose that the trichotomous distinction of outcome, performance and process goals may need to be refined.

Hardy and Nelson (1988) initially distinguished between three different types of goals. Outcome goals are based on the end-product of a specified event and may involve interpersonal comparison of some kind (e.g. a finishing place in a race, or winning and losing). Performance goals are self-referenced, and refer to a specific end-product of performance; they normally involve a numeric value (e.g. the total number of putts taken in the duration of a round of golf). Finally, process goals centre on the execution of behaviours, skills and strategies (e.g. technique, form, thought processes to regulate behaviour) that are integral to effective task execution. Outcome and performance goals are distinguishable because outcome goals are normatively referenced, whereas performance goals are self-referenced. Research has supported this distinction, and indeed they have been argued to have qualitatively different effects on performance and associated cognitions (e.g. Burton, 1989; Filby *et al.*, 1999; Kingston and Hardy, 1997; Zimmerman and Kitsantas, 1996).

Having clarified the delineation between the two types of self-referenced goals, a number of researchers have provided support from the use of process-based goals to facilitate sports performance (e.g. Filby et al., 1999; Kingston and Hardy, 1997; Zimmerman and Kitsantas, 1996). Such a directive, however, has been widely debated in the context of learning and coaching because instructing performers to consciously focus on their body movements during skill execution is not an effective learning strategy (Baumeister, 1984; Hardy et al., 1996b; Jackson et al., 2006; Masters, 1992; Wulf and Prinz, 2001). In their dart-throwing task, Zimmerman and Kitsantas (1996) failed to find support for the possible liabilities of awareness when learning motor skills. In attempting to explain this apparent confound, Kingston and Hardy (1997) proposed that process goals should be tailored according to the skill level of the performer, and further that they may actually serve qualitatively different functions for athletes. On the one hand, less-able performers may utilise process goals to focus attention on key elements of performance, while more-able performers may use them as holistic conceptual cues for the to-be-performed behaviour, which thus reduces the potential for performance disruption caused by explicit monitoring (Hardy et al., 1996b; Kingston and Hardy, 1994, 1997). While preliminary research has failed to illuminate this issue, the debate raises an interesting question: are there other self-referenced-type goals that facilitate perceptions of control and ownership, ensure a task focus, yet do not suffer because they encourage self-monitoring in the manner associated with process-oriented goals?

Zimmerman and Kitsantas (1996), using a learning paradigm, examined the effects of two goal types: process and product goals. Their operationalisation of process goals was in line with that forwarded by Hardy and Nelson (1988), while they described product-oriented goals as those that specify the outcomes of learning efforts. They suggested that 'product goals shift learners' attention away from the strategic means to task outcomes' (Zimmerman and Kitsantas, 1996: 62). Drawing upon the work of information-processing theorists (e.g. Carver and Scheier, 1981), which has shown that paying attention to other aspects of the task can be adaptable once elements of a complex skill become automatised, Zimmerman and associates suggested that product goals should assist learners when they are applying their routinised skills to natural conditions (cf. Zimmerman and Kitsantas, 1996). In terms of delineating between the different types of goal focus, it is apparent that their definition of product goals encapsulates both outcome (e.g. based on outperforming others) and performance (i.e. personal performance targets that are normally numeric) goals.

Within their review outlining a rationale supporting the use of process goals as a learning strategy, and based on the discussions of Singer et al. (1983), Zimmerman and Kitsantas (1996) outlined what they described as a 'non-awareness' strategy. This involved focusing on such things as the pre-planned form of the movement, a specific single situational cue (such as the seam of the ball or the centre of the target), and ignoring movement information and other situational cues as the task is executed. This notion of non-awareness ties in nicely with the recent work of Gabrielle Wulf and associates (e.g. Wulf and Prinz, 2001). Reflecting on Singer's (1985, 1988) five-step approach to skill learning (which encourages a task focus while distracting them from their own movements), Wulf and associates argued that cues used to focus attention need to be 'external' (e.g. on the dimples of the golf ball, the anticipated trajectory, or the target) rather than 'internal' (e.g. on body movements themselves), thus taking attention away from the required movement pattern (Wulf *et al.*, 2000). More specifically, Wulf and colleagues found that directing attention to the anticipated environmental effects of the movement (e.g. the consequence of kicking a ball) was more effective than focusing on the action itself (Lawrence and Kingston, 2008). This supports Prinz's (1997) action–effect hypothesis that suggests that actions are planned and controlled most effectively by their intended effects.

Based on this notion of 'effect goals', we would propose that such a strategy or focus represents a practically relevant and qualitatively distinguishable goal type that, while self-referenced (in so far that they do not involve social comparison) and task-based, do not promote conscious control of the skill itself (which is likely to undermine skill execution, especially when it is largely automated). 'Effect' goals might thus be defined as those where the primary focus is on the physical and environmental effects of task execution. While self-referenced, they are distinct from process goals because they are consequences of movements rather than an integral component of the skill. Examples of 'effect' goals might include the target, or the anticipated line, flight or trajectory of the ball. These goals are distinguishable from process goals which focus on such aspects as technique, form, thought processes and/or strategies that are integral to effective task execution.

Figure 3.2 provides an illustration of how 'effect' goals might be represented in a pictorial delineation of the different goal types. We have also shown how these types of goals might be distinguishable from other goal types in terms of the degree of personal control the individual exerts in pursuit of goal attainment; and, in team situations, the degree to which fellow team members need to be involved in the setting and planning of such goals.

It can also be seen that we have distinguished between three types of process-based goals: (a) those associated with technical aspects (e.g. focusing on the movement of the hands or shoulders while making a stroke); (b) those associated with self-regulation (e.g. adhering to a performance routine or maintaining a regular breathing pattern); and (c) those associated with strategic aspects (e.g. staying within two yards of an opposing player when their team is on the offence). This distinction reflects research (e.g. Wilson and Mellalieu, 2007) and anecdotal accounts of the nature of goals utilised by athletes that fall under the broader category of process-based goals.

Applied implications

Throughout this review, we have attempted to bridge the theory–practice link by illustrating how the evolving knowledge base might be effectively applied to the domain of sport. Before drawing some conclusions and identifying explicitly a number of potential avenues for future research, we would like to illustrate how a number of the research findings to date, the logical proposals based on work

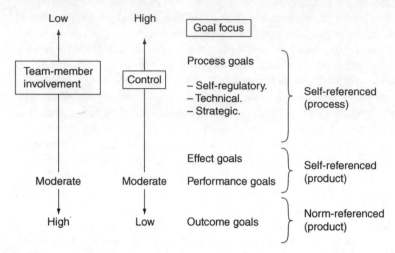

Figure 3.2 Delineation of goal types.

within teams at a sport and business level, and the refined distinction between the different goal types, can be used to guide goal setting at an individual and a team level. It should be noted, however, that these proposals represent 'best judgements' founded on the information to hand – clearly intervention-based studies utilising all or part of these suggestions are required to validate these proposals.

Application at an individual level

There is considerable empirical and anecdotal support for the use of process-based goals as a primary focus in competitive situations, mainly because they promote a task focus. Additionally, however, they can serve as controllable and flexible stepping stones in pursuit of performance and outcome goal 'achievement'. The caveat to these suggestions is that the process goals pursued by individual performers should be tailored according to the context (e.g. practice or competition) and their skill level. As alluded to previously, according to the 'reinvestment' hypothesis (Baumeister, 1984; Masters, 1992), the explicit focus elicited through attending to bodily movement while executing tasks is likely to disrupt performance in more capable performers. However, while this notion of 'skill' level as a moderator of the process goal–performance relationship has still to be supported in sport-based research, a number of researchers (e.g. Kingston and Hardy, 1997; Zimmerman and Kitsantas, 1996) proposed that process goals of a more holistic nature, for example those that focus on a single context-relevant conceptual cue (e.g. smooth, extend or tempo), would avoid the potential interference highlighted in Master's hypothesis.

Many skilled performers, particularly in closed-skill sport tasks (e.g. a golf swing, a place kick in rugby union or a basketball free-throw), describe focusing on the target, or imagining seeing the ball follow a desired path, as their primary focus. This focus on 'effects' might ensure a task focus, yet guard against the potential for conscious processing, and so be highly pertinent as an objective. The important point here is that there may need to be some sort of automated routinised behaviour before adopting an 'effect' focus to ensure that the individual is absorbed fully into the task and not liable to distraction. However, this idea requires empirical support.

The use of performance goals (numeric objectives) to evaluate performance levels is an integral component of many sports. Burton's (1989) study broadly supported their adoption; however, he also added that available research (Roberts, 1984) and anecdotal evidence suggested that most athletes do not spontaneously evaluate their competence based on performance goals. Nevertheless, performance tracking through numeric criteria is widespread. While some research suggests that such goals can have a positive motivational effect (Burton, 1989), and thus may be used as intermediate stepping stones in the pursuit of, for example outcome goals, they should not be used as a primary focus because, although being self-referenced, they may be undermined by external factors such as the environment or the quality of the opposition (Beggs, 1990; Kingston and Hardy, 1997).

The value placed upon outcome goals such as winning are clearly emphasised in our modern sport culture, and there is no doubt that the advent of professionalism and the tremendous rewards available in sport ensure that the importance of winning will continue to be emphasised. Consequently, there is little doubt as to the positive motivational function of such goals – as we pointed out earlier, such goals may give athletes an overall direction for their personal resources (e.g. 'I want to become world number one'). Indeed, research has supported the value placed upon outcome goals (Weinberg *et al.*, 2001); however, according to Burton and Naylor (2002), athletes have become more sophisticated in their use of process and performance goals to realise their desired outcome goals – whose importance lies in their long-term motivational function.

The preceding paragraphs have outlined a possible framework for utilising goals in sport. However, what has become apparent within our critique is that, in order to explain inter- and intra-individual differences in goal-setting practices and fluctuations in the nature of discrete goals used, it may be important to consider individual achievement goals (i.e. the meaning that individuals give to their goals). We would like to outline this case a little more explicitly and provide an applied illustration.

It has often been posited that high-level athletes may hold simultaneously high levels of task and ego orientations; that is, they have similarly high tendencies to be both task and ego involved in achievement settings (e.g. Hardy, 1997). This is because these goal orientations are viewed as orthogonal, or independent. Although there remains some conceptual confusion, Harwood and associates provide a compelling argument that, while it is quite possible for an individual to have simultaneous 'tendencies' for task and ego involvement (i.e. to be high task and high oriented), in a moment-to-moment sense 'one cannot be task and ego involved at the same time' (Harwood *et al.*, 2000: 240). Consequently, if we adopt this viewpoint, at an applied level it is critical to consider both the antecedents to moment-to-moment fluctuations in states of involvement, and the motivational, behavioural and affective consequences of judging competence and defining success and failure along the associated lines.

As we have outlined in the previous paragraphs, coaches are likely (and quite rightly in our view) to promote the value of goals that do not emphasise social comparison during competition, as it is unlikely that focusing on such would be the most effective goal-setting strategy in comparison to a process- or task-based focus. However, if we consider an individual athlete who in a general sense has a potentially (for an athlete who has multiple ways through which to judge competence) motivationally adaptive high task/high ego orientation profile, such a person (by definition) has tendencies to judge competence and define success in terms of both personal aspect of performance and social comparison. Consequently, at a situational level, especially in a competitive environment (as opposed to a training situation) where direct comparison can become salient, it is not surprising that the athlete may be susceptible to judging competence and evaluating success and failure based on social comparison – i.e. outperforming an opponent. The following hypothetical scenario illustrates how this may occur.

Let us consider an athlete who has both a high task and a high ego orientation 'goal profile' in a competitive sporting environment (i.e. an important game). The coach, throughout the season and the lead up to the game, has illustrated and emphasised the team's goals, and how unit (small group, e.g. offensive or defensive groups) and personal goals regarding strategy and execution of skills facilitate performance and team/unit goal achievement. The important point is that the player is in no doubt of the value of focusing on the task, rather than focusing on judging his competence based on social comparison. During the game, however, his immediate opposing player attempts to undermine his focus by fouling him off the ball and this is goes unseen by the officials. Annoyed and frustrated, his focus changes from his particular task-based goals (individual and unit goals perhaps) to a personal crusade to outperform his opposing player – from a goal perspectives view, he has moved from a task to an ego-involved state of involvement. Consequently, his lost focus on his specific role within the team undermines both the unit and the team goals, and ultimately team performance.

Such a situation shows how goal states have the potential to fluctuate from moment to moment in 'normal' situations experienced within the sporting arena. More importantly for practitioners, however, it illustrates how inter-individual differences might make athletes differentially susceptible to potentially performance-inhibiting changes in their goal-setting practices. This can occur despite individuals fully buying into the team, unit and individual philosophy of a task or process focus while engaging in competition because this is perceived as a route through which to achieve their broader comparison-based objectives (e.g. winning the league). For the coach or sport psychologist who has advocated a task focus in competitive situations, this type of scenario provides a teachable moment whereby the potential hazards of adopting a social comparison-based focus, even at a moment-to-moment level, can be illustrated. Further, it will facilitate understanding of the importance of prioritising goals according to the demands of the situation. Thus the role for practitioners is to recognise both inter- and intra-individual differences in 'tendencies' to be task and ego involved, and to educate athletes in how best to utilise or control possessing multiple criteria for judging competence and defining success and failure.

To summarise the application of goals at an individual level, we suggest that process (e.g. self-regulatory, technical or strategic) and effect (e.g. target or trajectory) goals should be used as a primary focus (with due consideration for personal and contextual factors), and as flexible and controllable stepping stones to realise intermediate performance-based goals (e.g. numeric targets). A structured and strategic programme of such goals should provide the performer with a route to realise his or her longer-term outcome-based objectives. Further, in organising and evaluating individual goal-setting practices, practitioners should give due consideration for the fact that athletes might reasonably possess multiple ways through which to judge competence and define success and failure, and that these have specific antecedents as well as varying behavioural, cognitive and affective consequences.

Application in a team context

When applying the goal-setting framework to teams, the control continuum is particularly salient. For example, teams will naturally set outcome (normatively referenced product) goals (e.g. to finish in the top four in the league) over which they have has limited control due to, for example, the performance of opposition teams. However, teams have also set team self-referenced performance goals (e.g. 'Win 80 per cent of our first-phase possession') and self-referenced process goals (e.g. 'Keep our depth after first phase'), for which teams have increasing amounts of control over attainment. In addition to the control continuum, when using this framework with teams, practitioners might also consider an involvement continuum (see Figure 3.2).

The involvement continuum reflects the degree to which goals need to be developed, discussed and agreed upon by all members of the team. For product-type goals (performance and outcome goals), these should generally have a high level of involvement by all team members, while process goals may require less involvement as they may (a) be more relevant to certain sub-units within a team (therefore only that unit need to discuss, develop and agree the goal); and (b) be more important for certain individuals who have distinct roles and responsibilities (e.g. hockey goalkeeper, striker in football, hooker in rugby union). In an applied context, practitioners should endeavour to ensure team product goals (normative and self-referenced) are developed, discussed and agreed by the coach and all team members (or relevant units for specific unit self-referenced product goals). Self-referenced process goals might be developed, discussed and agreed between pertinent individuals (i.e. defence, forwards) or the specific person for whom that goal is relevant. This increased level of shared knowledge should result in enhanced coordination, which is hypothesised to lead to increased performance levels in teams (Eccles and Tenenbaum, 2004). When team members set individual self-referenced process goals, at minimum they should be developed, discussed and agreed between player and coach (maybe through the use of performance profiling; see Butler, 1989; Dale and Wrisberg, 1996; Munroe et al., 2002). However, sharing (which does not necessarily imply agreement) individual goals (with relevant team members) may also enhance goal achievement, as it allows for increased understanding between team members, which should result in a greater degree of shared knowledge (Stout et al., 1999).

Conclusions

Our original desire was to provide the informed reader with a critical appraisal of the current 'state of play' with regard to work in the area of goal setting and its application to sport. Second, we sought to critique this work based on the large gaps that exist between goal setting at a theoretical and research level and the application of that work. The central emphasis became the consideration of individual and team-based research into goals and goal setting, and its application and implications for sport. However, we also sought to consider inter- and intra-individual differences, for example in terms of achievement goals, which were argued to give psychological meaning to the goals used.

At an individual level, it is clear that there is great disparity in findings between business and I/O settings and sport. At a team level, while currently there is a relative dearth of literature examining the effects of goals, this is beginning to be addressed. In carrying out our review, a number of messages came to the fore:

- While considerable debate surrounds the lack of transferability of goal-setting findings and principles from industrial/organisational settings to sport, this has tended to focus on methodological confounds. Our review, however, suggests that consideration for the unique sporting environment as well as inter- and intra-individual differences may be equally attributable.
- Moderately difficult goals are more desirable than very easy or very difficult goals; however, even in the face of such goals, sport participants by default engage in individual goal setting at a specific level.
- A structured framework of goals may help to optimise positive effects. This framework should include self-referenced, process or effect-based goals at the immediate level (depending on skill level and the context). These process goals should be flexible to provide for maximal learning and optimal task focus, and serve as stepping stones within a framework of

achieving intermediate performance and outcome goals. Coaches need also to consider the personal meaning of goals.

- Performers should perceive a high degree of choice and ownership of goals and the strategies to achieve them to maximise their motivational effects.
- While many of the methodological limitations identified in individual goal setting have been argued to apply equally to teams, the issues of cooperation and coordination are pivotal to the effects of goals in this environment.
- Team goal setting and the processes therein are unique and more challenging because several individual goals exist simultaneously.
- There is a lack of predictive validity in the models applied to goal setting within teams, but researchers have identified several ways in which goals impact on performance in teams (e.g. team focus, communication, individual commitment to the team, satisfaction and cohesion).
- The systematic development of goals and strategic planning and the use, at an individual level, of cooperative interdependent goals which facilitate unit and team goals are pivotal motivationally, and to minimise confounding effects of individual team member goals.
- Coaches utilise both long- and short-term goals, and link individual process goals with unit performance goals and team performance and outcome goals. Outcome goals are only used explicitly in the long term.
- The relationship between achievement goals (states of involvement or dispositional motives) and discrete (state) goals is unclear. However, despite questionable theoretical basis, the links appear logical and thus more research attention needs to consider the relationship between cognitive drivers and specific goal-setting practices.
- Ames' (1992) TARGET framework for developing a mastery-based motivational climate can effect positive motivational change, and the use of process-based goals that involve self-monitoring and ongoing evaluation promotes a mastery-based motivational climate.

Future research questions

Throughout this review we have attempted, as an ongoing process, to highlight where a specific line of research might help to illuminate the theoretical or applied knowledge base. The purpose of this final section is to give an overview of the questions raised across the whole chapter and which, in our opinion, require attention in order to develop in the area of goal setting. Furthermore, a number of the applied research questions will, we anticipate, help to close the gap between the research process and the application of those findings.

The early part of this chapter, covering individual goal setting, examined past research that focused on the attributes of goals that have been argued to moderate the goal setting–performance relationship. While we highlighted a number of contentious findings, several key future research questions emerged from this section. With regards to goal difficulty, we suggested that, in addition to questions surrounding the operationalisation of 'difficulty' across varying goal types, further research was required to understand the motivational consequences of athletes realising their inability to achieve their initial goal. Past research has suggested that if goals become too difficult, athlete performance levels plateau (Weinberg, 1994). In reality, however, athletes may redefine their goal to be more realistic and achievable, and continue in the pursuit of the new goal (Burton and Naylor, 2002). In addition, in terms of goal proximity, and with the objective of building a coherent framework for organising a long-term goal-setting strategy, it is important to identify the 'recipe' or combination of long- and short-term goals that most effectively support sports performers. This may well involve consideration for the specific focus of those long-, intermediate and short-term goals. Touching on this notion of goal focus, there is an emerging, yet under-developed, body of literature that has given rise to a number of contentious issues. Consequently, we suggest that possible directions for further work in this area might include: investigations into the nature of different process-based goals used by performers, and examination of the potential moderating (e.g. self-efficacy, concentration) or mediating (e.g. skill level) variables influencing their application in sport.

Hall and Kerr (2001) identified feedback and commitment as potential moderators of the goal setting–performance relationship in sport. To move this area forward, we suggest that researchers should examine the influence of feedback which highlights to the performer a wide discrepancy between current levels of performance and personal goals (e.g. the coach telling a performer he or she is not achieving set performance targets), and the effects on, for example, self-efficacy, motivational variables and performance. With regards to goal commitment, we propose that future research should examine the impact of athlete involvement (i.e. self-set versus other-set) in the setting of goals on commitment to goal achievement.

As we highlighted previously, relative to goal-setting research focusing on individual athletes, team goal-setting research in sport is in its infancy. Consequently, this area requires sustained research attention to facilitate understanding of the use of goal setting in team contexts. Particularly with respect to the notions of coordination and cooperation, we propose the following directions for future research:

1   Examine the impact of personal goal sharing and personal inter-team-member goal agreement upon team performance and coordination-related behaviours (i.e. communication) and performance.
2   Identify the extent to which effective performance in highly interdependent teams is associated with the adoption of goals that facilitate cooperative strategies.
3   Examine whether the congruence of team goals with individual goals increases motivation to coordinate within teams.
4   Assess whether performance and associated cognitions are supported when team members have an adequate representation of their fellow team members' individual goals.

5   Examine which types of personal goals (i.e. self-referenced product goals versus self-referenced process goals) allow team players to maintain a focus on individual processes during performance while avoiding compromising team goals.

6   Identify whether team members setting interdependent cooperative goals have increased accountability over their goal achievement (which is suggested to lead to effective decision-making, coordination and performance).

7   Examine whether coaches that promote cooperative interdependent goals for/with their athletes are perceived as more effective leaders by their players.

8   Identify the extent to which cooperative strategies (e.g. communication plans, problems solving and coping with setbacks) facilitate goal achievement within teams.

An overarching challenge for researchers examining goal setting within teams is to maintain the ecological validity of research utilising sports teams while aiming to control for potential confounding variables (i.e. control groups setting team goals).

Throughout our review we have also been keen to emphasise the importance that should be placed on considering inter- and intra-individual differences when planning and evaluating the use of specific types of goals. Specifically, with regard to achievement goals, we suggest that there is a need to clarify the relationship between goal perspectives, for example states of involvement and goal orientations, and the types of goals performers set. This would allow researchers and practitioners to more fully understand the link between the meaning athletes place on achievement contexts and the resulting types of goals they are likely to set. With regard to the psychological environment in which athletes develop and execute their skills, future research should explore manipulation of the motivational climate (via a manipulation of the TARGET structures), and its effects on (a) changing their goals; and/or (b) changing the meaning of their goals. Staying with achievement motivation, given Deci and Ryan's (2000) arguments that needs give goals their psychological potency, we believe that future research should consider the mediating role of the basic human needs of autonomy, competence and relatedness (Self-Determination Theory; Deci and Ryan, 1985) on the goal setting–performance relationship, and perhaps more specifically on the relationship between goal type and performance.

Finally, on several occasions throughout this chapter we have highlighted that a major limitation within goal-setting research (both individual and team) is the lack of adequate theoretical models to guide researchers and aid practitioners when applying goals within sport. Further examination of the predictive ability of Burton and Naylor's (2002) revised competitive goal-setting model would be a good starting point. In a team context, examining the predictive ability of Zanders' (1971) hypothesised relationships within contemporary team-sport contexts, and the role of goal setting as posited within Eccles and Tenenbaum's (2004) conceptualisation of team coordination and cooperation in sport, will again begin to inform both further research and applied practice.

Acknowledgement

We would like to thank Professor Dave Gilbourne for his advice and insightful comments throughout the production of this chapter.

Note

1 While detailed meta-analytic procedures have the potential to smooth-out data to identify trends, they have similar effects in shielding potential methodological flaws.

References

Albinson, J. G. and Bull, S. J. (1988). *The mental game plan: a training programme for all sports*. Melbourne: Sports Dynamics.

Ames, C. (1992). Classrooms: goals, structures, and student motivation. In G. C. Roberts (ed.), *Motivation in sport and exercise* (pp. 161–176). Champaign, IL: Human Kinetics.

Anderson, C. D., Crowell, C. R., Doman, M. and Howard, G. S. (1988). Performance posting, goal setting, and activity-contingent praise as applied to a university hockey team. *Journal of Applied Psychology*, 73, 87–96.

Bandura, A. (1986). *Social foundations of thoughts and actions: a social cognitive theory*. Englewood Cliffs, NJ: Prentice Hall.

Bandura, A. and Cervone, D. (1983). Self-evaluative and self-efficacy mechanisms governing the motivational effects of goal systems. *Journal of Personality and Social Psychology*, 45, 1017–1028.

Bandura, A. and Simon, K. M. (1977). The role of proximal intentions in self-regulation of refractory behaviour. *Cognitive Therapy and Research*, 1, 177–193.

Baron, R. M. and Kenny, D. A. (1986). The moderator–mediator variable distinction in social psychological research: conceptual, strategic, and statistical considerations. *Journal of Personality and Social Psychology*, 51, 1173–1182.

Baumeister, R. F. (1984). Choking under pressure: self-consciousness and paradoxical effects of incentives on skilful performance. *Journal of Personality and Social Psychology*, 46, 610–620.

Beggs, A. (1990). Goal setting in sport. In G. Jones and L. Hardy (eds), *Stress and performance in sport* (pp. 135–170). New York: Wiley.

Bowers, C. A., Braun, C. C. and Morgan, B. B. (1997). Team workload: its meaning and measurement. In M. T. Brennick, E. Salas and C. Prince (eds), *Team performance assessment and measurement: theories, methods and applications* (pp. 85–105). Mahwah, NJ: Earlbaum.

Boyce, B. A. (1992). Effects of assigned versus participant-set goals on skill acquisition and retention of a selected shooting task. *Journal of Teaching in Physical Education*, 11, 220–234.

Boyce, B. A. (1994). The effects of goal setting on performance and spontaneous goal setting behaviour of experienced pistol shooters. *The Sport Psychologist*, 8, 87–93.

Boyce, B. A. and Wayda, V. K. (1994). The effects of assigned and self-set goals on task performance. *Journal of Sport Exercise Psychology*, 16, 258–269.

Brawley, L. R., Carron, A. V. and Widmeyer, W. N. (1992). The nature of group goals in sport teams: a phenomenological analysis. *The Sport Psychologist*, 6, 323–333.

Brawley, L. R., Carron, A. V. and Widmeyer, W. N. (1993). The influence of the group and its cohesiveness on perceptions of group goal-related variables. *Journal of Sport and Exercise Psychology*, 15, 245–260.

Bray, S. R., Dawson, K. A. and Widmeyer, W. N. (2002). Goal setting by intercollegiate sport teams and athletes. *AVANTE*, 8, 14–23.

Brunel, P. C. (1999). Relationship between achievement goal orientation and perceived motivational climate on intrinsic motivation. *Scandinavian Journal of Medicine and Science in Sport*, 6, 365–374.

Burton, D. (1989). Winning isn't everything: examining the impact of performance goals on collegiate swimmers' cognitions and performance. *The Sport Psychologist*, 3, 105–132.

Burton, D. (1992). The Jekyll/Hyde nature of goals: reconceptualising goal setting in sport. In T. Horn (ed.), *Advances in sport psychology* (pp. 267–297). Champaign, IL: Human Kinetics.

Burton, D. (1993). Goal setting in sport. In R. N. Singer, M. Murphy and L. K. Tennant (eds), *Handbook of research on sport psychology* (pp. 467–491). New York: Macmillan.

Burton, D. and Naylor, S. (2002). The Jekyll/Hyde nature of goals: revisiting and updating goal setting research. In T. Horn (ed.), *Advances in sport psychology* (pp. 459–499). Champaign, IL: Human Kinetics.

Burton, D., Weinberg, R. S., Yukleson, D. and Weigand, D. (1998). The goal effectiveness paradox in sport: examining the goal practices of collegiate athletes. *The Sport Psychologist*, 12, 404–418.

Butler, R. J. (1989). Psychological preparation of Olympic boxers. In J. Kremer and W. Crawford (eds), *The psychology of sport: theory and practice* (pp. 74–84). BPS Northern Ireland Branch: Occasional Paper.

Cannon-Bowers, J. A. and Bowers, C. (2006). Applying work team results to sport teams: opportunities and cautions. *International Journal of Sport and Exercise Psychology*, 4, 363–369.

Cannon-Bowers, J. A., Salas, E. and Converse, S. (1993). Shared mental models in expert team decision making. In N. J. Castellan, Jr. (ed.), *Individual and group decision making* (pp. 221–246). Hillsdale, NJ: LEA.

Carron, A. V. (1982). Cohesiveness in sport groups: interpretations and considerations. *Journal of Sport Psychology*, 4, 123–138.

Carron, A. V. and Hausenblas, H. A. (1998). *Group dynamics in sport*. Morgantown, WV: Fitness Information Technology.

Carron, A. V., Brawley, L. R., Eys, M. A., Bray, S. R., Dorsh, K., Estabrook, P., Hall, C. R., Hardy, J., Hausenblas, H., Madison, R., Paskevich, D., Patterson, M. M., Prapavessis, H., Spink, K. S. and Terry, P. C. (2003). Do individual perceptions of group cohesion reflect shared beliefs? An empirical analysis. *Small Group Research*, 34, 468–496.

Carron, A. V., Coleman, M. M., Wheeler, J. and Stevens, D. (2002). Cohesion and performance in sport: a meta-analysis. *Journal of Sport and Exercise Psychology*, 24, 168–188.

Carron, A. V., Spink, K. S. and Prapavessis, H. (1997). Team building and cohesiveness in the sport and exercise setting: use of indirect interventions. *Journal of Applied Sport Psychology*, 9, 61–72.

Carver, C. S. and Scheier, M. F. (1981). Attention and self-regulation: a control-theory approach to human behaviour. New York: Springer-Verlag.

Carver, C. S. and Scheier, M. F. (1998). *On the self-regulation of behaviour*. New York: Cambridge University Press.

Cresswell, S. L., Hodge, K. P. and Kidman, L. (2003). Intrinsic motivation in youth sport: The effect of goal orientations and motivational climate. *Journal of Physical Education in New Zealand*, 36, 15–26.

Cury, F., Biddle, S. H., Famose, J. P., Goudas, M., Sarrazin, P. and Durand, M. (1996). Personal and situational factors influencing intrinsic interest of adolescent girls in physical education: a structural equation modelling analysis. *Educational Psychology*, 67, 293–309.

Dale, G. A. and Wrisberg, C. A. (1996). The use of performance profiling technique in a team setting: getting the athletes and coach on the 'same page'. *The Sport Psychologist*, 10, 261–277.

Deci, E. L. and Ryan, R. M. (1985). *Intrinsic motivation and self-determination in human behaviour*. New York: Plenum Press.

Deci, E. L. and Ryan, R. M. (2000). The 'what' and 'why' of goal pursuits: human needs and the self-determination of behaviour. *Psychological Inquiry*, 11, 227–268.

Ducharme, K. A., Bray, S. R. and Widmeyer, W. N. (1996). Goal setting by intercollegiate teams and athletes. *Journal of Sport and Exercise Psychology*, 18 (Suppl.), S26.

Duda, J. L. (1992). Motivation in sports settings: a goal perspective approach. In G. Roberts (ed.), *Motivation in sport and exercise* (pp. 57–91). Champaign, IL: Human Kinetics.

Duda, J. L. (1997). Perpetuating myths: a response to Hardy's 1996 Coleman Griffith Address. *Journal of Applied Sport Psychology*, 9, 303–309.

Duda, J. L. (2001). Achievement goal research in sport: pushing the boundaries and clarifying some misunderstandings. In G. C. Roberts (ed.), *Advances in motivation in sport and exercise* (pp. 129–182). Champaign, IL: Human Kinetics.

Duda, J. L., Olsen, L. K. and Templin, T. (1991). The relationship of task and ego orientation to sportsmanship attitudes and the perceived legitimacy of injurious acts. *Research Quarterly for Exercise and Sport*, 62, 79–87.

Deutsch, M. (1949). An experimental study of the effects of cooperation and competition upon group processes. *Human Relations*, 2, 199–231.

Deutsch, M. (1973). *The resolution of conflict*. New Haven, CT: Yale University Press.

Deutsch, M. (1980). Over fifty years of conflict research. In L. Festinger (ed.), *Four decades of social psychology* (pp. 46–77). New York: Oxford University Press.

Earley, P. C. and Northcraft, G. B. (1989). Goal setting, interdependence, and conflict management. In M. S. Rahim (ed.), *Managing conflict: an interdisciplinary perspective* (pp. 161–170). New York: Praeger Publishers.

Eccles, D. W. and Tenenbaum, G. (2004). Why an expert team is more than a team of experts: a social-cognitive conceptualization of team coordination and communication in sport. *Journal of Sport and Exercise Psychology*, 26, 542–560.

Epstein, J. (1989). Family structures and student motivation: a developmental perspective. In C. Ames and R. Ames (eds), *Research on motivation in education* (pp. 259–295). New York: Academic Press.

Filby, W. C. D., Maynard, I. W. and Graydon, J. K. (1999). The effect of multiple-goal strategies on performance outcomes in training and competition. *Journal of Applied Sport Psychology*, 11, 230–246.

Fiore, S. M., Salas, E. and Cannon-Bowers, J. A. (2001). Group dynamics and shared mental model development. In M. London (ed.), *How people evaluate others in organisations: person perception and interpersonal judgement in I/O psychology* (pp. 309–336). Mahwah, NJ: Erlbaum.

Fuoss, D. E. and Troppman, R. J. (1981). *Effective coaching: a psychological approach*. New York: Wiley.

Germain, S. J. (2005). Shared mental model utilization among high school basketball players. Masters Thesis, Florida State University.

Gully, S. M., Incalcaterra, K. A., Joshi, A. and Beaubein, J. M. (2002). A meta-analysis of team efficacy, potency, and performance: interdependence and level of analysis as moderators of observed relationships. *Journal of Applied Psychology*, 87, 819–832.

Hall, H. K. and Byrne, T. J. (1988). Goal setting in sport: clarifying recent anomalies. *Journal of Sport and Exercise Psychology*, 10, 184–198.

Hall, H. K. and Kerr, A. W. (2001). Goal-setting in sport and physical activity: tracing empirical developments and establishing conceptual direction. In G. C. Roberts (ed.), *Advances in motivation in sport and exercise*. Champaign, IL: Human Kinetics.

Hall, H. K., Weinberg, R. S. and Jackson, A. W. (1987). Effects of goal specificity, goal difficulty, and information feedback on endurance performance. *Journal of Sport Psychology*, 9, 43–54.

Hardy, L. (1997). The Coleman Roberts Griffiths Address: three myths about applied consultancy work. *Journal of Applied Sport Psychology*, 9, 277–294.

Hardy, L. (1998). Responses to the reactants on three myths in applied consultancy work. *Journal of Applied Sport Psychology*, 10, 212–219.

Hardy, L. and Nelson, D. (1988). Self control training in sport and work. *Ergonomics*, 31, 1573–1585.

Hardy, L., Jones, G. and Gould, D. (1996a). *Understanding psychological preparation for sport: theory and practice of elite performers*. Chichester: Wiley.

Hardy, L., Mullen, R. and Jones, G. (1996b). Knowledge and conscious control of motor actions under stress. *British Journal of Psychology*, 87, 621–636.

Harwood, C., Hardy, L. and Swain, A. (2000). Achievement goals in sport: a critique of conceptual and measurement issues. *Journal of Sport and Exercise Psychology*, 22, 235–255.

Hollenbeck, J. R. and Klein, H. J. (1987). Goal commitment and the goal setting process: problems, prospects and proposals for future research. *Journal of Applied Psychology*, 72, 212–220.

Jackson, J. M. and Williams, K. D. (1985). Social loafing on difficult tasks. *Journal of Personality and Social Psychology*, 49, 937–942.

Jackson, R. C., Ashford, K. J. and Norsworthy, G. (2006). Attentional focus, dispositional reinvestment, and skilled motor performance under pressure. *Journal of Sport and Exercise Psychology*, 28, 49–68.

Johnson, D. W. and Johnson, F. P. (1985). Motivational processes in cooperative, competitive and individualistic learning situations. In C. Ames and R. Ames (eds), *Research on motivation in education* (pp. 249–289). Orlando, FL: Academic Press.

Johnson, S. R., Ostrow, A. C., Perna, F. M. and Etzel, E. F. (1997). The effect of group versus individual goal setting on bowling performance. *The Sport Psychologist*, 11, 190–200.

Jones, G. and Hanton, S. (1996). Interpretation of competitive anxiety symptoms and goal attainment expectancies. *Journal of Sport and Exercise Psychology*, 18, 144–157.

Kidman, L. (2001). *Developing decision-makers: an empowerment approach to coaching*. Christchurch: Innovative Print.

Kingston, K. M. and Goldea, A. (2007). Goals and flow. Paper presented at the Annual Conference of the Association for Applied Sport Psychology, Louisville, Kentucky, USA.

Kingston, K. M. and Hardy, L. (1994). Factors affecting the salience of outcome, performance, and process goals in golf. In A. J. Cochran and M. Farrally (eds), *Science* and Golf II: Proceedings of the 1994 World Scientific Congress of Golf (pp. 144–149). London: Chapman-Hill.

Kingston, K. M. and Hardy, L. (1997). Effects of different types of goals on processes that support performance. The Sport Psychologist, 11, 277–293.

Kingston, K. and Swain, A. (1999). Goal orientations and state goals: research in golf and implications for performance. In M. R. Farrally and A. J. Cochran (eds), Science and Golf III: Proceedings of the 1998 World Scientific Congress of Golf (pp. 150–157). Champaign, IL: Human Kinetics.

Kingston, K. M., Hanton, S. and Horrocks, C. S. (2006). Do multidimensional intrinsic and extrinsic motivational profiles discriminate between athlete scholarship status and gender? European Journal of Sport Science, 6, 53–63.

Kingston, K. M., Hardy, L. and Markland, D. (1992). Study to compare the effect of two different goal orientations and stress levels on a number of situationally relevant performance subcomponents. Journal of Sports Sciences, 10, 610–611.

Kingston, K. M., Harwood, C. G. and Spray, C. M. (2006). Contemporary approaches to motivation in sport. In S. Hanton and S. D. Mellalieu (eds), Literature reviews in sport psychology (pp. 159–197). New York: Nova Science Publishers.

Kingston, K., King, H. D. and Wilson, K. (in preparation). The influence of a participative group goal setting intervention on team cohesion and performance.

Kirschenbaum, D. S. (1985). Proximity and specificity of planning: a position paper. Cognitive Therapy and Research, 9, 489–506.

Kyllo, L. B. and Landers, D. M (1995). Goal setting in sport and exercise: a research synthesis to resolve the controversy. Journal of Sport and Exercise Psychology, 17, 117–137.

Larson, J. R. and Schaumann, L. J. (1993). Group goals, group coordination, and group membership motivation. Human Performance, 6, 49–69.

Lawrence, G. and Kingston, K. (2008). Skill acquisition for coaches. In R. L. Jones, M. Hughes and K. Kingston (eds), An introduction to sports coaching: from science and theory to practice (pp. 16–27). New York: Routledge.

Lee, C. (1988). The relationship between goal setting, self-efficacy, and female field hockey team performance. International Journal of Sport Psychology, 20, 147–161.

Lee, C., Earley, C. P., Lituchy, T. R. and Wagner, M. (1991). Relation of goal setting and goal sharing to performance and conflict for interdependent tasks. British Journal of Management, 2, 33–39.

Locke, E. A. (1968). Toward a theory of task motivation and incentives. Organisational Behaviour and Human Performance, 3, 157–189.

Locke, E. A. (1991). Problems with goal setting research in sport – and their solutions. Journal of Sport and Exercise Psychology, 8, 311–316.

Locke, E. A. (1994). Comments on Weinberg and Weigand. Journal of Sport and Exercise Psychology, 16, 212–215.

Locke, E. A. and Henne, D. (1986). Work motivation theories. In C. L. Copper and I. Robertson (eds), Review of industrial and organisational psychology. Chichester: Wiley.

Locke, E. A. and Latham, G. P. (1984). Goal setting: a motivational technique that works. Englewood Cliffs, NJ: Prentice-Hall.

Locke, E. A. and Latham, G. P. (1985). The application of goal setting to sports. Journal of Sports Psychology, 7, 205–222.

Locke, E. A. and Latham, G. P. (1990). A theory of goal setting and task motivation. Englewood Cliffs, NJ: Prentice-Hall.

Locke, E. A., Shaw, K. N., Saari, L. M. and Latham, G. P. (1981). Goal setting and task performance: 1969–1980. Psychological Bulletin, 90, 125–152.

McGrath, J. E. (1984). *Groups: interaction and performance*. Englewood Cliffs, NJ: Prentice-Hall.

McIntyre, R. M. and Salas, E. (1995). Measuring and managing team performance: emerging principles form complex environments. In R. Guzzo and E. Salas (eds), *Team effectiveness and decision making in organisations* (pp. 9–45). Washington, DC: American Psychological Association.

Masters, R. S. W. (1992). Knowledge, knerves and know-how: the role of explicit versus implicit knowledge in the breakdown of a complex motor skill under pressure. *British Journal of Psychology*, 83, 343–358.

Mento, A. J., Steele, R. P. and Karren, R.J. (1987). A meta-analytic study of the effects of goal-setting on task performance: 1966–1984. *Organizational Behaviour and Human Decision Processes*, 39, 52–83.

Morgan, K. and Carpenter, P. J. (2002). Effects of manipulating the motivational climate in physical education lessons. *European Journal of Physical Education*, 8, 209–232.

Morgan, K. and Kingston, K. M. (2008). Development of a self-observation mastery intervention programme for teacher education. *Physical Education and Sport Pedagogy*, 13, 1–21.

Munroe, K., Terry, P. and Carron, A. (2002). Cohesion and teamwork. In B. Hale and D. Collins (eds), *Rugby tough* (pp. 137–154). Champaign, IL: Human Kinetics.

Munroe-Chandler, K. J., Hall, C. R. and Weinberg, R. S. (2004). A qualitative analysis of the types of goals athletes set in training and competition. *Journal of Sport Behaviour*, 27, 58–74.

Newton, M. and Duda, J. L. (1999). The interaction of motivational climate, dispositional goal orientations, and perceived ability in predicting indices of motivation. *International Journal of Sport Psychology*, 30, 63–82.

Nicholls, J. G. (1984). Achievement motivation: conceptions of ability, subjective experience, task choice, and performance. *Psychological Review*, 91, 328–346.

Nicholls, J. G (1989). *The competitive ethos and democratic education*. Cambridge, MA: Harvard University Press.

Ntoumanis, N. (2001). Empirical links between achievement goal theory and self-determination theory in sport. *Journal of Sports Sciences*, 19, 397–409.

O'Leary-Kelly, A. M., Martocchio, J. J. and Frink, D. D. (1994). A review of the influence of group goals on group performance. *Academy of Management Journal*, 37, 1285–1301.

Prinz, W. (1997). Perceptions and action planning. *European Journal of Cognitive Psychology*, 9, 129–154.

Reinboth, M. and Duda, J. L. (2006). Perceived motivational climate, need satisfaction and indices of well-being in team sports: a longitudinal perspective. *Psychology of Sport and Exercise*, 7, 269–286.

Roberts, G. C. (2001). *Advances in motivation in sport and exercise*. Champaign, IL: Human Kinetics.

Singer, R. N. (1985). Sport performance: a five-step approach. *Journal of Physical Education and Recreation*, 57, 82–84.

Singer, R. N. (1988). Strategies and metastrategies in learning and performing self-paced athletic skills. *The Sport Psychologist*, 2, 49–68.

Singer, R. N., Lidor, R. and Cauraugh, J. H. (1983). To be aware or not aware? What to think about while learning and performing a motor skill. *The Sport Psychologist*, 7, 19–30.

Smith-Jentsch, K. A., Zeisig, R L., Acton, B. and McPhearson, J. A. (1998). Team dimensional training: a strategy for guided team self-correction. In J. A. Cannon-Bowers and E. Salas (eds), *Making decisions under stress: implication for individual and team training* (pp. 271–297). Washington, DC: American Psychology Society.

Standage, M., Duda, J. L. and Ntoumanis, N. (2003). A model of contextual motivation in physical education: using constructs from self-determination and achievement goal theory to predict physical activity intentions. *Journal of Educational Psychology*, 95, 97–110.

Steiner, I. D. (1972). *Group processes and group productivity*. New York: Academic Press.

Stout, R. J., Cannon-Bowers, J. A., Salas, E. and Milanovich, D. M. (1999). Planning, shared mental models, and coordinated performance: an empirical link is established. *Human Factors*, 41, 61–71.

Swezey, R. W. and Salas, E. (1992). *Teams: their training and performance*. Norwood, NJ: Ablex.

Tenenbaum, G., Pinchas, S., Elbaz, G., Bar-Eli, M. and Weinberg R. (1991). Effect of Goal Proximity and goal specificity on muscular endurance performance: a replication and extension. *Journal of Sport and Exercise Psychology*, 13, 160–173.

Theeboom, M., DeKnop, P. and Weiss, M. R. (1995). Motivational climate, psychological responses, and motor skill development in children's sport: a field-based intervention study. *Journal of Sport and Exercise Psychology*, 17, 294–311.

Tjosvold, D. (2001a). Effects of shared responsibility and goal interdependence on controversy and decision making between departments. *The Journal of Social Psychology*, 128, 7–18.

Tjosvold, D. (2001b). Dynamics and outcomes of goal interdependence in organisations. *The Journal of Psychology*, 120, 101–112.

Tjosvold, D. and Halco, J. A. (2001). Performance appraisal of managers: goal interdependence, ratings, and outcomes. *The Journal of Social Psychology*, 132, 629–639.

Tjosvold, D., Andrews, R. I. and Struthers, J. T. (2001). Leadership influence: goal interdependence and power. *The Journal of Social Psychology*, 132, 39–50.

Tjosvold, D., Yu, Z. Y. and Hui, C. (2004). Team learning from mistakes: the contribution of cooperative goals and problem solving. *Journal of Management Studies*, 41, 1223–1245.

Ward, P. and Eccles, D. W. (2006). A commentary on 'Team cognition and expert teams: emerging insights into performance for exceptional teams'. *International Journal of Sport and Exercise Psychology*, 4, 463–483.

Weinberg, R. S. (1992). Goal setting and motivational performance: a review and critique. In G. Roberts (ed.), *Motivation in sport and exercise* (pp. 177–197). Champaign, IL: Human Kinetics.

Weinberg, R. S. (1994). Goal setting and performance in sport and exercise settings: a synthesis and critique. *Medicine and Science in Sports and Exercise*, 26, 469–477.

Weinberg, R. S. and Weigand, D. (1993). Goal setting in sport and exercise: a reaction to Locke. *Journal of Sport and Exercise Psychology*, 15, 88–96.

Weinberg, R. S., Bruya, L. D., Jackson, A. and Garland, H. (1986). Goal difficulty and endurance performance: a challenge to the goal attainability assumption. *Journal of Sport Behaviour*, 10, 82–92.

Weinberg, R. S., Bruya, L. D., Longino, J. and Jackson, A. (1988). Effect of goal proximity and specificity on endurance performance of primary-grade children. *Journal of Sport and Exercise Psychology*, 10, 81–91.

Weinberg, R. S., Butt, J., Knight, B. and Perritt, N. (2001). Collegiate perceptions of their goal setting practices: a qualitative investigation. *Journal of Applied Sport Psychology*, 13, 374–398.

West, M. A. (1996). Reflexivity and work group effectiveness: a conceptual integration. In M. A. West (ed.), *Handbook of work group psychology* (pp. 555–579). Chichester: Wiley.

Widmeyer, W. N. and Ducharme, K. (1997). Team building through team goal setting. *Journal of Applied Sport Psychology*, 9, 97–113.

Widmeyer, W. N., Brawley, L. R. and Carron, A. V. (1985). *The measurement of cohesion in sports teams: the group environment questionnaire*. London, ON: Sports Dynamics.

Widmeyer, W. N., Silva, J. M. and Hardy, C. J. (1992). The nature of group cohesion in sport teams: a phenomenological approach. Paper presented at the Association for the Advancement of Applied Sport Psychology Conference, Colorado Springs, CO.

Wilson, K. M. and Brookfield, D. (in press). The effect of goal setting on motivation and adherence in a six-week exercise programme. *International Journal of Sport and Exercise Psychology*.

Wilson, K. M. and Mellalieu, S. (2007). Investigating the processes that contribute to enhanced coordination in rugby union teams (Abstract). *Journal of Sport and Exercise Psychology*, 29, S216.

Wilson, K. M., Hardy, L. and Harwood, C. G. (2006). Investigating the relationship between achievement goal orientations and process goals in rugby union players. *Journal of Applied Sport Psychology*, 18, 297–311.

Wong, A., Tjosvold, D. and Yu, Z.-Y. (2005). Organisational partnerships in China: self-interest, goal interdependence, and opportunism. *Journal of Applied Psychology*, 90, 782–791.

Woodman, T. and Hardy, L. (2001). A case study of organisational stress in elite sport. *Journal of Applied Sport Psychology*, 13, 207–238.

Wulf, G. and Prinz, W. (2001). Directing attention to movement effects enhances learning: a review. *Psychonomic Bulletin and Review*, 8, 648–660.

Wulf, G., McNevin, N. H., Fuchs, T., Ritter, F. and Toole, T. (2000). Attentional focus in complex skill learning. *Research Quarterly for Exercise and Sport*, 71, 229–239.

Zander, A. (1971). *Motives and goals in groups*. New York: Academic Press.

Zimmerman, B. J. and Kitsantas, A. (1996). Self-regulated learning of a motoric skill: the role of goal setting and self-monitoring. *Journal of Applied Sport Psychology*, 8, 60–75.

4 Stress management in applied sport psychology

Owen Thomas, Stephen D. Mellalieu and Sheldon Hanton

Introduction

The areas of competitive stress and anxiety have received considerable attention within the sport psychology literature, and are often cited as one of the most prominent topics of the discipline (Biddle, 1997; Hanton *et al.*, 2008; Jones, 1995a; Mellalieu *et al.*, 2006a; Woodman and Hardy, 2001). This interest is undoubtedly associated with the stressful nature of elite sport, and the numerous demands placed upon performers as a consequence of the pressurised environment within which they operate (Hardy *et al.*, 1996; Jones, 1995a, b; Woodman and Hardy, 2001). Indeed, several reviews have been published addressing: the measurement and design developments within competitive anxiety research (Burton, 1998; Jones, 1995a); the re-conceptualisation of trait anxiety in sport (Smith *et al.*, 1998); the cognitive aspects of the anxiety–performance relationship (Woodman and Hardy, 2001); an integrated overview of the measurement of arousal, activation, anxiety and performance (Gould *et al.*, 2002); the mechanisms by which competitive anxiety responses may positively impact on performance (Mellalieu *et al.*, 2006a); and how the study of directional interpretations has advanced understanding of the competitive anxiety response (Hanton *et al.*, 2008).

Although these reviews provide an informative overview of the study of competitive stress and anxiety, the prominent thread of debate has focused on theoretical, conceptual and measurement issues. While it remains commonplace for reviews to conclude with a section on implications for practitioners, no single body of work has focused entirely on this theme. Therefore, in this chapter we consider the literature surrounding the study and application of stress management in sport. We explore the two major treatment philosophies upon which stress management interventions in sport have been based; namely, the *reduction* and *restructuring* approaches. To the best of our knowledge, this is the first review to focus specifically on this topic and provide a 'theory-to-practice' overview of the area.

This chapter contains six main sections. The first defines key terms used within competitive stress and anxiety research. The second section then considers the importance of making certain distinctions for researchers and practitioners interested in studying and applying stress management interventions. In the third section, we highlight the salient conceptual and theoretical developments within the competitive stress and anxiety literature. The fourth section then focuses on how these developments have informed the content and application of stress management interventions in sport. Here we discuss the traditional *reduction* approach to stress management interventions and the contemporary *restructuring* approach to the treatment of anxiety symptoms. Specifically, we consider the evidence underpinning the content of each approach, the relevant psychological skills and strategies associated with the treatment, and the studies that have examined the efficacy of these stress management interventions in sport. Throughout this section we also consider one of the major issues that has guided stress management interventions: the study of the temporal patterning of the competitive stress response in the time-to-event. The fifth and penultimate section of this chapter then outlines implications for practitioners grounded in the relevant stress management literature. Finally, we conclude by highlighting areas that we consider pertinent for future investigation into stress management in sport.

Definition of terms

Inconsistency in the use of key terms within the areas of competitive stress and anxiety has often been cited as one of the primary factors limiting theoretical understanding and advancement of knowledge (see Burton, 1998; Fletcher *et al.*, 2006; Hanton *et al.*, 2008; Hardy *et al.*, 1996; Jones, 1995a; Jones and Hardy, 1990; Mellalieu *et al.*, 2006a; Woodman and Hardy, 2001). Indeed, the lack of clarity has frequently influenced the recommendations provided for the use of stress management interventions. It is not the intention of this section to provide an in-depth discussion of these issues (the reader is directed to reviews by Fletcher *et al.*, 2006, and Mellalieu *et al.*, 2006a, for a full synopsis). However, given the direct relationship between theory and practice in sport psychology, we feel it is important to identify and define the key terms and concepts that influence the design and application of stress management interventions. These include the operationalisation of the terms 'competitive stress', 'stressors', 'strain', 'anxiety' and 'activation'. The definitions presented here draw closely on recent reviews by Fletcher *et al.* and Mellalieu *et al.*, which, in turn, derive from the works of Lazarus (1981, 1982, 1999, 2000).

The contemporary conceptualisation of stress within psychology suggests it is not a factor that resides solely within the individual, or one that resides solely within the environment (Lazarus, 1999); rather it is a process that explains the relationship between the two. Specifically, stress has been defined as: 'An on going process that involves individuals transacting with their environments, making appraisals of the situations they find themselves in, and endeavoring to cope with any issues that may arise' (Fletcher *et al.*, 2006: 329).

Based upon this conceptualisation of stress, the following definitions are offered (cf. Fletcher *et al.*, 2006; Mellalieu *et al.*, 2006a) which are pertinent to the stress management context of this chapter:

- *Competitive stress*: an ongoing transaction between an individual and the environmental demands associated primarily and directly with competitive performance.
- *Competitive stressors*: the environmental demands (i.e. stimuli) associated primarily and directly with competitive performance.
- *Competitive strain*: an individual's negative psychological, physical and behavioural responses to competitive stressors.
- *Competitive anxiety*: a specific negative emotional response to competitive stressors.
- *Activation*: specific cognitive and physiological activity geared towards preparing a planned response applicable to the task demands facing the performer (cf. Hardy *et al.*, 1996; Pribram and McGuinness, 1975; Woodman and Hardy, 2001).

While the provision of a definition of activation goes beyond the concepts outlined by Fletcher *et al.* (2006) and Mellalieu *et al.* (2006a), the justification for its inclusion here rests with the direct relevance of activation to stress management interventions. We expand upon this reasoning in the next section that clarifies the importance of these conceptual distinctions within the stress management literature.

Contextualisation of concepts within stress management settings

Having defined the key conceptual terms relevant to the study of stress management interventions, we now consider how several of these concepts underpin much of the forthcoming detail and discussion in the chapter regarding the development and study of treatment frameworks. This section outlines the transactional perspective of stress, including the notion of stress as a process, the role of appraisal in this process and the importance of considering the activation state of the performer within applied settings.

One of the key features of the transactional perspective of stress relevant to this chapter is the premise that stress is an *ongoing process* (Lazarus, 1981, 1982, 1999, 2000). Here, we can consider a particular sequence or 'snap shot' of this process by examining the stressor, appraisal, response and behaviour that accounts for specific competitive stress situations (e.g. the demands associated with taking or attempting to save a penalty kick in football). Equally, we can consider the broader recurring nature of the stress process whereby an individual's responses to performance-related stressors are likely to fluctuate throughout the transaction (i.e. over the duration of a match, week or even longer period of time). Consequently, in light of the recurring or reciprocal nature of this process, the key implication for the design and study of stress management interventions in sport is that practitioners need to view stress management interventions in a temporal context. Stress can therefore be considered at the macro-, meso- and micro-level. A 'macro'-level perspective considers a performer's experiences of competitive stress over the duration of their sporting career (cf. Hanton and Jones, 1999a; Hanton *et al.*, 2007). 'Meso'-level perspectives examine competitive stress experiences over a more finite time period, such as directly in the lead up to the start of a specific competition or event (cf. Hanton *et al.*, 2002, 2004a; Thomas *et al.*, 2004, 2007a, b). Finally, a 'micro'-level perspective to the study of competitive stress explores the specific 'snap shot' of a performer's experiences at any one given moment or time (e.g. the exact sequence of demand, appraisal, emotion and behavioural response experienced).

Central to the reciprocal nature of stress as a process over time is the role of cognitive appraisal. According to Lazarus (1966), appraisal describes a person's cognitive evaluation of the meaning or significance of a perceived demand (i.e. the stressor). Therefore, appraisal remains a critical component of the stress process because individuals continuously evaluate their transactions with the environment. In a sporting context, appraisal involves the performer initially evaluating the relevance of a stressor (e.g. the perceived competence of the opposition) and the significance of this demand on their well-being (cf. Fletcher *et al.*, 2006). If, for example, the individual considers the perceived competence of the opposition as meaningful to them, they proceed to evaluate whether they possess the resources to cope with this demand. Lazarus labelled these two cognitive processes as 'primary' and 'secondary' appraisal, and suggested that primary appraisal related to the evaluation of the relevance of an encounter, with secondary appraisal only occurring if the individual ascribes some meaning to the encounter. If meaning is assigned, then secondary appraisal takes place via the individual identifying the availability of coping resources to deal with the potential harm/loss, threat and challenge (cf. Fletcher *et al.*, 2006).

The notion of appraisal is critical to the design of stress management interventions in that how an individual evaluates a performance-related stressor determines whether they will experience strain as the precursor to emotional symptoms such as competitive anxiety. Moreover, as stress is a reciprocal process occurring over time, changes in the demands imposed by sporting performance and the individual's subsequent appraisals of them dictate that a range of psychological skills and strategies require implementation at various intervals. For further detail on the role of appraisal in the competitive stress process, the reader is directed to the conceptual and theoretical reviews of Fletcher *et al.* (2006) and Mellalieu *et al.* (2006a).

The final concept that requires clarification with regard to its influence upon the study and design of stress management interventions is that of the activation state of the performer. As highlighted in the previous section, activation refers to the desired level of cognitive and physical activity individuals require in order to perform optimally in relation to the task demands they face in sport (Hardy *et al.*, 1996; Pribram and McGuinness, 1975; Woodman and Hardy, 2001). For example, the level of cognitive and physiological activity required to demonstrate readiness to perform in weight lifting contrasts greatly to that required to complete the skill of putting in golf (Hanton *et al.*, in press; Hardy *et al.*, 1996). Consequently, as Hardy *et al.* (1996) suggested, it would be more logical for theorists and practitioners to consider *appropriate* activation states for a given task rather than focus solely on *levels* of activation as such. Within their commentary, Hardy *et al.* also highlighted the need for sport psychologists to differentiate between activation and competitive anxiety. This position may lead the reader to question why we have included reference to activation within our chapter on stress management. The answer resides in the fact that, although we concur with Hardy *et al.* on the importance of this conceptual distinction, early literature on stress management has neglected this difference (cf. Mellalieu *et al.*, 2008). Specifically, only recently have researchers begun to consider the importance of task demands on the cognitive and physiological states required for performance, and its subsequent role in the competitive stress process. This distinction has direct relevance for the potential stress management interventions practitioners may prescribe in an attempt to ensure the performer enters the competition arena in the desired state of readiness to perform (Mellalieu *et al.*, 2008).

The significance of the concepts outlined in this section for the study and design of stress management interventions become fully apparent as we progress through the stress management content of the chapter. However, it is first necessary to review the key conceptual developments that have directly contributed to shaping existing stress management treatment philosophies in sport.

Conceptual developments pertinent to the context of stress management interventions

This section provides an overview of the conceptual advances that have impacted upon stress management research in sport. It is not our aim to provide a complete review of every conceptual development within the literature (see e.g. Burton, 1998; Jones, 1995a; Mellalieu *et al.*, 2006a; Smith *et al.*, 1998, for in-depth theoretical descriptions of the literature). Instead, we intend to discuss the developments that have directly underpinned the study and use of stress management interventions in sport. Specifically, this section considers developments that have provided the rationale for the reduction and restructuring approaches to stress management respectively, together with the literature that advocates the adoption of a temporal context to the content and delivery of stress management interventions in sport.

Competitive anxiety: early developments and a conceptual rationale for the reduction approach

One of the first major developments relevant to the application of stress management programmes was the identification of anxiety as a situation-specific response as opposed to a single unitary (general) phenomenon that exits across a range of settings (Mandler and Sarason, 1952). Spielberger (1966) expanded this distinction with his proposal of the state-trait theory of anxiety. State anxiety was viewed as a relatively transitory phenomenon that varied from one moment to another in relation to the perceived threat of the situation. Trait anxiety was termed a more general phenomena related to a predisposition to appraise a range of threatening or unthreatening situations with elevated levels of anxiety. The principle implication that emerged from this distinction was that stress management interventions needed to account for the influence of situation-specific factors within the competitive environment (Martens et al., 1990a).

Another salient conceptual advance in the competitive anxiety literature was the notion that responses were multidimensional in nature (Borkovec, 1976; Davidson, 1978; Davidson and Schwartz, 1976; Liebert and Morris, 1967; Schwartz et al., 1978; Wine, 1971). This distinction separated anxiety symptoms into cognitive and somatic components. Cognitive anxiety was defined as 'the cognitive elements of anxiety, such as negative expectations and cognitive concerns about oneself, the situation at hand and potential consequences' (Morris et al., 1981: 541). Somatic anxiety was identified as 'one's negative perception of the physiological-affective elements of the anxiety experience, that is, indications of autonomic arousal and unpleasant feeling states such as nervousness and tension' (Morris et al., 1981: 541). This distinction was introduced into the sport psychology literature by Martens and colleagues with their proposal of Multidimensional Anxiety Theory (MAT), and the development of the Competitive State Anxiety Inventory-2 (CSAI-2; Martens et al., 1990b) to measure the intensity of cognitive and somatic anxiety symptoms experienced in response to competition.[1] Subsequent research employing this multidimensional approach has provided evidence to support the different components of the CSAI-2 when investigating competitive anxiety as a function of its antecedents (Gould et al., 1984; Jones et al., 1990, 1991), temporal characteristics (Gould et al., 1984; Jones et al., 1991; Martens et al., 1990a), performance outcomes (Burton, 1988; Gould et al., 1987; Jones and Cale, 1989; Parfitt and Hardy, 1987, 1993), goal attainment expectancies (Krane et al., 1992) and in response to interventions (Burton, 1990; Maynard and Cotton, 1993).

Inherent within Martens et al.'s (1990a) MAT was the suggestion that the constructs of cognitive and somatic anxiety would have independent and differential influences over competitive performance. Martens et al. posited that cognitive anxiety displayed a negative linear relationship with performance and somatic anxiety a quadratic, or inverted-U, relationship (i.e. increases in somatic anxiety to a certain point will benefit performance). Martens et al. also theorised that, of the two constructs, cognitive anxiety would provide the principle influence on performance because somatic anxiety would dissipate once performance commenced (cf. Burton, 1990). Although empirical support for these predictions has remained equivocal (see Burton, 1998; Craft et al., 2003; Woodman and Hardy, 2003), several of the theoretical assumptions implicit within the original multidimensional framework have helped to shape the rationale for the *reduction* approach to stress management interventions. Specifically, the fundamental principle of MAT was that high levels of competitive anxiety had a negative influence upon performance (Burton, 1990; Hardy, 1990). This assumption fostered the general philosophy of the reduction framework, such that practitioners should seek to decrease the level of anxiety symptoms performers experienced.

Further, the separation of anxiety into cognitive and somatic constructs helped to promote the notion that certain stress management techniques are more applicable for certain anxiety responses (Burton, 1990; Davidson and Schwartz, 1976), a premise that underpinned Morris *et al.*'s (1981) proposal of the 'Matching Hypothesis' as a treatment framework within the reduction approach.

Up to this point in the competitive anxiety literature, researchers and practitioners had focused their attention on assessing only the *intensity* of performers' cognitive and somatic anxiety (i.e. the level or amount of symptoms experienced). Furthermore, high intensity levels were also viewed as invariably detrimental to performance. The following sub-section outlines how this 'intensity alone' conceptualisation of competitive anxiety has been viewed as limiting when attempting to understand the stress management process.

Directional interpretation of competitive anxiety symptoms: a conceptual rationale for the restructuring approach

One of the first indications that suggested experiencing anxiety did not always result in negative consequences for sports performance came from Mahoney and Avener's (1977) comparison of psychological skill usage between unsuccessful and successful qualifiers for the United States 1976 Olympic gymnastics team. Mahoney and Avener noted that those gymnasts who qualified were able to use their anxiety as a stimulant for better performance. This finding, and the proposition that symptoms associated with competitive anxiety are not always detrimental towards performance, was in line with the beliefs held in other domains of psychology. For example, in the test anxiety literature, Alpert and Haber (1960) indicated that a psychometric scale designed to assess both the intensity and direction (i.e. debilitating and facilitating effects of anxiety) of symptoms was a stronger predictor of academic performance than traditional intensity-only scales.

The work of Jones and associates in the early 1990s then questioned the traditional view within sport that increases in anxiety symptom intensities were always detrimental to performance, subsequently proposing the notion of directional interpretations (Jones, 1991; Jones and Swain, 1992). Jones and colleagues defined directional interpretations as the extent to which a performer viewed their anxiety levels as positive (facilitative) or negative (debilitative) towards upcoming performance (Jones, 1991; Jones and Swain, 1992). Central to the understanding of the concept of anxiety direction is Jones' (1995a) control model. This model, based on the work of Carver and Scheier (1986, 1988), suggests that a performer's ability to control a stressor determines how he or she will interpret anxiety symptoms (i.e. as facilitative or debilitative to performance). Indeed, individuals who appraise that they possess a degree of control over the situation, perceive they are able to cope with their anxiety symptoms and believe that they are likely to achieve their goals (i.e. coping or positive expectancy of goal achievement), are predicted to interpret symptoms as facilitative to performance. In comparison, performers who appraise that they are not in

control, cannot cope with the situation at hand, and possess negative expectancies regarding goal attainment are predicted to interpret such symptoms in a
negative manner (Jones, 1995a).

From an applied perspective, the explanation for the cognitive processes associated with control and a performer's ability to interpret anxiety symptoms as facilitative is a salient factor in determining intervention choice. Specifically, it helps to
underpin the basis of the *restructuring* approach to stress management in that it
focuses on the performer creating appraisals that foster perceptions of control over
the demands they face and a subsequent facilitative interpretation of their symptoms experienced. Based on the works of Lazarus (Lazarus, 1966, 1981, 1993,
1999), Fletcher and Fletcher (2005) and Fletcher *et al.* (2006) proposed a meta-
model of stress, emotion and performance to further detail the cognitive processes
associated with perceptions of control and facilitating anxiety symptom interpretations. Fletcher and colleagues' three-stage model proposes an extension to Lazarus'
use of primary and secondary appraisal types to include tertiary and quaternary
appraisals. The first stage of the model, the person–environment (P–E) fit, represents what would be commonly associated with a competitive anxiety response.
Specifically, incongruence occurs during primary and secondary appraisal between
the perceived resources available to the performer and the demands they face
(i.e. appraisals of the stressor(s)).

The second stage of the model is based upon the notion of directional interpretations of symptom responses and helps to underpin the theoretical rationale
for the restructuring approach. Here, the processes of tertiary and quaternary
appraisal are suggested to sequentially reflect an evaluation by the individual of
whether the emotion they experience (e.g. competitive anxiety) as a consequence of the incongruence in the first stage of the model is relevant to subsequent performance, and the utility of the coping options available. These
additional appraisals are considered mediators of directional interpretations and
are proposed to dictate whether the individuals' responses are interpreted as
facilitative or debilitative towards performance (Fletcher and Fletcher, 2005;
Fletcher *et al.*, 2006; Mellalieu *et al.*, 2006a). In the context of stress management, it is these tertiary and quaternary appraisals that form the target of interventions designed under the restructuring approach. Specifically, the labels a
performer ascribes to their anxiety and associated cognitive and somatic symptoms determine their overall affective state, rather than the initial experience of
the anxiety response. Performers can therefore experience a negative emotion
such as competitive anxiety (i.e. through primary and secondary appraisal
processes) and then follow this experience with further appraisals (i.e. tertiary
and secondary) that provide them with an overall positive emotional interpretation towards performance (cf. Mellalieu *et al.*, 2006a). Therefore, strategies
designed to target the appraisal of *anxiety symptoms* experienced are promoted
within the directional interpretation literature and the restructuring approach
to stress management interventions.

A common element within both the control model proposed by Jones (1995a)
and the meta-model of Fletcher and colleagues is the moderating influence of

individual difference variables. Indeed, considerable research has investigated the impact of moderating characteristics on individuals' capacity to interpret their symptoms associated with competitive anxiety in a facilitative manner. In their recent review of theoretical advances within the competitive anxiety direction literature, Mellalieu *et al.* (2006a) identified: cognitive bias, positive and negative affect, self-confidence, neuroticism and extroversion, hardiness, coping strategy use, psychological skill use, achievement motivation, competitiveness, gender, skill level, competitive experience, sport type, team cohesion, control, performance level, and temporal patterning as prominent personal or situational moderators of the ability to interpret anxiety symptoms as positive for performance. A complete review of these is beyond the scope of this chapter. However, a summary of the effects of these variables suggests that individuals who possess facilitative interpretations of their anxiety symptoms have been observed to: execute better performance (Jones *et al.*, 1993), be more elite in competitive status (Eubank *et al.*, 1995; Jones *et al.*, 1994; Jones and Swain, 1992; Perry and Williams, 1998), exert greater perceived control over the self and the environment (Hanton *et al.*, 2003b; Jones and Hanton, 1996; Ntoumanis and Jones, 1998; O'Brien *et al.*, 2005), exhibit higher levels of self-confidence (Hanton and Jones, 1997; Hanton *et al.*, 2004b; Thomas *et al.*, 2004), use greater levels of psychological skills (Fletcher and Hanton, 2001), adopt more effective coping strategies (Eubank and Collins, 2000; Jerome and Williams, 2000; Ntoumanis and Biddle, 2000), display more hardy and resilient personality characteristics (Hanton *et al.*, 2003a), possess more competitive experience (Hanton and Jones, 1999a; Mellalieu *et al.*, 2004), demonstrate a more competitive orientation (Jones and Swain, 1992), present greater task cohesion in group settings (Eys *et al.*, 2003), and experience greater positive affect (Jones *et al.*, 1996; Mellalieu and Hanton, 2008) than athletes who interpret their anxiety symptoms as debilitative. Several of these individual difference variables are particularly relevant to informing the design and content of stress management programmes within the restructuring approach. Specifically, the skill level of the performer, the type of sport participated in, the level of self-confidence experienced and the amount of psychological skill use undertaken.

Focusing on the influence of skill level, a consistent finding within the anxiety direction literature has been the relationship between the competitive level of the performer (i.e. elite or non-elite) and their subsequent symptom interpretations. While elite and non-elite performers have been found to display no differences in the intensity of cognitive and somatic anxiety symptoms experienced, elite individuals consistently interpret these levels as more facilitative towards performance than their non-elite counterparts (Eubank *et al.*, 1995; Hanton and Connaughton, 2002; Jones and Swain, 1995; Jones *et al.*, 1994). Similar patterns have also emerged with respect to the moderating influence of skill level at the trait level (Hanton *et al.*, 2003b; Perry and Williams, 1998). Interestingly, both these sets of findings appear constant across a range of sporting activities, including swimming (Hanton and Connaughton, 2002; Jones *et al.*, 1994), cricket (Jones and Swain, 1995), badminton (Eubank *et al.*, 1995) and tennis (Perry and Williams, 1998). However, sport type, or the nature of the sporting activity engaged in, has also been noted to moderate anxiety interpretation, particularly when the activation demands of the sport contrast in their motor skill requirements. For example, while Hanton *et al.* (2000) and Mellalieu *et al.* (2004) found no differences in the intensity of anxiety symptoms experienced (cognitive and somatic), individuals involved in gross muscular activities (e.g. rugby union and rugby league) interpreted their pre-performance anxiety as more beneficial towards upcoming performance than participants competing in sports that required higher levels of fine muscular control (e.g. pistol shooting and golf).

Perhaps one of the most robust findings to emerge from the direction literature on moderating variables relates to the influence of self-confidence upon performers' anxiety symptom interpretations. Individuals with facilitative interpretations of their symptoms (i.e. facilitators) consistently report greater levels of self-confidence than those with debilitative interpretations (i.e. debilitators; Hanton and Jones, 1997; Hanton *et al.*, 2000; Jones and Swain, 1995; Jones *et al.*, 1994; Perry and Williams, 1998; Thomas *et al.*, 2004). This has led researchers to propose that self-confidence serves as a protection mechanism against the potential debilitative effects of anxiety symptom experiences (Hanton *et al.*, 2004a; Hardy *et al.*, 1996; Hays *et al.*, 2007; Mellalieu *et al.*, 2006b). Finally, an additional personal variable suggested to moderate the relationship between the intensity and direction of the symptoms associated with competitive anxiety is the performers' psychological skill use. Studies have identified those individuals with more facilitative interpretations of symptoms report greater use of psychological skills than their debilitating counterparts (Fletcher and Hanton, 2001; Hale and Whitehouse, 1998; Neil *et al.*, 2006; Page *et al.*, 1999).

Taken collectively, the findings of these studies highlight the moderating effects of individual difference variables upon facilitative interpretations of anxiety symptoms and the experience of an overall positive affective state in relation to performance. Researchers within the direction literature have recently drawn on these findings to justify a shift away from research predominantly focused on assessing the moderating influence of personal and situational characteristics towards the exploration of a more fundamental understanding of the underlying skills performers use to attain facilitative interpretations. This shift has seen a trend towards the adoption of qualitative methods to provide detailed evidence to inform the content and structure of stress management intervention programmes. Commentary on these qualitative studies occurs later in the chapter when we summarise the specific content of stress management intervention approaches used in the sport psychology literature.

Frequency of cognitive intrusions: a conceptual rationale for temporal-based interventions

In addition to highlighting the need to move beyond the measurement of solely the intensity of competitive anxiety responses, via the consideration of directional symptom interpretations, Jones and associates also advocated the study of the frequency of cognitive intrusions experienced by performers (Swain and Jones, 1993). In this context, frequency of intrusions referred to the amount of time (i.e. percentage amount of occurrence) that anxiety-related thoughts or feelings occupied the performer's mind. The conceptual rationale for frequency derives from the transactional perspective of stress that suggests an individual's responses to the demands (i.e. stressors) placed upon them should be viewed as products over time (i.e. are temporal in nature; Lazarus, 1999; Lazarus and Folkman, 1984). In a practical context, stress should therefore be viewed as a dynamic process whereby responses are assessed in a temporal context (i.e. temporal patterns) in order to identify prescriptive points for any form of intervention as the competitive event approaches (Hanton *et al.*, 2004b; Mellalieu *et al.*, 2006a; Thomas *et al.*, 2004). The study of the temporal patterning of the experiences of competitive stress was originally based in the early multidimensional anxiety research that examined responses from an intensity only perspective (for a review, see Cerin *et al.*, 2000). Traditionally, 'meso'-level anxiety responses were collected within the seven-day pre-performance period leading up to the competitive event (e.g. 7 days, 5 days, 48 hours, 24 hours and 1 hour). Based on the original work of Martens *et al.* (1990a), predictions for competitive anxiety indicated that if the evaluation of performance expectancy remained unchanged, the intensity of cognitive anxiety and self-confidence symptoms would remain constant during the time leading up to the competitive event. The intensity of somatic anxiety was proposed to initially remain stable, but show a sharp rise to its peak at the onset of competition, before dissipating once the event commenced. Although some support for these predictions was initially forthcoming (e.g. Gould *et al.*, 1984), the literature base has remained equivocal (see Cerin *et al.*, 2000, for a review).

The lack of support for Martens *et al.*'s (1990a) original predictions led Swain and Jones (1993) to question the sole use of intensity within a temporal approach. Swain and Jones (1993) indicated that the same level or intensity of cognitive anxiety symptoms experienced at seven days and one hour before performance did not provide a complete representation of the athlete's overall emotional state. Indeed, it merely represented the same intensity at two different time periods without providing reference to how often these symptoms occupied the athlete's mind (i.e. frequency of cognitive intrusions). In line with Lazarus' view of stress as a dynamic process (Lazarus and Folkman, 1984), Swain and Jones (1993) added a frequency continuum to each item of the CSAI-2 asking, 'How frequently do you experience this thought or feeling at this stage?' The findings established that, while the intensity of cognitive anxiety responses remained constant, frequencies of cognitive anxiety intrusions differed significantly during the two days preceding competition (48 hours, 24 hours, 2 hours and 30 minutes). Swain and Jones concluded that states where cognitive anxiety symptoms occur for 5 per cent of the time are considerably different from those where they are experienced for 90 per cent of the time, even though the intensity of the responses may remain constant. The importance of frequency as a dimension to assess temporal changes in symptom experiences has been emphasised in the work of Hanton *et al.* (2004b) and Thomas *et al.*

(2004). These studies indicated that the frequency of symptoms experienced (both cognitive and somatic anxiety) appear to be a more sensitive indicator of anxiety responses as the individual neared the competitive event. Coupled with the existing beliefs held in clinical psychology that humans are able to recall and encode more information of emotion frequency as opposed to information of emotion intensity (Diener *et al.*, 1991; Kardum, 1999), Thomas *et al.* have suggested that frequency information should be used to help practitioners devise meso-level interventions within stress management programmes.

Research evidence underpinning the content of stress management interventions

The preceding commentary has provided a brief overview of the key conceptual issues relevant to the application of stress management interventions. Distinctions were made in respect to the conceptual rationale for the reduction and restructuring approaches, and the need for interventions to consider the temporal nature of the stress process. In this section we now focus explicitly on the empirical evidence behind the rationale for the content of the interventions under the reduction and restructuring approaches, and the actual psychological skills utilised within each stress management programme.

Research evidence for the content of stress management interventions within the reduction approach

The treatment philosophy of the reduction approach is based on the premise that increases in anxiety levels are considered detrimental to performance, suggesting practitioners should aim to lower performers' intensity of symptom responses (cf. Jones, 1995a). The evidence base that has driven the content of these intervention programmes in sport psychology was highly dependent on developments of the time within the clinical and test anxiety literature (e.g. Borkovec, 1976; Davidson and Schwartz, 1976; Meichenbaum, 1975, 1985). Early approaches proposed that independent or unimodal strategies should be used to treat cognitive and somatic anxiety separately (e.g. Borkovec, 1976). An extension to this perspective occurred with the proposals of Morris *et al.*'s (1981) Matching Hypothesis and Davidson and Schwartz's (1976) Psychophysiological Relaxation Model (see Burton, 1990, for a review). These two approaches were based on the notion that anxiety reduction techniques should be 'compatible' with or 'matched' to the client's dominant anxiety response. Davidson and Schwartz (1976) highlighted that anxiety problems demonstrated variable response rates to different anxiety-management approaches, and that specific anxiety-management techniques (i.e. cognitive or somatic) had a more significant impact on reducing the specific types of anxiety (i.e. cognitive or somatic). This led to the proposal of Davidson and Schwartz's multi-process theory, and the notion that relaxation interventions would be more effective if they were directed at the dominant symptoms experienced. Consequently, a cognitive relaxation procedure would have a primary impact on reducing cognitive anxiety, while a somatic technique would have the greatest influence on reducing unwanted somatic anxiety. In their review of the test anxiety literature, Morris *et al.* (1981) supported these findings and the notion of the matching hypothesis. However, they also concluded that improvements in actual examination performance were only observed when both cognitive *and* somatic anxiety was reduced. Further, several studies that have used incompatible treatment frameworks (i.e. cognitive techniques to treat dominant somatic responses and vice versa) have also shown positive results in comparison to the compatible treatment approach (Burton, 1990). These findings are to some extent paradoxical in relation to the conceptual foundations of the psychophysiological relaxation model/matching hypothesis and question the accuracy of their construction and effectiveness as frameworks to drive intervention choice (Maynard *et al.*, 1998). 'Cross-over effects' have been used as possible explanations for these anomalies due to the fact that cognitive anxiety and somatic anxiety display a level of shared variance (i.e. any attempt to reduce one of the anxiety components is likely to influence the other).

The preceding literature provided two contradictory viewpoints of the time for the choice of stress management intervention. The first was based on the notion that the intervention should be 'matched' to the prominent anxiety response displayed by the client. However, the second suggested that interventions should be designed to treat both cognitive and somatic anxiety simultaneously. Here, one school of thought argued that the matched interventions would reduce both forms of anxiety due to cross-over effects (Davidson and Schwartz, 1976), whereas the second view proffered support for treatments that combined cognitive and somatic treatments through the use of multimodal treatment packages (Meichenbaum, 1975, 1985; Smith, 1980).

Fundamental psychological skills and techniques associated with the reduction approach

Several psychological skills have been primarily associated with the reduction approach. The use of these skills has developed from their adoption in unimodal applications of relaxation methods to more complex approaches that have advocated combining the techniques into multimodal interventions. The final progression has seen the adoption of strategies that enable athletes to 'inoculate' themselves against the negative effects of the stress process or 'simulate' stressful situations, thereby enabling performers to more successfully manage their competitive environments. This sub-section briefly reviews these techniques and their use within applied contexts. Practical guides on the techniques covered in this sub-section can be found in the work of Burton (1990), Hanton *et al.* (in press), Hardy *et al.* (1996) and Williams and Harris (2006).

One of the fundamental psychological skills primarily associated with the reduction approach is the use of relaxation techniques. Following the distinction of competitive anxiety responses into cognitive and somatic elements, and the proposal of the matching hypothesis, relaxation skills have traditionally been grouped into physical and mental relaxation techniques (cf. Hardy *et al.*, 1996). Derivatives of Jacobson's (1938) Progressive Muscular Relaxation programmes have formed the basis of many of the physical relaxation techniques applied in sport. Indeed, Ost's (1988) applied relaxation technique has become synonymous with stress management in sport due to its diverse application to stressful situations that occur before, during and after performance (Hanton *et al.*, in press; Hardy *et al.*, 1996; Rotella, 1985). The primary goal of an applied relaxation programme is to transfer the athlete through a series of progressive stages towards an end-point where a physically relaxed state can be rapidly attained in any given situation.

In comparison to physical relaxation techniques, cognitive relaxation strategies have received less exposure within the stress management literature. One technique, transcendental meditation, has begun to be adopted within stress management interventions. However, Jones' (1993) progressive meditative relaxation programme, based on the philosophy of Ost (1988) for use with physical relaxation techniques, remains one of the few structured applications of cognitive meditation. Performers using this type of strategy adopt a focused breathing technique combined with the use of a 'mantra' word through self-talk (Benson, 1975; Hanton *et al.*, in press; Hardy *et al.*, 1996; Jones, 1993; Williams and Harris, 2006). Here, the goal of the practitioner is to develop a programme that enables the performer to transcend to a deeper level of cognitive relaxation. Additional techniques synonymous with the reduction of cognitive anxiety that fall outside the classification of relaxation include thought-stopping, Suinn's (1987) positive thought control technique, calming imagery and autogenic training (cf. Hanton *et al.*, in press; Meyers and Schlesser, 1980; Zinsser *et al.*, 2006).

As alternatives to the techniques outlined above, more complex advanced multimodal stress treatment frameworks have been proposed and tested (see Burton, 1990; Hardy *et al.*, 1996), including stress inoculation training (Meichenbaum, 1975, 1985) and stress management training (Smith, 1980). Stress inoculation training combines the skills of imagery, self-talk and relaxation to develop a coping skills programme. These programmes initially use imagery to rehearse exposure to increasingly stressful encounters in order to develop an adaptive coping behaviour pattern. The athlete is then exposed to challenging but manageable stressful environments where these coping skills are tested in real life. The intensity of the demands placed on the performer is steadily increased so that their coping skills are built up to effectively deal with the most stressful situation they may encounter, thereby 'inoculating' the athlete to the effects of the stressors (Burton, 1990; Hardy *et al.*, 1996). Stress management training (Smith, 1980; Smith and Ascough, 1985; Smith and Rohsenhow, 1987) adheres to similar underlying principles of stress inoculation training. However, the distinguishing factor of stress management training is the focus on coping with emotional and affective responses to the stressor(s). Specifically, during the imagery rehearsal phase of the technique the athlete is asked to acutely focus on their emotional and affective responses to the stressor(s) they are visualising. Then, during the rehearsal phase the practitioner encourages a strong and intense emotional response through the use of verbal propositions (Burton, 1990; Smith and Ascough, 1985). Once experienced, the athlete is instructed to 'turn off' their intense emotional and affective response by implementing coping responses in the form of relaxation and self-instruction skills (Burton, 1990). These skills are then transferred from imagined rehearsal scenarios to real-life settings of a steadily increasing stressful nature.

Research evidence for the content of stress management interventions under the restructuring approach

The evidence base for the content of interventions under the restructuring approach has developed through a series of qualitative-based studies investigating the mechanisms that lead to facilitative interpretations of anxiety symptoms. The first of these was Hanton and Jones' (1999a) adoption of a 'macro-level' perspective to study the temporal nature of the competitive stress process through the exploration of how performers had developed the ability to interpret anxiety-related symptoms across their competitive careers. Specifically, Hanton and Jones examined how ten elite-level swimmers who consistently experienced their interpretations of anxiety as facilitative had acquired the cognitive skills and strategies that enabled them to view symptoms with positive performance consequences. At the early stages of their career, negative performance consequences associated with their pre-performance anxiety symptoms were experienced. However, as the swimmers developed over time, they reported learning to interpret these symptoms as having positive performance impact. Specifically, natural learning experiences and educational methods, such as seeking advice from critical others, were adopted to build refined pre-competition and pre-race routines that enabled pre-race symptoms to be viewed as facilitative towards performance.

Hanton and Connaughton (2002) expanded on these initial findings by conducting a qualitative examination of Jones' (1995a) control model of facilitative and debilitative anxiety. In supporting the model, Hanton and Connaughton reported elite and sub-elite swimmers interpreted pre-race symptoms as debilitative or facilitative based on their perception of control over the anxiety responses experienced and in relation to the situation they faced. Hanton and Connaughton also noted the elite group were able to trigger self-regulatory psychological skills which resulted in the re-interpretation of anxiety symptoms originally appraised and perceived as negative, uncontrollable and debilitative to performance into symptoms that were appraised and perceived as positive, controllable and facilitative. This process supports the second stage of Fletcher and Fletcher's (2005) meta-model of stress, emotion and performance described earlier in the chapter. Specifically, it highlights the contribution of tertiary and quaternary appraisal to the processes of anxiety symptom interpretation and the mechanisms by which individuals may experience an overall subsequent emotional or affective experience in relation to performance (cf. Fletcher *et al.*, 2006).

Hanton *et al.* (2004a) then further extended research into facilitating anxiety mechanisms by examining the relationship between elite performers' levels of self-confidence and their subsequent interpretation of competitive anxiety symptoms. The rationale for their study derived from the quantitative findings that have consistently demonstrated an association between facilitative interpretations of competitive anxiety-related symptoms and increased levels of self-confidence (Hanton and Jones, 1997; Hanton *et al.*, 2000; Jones and Swain, 1995; Jones *et al.*, 1994; Perry and Williams, 1998; Thomas *et al.*, 2004). Following interviews with ten elite performers from a range of sports, high self-confidence was reported to be associated with facilitative interpretations of anxiety symptoms that led to enhanced levels of motivation and task-related effort. Conversely, low self-confidence was associated with debilitative interpretations of anxiety symptoms, leading to losses in focus and concentration. In providing evidence to support the protective nature of self-confidence over the potential debilitative effects of anxiety symptoms, Hanton *et al.* indicated that cognitive confidence management strategies were pivotal for performers requiring stress management interventions designed to restructure debilitative anxiety interpretations and/or maintain facilitative interpretations of anxiety-related symptoms.

The psychological skills used to maintain facilitating symptom interpretations have also been considered in a meso-level context (i.e. in the time to competition). For example, using the time period of 24 hours prior to competition, Hanton *et al.* (2002) highlighted the dynamic properties of the anxiety response in a sample of elite athletes. Their findings also suggested that self-confidence management strategies were particularly important in protecting against debilitative interpretations of competitive anxiety symptoms. Thomas *et al.* (2007a) complemented these findings by comparing the elite female field-hockey performers' anxiety experiences during the seven-day competitive cycle associated with many elite-level team sports. The findings supported the dynamic properties of the competitive stress process during the seven days between competitive fixtures – specifically, anxiety responses (intensity and frequency of intrusions) fluctuated across the seven-day cycle through three phases: a post-performance phase (one-to-two days post-performance) and two pre-performance phases (two-to-one day pre-performance and match day respectively). The study also highlighted the differential application of psychological skills by the facilitators and debilitators of symptoms during the tertiary and quaternary phases of the appraisal process that resulted in either positive or negative performance consequences of anxiety symptoms (i.e. directional interpretations). Specifically, facilitators possessed a refined repertoire of psychological skills that they could draw upon during the seven-day cycle, enabling them to interpret anxiety symptoms as facilitative towards performance. In comparison, debilitators attempted to implement psychological skills, but did not possess the control over these skills, leading to a continued debilitative interpretation of their pre-performance anxiety symptoms.

The final qualitative study that has helped to support the rationale for the restructuring approach also focused on the performer's use of psychological skills within a meso-level temporal context. Specifically, Mellalieu *et al.* (2008) examined elite rugby union players' emotional experiences, behavioural responses and affective states throughout the pre-competition period, with a focus on times directly prior to performance. Mellalieu *et al.* also considered the psychological strategies performers used to achieve desirable activation states rather than a focus on anxiety responses per se. Mellalieu *et al.*'s findings supported the dynamic nature of performers' responses to stressors as the competition moved closer and indicated that a wide range of emotions were experienced in the time leading up to competition. Further, the elite performers reported using a number of psychological skills, including imagery and verbal persuasion, in order to interpret their pre-competition symptoms as facilitative and create an optimal activation state to enter the competitive arena.

Collectively, the evidence that has emerged from these qualitative studies has helped to identify the psychological skills and strategies associated with the restructuring approach to stress management. Specifically, a number of psychological skills and techniques appear to be used to help maintain a facilitative interpretation of pre-competitive anxiety symptoms, and protect against the potential debilitative performance consequences of competitive anxiety. The following sub-section proceeds to outline these specific skills and techniques.

Fundamental psychological skills and techniques associated with the restructuring approach

The literature outlined in the previous sub-section has highlighted a number of psychological skills that are synonymous with the restructuring approach to stress management. Specifically, imagery, goal setting, positive self-talk and rationalisation/restructuring skills (underpinned by self-talk) have been identified as the key strategies performers employ to foster facilitative interpretations of competitive anxiety symptoms (Hanton and Connaughton, 2002; Hanton and Jones, 1999a; Hanton *et al.*, 2002, 2004a; Mellalieu *et al.*, 2008; Thomas *et al.*, 2007a). The literature has also highlighted that performers use external sources of information such as verbal persuasion from significant others (Hanton and Jones, 1999a; Hanton *et al.*, 2004a; Mellalieu *et al.*, 2008; Thomas *et al.*, 2007a), an applicable team climate (Mellalieu *et al.*, 2008) and superior warm-up routines (Hanton and Jones, 1999a; Thomas *et al.*, 2007a; Mellalieu *et al.*, 2008) to help develop or maintain facilitative interpretations. This sub-section will review the contribution of a number of these techniques towards the self-regulatory skills associated with the restructuring approach.

It is important to emphasise at this point that, if prescribed, the aim of these skills is to promote control over anxiety symptoms and the competitive environment without attempting to reduce the level of symptoms experienced. Consequently, the range of skills summarised here focus on techniques that create positive interpretations of symptoms and high levels of self-confidence to offer protection against potential debilitative effects of anxiety symptoms experienced. Practical guides on execution of the techniques covered in this sub-section can be found in the work of Hanton *et al.* (in press), Hardy *et al.* (1996) and Williams and Harris (2006).

The most consistent skill to emerge from the literature associated with the restructuring approach is that of imagery. Indeed, all the qualitative studies reviewed in this chapter have indicated the prominent role of effective imagery routines in maintaining facilitative interpretations of anxiety symptoms. However, only recently has the literature base provided any substantial information on the precise form and function of these imagery routines. Specifically, imagery routines that use cognitive-specific and cognitive-general functions appear to be more suited to developing facilitative interpretations of anxiety (Mellalieu *et al.*, 2008; Thomas *et al.*, 2007a). Additionally, both the cognitive and motivational mastery functions of imagery have emerged as key skills associated with the techniques that manage self-confidence in order to protect against potential debilitative anxiety effects (Hanton *et al.*, 2004a; Mellalieu *et al.*, 2008).

Cognitive rationalisation and restructuring of an athlete's thoughts and perceived feelings have also been identified as key psychological skills within the restructuring approach (Hanton and Connaughton, 2002; Hanton and Jones, 1999a; Hanton *et al.*, 2004a; Thomas *et al.*, 2007a). The basis for the adoption of these skills derives from the use of effective self-talk, and has close links to Rational Emotive Behaviour Therapy (REBT) within clinical psychology (Ellis, 1962, 1970, 1994). According to Ellis's cognitive theory, people experience situations that lead to rational and/or irrational or negative beliefs. These beliefs then lead to cognitive, emotional and behavioural consequences. Rational beliefs lead to functional consequences for the individual and are associated with a positive interpretation of anxiety-related symptoms. In contrast, irrational beliefs lead to dysfunctional consequences and are associated with a negative interpretation of anxiety-related symptoms (cf. David *et al.*, 2002; Ellis, 1962, 1970, 1994). As a therapeutic approach, REBT involves individuals disputing irrational beliefs and incorporating rationale ones, with the aim of realising a positive influence over cognitive, emotional and behavioural responses. Therefore, individuals rationalise and restructure any negative symptoms experienced (David *et al.*, 2002). In line with Lazarus' perspective of stress (Lazarus, 1999), this approach suggests a performer's thoughts directly affect their feelings, which in turn affect their behaviour at that time (i.e. preparation for performance and/or performance). When these thoughts and associated feelings are appraised as negative or irrational (i.e. a debilitative interpretation), dysfunctional preparation for performance or performance consequences will arise. However, through the process of REBT, these negative or irrational thoughts can be restructured (i.e. reinterpreted using tertiary or quaternary appraisal), to create rational or restructured beliefs that promote functional consequences for performance preparation and/or performance (i.e. a facilitative interpretation). The application of REBT within sport psychology has tended to utilise the fundamental questioning approach that enables athletes to 'identify', 'dispute' and 'replace' their negative initial appraisal of anxiety-related symptoms (see Hanton and Jones, 1999b; Thomas *et al.*, 2007b).

In addition to using self-talk skills during the process of cognitive rationalisation and restructuring, the autonomous use of positive self-talk has also been associated with the restructuring approach (Hanton *et al.*, 2002, 2004a; Mellalieu *et al.*, 2008; Thomas *et al.*, 2007a). For example, the use of self-talk is synonymous with strategies that use cognitive confidence management techniques to create a protection mechanism against debilitative anxiety symptoms (Hanton *et al.*, 2004a; Mellalieu *et al.*, 2008; Thomas *et al.*, 2007a). Specifically, findings have highlighted the positive effect that a phonetically brief positive self-talk statement can have over debilitative competitive anxiety symptom interpretation (Hanton *et al.*, 2002, 2004a; Thomas *et al.*, 2007a). Self-talk skills have also been associated with the use of thought-stopping in this process, aiding performers in their attempts to protect confidence by repressing negative self-statements experienced (Hanton *et al.*, 2002, 2004a). Further, positive verbal persuasion from credible and significant external sources (e.g. coach and team-mates) have also been found to help manipulate confidence and protect against the debilitative performance consequences of symptoms associated with competitive anxiety (Hanton *et al.*, 2004a; Mellalieu *et al.*, 2008; Thomas *et al.*, 2007a).

Goal setting is the final self-regulation skill that has emerged as critical within the restructuring approach (cf. Hanton and Jones, 1999a; Thomas *et al.*, 2007a). Interestingly, in both these studies, performance and process goals have been cited as effective goal types for performers to adopt as the competitive event draws nearer. This finding has direct links to the notion of goal attainment expectancy within Jones' (1995a) control model of facilitative and debilitative anxiety, and the suggestion within the goal-setting literature that effective performance and process goals are easier for performers to control, due to their self-referenced nature (see Kingston *et al.*, 2006). Specifically, goals of a more controllable nature (i.e. performance and process) become more effective at helping to maintain a facilitative interpretation of anxiety-related symptoms. However, caution is advised here in relation to presenting the perspective that outcome goals are directly associated with debilitative interpretations of competitive anxiety symptoms and should therefore be avoided in stress management interventions. The preliminary position that has emerged from the anxiety literature, in addition to the perspective voiced in some areas of the sports motivation literature (see Kingston *et al.*, 2006), indicates that although perceived controllability of outcome goals can be an issue, and that unrealistic outcome goals may actually create anxiety for the performer, their powerful motivational properties cannot be ignored. Therefore, we would advocate a combined goal-setting programme (outcome, performance and process) where the performer is encouraged to focus on performance and process goals at anxious times close to competition (cf. Thomas *et al.*, 2007a).

The application of the psychological skills outlined under the restructuring approach has tended to occur in the form of athlete education, with the creation of structured pre-competition and pre-race routines where the strategies taught are predominantly designed for use immediately prior to performance (Hanton and Jones, 1999b; Mamassis and Doganis, 2004). However, recent studies have provided evidence of how psychological skills can be used differentially at a meso-level during the seven days preceding performance (e.g. Mellalieu *et al.*, 2008; Thomas *et al.*, 2007a, b). For example, Thomas *et al.* (2007a) examined how psychological skills were employed by facilitators of symptom interpretations across three phases of the seven-day competitive cycle. During Phase I (post-performance), imagery skills were used by the facilitators to replace naturally occurring negative post-performance images (e.g. skill execution) with counter images that were positive in nature. During Phase II (two-to-one day pre-performance), imagery skills focused on best performance imagery routines associated with the cognitive-general and motivational-general-mastery functions (Hall, 2001; Paivio, 1985). Finally, in Phase III (match day), imagery skills focused on snap-shot best performance imagery routines of cognitive-specific functions related to the player's role within the team (e.g. shooting skills for a forward). This differential application of techniques was also found to be extended to the cognitive rationalisation and restructuring, goal setting and self-talk skills employed within the seven-day competitive cycle providing a clearer evidence base for the timing, structure and specific content of stress management programmes within the restructuring approach (see Thomas *et al.*, 2007a). Mellalieu *et al.* (2008) have supported these findings in their examination of the psychological skills elite rugby union players used to attain desirable activation states and facilitating interpretations of emotional and affective symptoms prior to performance. Specifically, players reported differential use of imagery skills as competition moved closer, and the salience of the use of the mastery function of imagery to maintain and protect against the potential debilitative effects of anxiety symptoms immediately prior to performance.

The qualitative literature reviewed in this section provides an insight into the fundamental psychological skills associated with the restructuring approach. A number of studies have also empirically tested the efficacy of different multi-modal cognitive behavioural interventions on pre-competitive anxiety responses and performance. Consequently, in the penultimate section of the chapter we review these studies, together with the body of literature that has tested the efficacy of interventions designed under the reduction-based approach to stress management.

Applied research testing the efficacy of stress management interventions

This section reviews the research that has tested the efficacy of stress management interventions in sport under the label of either the reduction or restructuring approach. Investigations using the reduction approach have adopted three main practice philosophies: the matching hypothesis (e.g. Maynard *et al.*, 1995a, b, 1998), techniques associated with stress management training (e.g. Crocker, 1989; Crocker *et al.*, 1988; Kenney *et al.*, 1987; Smith, 1980; Smith and Ascough, 1985) and interventions associated with stress inoculation training (e.g. DeWitt, 1980; Hamilton and Fremouw, 1985; Kerr and Leith, 1993; Mace and Carroll, 1985, 1989; Mace *et al.*, 1986, 1987; Meyers and Schleser, 1980; Meyers *et al.*, 1982; Zeigler *et al.*, 1982). In contrast to the literature on the reduction approach, only a limited number of studies have empirically tested the effectiveness of interventions under the label of the restructuring approach (i.e. Hanton and Jones, 1999b; Mamassis and Doganis, 2004; Thomas *et al.*, 2007b).

Research testing the efficacy of stress management interventions under the reduction approach

Investigations testing the efficacy of stress management interventions in sport based on the tenets of the matching hypothesis have come from a programme of research conducted by Maynard and associates. Initially, Maynard *et al.* (1995b) examined the impact of a somatic intervention in the form of an applied relaxation technique with 17 semi-professional football players. The eight players most debilitated by their somatic anxiety symptoms formed the intervention group, whilst the remaining nine players comprised the control group. Following an eight-week period of applied relaxation, the intervention group showed significant decreases in cognitive and somatic anxiety intensity, and significantly more facilitative interpretations of somatic anxiety symptoms. In comparison, no significant pre-post-intervention changes were noted across anxiety symptoms in the control group.

Using a similar sample, Maynard *et al.* (1995a) replicated their original study, but replaced the somatic intervention with a cognitive strategy based on the application of Suinn's (1987) positive thought control technique. Participants were assigned to a cognitive debilitative, somatic debilitative or control group based on their competitive anxiety direction scores. To examine issues of 'crossover effects' within the matching hypothesis, both the cognitive and somatic debilitated groups received the cognitive intervention. The findings indicated that the cognitive intervention decreased both cognitive and somatic intensity, and created more facilitative interpretations of both cognitive and somatic anxiety symptoms in both intervention groups. These findings added further uncertainty to the premise of the matching hypothesis that the selection of treatments should be made compatible with the performers' dominant anxiety response. Indeed, Maynard *et al.* suggested their findings corroborated the 'crossover' argument proffered to explain the questionable conceptual accuracy of the original predictions of the matching hypothesis.

In a direct extension to these conclusions, Maynard *et al.* (1998) proceeded to examine the efficacy of what they termed 'unimodal compatible', 'unimodal non-compatible' and 'multimodal' stress management interventions over performers' intensity and direction of anxiety responses. Unimodal compatible treatments comprised a single treatment technique that matched the athletes' dominant anxiety response. Unimodal non-compatible constituted a single treatment technique that was the opposite of the athletes' dominant response, while the multimodal intervention adhered to the stress management principles within Smith's (1980) approach. Using a matched pairs design, 44 athletes with debilitative interpretations of cognitive anxiety symptoms were assigned to either one of the treatment groups or a control group. The results indicated the unimodal-matched and the multimodal intervention programmes decreased cognitive anxiety intensity. Somatic anxiety and self-confidence intensity were decreased within multimodal intervention only. For the direction of symptom responses, the unimodal-matched and multimodal intervention programmes increased facilitative interpretations of cognitive anxiety, the unimodal-unmatched and multimodal intervention increased facilitative interpretations of somatic anxiety, and the multimodal intervention increased facilitative interpretations of self-confidence. These findings led Maynard *et al.* to conclude that multimodal interventions appeared to be the most robust design for stress management interventions, and highlighted the lack of sensitivity with some of the theoretical predictions of the matching hypothesis.

Several additional conceptual issues have been identified within Maynard and associates' research (cf. Hanton and Jones, 1999a, b). Specifically, in all three of their applied studies, Maynard and colleagues utilised directional interpretations (in addition to the intensity of symptoms) as a dependent variable. Further, Maynard and colleagues used the direction scores of the participants (i.e. the interpretation of their anxiety responses) as the screening variable that dictated intervention application (i.e. their cognitive or somatic dominant response). This is somewhat paradoxical in relation to the underlying principles we outlined previously within the chapter regarding the conceptual basis for the intervention choice that is associated with the matching hypothesis. Specifically, the propositions of matching hypothesis that indicate treatments should be designed to reduce competitive anxiety symptom responses, and that intervention choice (i.e. cognitive versus somatic) should be dictated by the athletes' dominant response (in terms of the level or intensity of symptoms experienced), appear to have been overlooked. The conceptual rationale for utilising direction in this way within these studies has never been fully explained and it appears that inclusion within these research questions may have been associated more with the contemporary thinking of the time (i.e. the recognition of directional interpretations within stress-related research) rather than on the underlying tenets of the matching hypothesis. However, although the theoretical foundation of these studies can be questioned, the findings regarding the utility of the multimodal interventions investigated have helped inform the stress management literature at both an individual and collective level.

Several studies have empirically tested the efficacy of multimodal interventions associated with stress management and stress inoculation training respectively (see Burton, 1990; Cox, 1998; Smith and Smoll, 2004). Although the majority of these studies were conducted approximately 20 years ago, their practical relevance to the treatment of stress-related issues remains applicable within the contemporary sport psychology literature. Due to their clinical foundation, stress management training and stress inoculation training have been successfully applied across a wide range of settings and populations. For example, stress management training has been shown to be an effective treatment approach in test-anxious students (Smith and Nye, 1989), heavy alcohol drinkers (Rohensenow *et al.*, 1985) and stressed student populations (Holtzworth-Munroe *et al.*, 1985). In comparison, stress inoculation training has emerged as an effective approach with individuals in the stressful occupations of nursing, teaching, policing, social working, probationary working and the military (see Burchfield *et al.*, 1985; O'Leary and Wilson, 1998; Spiegler and Guevremont, 1998).

Researchers in sport have transferred the application of these frameworks into the treatment of stress-related issues within athletic populations. For example, derivatives of Smith's (1980) stress management training have been found to be successful in reducing anxiety-related symptoms across the sports of football (Smith and Smoll, 1978), figure skating (Smith, 1980), running (Kenney *et al.*, 1987; Zeigler *et al.*, 1982) and volleyball (Crocker, 1989; Crocker *et al.*, 1988). In comparison, adaptations of Meichenbaum's (1975, 1985) stress inoculation training have been successfully applied across the sporting populations of basketball (DeWitt, 1980; Hamilton and Fremouw, 1985; Meyers and Schleser, 1980; Meyers *et al.*, 1982), abseiling (Mace and Carroll, 1985; Mace *et al.*, 1986), running (Ziegler *et al.*, 1982) and gymnastics (Mace and Carroll, 1989; Mace *et al.*, 1987). Although these studies point to the obvious benefits of stress management training and stress inoculation training in relation to lowering levels of anxiety symptom intensity, limited information can be gleaned from the studies in relation to the performance enhancing effects of the techniques. Further, the multimodal nature of the interventions applied renders it difficult to ascertain which specific component parts (versus the total programme used) provide the beneficial reducing influence over anxiety-related symptoms (cf. Burton, 1990).

Research testing the efficacy of stress management interventions under the restructuring approach

A limited number of studies have empirically tested the effectiveness of interventions formulated under the umbrella of the restructuring approach (i.e. Hanton and Jones, 1999b; Mamassis and Doganis, 2004; Thomas *et al.*, 2007b). All of these studies have used derivatives of single-subject multiple-baseline designs together with some form of multimodal intervention as the stress management programme associated with their work. The first of these was Hanton and Jones' (1999b) application of a psychological skills programme with elite swimmers who interpreted their pre-competitive anxiety symptoms as debilitative towards upcoming performance. In line with the conceptual standpoint of the restructuring approach, the primary goal of the intervention was to restructure debilitative interpretations of anxiety-related symptoms (cognitive and somatic), increase levels of self-confidence experienced and, in turn, elicit positive effects on performance. The content of the multimodal psychological skills programme was based on in-depth qualitative interviews with elite swimmers who had utilised psychological skills to control their stress-related symptoms (see Hanton and Jones, 1999a) and included goal setting, imagery and positive self-talk. The findings indicated no effect on the intensity of cognitive and somatic anxiety. However, swimmers reported increases in self-confidence and changes in symptom interpretations (both cognitive and somatic) from debilitative to facilitative. Increases in swimming performance of between 2 to 3 per cent were also recorded.

In the next study to assess the efficacy of the restructuring approach, Mamassis and Doganis (2004) used a multimodal psychological skill package similar to that adopted by Hanton and Jones (1999b) to influence the intensity and directional interpretations of tennis players' pre-competitive cognitive, somatic and self-confidence responses. Although Mamassis and Doganis' rationale for their intervention was primarily based on their experiences of the use of mental training programmes with the sample used within in their study (junior elite tennis players), the content of their season-long intervention programme was linked to a number of skills advocated within the restructuring approach. These included imagery, goal setting, positive thinking and self-talk, arousal regulation and concentration skills. The results provided support for the efficacy of the restructuring approach in that no changes were reported in levels of cognitive and somatic anxiety experienced, levels of self-confidence increased, and interpretations of cognitive and somatic anxiety symptoms became more facilitative. Improvements in players' subjective (self-reported) tennis performance scores were also supported (see Mamassis and Doganis, 2004).

The most recent study to test the efficacy of stress management programmes designed under the umbrella of the restructuring approach is that of Thomas *et al.* (2007b). In line with the theory-to-practice philosophy adopted by Hanton and Jones (1999a, b), Thomas *et al.* derived the content of their restructuring intervention from interviews with facilitators of anxiety symptoms (Thomas *et al.*, 2007a). Adopting a focus on the reciprocal process of stress, Thomas *et al.* tested the efficacy of a meso-level temporal intervention programme over a seven-day competitive cycle commonly associated with team sports (i.e. Saturday to Saturday). The intervention consisted of the psychological skills of imagery, rationalisation and restructuring, goal setting and self-talk. However, the specific form and function of each skill was applied differentially within the temporal period of the intervention (see Figure 4.1; Thomas *et al.*, 2007a, b). For example, imagery routines used seven-to-five days prior to performance were described as 'counter imagery routines' and were structured around replacing negative post-performance images that players naturally experienced following performance with positive images of similar scenarios that depicted accomplishment of skills and tasks. Imagery routines used two-to-one day prior to performance focused upon mastery elements through the integration of cognitive general and cognitive specific functions in routines that were rehearsed for some length of time (see Figure 4.1). Finally, imagery routines utilised on match day focused on positive performance scenarios based solely on cognitive specific functions and utilised routines that were short in time and described as 'snap-shot' in nature (see Figure 4.1). Similar variation in the implementation of rationalisation and restructuring, goal setting and self-talk skills was applied throughout the seven-day intervention period. The results of the study indicated that the temporal

Temporal phase I (Post-performance – seven days to five days preceding next match)		Participant time commitment	Consultant time commitment (per participant)
Preparation booklets	• Review of individual performance errors. • Review of countering performance accomplishments.	~1 hr	~1 hr
Intervention (one-on-one consultation)	• Replacing negative post-performance images with countering positive images. • Rationalising and restructuring negative post-performance symptoms.	~5 hrs (including skill practice time)	~3 hrs

Temporal phase II (Two days to one day preceding match)		Participant time commitment	Consultant time commitment (per participant)
Preparation booklets	• Review of best performances. • Recording of negative pre-performance symptoms.	~1 hr	~1 hr
Intervention (one-on-one consultation)	• Best performance imagery (CG function) . • Rationalising and restructuring of negative pre-performance symptoms. • Performance and process goals.	~7 hrs (including skill practice time)	~4 hrs

Temporal phase III (Match day pre-performance)		Participant time commitment	Consultant time commitment (per participant)
Preparation booklets	• Review of key skills for position.role (examples of recent best performance of these skills). • Recording of key technical words/ statements. • Recording of negative pre-performance symptoms.	~1.5 hrs	~2 hrs
Intervention (one-on-one consultation)	• Best performance imagery (CS function) . • Rationalising and restructuring of negative pre-performance symptoms. • Integrated self-talk programme (positive self-statements and performance and process goals).	~3 hrs (including skill practice time)	~4 hrs

Figure 4.1 Holistic representation of a temporal intervention programme (source: Thomas *et al.*, 2007b).

intervention successfully restructured interpretations of cognitive and somatic anxiety, increased levels and frequency of occurrences of self-confidence symptoms, and decreased frequency of occurrences of cognitive and somatic anxiety-related symptoms. In addition, in line with the conceptual standpoint of the direction approach, these changes occurred without affecting the levels of cognitive and somatic anxiety experienced. These effects were also associated with increased levels of performance across all three field-hockey players.

Practical implications

In this section, we draw together a number of issues discussed in the chapter to give a summary of the status on the efficacy of stress management interventions. We also present several recommendations for practitioners that are grounded in the relevant findings from the literature.

Although we have considered both approaches to stress management in this review so far (i.e. reduction versus restructuring), issues have arisen with the application of techniques under the matching hypothesis that question the 'compatibility' stance adopted within that approach. Consequently, the recommendations presented in this section cement our position that it is the situational and personal variables that have been identified to moderate performers' symptom responses and interpretations that should determine the stress management techniques employed. The simplification of the debate to a straight comparison of 'reduce' versus 'restructure' would, in our opinion, present a rather naive and futile position at this point in time given the emerging knowledge base surrounding the study of stress management in sport.

In relation to the need to consider the moderating influence of situation variables when designing stress management interventions, thereby choosing between a 'reduce' or 'restructure' approach to adopt, one of the key findings highlighted in the literature is that the relative activation demands of the sport should form a prime factor underpinning intervention choice (cf. Mellalieu *et al.*, 2008). For example, techniques designed to reduce anxiety intensity may also decrease a performer's activation state and subsequent mental and physical readiness to compete. For sports with higher activation demands, the application of techniques designed to reduce anxiety-related symptoms may, therefore, be more harmful than beneficial to the overall psychological preparation of the individual (Hanton *et al.*, 2000; Mellalieu *et al.*, 2008). In these situations practitioners should strive to alter the performers' interpretation of anxiety-related symptoms via the cognitive and confidence management strategies associated with the restructuring approach (cf. Hanton and Jones, 1999a, b; Hanton *et al.*, 2000; Mellalieu *et al.*, 2008; Thomas *et al.*, 2007a, b). Conversely, for sports with low activation demands, techniques associated with reducing anxiety-related symptoms would appear more applicable (Hanton *et al.*, 2000; Mellalieu *et al.*, 2008).

One personal variable that also appears to have direct implications for intervention choice is the consistent finding related to the moderating effects of skill level upon experiences of, and techniques for, coping with competitive stress.

Indeed, whether the status of the performer is elite or non-elite appears to dictate the type of psychological skills that should be adopted. Specifically, when compared to their non-elite counterparts, elite performers not only view their symptom responses as more facilitating to performance, but also appear to have a more salient understanding and controlled application of the advanced psychological skills associated with the restructuring approach (Fletcher and Hanton, 2001; Hanton and Jones, 1999a, b; Jones *et al.*, 1994; Thomas *et al.*, 2007a). Therefore, when working with non-elite performers, it may be more applicable to initially attempt to reduce anxiety-related symptoms experienced, and then proceed to restructure interpretations of responses before returning activation states to the levels required for the specific demands of the sport (cf. Mellalieu and Hanton, 2008; Mellalieu *et al.*, 2006a). In contrast to their non-elite debilitating counterparts, however, and due to the potential capacity to adopt advance psychological skills, elite performers debilitated by anxiety responses should adopt techniques that restructure interpretations, with a focus on combining the psychological skills of imagery, goal setting, cognitive rationalisation and restructuring and self-talk (Hanton and Jones, 1999 a, b; Hanton *et al.*, 2005b; Thomas *et al.*, 2007a, b).

The literature highlighted throughout this chapter has also emphasised the importance of accounting for the temporal nature of performers' responses to the demands they face, particularly the need to consider macro-, meso- and micro-level perspectives when designing stress management interventions (cf. Mellalieu *et al.*, 2006a). For example, at a macro-level, Hanton and Jones (1999a) described how the temporal responses of elite swimmers and the strategies employed to cope with competitive demands shifted as their career progressed. Specifically, positive interpretations of pre-race symptoms developed via natural learning experiences and educational input from several sources. These findings suggest that early career interventions should be orientated towards educating performers to accept that the thoughts and feelings they experience are an intrinsic part of elite performance (see also Hanton *et al.*, 2007). Indeed, while these symptoms may initially appear unpleasant and discomforting, they may not necessarily be debilitative towards performance.

Although some attention has focused on the macro-level perspective regarding how performers manage competition stress over time, the majority of research has examined how stress management interventions can be applied at the meso- and micro-level. Indeed, the studies reviewed in this chapter suggest the core psychological skills of relaxation, imagery, goal setting, cognitive rationalisation, and restructuring and self-talk should be applied differentially within the time leading up to individual competitive events (Hanton and Jones, 1999b; Mellalieu *et al.*, 2008; Thomas *et al.*, 2007a, b). Specifically, Mellalieu *et al.*'s (2008) findings suggested that, during the early preparation period, where lower activation states are more desirable (e.g. five-to-seven days pre-performance), performers use strategies that regulate or reduce emotional responses (i.e. anxiety). However, closer to the event (e.g. 30-to-60 minutes pre-performance), strategies are adopted that focused on energising the performer to achieve the higher activation state required for the demands of the competition. Mellalieu *et al.*'s findings also support Thomas and colleagues' differential application of psychological skills during the time leading up to competition. However, it is interesting to note that individual difference variables again provide an influence over the potential application of these findings from these studies. Indeed, both Thomas and colleagues, and Mellalieu *et al.* investigated team sports that required relatively high levels of activation. Therefore, practitioners should consider the salient individual difference variables applicable to their client(s) when constructing temporal interventions.

The final key implication to emerge from the studies assessing temporal change at the meso-level is that, in line with the current trend of research, a fine-grained measurement approach should be adopted when assessing pre-competitive responses. Here, practitioners need to consider assessing not only the intensity of symptom responses performers experience in relation to the time to event, but also the directional interpretations and frequency of intrusions reported.

Future research directions

In light of the body of research that has considered the study and application of stress management programmes in sport we now present several areas where we believe future research efforts may wish to focus. This includes investigations that seek to compare the situations where reduction or restructuring techniques are most applicable, further the understanding of the application of stress management techniques across temporal contexts and attempt to clarify the contribution of individual psychological skills in the stress management process.

In discussing the chronological developments within the stress management literature, this chapter has identified that research to date has examined the efficacy of interventions designed either under the umbrella of the reduction (e.g. Maynard *et al.*, 1995a, b, 1998) or restructuring approach (e.g. Hanton and Jones, 1999b; Thomas *et al.*, 2007b). An obvious extension to this body of literature is one that directly compares the effectiveness of these approaches to provide more conclusive answers regarding the efficacy of interventions to specific groups (cf. Thomas *et al.*, 2007b). For example, a comparison of the effectiveness of the psychological skills used within the reduction approach to those associated with the restructuring approach in groups of elite versus non-elite performers would reveal the efficacy of the interventions relative to a key individual difference variable (i.e. skill level). A further extension to this work would be to test the efficacy of interventions of the two approaches relative to the activation or task demands of different sports (cf. Hanton *et al.*, 2000; Mellalieu *et al.*, 2008).

The adoption of a temporal perspective to the stress process (i.e. at the macro-, meso- and micro-level) is also important for future research in stress management (Hanton and Jones, 1999a; Hanton *et al.*, 2002; Mellalieu *et al.*, 2008; Thomas *et al.*, 2007a). As this body of research remains in its infancy within sport psychology, investigation is required to corroborate the findings of Hanton and Jones (1999a) relative to developing macro-level educational interventions that foster facilitative symptom interpretations in performers during early career development. This should be supplemented with research at a meso-level that extends information relative to the use of psychological skills in the time leading up to specific events (Mellalieu et al., 2008; Thomas et al., 2007a). Indeed, these studies have already indicated distinct uses for several psychological skills during the week leading up to competitive events in team sports that tend to operate within a competitive seven-day cycle. Consequently, there is obvious scope to explore the activities and disciplines that fall outside the seven-day competitive cycle commonly associated with team sports. In addition, to date, studies have only focused on how elite performers utilise psychological skills in the time period preceding competition. Research assessing how non-elite performers utilise psychological skills will help to provide a more comprehensive picture of this particular population. Research of this type could serve to strengthen the proposal that stress management interventions are more suited to the application of skills associated with the reduction approach in non-elite performers (cf. Fletcher and Hanton, 2001; Hanton and Jones, 1999a, b; Jones et al., 1994; Maynard et al., 1998; Thomas et al., 2007a).

Studies that examine the direct influence of each psychological skill upon the competitive stress process should also be encouraged. With the exception of Maynard and colleagues' work testing the matching hypothesis, research considering the efficacy of stress management interventions using stress inoculation and stress management training and restructuring interventions has tended to examine the efficacy of multimodal intervention programmes. Although recent qualitative studies have provided more detail regarding perceived explanations of how facilitative symptoms interpretations are developed and maintained, these studies have provided general guidance for the application of psychological strategies. Future research should therefore attempt to use this information as the basis to generate more specific knowledge regarding the use and application of each psychological skill. For example, the use of self-talk and cognitive rationalisation has emerged as a particularly pertinent psychological skill within the restructuring approach, but no study has yet to address a specific research question on its role and mechanism in fostering facilitative symptom interpretations. As Fletcher and Hanton (2001) suggested, research should be encouraged that elicits clear information on the success of individual psychological skills or that directly compares the efficacy of one strategy versus another to gain a clearer understanding of the successful deployment of psychological skills in the stress management process.

Finally, although the content of this chapter has focused on the study of the application of techniques to deal with competitive stress, the notion of organisational stress and, more specifically, organisational stress management has recently begun to emerge as a topic of interest within sport psychology. Specifically, Fletcher and colleagues have attempted to define and contextualise organisational stress within a sporting environment (see Fletcher et al., 2006), generating an initial conceptual framework for classifying groups of organisational stressors experienced (see Fletcher and Hanton, 2003; Hanton and Fletcher, 2005; Hanton et al., 2005a). However, in comparison to the wealth of research that exists in competitive stress management, developments within the organisational stress management literature in sport remain in their infancy. To date, no research has considered or tested the efficacy of organisational stress management interventions in sport. Fletcher *et al.* (2006) have provided a framework for the treatment of organisational stress through their proposal of primary, secondary and tertiary level interventions. This framework requires rigorous testing in order to develop a theory-to-practice rationale for the content of organisational stress management interventions. Intuitively, this would appear a fruitful area for research to develop holistic intervention strategies that enable individuals and groups to deal with the effects of both competitive and organisational stress.

Concluding remarks

This chapter has discussed the conceptually distinct treatment frameworks associated with the *reduction* and *restructuring* stress management approaches used in sport psychology. In addition, these different positions have been underpinned by reference to the body of literature highlighting the temporal elements of the competitive stress process. We conclude our chapter, therefore, with a series of statements summarising what we consider are the salient points at present within this research area. Specifically, the current findings into stress management in competitive sport highlighted within this review suggest:

1   Stress is an ongoing transaction for the performer and as such, subsequent research and interventions should consider the temporal facets of the stress process. This can be considered at the macro-, meso- or micro-level.
2   When dealing with an individual's emotional response within this transaction, the intensity (i.e. level), direction (i.e. interpretation) and frequency (i.e. occurrence) of performers' anxiety symptoms experiences should be considered to elicit a more complete understanding of the responses to the demands of competition.
3   Within the transaction process, the role of individual difference variables (e.g. the activation demands of the sport and the skill level of the performer) should be used as the pivotal criteria when selecting psychological skills either aligned to the reduction or restructuring approach for stress management interventions.

We hope these statements provide a clearer understanding of some of the pertinent issues facing researchers and practitioners when attempting to develop and investigate stress management interventions in sport.

Note

1   Martens *et al.*'s (1990a) MAT also included the construct of self-confidence. Given the stress management focus of this review we have omitted detail on this issue within this chapter.

References

Alpert, R. and Haber, N. N. (1960). Anxiety in academic achievement situations. *Journal of Abnormal Social Psychology*, 61, 207–215.

Benson, H. (1975). *The relaxation response*. New York: Avon Books.

Biddle, S. J. H. (1997). Current tends in sport and exercise psychology research. *The Psychologist*, 46, 63–69.

Borkovec, T. D. (1976). Physiological and cognitive processes in the regulation of anxiety. In G. E. Schwartz and D. Shapiro (eds), *Consciousness and self-regulation: advances in research* (Vol. 1, pp. 261–312). New York: Plenum.

Burchfield, S. R., Stein, L. J. and Hamilton, K. L. (1985). Test anxiety: a model for studying psychological and physiological interrelationships. In S. R. Burchfield (ed.), *Stress: psychological and physiological interaction* (pp. 35–63). New York: Hemisphere.

Burton, D. (1988). Do anxious swimmers swim slower? Re-examining the elusive anxiety performance relationship. *Journal of Sport and Exercise Psychology*, 10, 45–61.

Burton, D. (1990). Multimodal stress management in sport: current status and future directions. In G. Jones and L. Hardy (eds), *Stress and performance in sport* (pp. 171–201). Chichester: Wiley.

Burton, D. (1998). Measuring competitive state anxiety. In J. L. Duda (ed.), *Advances in sport and exercise psychology measurement* (pp. 129–148). Morgantown, WV: Fitness Information Technology Inc.

Carver, C. S. and Scheier, M. F. (1986). Functional and dysfunctional approaches to anxiety: the interaction between expectancies and self-focused attention. In R. Schwarzer (ed.), *Self-related cognitions in anxiety and motivation* (pp. 111–146). Hillsdale, NJ: Erlbaum.

Carver, C. S. and Scheier, M. F. (1988). A control-process perspective on anxiety. *Anxiety Research*, 1, 17–22.

Cerin, E., Szabo, A., Hunt, N. and Williams, C. (2000). Temporal patterning of competitive emotions: a critical review. *Journal of Sports Sciences*, 18, 605–626.

Cox, R. H. (1998). *Sport psychology: concepts and applications* (4th edn). Boston, MA: McGraw-Hill.

Craft, L. L., Magyar, M., Becker, B. J. and Feltz, D. L. (2003). The relationship between competitive state anxiety inventory-2 and sport performance: a meta-analysis. *Journal of Sport and Exercise Psychology*, 25, 44–65.

Crocker, P. R. E. (1989). A follow-up of cognitive-affective stress management training. *Journal of Sport and Exercise Psychology*, 11, 236–242.

Crocker, P. R. E., Alderman, R. B. and Smith, F. M. R. (1988). Cognitive affective stress management training with high performance youth volleyball players: effects on affect, cognition and performance. *Journal of Sport and Exercise Psychology*, 10, 448–460.

David, D., Schnur, J. and Belloiu, A. (2002). Another search for the 'Hot' cognitions: appraisal, irrational beliefs, attributions, and their relation to emotion. *Journal of Rational-Emotive and Cognitive-Behaviour Therapy*, 20, 93–131.

Davidson, R. J. (1978). Specificity and patterning in biobehavioural systems. *American Psychologist*, 33, 430–436.

Davidson, R. J. and Schwartz, G. E. (1976). The psychobiology of relaxation and related stress: a multiprocess theory. In D. I. Mostofsky (ed.), *Behavioural control and modification of physiological activity* (pp. 399–442). Englewood Cliffs, NJ: Prentice Hall.

DeWitt, D. J. (1980). Cognitive and biofeedback training for stress reduction with university athletes. *Journal of Sport Psychology*, 2, 288–294.

Diener, E., Sandvik, E. and Pavot, W. G. (1991). Happiness is the frequency, not the intensity, of positive vs. negative affect. In F. Strack, M. Argyle and N. Schwarz (eds), *Subjective well being: an interdisciplinary perspective* (pp. 119–139). Oxford: Pergamon Press.

Ellis, A. (1962). *Reason and emotion in psychotherapy*. New York: Stuart.

Ellis, A. (1970). *The essence of rationale psychotherapy: a comprehensive approach to treatment*. New York: Institute for Rational Living.

Ellis, A. (1994). *Reason and emotion in psychotherapy*. New Jersey: Secaucus.

Eubank, M. and Collins, D. (2000). Coping with pre- and in-event fluctuations in competitive state anxiety: a longitudinal approach. *Journal of Sports Sciences*, 18, 121–131.

Eubank, M. R., Smith, N. C. and Smethhurst, C. J. (1995). Intensity and direction of multidimensional competitive state anxiety: relationships to performance in racket sports. *Journal of Sports Sciences*, 13, 30–35.

Eys, M. A., Hardy, J., Carron, A. V. and Beauchamp, M. R. (2003). The relationship between task cohesion and competitive state anxiety. *Journal of Sport and Exercise Psychology*, 25, 66–76.

Fletcher, D. and Fletcher, J. (2005). A meta-model of stress, emotions and performance: conceptual foundations, theoretical framework, and research directions. *Journal of Sports Sciences*, 23, 157–158.

Fletcher, D. and Hanton, S. (2001). The relationship between psychological skills usage and competitive anxiety responses. *Psychology of Sport and Exercise*, 2, 89–101.

Fletcher, D. and Hanton, S. (2003). Sources of organisational stress in elite sports performers. *The Sport Psychologist*, 17, 175–195.

Fletcher, D., Hanton, S. and Mellalieu, S. D. (2006). An organisational stress review: conceptual and theoretical issues in competitive sport. In S. Hanton and S. D. Mellalieu (eds), *Literature reviews in sport psychology* (pp. 321–374). Hauppauge, NY: Nova Science.

Gould, D., Greenleaf, C. and Krane, V. (2002). Arousal-anxiety and sport behaviour. In T. S. Horn (ed.), *Advances in sport psychology* (pp. 207–241). Champaign, IL: Human Kinetics.

Gould, D., Petlichkoff, L., Simons, J. and Vevera, M. (1987). Relationships between CSAI-2 sub-scales scores and pistol shooting performance. *Journal of Sport Psychology*, 9, 33–42.

Gould, D., Petlichkoff, L. and Weinberg, R. S. (1984). Antecedents of temporal changes in and relationships between CSAI-2 subcomponents. *Journal of Sport Psychology*, 6, 289–304.

Hale, B. D. and Whitehouse, A. (1998). The effects of imagery-manipulated appraisal on intensity and direction of competitive anxiety. *The Sport Psychologist*, 12, 40–51.

Hall, C. R. (2001). Imagery in sport and exercise. In R. Singer, H. A. Hausenblas and C. M. Janelle (eds), *Handbook of research on sport psychology* (2nd edn, pp. 529–549). New York: Wiley.

Hamilton, S. A. and Fremouw, W. J. (1985). Cognitive-behavioural training for college basketball free-throw performance. *Cognitive Therapy and Research*, 9, 479–483.

Hanton, S. and Connaughton, D. (2002). Perceived control of anxiety and its relationship with self-confidence and performance: a qualitative explanation. *Research Quarterly for Exercise and Sport*, 73, 87–97.

Hanton, S. and Fletcher, D. (2005). Organisational stress in competitive sport: more than we bargained for? *International Journal of Sport Psychology*, 36, 273–283.

Hanton, S. and Jones, G. (1997). Antecedents of competitive state anxiety as a function of skill level. *Psychological Reports*, 81, 1139–1147.

Hanton, S. and Jones, G. (1999a). The acquisition and development of cognitive skills and strategies. I: Making the butterflies fly in formation. *The Sport Psychologist*, 13, 1–21.

Hanton, S. and Jones, G. (1999b). The effects of a multimodal intervention programme on performers. II: Training the butterflies to fly in formation. *The Sport Psychologist*, 13, 22–41.

Hanton, S., Cropley, B., Miles, A., Mellalieu, S. D. and Neil, R. (2007). Experience in sport and its relationship with competitive anxiety. *International Journal of Sport and Exercise Psychology*, 5, 28–53.

Hanton, S., Evans, L. and Neil, R. (2003a). Hardiness and the competitive trait anxiety response. *Anxiety, Stress, and Coping*, 16, 167–184.

Hanton, S., Fletcher, D. and Coughlan, G. (2005a). Stress in elite sport performers: a comparative study of competitive and organisational stressors. *Journal of Sports Sciences*, 10, 1129–1141.

Hanton, S., Jones, G. and Mullen, R. (2000). Intensity and direction of competitive anxiety as interpreted by rugby players and rifle shooters. *Perceptual and Motor Skills*, 90, 513–521.

Hanton, S., Mellalieu, S. D. and Hall, R. (2004a). Self-confidence and anxiety interpretation: a qualitative investigation. *Psychology of Sport and Exercise*, 5, 379–521.

Hanton, S., Mellalieu, S. D. and Young, S. (2002). A qualitative investigation into temporal patterning of the precompetitive anxiety response and its effects on performance. *Journal of Sports Sciences*, 20, 911–928.

Hanton, S., Neil, R. and Mellalieu, S. D. (2008). Recent developments in competitive anxiety direction and competition stress research. *International Review of Sport and Exercise Psychology*, 1, 45–57.

Hanton, S., O'Brien, M. and Mellalieu, S. D. (2003b). Individual differences, perceived control and competitive trait anxiety. *Journal of Sport Behaviour*, 26, 39–55.

Hanton, S., Thomas, O. and Maynard, I. (2004b). Competitive anxiety responses in the week leading up to competition: the role of intensity, direction and frequency dimensions. *Psychology of Sport and Exercise*, 15, 169–181.

Hanton, S., Thomas, O. and Mellalieu, S. D. (in press). Management of competitive stress in elite sport. In B. Brewer (ed.), *International Olympic Committee (IOC) sport psychology handbook*. Blackwell Publishing.

Hanton, S., Wadey, R. and Connaughton, D. (2005b). Debilitative interpretations of competitive anxiety: a qualitative examination of elite performers. *European Journal of Sport Science*, 5, 123–136.

Hardy, L. (1990). A catastrophe model of anxiety and performance. In J. G. Jones and L. Hardy (eds), *Stress and performance in sport* (pp. 81–106). Chichester: Wiley.

Hardy, L., Jones, G. and Gould, D. (1996). *Understanding psychological preparation for sport: theory and practice of elite performers*. Chichester: Wiley.

Hays, K., Maynard, I., Thomas, O. and Bawden, M. (2007). Sources and types of confidence identified by world-class performers. *Journal of Applied Sport Psychology*, 19, 434–456.

Holtzworth-Munroe, A., Munroes, M. S. and Smith, R. E. (1985). Effects of a stress management training programme on first and second year medical students. *Journal of Medical Education*, 60, 417–419.

Jacobson, E. (1938). *Progressive relaxation* (2nd edn). Chicago, IL: University of Chicago Press.

Jerome, G. J. and Williams, J. M. (2000). Intensity and interpretation of competitive anxiety: relationship to performance and repressive coping. *Journal of Applied Sport Psychology*, 12, 236–250.

Jones, G. (1991). Recent issues in competitive state anxiety research. *The Psychologist*, 4, 152–155.

Jones, G. (1993). The role of performance profiling in cognitive behavioural interventions in sport. *The Sport Psychologist*, 7, 160–172.

Jones, G. (1995a). More than just a game: research developments and issues in competitive state anxiety in sport. *British Journal of Psychology*, 86, 449–478.

Jones, G. (1995b). Competitive anxiety in sport. In S. J. H. Biddle (ed.), *European perspectives on exercise and sport psychology* (pp. 128–153). Champaign, IL: Human Kinetics.

Jones, G. and Cale, A. (1989). Relationships between multidimensional competitive state anxiety and motor subcomponents of performance. *Journal of Sports Sciences*, 7, 129–140.

Jones, G. and Hanton, S. (1996). Interpretation of anxiety symptoms and goal attainment expectations. *Journal of Sport and Exercise Psychology*, 18, 144–158.

Jones, G. and Hardy, L. (1990). *Stress and performance in sport*. Chichester: Wiley.

Jones, G. and Swain, A. B. J. (1992). Intensity and direction dimensions of competitive state anxiety and relationships with competitiveness. *Perceptual and Motor Skills*, 74, 467–472.

Jones, G. and Swain, A. B. J. (1995). Predispositions to experience facilitating and debilitating anxiety in elite and non-elite performers. *The Sport Psychologist*, 9, 201–211.

Jones, G., Hanton, S. and Swain, A. B. J. (1994). Intensity and interpretation of anxiety symptoms in elite and non-elite sports performers. *Personality and Individual Differences*, 17, 657–663.

Jones, G., Swain, A. B. J. and Cale, A. (1990). Antecedents of multidimensional competitive state anxiety and self-confidence in elite intercollegiate middle distance runners. *The Sport Psychologist*, 4, 107–118.

Jones, G., Swain, A. B. J. and Cale, A. (1991). Gender differences in precompetition temporal patterning and antecedents of anxiety and self-confidence. *Journal of Sport and Exercise Psychology*, 13, 1–15.

Jones, G., Swain, A. B. J. and Hardy, L. (1993). Intensity and direction dimensions of competitive state anxiety and relationships with performance. *Journal of Sports Sciences*, 11, 533–542.

Jones, G., Swain, A. B. J. and Harwood, C. (1996). Positive and negative affect as predictors of competitive anxiety. *Personality and Individual Differences*, 20, 109–114.

Kardum, I. (1999). Affect intensity and frequency: their relation to mean level and variability of positive and negative affect and Eysenck's personality traits. *Personality and Individual Differences*, 26, 33–47.

Kenney, E. A., Rejeski, W. J. and Messier, S. P. (1987). Managing exercise distress: the effect of broad spectrum intervention on affect, R.P.E. and running efficiency. *Canadian Journal of Sports Sciences*, 2, 97–105.

Kerr, G. and Leith, L. (1993). Stress management and athletic performance. *The Sport Psychologist*, 7, 221–231.

Kingston, K. M., Spray, C. M. and Harwood, C. G. (2006). Motivation in sport: a goal directed intention approach. In S. Hanton and S. D. Mellalieu (eds), *Literature reviews in sport psychology* (pp. 159–197). Hauppauge, NJ: Nova Science.

Krane, V., Williams, J. M. and Feltz, D. (1992). Path analysis examining relationships among cognitive anxiety, somatic anxiety, state confidence, performance expectations, and golf performance. *Journal of Sport Behaviour*, 15, 279–295.

Lazarus, R. S. (1966). *Psychological stress and coping process*. New York: McGraw-Hill.

Lazarus, R. S. (1981). The stress and coping paradigm. In C. Eisdorfer, D. Cohen, A. Kleinman and P. Maxim (eds), *Models for clinical psychopathology* (pp. 177–214). New York: Spectrum.

Lazarus, R. S. (1982). Thoughts on the relation between emotion and cognition. *American Psychologist*, 37, 1019–1024.

Lazarus, R. S. (1993). From psychological stress to the emotions: a history of changing outlooks. *Annual Review of Psychology*, 44, 1–22.

Lazarus, R. S. (1999). *Stress and emotion: a new synthesis*. London: Free Association Books.

Lazarus, R. S. (2000). How emotions influence performance in competitive sports. *The Sport Psychologist*, 14, 229–252.

Lazarus, R. S. and Folkman, S. (1984). *Stress, appraisal and coping*. New York: Erlbaum.

Liebert, R. M. and Morris, L. W. (1967). Cognitive and emotional components of test anxiety: a distinction and some initial data. *Psychological Reports*, 20, 975–978.

Mace, R. D. and Carroll, D. (1985). The control of anxiety in sport: stress inoculation training prior to abseiling. *International Journal of Sport Psychology*, 16, 165–175.

Mace, R. D. and Carroll, D. (1989). The effect of stress inoculation training on self-reported stress, observer's rating of stress, heart rate and gymnastic performance. *Journal of Sports Sciences*, 7, 257–266.

Mace, R. D., Carroll, D. and Eastman, C. (1986). Effects of stress inoculation training on self-report, behavioural and psycho-physiological reactions to abseiling. *Journal of Sports Sciences*, 4, 229–236.

Mace, R. D., Eastman, C. and Carroll, D. (1987). The effects of stress inoculation training on gymnastics performance on the pommel horse: a case study. *Behavioural Psychotherapy*, 15, 272–279.

Mahoney, M. J. and Avener, M. (1977). Psychology of the elite athlete: an exploratory study. *Cognitive Therapy and Research*, 1, 135–141.

Mamassis, G. and Doganis, G. (2004). The effects of a mental training programme on juniors' precompetitive anxiety, self-confidence and tennis performance. *Journal of Applied Sport Psychology*, 16, 118–137.

Mandler, G. and Sarason, S. B. (1952). A study of anxiety and learning. *Journal of Abnormal and Social Psychology*, 47, 166–173.

Martens, R., Vealey R. S. and Burton D. (eds). (1990a). *Competitive anxiety in sport*. Champaign, IL: Human Kinetics.

Martens, R., Burton, D., Vealey, R. S., Bump, L. and Smith, D. E. (1990b). Development and validation of the Competitive State Anxiety Inventory-2 (CSAI-2). In R. Martens, R. S. Vealey and D. Burton (eds), *Competitive anxiety in sport* (pp. 117–213). Champaign, IL: Human Kinetics.

Maynard, I. W. and Cotton, P. C. J. (1993). An investigation of two stress management techniques in a field setting. *The Sport Psychologist*, 7, 375–387.

Maynard, I. W., Hemmings, B., Greenlees, I. A., Warwick-Evans, L. and Stanton, N. (1998). Stress management in sport: a comparison of unimodal and multimodal interventions. *Anxiety, Stress and Coping*, 11, 225–246.

Maynard, I. W., Hemmings, B. and Warwick-Evans, L. (1995a). The effects of a somatic intervention strategy on competitive state anxiety and performance in semi-professional soccer players. *The Sport Psychologist*, 9, 51–64.

Maynard, I. W., Smith, M. J. and Warwick-Evans, L. (1995b). The effects of a cognitive intervention strategy on competitive state anxiety and performance in semi-professional soccer players. *Journal of Sport and Exercise Psychology*, 17, 428–446.

Meichenbaum, D. (1975). A self-instructional approach to stress management: a proposal for stress inoculation training. In C. D. Spielberger and I. G. Sarason (eds), *Stress and anxiety* (pp. 65–78), Vol. 1. Washington, DC: Hemisphere.

Meichenbaum, D. (1985). *Stress inoculation training*. New York: Pergamon.

Mellalieu, S. D. and Hanton, S. (2008). Facilitative anxiety: myth or mislabelled? The relationship between interpretations of competitive anxiety symptoms and positive affective states. In. M. P. Simmons and L. A. Foster (eds), *Sport and exercise psychology research advances* (pp. 222–246). Hauppauge, NY: Nova Science.

Mellalieu, S. D., Hanton, S. and Fletcher, D. (2006a). A competitive anxiety review: recent directions in sport psychology. In S. Hanton and S. D. Mellalieu (eds), *Literature reviews in sport psychology* (pp. 1–45). Hauppauge, NY: Nova Science.

Mellalieu, S. D., Hanton, S. and O'Brien, M. (2004). Intensity and direction dimensions of competitive anxiety as a function of sport type and experience. *Scandinavian Journal of Science and Medicine in Sport*, 14, 326–334.

Mellalieu, S. D., Hanton, S. and Shearer, D. A. (2008). Hearts in the fire, heads in the fridge: a qualitative investigation into the temporal patterning of precompetitive psychological response in elite performers. *Journal of Sports Sciences*, 26, 854–867.

Mellalieu, S. D., Neil, R. and Hanton, S. (2006b). An investigation of the mediating effects of self-confidence between anxiety intensity and direction. *Research Quarterly for Sport and Exercise*, 77, 263–270.

Meyers, A. W. and Schleser, R. (1980). A cognitive behavioural intervention for improving basketball performance. *Journal of Sport Psychology*, 2, 69–73.

Meyers, A. W., Schleser, R. and Okwumabua, T. M. (1982). A cognitive behavioural intervention for improving basketball performance. *Research Quarterly for Exercise and Sport*, 53, 344–347.

Morris, L. W., Davis, M. A. and Hutchings, C. H. (1981). Cognitive and emotional components of anxiety: literature review and a revised worry-emotionality scale. *Journal of Educational Psychology*, 73, 541–555.

Neil, R., Mellalieu, S. D. and Hanton, S. (2006). Psychological skills usage and the competitive trait anxiety response as a function of skill level in rugby union. *Journal of Sports Science and Medicine*, 5, 415–423.

Ntoumanis, N. and Biddle, S. J. H. (2000). Relationship of intensity and direction of competitive anxiety with coping strategies. *The Sport Psychologist*, 14, 360–371.

Ntoumanis, N. and Jones, G. (1998). Interpretation of competitive trait anxiety symptoms as a function of locus of control beliefs. *International Journal of Sport Psychology*, 29, 99–114.

O'Brien, M., Hanton, S. and Mellalieu, S. D. (2005). Intensity and direction of competitive state anxiety as a function of perceived control and athlete input into the generation of competition goals. *Australian Journal for Science and Medicine in Sport*, 8, 418–427.

O'Leary, K. D. and Wilson, G. T. (1998). *Behaviour therapy: applications and outcome*. Paramus, NJ: Prentice-Hall.

Ost, L. G. (1988). Applied relaxation: description of an effective coping technique. *Scandinavian Journal of Behaviour Therapy*, 17, 83–96.

Page, S. J., Sime, W. and Nordell, K. (1999). The effects of imagery on female college swimmers' perceptions of anxiety. *The Sport Psychologist*, 13, 458–469.

Paivio, A. (1985). Cognitive and motivational functions of imagery in human performance. *Canadian Journal of Applied Sport Science*, 10, 22–28.

Parfitt, C. G. and Hardy, L. (1987). Further evidence for the differential effect of competitive anxiety on a number of cognitive and motor sub-systems. *Journal of Sports Sciences*, 5, 517–524.

Parfitt, C. G. and Hardy, L. (1993). The effects of competitive anxiety on the memory span and rebound shooting tasks in basketball players. *Journal of Sports Sciences*, 11, 517–524.

Perry, J. D. and Williams, J. M. (1998). Relationship of intensity and direction of competitive trait anxiety to skill level and gender in tennis. *The Sport Psychologist*, 12, 169–179.

Pribram, K. H. and McGuiness, D. (1975). Arousal, activation and effort in the control of attention. *Psychological Review*, 82, 116–149.

Rohensenow, D. J., Smith, R. E. and Johnson, S. (1985). Stress management training as a prevention for heavy social drinkers: cognitions, affect, drinking and individual differences. *Addictive Behaviours*, 10, 45–54.

Rotella, R. J. (1985). Strategies for controlling anxiety and arousal. In L. K. N. Bunker, R. J. Rotella and A. Reilly (eds), *Sport psychology*. Michigan: McNaughton and Gunn.

Schwartz, G. E., Davidson, R. J. and Goleman, D. J. (1978). Patterning of cognitive and somatic processes in self-regulation of anxiety: effects of meditation versus exercise. *Psychosomatic Medicine*, 40, 321–328.

Smith, R. E. (1980). Development of an integrated coping response through cognitive-affective stress management training. In I. G. Sarason and C. D. Spielberger (eds), *Stress and Anxiety* (Vol. 7, pp. 265–280). Washington, DC: Hemisphere.

Smith, R. E. and Ascough, J. C. (1985). Induced affect in stress management training. In S. R. Burchfield (ed.), *Stress: psychological and physiological interaction*. New York: Hemisphere.

Smith, R. E. and Nye, S. L. (1989). Comparison of induced affect and covert rehearsal in the acquisition of stress management coping skills. *Journal of Counselling Psychology*, 36, 17–23.

Smith, R. E. and Rohesenow, D. J. (1987). Cognitive-affective stress management training: a treatment and resource manual. *Social and Behavioural Sciences Documents*, 17, 2.

Smith, R. E. and Smoll, F. L. (1978). Psychological intervention and sports medicine: stress management training and coach effectiveness training. *University of Washington Medicine*, 5, 20–24.

Smith, R. E. and Smoll, F. L. (2004). Anxiety and coping in sport: theoretical models and approaches to anxiety reduction. In T. Morris and J. Summers (eds), *Sport psychology: theory, applications and issues* (2nd edn, pp. 294–321). Queensland: Wiley and Sons.

Smith, R. E., Smoll, F. L. and Weichman, S. A. (1998). Measurement of trait anxiety in sport. In J. Duda. (ed.), *Advances in sport and exercise psychology measurement* (pp. 129–148). West Virginia: Fitness Information Technology.

Spiegler, M. D. and Guevremont, D. C. (1998). *Contemporary behaviour therapy*. Forest Grove, CA: Brooks-Cole.

Spielberger, C. D. (1966). Theory and research on anxiety. In C. D. Spielberger (ed.), *Anxiety and behaviour* (pp. 3–20). New York: Academic Press.

Suinn, R. M. (1987). Behavioural approaches to stress management in sport. In J. R. May and M. J. Asken (eds), *Sport psychology* (pp. 59–75). New York: PMA.

Swain, A. B. J. and Jones, G. (1993). Intensity and frequency dimensions of competitive state anxiety. *Journal of Sports Sciences*, 11, 533–542.

Thomas, O., Hanton, S. and Maynard, I. (2007a). Anxiety responses and psychological skill use during the time leading up to competition: theory to practice I. *Journal of Applied Sport Psychology*, 19, 379–397.

Thomas, O., Maynard, I. and Hanton, S. (2004). Temporal aspects of competitive anxiety and self-confidence as a function of anxiety perceptions. *The Sport Psychologist*, 18, 172–188.

Thomas, O., Maynard, I. and Hanton, S. (2007b). Intervening with athletes during the time leading up to competition: theory to practice II. *Journal of Applied Sport Psychology*, 19, 398–418.

Williams, J. M. and Harris, D. V. (2006). Relaxation and energizing techniques for regulation of arousal. In J. M. Williams (ed.), *Applied sport psychology: personal growth to peak performance* (5th edn, pp. 285–305). Boston, MA: McGraw-Hill.

Wine, J. D. (1971). Test anxiety and direction of attention. *Psychological Bulletin*, 76, 92–104.

Woodman, T. and Hardy, L. (2001). Stress and anxiety. In R. Singer, H. A. Hausenblas and C. M. Janelle (eds), *Handbook of research on sport psychology* (pp. 290–318). New York: Wiley.

Woodman, T. and Hardy, L. (2003). The relative impact of cognitive anxiety and self-confidence upon sport performance: a meta-analysis. *Journal of Sports Sciences*, 21, 443–457.

Zeigler, S. G., Klinzing, J. and Williamson, K. (1982). The effects of two stress management training programmes on cardio respiratory efficiency. *Journal of Sport Psychology*, 4, 280–289.

Zinsser, N., Bunker, L. and Williams, J. M. (2006). Cognitive techniques for building confidence and enhancing performance. In J. M. Williams (ed.), *Applied sport psychology: personal growth to peak performance* (5th edn, pp. 349–381). Boston, MA: McGraw-Hill.

5 Getting a grip on emotion regulation in sport

Conceptual foundations and practical application

Mark A. Uphill, Paul J. McCarthy and Marc V. Jones

Introduction

Emotions figure so pervasively within our lives generally, and within sport in particular, that it is difficult to imagine sport bereft of emotion (cf. Zajonc, 1998). Indeed, an increasing body of research illustrates that athletes experience positive and negative emotions before, during and after sport competition (e.g. Hanin, 2000; Uphill and Jones, 2007a). It is perhaps unsurprising then, that the ability to regulate one's emotions is regarded by many sport psychologists as an important psychological skill (e.g. Orlick, 2000; Thomas et al., 1999) and that the role of the applied sport psychologist often includes assisting athletes in the control or regulation of emotions.

Delivering psychological interventions (and, by implication, strategies to assist athletes in emotional control) should be founded upon a sound theoretical and empirical base (e.g. Biddle et al., 1992; Chambless and Ollendick, 2001). Historically however, there has been an uneasy alliance between theory and practice. Practitioners, for example, are challenged with keeping abreast of a burgeoning literature on emotion generally, and emotion regulation particularly. To illustrate, a literature search limited to the English language and the term 'emotion' using PsycInfo® returned 4,086, 30,249 and 43,645 citations for the periods 1971–1980, 1981–1990, and 1991–2000 respectively. On average, from 2001 to 2007, about 2,100 citations per year were published.

In addition to the burgeoning literature, concerns have been voiced about difficulty in translating theory and research to practice (cf. Folkman and Moskowitz, 2004). For example, just as politicians and policy-makers may not make decisions based on empirical evidence alone, practitioners and athletes may not make decisions about which strategy to use based solely on empirical evidence. In what has sometimes been called 'collaborative empiricism' practitioners often work *with* clients to arrive at a solution based in part on empirical evidence, but also individual preferences and situational constraints. Accordingly, our chapter focuses primarily on illuminating the theoretical and empirical basis upon which certain interventions (e.g. goal setting, self-talk, imagery) are founded. Without diminishing the complexity of the applied practitioner's role, we would contend that the interrelated tasks of assessment, problem formulation, intervention and evaluation may be facilitated by understanding in more detail (a) the characteristics of emotion; (b) how emotions are elicited and sustained; and (c) the consequences of emotions. In attempting to accomplish this endeavour, we draw upon literature on the 'social-neuroscience' of emotion regulation (e.g. Ochsner and Gross, 2007) to provide a framework for the range of strategies that applied sport psychologists may draw upon to assist athletes in emotion regulation. As expanded upon below, emotion regulation refers to attempts to evoke, diminish, prolong or intensify emotions. By illustrating how a range of interventions can be located within this framework, we hope to assist in bridging the divide between theory and practice. We conclude the chapter by considering some implications associated with the proposed framework and suggestions for further research.

Defining emotion

Intuitively, we all know what it is like to experience an emotion towards something or somebody, whether it is guilt about making a mistake, disappointment at not attaining one's goals or anger at a malicious tackle. Emotions are typically conceived as being bound up with feeling, possibly accompanied by physiological and behavioural change (Strongman, 1987). Oatley (1992) remarked that emotions are consciously preoccupying, they claim our attention and direct our interest, and are both private and public affairs. On the one hand, private, conscious experience of emotion can be available to us and no one else. On the other, public displays of emotion (e.g. postural and facial expression of anger) may be available to others but not fully accessible to our own awareness. However, despite this intuitive understanding of emotion, efforts to derive a more concise definition of the term have eluded philosophers and psychologists alike (Lazarus, 1995). Because emotion is a term derived from everyday language, arriving at a list of necessary and sufficient conditions for something to qualify as an emotion has been plagued with difficulty (Gross, 2007). Increasingly, then, emotion researchers are reliant upon prototype conceptions of emotion (e.g. Russell and Fehr, 1994). From this perspective, what separates an emotion from non-emotion (at a macro-level) and, for example, anger from non-anger, or anxiety from non-anxiety (at a micro-level) is a matter of degree, ill-defined and 'fuzzy' (Russell, 1991; Russell and Fehr, 1994). The presence of more of these prototypical features makes it increasingly probable that what one is referring to is an emotion (Gross, 2007).

Prototypically, emotions are typically conceived as being more transient and intense than moods (Jones *et al.*, 2000). Although the duration and magnitude of an emotional response are essentially descriptive markers (Davidson, 1994), mood and emotion are often differentiated concerning their respective antecedents. Specifically, although both mood and emotion are posited to possess a cognitive origin (e.g. Lazarus, 1991), unlike an emotion, mood is thought to lack a relationship with an object (Beedie *et al.*, 2005; Vallerand and Blanchard, 2000). Specifically, 'moods refer to the larger, pervasive, existential issues of one's life, whereas *acute emotions refer to an immediate piece of business, a specific and relatively narrow goal in an adaptational encounter with the environment*' (Lazarus, 1991: 48; emphasis added). The essence of emotion is encapsulated by Frederickson (2001), who suggests that an emotion is a cognitively appraised reaction to an event, either conscious or unconscious, which 'triggers a cascade of response tendencies across loosely coupled component systems, such as subjective experience, facial expression, cognitive processing, and physiological changes' (2001: 218). Researchers often include a behavioural component (e.g. action tendencies) in the emotional response (e.g. Gross, 1998; Russell, 2003). In summary, the inclusion of more of these prototypical features in athletes' responses, the more confident one can be that what one is referring to is emotion.

Of course, researchers typically attempt to apply greater precision in their use of terms than athletes and coaches. In reporting feelings of doubt, lowered expectations and a degree of nervousness, symptoms are arguably indicative of heightened anxiety and lowered confidence. That emotions are not experienced in isolation is recognised by Hanin (1997, 2000), who conceptualised emotions as occurring as part of a more generalised psychobiosocial state. A strength of Hanin's (2000) approach is that attention is directed towards understanding athletes' use of adjectives to describe their feeling states. While this approach may 'muddy the waters' theoretically, in practice, greater rapport and adherence is likely by 'talking the athletes' language'. Besides making use of appropriate terminology to assess athletes' emotional response, interventions to assist athletes in both regulating emotions and enhancing performance are logically founded on a thorough understanding of eliciting and sustaining conditions. It is to the characteristics of emotions and their eliciting and sustaining conditions that the chapter now turns.

Characteristics of the emotional response

Appraisal

It is the appraisal of the situation, rather than the situation per se, that influences the quality and intensity of the emotional response. The basic premise of appraisal theories of emotion is simple: emotions by and large appear to be related to how people evaluate events in their lives (Parrott, 2001). For example, imagine that you have just lost a soccer match by one goal to nil and are being criticised by your coach for your poor positioning, which allowed an opponent to score the critical goal. You might respond with anger if you perceive the criticism to be unwarranted, and that you were in a poor position because a teammate had lost possession. Alternatively, if you consider that your error contributed to your loss, you might feel guilty or disappointed. Appraisal theories then, suggest that (a) the meaning of a situation or event to an individual influences that individual's emotional reaction; and (b) the meaning that an individual ascribes to a situation or event can be regarded as a composite of individual appraisal components (Bennett *et al.*, 2003). Accordingly, interventions that impact athletes' appraisal of situations or events are likely to impact the quality and intensity of athletes' emotional response.

One appraisal theory, cognitive motivational relational theory (CMR: Lazarus, 1991) has been purported as being applicable to sport (Lazarus, 2000), is increasingly being used to inform research (e.g. Skinner and Brewer, 2004) and has received support for some of its tenets (Uphill and Jones, 2004, 2007). From a CMR perspective, appraisals of events are suggested to comprise primary and secondary appraisals. Primary appraisals refer to whether an event or situation is personally relevant to the athlete and comprise three components: goal relevance, goal congruence and type of ego involvement. Goal relevance reflects the degree to which an athlete has something important at stake in an encounter (Lazarus, 1991). If an athlete appraises an event as having no relevance, no emotions will arise. Goal congruence (or incongruence) describes the extent to which an event facilitates (or impedes) the attainment of particular goals. If an event is congruent with an athlete's goals, positive emotions are elicited, while the converse is true for incongruent events. The final component of primary appraisal consists of the type of ego-involvement invested in a particular encounter. Lazarus (1991) suggests that there are six types of goal to which an athlete might be committed, namely: enhancement of self and/or social esteem, maintenance of moral values, ego-ideals, meaning and ideas, other persons and their well-being, and life goals. The type of goal to which an athlete is committed will reflect the emotions that are experienced. As Lazarus (1991) notes, multiple goals may be present in any particular encounter and consequently consideration of athletes' goal hierarchies, or how athletes prioritise, may be beneficial in understanding the emotions that individual athletes experience. For example, a female gymnast who falls off a beam during the course of an Olympic trial may be concerned about not reaching the Olympics (life goal), preserving self-esteem and even the influence on significant others who have invested much time in her success. In addition to athletes' goal hierarchies, the importance of a particular goal will influence the intensity of emotions experienced. For instance, a 400m runner is likely to attach far more importance (and thus experience a greater intensity of emotion) to running well in the final of the Olympics than to performing well in a Grand Prix competition in the first year of an Olympic training cycle.

Secondary appraisals are concerned with an athlete's perceived coping options and similarly consist of three components: an evaluation about blame or credit for a particular occurrence, coping potential and future expectancy (Lazarus, 1991). According to Lazarus (1991), an appraisal of blame or credit (both of which can be directed towards oneself or others) influences the specific emotions that athletes experience. For example, a badminton doubles player may give credit to his/her partner for success, perhaps reducing his or her own sense of happiness and pride in success.

Coping potential refers to whether the athlete can manage the demands of the situation. Coping potential does not refer to *actual* coping, but an evaluation by the athlete about his/her prospects for coping (Lazarus, 1991). A golfer who hits a drive into the deep rough may have either a favourable or unfavourable coping expectancy depending on, for example, previous outcomes of similar shots. The third and final secondary appraisal is that of future expectancy, an evaluation of whether things are likely to get better or worse for an athlete (Lazarus, 1991). For instance, after a try by the opposing team which equals the score, a rugby union player may consider that this was a lack of concentration and that this deficit can be easily overturned, or perceive that the opposition may be too strong and overwhelm his/her side. In summary, then, each of these six individual appraisals is suggested by Lazarus (1991) to differentiate a number of discrete emotions.

The third component of Lazarus's CMR theory influencing the emotions that athletes experience is *coping*. In particular, Lazarus and colleagues (Folkman and Lazarus, 1988; Lazarus, 1991, 2000) suggest that coping behaviours can be classified into one of either two categories. Problem-focused coping involves taking action to change an aspect of the person–environment relationship, either by altering an aspect of the environment itself or by changing one's situation within it. In training, a high jumper could reduce the height of the bar, or alternatively remove him/herself from the training environment to try to cope with his/her anger or disappointment. Importantly, coping behaviours act to mediate and change the emotional experience of athletes. Thus, reducing the bar height may engender more positive feelings of relief or happiness at subsequent success, while leaving the training environment may elicit feelings of embarrassment or shame.

Emotion-focused coping, on the other hand, influences only what is in the mind of an athlete (Lazarus, 2000). Specifically, strategies to cope with a particular event may involve either a re-direction of attention or a re-interpretation (re-appraisal) of the person–environment relationship. A golfer who is distracted by a shout from a crowd may feel some semblance of annoyance or anger. In this scenario, anger may be reduced by re-focusing attention to task-relevant cues or by re-appraising the situation more as a challenge to his/her mental skills than as a threat to achieving his/her target for the round. Similarly, how athletes' use emotion-focused coping behaviours is posited to influence the specific emotions experienced. Because there are strong conceptual parallels between coping and emotion regulation, we elaborate on the similarities and differences later in the chapter when we provide a framework for the regulation of emotions in sport.

Critics of appraisal approaches have questioned the likelihood that elaborate evaluations about the significance of an event for one's well-being are formed during the few milliseconds it can take for an emotion to arise (Scherer, 1999). Indeed, past decades saw a protracted debate regarding the role of appraisal in the generation of emotion (e.g. Lazarus, 1984; Zajonc, 1984). This historical debate has become largely superfluous, however, with the answer to the question of whether appraisals are involved in emotion, dependent upon how appraisal and emotion are defined (e.g. Lazarus, 1999; Scherer, 1999). Moreover, this debate has been superseded by studies regarding the neurobiology of emotion (e.g. Le Doux, 2000; Ochsner and Gross, 2007; Quirk, 2007). Indeed, converging lines of evidence from both animal studies and those involving humans supports the role of (a) processes that rapidly detect the affective relevance of a stimulus; and (b) processes that provide a more elaborate, context-dependent evaluation (e.g. Le Doux, 1996; Ochsner and Gross, 2004, 2007). Although a thorough review of the neurobiological substrate underpinning emotion generation is outside the remit of this chapter, we draw upon a neural architectural model of emotion regulation posited by Ochsner and Gross (2007) to provide a framework for emotion regulation strategies that follows. This model posits that emotion generation and regulation involve the interaction of bottom-up and top-down processing systems.

The bottom-up generation of an emotion may be triggered by the perception of stimuli with intrinsic or learned affective value. Concerning the former, a racing driver need not *learn* that the rapidly enlarging image of the car in front is something to be anxious about. Concerning the latter, learning that errors are punished may generate a sense of anxiety after making a mistake. Areas such as the amygdala, ventral portions of the striatum and insula encode the properties of both positive and negatively toned stimuli (Adolphs and Tranel, 1999; Hamann *et al.*, 1999; Ochsner and Gross, 2004). These areas in turn propagate signals to the hypothalamic and brainstem nuclei that control autonomic and behavioural responses, and also to cortical systems that may represent in awareness the various characteristics of the emotional response.

The top-down generation of an emotional response begins with the perception of situational cues that (a) lead an individual to anticipate the occurrence of a stimulus with emotional properties (e.g. a gymnast anticipating falling off a beam); or (b) thinking about a neutral stimulus in emotional terms (e.g. thinking about a coach's tactical decision to substitute you as a signal that you are performing poorly). Top-down processes can be used to place particular stimuli in the focus of attention and in so doing have the potential to generate and regulate emotions by influencing which stimuli have access to bottom-up processes involved in emotion generation. Once bottom-up processing has begun (and perhaps before if one anticipates a certain event), top-down processes can regulate, re-direct and alter the way in which stimuli are being (or will be) appraised. Top-down processes then, can begin emotion generation directly as beliefs, expectations and memory, for example, may guide the appraisal and interpretation of stimuli (cf. Ochsner and Gross, 2007). From this perspective it may be that no external stimulus may need to be present for an emotion to be generated – an individual can generate an emotion using (re)constructions of past and possible future events.

For fear, and possibly other emotions too (e.g. anger, shame), the neural connections emanating from the amygdala to the cortex are considerably greater than from the cortex to the amygdala (Le Doux, 1996), and may account in part for the change in one's direction of attention when experiencing an emotion, but also the possibility, through top-down processing, of influencing the physiological response.

Physiological and behavioural correlates

It has long been assumed that peripheral physiological arousal is essential to the subjective experience of emotion (e.g. Damasio, 1999; James, 1884; Schachter and Singer, 1962) whether one is concerned with the feedback from the muscles and viscera (James, 1884) or the vasomotor system (Lange, 1885). Perhaps because the autonomic nervous system is thought to have evolved primarily to provide the metabolic supports for action, the idea that there is emotion-specific autonomic patterning has considerable intuitive appeal (Davidson, 1994; Levenson, 1994). There are nevertheless some difficulties associated with this position. First, autonomic differences between positive emotions may, at the very least, not be easily differentiated, and possibly may not exist (LeDoux, 1996; Levenson, 1994). As Davidson (1994) acknowledges, difficulties further arise when the same emotion is associated with different patterns of autonomic activity. For example, fear may be associated with both fleeing and freezing.

However, although there are undoubted inconsistencies inherent in research exploring the patterns of physiological responses associated with emotion, the evidence *against* bodily feedback playing a role in subjective emotional experience is weak. According to LeDoux (2000) there is plenty of feedback available during emotional responses, and some is fast and specific enough to play a role in subjective experiences.

That unique patterns of physiological arousal have not been strongly associated with emotion also suggests that unique action tendencies (or urges to act) may not be as evident as once initially thought (Clore, 1994). Emotions may help actions in a general way, such as increasing muscle tension, redistributing blood without activating specific motor programmes (Clore, 1994). Thus rather than being 'programmed' to run when afraid, or hit when angry, we are prepared to engage in action more forcefully or rapidly. Action tendencies for positively valenced emotions are similarly difficult to 'pin down', although it has been contended that positive emotions might facilitate a 'broadening and building' of behaviours (Frederickson, 2001). Regardless of the relationship between physiological patterns and action tendencies, whether such 'urges' are manifested behaviourally depends on a complex interplay among coping styles, impulse control and cultural norms as well as affordances inherent in specific contexts (Frederickson, 1998).

Subjective experience

Intuitive conceptions of emotion place the subjective or phenomenal experience at its heart. Although our introspection suggests that anger *feels* different from anxiety, which *feels* different from happiness, which *feels* different from shame, there is surprisingly little research concerning the differences (from a first-person, subjective perspective) between these states and differences within a family of related terms, such as anger, irritation, rage (Barrett *et al.*, 2007). According to Barrett *et al.*, a theory of emotion must do justice to both understanding how emotions arise and understanding the content of different emotional states. Interestingly, there is a large variability among individuals in their capacity to differentiate among emotion terms (Barrett *et al.*, 2001). Individuals may not always be able to differentiate between shame and guilt, for example. For practising sport psychologists, acknowledging this variability may be important in designing interventions to assist athletes in emotional control, particularly as it is the subjective experience of emotion that frequently underpins individualised (e.g. Hanin, 1997) and group-oriented (e.g. Jones *et al.*, 2005; Martens *et al.*, 1990) emotional measures.

These measures share a common limitation in that they typically only assess the intensity of subjective emotion. As some have acknowledged however (Fernandez and Beck, 1992; Jones *et al.*, 1993; Swain and Jones, 1993; Uphill and Jones, 2005), not only can the intensity of subjective experience be assessed, but also the duration, frequency and direction. Such indices may be indicative of effective psychological intervention, independent of any change in the intensity of experienced emotion.

In summary, how athletes appraise and cope with certain events is thought to be associated with the elicitation and regulation of the emotional response. That is, how we evaluate certain events may impact how we physiologically and behaviourally respond, as well as influence how we 'feel'. These interrelated characteristics of emotion may be associated with facilitating and/or debilitating effects upon sport performance (Hanin, 2000). However, merely observing that certain emotions are associated with particular performance levels is not as important as understanding why that might be the case, in theory and practice. Consider for example a golfer becoming angry at a careless mistake, and performance on subsequent holes starts to decline. Understanding (in theory and practice) the mechanisms by which this occurs is likely to yield efficacious intervention outcomes. In the section below we outline the processes by which emotions may influence performance, given the implications this may have for practitioners assisting athletes in emotion regulation.

Consequences of emotions

Consequences of emotions can be recognised in both the short term (e.g. behavioural response) and long term (e.g. health outcomes), and at the intra-personal and inter-personal levels. In this review we focus exclusively on the short-term consequences of emotions in sport, primarily because there is little published research on the long-term consequences.

Intrapersonal consequences

In general, consequences of emotions for individual athletes can be categorised as cognitive, physiological and motivational (Jones, 2003; Lazarus, 2000; Vallerand and Blanchard, 2000), with clear parallels associated with the emotional response and the effect(s) emotion engenders.

Physiological consequences

Although precise patterns accompanying discrete emotions are, at the least, difficult to identify, particularly concerning positive emotions, it is plausible that the arousal accompanying some emotions may, on occasion, if not more frequently, be of sufficient intensity to influence sport performance. For instance, heightened arousal accompanies both excitement and anxiety (Kerr, 1997). Such heightened physiological arousal may influence athletes' power, muscular tension and coordination. Perhaps unsurprisingly, a simple relationship between the physiological arousal accompanying emotions and athletes' performance is unlikely. First, differential effects may be observed depending on the characteristics of the task the athlete is undertaking (Parfitt *et al.*, 1990).

High levels of arousal accompanying some emotions (e.g. anger, anxiety) can increase anaerobic power, which may enhance performance on simple tasks (Parfitt *et al.*, 1990, 1995). Parfitt *et al.* (1995) for example, found that increased physiological arousal was positively related to height jumped in university-age basketball players. Interestingly, Perkins *et al.* (2001) observed that the effect of arousal on strength performance depended on which emotion it accompanied. After physiological arousal had been manipulated via a guided imagery script and paced respiration, a measure of hand-grip strength was taken. Results suggested that hand-grip strength was significantly higher in the excited compared to anxious condition, which in turn was significantly higher compared to a control condition. It is problematic to assume however that physiological arousal accompanying some emotions could be positive for sports requiring anaerobic power. First, high arousal is not unequivocally associated with enhanced anaerobic power. Murphy *et al.* (1988) found that fear and anger were not associated with an increase in hand-grip dynamometer performance. Second, there are few if any sport tasks whereby success is determined solely by strength; even skills such as weightlifting require attention and coordination to be successful.

Enhanced arousal could also increase muscular tension leading to a decrement in fine motor control (Noteboom *et al.*, 2001a, b; Parfitt *et al.*, 1990). Arousal was increased through the receipt of electric shocks (Noteboom *et al.*, 2001a, b) or engagement in a mental arithmetic task (Noteboom *et al.*, 2001b), and participants were required to perform a submaximal isometric pinch task, specifically exerting a force of four newtons with the thumb and index finger of the right hand. Increased arousal from the electric shocks was associated with a decrease in steadiness – that is, increased variation in force exerted (Noteboom *et al.*, 2001a, b), although increased arousal from the mental arithmetic task did not affect performance (Noteboom *et al.*, 2001b).

Perhaps a corollary of increased muscle tension (Van Gemmert and Van Galen, 1997), increased arousal may also result in difficulties in muscular coordination (Oxendine, 1970), affecting the movement patterns of athletes. Collins *et al.* (2001) reported that anxiety, which is often associated with an increase in arousal, influenced the movement pattern of soldiers required to perform a stepping task on two parallel bars 20 metres off the ground and weightlifters performing the snatch lift. Similarly, Beuter and Duda (1985), in a study of stepping motion over low obstacles in eight-year-old children, observed that under conditions of high arousal (manipulated by evaluative threat and competition), stepping motion which was once smooth and automatic became jerky and less smooth. The influence of emotions upon components of performance influenced by levels of physiological arousal is an appealing one, albeit predominantly for those emotions characterised by heightened physiological arousal. However, it is uncertain (a) exactly how many emotions are accompanied by high levels of arousal; and (b) whether emotions characterised by comparatively low levels of physiological arousal (e.g. embarrassment, sadness) are associated with actual decrements in muscle coordination.

Cognitive consequences

Emotions may lead to changes in a range of (interrelated) cognitive functions that could influence sport performance, including attentional focus and decision-making. Emotions may impact attention in two ways. Easterbrook (1959) suggested that, under conditions of high physiological arousal, attention is supposed to be narrower than under conditions of low physiological arousal. While increasing levels of arousal may have a positive influence on performance if irrelevant cues are unattended to, if task-relevant cues are missed, a negative influence on performance may occur. Some support for a peripheral narrowing effect associated with increased arousal has been obtained (Janelle *et al.*, 1999; Landers *et al.*, 1985).

Somewhat contrary to Easterbrook's hypothesis, it has also been suggested that anxious individuals may display an increased tendency to be distracted by irrelevant peripheral cues (Janelle, 2002). Some sport-specific evidence supports this proposition. Members of a gymnastic squad were presented with three slides showing a gymnast performing a back flip (Moran *et al.*, 2002). In the low-anxiety slide, the back flip was performed on a low beam with safety mats; the medium-anxiety condition comprised a low beam with no safety mats; and in the high-anxiety condition it was performed on a high beam with no safety mats. The gymnasts were asked to imagine they were the gymnast in each slide and their point of gaze was measured. Results suggested that the high-anxiety condition was associated with significantly more fixations to peripheral areas compared to low- and medium-anxiety conditions. Moran *et al.* (2002) provided two possible explanations for the observation. First, and illustrating that the narrowing and distractibility hypotheses may not be incompatible, anxious athletes may attempt to compensate for an attentional narrowing effect by including more fixations on peripheral cues. Alternatively, the subjective importance of cues rather than their location in the visual field may govern attention (e.g. Eysenck, 1992; Hardy *et al.*, 1996). Previous research has suggested that individuals high in anxiety selectively attend to threatening stimuli (Mathews and MacLeod, 1994). In the Moran *et al.* (2002) study, the peripheral aspects of the slide (e.g. absence of crash mats) was found threatening by the gymnasts and they focused their attention more on this aspect.

Besides anxiety, emotions generally may influence attention by encouraging task-irrelevant processing (Moran, 1996). For example, a tennis player, instead of focusing on where to hit his/her serve, may be angry and focusing on a contentious decision by a line-judge. Niedenthal *et al.* (1994) observed that the thoughts associated with shame and guilt were distinctive. Specifically, shame was associated with fairly global self-condemnation in which aspects of the self are seen as the cause of the transgression, in comparison to guilt which involved condemning actual behaviours. Global condemnation ('I'm useless at rugby') versus condemnation of behaviours ('I mistimed my tackle') might be associated with a novice rugby union player's experience of shame and guilt respectively. From this perspective, cognitions associated with specific emotions deplete performers' resources of working memory (Moran, 1996). Specifically, working memory represents a transient store of perceptual information important for pattern recognition and the initiation of appropriate action (Moran, 1996). Consequently, task performance that is reliant on processing information in the sports environment will deteriorate if working memory resources are reduced. For example, a cricketer who is angry and ruminating over a previous dangerous delivery is less able to process information relating to the position of fielders and perhaps obtain pre-flight cues about the bowler's delivery.

Schwarz (2000) alludes to the possibility that *decision-making* may be influenced by the impact of emotions upon (working) memory. Specifically, Schwarz notes emotions may influence decision-making by influencing the retrieval, accessibility and evaluation of features within the sporting environment. In support of the influence of emotions upon decision-making, Lerner and Keltner (2001) indicated that angry people were more inclined to seek risk than their fearful counterparts. In sport, a happy (as opposed to disappointed) snooker player may be more likely to recollect previous shots with favourable outcomes, and perceive a difficult scoring opportunity more favourably.

Motivational consequences

Emotions may also influence athletes' motivation (Hanin, 2000; Izard, 1993), or what Deci (1980) calls action tendencies. Hanin (2000) suggested that dysfunctional emotions result in an inappropriate amount of energy being deployed, whereas optimal emotions for performance generate enough energy to begin and maintain the required amount of effort for a task. For example, anxiety may contribute to enhanced cognitive effort in some circumstances (Eysenck and Calvo, 1992; Smith *et al.*, 2001). Despite researchers commenting on the motivational effect of emotions upon sport performance (Hanin, 2000; Isberg, 2000), research examining the influence of emotions on motivation is scarce. Indeed, the processes by which emotions may influence motivation are unclear, although it is plausible that self-talk associated with certain emotions may serve a motivational function (Hardy, 2006).

More generally, positive emotions associated with task enjoyment could influence persistence and commitment. Specifically, within general psychology, enjoyment does not appear as a discrete emotion within the emotion research literature; rather, researchers have classified enjoyment within joy which commonly appears as a primary positive emotion (e.g. Shaver *et al.*, 1987). Indeed, enjoyment may be a more diffuse state than discrete emotions, with positive emotions representing one facet of enjoyment.

Sport enjoyment is typically defined as 'a positive affective response to the sport experience that reflects generalised feelings such as pleasure, liking and fun' (Scanlan and Simons, 1992: 202), with enjoyment in a sport context reflecting a multifaceted construct consisting of intrinsic and extrinsic sources that are both achievement and non-achievement related (Scanlan and Lewthwaite, 1986; Scanlan *et al.*, 1989). These sources of enjoyment can be grouped into three categories: intrapersonal, situational and significant others, and may operate independently or interactively with another source (Scanlan *et al.*, 2005). Intrapersonal sources of enjoyment include perceived ability and a sense of being special, mastery, task-goal orientation, personal movement experiences, coping and emotional release. Situational sources comprise competitive outcomes and processes, social recognition and opportunities associated with competitive sport such as travel. Significant other sources of enjoyment consist of positive perceptions of parental and coach influence and positive social interaction with team-mates and peers (Scanlan *et al.*, 2005).

Indeed, researchers have also identified enjoyment as a key predictor of sport commitment and a primary reason for initiating and maintaining involvement in youth (Carpenter and Scanlan, 1998; Scanlan *et al.*, 1993; Weiss *et al.*, 2001) and elite sport (Scanlan *et al.*, 1989, 2003). For example, Scanlan *et al.*'s (2003) examination of sport commitment among New Zealand All-Black rugby union players portrayed the importance of enjoyment for intense persistence to rugby union over time.

Interpersonal consequences of emotion

According to Parkinson (1995), other people's emotions help to shape interpretations and ensuing emotions associated with a shared situation. For example, how one's team-mates respond to a late tackle in football may shape a player's impression that the tackle, was not only late, but malicious. The expression of emotions may also influence others' judgements (e.g. Knutson, 1996), including competitors'. This intuitively appealing prospect has yet to be examined in sport, although Greenlees and colleagues have, in a series of studies, suggested that one's body language may play a role in influencing performance-outcome expectancies (e.g. Greenlees *et al.*, 2005a, b). When experiencing embarrassment or guilt following a personal error, one can feel like they are 'sticking out like a sore thumb'. However, these interpersonal judgements may not be as harsh as one imagines. For example, some research suggests that individuals (a) overestimate the extent to which others can discern our internal state (Gilovich *et al.*, 1998); and (b) believe that their mishaps and errors will be judged more harshly than indeed they are (Savitsky *et al.*, 2001).

In part, perhaps because it is difficult to intentionally manipulate emotionally expressive behaviour, research on interpersonal aspects of emotion has been less prevalent compared to intrapersonal facets of emotion (see also Ambady *et al.*, 2001). Yet this is an important avenue for researchers to address. In sport, a coach who is visibly anxious or agitated before an important game may then communicate this anxiety to his/her players. Other people's emotions, then, may be communicated to oneself via processes of which we are not consciously aware, perhaps through reciprocating facial expressions, bodily postures or vocal responses. This process has been labelled 'emotional contagion' (Neumann and Strack, 2000; Parkinson, 2000). In sport, some evidence for the transmission of emotions among cricketers is provided by Totterdell (2000), who demonstrated that players' happiness was related to their team-members' happiness independently of the match situation and 'hassles' (i.e. minor negative experiences). Moreover, research on the *intergenerational* transmission of the fear of failure (Elliott and Thrash, 2004) suggests that our own emotional responding is likely to be acquired from others' emotional responses and attitudes towards stimuli.

In summary, emotions are likely to be indirectly rather than directly associated with sport performance (cf. Baumeister *et al.*, 2007). By comprehensively considering the intra- and interpersonal consequences of emotions for individual athletes in the assessment stage, it is contended that practitioners may provide a more nuanced and individually tailored strategy. Having outlined the prototypical components of the emotional response, and the consequences of emotion, we now provide a framework for the regulation of emotions before considering the efficacy of specific intervention strategies that can be located within this framework.

A framework for the regulation of emotions in sport

Emotion regulation refers to the evocation of thoughts or behaviours that influence which emotions people have, when people have them and how people experience or express these emotions (Richards and Gross, 2000). Thus, emotion regulation includes attempts to evoke, diminish, prolong or intensify emotional experience, cognitions, expression and/or physiology (cf. Gross, 1999; Gross and Thompson, 2007). Historically, whether in psychology generally or sport psychology specifically, there has been an emphasis on the amelioration of negative psychological states (e.g. Seligman, 2002). Recent years have seen an explosion of interest in what's been labelled positive psychology. In relation to emotion regulation, it recognises that sport psychologists may not only wish to reduce negatively toned emotions such as anxiety or anger, but enhance the frequency or intensity of emotions such as happiness or excitement. Phrased slightly differently, athletes may not just want to experience less sadness and worry, but greater happiness and excitement. Importantly the attainment of positively toned emotions such as happiness may serve as a protective mechanism or buffer, such that individuals show greater resilience to, and experience fewer pejorative outcomes in the presence of, stressful stimuli (Duckworth *et al.*, 2005; Frederickson, 2001).

The ways in which emotions can be regulated are almost limitless (Richards and Gross, 2000), and for this reason it is desirable for practitioners to have an organising framework, based on theory and research, from which one or a combination of intervention strategies can be used to assist athletes in emotion regulation. We draw upon the model of emotion regulation postulated by Gross and colleagues (Gross, 1998; Gross and Thompson, 2007), given that (a) it recognises the temporal characteristic of emotion; and (b) highlights the possibility of both influencing the generation and amelioration/augmentation of emotions.

In their framework Gross and Thompson (2007) identify five classes of emotion-regulation strategies: situation selection, situation modification, attentional deployment, cognitive change and response modulation (see Figure 5.1). The first two of these strategies (situation selection and modification) closely approximate the notion of problem-focused coping described earlier. Attention deployment, cognitive change and response modulation collectively bear close resemblance to emotion-focused coping. However, Gross' model of emotion regulation includes processes not traditionally considered in the coping literature, such as maintaining or augmenting positive emotions (Gross, 1998). Also, while coping behaviours are typically defined as conscious cognitive and behavioural activities to manage sources of stress identified as taxing or exceeding individuals' resources, Gross' model of emotion regulation acknowledges that strategies may exist on a continuum, differing in the degree to which they are automatic and/or conscious (Gross and Thompson, 2007). Similarly, while Lazarus (1991) contended that coping can either flow from or temporally precede an emotion, Gross and Thompson recognise both antecedent-focused strategies (situation selection and modification, attention deployment and cognitive change), and response-focused strategies. The former are proposed to 'shut down' an emotion, reducing the likelihood of an emotional response, whereas response-focused strategies are suggested to 'mop-up' the emotion once it has arisen (Gross, 1998).

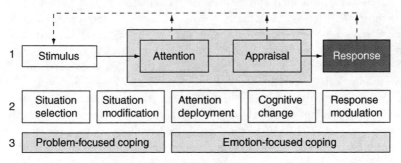

Figure 5.1 A framework for emotion regulation (source: adapted from Gross and Thompson, 2007).

Note
Level 1 provides a schematic illustration of the emotion response. Given a particular stimulus, the emotional response is influenced by how we attend to and evaluate that stimulus. Level 2 depicts the framework of emotion regulation provided by Gross and Thompson, in which some specific intervention strategies can be used. Finally, Level 3 illustrates the conceptual overlap between aspects of Gross' emotion-regulation framework and literature on coping.

Situation selection and modification

Situation selection refers to the process of actively choosing to place oneself in a certain situation or context, rather than others (Gross, 1998). By selecting some situations as opposed to others, one may be able make it more or less likely that a desirable emotional state is attained. A runner, for example, may select to run at the front of the group to minimise anxiety associated with being 'boxed in' or tripped by a fellow competitor. By 'controlling the controllable', athletes and coaches have the capacity to change, in part, the situation to influence emotional outcomes. A football player may (if given the option) choose not to take a penalty, lest s/he feels guilty or disappointed at missing. One barrier to using situation selection, however, is weighing short-term benefits against longer-term costs. In the latter example, the football player may feel regret about having forsaken the opportunity to take a penalty, and/or a loss of self-esteem. Selecting one situation as opposed to another may also help to attenuate or exaggerate emotions after they have arisen. Joy at winning a medal may be augmented by choosing to celebrate with friends and family, while anger at a contentious referee decision may be alleviated by taking a 'comfort break' in tennis.

As Gross and Thompson (2007) acknowledge, it is sometimes difficult to draw the boundaries between situation selection and situation modification, given the vagueness of the term 'situation'. However, whereas the former might refer to changing aspects of one's self in relation to an environment, the latter may involve attempts to modify external aspects of the environment or the people therein. For example, intervention studies that have included enjoyment as an outcome variable typically focused on modifying aspects of the task or situation to modify the psychological environment (Goudas *et al.*, 1995; Papaioannou and Kouli, 1999; Theeboom *et al.*, 1995). Indeed, strategies designed to enhance enjoyment are by definition likely to increase one or more positively toned emotions such as happiness or excitement.

Either in anticipation of, or actually during, challenging interpersonal situations that may require aspects of the situation to be modified, athletes' problem-solving skills are likely to be important for emotion regulation (cf. Platt *et al.*, 1986). Although space precludes a thorough consideration of problem-solving skills in relation to emotion regulation, problem-solving has been differentiated into two partially independent processes: problem orientation and problem-solving 'proper' (D'Zurilla and Nezu, 1999; Rodríguez-Fornells and Maydeu-Olivares, 2000). Whereas the former largely comprise a set of predispositions associated with how individuals approach situations (D'Zurilla and Nezu, 1999), the latter suggests the development of strategies to define the problem, formulate alternative responses and apply solutions. Because the ability to generate a variety of response alternatives will increase the likelihood that an athlete is able to select an effective response from these alternatives, it is hypothesised that the acquisition of problem-solving skills will enhance an athlete's appraised or actual ability to cope with a situation, conferring a more adaptive emotional response (cf. Jones, 2003).

Attention deployment

Attention deployment refers to how an individual directs their attention within a given situation to influence their emotions. When it is not possible, or at least extremely difficult, to change aspects of the situation, what one attends to is theorised to influence the emotional response. Although the results are equivocal, and the mechanisms and processes remain unclear, some evidence suggests that either attending to, or distracting one's attention from, emotional cues will either facilitate or enhance the emotional response respectively (Ochsner and Gross, 2005, 2007). In some circumstances it might be desirable to concentrate on or attend to emotional features of a stimulus (either internal or external), what Wegner and Bargh (1998) term the controlled starting of an emotion. For example, an image of a past encounter with an opponent who made some 'dubious' line calls in badminton may evoke a sense of anger. Attention, when directed repetitively to our feelings and their consequences, is often called 'rumination' (e.g. Nolen-Hoeksema, 1991). Maxwell (2004) highlighted that ruminating about anger was a significant predictor of aggression. Providing that the aggression is instrumental in nature (Anderson and Bushman, 2002) and associated with enhanced performance, the strategy of focusing on the thoughts and feelings associated with anger may be desirable in some circumstances (e.g. in contact sports such as rugby union).

Alternatively, one can use *distraction* to focus on non-emotional aspects of the situation. Pre-performance routines consist of a 'sequence of task-relevant thoughts and actions which an athlete engages in systematically prior to his or her performance of a specific sport skill' (Moran, 1996: 177). The cognitive component of pre-shot routines may include relaxation, imagery, cognitive restructuring, self-talk and decision-making processes, while behavioural strategies may include a practice swing, alignment of the body, 'waggling' the club and glancing at the target (Cohn, 1990; Cohn et al., 1990). Research investigating the use of routines has focused primarily on directly measurable behavioural components (Jackson, 2003), and less is known about the influence of pre-performance routines on the regulation of athletes' emotions. However, when used as part of a multimodal intervention, pre-performance routines have been associated with adaptive emotional and performance outcomes (e.g. Uphill and Jones, 2005, 2007b).

Cognitive change

Cognitive change involves changing the meaning or significance of an event or situation. For instance, a football player who has just missed a penalty may reappraise the extent to which self-blame is attached; for example, 'I didn't deliberately miss.' As described previously, how one appraises a situation is thought to alter the quality and intensity of the emotional response. In this section we provide some strategies that practitioners may use to assist athletes change cognitions associated with an emotional response.

Goal setting

Because of the multiple goals in competition (e.g. outcome, performance and process goals; Kingston and Hardy, 1997), the skilful use of goal setting and monitoring procedures may create a range of emotional responses. By altering the significance of particular cues, prioritising some goals rather than others, it is plausible that goal setting may be used constructively to assist athletes either in enhancing the experience of positive emotions (e.g. when athletes meet challenging goals), or increasing the likelihood of generating negatively toned emotions such as dejection or anger (e.g. when goals remain unfulfilled or 'blocked'). Interestingly, practitioners have typically discouraged the use of 'do-your-best' goals with regards to performance enhancement (Burton *et al.*, 2001). In the context of emotion regulation, however, 'doing your best' may alleviate potentially negative ramifications of failing to meet outcome, performance or process goals and, at least as a short-term strategy, reduce the emotional salience of a particular competition.

Reappraisal

In essence, reappraisal entails reinterpreting a stimulus in ways that change its emotional 'punch'. Although reappraisal is typically used to ameliorate or diminish the intensity of an emotional response (cf. Ochsner and Gross, 2007), reappraisal may be used to heighten or augment an emotional response. For example, research demonstrates that the physiological response of an individual before performing a task differs depending on whether it is perceived as challenging or threatening (Blascovich *et al.*, 1999). Besides evaluating current events, athletes' emotions may be influenced by consideration of past (or indeed future) events. For example, 'counterfactual thinking' describes the process of thinking about how past events could have turned out differently (Roese, 1997). An athlete finishing in fourth place in a 100 m final might think, 'If only I had a better start', or 'I shouldn't have competed in the 200 m as well'. The reflection and evaluation model (Markman and McMullen, 2003) highlights how thinking about how the past could have turned out better or worse than what *actually* occurred can influence the generation of positively or negatively toned emotions, depending on how the comparison is processed (see Markman and McMullen, 2003, for a review).

One's appraised ability to regulate emotion may also influence the emotional response. Individuals hold different beliefs about the malleability of personal constructs such as emotion (Dweck, 1999). Individuals holding *entity beliefs* view attributes as fixed and impossible to control, whereas individuals holding *incremental beliefs* view attributes as malleable and controllable. Tamir *et al.* (2007) found that only a small majority (60 per cent) of people favoured the belief that emotions were more malleable than fixed. If individuals have little appraised ability in their capacity to regulate emotions, it follows that they will be unlikely to make use of strategies, or effectively use strategies, to regulate emotions. Accordingly, strategies that educate athletes regarding the characteristics of stimuli, their emotional responses and associated consequences of secondary appraisals (e.g. coping potential, future expectations) may yield a more adaptive response.

The didactic approach involves clients being educated about their 'problem' (Jones, 2003). It is anticipated that increased awareness of the circumstances in which emotions are elicited and associated consequences will facilitate a more adaptive emotional response. Enhancing an athlete's awareness, although typically not considered a psychological skill (e.g. Hardy *et al.*, 1996), often forms a component of psychological skills training as part of an education phase (e.g. Mace, 1990; Uphill and Jones, 2007b). Indeed, attaining awareness of one's ideal emotional state may be considered the first step in attaining emotional control (Barrett *et al.*, 2001; Ravizza, 2001), and perhaps through increasing participants' cognisance of conscious and unconscious thoughts (Meichenbaum and Gilmore, 1984), lead to a change in emotional state. Similarly, Socratic dialogue involves asking thought-provoking questions with the intent of getting athletes to re-evaluate self-defeating ideas, perceptions and behaviours (Jones, 2003). Jones (1993), for example, asked a racquet sport player to compare the number of times she'd contested an official's decision to the number of times the official had changed the decision, in order to highlight the futility of such action.

Storytelling and metaphors provide a further strategy by which practitioners may influence athletes' appraisals to particular events (Jones, 2003; Niederhoffer and Pennebaker, 2005). Not only is the act of disclosure through writing a powerful therapeutic agent, stories may assist participants to re-construct past experiences and perhaps encourage athletes to consider alternative ways of dealing with emotive stimuli. Using quotes or stories by relevant sports stars might be one example of how stories could assist athletes reconsider their emotional response. In addition, Beswick (2001) reported the successful use of a traffic-light metaphor to maintain emotional control in a potentially hostile environment. While 'red' represented a loss of control and 'green' perfect control, 'amber' was taken to be the point at which an athlete could decide to go red or green. The importance of staying in the green was emphasised and accompanied by several strategies to assist players 'in the amber'.

Other strategies such as cognitive paradox, corrective experiences, role play and vicarious learning may all assist in helping athletes' to attain an adaptive emotional response to competition theoretically by manipulating the thoughts that mediate between stimuli and behaviours (see Jones, 2003, for a review).

Imagery

At least two types of imagery may be associated with attaining a more adaptive emotional state (cf. Martin *et al.*, 1999). Motivational general mastery (MG-M) imagery represents effective coping and mastery of situations, whereas motivational general arousal (MG-A) imagery involves images of stress, arousal and anxiety in relation to competition. Citing Lang's (1977, 1979) bioinformational theory, Martin *et al.* (1999) suggested that the imagination of a situation activates both stimulus characteristics (which describe the situation) and response propositions (which represent physiological and behavioural responses to the imaged situation). Because response propositions are malleable, by encouraging athletes to imagine effectively mastering challenging situations (MG-M) and associated emotional reactions (MG-A), they may be able to change undesired emotional responses. For example, the use of MG-M and MG-A imagery was found to be effective in reducing stress and raising self-efficacy in novice climbers, before and during an ascent of an indoor climbing wall (Jones *et al.*, 2002).

Self-statement modification

The use of self-talk as a motivational tool to control arousal, relaxation and 'psyching up' has been widely acknowledged (e.g. Hardy, 2006; Hardy *et al.*, 2001). Jones (2003) proposed that self-statements could alter emotional states in two ways: first, by replacing a maladaptive thought with a positive or neutral statement, a stimulus is removed that may result in a negative emotional state; second, self-statements could be used as stimuli to generate an appropriate emotional state. In combination with other techniques (e.g. relaxation training), positive self-statements have been used to reduce levels of anxiety (e.g. Prapavessis *et al.*, 1992) and stimulate a more positive perception of anxiety symptoms (e.g. Hanton and Jones, 1999).

Response modulation

Strategies designed to change the emotional response are proposed by Gross and Thompson (2007) to occur relatively late in the emotion-generative process. Response modulation refers to strategies designed to regulate the physiological, behavioural, cognitive and experiential aspects of emotion as directly as possible (Gross and Thompson, 2007).

Attempts to regulate the behavioural expression of emotion can occur in several forms. When experiencing an emotion, initiating emotionally expressive behaviour is suggested to slightly increase the feeling of that emotion (Izard, 1990; Matsumoto, 1987). However, whether merely expressing emotion will generate the emotion associated with that expression is a little more contentious, although there is some possibility that the physiological mechanisms supporting emotion may contribute to the felt experience of that emotion. In contrast, attempts to suppress or inhibit behavioural expression appear to have mixed effects on emotion experience (decreasing experience of positive but not negative emotion) and increasing sympathetic activation (Gross, 1998; Gross and Levenson, 1993, 1997). In addition, compared to reappraisal, there may be cognitive costs associated with suppressing emotion (Richards and Gross, 2000), affecting the resources available for a given task.

Regulating the physiological arousal associated with emotion makes intuitive sense given the potential effect of the intensity of emotions experienced (Zillman, 1971) and its potential impact on performance (Parfitt *et al.*, 1990).

Some strategies (e.g. progressive muscular relaxation, centring, quiet place, emotive imagery, up-beat music and exercise) have been proposed to regulate the physiological arousal levels of individuals, and concomitantly influence the experience of emotion (Jones, 2003). According to Jones (2003), increasing or decreasing physiological arousal may have a 'blanket effect' on the intensity of all emotions experienced by the individual (Zillman, 1971; Zillman *et al.*, 1972), and thus should be used carefully by practitioners.

Attempts to suppress thoughts associated with emotions may also have paradoxical effects. Specifically, when one attempts to suppress thoughts, particularly under cognitive load, the thoughts one is attempting to suppress may be exacerbated (Wegner, 1994; Wegner *et al.*, 1987, 1993). Indeed, efforts to reduce exciting thoughts, for example, may not only increase the intrusion of such thoughts but also intensify physiological arousal (Wegner *et al.*, 1998).

Perhaps unsurprisingly, then, strategies designed to inhibit emotions arising may be more efficacious than attempts to modulate emotional responses. For example, in contrast to reappraisal strategies, there is a cognitive cost to engaging in suppression (Richards and Gross, 2000; Gross and John, 2003) which may influence sport performance. Furthermore, a conscious attempt to suppress a negative emotion, such as anger, may mean that, in line with Wenger's (1994) ironic process theory, greater attention is paid to anger-related cognitions and effects (Quartana and Burns, 2007). Thus, although research in this area is in its infancy, there is enough evidence to suggest that practitioners should use strategies that affect the appraisal of the situation to create the most appropriate state for competition, rather than suppress unwanted emotions. In short, and not surprisingly, prevention is better than cure.

Implications for practice

There is evidence that athletes are capable of competing in the most important, and potentially stressful, competitions in a positive emotional state without having to suppress any unwanted emotions. For example, more than 25 per cent of 110 Norwegian and Danish Olympic athletes experienced no dysfunctional emotions during performance (Pensgaard and Duda, 2003). How athletes enter such an important and potentially stressful competition without having to deal with unwanted emotions is clearly of interest, particularly given that there are costs and benefits attached to the use of certain emotion-regulation strategies (cf. Mauss *et al.*, 2006).

Strategies designed to influence athletes' appraisal of particular situations seem adaptive at changing the experiential, physiological and expressive dimensions of emotion, compared to suppression that, at least in laboratory studies, appears to confer both physiological and cognitive costs. Not only might practitioners assist in modulating athletes' appraisal of a given *stimulus*, it was suggested that educating athletes' perceptions about the characteristics and consequences of emotions may be desirable in changing athletes' self-efficacy and/or perceived ability to cope with a situation.

Self-efficacy is 'a belief in one's capabilities to organise and execute the courses of action required to produce given attainments' (Bandura, 1997: 3), and increasing athletes' beliefs in their ability to cope with the demands of competition appears to regulate emotions in a manner that is adaptive for athletic performance. For example, with regard to anxiety, athletes with a positive belief in their ability to cope, and of goal attainment, typically interpret their symptoms as facilitative to performance, whereas those with negative expectancies will typically interpret their symptoms as debilitative to performance (Jones, 1995). More recent work by Jones and Hanton (2001) and Mellalieu *et al.* (2003) has extended this line of inquiry to consider a broader range of emotions. Athletes who perceived their anxiety symptoms as facilitative to performance (i.e. had a positive belief in their ability to cope, and of goal attainment) reported more positive feelings (e.g. excitement) and fewer negative feelings (e.g. tension) than athletes who perceive their anxiety symptoms as debilitative to performance.

Many people take part in competitive sport at a recreational level and, while most, if not all, athletes strive to win, emotion regulation is not just about performance enhancement. It is also about creating a positive emotional experience which has a range of benefits (cf. Fredrickson and Losada, 2005), not least of which is that enjoyment is a key predictor of sport commitment and a primary reason for initiating and maintaining involvement in sport (e.g. Carpenter and Scanlan, 1998; Scanlan *et al.*, 1989, 1993, 2003). Thus, the regulation of emotions should not solely be concerned with managing negative or unwanted emotions but also, where possible, to be focused on enhancing the positive emotional experience of participation in sport. Much of the literature reviewed, however, has been concerned primarily with reducing negatively toned emotions, although literature does suggest that individuals engage in processes to alter positive emotion experience (Gross *et al.*, 2006). This is particularly salient given that positive emotions may assist individuals in coping with adversity and stressors experienced as part of competitive sport (e.g. Fletcher and Hanton, 2003).

Typically a common goal of psychological skills training is to facilitate athletes' automatic execution of skills in competition. However, the extent to which outcomes would differ depending on their conscious or unconscious use remains debatable, as does the efficacy of trying to change athletes' possibly maladaptive strategies. On the one hand, the automatic compared to the relatively controlled use of reappraisal has been demonstrated to confer some advantages for the successful regulation of emotion (Mauss *et al.*, 2007, in press). On the other hand, individuals who habitually repress/suppress anxiety demonstrate a quicker and larger physiological response to threatening stimuli, and may find it difficult to recognise their own anxiety (Derakshan and Eysenck, 1998, 1999).

As illustrated, the evidence base upon which practitioners may draw is far from unequivocal, although there is evidence to support various strategies in assisting athletes' regulation of emotions. Indeed, although the framework provided above considered strategies in isolation, multimodal interventions drawing upon several of these strategies have shown efficacy in assisting athletes in emotion regulation and/or enhancing performance (e.g. Uphill and Jones, 2005, 2007).

Future of the area

Because sport is an achievement setting in which skilled performers compete for meaningful rewards, it provides an excellent environment to study emotion regulation, and findings from sport have relevance to other achievement domains (e.g. the performing arts, military and organisational settings). Jones *et al.* (2004) identified several areas relating to the study of emotion in sport worthy of future research, including the role of conscious and unconscious processing, regulating positive events and emotions, and the role of culture and team environment in emotion regulation. In addition, enquiry and reflection based on practitioners' interests and dilemmas needs to complement and inform the researchers' efforts.

Emotion regulation can include both conscious and unconscious strategies (Gross, 1999). Understanding the role that conscious and unconscious processing plays in emotion generation (and, accordingly, regulation) is an important avenue for sport psychologists (Jones, 2003). For example, a football player may accept that a referee made an honest mistake in awarding a dubious penalty to the opposition, yet still feel angry towards the referee, and his performance suffers accordingly. Understanding what types of strategies can be used in a situation where an athlete's conscious appraisal should be enough to regulate an emotion, but is not, and understanding how multiple appraisals of an event or situation in sport can lead to multiple and contrasting emotions, is clearly an area worthy of further research.

The application of emotion-regulation strategies to enhancing positive emotions has already been discussed in this chapter. Not surprisingly, experiencing positive emotions is, by their nature, a pleasant experience. Examining and reducing the effects of negative emotions on performance has been a core function of sport psychology research, perhaps to the detriment of exploring the benefits of positive emotions on performance and psychological well-being. With the advent of positive psychology, however, positive emotions are suitable for investigation, and enjoyment is central to that enquiry. Paying attention to Seligman *et al.*'s (2005) direction, interventions to enhance positive emotions are the bottom line of positive psychology, and recent investigations into positive affect have provided a wealth of empirical evidence documenting the adaptive value of positive affect. Although positive emotions carry multiple, interrelated benefits (Frederickson and Branigan, 2005; Fredrickson and Losada, 2005; Frederickson *et al.*, 2003), and are often experienced by athletes, positive emotions may also be associated with performance decrements (Hanin, 2000). While, for many of us, positive emotions are to be 'enjoyed', the reality for athletes, particularly during competition, may be different. For example, happiness at breaking an opponent's serve in an important tennis match may immediately be tempered by a need to 'focus on the next game and serve out the set'. Accordingly, understanding how athletes regulate positive emotions (see Jackson *et al.*, 1998; Kreiner-Phillips and Orlick, 1993) is both an interesting and applicable topic, and one that is worthy of further research.

The social and cultural environment of the athlete has an important role to play in the way emotions are regulated individually and interpersonally. Emotions have display rules (Ekman, 1973) that not only outline which emotions should be experienced but how they should be expressed. Thus, emotions do not only indicate to others how an individual is feeling, but also affect others' judgements regarding our likely intentions, attitudes and the appropriateness of the response for a situation (Shields, 2005). These rules can change across cultures, countries and sports, and also across time. Consider, for example, the reserved way in which success was greeted in the early twentieth century compared to how athletes react to scoring a touchdown, football goal or winning an Olympic medal in the twenty-first century. These social and cultural norms are important because they affect the types of emotion-regulation strategies used by an athlete. For example, in most sports it is not acceptable to appear anxious, and accordingly athletes may engage in the cognitively effortful task of trying to suppress any anxiety experienced. In sum, the specific culture, or ethos, of the sport that defines acceptable and appropriate behaviour may have a significant influence on the way athletes regulate emotions. Interestingly the consequences of emotion suppression may also differ across cultures. Butler *et al.* (2007) found that negative consequences of emotion suppression were found among Americans holding Western-European values but not among individuals with Asian values. In short, the effect of emotion-regulation strategies may differ across cultures. Exploring the types, and effects, of emotion-regulation strategies across different sports and cultures is clearly an area worthy of future research.

While emotion-regulation strategies may be shaped by the environment, athletes may also look to the environment for support in regulating emotions. Athletes may rely on other individuals to help regulate emotions, and current research in the area of social support by Rees and colleagues is relevant in this regard (e.g. Rees and Hardy, 2000; Rees *et al.*, 2003). The time at which certain strategies are used to regulate emotion may also be explored. Although Figure 5.1 depicts appraisal and suppression as an antecedent- and response-focused emotion-regulation strategy respectively, it is logical that the processual nature of emotion dictates that reappraisal could be attempted when a 'full-blown' emotion has occurred, and suppression may be used by the individual as s/he recognises the beginnings of an angry response, for example. Some research suggests that the time at which the strategy is used, rather than its categorisation per se, influences the efficacy of the outcome (Sheppes and Meiran, 2007). Besides examining short-term consequences, little is known about the long-term costs (e.g. health) associated with using certain emotion-regulation strategies in sport, or the interpersonal outcomes such as team cohesion and coach–athlete relations.

As is evident from above, using a range of research designs (e.g. qualitative research, single-subject, prospective studies, experimental research) is desirable for pursuing answers to the many questions that remain concerning the regulation of emotion in sport. Indeed, greater collaboration between researchers and practitioners may witness research developments that not only have theoretical utility, but provide practical solutions. Although the model depicted in Figure 5.1 is intended to organise the strategies that can be used to help athletes to regulate emotions, the wealth of research that could conceivably be conducted from both a basic and applied perspective cannot be done justice by the simplicity of the diagram. Nonetheless, *from an applied perspective* by illustrating the dynamic unfolding of emotion, the figure is intended to facilitate practitioners' use of a range of strategies to assist athletes in emotion regulation, and help to provide some coherence to the evidence base upon which practitioners may base their interventions.

Conclusion

In this chapter we have attempted to describe the characteristics of the emotional response and associated consequences. Based on a distillation of converging viewpoints, we provided a framework for the regulation of emotions, and briefly considered the efficacy of some strategies within this framework. Much of the evidence for the efficacy of emotion-regulation in sport comes from (a) literature on emotion regulation generally, much of which is informed by laboratory methods; or (b) the regulation of anxiety in sport. Extrapolating from either of these two positions to consider the regulation of emotions generally in sport is somewhat problematic, but we hope to have made some 'in-roads' in this regard. The process of interconnecting differing islands of research, of building bridges between them, may sometimes yield critical advances (see Barrow, 1998). We are conscious that at times these bridges may not be as strong as one would like, or perhaps need to be re-positioned or even removed as new evidence emerges. That said, the area of emotion regulation in sport is one that is ripe for the nascent literature to grow. To this end, we hope this chapter has stimulated some critical reflection for practitioners regarding their use of strategies to assist athletes in emotion regulation and, perhaps, even sown some seeds for the further development of research in this area.

References

Adolphs, R. and Tranel, D. (1999). Preferences for visual stimuli following amygdale damage. *Journal of Cognitive Neuroscience*, 11, 610–616.

Ambady, A., Bernieri, F. J. and Richeson, J. A. (2001). Toward a histology of social behaviour: judgemental accuracy from thin slices of the behavioural stream. In M. P. Zanna (ed.), *Advances in experimental social psychology*, Vol. 32, 201–271.

Anderson, C. A. and Bushman, B. J. (2002). Human aggression. *Annual Review of Psychology*, 53, 27–51.

Bandura, A. (1997). *Self-efficacy: the exercise of control.* New York: W. H. Freeman.

Barrett, L. F., Gross, J. J., Christenson, T. C. and Benvenuto, M. (2001). Knowing what you're feeling and knowing what to do about it: mapping the relation between emotion differentiation and emotion regulation. *Cognition and Emotion*, 15, 713–724.

Barrett, L. F., Mesquita, B., Ochsner, K. N. and Gross, J. J. (2007). The experience of emotion. *Annual Review of Psychology*, 58, 373–403.

Barrow, J. D. (1998). *Impossibility: limits of science and the science of limits*. Oxford: Oxford University Press.

Baumeister, R. F., Vohs, K. D., DeWall, C. N. and Zhang, L. (2007). How emotion shapes behaviour: feedback, anticipation, and reflection, rather than direct causation. *Personality and Social Psychology Review*, 11, 167–203.

Beedie, C. J., Terry, P. C. and Lane, A. M. (2005). Distinctions between mood and emotion. *Cognition and Emotion*, 19, 847–878.

Bennett, P., Lowe, R. and Honey, K. (2003). Appraisals and emotions: a test of the consistency of reporting and their associations. *Cognition and Emotion*, 17, 511–520.

Beswick, B. (2001). *Focused for soccer*. Champaign, IL: Human Kinetics.

Beuter, A. and Duda, J. L (1985). Analysis of the arousal/motor performance relationship in children using movement kinematics. *Journal of Sport Psychology*, 7, 229–243.

Biddle, S. J. H., Bull, S. J. and Seheult, C. L. (1992). Ethical and professional issues in contemporary British sport psychology. *The Sport Psychologist*, 6, 66–76.

Blascovich, J., Mendes, W. B., Hunter, S. and Salomon, K. (1999). Social facilitation as challenge and threat. *Journal of Personality and Social Psychology*, 77, 68–77.

Burton, D., Naylor, S. and Holliday, B. (2001). Goal setting in sport: investigating the goal effectiveness paradox. In R. Singer, H. A. Hausenblas and C. M. Janelle (eds), *Handbook of research on sport psychology* (pp. 497–528). New York: Wiley.

Butler, E. A., Lee, T. L. and Gross, J. J. (2007). Emotion regulation and culture: are the social consequences of emotion suppression culture-specific? *Emotion*, 7, 30–48.

Carpenter, P. J. and Scanlan, T. K. (1998). Changes over time in the determinance of sport commitment. *Pediatric Exercise Science*, 10, 356–365.

Chambless, D. L. and Ollendick, T. H. (2001). Empirically supported psychological interventions: controversies and evidence. *Annual Review of Psychology*, 52, 685–716.

Clore, G. L. (1994). Why emotions are felt. In P. Ekman and R. J. Davidson (eds), *The nature of emotion: fundamental questions* (pp. 103–111). Oxford: Oxford University Press.

Cohn, P. J. (1990). Pre-performance routines in sport: theoretical support and practical applications. *The Sport Psychologist*, 4, 301–312.

Cohn, P. J., Rotella, R. J. and Lloyd, J. W. (1990). Effects of a cognitive behavioural intervention on the pre-shot routine and performance in golf. *The Sport Psychologist*, 4, 33–47.

Collins, D., Jones, B., Fairweather, M., Doolan, S. and Priestley, N. (2001). Examining anxiety associated changes in movement patterns. *International Journal of Sport Psychology*, 31, 223–242.

Damasio, A. R. (1999). *The feeling of what happens: body and emotion in the making of consciousness*. New York: Harcourt Brace.

Davidson, R. J. (1994). On emotion, mood, and related affective constructs. In P. Ekman and R. J. Davidson (eds), *The nature of emotion: fundamental questions* (pp. 51–55). Oxford: Oxford University Press.

Deci, E. L. (1980). *The psychology of self-determination*. Lexington, MA: Heath.

Derakshan, N. and Eysenck, M. W. (1998). Working memory capacity in high trait anxious and repressor groups. *Cognition and Emotion*, 12, 697–713.

Derakshan, N. and Eysenck, M. W. (1999). Are repressors self-deceivers or other-deceivers? *Cognition and Emotion*, 13, 1–18.

Duckworth, A. L., Steen, T. A. and Seligman, M. E. P. (2005). Positive psychology in clinical practice. *Annual Review of Clinical Psychology*, 1, 629–651.

Dweck, C. S. (1999). *Self-theories: their role in motivation, personality, and development*. Philadelphia, PA: Taylor and Francis.

D'Zurilla, T. J. and Nezu, A. M. (1999). *Problem-solving therapy: a social competence approach to clinical intervention* (2nd edn). New York: Springer.

Easterbrook, J. A. (1959). The effect of emotion on cue utilisation and the organisation of behaviour. *Psychological Review*, 66, 183–201.

Ekman, P. (1973). Darwin and cross cultural studies of facial expression. In P. Ekman (ed.), *Darwin and facial expression: a century of research in review*. New York: Academic Press.

Elliott, A. J. and Thrash, T. M. (2004). The intergenerational transmission of fear of failure. *Personality and Social Psychology Bulletin*, 30, 957–971.

Eysenck, M. W. (1992). *Anxiety: the cognitive perspective*. Hove: Lawrence Erlbaum Associates.

Eysenck, M. W. and Calvo, M. G. (1992). Anxiety and performance: the processing efficiency theory. *Cognition and Emotion*, 6, 409–434.

Fletcher, D. and Hanton, S. (2003). Sources of organisational stress in elite sports performers. *The Sport Psychologist*, 17, 175–195.

Folkman, S. and Lazarus, R. S. (1988). Coping as a mediator of emotion. *Journal of Personality and Social Psychology*, 54, 466–475.

Folkman, S. and Moskowitz, J. T. (2004). Coping: pitfalls and promise. *Annual Review of Psychology*, 55, 745–774.

Frederickson, B. L. (1998). What good are positive emotions? *Review of General Psychology*, 2, 300–319.

Frederickson, B. L. (2001). The role of positive emotions in positive psychology. *American Psychologist*, 56, 218–226.

Frederickson, B. L. and Branigan, C. (2005). Positive emotions broaden the scope of attention and thought-action repertoires. *Cognition and Emotion*, 19, 313–332.

Frederickson, B. L. and Losada, M. F. (2005). Positive affect and the complex dynamics of human flourishing. American Psychologist, 60, 678–686.

Frederickson, B. L., Tugade, M. M., Waugh, C. E. and Larkin, G. (2003). What good are positive emotions in crises? A prospective study of resilience and emotions following the terrorist attacks on the United States on September 11th 2001. *Journal of Personality and Social Psychology*, 84, 365–376.

Gilovich, T., Savitsky, K. and Medvec, V. H. (1998). The illusion of transparency: biased assessments of others' ability to read one's emotional states. *Journal of Personality and Social Psychology*, 75, 332–346.

Goudas, M., Biddle, S., Fox, K. and Underwood, M. (1995). It ain't what you do, it's the way that you do it! Teaching style affects children's motivation in track and field lessons. *The Sport Psychologist*, 9, 254–264.

Greenlees, I. A., Bradley, A., Thelwell, R. C. and Holder, T. P. (2005a). The impact of two forms of opponents' non-verbal communication on impression formation and outcome expectations. *Psychology of Sport and Exercise*, **6,** 103–115.

Greenlees, I. A., Buscombe, R., Thelwell, R., Holder, T. and Rimmer, M. (2005b). Impact of opponents' clothing and body language on impression formation and outcome expectations. *Journal of Sport and Exercise Psychology*, 27, 39–52.

Gross, J. J. (1998). Antecedent- and response-focused emotion regulation: divergent consequences for experience, expression and physiology. *Journal of Personality and Social Psychology*, 74, 224–237.

Gross, J. J. (1999). Emotion regulation: past, present, future. *Cognition and Emotion*, 13, 551–573.

Gross, J. J. (2007). *Handbook of emotion regulation*. London: Guilford Press.

Gross, J. J. and John, O. P. (2003). Individual differences in two emotion regulation processes: implications for affect, relationships and well-being. *Journal of Personality and Social Psychology*, 85, 348–362.

Gross, J. J. and Levenson, R. W. (1993). Emotional suppression: physiology, self-report, and expressive behaviour. *Journal of Personality and Social Psychology*, 64, 970–986.

Gross, J. J. and Levenson, R. W. (1997). Hiding feelings: the acute effects of inhibiting positive and negative emotions. *Journal of Abnormal Psychology*, 106, 95–103.

Gross, J. J. and Thompson, R. A. (2007). Emotion regulation: conceptual foundations. In J. J. Gross (ed.), *Handbook of emotion regulation* (pp. 3–24). London: Guilford Press.

Gross, J. J., Richard, J. M. and John, O. P. (2006). Emotion regulation in everyday life. In D. K. Snyder, J. A. Simpson and J. N. Hughes (eds), *Emotion regulation in couples and families: pathways to dysfunction and health*. Washington, DC: American Psychological Association.

Hamann, S. B., Ely, T. D., Grafton, S. T. and Kilts, C. D. (1999). Amygdala activity related to enhanced memory for pleasant and aversive stimuli. *Nature Neuroscience*, 2, 289–293.

Hanin, Y. L. (1997). Emotions and athletic performance: individual zones of optimal functioning model. *European Yearbook of Sport Psychology*, 1, 29–72.

Hanin, Y. L. (2000). Individual zones of optimal functioning (IZOF) model: emotion–performance relationships in sport. In Y. L. Hanin (ed.), *Emotions in sport* (pp. 65–89). Champaign, IL: Human Kinetics.

Hanton, S. and Jones, G. (1999). The effects of a multimodal intervention programme on performers: II. Training the butterflies to fly in formation. *The Sport Psychologist*, 13, 22–41.

Hardy, J. (2006). Speaking clearly: a critical review of the self-talk literature. *Psychology of Sport and Exercise*, 7, 81–97.

Hardy, J., Gammage, K. and Hall, C. R. (2001). A description of athlete self-talk. *The Sport Psychologist*, 15, 306–318.

Hardy, L., Jones, G. and Gould, D. (1996). *Understanding psychological preparation for sport: theory and practice of elite performers*. Chichester: John Wiley and Sons.

Isberg, L. (2000). Anger, aggressive behaviour, and athletic performance. In Y. L. Hanin (ed.), *Emotions in sport* (pp. 113–133). Champaign, IL: Human Kinetics.

Izard, C. E. (1990). Facial expressions and the regulation of emotions. *Journal of Personality and Social Psychology*, 58, 487–498.

Izard, C. E. (1993). Four systems for emotion activation: cognitive and noncognitive processes. *Psychological Review*, 100, 68–90.

Jackson, R. C. (2003). Pre-performance routine consistency: temporal analysis of goal kicking in the Rugby Union World Cup. *Journal of Sports Sciences*, 21, 803–814.

Jackson, S. A., Mayocchi, L. and Dover, J. D. (1998). Life after winning gold II: coping with change as an Olympic gold-medallist. *The Sport Psychologist*, 12, 137–155.

James, W. (1884). What is emotion? *Mind*, 9, 188–205.

Janelle, C. M. (2002). Anxiety, arousal and visual attention: a mechanistic account of performance variability. *Journal of Sports Sciences*, 20, 237–251.

Janelle, C. M., Singer, R. N. and Williams, A. M. (1999). External distraction and attentional narrowing: visual search evidence. *Journal of Sport and Exercise Psychology*, 21, 70–91.

Jones, G. (1993). The role of performance profiling in cognitive behavior interventions in sport. *The Sport Psychologist*, 7, 160–172.

Jones, G. (1995). More than just a game: research developments and issues in competitive anxiety in sport. *British Journal of Psychology*, 86, 449–478.

Jones, G. and Hanton, S. (2001). Pre-competition feeling states and directional anxiety interpretations. *Journal of Sports Sciences*, 19, 385–395.

Jones, G., Swain, A. B. J. and Hardy, L. (1993). Intensity and direction dimensions of competitive state anxiety and relationships with performance. *Journal of Sports Sciences*, 11, 525–532.

Jones, M. V. (2003). Controlling emotions in sport. *The Sport Psychologist*, 17, 471–486.

Jones, M. V., Lane, A. M., Bray, S. R., Uphill, M. and Catlin, J. (2005). Development and validation of the Sport Emotion Questionnaire. *Journal of Sport and Exercise Psychology*, 27, 407–431.

Jones, M. V., Lavallee, D. and Thatcher, J. (2004). Coping and emotion in sport: future directions. In D. Lavallee, J. Thatcher and M. V. Jones (eds), *Coping and emotion in sport* (pp. 273–280). New York: Nova Science Publishers.

Jones, M. V., Mace, R. D., Bray, S. R., MacRae, A. and Stockbridge, C. (2002). The impact of motivational imagery on the emotional state and self-efficacy of novice climbers. *Journal of Sport Behaviour*, 25, 57–73.

Jones, M. V., Mace, R. D. and Williams, S. (2000). Relationship between emotional state and performance during international field hockey matches. *Perceptual and Motor Skills*, 90, 691–701.

Kerr, J. J. (1997). *Motivation and emotion in sport: reversal theory*. Hove: Psychology Press.

Kingston, K. and Hardy, L. (1997). Effects of different types of goals on processes that support performance. *The Sport Psychologist*, 11, 277–293.

Knutson, B. (1996). Facial expression of emotion influence interpersonal trait inferences. *Journal of Nonverbal Behaviour*, 20, 165–182.

Kreiner-Phillips, K. and Orlick, T. (1993). Winning after winning: the psychology of ongoing excellence. *The Sport Psychologist*, 7, 31–48.

Landers, D. M., Wang, M. Q. and Courtet, P. (1985). Peripheral narrowing among experienced and inexperienced rifle shooters under low- and high-stress conditions. *Research Quarterly for Exercise and Sport*, 56, 122–130.

Lang, P. J. (1977). Imagery in therapy: an information processing analysis of fear. *Behaviour Therapy*, 8, 862–886.

Lang, P. J. (1979). A bioinformational theory of emotional imagery. *Psychophysiology*, 17, 495–512.

Lange, C. (1885 [1922]). Om sindsbevaegelser. English trans. in K. Dunlap (ed.), *The emotions*. Baltimore, MD: Williams and Wilkins.

Lazarus, R. (1984). On the primacy of cognition. *American Psychologist*, 37, 124–139.

Lazarus, R. S. (1991). *Emotion and adaptation*. Oxford: Oxford University Press.

Lazarus, R. S. (1995). Vexing research problems inherent in cognitive-mediational theories of emotion and some solutions. *Psychological Inquiry*, 6, 183–196.

Lazarus, R. S. (1999). The cognition-emotion debate: a bit of history. In T. Dalgleish and M. J. Power (eds), *Handbook of cognition and emotion* (pp. 3–19). Chichester: Wiley.

Lazarus, R. S. (2000). How emotions influence performance in competitive sports. *The Sport Psychologist*, 14, 229–252.

Le Doux, J. E. (1994). Emotion-specific physiological activity: don't forget about CNS physiology. In P. Ekman and R. J. Davidson (eds), *The nature of emotion: fundamental questions* (pp. 248–252). Oxford: Oxford University Press.

LeDoux, J. E. (1996). *The emotional brain*. New York: Simon and Schuster.

Le Doux, J. E. (2000). Cognitive-emotional interactions: listen to the brain. In R. D. Lane and L. Nadel (eds), *Cognitive neuroscience of emotion* (pp. 129–155). Oxford: Oxford University Press.

Lerner, J. S. and Keltner, D. (2001). Fear, anger, and risk. *Journal of Personality and Social Psychology*, 81, 146–159.

Levenson, R. W. (1994). The search for autonomic specificity. In P. Ekman and R. J. Davidson (eds), *The nature of emotion: fundamental questions* (pp. 252–257). Oxford: Oxford University Press.

Mace, R. (1990). Cognitive behavioural interventions in sport. In J. G. Jones and L. Hardy (eds), Stress *and performance in sport* (pp. 203–230). Chichester: Wiley.

Markman, K. D. and McMullen, M. N. (2003). A reflection and evaluation model of comparative thinking. *Personality and Social Psychology Review*, 7, 244–267.

Martens, R., Burton, D., Vealey, R. S., Bump, L. A. and Smith, D. E. (1990). Development and validation of the Competitive State Anxiety Inventory-2. In R. Martens, R. S. Vealey and D. Burton (eds), *Competitive anxiety in sport* (pp. 117–190). Champaign, IL: Human Kinetics.

Martin, K. A., Moritz, S. E. and Hall, C. R. (1999). Imagery use in sport: a literature review and applied model. *The Sport Psychologist*, 13, 245–268.

Mathews, A. and MacLeod, C. (1994). Cognitive approaches to emotion and emotional disorders. *Annual Review of Psychology*, 45, 25–50.

Matsumoto, D. (1987). The role of facial response in the experience of emotion: more methodological problems and a meta-analysis. *Journal of Personality and Social Psychology*, 52, 769–774.

Mauss, I. B., Cook, C. L., Cheng, J. Y. J. and Gross, J. J. (in press). Individual differences in cognitive reappraisal: Experiential and physiological responses to an anger provocation. *International Journal of Psychophysiology*.

Mauss, I. B., Cook, C. L. and Gross, J. J. (2007). Automatic emotion regulation during an anger provocation. *Journal of Experimental Social Psychology*, 43, 698–711.

Mauss, I. B., Evers, C., Wilhelm, F. H. and Gross, J. J. (2006). How to bite your tongue without blowing your top: implicit evaluation of emotion regulation predicts affective responding to anger provocation. *Personality and Social Psychology Bulletin*, 32, 589–602.

Maxwell, J. (2004). Anger rumination: an antecedent of aggression? *Psychology of Sport and Exercise*, 5, 279–289.

Meichenbaum, D. and Gilmore, J. D. (1984). The nature of unconscious processes: a cognitive-behavioural perspective. In K. S. Bowers and D. Meichenbaum (eds), *The unconscious reconsidered* (pp. 273–297). Chichester: Wiley.

Mellalieu, S. D., Hanton, S. and Jones, G. (2003). Emotional labelling and competitive anxiety in preparation and competition. *The Sport Psychologist*, 17, 157–174.

Moran, A. P. (1996). *The psychology of concentration in sports performers: a cognitive analysis*. East Sussex: Psychology Press.

Moran, A., Byrne, A. and McGlade, N. (2002). The effects of anxiety and strategic planning on visual search behaviour. *Journal of Sports Sciences*, 20, 225–236.

Murphy, S. M., Woolfolk, R. L. and Budney, A. J. (1988). The effects of emotive imagery on strength performance. *Journal of Sport and Exercise Psychology*, 10, 334–345.

Neumann, R. and Strack, F. (2000). 'Mood contagion': the automatic transfer of mood between persons. *Journal of Personality and Social Psychology*, 79, 211–223.

Niedenthal, P. M., Tangney, J. P. and Gavansky, I. (1994). 'If only I weren't' versus 'If only I hadn't': distinguishing shame and guilt in counterfactual thinking. *Journal of Personality and Social Psychology*, 67, 585–595.

Niederhoffer, K. G. and Pennebaker, J. W. (2005). Sharing one's story: on the benefits of writing or talking about emotional experience. In C. R. Snyder and S. J. Lopez (eds), *Handbook of positive psychology* (pp. 573–583). Oxford: Oxford University Press.

Nolen-Hoeksema, S. (1991). Responses to depression and their effects on the duration of depressive episodes. *Journal of Abnormal Psychology*, 100, 569–582.

Noteboom, J. T., Barnholt, K. R. and Enoka, R. M. (2001a). Activation of the arousal response and impairment of performance increase with anxiety and stressor intensity. *Journal of Applied Physiology*, 91, 2093–2101.

Noteboom, J. T., Fleshner, M. and Enoka, R. M. (2001b). Activation of the arousal response can impair performance on a simple motor task. *Journal of Applied Physiology*, 91, 821–831.

Oatley, K. (1992). *Best laid schemes: the psychology of emotions*. Cambridge: Cambridge University Press.

Ochsner, K. N. and Gross, J. J. (2004). Thinking makes it so: a social cognitive neuroscience approach to emotion regulation. In R. F. Baumeister and K. D. Vohs (eds), *Handbook of self-regulation: research, theory and applications* (pp. 229–255). New York: Guilford Press.

Ochsner, K. N. and Gross, J. J. (2005). The cognitive control of emotion. *Trends in Cognitive Sciences*, 9, 242–249.

Ochsner, K. N. and Gross, J. J. (2007). The neural architecture of emotion regulation. In J. J. Gross (ed.), *Handbook of emotion regulation* (pp. 87–109). London: Guilford Press.

Orlick, T. (2000). *In pursuit of excellence: how to win in sport and life through mental training* (3rd edn). Champaign, IL: Human Kinetics.

Oxendine, J. B. (1970). Emotional arousal and motor performance. *Quest*, 13, 23–32.

Papaioannou, A. and Kouli, O. (1999). The effect of task structure, perceived motivational climate and goal orientations on students' task involvement and anxiety. *Journal of Applied Sport Psychology*, 11, 51–71.

Parfitt, G., Hardy, L. and Pates, J. (1995). Somatic anxiety and physiological arousal: their effects upon a high anaerobic, low memory demand task. *International Journal of Sport Psychology*, 26, 196–213.

Parfitt, G., Jones, J. G. and Hardy, L. (1990). Multidimensional anxiety and performance. In J. G. Jones and L. Hardy (eds), *Stress and performance in sport* (pp. 43–80). Chichester: Wiley.

Parkinson, B. (1995). *Ideas and realities of emotion*. London: Routledge.

Parkinson, B. (2000). Emotions are social. *British Journal of Psychology*, 87, 663–683.

Parrott, W. G. (2001). *Emotions in social psychology*. Hove: Psychology Press.

Pensgaard, A. M. and Duda, J. L. (2003). Sydney 2000: the interplay between emotions, coping and the performance of Olympic-level athletes. *The Sport Psychologist*, 17, 253–267.

Perkins, D., Wilson, G. V. and Kerr, J. H. (2001). The effects of elevated arousal and mood on maximal strength performance in athletes. *Journal of Applied Sport Psychology*, 13, 239–259.

Platt, J. J., Prout, M. F. and Metzger, D. S. (1986). Interpersonal cognitive problem-solving therapy (ICPS). In W. Dryden and W. L. Golden (eds), *Cognitive-behavioural approaches to psychotherapy* (pp. 261–289). London: Harper and Row.

Prapavessis, H., Grove, J. R., McNair, P. J. and Cable, N. T. (1992). Self-regulation training, state anxiety and sport performance: a psychophysiological case study. *The Sport Psychologist*, 6, 213–229.

Quartana, P. J. and Burns, J. W. (2007). Painful consequences of anger suppression. *Emotion*, 7, 400–414.

Quirk, G. J. (2007). Prefrontal-amygdala interactions in the regulation of fear. In J. J. Gross (ed.), *Handbook of emotion regulation* (pp. 27–46). London: Guilford Press.

Ravizza, K. (2001). Increasing awareness for sport performance. In J. M. Williams (ed.), *Applied sport psychology: personal growth to peak performance* (pp. 179–187). London: Mayfield.

Rees, T. and Hardy, L. (2000). An examination of the social support experiences of high-level sports performers. *The Sport Psychologist*, 14, 327–347.

Rees, T., Smith, B. and Sparkes, A. (2003). The influence of social support on the lived experiences of spinal cord injured sportsmen. *The Sport Psychologist*, 17, 135–156.

Richards, J. M. and Gross, J. J. (2000). Emotion regulation and memory: the cognitive costs of keeping one's cool. *Journal of Personality and Social Psychology*, 79, 410–424.

Rodríguez-Fornells, A. and Maydeu-Olivares, A. (2000). Impulsive/careless problem solving style as predictor of subsequent academic achievement. *Personality and Individual Differences*, 28, 639–645.

Roese, N. R. (1997). Counterfactual thinking. *Psychological Bulletin*, 121, 133–148.

Russell, J. A. (1991). In defence of a prototype approach to emotion concepts. *Journal of Personality and Social Psychology*, 60, 37–47.

Russell, J. A. (2003). Core affect and the psychological construction of emotion. *Psychological Review*, 110, 145–172.

Russell, J. A. and Fehr, B. (1994). Fuzzy concepts in a fuzzy hierarchy: varieties of anger. *Journal of Personality and Social Psychology*, 67, 186–205.

Savitsky, K., Epley, N. and Gilovich, T. (2001). Do others judge us as harshly as we think? Overestimating the impact of our failures, shortcomings, and mishaps. *Journal of Personality and Social Psychology*, 81, 44–56.

Scanlan, T. K. and Lewthwaite, R. (1986). Social psychological aspects of competition for male youth sport participants: IV. Predictors of enjoyment. *Journal of Sport Psychology*, 8, 25–35.

Scanlan, T. K. and Simons, J. P. (1992). The construct of sport enjoyment. In G. C. Roberts (ed.), *Motivation in sport and exercise* (pp. 199–215). Champaign, IL: Human Kinetics.

Scanlan, T. K., Babkes, M. L. and Scanlan, L. A. (2005). Participation in sport: a developmental glimpse at emotion. In J. L. Mahoney, R. W. Larson and J. S. Eccles (eds), *Organised activities as contexts of development: extracurricular activities, after-school, and community programmes* (pp. 275–309). Mahwah, NJ: Lawrence Erlbaum Associates.

Scanlan, T. K., Carpenter, P. J., Lobel, M. and Simons, J. P. (1993). Sources of enjoyment of youth sport athletes. *Pediatric Exercise Science*, 5, 275–285.

Scanlan, T. K., Russell, D. G., Beals, K. P. and Scanlan, L. A. (2003). Project on elite athlete commitment (PEAK): II. A direct test and expansion of the sport commitment model with elite amateur sportsmen. *Journal of Sport and Exercise Psychology*, 25, 377–401.

Scanlan, T. K., Stein, G. L. and Ravizza, K. (1989). An in-depth study of former elite figure skaters: II. Sources of enjoyment. *Journal of Sport and Exercise Psychology*, 11, 65–83.

Schachter, S. and Singer, J. E. (1962). Cognitive, social, and physiological determinants of emotional state. *Psychological Review*, 69, 379–399.

Scherer, K. R. (1999). Appraisal theory. In M. Lewis and J. M. Haviland-Jones (eds), *Handbook of emotions* (2nd edn, pp. 637–663). Chichester: Wiley.

Schwarz, N. (2000). Emotion, cognition, and decision making. *Cognition and Emotion*, 14, 433–440.

Seligman, M. E. P. (2002). Positive psychology, positive prevention, and positive therapy. In C. R. Snyder and S. J. Lopez (eds), *The handbook of positive psychology* (pp. 3–12). New York: Oxford Press.

Seligman, M. E. P., Steen, T. A., Park, N. and Peterson, C. (2005). Positive psychology progress: empirical validation of interventions. *American Psychologist*, 60, 410–421.

Shaver, P., Schwarz, J., Kirson, D. and O'Connor, C. (1987). Emotion knowledge: further explorations of a prototype approach. *Journal of Personality and Social Psychology*, 52, 1061–1086.

Sheppes, G. and Meiran, N. (2007). Better late than never? On the dynamics of online regulation of sadness using distraction and cognitive reappraisal. *Personality and Social Psychology Bulletin*, 33, 1518–1532.

Shields, S. A. (2005). The politics of emotion in everyday life: 'appropriate' emotion and claims on identity. *Review of General Psychology*, 9, 3–15.

Skinner, N. and Brewer, N. (2004). Adaptive approaches to competition: challenge appraisals and positive emotion. *Journal of Sport and Exercise Psychology*, 26, 283–305.

Smith, N. C., Bellamy, M., Collins, D. J. and Newell, D. (2001). A test of processing efficiency theory in a team sport context. *Journal of Sports Sciences*, 19, 321–332.

Strongman, K. T. (1987). *The psychology of emotion*. Chichester: John Wiley and Sons.

Swain, A. B. J. and Jones, G. (1993). Intensity and frequency dimensions of competitive state anxiety. *Journal of Sports Sciences*, 11, 533–542.

Tamir, M., John, O. P., Srivastava, S. and Gross, J. J. (2007). Implicit theories of emotion: affective and social outcomes across a major life transition. Journal of Personality and Social Psychology, 92, 731–744.

Theeboom, M., De Knop, P. and Weiss, M.R. (1995). Motivational climate, psychological responses, and motor skill development in children's sport: a field-based intervention study. *Journal of Sport and Exercise Psychology*, 17, 294–311.

Thomas, P. R., Murphy, S. M. and Hardy, L. (1999). Test of performance strategies: development and preliminary validation of a comprehensive measure of athletes' psychological skills. *Journal of Sports Sciences*, 17, 697–711.

Totterdell, P. (2000). Catching moods and hitting runs: mood linkage and subjective performance in professional sport teams. *Journal of Applied Psychology*, 85, 848–859.

Uphill, M. A. and Jones, M. V. (2004). Coping with emotions in sport: a cognitive motivational relational theory perspective. In D. Lavallee, J. Thatcher and M. V. Jones (eds), *Coping and emotion in sport* (pp. 75–89). New York: Nova Science Publishers.

Uphill, M. A. and Jones, M. V. (2005). Coping with, and reducing the number of careless shots: a case study with a county golfer. *Sport and Exercise Psychology Review*, 2, 14–22.

Uphill, M. A. and Jones, M. V. (2007a). Antecedents of emotions in elite athletes: a cognitive motivational relational perspective. *Research Quarterly for Exercise and Sport*, 78, 79–89.

Uphill, M. A. and Jones, M. V. (2007b). 'When running is something you dread': a cognitive-behavioural intervention with a club runner. In A. M. Lane (ed.), *Mood and human performance: conceptual, measurement and applied issues* (pp. 271–295). New York: Nova Science Publishers.

Vallerand, R. J. and Blanchard, C. M. (2000). The study of emotion in sport and exercise: historical, definitional, and conceptual perspectives. In Y. L. Hanin (ed.), *Emotions in sport* (pp. 3–37). Champaign, IL: Human Kinetics.

Van Gemmert, A. W. A. and Van Galen, G. P. (1997). Stress neuromotor noise, and human performance: a theoretical perspective. *Journal of Experimental Psychology*, 23, 1299–1313.

Wegner, D. M. (1994). Ironic processes of mental control. *Psychological Review*, 101, 34–52.

Wegner, D. M. and Bargh, J. A. (1998). Control and automaticity in social life. In D. Gilbert, S. T. Fiske and G. Lindzey (eds), *Handbook of social psychology* (4th edn, pp. 446–496). New York: McGraw-Hill.

Wegner, D. M., Ansfield, M. and Pilloff, D. L. (1998). The putt and the pendulum: ironic effects of the mental control of action. *Psychological Science*, 9, 196–199.

Wegner, D. M., Erber, R. and Zanakos, S. (1993). Ironic processes in the mental control of mood and mood-related thought. *Journal of Personality and Social Psychology*, 65, 1093–1104.

Wegner, D. M., Schneider, D. J., Carter, S. and White, T. (1987). Paradoxical effects of thought suppression. *Journal of Personality and Social Psychology*, 53, 5–13.

Wegner, D. M., Shortt, J. W., Blake, A. W. and Page, M. S. (1990). The suppression of exciting thoughts. *Journal of Personality and Social Psychology*, 28, 409–418.

Weiss, M. R., Kimmel, L. and Smith, A. L. (2001). Determinants of sport commitment among junior tennis players: enjoyment as a mediating variable. *Pediatric Exercise Science*, 13, 131–144.

Zajonc, R. B. (1984). On the primacy of affect. *American Psychologist*, 39, 117–123.

Zajonc, R. B. (1998). Emotions. In D. T. Gilbert, S. T. Fiske and G. Lindzey (eds), *The handbook of social psychology* (4th edn, pp. 591–632). Boston, MA: McGraw-Hill.

Zillmann, D. (1971). Excitation transfer in communication-mediated aggressive behaviour. *Journal of Experimental Social Psychology*, 7, 419–434.

Zillmann, D., Katcher, A. H. and Milavsky, B. (1972). Excitation transfer from physical exercise to subsequent aggressive behaviour. *Journal of Experimental Social Psychology*, 8, 247–259.

6   Attention in sport

Aidan Moran

Introduction

Concentration, or the ability to pay attention to what is most important in any situation while ignoring distractions, is a vital ingredient of successful performance in sport. Evidence to support this claim comes from at least three sources. First, reviews of research on athletes' "flow states" and peak performance experiences in sport (e.g. Harmison, 2007) highlight the importance to optimal performance of total absorption in the task at hand. Second, there is growing evidence of a link between athletes' focus of attention and the quality of their performance. Specifically, a recent review by Wulf (2007) concluded that an *external* focus of attention (in which performers direct their attention at the effects that their movements have on the environment) is usually more effective than an *internal* one (in which performers focus on their own body movements) in improving the learning and performance of various motor skills. This conclusion seems to apply generally across a range of tasks (e.g. balance activities, jumping, golf, American football), levels of experience (i.e. whether the performers are experts or novices) and participant populations (including those with motor impairments). Finally, a variety of anecdotal testimonials and sporting incidents emphasise the significance of focusing skills in determining athletic performance. To illustrate, Petr Cech, the Czech Republic goalkeeper who set a remarkable record for his club, Chelsea, by keeping 24 "clean sheets" in the UK Premier League in 2005, revealed that, "everything is about concentration" (cited in Szczepanik, 2005: 100). This comment was prompted by Cech's observation that opposing teams invariably get at least one chance to score during a game and "it's difficult to be concentrated for the right moment" (ibid.). Clearly, lapses in attention can mean the difference between success and failure in competitive sport. For example, at the 2004 Olympic Games in Athens, the American rifle shooter Matthew Emmons missed an opportunity to win a gold medal in the 50 m three-position target event when he shot at the wrong target. Leading his nearest rival Jia Zhambo (China) by three points as he took his last shot, Emmons lost his focus momentarily and shot at the target of a competitor in the next lane – thereby squandering his chance of victory.

Despite the preceding converging evidence on the importance of concentration processes in athletes, many research questions remain unresolved in this field. For example, what exactly is "concentration"? Why do athletes seem to lose their focus so easily and what kinds of distractions do they encounter in competitive sport? What psychological principles govern effective concentration in athletes? How is concentration affected by emotions such as anxiety? What practical techniques can sports performers use in order to improve their concentration skills? And, perhaps most importantly of all, how effective are these techniques? The purpose of this chapter is to answer these questions by reviewing the psychological research literature on attentional processes in athletes. Unfortunately, there has been a dearth of evaluative studies in this field. To illustrate, a search of the PsycINFO electronic database located no references using either the keywords "attentional skills training" or "concentration skills training" in sport. We shall return to this issue briefly later in the chapter, but at this stage it is important to clarify our terminology. Specifically, we need to explore the meaning of, and relationship between, the terms "attention" and "concentration".

Exploring attention and concentration: theoretical distinctions

Research on attention is one of the most important fields in cognitive psychology and cognitive neuroscience because it addresses such fundamental questions as how "voluntary control and subjective experience arise from and regulate our behaviour" (Posner and Rothbart, 2007: 1). This question of meta-cognitive regulation is especially relevant to elite-level athletic performance because, to be successful, sports performers need accurate insights into, and control over, their own concentration system. So, what exactly is the relationship between attention and concentration?

For psychologists, the term "attention" is at once familiar yet mysterious. Its familiarity stems from the fact that it is widely used in everyday situations. For example, a tennis coach may ask her students to "pay attention" to the way she tosses the ball as she demonstrates a serve to her players. Based on such familiarity, we can readily identify with William James's assertion that intuitively:

> Millions of items ... are present to my senses which never properly enter my experience. Why? Because they have no interest for me. My experience is what I agree to attend to. ... Everyone knows what attention is. It is the taking possession by the mind, in clear and vivid form, of one of what may seem several simultaneously possible objects or trains of thought. Focalization, concentration, of consciousness are of its essence. It implies withdrawal from some things in order to deal effectively with others.
>
> (1890: 403–404)

But does everyone *really* know what attention is? The problem here is that the construct of attention incorporates a wide variety of different types of psychological processes, ranging from low-level alertness or arousal to high-level conscious awareness. Indeed, Ashcraft (2006) identified *six* different meanings of this term. More precisely, his definitions of attention refer to: (a) biological alertness or arousal (a state of readiness to respond to the environment); (b) the orienting response (whereby attention is captured reflexively by an unexpected stimulus); (c) visual search (a shift in attention towards a specific region of visual space); (d) selective attention (the ability to attend to a particular source of information while ignoring other material); (e) mental resources (a form of mental effort that fuels cognitive activity); and (f) a supervisory process that regulates conscious cognitive activity. This heterogeneity of definitions reinforces Pashler's (1998) quip that, perhaps, "*no one* knows what attention is"! However, this latter conclusion seems unduly pessimistic because considerable agreement exists among attention researchers about certain theoretical assumptions. For example, it is now widely accepted that attention involves the concentration of mental activity on sensory or cognitive events. Thus, Goldstein defined it as, "the process of concentrating on specific features of the environment, or on certain thoughts or activities" (2008: 100). In addition, attention researchers agree that it is a *multidimensional* construct with at least three separate components (Moran, 2004).

The first dimension of attention is what is commonly known as "concentration" and refers to people's deliberate decision to invest mental effort in things that seem important to them at a given moment. For example, during a team-talk before an important match, athletes usually make a big effort to listen carefully to their coach's instructions. By contrast, when there is little at stake (e.g. during a routine training session), sports performers may find it difficult to concentrate on the task at hand. The second dimension of attention denotes a skill in selective perception whereby athletes become adept at "zooming in" on task-relevant information while ignoring distractions. This latter ability to discriminate relevant targets from irrelevant distractions is crucial in sport. For example, a football goalkeeper who is preparing to defend against a corner-kick has to learn to focus only on the flight of the incoming ball rather than on the movements of players in the penalty area. The third dimension involves "divided attention" and refers to a form of mental time-sharing ability whereby athletes learn from extensive practice to perform two or more concurrent actions equally well. For example, a skilled hockey player can dribble with the ball while simultaneously looking around for a team-mate who is in a good position to receive a pass. In summary, the construct of attention refers to at least three different cognitive processes – concentration or effortful awareness, selectivity of perception, and/or the ability to coordinate two or more actions at the same time. Having explained the multi-dimensional nature of attention, let us now consider how this construct has been conceptualised historically.

Approaches to attention: metaphor, theories and implications

Scientists try to understand the unknown in terms of the known. Influenced by this dictum, cognitive psychologists since the 1950s have postulated a variety of metaphors and theories in an effort to explain the mechanisms underlying attention (for a review, see Fernandez-Duque and Johnson, 1999). These metaphors and their implications for sport psychology can be summarised as follows.

The first information-processing theory of attention was developed by Broadbent (1958) as a result of a series of laboratory experiments in which people were required to engage in selective listening tasks. Assuming that people are limited in their ability to process information, he postulated a mechanism in the mind that facilitates the selection of some information while inhibiting that of competing information. This assumption led Broadbent to envisage attention as a mechanical bottleneck that serves to screen the flow of information into the mind in accordance with various criteria. Just as the neck of a bottle restricts the flow of liquid into or out of it, Broadbent's hypothetical filtering mechanism was believed to curtail the quantity of information which people can pay attention to at any given time. Furthermore, Broadbent proposed that, although multiple channels of sensory information (e.g. hearing, vision) can reach the filter, only *one* channel is allowed through to the next stage of information processing (where perceptual analysis is performed). The selection undertaken by this filtering mechanism was believed to occur on the basis of physical characteristics of the incoming information such as its pitch or loudness. Although Broadbent's (1958) model was plausible, it soon encountered many conceptual and methodological criticisms. For example, subsequent researchers failed to agree on either the location or temporal characteristics of the filter. Another blow to Broadbent's filter theory came from everyday experience whereby in certain social settings (e.g. a party) people report the ability to hear their names spoken in conversations to which they had not being paying attention. How can Broadbent's theory explain this "cocktail party effect"? The problem here is that people seem to be able to process sounds to which they had not been paying conscious attention. In the light of such problems, filter theory was shown to be incapable of accounting for the flexibility and sophistication of human attention. Another development that hastened the demise of filter theory was the switch from an auditory to a visual methodological paradigm in attention research. This switch occurred principally because experimenters found it easier to measure the presentation times of visual stimuli than their auditory equivalents. Taken together, these developments paved the way for a cluster of visual approaches of attention such as the "spotlight" and "zoom lens" metaphors.

According to the spotlight metaphor (e.g. Posner, 1980), selective attention resembles a mental beam that illuminates a circumscribed part of the visual field. The assumption is that information lying outside the illuminated region is ignored. Spotlight theorists also suggested that people's attentional beam can be re-directed voluntarily to other locations in space. A related visual metaphor of attention is the "zoom lens" (Eriksen and St James, 1986). This metaphor proposed that the one's attentional focus can be increased or decreased at will, as if one were adjusting the zoom lens of a camera.

For athletes and applied sport psychologists, these visual metaphors of attention have several practical implications. First, they highlight the fact that sports performers' beam of concentration is never truly "lost" but can be directed at the "wrong" target – namely, one that is irrelevant to the task at hand or outside one's control. We shall return to this idea later in the chapter when we identify some key principles of effective concentration. In passing, it is notable that few studies have been published on the question of what exactly athletes should focus on when they are exhorted to "concentrate" by their coaches (but for an exception, see Castaneda and Gray, 2007). A related benefit of visual metaphors of attention is that they suggest to athletes that they have control over where they choose to "shine" their concentration beam at any given moment. This principle forms the basis of Nideffer's (1976) model of attention in sport psychology. Briefly, this model postulates that athletes' attentional focus can vary simultaneously along two independent dimensions – "width" and "direction". With regard to width, attention is believed to range along a continuum from a broad focus (where athletes are generally aware of many different stimulus features at the same time) to a narrow one (where athletes can exclude irrelevant information). Attentional "direction" refers to the target of an athlete's focus – namely, whether it is external or internal. According to Nideffer, these dimensions of width and direction may be combined factorially to yield four hypothetical attentional styles that are valuable in different sport situations. For example, a narrow *external* attentional focus in sport is required when a golfer looks at the hole before putting. By contrast, a narrow *internal* focus is required when a gymnast mentally rehearses a skill such as a back-flip in her mind's eye before performing it. Unfortunately, attempts to validate Nideffer's (1976) model have encountered mixed success and the status of his model remains equivocal (Moran and Summers, 2004).

Although the spotlight metaphor of attention has been helpful in applied settings, it is plagued by a number of conceptual and empirical problems. First, spotlight theorists have not adequately explained the mechanisms by which executive control of attentional focus is achieved. Put simply, what processes govern *direction* of the spotlight? Second, the spotlight model assumes that people's attentional beam sweeps through space en route to its target. However, if that were true, then one might expect that if an obstacle were encountered during the sweep, attention would be hampered or delayed. But research shows that "attention is not influenced by the presence of spatially intervening information" (Smith and Kosslyn, 2007: 131). Third, the spotlight metaphor neglects the issue of what lies *outside* the beam of our concentration. In other words, it ignores the possibility that *unconscious* factors can affect people's attentional processes. Interestingly, such factors have attracted increasing interest from cognitive scientists in recent years. Indeed, Nadel and Piattelli-Palmarini remarked that, although researchers had originally assumed that cognition was limited to conscious processes, "much of the domain is now concerned with phenomena that lie behind the veil of consciousness" (2002: xxvi). This observation is especially true of contemporary research in attention, perception and implicit learning where there has been a resurgence of interest in unconscious influences on people's experience (Claxton, 2006). For example, Merikle (2007) recently reviewed research on perception without awareness in vision. Fourth, the spotlight model of attention has been concerned mainly with *external* targets – not internal ones. A fifth weakness of the spotlight metaphor is that it neglects emotional influences on attentional processes. We shall return to this issue later when we summarise some key principles of effective concentration. For example, it seems that anxiety can narrow one's mental spotlight and encourage performers to shine it inwards. Interestingly, Eysenck *et al.* (2007) have recently developed a theoretical model called "attentional control theory" in an effort to account for the effects of anxiety on cognitive performance.

A third influential approach to attention is based on "resource" or "capacity" metaphors (e.g. Kahneman, 1973). This approach was developed in order to explain the mechanisms underlying divided attention or people's ability to perform two or more tasks at the same time. These metaphors suggested that attention is a limited pool of undifferentiated mental energy that can be allocated to concurrent tasks depending on various strategic principles. For example, motivation, practice and arousal are held to *increase* spare attentional capacity, whereas task difficulty is believed to reduce it. Most resource theorists (e.g. Baddeley, 1986) believe that divided attentional performance is regulated by a limited central capacity system such as the "central executive" of the working memory model (Baddeley, 2003). The extent to which two tasks can be performed concurrently depends on their combined demands on available attentional resources.

What are the strengths and weaknesses of the resource model for performance psychologists? Perhaps its biggest strength is its proposal that, although dual-task performance is constrained by available mental resources, extensive practice can reduce the attentional demands of any task. Unfortunately, the resource metaphor of divided attention has encountered criticism. For example, Navon and Gopher (1979) have argued that people can have multiple attentional resources rather than a single pool of undifferentiated mental energy. Each of these multiple pools may have its own functions and limits. For example, Schmidt and Lee (1999) suggested that the attentional resources required for a motor skill such as selecting a finger movement may be separate from those which regulate a verbal skill such as the pronunciation of a word. This idea of multiple attentional resources casts doubt on the possibility of a single definition of the construct. Thus, Luck and Vecera suggested that "the term attention applies to many separable processes, each of which operates within a different cognitive subsystem" (2002: 261). An additional problem for multiple resource theories of attention is that they may be "inherently untestable" (Palmeri, 2002: 298). To explain, virtually any pattern of task interference can be "explained" *post hoc* by attributing it to the existence of multiple pools of attentional resources.

So far, we have explored three different metaphors of attention – the filter, spotlight and resource approaches. Whereas filter theories of attention were concerned mainly with identifying *how* and *where* selective attention occurred in the information-processing system, resource theories explored divided attention.

When they are evaluated critically, spotlight and resource models of attention have two major limitations. First, they have dealt mainly with *external* (or environmental) determinants of attention and have largely overlooked internal factors (e.g. thoughts and feelings). Interestingly, Posner and Rothbart acknowledged this gap in the research literature on attention when they concluded that people "differ in their ability to concentrate for long periods on internal trains of thought" (2007: 9). Of course, performers' insights into their own mental processes are not always reliable or valid from a researcher's perspective. The second weakness of cognitive models of attention is that they ignore the influence of emotional states. This neglect of the affective dimension of behaviour is unfortunate because it is widely known that anxiety impairs attentional processes. For example, the phenomenon of "choking under pressure" (whereby nervousness causes a sudden deterioration of athletic performance) illustrates how the beam of one's attentional spotlight can be directed *inwards* when it should be focused on the task at hand. For a comprehensive account of the role of emotional factors in skilled performance, see Hanin (2000) and Eysenck *et al.* (2007).

Why do athletes lose their concentration? Distractions in sport

Competitive sport is replete with a variety of distractions that can disrupt athletes' concentration. In general, these distractions fall into two main categories – external and internal (Moran, 1996, 2004). Whereas external distractions are objective stimuli that divert our attentional spotlight away from its intended target, internal distractions include a vast array of thoughts, feelings and/or bodily sensations (e.g. pain, fatigue) that impede athletes' efforts to concentrate on the job at hand.

Typical external distractions include such factors as crowd movements, sudden changes in ambient noise levels (e.g. the click of a camera), gamesmanship by opponents (e.g. at corner-kicks in football, opposing forwards often stand in front of the goalkeeper to prevent him/her from tracking the incoming ball) and unpredictable playing surfaces or weather (e.g. a golfer may become distracted by windy conditions). Often, these distractions lead to impaired performance at the worst possible moment for the performer concerned. For example, the Brazilian marathon-runner Vanderlei De Lima was leading the race in the 2004 Olympics in Athens when an unstable spectator suddenly jumped out from the crowd and wrestled him to the ground. Stunned and naturally distracted, De Lima eventually finished third in the event (Goodbody and Nichols, 2004). By contrast, internal distractions are self-generated concerns arising from one's own thoughts and feelings. Typical factors in this category include wondering what might happen in the future, regretting what has happened in the past, worrying about what other people might say or do and/or feeling tired, bored or otherwise emotionally upset. A classic example of a costly internal distraction occurred in the case of the golfer Doug Sanders who missed a putt of less than three feet that would have earned him victory at the 1970 British Open championship in St Andrews, Scotland. This error not only prevented him from winning his first major tournament – but also deprived him of an estimated ten million pounds in prize-money, tournament invitations and advertising endorsements. Remarkably, Sanders' attentional lapse was precipitated by a cognitive error – thinking too far ahead or in this case, making a victory speech before the putt had been taken. Intriguingly, over 30 years later, he revealed what had gone through his mind at the time, "I made the mistake about thinking which section of the crowd I was going to bow to" (cited in Gilleece, 1999: 23). Clearly, Sanders had inadvertently distracted *himself* by allowing his mental spotlight to shine into the future instead of at the task in hand. As he explained,

> I had the victory speech prepared before the battle was over. ... I would give up every victory I had to have won that title. It's amazing how many different things to my normal routine I did on the 18th hole. There's something for psychologists there, the way that the final hole of a major championship can alter the way a man thinks.
>
> (Cited in Moran, 2005: 21)

Unfortunately, despite such vivid accounts of attentional lapses in sport, little research has been conducted on the phenomenology of distractibility – although a recent paper by Gouju *et al.* (2007) explored athletes' attentional experiences in a hurdle race. This general neglect of distractibility is attributable to a combination of theoretical and methodological factors. First, since the 1960s, cognitive researchers have assumed falsely that information flows into the mind in only one direction – from the outside world inwards. In so doing, they ignored the possibility that information (and, hence, distractions) could travel in the opposite direction – from long-term memory into working memory or current awareness. A second reason why researchers focused on external distractions is simply because they were easier to measure than their self-generated equivalents. As a result of this combination of factors, the theoretical mechanisms by which internal distractions disrupt concentration are still rather mysterious. Nevertheless, a promising approach to this problem may be found in Wegner's (1994) "ironic processes" model. This model is interesting because it addresses the question of why people often lose their concentration at the most *inopportune* moment. Briefly, Wegner's (1994) theory proposed that the mind wanders *because* we try to control it. Put simply, when we are anxious or tired, the decision *not* to think about something may paradoxically increase the prominence of that phenomenon in our consciousness. In such circumstances, the attempt to block out a certain thought from one's mind may lead to a "rebound" experience whereby the suppressed thought becomes even more prominent in consciousness. This tendency for a suppressed thought to come to mind more readily than a thought that is the focus of intentional concentration is called "hyperaccessibility" and is especially likely to occur under conditions of increased mental load. What theoretical mechanisms could account for this ironic experience?

According to Wegner (1994), when people try to suppress a thought, they engage in a controlled (conscious) search for thoughts that are different from the unwanted thought. At the same time, however, our minds conduct an automatic (unconscious) search for any signs of the unwanted thought. In other words, the intention to suppress a thought activates an automatic search for that very thought in an effort to monitor whether or not the act of suppression has been successful. Normally, the conscious intentional system dominates the unconscious monitoring system. Under certain circumstances (e.g. when our working memories are overloaded or when our attentional resources are depleted by fatigue or stress), however, the ironic system prevails and an ironic intrusion of the unwanted thought occurs. Wegner attributes this rebound effect to cognitive load. But, although this load is believed to disrupt the conscious mechanism of thought control, it does not interfere with the automatic (and ironic) monitoring system. Thus, Wegner proposed that "the intention to concentrate creates conditions under which mental load enhances monitoring of irrelevancies" (1994: 7). To summarise, Wegner's research helps us to understand why performers may find it difficult to suppress unwanted or irrelevant thoughts when they are tired or anxious. Intriguingly for sport psychology, Wegner and his colleagues have investigated ironies of *action* (i.e. making movement or skill errors that represent the *opposite* of what they had intended to do) as well as those of thought. For example, Wegner *et al.* (1998) explored the extent to which a mental load task (attempting to keep a six-digit number in their minds) can precipitate an ironic effect in the execution of a golf putt. They found that, as predicted by ironic processes theory, trying *not* to overshoot the hole in a putting task caused precisely such an outcome when participants were required to perform under the imposition of a mental load. Such experimental findings have significant implications for understanding why athletes sometimes unwittingly perform actions that are the exact opposite of those they had intended (see also Janelle, 1999; Moran, 1996; Woodman and Davis, 2008).

Principles of effective concentration

Based on reviews of relevant research (e.g. Abernethy, 2001; Moran, 1996), Figure 6.1 summarises at least five theoretical principles of effective concentration in sport. Three of these principles describe the establishment of an optimal focus, whereas the other two indicate how it may be disrupted (see Figure 6.1).

Athletes have to decide to concentrate – it will not happen accidentally

The first principle of effective concentration is the idea that athletes must prepare to concentrate by making a deliberate decision to invest mental effort in their performance. This link between *deciding* to concentrate and subsequently performing to one's full potential is well known in sport. For example, Ronan O'Gara, the Irish and Lions rugby union out-half, claimed that:

> I have to be focused. I have to do my mental preparation. I have to feel that I'm ready. I don't want to be putting myself out there for credit but I have a

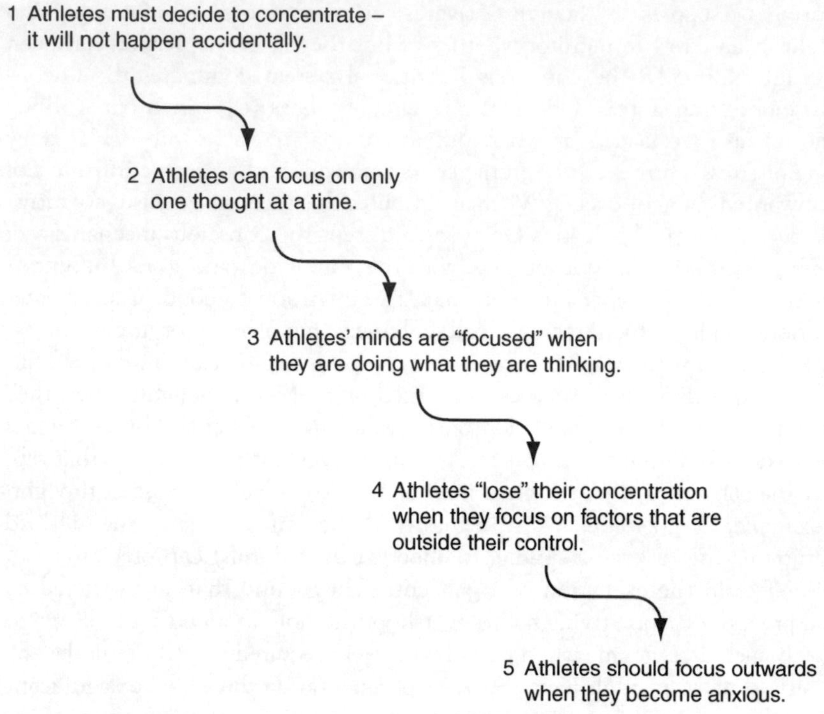

1 Athletes must decide to concentrate –
it will not happen accidentally.

2 Athletes can focus on only
one thought at a time.

3 Athletes' minds are "focused" when
they are doing what they are thinking.

4 Athletes "lose" their concentration
when they focus on factors that are
outside their control.

5 Athletes should focus outwards
when they become anxious.

Figure 6.1 Concentration principles (source: based on Moran, 1996).

big impact on how Munster perform. When it's coming up to a big match, rugby is the only thing in my head. Driving around, I visualise certain scenarios, different positions on the pitch, different times when the ball is coming to me.

(Cited in English, 2006: 70)

Not surprisingly, many athletes use imaginary "switch on" and "switch off" zones in their sports. For example, when top tennis players look for towels behind the baseline during a game to mop up perspiration, they are in their "switch off" zone. But when they step forward to begin their pre-service routine, they move into their "switch on" zone. Interestingly, this idea of switching one's concentration on and off was raised by Sir Garry Sobers, the famous cricket star, when he observed that:

Concentration's like a shower. You don't turn it on until you want to bathe. ... You don't walk out of the shower and leave it running. You turn it off, you turn it on. ... It has to be fresh and ready when you need it.

(Cited in White, 2002: 20)

Athletes can focus on only one thought at a time

A second building block of effective concentration is the "one thought" principle – the idea that you can focus consciously on only one thing at a time. Theoretically, it has long been believed (e.g. as far back as James, 1890) that the information-processing resources that give rise to consciousness are limited (Smith and Kosslyn, 2007). Based on this assumption, some researchers (e.g. McElree and Dosher, 1989) have postulated that we can be conscious of only one thing at a time. Of course, this limitation of consciousness does not apply to skill execution. Thus, as we mentioned earlier in our discussion of divided attention, people can perform several actions simultaneously – as long as one or more of these skills has been practised to the point where it no longer requires conscious control (a state of automaticity). Returning to focused attention, single-mindedness has produced some unusual theories among athletes. For example, Retief Goosen, who won the 2004 US Open golf championship in New York, claimed that he plays his best when pressure situations force him to concentrate on what he has to do:

> I've reached a point where I feel like I can only play my best golf when I'm really under the cosh. When you're under pressure, it's a sort of "must" thing. You must focus and you must make the putt. That's what I feel.
>
> (Cited in Mair, 2004: S10)

Athletes' minds are focused when they are doing what they are thinking

A third principle of effective concentration is that athletes' minds are truly focused when there is no difference between what they are *thinking* about and what they are *doing*. This congruence between thought and action is characteristically evident in peak performance experiences in sport. For example, after Roger Bannister had run the first sub-4-minute mile in May 1954 in Oxford, he revealed that, "There was no pain, only a great unity of movement and aim" (Bannister, 2004: 12). Similarly, after the golfer Pádraig Harrington won the 2007 Open Championship in Carnoustie after a play-off against Sergio Garcia, he described what had gone through his mind as he sank the winning putt:

> no conscious effort whatsoever went into that putt. There were no thoughts about "this is for the Open". ... This was as pure as you like. I stroked it in. It might just be the most fluid putt I'll ever hit in my life.
>
> (Cited in Jones, 2007: 12)

Based on such insights from peak performance experiences, it seems clear that in order to increase one's chances of achieving this state of mind, one has to concentrate on actions that are specific, relevant and, above all, under one's own control.

Athletes "lose" their concentration when they focus on factors outside their control

Fourth, as we indicated earlier in the case of the unfortunate Doug Sanders, athletes are likely to "lose" their concentration whenever they focus on factors that are outside their control, irrelevant to the job at hand or too far in the future.

Athletes should focus outwards when they become anxious

The final building block of effective concentration is that when athletes get nervous, they should focus *outwards* on actions – not inwards on doubts. This outward focus is necessary because anxiety tends to make people self-conscious and self-critical. This advice is consistent with Wulf's (2007) analysis of a decade of research on attentional aspects of motor learning. Briefly, this review examined a range of studies on the influence of a person's focus of attention (i.e. either external or internal) on the learning and performance of motor skills. She concluded that an external focus of attention (one that targets the *effects* of a given motor movement) is typically associated with higher levels of performance and longer retention of the skill in question. Wulf's conclusion is questionable, however. For example, there is evidence that attentional focus interacts with the level of expertise of the performer. Thus, Perkins-Ceccato *et al.* (2003) found that whereas highly skilled golfers performed a pitch shot better with external than with internal attentional focus instructions, the opposite held for less skilled counterparts. Specifically, the latter golfers performed better with an *internal* than an external focus of attention. Clearly, the effect of attentional focus on skilled performance is a complex issue.

Anxiety, concentration and skilled performance

As explained earlier, cognitive researchers have traditionally ignored the influence of emotional factors on skilled performance – mainly because of the primacy of rational computational models which did not take account of the affective side of mental life. As Smith and Kosslyn observed, "emotion was not considered an appropriate domain of inquiry within the study of cognition until very recently" (2007: 326). Fortunately, this oversight has been corrected and, over the past two decades, the phenomenon of "choking under pressure" has attracted considerable interest from cognitive as well as sport psychologists (e.g. see Beilock and Carr, 2001; Gucciardi and Dimmock, 2008; Wilson *et al.*, 2007).

The term "choking under pressure" refers to the failure of normally expert skills under pressure (Masters, 1992). What makes this phenomenon intriguing for athletes and sport psychologists alike is that it seems to involve a motivational paradox. Specifically, the more effort the athlete expends in trying to do well, the worse the performance becomes. Therefore, choking is a form of "paradoxical performance" (Gucciardi and Dimmock, 2008) because it happens in situations where people *try too hard* to perform well.

In general, sport psychologists regard choking as an anxiety-based attentional problem rather than a personality weakness. This distinction is important because it suggests that *anyone* can choke under certain circumstances, not just those performers who have a nervous disposition. Thus, all athletes – regardless of their ability or experience – can choke if they focus on the "wrong" target, such as the importance of the occasion or the mechanics of the skill or movement being executed.

What cognitive mechanisms underlie choking under pressure? Two main attentional models have been postulated to account for the debilitative effects of anxiety on skilled performance. On the one hand, the "self-consciousness" approach (Baumeister, 1984) proposes that, when people experience pressure to perform well, they tend to think more about themselves and the importance of the skill that they are performing than they would normally. This excessive self-consciousness causes people to try to exert conscious control over skills that had previously been automatic – hence leading to an unravelling process known commonly as "paralysis by analysis". Recent support for this approach comes from Gucciardi and Dimmock (2008) who tested golfers' putting skills in three attentional conditions in low- and high-anxiety situations. In the first condition, the golfers had to focus on three words that represented aspects of their technique (e.g. "arms", "head"). In the second, they had to focus on three irrelevant words (e.g. colours). In the third, they had to focus on just one word that described their putting action (e.g. "smooth"). Results showed that the golfers' putting skills were most accurate when they focused on a single generic word that encapsulated their putting action – rather than on several words representing other aspects of their technical action.

An alternative approach to understanding the effects of choking under pressure comes from "processing-efficiency" theory (Eysenck and Calvo, 1992). Briefly, this model distinguishes between processing "effectiveness" (the quality of task performance) and processing "efficiency" (the relationship between the effectiveness of performance and the effort or processing resources invested in task performance). Based on this distinction, it predicts that the adverse effects of anxiety on performance effectiveness tend to be less than those on processing efficiency. Further, it postulates that anxiety impairs the processing efficiency of the central executive component of working memory – that part of the memory system that stores and manipulates currently relevant information for short periods of time (Baddeley, 2003). The theory also proposes that anxious performers may try to maintain their level of performance by investing additional effort in it. Although this increased investment of effort seems to pay off initially, it soon reaches a point of diminishing return. When this point is reached, the performer may conclude that too much effort is required so s/he gives up. Thus, processing-efficiency theory highlights a major cost of anxiety – the fact that its effects on performance only become evident when processing *efficiency* is assessed along with task outcome. Theoretically, a notable aspect of the processing-efficiency model is its assumption that the effects of anxiety on performance are mediated by the central executive component of working memory (Baddeley, 2003). Unfortunately, Eysenck and Calvo (1992) fail to specify precisely how this mediation occurs. In an effort to address this deficiency, however, Eysenck *et al.* (2007) recently revised processing-efficiency theory and postulated a new theoretical model called "attentional-control theory". According to this latter theory, two key mechanisms by which anxiety impairs skilled performance are the inhibition function and the attentional-shifting function of the central executive. Specifically, Eysenck *et al.* (2007) suggest that highly anxious performers not only experience great difficulty in inhibiting the effects of distracting stimuli, but also encounter problems in shifting their attentional resources efficiently to meet task demands. Put simply, anxiety is postulated to hamper attentional control – which in turn curtails the efficiency of task processing. Interestingly, a recent study by Wilson and Smith (2007) supported a key prediction of both processing-efficiency theory and attentional-control theory – namely, that the adverse effects of anxiety were more apparent on processing efficiency than on performance effectiveness for a team of elite female hockey players.

Concentration training exercises and techniques

Sport psychology researchers have developed a variety of practical strategies that purport to improve concentration skills in athletes (see Greenlees and Moran, 2003). Unfortunately, as mentioned earlier in the chapter, little evaluative research has been conducted to assess the efficacy of these techniques – either alone or in combination – as focusing tools in competitive situations. What these cognitive-behavioural strategies have in common, however, is that they purport to help sports performers to achieve a focused state of mind in which there is no difference between what they are thinking about and what they are doing. When this happens for an individual, the performer's mind is "cleared of irrelevant thoughts, the body is cleared of irrelevant tensions, and the focus is centred only on what is important at that moment for executing the skill to perfection" (Orlick, 1990: 18).

In general, two types of psychological activities are recommended to enhance focusing skills – concentration training exercises and concentration techniques (Moran, 1996, 2003). Whereas the former are intended for use mainly in athletes' training sessions, the latter are designed primarily for use in competitive situations.

One of the most widely recommended concentration exercises is the "concentration grid" – a visual search task endorsed by Schmid and Peper (1998) in which the participant is required to scan as many digits as possible within a given time limit. Unfortunately, this exercise does not seem to have a coherent theoretical rationale. Furthermore, no references were cited by Weinberg and Gould to support their claim that this exercise was used "extensively in Eastern Europe as a pre-competition screening device" (1999: 347) or that it "will help you learn to focus your attention and scan the environment for relevant cues" (ibid.). Despite the absence of such evidence, the concentration grid is recommended unreservedly by Schmid and Peper as a "training exercise for practising focusing ability" (1998: 324) and also by Weinberg and Gould (2007). Interestingly, Greenlees *et al.* (2006) recently examined the validity of the grid as a concentration exercise over a nine-week period with a sample of collegiate football players. Results showed no significant effects of the grid on the athletes' concentration skills relative to a control group. Therefore, these authors concluded that the grid "lacks the efficacy that has been ascribed to it in previous literature and anecdotal accounts" (2006: 36).

To summarise, there seems to be little empirical justification for the use of generic visual search and/or vigilance tasks in an effort to improve performers' concentration skills. Nevertheless, generic perceptual training may have other benefits for sports performers. For example, recent evidence suggests that perceptual-cognitive skills training can improve senior (over 50 years old) tennis players' response speed and decision-making on court (Caserta *et al.*, 2007). By contrast with the concentration grid, however, "simulation training" (Orlick, 1990) appears to have a satisfactory theoretical rationale. This latter exercise, which is also known as "dress rehearsal" (Schmid and Peper, 1998), "simulated practice" (Hodge and McKenzie, 1999) and "distraction training" (Maynard, 1998), proposes that performers can learn to concentrate more effectively in real-life pressure situations by simulating them in practice conditions.

Interestingly, a number of anecdotal testimonials to the value of this practice have emerged in sport psychology in recent years. To illustrate, the late Earl Woods, the father and initial coach of Tiger Woods, used such methods on him when he was a boy. Indeed, Woods senior claimed that:

> all the strategies and tactics of distraction I'd learned I threw at that kid and he would just grit his teeth and play ... and if anyone tries pulling a trick on him these days he just smiles and says, "My dad used to do that years ago."
>
> (Cited in *Evening Herald*, 2001: 61)

Similarly, Javier Aguirre, the coach of the 2002 Mexican national football team, instructed his players to practise penalty-taking after every friendly match in the year leading up to the 2002 World Cup in an effort to prepare for the possibility of penalty shoot-outs in that competition. As he explained: "there will always be noise and that is the best way to practise" (cited in Smith, 2002: S3).

Unfortunately, although laboratory and field simulations have been used extensively to measure expert–novice differences in athletic performance (for a recent review of the scientific literature on this topic, see Ward *et al.*, 2006), no published research could be located on the efficacy of simulation *training* as a concentration strategy. Despite this gap in the literature, some support for the theoretical rationale of simulation training may be found in cognitive psychology. For example, research on the "encoding specificity" principle of learning shows that people's recall of information is facilitated by conditions which resemble those in which the original encoding occurred (Matlin, 2005). Based on this principle, the simulation of competitive situations in practice should lead to positive transfer effects to the competition itself. In addition, adversity training may counteract the tendency for novel or unexpected stimuli to distract performers in competition. The simulation of these factors in training should reduce their attention-capturing qualities subsequently. In summary, there is some theoretical justification for the belief that simulation training could enhance performers' concentration skills. However, this conclusion is tentative for one important reason. Specifically, most sports performers realise that even the most ingenious simulations cannot replicate completely the *actual* arousal that they experience in competitive situations. For example, Ronan O'Gara, the Ireland and Lions rugby union out-half, admitted that although he can practise taking penalty kicks in training, "it's completely different in a match where my heartbeat is probably 115 beats a minute whereas in training it's about 90–100" (cited in Fanning, 2002: 6). Clearly, it is difficult to simulate accurately the emotional aspects of competitive action.

Having reviewed some popular concentration exercises, let us now turn to the second type of attentional skills intervention used in performance psychology – namely, concentration techniques.

Specifying performance and process goals

"Goals" are future valued outcomes (Locke and Latham, 2006). Psychologists (e.g. Hardy and Jones, 1994) commonly distinguish between result goals (e.g. the outcome of a sporting contest), performance goals (or specific end-products of performance that lie within the athlete's control, such as attempting to achieve 90 per cent accuracy in one's serve in tennis) and "process" goals (or specific behavioural actions that need to be undertaken to achieve a goal – such as tossing the ball up high for greater service accuracy). Arising from these distinctions, some sport psychologists suggest that performance goals can improve athletes' concentration skills. For example, it is plausible that tennis players could improve their concentration on court by focusing solely on such performance goals as seeking 100 per cent accuracy on their first serves. Theoretically, this idea seems valid because performance goals encourage athletes to focus on task-relevant information and on controllable actions. Additional support for this idea stems from studies on the correlates of people's best and worst athletic performances. For example, Jackson and Roberts (1992) found that collegiate athletes produced their best displays when they focused explicitly on performance goals. By contrast, their worst performances tended to happen when they were preoccupied with result goals. Interestingly, there is some evidence that process-oriented goals are helpful for competitive athletes. For example, Kingston and Hardy (1997) reported that for golfers, process goals facilitated faster changes in performance than performance goals and were associated with greater control of cognitive anxiety and increased concentration. In summary, there seems to be some empirical support for the principle that performance and process goals can facilitate concentration skills in athletes.

Using pre-performance routines

Most top-class athletes display characteristic and consistent sequences of preparatory actions before they perform key skills. For example, golfers tend to "set up" in self-consistent ways and waggle their clubs and take the same number of practice swings before striking the ball on the course. These preferred action sequences and/or repetitive behaviours are called "pre-performance routines" and are typically performed prior to the execution of "self-paced" skills (i.e. actions that are carried out largely at one's own speed and without interference from other people).

At least three types of routines are common among athletes. First, pre-event routines are preferred sequences of actions in the run up to competitive events. Included here are stable preferences for what to do on the night before, and on the morning of, the competition itself. Second, as we have just explained, pre-performance routines are characteristic sequences of thoughts and actions which performers adhere to prior to skill execution – as in the case of tennis players bouncing the ball before serving. Finally, post-mistake routines are action sequences that may help performers to leave their errors in the past so that they can re-focus on the task at hand. For example, a golfer may "shadow" the correct swing of a shot that had led to an error.

Support for the value of pre-performance routines as concentration techniques comes from both theoretical and empirical sources. Theoretically, pre-performance routines are intended to encourage performers to develop an appropriate mental set for skill execution by helping them to focus on task-relevant information. For example, many football goalkeepers follow pre-kick routines in an effort to block out any jeering that is directed at them by supporters of opposing teams. Similarly, routines may enable performers to concentrate on the present moment rather than on past events or on possible future outcomes. Finally, pre-performance routines may prevent performers from devoting too much attention to the mechanics of their well-learned skills – a habit that can unravel automaticity (see Beilock and Carr, 2001). Thus, routines may help to suppress the type of inappropriate conscious control that often occurs in pressure situations. A useful five-step pre-performance routine for self-paced skills is described by Singer (2002).

A key issue in research on the efficacy of pre-performance routines concerns the degree to which they are *actually* consistent in competitive situations. Some studies have raised doubts about such consistency. For example, Jackson and Baker (2001) analysed the pre-strike routine of the prolific former Welsh international and Lions rugby union kicker, Neil Jenkins, who scored 1,049 points in 87 games for his country. As expected, this player reported using a variety of concentration techniques (such as thought-stopping and mental imagery) as part of his pre-kick routine. However, what surprised Jackson and Baker was that Jenkins *varied* the timing of his pre-kick behaviour as a function of the difficulty of the kick he faced. This finding shows that routines are not as rigid or stereotyped as was originally believed. Subsequently, Jackson (2003) reported that goal-kickers at the 1999 rugby union World Cup varied the duration of their pre-kick routine in accordance with the perceived difficulty of the task. More recently, Lonsdale and Tam (2008) examined the consistency of the pre-performance routines of a sample of elite National Basketball Association (NBA) players whose "free-throw" behaviour was analysed from television footage. Results showed that, contrary to expectations, the temporal consistency of the basketball players' pre-performance routines was not associated with accurate skill execution. However, there was evidence that behavioural consistency was related to accurate performance. Specifically, Lonsdale and Tam (2008) found that the basketball players were more successful when they adhered to their dominant behavioural sequence prior to their free throws. Having considered research on the relationship between pre-performance behaviour and skilled performance, is there any empirical evidence on the attentional importance of pre-shot routines? Unfortunately, there is a dearth of studies on this issue. However, a case study by Shaw reported that a professional golfer experienced some attentional benefits arising from the use of a pre-shot routine. Although this evidence is anecdotal, the golfer reported that "the new routine had made him more focused for each shot and therefore less distracted by irrelevancies" (2002: 117).

Apart from their apparent variability in different situations, pre-performance routines give rise to two other practical issues that need to be addressed here. First, they may lead to superstitious rituals on the part of the athlete concerned. Interestingly, a recent study by Schippers and Van Lange (2006) analysed the psychological benefits of superstitious rituals among elite athletes. Based on an examination of the circumstances in which such rituals are displayed before games, these investigators concluded that superstitious behaviour was most likely to occur when games were perceived as especially important. In addition, Schippers and Van Lange (2006) reported that players with an external locus of control tended to display more superstitious rituals than those with an internal locus of control. A second problem with routines is that they need to be reviewed and revised regularly in order to avoid the danger of automation. To explain, if sports performers maintain the same pre-performance routines indefinitely, their minds may begin to wander as a consequence of tuning out. Clearly, an important challenge for applied sport psychologists is to help performers to attain an appropriate level of conscious control over their actions before skill execution.

Using "trigger words" as cues to concentrate

Many athletes talk to themselves covertly when they compete – usually in an effort to motivate themselves. This silent cognitive activity, or "self-talk", may involve praise (e.g. "Well done! That's good"), criticism ("You idiot – that's a stupid mistake") and/or instruction ("Swing slowly"). A self-report scale designed to measure athletes' use of such self-talk was developed recently by Zervas et al. (2007).

Instructional self-talk – or the use of trigger words – is widely used by elite sports performers. For example, the British Olympic athlete Paula Radcliffe, who won the 2007 New York City Marathon, reported counting her steps silently to herself in an effort to maintain her concentration in a race. As she explains:

> when I count to 100 three times, it's a mile. It helps me to focus on the moment and not to think about how many miles I have to go. I concentrate on breathing and striding, and I go within myself.
>
> (Cited in Kolata, 2007: 1)

Similarly, consider the use of covert verbal cues by Michael Lynagh, the former Australian international rugby union player, as he prepared to take a penalty kick during the World Cup final against England in 1991: "Five steps back, three to the left, and kick through the ball" (cited in Brolly, 2007: 93). Clearly, such words are intended to improve athletes' focusing skills. A similar use of trigger words occurred during the 2002 Wimbledon ladies' singles tennis final between the Williams sisters. In this match, Serena Williams (who defeated Venus 7–6, 6–3) was observed by millions of viewers to read something as she sat down during the change-overs between games. Afterwards, she explained that she had been reading notes that she had written to herself as trigger words or instructional cues to remind her to "hit in front" or "stay low" (R. Williams, 2002: 6). She used a similar strategy in 2007 in Wimbledon when she defeated Daniela Hantuchova in the fourth round of the tournament. On this occasion, she used phrases like "get low", "add spin" and "move up" (Martin, 2007).

As a cognitive self-regulatory strategy, self-talk may enhance concentration skills (Williams and Leffingwell, 2002). In particular, Landin and Herbert (1999) discovered that tennis players who had been trained to use instructional cues or trigger words (such as "split, turn") attributed their improved performance to enhanced concentration on court. Unfortunately, only a few studies have been conducted on the impact of self-talk on concentration processes in athletes. In one of these studies, Hatzigeorgiadis *et al.* (2004) encouraged participants to use instructional self-talk (e.g. "ball, target") in an effort to concentrate on the most important elements of the execution of an open skill (e.g. water-polo ball throwing). They found that this use of self-talk not only improved skilled performance in water-polo but also decreased the prevalence of intrusive thoughts among the players concerned.

Theoretically, it seems plausible that instructional self-statements enhance attentional skills by reminding performers on what to focus on in a given situation. For example, total novices in golf may miss the ball completely on the fairway in the early stages of learning to swing the club properly. So, in an effort to overcome this problem, golf instructors may advise learners to concentrate on sweeping the grass rather than hitting the ball. This trigger phrase ensures that learners stay "down" on the ball instead of looking up to see where it went.

In general, sport-psychology textbooks (e.g. Moran, 2004) recommend that trigger words should be short, vivid and positively phrased to yield maximum benefits. Ideally, these words should also emphasise positive targets (what to aim for) rather than negative ones (what to avoid).

Engaging in mental practice

The term mental practice (MP) or "visualisation" refers to the systematic use of mental imagery in order to rehearse physical actions. It involves "seeing" and "feeling" a skill in one's imagination before actually executing it (Driskell et al., 1994). Although there is considerable empirical evidence that MP facilitates skill learning and performance, its status as a concentration technique remains uncertain. Anecdotally, however, mental imagery is used widely by performers for the purpose of focusing optimally. For example, visualisation can be valuable in blocking out negative thoughts, as Darren Clarke, the Irish Ryder Cup golfer, revealed recently:

> Visualising things is massively important. If you don't visualise, then you allow other negative thoughts to enter your head. Not visualising is almost like having a satellite navigation system in your car, but not entering your destination into it. The machinery can only work if you put everything in there.
>
> (Clarke, 2005: 3)

A more conventional use of imagery was reported by Mike Atherton, the former England cricket captain, who used to prepare mentally for test matches by actually going to the match venue and visualising, "who's going to bowl, how they are going to bowl ... so that nothing can come as a surprise" (cited in Selvey, 1998: 2). From this quotation, it seems that imagery helps performers to prepare for various hypothetical scenarios, thereby ensuring that they will not be distracted by unexpected events. However, this hypothesis has not been tested empirically to date. Therefore, despite the fact that mental imagery is known to improve athletic performance, its status as a concentration technique is uncertain.

In summary, we have reviewed four psychological techniques that are used regularly by coaches, athletes and sport psychologists in an effort to improve concentration skills. Although each of these techniques seems plausible and has some empirical support, no published research is available in which these techniques have been evaluated in combination as an intervention pro-gramme to enhance athletes' focusing skills. Accordingly, an urgent priority for future researchers in this field is a study designed to evaluate an atten-tional skills programme for elite athletes in field settings using some or all of the preceding four psychological techniques. It is only through such research that the relative efficacy of focusing techniques in sport can be assessed adequately.

New directions in research on concentration processes

Despite a considerable amount of research on attentional processes in athletes, some thorny old problems remain. The purpose of this section of the chapter is to identify these unresolved issued and to sketch some potentially fruitful new directions for research in this field.

To begin with, as is evident from the insights of athletes such as Petr Cech earlier in this chapter, further research is required on the "meta-attentional" processes of athletes – namely, their intuitive theories about how their own concentration systems work. As yet, however, we know very little about the nature and accuracy of athletes' theories of how their own mental processes operate. Next, we need to address the question of why athletes lose their concentration so easily in competitive situations. Unfortunately, until recently, few studies addressed this topic. As a consequence, little empirical evidence has accumulated on the influence of internal distractions (i.e. those which arise from athletes' own thoughts and feelings) on athletic performance. However, with the advent of Wegner's (1994, 2002) ironic processes model and the development of self-report measures of athletes' susceptibility to cognitive interference (e.g. see the test developed by Hatzigeorgiadis and Biddle, 2000), useful theories and measurement tools have emerged to help researchers to explore the mechanisms underlying athletes' internal distractions. Third, Simons (1999) raised the old question of whether or not sport performers *really* know precisely what they should be concentrating on in different sport situations. This question is often neglected by sport psychologists in their enthusiasm to provide practical assistance to athletes. As a possible solution to this problem, Simons (1999) recommended that instead of exhorting players to "watch the ball", sport psychology consultants should ask questions such as "What way was the ball spinning as it came to you?" or "Did you guess correctly where it would land"? Fourth, additional research is required on the relationship between the *structure* of various athletic activities and their attentional demands. For example, do untimed games such as golf place different cognitive demands on athletes' concentration systems as compared with those imposed by timed activities (e.g. football)? If so, what theoretical mechanisms could account for such differences? A related issue concerns the *type* of concentration required for success in various sports. Intuitively, it seems reasonable to expect that sports such as weightlifting may require short periods of intense concentration, while others (e.g. cycling) may demand sustained alertness for a longer duration. If this idea is supported by empirical research, is it reasonable to expect that the same concentration intervention packages should work equally well in all sports? Unfortunately, many applied sport psychologists advocate a "one size fits all" approach in promoting the same toolbox of psychological strategies (e.g. goal setting, self-talk) for a variety of different athletic problems. Next, what is the best way to measure concentration skills in athletes? Although a number of approaches to this question have been proposed in sport psychology (e.g. the psychometric, neuroscientific and experimental paradigms; see Moran, 2004: 108–113), there is a dearth of validation data on tests of concentration in sport. This situation needs to be addressed urgently because without adequate measures of concentration skills, it is impossible to evaluate the efficacy of intervention programmes purporting to improve athletes' attentional skills. Finally, additional theoretically driven research is needed to establish the precise mechanisms by which emotions (such as anxiety) affect athletes' concentration processes. An interesting recent example of such research is Wilson et al.'s (2007) attempt to arbitrate empirically between different theoretical accounts of choking in athletes.

References

Abernethy, B. (2001). Attention. In R. N. Singer, H. A. Hausenblas and C. M. Janelle (eds), Handbook of sport psychology (2nd edn, pp. 53–85). New York: John Wiley.

Ashcraft, M. (2006). Cognition (4th edn). New Jersey: Pearson.

Baddeley, A. D. (1986). Working memory. Oxford: Clarendon Press.

Baddeley, A. (2003). Working memory: looking back and looking forward. Nature Reviews Neuroscience, 4, 829–839.

Bannister, R. (2004). Fear of failure haunted me right to the last second. The Guardian, 1 May, p. 12 (Sport).

Baumeister, R. F. (1984). Choking under pressure: self-consciousness and the paradoxical effects of incentives on skilled performance. Journal of Personality and Social Psychology, 46, 610–620.

Beilock, S. L. and Carr, T. H. (2001). On the fragility of skilled performance: what governs choking under pressure? Journal of Experimental Psychology: General, 130, 701–725.

Broadbent, D. E. (1958). Perception and communication. London: Pergamon Press.

Brolly, J. (2007). How to win Sam or Liam? Start as you aim to finish. The Irish Mail on Sunday, 14 January, p. 93.

Caserta, R. J., Young, J. and Janelle, C. M. (2007). Old dogs, new tricks: perceptual skills of senior tennis players. Journal of Sport and Exercise Psychology, 29, 479–497.

Castaneda, B. and Gray, R. (2007). Effects of focus of attention on baseball performance in players of differing skill levels. Journal of Sport and Exercise Psychology, 29, 60–77.

Clarke, D. (with K. Morris). (2005). Golf – the mind factor. London: Hodder and Stoughton.

Claxton, G. (2006). The wayward mind: an intimate history of the unconscious. London: Abacus.

Driskell, J. E., Copper, C. and Moran, A. (1994). Does mental practice enhance performance? Journal of Applied Psychology, 79, 481–492.

English, A. (2006). Munster: our road to glory. Dublin: Penguin.

Eriksen, C. W. and St James, J. D. (1986). Visual attention within and around the field of local attention: a zoom lens model. Perception and Psychophysics, 40, 225–240.

Evening Herald (2001). One Tiger that will never crouch. Evening Herald, 9 April, p. 61.

Eysenck, M. W. and Calvo, M. (1992). Anxiety and performance: the processing efficiency theory. Cognition and Emotion, 6, 409–434.

Eysenck, M. W., Derakshan, N., Santos, R. and Calvo, M. G. (2007). Anxiety and cognitive performance: attentional control theory. Emotion, 7, 336–353.

Fanning, D. (2002). Coping with a stress factor. Sunday Independent, 6 October, p. 6 (Sport).

Fernandez-Duque, D. and Johnson, M. L. (1999). Attention metaphors: how metaphors guide the cognitive psychology of attention. *Cognitive Science*, 23, 83–116.

Gilleece, D. (1999). So near and yet so far. The *Irish Times*, 6 July, p. 23.

Goldstein, E. B. (2008). *Cognitive psychology: connecting mind, research, and everyday experience* (2nd edn). Belmont, CA: Thompson/Wadsworth.

Goodbody, J. and Nichols, P. (2004). Marathon marred by invader's attack on race leader. *The Times*, 30 August, p. 1 (Sport).

Gouju, J.-L., Vermersch, P. and Bouthier, D. (2007). A psycho-phenomenological approach to sport psychology: the presence of the opponents in hurdle races. *Journal of Applied Sport Psychology*, 19, 173–186.

Greenlees, I. and Moran, A. (eds). (2003). *Concentration skills training in sport*. Leicester: The British Psychological Society (Sport and Exercise Psychology Division).

Greenlees, I., Thelwell, R. and Holder, T. (2006). Examining the efficacy of the concentration grid exercise as a concentration enhancement exercise. *Psychology of Sport and Exercise*, 7, 29–39.

Gucciardi, D. F. and Dimmock, J. A. (2008). Choking under pressure in sensorimotor skills: conscious processing or depleted attentional resources? *Psychology of Sport and Exercise*, 9, 45–59.

Hanin, Y. (ed.). (2000). *Emotions in sport*. Champaign, IL: Human Kinetics.

Hardy, L. and Jones, J. G. (1994). Current issues and future directions for performance-related research in sport psychology. *Journal of Sports Sciences*, 12, 61–92.

Harmison, R. J. (2007). Peak performance in sport: identifying ideal performance states and developing athletes' psychological skills. *Professional Psychology: Research and Practice*, 37, 233–243.

Hatzigeorgiadis, A. and Biddle, S. J. H. (2000). Assessing cognitive interference in sport: development of the Thought Occurrence Questionnaire for Sport. *Anxiety, Stress, and Coping*, 13, 65–86.

Hatzigeorgiadis, A., Theodorakis, Y. and Zourbanos, N. (2004). Self-talk in the swimming pool: the effects of self-talk on thought content and performance on water-polo tasks. *Journal of Applied Sport Psychology*, 16, 138–150.

Hodge, K. and McKenzie, A. (1999). *Thinking rugby: training your mind for peak performance*. Auckland: Reed.

Jackson, R. C. (2003). Pre-performance routine consistency: temporal analysis of goal kicking in the Rugby Union World Cup. *Journal of Sports Sciences*, 21, 803–814.

Jackson, R. C. and Baker, J. S. (2001). Routines, rituals, and rugby: case study of a world class goal kicker. *The Sport Psychologist*, 15, 48–65.

Jackson, R. C. and Roberts, G. C. (1992). Positive performance states of athletes: toward a conceptual understanding of peak performance. *The Sport Psychologist*, 6, 156–171.

James, W. (1890). *Principles of psychology*. New York: Holt, Rinehart and Winston.

Janelle, C. M. (1999). Ironic mental processes in sport: implications for sport psychologists. *The Sport Psychologist*, 13, 201–220.

Jones, M. (2007). Open minded. *Mad About Sport* (issue 9), pp. 10–13 (supplement to the *Sunday Tribune*, 23 December).

Kahneman, D. (1973). *Attention and effort*. New York: Prentice-Hall.

Kingston, K. and Hardy, L. (1997). Effects of different types of goals on processes that support performance. *The Sport Psychologist*, 11, 277–293.

Kolata, P. (2007). I'm not really running, I'm not really running ... The *New York Times*. Retrieved 6 December 2007, from www.nytimes.com/2007/12/06/health/nutrition/06Best.html.

Landin, D. and Herbert, E. P. (1999). The influence of self-talk on the performance of skilled female tennis players. *Journal of Applied Sport Psychology*, 11, 263–282.

Locke, E. A. and Latham, G. P. (2006). New directions in goal-setting theory. *Current Directions in Psychological Science*, 15, 265–278.

Lonsdale, C. and Tam, J. T. M. (2008). On the temporal and behavioural consistency of pre-performance routines: an intra-individual analysis of elite basketball players' free throw shooting accuracy. *Journal of Sports Sciences*, 26, 259–266.

Luck, S. J. and Vecera, S. P. (2002). Attention. In H. Pashler (ed.), *Stevens' Handbook of experimental psychology* (3rd edn, Vol. 1, pp. 235–286). New York: John Wiley.

McElree, B. and Dosher, B. A. (1989). Serial position and set size in short-term memory: the time course of recognition. *Journal of Experimental Psychology: General*, 118, 346–373.

Mair, L. (2004). Cool Goosen rides the storm. The *Daily Telegraph*, 22 June, p. S10 (Sport).

Martin, A. (2007). More than words: Book of Serena the answer to Williams' prayers. The *Guardian*, 3 July, p. 5 (Sport).

Masters, R. S. W. (1992). Knowledge, "knerves" and know-how: the role of explicit versus implicit knowledge in the breakdown of complex motor skill under pressure. *British Journal of Psychology*, 83, 343–358.

Matlin, M. (2005). *Cognition* (6th edn). New York: Holt Rinehart Winston.

Maynard, I. (1998). *Improving concentration*. Headingley: The National Coaching Foundation.

Merikle, P. (2007). Preconscious processing. In M. Velmans and S. Schneider (eds), *The Blackwell companion to consciousness* (pp. 512–524). Oxford: Blackwell.

Moran, A. P. (1996). *The psychology of concentration in sport performers: a cognitive analysis*. Hove: Psychology Press.

Moran, A. P. (2003). The state of concentration skills training in applied sport psychology. In I. Greenlees and A. Moran (eds), *Concentration skills training in sport* (pp. 7–19). Leicester: The British Psychological Society (Division of Sport and Exercise Psychology).

Moran, A. P. (2004). *Sport and exercise psychology: a critical introduction*. London: Psychology Press/Routledge.

Moran, A. P. and Summers, J. (2004). Attention in sport. In T. Morris and J. Summers (eds), *Sport psychology: theory, applications and issues* (2nd edn, pp. 101–120). Brisbane: John Wiley.

Moran, G. (2005). Oh dear, so near but yet so far away. The *Irish Times*, 12 July, p. 21.

Nadel, L. and Piattelli-Palmarini, M. (2002). What is cognitive science? In L. Nadel (ed.), *Encyclopaedia of cognitive science* (Vol. 1, pp. xiii–xli). London: Nature Publishing Group.

Navon, D. and Gopher, D. (1979). On the economy of the human-processing system. *Psychological Review*, 86, 214–255.

Nideffer, R. (1976). Test of attentional and interpersonal style. *Journal of Personality and Social Psychology*, 34, 394–404.

Orlick, T. (1990). *In pursuit of excellence*. Champaign, IL: Leisure Press.

Palmeri, T. J. (2002). Automaticity. In L. Nadel (ed.), *Encyclopaedia of cognitive science* (Vol. 1, pp. 290–301). London: Nature Publishing Group.

Pashler, H. (ed.). (1998). *Attention*. Hove: Psychology Press.

Perkins-Ceccato, N., Passmore, S. R. and Lee, T. D. (2003). Effects of focus of attention depend on golfers' skill. *Journal of Sports Sciences*, 21, 593–600.

Posner, M. I. (1980). Orienting of attention: the VIIth Sir Frederic Bartlett lecture. *Quarterly Journal of Experimental Psychology*, 32A, 3–25.

Posner, M. I. and Rothbart, M. K. (2007). Research on attention networks as a model for the integration of a psychological science. *Annual Review of Psychology*, 58, 1–23.

Schippers, M. C. and Van Lange, P. A. (2006). The psychological benefits of superstitious rituals in top sport: a study among top sportspersons. *Journal of Applied Social Psychology*, 36, 2532–2553.

Schmid, A. and Peper, E. (1998). Strategies for training concentration. In J. M. Williams (ed.), *Applied sport psychology: personal growth to peak performance* (pp. 316–328). Mountain View, CA: Mayfield.

Schmidt, R. A. and Lee, T. D. (1999). *Motor control and learning: a behavioural emphasis* (3rd edn). Champaign, IL: Human Kinetics.

Selvey, M. (1998). Getting up for the Ashes. The *Guardian*, 20 November, p. 2 (Sport).

Shaw, D. (2002). Confidence and the pre-shot routine in golf: a case study. In I. Cockerill (ed.), *Solutions in sport psychology* (pp. 108–119). London: Thomson.

Simons, J. (1999). Concentration. In M. A. Thompson, R. A. Vernacchia and W. E. More (eds), *Case studies in applied sport psychology: an educational approach* (pp. 89–114). Dubuque, IA: Kendall/Hunt.

Singer, R. N. (2002). Preperformance state, routines and automaticity: what does it take to realize expertise in self-paced tasks? *Journal of Sport and Exercise Psychology*, 24, 359–375.

Smith, E. E. and Kosslyn, S. M. (2007). *Cognitive psychology: mind and brain.* Upper Saddle River, NJ: Pearson Prentice-Hall.

Smith, M. (2002). Practice makes perfect. The *Daily Telegraph*, 15 February, p. 3 (Sport).

Szczepanik, N. (2005). Focused Cech puts records low on his list of priorities. *The Times*, 30 April, p. 100.

Ward, P., Williams, A. M. and Hancock, P. A. (2006). Simulation for performance and training. In K. A. Ericsson, P. J. Feltovich and R. R. Hoffman (eds), *The Cambridge handbook of expertise and expert performance* (pp. 243–262). New York: Cambridge University Press.

Wegner, D. M. (1994). Ironic processes of mental control. *Psychological Review*, 101, 34–52.

Wegner, D. M. (2002). Thought suppression and mental control. In L. Nadel (ed.), *Encyclopaedia of cognitive science* (Vol. 4, pp. 395–397). London: Nature Publishing Group.

Wegner, D. M., Ansfield, M. and Pilloff, D. L. (1998). The putt and the pendulum: ironic effects of the mental control of action. *Psychological Science*, 9, 196–199.

Weinberg, R. S. and Gould, D. (1999). *Foundations of sport and exercise psychology* (2nd edn). Champaign, IL: Human Kinetics.

Weinberg, R. S. and Gould, D. (2007). *Foundations of sport and exercise psychology* (4th edn). Champaign, IL: Human Kinetics.

White, J. (2002). Interview: Garry Sobers. The *Guardian*, 10 June, pp. 20–21 (Sport).

Williams, J. M. and Leffingwell, T. R. (2002). Cognitive strategies in sport and exercise psychology. In J. Van Raalte and B. W. Brewer (eds), *Exploring sport and exercise psychology* (2nd edn, pp. 75–98). Washington, DC: American Psychological Association.

Williams, R. (2002). Sublime Serena celebrates the crucial difference. The *Guardian*, 8 July, p. 6 (Sport).

Wilson, M. and Smith, N. C. (2007). A test of the predictions of processing efficiency theory during elite team competition using the Thought Occurrence Questionnaire for Sport. *International Journal of Sport Psychology*, 38, 245–262.

Wilson, M., Chattington, M., Marple-Horvat, D. and Smith, N. C. (2007). A comparison of self-focus versus attentional explanations of choking. *Journal of Sport and Exercise Psychology*, 29, 439–456.

Woodman, T. and Davis, P. (2008). The role of repression in the incidence of ironic errors. *The Sport Psychologist*, 22, 183–196.

Wulf, G. (2007). Attentional focus and motor learning: a review of 10 years of research. In E. J. Hossner and N. Wenderoth (eds), *Bewegung und Training*, 1, 4–14.

Zervas, Y., Stavrou, N. A. and Psychountaki, M. (2007). Development and validation of the Self-Talk Questionnaire (S-TQ) for Sports. *Journal of Applied Sport Psychology*, 19, 142–159.

7 A review of self-efficacy based interventions

Sandra Short and Lindsay Ross-Stewart

Introduction

After reading a couple of chapters on self-efficacy in sport, any reader should be able to note several similarities in content – even if the chapters have been written by different authors. These similarities are because the tenets of self-efficacy theory have withstood the test of time. What has changed, however, is the amount of research that has tested the theoretical propositions of self-efficacy theory, and how this research has been used as a guide for the development of effective interventions.

Self-efficacy beliefs in sport have been studied for over 30 years (Feltz *et al.*, 2008). This chapter includes a brief overview of the development of self-efficacy theory and its introduction into sport research. Next, we outline the sources and effects of self-efficacy beliefs in sport. The literature review is focused primarily on research that investigated the sources of self-efficacy beliefs. This focus is intentional, as it is this part of the theory that should generate the techniques that are used in applied sport psychology. As noted by Kanfer (1984), few theories or models provide explicit step-by-step guidelines for developing interventions, but a good theory should provide the practitioner with a conceptual framework that can serve as a general guide for understanding and conducting interventions. According to Maddux and Lewis, "a self-efficacy approach to psychological interventions is based on the assumption that the individual seeking assistance is experiencing a low and ineffective sense of personal control and that one of the major goals of the intervention is its restoration" (1995: 55). Thus, while the sources of self-efficacy suggest strategies for constructing effective interventions, the emphasis is on the importance of arranging experiences designed to increase the individual's sense of self-efficacy or mastery in the specific domains that have resulted in distress (Maddux and Lewis, 1995). This emphasis on providing opportunities for people to engage in new and more effective behaviours results in behavioural changes and initiates cognitive and affective changes that support the behavioural changes and encourage their durability (Maddux and Lewis, 1995). We believe that the autonomy that self-efficacy theory provides a practitioner with respect to the techniques that can be used is an asset, and that the lack of "cookbook" intervention strategies is more practical for those working within the field of applied sport psychology.

The conceptualisation of self-efficacy theory

It was in 1977 that Albert Bandura wrote his seminal article introducing the self-efficacy construct. In this article he proposed that psychological procedures, whatever their form, alter self-efficacy beliefs. This proposition was the result of Bandura's 20 years of personal research (see www.des.emory.edu/mfp/Bandura-Pubs.html) and clinical experience. Bandura (1977) proposed an "integrative theoretical framework" as a means to explain and predict psychological changes achieved by different modes of treatment. He described several sources of self-efficacy, hypothesised outcomes and various factors that were thought to influence the cognitive processing of efficacy information.

Self-efficacy theory was actually an addition to social-cognitive theory (Bandura, 2006). In social-cognitive theory, people are viewed as agents – capable of using forethought, self-reactiveness (or self-regulation) and self-reflection (Bandura, 2001). To be an agent is to intentionally make things happen by one's actions. Bandura's views differed significantly from behaviourism which characterised people as reactors to their environment and focused only on observable behaviour. In fact, his work can be considered a part of the cognitive revolution in psychology. He was listed as one of the ten most eminent psychologists of the twentieth century (Haggbloom et al., 2002).

In his social-cognitive theory, Bandura (2001) identified a network of causal structures that depend on people's own agentic behaviours (e.g. persistence), personal factors (e.g. knowledge and beliefs) and environmental conditions (e.g. interactions with others). This network represents a reciprocal process in which the triadic factors all operate as interacting determinants of one another to explain motivation and behaviour. It was Bandura's interest in the self-regulatory mechanisms by which people exercise control over their motivation, styles of thinking, emotional life and personal accomplishments that spawned the self-efficacy construct (Bandura, 2006). During this time, he was devising new methods of treatment using mastery experiences as the principal vehicle of change. According to Bandura, "the addition of the self-efficacy belief system to the agentic features of social-cognitive theory was an outgrowth of our research aimed at building resilience to phobic threats" (2006: 65).

Self-efficacy is defined as "beliefs in one's capabilities to organise and execute the courses of action required to produce given attainments" (Bandura, 1997: 3). It is considered to be the foundation of human agency (Bandura, 2001). According to Bandura (1997), nothing is more central or pervasive than people's beliefs in their capability to exercise some measure of control over their own functioning and over environmental events. Given the complexity of self-efficacy beliefs, we elaborate on certain characteristics below:

1   Self-efficacy beliefs vary along three dimensions: level, strength and generality (Feltz et al., 2008). "Level" refers to people's expected performance attainments at different levels of difficulty. For example, kickers in American football with differing levels of self-efficacy would judge how many

kicks they could make successfully from varying distances (e.g. from none to 100 per cent). "Strength" refers to the certainty of people's beliefs that they can attain these different levels of performance. For example, two kickers may both believe they can be successful from the 35-yard line; however, one may be more certain in this belief than the other. "Generality" refers to the number of domains of functioning that people judge themselves to be efficacious in and the transferability of one's efficacy judgements across different tasks or activities. For example, one kicker may be efficacious in his or her ability to kick, while another kicker may generalise his or her exceptional skills and high efficacy beliefs in an ability to punt as well. These different dimensions are important for self-efficacy assessment (see Feltz *et al.*, 2008).

2   Self-efficacy beliefs are considered to be specific to distinct domains of functioning rather than an overall global trait or personality characteristic (Bandura, 1997). Thus, it would be misleading to label an athlete as self-efficacious without referring to a specific domain of functioning. For example, ice-hockey superstar Wayne Gretzky likely has higher self-efficacy beliefs in his ability to play ice hockey compared to golf or basketball. Going further into one specific domain, Gretzky has been known to quip about his lack of self-efficacy for shooting and scoring on breakaways. It is important to note that although these examples are focused on physical skills, self-efficacy beliefs within a particular area are multifaceted. An athlete may possess high self-efficacy for executing physical skills, but lower self-efficacy when psychological tasks, like maintaining focus or using imagery, are considered. The bulk of sport research has focused on physical task performance as opposed to these other areas of functioning (Feltz *et al.*, 2008).

3   Self-efficacy beliefs are judgements about what one thinks one can do with one's skills (e.g. "I think I can…") and not judgements about what one has (e.g. "I have…"). They are also not behavioural intentions ("I will…").

4   There are different types of efficacy beliefs. Feltz *et al.* (2008) described eight of them relevant to sport. Ameliorative or coping efficacy refers to athletes' beliefs regarding their ability to cope with diverse threats (e.g. stress, unwanted thoughts, difficult situations, pain). Collective efficacy (or team efficacy) refers to beliefs that group members have about their group's capabilities to organise and execute successful group actions. Competitive efficacy refers to beliefs about performing successfully against an opponent. Learning efficacy refers to beliefs in one's learning capabilities. Performance efficacy refers to one's efficacy beliefs at the time of performance or competition. Preparatory efficacy beliefs are those during acquisition phases of learning skills or during preparation time for a competition. Self-regulatory efficacy refers to beliefs in one's ability to exercise influence over one's own motivation, thought processes, emotional states and patterns of behaviour. Task efficacy refers to beliefs in capabilities to perform particular tasks. Additional research has also attested to the multidimensional nature of confidence in sport (see Hays *et al.*, 2007; Vealey and Knight, as cited in Vealey, 2005).

It is vital for researchers to understand the differences between efficacy beliefs and outcome expectations. They are not the same. Outcome expectations are a belief that a certain behaviour will lead to a certain outcome (e.g. physical, social and self-evaluative). For example, approval or disapproval and monetary compensation are potential social outcome effects. Self-efficacy beliefs, on the other hand, are beliefs that one can perform the behaviours that might produce the outcomes.

5   Self-efficacy is *not* considered, by Bandura (1977, 1986, 1997), to be a synonym for self-confidence. However, many people involved in sport psychology often use the terms interchangeably because the latter is more familiar to athletes and those not in the academic arena. Bandura (1997) prefers the use of self-efficacy over self-confidence. In his opinion, confidence is a catchword in sports, but self-efficacy is a construct embedded in a theoretical system. He considers confidence to be a non-descript term that refers to strength of belief but does not necessarily specify what the certainty is about (e.g. a person can be supremely confident that he/she will fail at an endeavour). Self-efficacy, on the other hand, refers to belief in one's power to produce given levels of attainment and includes both the affirmation of capability and the strength of the belief.

Self-efficacy theory in sport

Like other topics in sport psychology, the focus of self-efficacy research studies has varied over time and is reflective of the paradigmatic evolution of the field. An overview of self-efficacy theory is presented in Figure 7.1. This figure includes the sources of self-efficacy, the outcomes of self-efficacy beliefs and their relationships to self-efficacy beliefs. Although the focus of this chapter is on the sources of self-efficacy, we will briefly elaborate on the outcomes so that the reader is aware of the importance of self-efficacy beliefs. Self-efficacy beliefs affect behaviour (i.e. choice, effort, persistence), goals and self-regulation, thought patterns (e.g. attributions, decision-making, and optimistic and pessimistic thinking), and emotional reactions (i.e. anxiety, worries or fear). Feltz (1988a) commented that much of the sport research on self-efficacy had looked at it in relation to sport performance rather than in terms of the motivational behaviour actually specified by the theory, such as persistence or mastery attempts, choice of activities or skills, and effort expended. In their recent book, *Self-Efficacy in Sport*, Feltz et al. (2008) noted that this trend has continued. The study of self-efficacy beliefs in sport should not be limited to physical proficiency (Bandura, 1997); it can include all aspects of performance, like reading shifting game situations, selecting effective strategies, predicting opponents' actions, using imagery, managing pressure and distractions, etc. For a comprehensive review of the outcomes of self-efficacy, readers are directed to Feltz et al. (2008).

The study of self-efficacy within sport started with two systematic programmes of research (Feltz et al., 2008). Feltz and her colleagues focused on the causal relationships between self-efficacy and performance across time, which also included

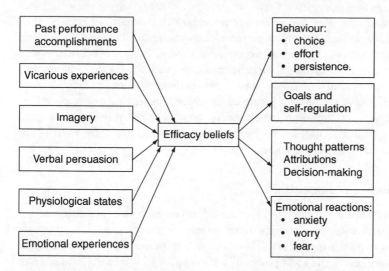

Figure 7.1 Overview of self-efficacy theory: sources and outcomes.

investigating the effectiveness of different sources of efficacy information (e.g. modelling; Feltz, 1982, 1988b; Feltz *et al.*, 1979; Feltz and Mugno, 1983), and Weinberg and his colleagues (Weinberg, 1985; Weinberg *et al.*, 1979, 1980, 1981) examined the effects of self-efficacy on persistence and performance within competitive situations. These research programmes, using college students as participants, were designed to test certain aspects of self-efficacy theory in sport. This theory-testing focus was consistent with the bulk of sport-psychology research being conducted during this time period (Landers, 1983), and this application of social-psychological theories to issues in sport and physical activity developed and sustained the systematic, theoretical research traditions that have continued to this day (Vealey, 2006).

During this same time period, there was also a call to study sport in context – that is, by conducting field research. Many people believed that the profession-alisation of sport psychology depended on providing scientific evidence to justify the use of psychological interventions in sport (Vealey, 2006). Thus, there was a call for applied or intervention research. Martens (1979) advocated for studying topics that were specifically relevant to sport contexts with a view towards constructing theories specific to sport. For example, Vealey (1986) developed a model of sport confidence that is also based in social-cognitive theory (we discuss this model near the end of this chapter).

The sources of self-efficacy

Self-efficacy beliefs, whether accurate or faulty, are a product of a complex process of self-appraisal and self-persuasion that relies on cognitive processing of diverse sources of efficacy information (Feltz et al., 2008). Bandura (1977, 1986, 1997) proposed four principal sources of information: past performance accomplishments (also called mastery or performance experiences or enactive mastery experience/attainment), vicarious experiences (also called comparisons, observational learning or modelling), verbal persuasion (and other social influences), and physiological and emotional states. Since then, others (Maddux, 1995; Schunk, 1995) have created a separate category for imaginal experiences (rather than including it in vicarious experiences), and have separated physiological states from emotional states. The next sections include literature reviews for each of these six categories of sources.

Past performance accomplishments

According to Bandura (1986, 1997), past performance accomplishments are the most influential source of efficacy information for athletes because they are based on their own experiences. Thus, the actual performance of behaviours that lead to success is the most powerful way to build self-efficacy (Maddux and Lewis, 1995). There is a considerable amount of sport research that has examined the past performance accomplishments–self-efficacy relationship. As pointed out by Feltz et al. (2008), the primary strategies that researchers have used include using performance measures to predict self-efficacy beliefs (in regression and path analyses), using success and failure as independent variables (in ANOVA-type analyses) with self-efficacy as a dependent variable, and examining the effects of mastery-based instructional methods.

Overall, there is overwhelming support for the influence of past performance accomplishments on self-efficacy beliefs. In their meta-analysis of the self-efficacy–performance relationship (using correlational data), Moritz et al. (2000) found slightly larger, but significantly different, correlations for those studies that assessed self-efficacy after performance (r = 0.39) compared to the studies that assessed self-efficacy before performance (r = 0.36). This type of assessment variable was also significant in their multiple moderator analysis (i.e. when all other moderators were controlled for). Thus, as a person gains experience on a task over time, performance becomes a stronger predictor of self-efficacy than self-efficacy is of performance. Examples of studies that have used athletes as participants and have shown this effect were completed by George (1994: baseball players), Kane et al. (1996: wrestlers), McAuley (1985: gymnasts), Barling and Abel (1983: tennis players) and Vealey (1986: gymnasts). Bandura (1997) has argued that the stronger effect of performance on self-efficacy is due to self-efficacy being embedded in performance results (for information on how to assess the reciprocal pattern of efficacy beliefs and performance, readers are directed to Feltz et al., 2008).

According to self-efficacy theory, successes should raise self-efficacy beliefs, and failures should lower them. Thus, researchers have used various types of success and failure manipulations to examine their effects on self-efficacy beliefs. For example, confederates have been used in experimental designs (e.g. Eyal et al.,

1995; Feltz and Riessinger, 1990; Shaw *et al.*, 1992; Weinberg, 1985; Weinberg *et al.*, 1979, 1980, 1981). In Weinberg's studies, participants completed a muscular endurance task where they were told to extend their leg and hold it for as long as possible. In the success condition, participants thought they were performing against a person with weak ligaments and a knee injury who had performed poorly on a related leg-strength task. Those in the failure condition thought they were performing against a track athlete who lifted weights to increase leg strength. This manipulation resulted in different self-efficacy scores between the groups.

Although feedback is best considered to be a communication-based confidence-building strategy more related to the source of verbal persuasion (Feltz *et al.*, 2008), it has also been used to create success and failure conditions, so we include it here. In such experiments, participants are told a fabricated performance score. For example, Escarti and Guzman (1999) had college students estimate how well they would perform a hurdle task after being shown the task. The participants then performed the task. A week later, the participants were "informed" of their first session results – one group was told that their task score was lower than the performance time they estimated, and another group was given a score higher than their previous estimation. This manipulation affected self-efficacy scores and future performance. Several other researchers have used this same type of manipulation to test the theoretical prediction that success raises self-efficacy beliefs and failure lowers them (e.g. Fitzsimmons *et al.*, 1991; Gernigon *et al.*, 2000; Grieve *et al.*, 1994; Weinberg, 1985; Weinberg *et al.*, 1979, 1980, 1981; Wells *et al.*, 1993; Yan Lan and Gill, 1984), but only one study has been conducted in the field with athletes as participants. Gernigon and Delloye (2003) showed that manipulated time feedback (which was used to create success/failure conditions) affected self-efficacy beliefs in national-level competitive sprinters. Self-efficacy scores increased over time in the success condition, and those participants also had higher self-efficacy scores than those in the failure condition.

Manipulating success and failure via feedback is similar to using "bogus" feedback. Minimising or exaggerating past performance accomplishments has been shown to affect self-efficacy beliefs. For example, intervention experiments with strength trainers have demonstrated that strength coaches can improve athletes' maximum press and increase athletes' self-efficacy scores by telling the athletes that they are lifting less weight than they actually are (e.g. Fitzsimmons *et al.*, 1991; Wells *et al.*, 1993; Yan Lan and Gill, 1984). According to Feltz (1994), this type of strategy is more appropriate for learners who lack experience with the task, are in the early stages of their skill acquisition and are not accurate judges of their own capabilities. Although bogus feedback strategies are one way to test the theoretical propositions of self-efficacy theory, Bandura (1997) advises against using deception as a performance-enhancement strategy because it could undermine the trust between coaches and athletes. He suggests using strategies that genuinely cultivate both skills and self-efficacy beliefs.

Using win/loss as an independent variable to assess the effects of success (i.e. win) and failure (i.e. loss) on self-efficacy beliefs is naturally a more popular research design in field research. In an interesting study, Feltz and Lirgg (1998) tracked self- (and collective) efficacy scores for six ice-hockey teams across a 32-game season. They found that self-efficacy beliefs were not affected by team-level win/loss (although team-efficacy beliefs were). In their study, Lane et al. (2002) examined changes in self-efficacy scores following defeat. Tennis players' self-efficacy scores decreased following tie-break losses. Moritz et al. (1996) showed that the more successful athletes in their study were also the most confident. Using the same sample of international competitive roller skaters, Vadocz et al. (1996), replicated their results using a different measure of confidence. Treasure et al. (1996) showed that self-efficacy beliefs were the only variable that differentiated winners from losers in a sample of male high-school wrestlers.

Examining the effects of mastery-based (and also vicariously based) instructional methods is another research design that has been used to investigate the effect of past performance accomplishments on self-efficacy beliefs. Participant modelling, as described by Bandura (1977), includes modelling, guided participation and success experiences. The model first demonstrates the task and then performs the task jointly with the learner, or offers physical support when needed to ensure success. The successful performance is considered to be the primary vehicle for psychological change in participant modelling (Feltz et al., 1979). Although we more fully consider the modelling research related to self-efficacy beliefs in the vicarious experiences section, researchers have shown that groups of non-athletes who received a participant modelling intervention to learn a sport-related task had higher self-efficacy scores than those who did not (e.g. Brody et al., 1988; Carnahan et al., 1990; Feltz et al., 1979; McAuley, 1985; Weiss et al., 1998), and that the increases in self-efficacy could be generalised to other similar activities (Brody et al., 1988).

Strategies for enhancing self-efficacy based on the past performance accomplishments source

Before presenting strategies for enhancing self-efficacy, it is important for the reader to understand that the most effective psychological interventions involve combinations of more than one source of self-efficacy information (Maddux and Lewis, 1995). For example, an effective intervention for an athlete may involve the following:

• having an athlete physically practise a certain skill (past performance accomplishments);
• having the athlete watch filmed or live models engaging in specific tasks (vicarious experiences);
• having the athlete image him/herself in similar situations (imaginal experiences);
• persuading the athlete to attempt a new task and challenging his/her expectations of failure (verbal persuasion);
• teaching the athlete to recognise and interpret their arousal and anxiety symptoms as facilitative (emotional and physiological states).

Related specifically to past performance accomplishments, there is support for the adage that "success builds confidence". Generalising from what the research has shown, in order to build confidence one should structure the sport experience so that athletes experience success, interpret their success as success, and feel as though their success was the result of their own doing (Feltz et al., 2008; Maddux and Lewis, 1995). For intervention purposes, there are several ways to ensure successes among participants. For example, instructional strategies like progressions, performance aids and physical guidance can be used (see Feltz et al., 2008). The idea behind these techniques is to think small and influence efficacy beliefs by gradual increases in skill improvement (Feltz and Weiss, 1982). It is important to remember that the ultimate goal is to facilitate self-directed mastery experiences for the learner, so the aids should be gradually removed and abandoned (Feltz, 1994; Feltz and Weiss, 1982): "Self-directed experiences indicate higher levels of self-efficacy to the athlete than do externally guided experiences because the performance is attributed to one's own ability rather than to external aids" (Feltz and Weiss, 1982: 24). Simulations can also be created so that athletes can practise their desired performance responses and coping strategies in situations made as real as possible (Orlick, 2000). Modifying equipment, like lowering the height of basketball nets and using oversized rackets, is another technique to reduce the difficulty or complexity of a task and consequently foster success in learning new skills (Harrison et al., 1996; Rink, 1992). Chase et al. (1994) showed that lowering the height of a basketball net had positive results on children's shooting performance and self-efficacy, and Pellett and Lox (1998) showed that undergraduate college students taking a beginning tennis course performed better and had higher self-efficacy scores when they used a racket with a larger head. These effects were found for those people learning new skills, which may not be the case for more experienced athletes. However, we believe that equipment modifications or changes may work to positively affect self-efficacy beliefs in experienced athletes if guised as being a performance enhancer by changing athletes' expectations of success, although this assertion has not been tested.

The phrase "seeing is believing" underscores the importance of providing people with tangible evidence of their successes (Maddux and Lewis, 1995). For this reason, many sport psychologists engage athletes in goal-setting interventions. Performance goals based on behavioural changes provide people with regular and meaningful feedback and can quantify behavioural changes that may otherwise go unnoticed. The key to the relationship between goal setting and self-efficacy has to do with the effect of reaching one's goals (Feltz et al., 2008). When people attain their goals they should experience enhanced feelings of self-efficacy (Bandura, 1997). Bandura (1997) considers practice goals to be the most effective because they provide more frequent evaluation of success, which stimulates the development of self-efficacy beliefs when goals are attained and stimulates motivation regardless of the outcome. This is thought to prevent procrastination and premature discouragement. Several studies have been conducted within sport examining the effect of goal setting on self-efficacy beliefs (Boyce and Bingham, 1997; Galloway, 2003; Hardy et al., 2005; Kane et al., 1996; Kitsantas and Zimmerman, 1998; Miller, 1993; Miller and McAuley, 1987; Theodorakis, 1995, 1996; Zimmerman and Kitsantas, 1996, 1997). These studies show support for assigned goals as a source of self-efficacy, and their results highlight the differential effectiveness of the types of goals during the various stages of the learning process (Feltz et al., 2008).

According to Feltz and Weiss, both process-related and outcome-related goals should be emphasised. They suggest defining success to include effort, form, and strategy (rather than winning and losing) because these goals are under the athlete's control:

> When athletes give their total effort in a game, there is not much more that coaches can ask of them. Thus, coaches must reinforce effort shown by players, even when winning is not the outcome. Similarly, performance measures, such as form and strategy, must be recognised and positively rewarded because the outcome may not always be successful.
>
> (1982: 25)

As an example, a tennis player may go for a shot down the line, but it may end up out of bounds. Feltz and Weiss suggest encouraging and rewarding the action (despite the outcome).

In some situations, athletes may need to relax their performance standards or goals (Feltz et al., 2008). The rationale behind this technique is that it will help slumping athletes view progress towards future performances, rather than attainment of previous performances, as successes. Doing so may be difficult, however. Burton (1989) showed that swimmers who previously had no difficulty adjusting goals upwards found it extremely difficult from a psychological perspective to adjust goals downward after an injury or illness. Weinberg and Gould (2003) suggested that athletes will feel less distress adjusting their goals if they are taught that it is a normal part of the goal-setting process from the outset. In addition, re-setting the goals so that the new goals surpass the original goal should help convince the athlete that the lowered goal is only a temporary setback.

Another important strategy related to past performance accomplishments involves changing one's causal attributions. Attributions are the reasons people give for their successes and failures (Weiner, 1985). Athletes should be encouraged to attribute success to their own effort and competence rather than to environmental circumstances or to the expertise and insights of their coaches, or sport psychologists (Maddux and Lewis, 1995). These attributions are thought to influence self-efficacy beliefs and vice versa (Maddux and Lewis, 1995). Research in sport has shown a relationship between the attributions athletes make and their self-efficacy beliefs. For example, Rudisill (1988) investigated the effect of attributional instructions on self-efficacy beliefs. Participants who were oriented to see their performance on a balance task as due to internal, controllable and unstable causes had higher self-efficacy and performed better than both those who were oriented to attribute their performance to internal, uncontrollable and stable causes, and those who were provided with no instructions. Orbach *et al.* (1999) showed that beginning tennis players who were instructed to attribute their failures in tennis-ball returns to unstable and controllable causes had higher self-efficacy scores than those instructed to attribute them to stable and uncontrollable causes. Kitsantas and Zimmerman (1998; and Zimmerman and Kitsantas, 1997) showed that participants who were taught to make strategy attributions for poor outcomes had higher self-efficacy scores than participants who attributed failure to a lack of ability or effort.

It is important to note that the influence of past performance experiences on self-efficacy beliefs also depends on other factors. However, these mediating/moderating variables have not been studied as thoroughly. For example, Bandura (1997) postulated that the perceived difficulty of the task would affect the past performance–self-efficacy relationship. Only one study (Slobounov *et al.*, 1997) has indirectly tested this assertion. Slobounov *et al.* showed that self-efficacy varied inversely as a function of dive difficulty. They measured movement variability, self-efficacy, satisfaction and performance in a small sample of six national-level divers. Divers performed five trials for three different dives that increased in difficulty. Results showed a progressive rise in self-efficacy over the trials which supported that self-efficacy could change during a single practice session. The authors concluded that divers acquire self-efficacy faster when practising less-difficult dives.

From an applied perspective, even though self-efficacy beliefs are postulated to increase after performance accomplishments on difficult tasks completed with minimal effort, there is limited research support for this assertion. It may be that successful completion of difficult tasks lowers self-efficacy beliefs because athletes could doubt that they have the ability to repeat the performance. Understanding the past performance–self-efficacy relationship relative to single game "bests" would be an interesting area for future research.

The temporal patterns of success and failure are another factor that can affect the past performance–self-efficacy relationship. Professional sport statistics show that, in 2003, the Detroit Tigers baseball team set an American League record by losing 118 games during the regular season. The Ottawa Senators ice hockey team in 1992–1993 had a record of ten wins, 70 losses and four ties and managed to win just one game on the road all season. The longest losing streaks in the National Basketball Association range from 17 to 24 consecutive games (out of 82). Theoretically, repeated performance failures are thought to lower self-efficacy beliefs, particularly if the failures occur early and do not reflect lack of effort or adverse external circumstances (Bandura, 1997; Feltz *et al.*, 2008). Similarly, a strong sense of self-efficacy is likely to be developed through repeated successes (and even the occasional failures will not have much of a debilitative effect in this situation; Bandura, 1997). It seems as though most of the longitudinal efficacy studies have been focused on collective (or team) efficacy beliefs rather than self-efficacy (e.g. Edmonds, 2003; Myers *et al.*, 2004a and b, 2007). Longitudinal studies would provide a fascinating look at the patterns of success and failure and their effects on self-efficacy beliefs, but it would also be vital to examine the athletes' perceptions of the performances. Self-efficacy beliefs are affected by the information that they convey about capability, not by the final score of a performance. That is, the increases in self-efficacy beliefs are a result of how successes are interpreted and processed (Feltz et al., 2008). Furthermore, to have a positive effect on self-efficacy beliefs, athletes must feel that they have "earned" their successes.

In concluding this section, we offer one final note of caution to practitioners. Despite the overwhelming evidence for a positive relationship between past performance accomplishments and self-efficacy beliefs, Bandura (1997) warns that successful athletes could become complacent because let-downs after easy successes and intensifications of effort after failures are also common sequences in competitive struggles in sport. For example, in their study, Weinberg et al. (1981) showed that their high self-efficacy group responded to manipulated failure feedback by exerting greater effort. Similarly, in their qualitative study on the sources of self-efficacy beliefs, Chase et al. (2003) showed that athletes often perceive a "bouncing back" or "we're due" effect after previous poor performances.

Vicarious experiences

The second source of self-efficacy is vicarious experiences. In self-efficacy theory, vicarious experiences are those that involve observing and comparing oneself with others or with norms. Thus, this source includes the relatively simple act of comparing oneself to another, as well as more advanced modelling-based interventions. According to Bandura, in ambiguous situations, "people must appraise their capabilities in relation to the attainments of others" (1997: 86). He gives an example of a student who achieves a score of 115 points on an examination. Without knowing the maximum number of points one could obtain or the scores of his classmates, the student would have no basis for judging whether it is a good or bad performance.

Self-efficacy beliefs in sport have been shown to vary depending on who is chosen for social comparison. Schultz and Short (2006) examined how the selection of the "standard of comparison" affected confidence ratings using the Trait Sport Confidence Inventory (Vealey, 1986). When completing this measure, athletes are instructed to "compare their confidence to the most confident athlete they know". The results from a sample of 190 high-school and college-aged student athletes showed that the higher the comparison athletes, the lower the confidence score. For example, high-school hockey players had lower confidence scores when their standard of comparison was a professional or college hockey player, compared to a fellow high-school player.

In sport, athletes are constantly "sizing themselves up" against other athletes. For example, based on the results from Weinberg et al. (1980), Bandura stated that "a formidable-looking opponent instils lower efficacy beliefs than does one who looks less impressive" (1997: 18). That is, an opponent who appears intimidating causes their opponent's efficacy beliefs to decrease in comparison to an opponent who did not exhibit those qualities. Bandura also noted that "the mere presence of an opponent exuding high confidence can undermine one's use of routine skills" (1997: 18). In their book, Feltz *et al.* (2008) suggested that one way athletes can build, maintain or regain confidence is by thinking and acting confident.

One of the things most people immediately notice about athletes is their uniform. As an example, tremendous media attention has been given to the clothing Serena Williams has worn while participating in various tennis tournaments (e.g. the "catsuit" during the 2004 United States Open tennis tournament). It may be that uniforms make people more "formidable" or "impressive looking", and as such affect efficacy beliefs. Greenlees and his colleagues have studied this type of impression formation. In their first study, Greenlees *et al.* (2005a) examined the effect of an opponent's body language (posture and eye contact) and clothing (sport-specific vs general sportswear) on participants' impressions of the opponent and their efficacy ratings (mislabelled as outcome expectations: see Feltz *et al.*, 2008). Their results showed that models who displayed positive body language were rated as more assertive, aggressive, competitive, experienced, confident, positive, focused, relaxed and fit than individuals displaying negative body language. Furthermore, the participants were more confident in their ability to defeat potential opponents who displayed negative body language rather than positive body language, and those wearing general sportswear rather than table-tennis specific clothing.

In a follow up study, Greenlees *et al.* (2005b) replicated the findings of their previous study with tennis players, rather than table-tennis players, showing that their findings were generalisable to a different sport context. In addition, they examined the impact of body language and clothing on "attributive responses" (i.e. judgements made concerning characteristics and goals of people perceived) and "expectancy responses" (i.e. the use of information received about a person to form expectations about behaviour and progress). Although their first study looked at judgements that individuals made of their opponents, they did not specify the types of judgements made. Therefore, in this second study, episodic judgements (i.e. judgements made about the states of a person at that moment in time) and dispositional judgements (i.e. judgements made about the enduring characteristics of an individual) were also assessed. The results for episodic judgements showed that when the target player was viewed wearing general sportswear and displaying positive body language, he received more positive ratings than in the other conditions. For dispositional judgements there was a body language by clothing interaction. When the target player was viewed wearing general sportswear and displaying positive body language, he was rated more positively than in the other conditions. The authors speculated that "when viewed with positive body language, general sportswear somehow creates the impression that the player is confident, and able enough, not to need to use clothing to augment how he or she is perceived by others" (Greenlees *et al.*, 2005b: 49). In addition, when the target player was viewed wearing tennis-specific clothing and displaying positive body language, he was rated more positively than when he displayed negative body language and wore either general sportswear or tennis-specific clothing.

In another study, Buscombe et al. (2006) investigated the effect of a male opponent's pre-match body language (positive vs negative) and clothing (general vs sports-specific clothing) on tennis players' ratings of their confidence in their ability to beat an opponent. This study was conducted to show that pre-match body language and clothing influenced expectancies of success even when participants viewed playing footage (which could be proposed to be more useful information on which to base expectancies), and to show that pre-match body language and clothing influenced the way in which the playing footage was evaluated by the participants. Four videos were used, consisting of three tennis players entering the competition venue, walking to a courtside seat and removing their racket from a bag, moving to the baseline area of the court, performing a series of stretches and warm-up exercises, removing their tracksuit/outer clothing in preparation to play, and playing seven rallies. Footage for the first and third players was the same, while four different versions were shown for the second (target) player. The target player was either viewed as: positive body language/tennis-specific sportswear, positive body language/general sportswear, negative body language/tennis-specific sportswear and negative body language/ general sportswear. Results indicated that those who were displaying positive body language and wearing general sportswear were rated more favourably and participants felt less confident in their ability to beat them compared to when the opponent was displaying negative body language and was wearing either tennis-specific sportswear or general sportswear.

In another study, Greenlees and Crosbie (2005) proposed that the initial impressions and expectancies that individuals form of their opponents can have an impact on sporting encounters. They hypothesised that ability level, as well as clothing worn by athletes, would influence how the athletes' performance was rated. Four videos were used, consisting of three football players performing ball skills. Footage for the first and third players was the same, while four different versions were shown for the second (target) player. The target player was either viewed as: smart dress/recreational, smart dress/semi-professional, scruffy dress/recreational and scruffy dress/semi-professional. "Smart" football clothing consisted of a clean and ironed kit with shirt tucked in and socks pulled up, while "scruffy" football clothing involved a dirty and crumpled kit with shirt not tucked in and socks rolled down to the ankles. A "semi-professional" player was one who was believed to play at a higher level, while "recreational" was a player performing at a lower level. Forty amateur football players viewed one of four videos of players performing a series of ball skills. They then rated five aspects of the performance (i.e. ball control, passing, dribbling, shooting, volleying and overall ability) on a ten-point Likert scale. Results of the study indicated that performances of individuals who were believed to perform in a semi-professional league were perceived as being better than the performances of individuals who were believed to perform in a recreational league. Results also showed that performances were more positively evaluated when the player was wearing "smart" clothing.

Recently, LeMaire et al. (2007) investigated the effect of uniform colour on athletes' readiness for competition and perceptions of opponents' attributes.

University-level softball players (*n* = 120) were given a packet containing a scenario and picture of an upcoming opponent. The pictures were digitally manipulated differing only in uniform base colour (i.e. black, navy blue, red, royal blue, yellow and kelly green). Participants made ratings relative to the perceptions they formed of the team and how they would feel if they were competing against them. Participants were specifically asked two questions about confidence: how confident do you think *the athletes* on this team are? And how confident do you think *the team* is? Data were first screened for differences according to the participants' playing position, win/loss record, division level of competition and the actual uniform colour they wore. For how the athletes would feel if they were competing against the team in the picture (i.e. athletes' readiness for competition), the results showed that athletes from winning teams felt more focused, more relaxed, less intimidated and less competitive than athletes on losing teams. There was no significant main effect or interaction for uniform colour. For the perceptions the participants formed of the team (i.e. perceptions of opponents' attributes), the yellow-colour-uniform team was given the highest ratings for "bad", and "not focused", was considered to be the "weakest" and had the highest ratings for "scruffy" dressed. They were also perceived as a losing team, the least impressive and the least intimidating. In addition, the red-colour-uniform team had the highest ratings for "winning", "impressive" and "intimidating", and the black-colour-uniform team was perceived to be the "meanest" (see also Frank and Gilovich, 1988). Results for the confidence items showed that the participants who perceived they were on losing teams rated the self- and team-confidence of the hypothetical opposing team higher than those who perceived they were on a winning team. The red-colour-uniform team was given higher ratings for self-confidence and team confidence compared to the royal-blue and yellow-colour-uniform teams, and the black-colour-uniform team had higher ratings for team confidence compared to the yellow-colour-uniform team. These results show that the colours of uniforms affect athletes' perceptions of opponents, that both uniform colour and athletes' own experiences (i.e. winning/losing) affect athletes' perceptions of opponents' confidence, and that athletes' experiences more strongly affect their feelings relative to upcoming competitions (i.e. past performance accomplishments).

Social comparisons are also part of the modelling process. As noted by Feltz *et al.* (2008), modelling provides efficacy information by providing instructional information, by showing that a task can be learned, and by showing that a challenging task is surmountable. From an applied perspective, models are used as a stimulus for behavioural or psychological change, and in that way, the use of modelling can be considered an intervention technique. Although vicarious experiences are considered to be less powerful compared to past performance accomplishments (Bandura, 1997; see also Wise and Trunnell, 2001), they are particularly useful in situations when people have limited knowledge about their own capability to perform a task (Feltz *et al.*, 2008).

Research on modelling within self-efficacy theory is plentiful. It started with a series of studies devoted to examining which characteristics of models were most important to observers, and has progressed to examining the effectiveness of different modelling types in enhancing self-efficacy beliefs and performance, and to comparison studies where different modelling conditions have been pitted against each other, or some other intervention technique (e.g. imagery). When self-efficacy has been considered, the research designs are typically experimental (using ANOVA-like data analysis techniques) where the independent variable is the modelling condition, and the dependent variable is self-efficacy.

The variables most often studied relative to model characteristics have been model status, competence and similarity (e.g. George et al., 1992; Gould and Weiss, 1981; Landers and Landers, 1973; Lirgg and Feltz, 1991). In general, the results have consistently shown that, when observers are trying to learn a new task, model competence has a greater influence than other model attributes such as age, sex or status (Bandura, 1997). Specific to self-efficacy beliefs, Gould and Weiss (1981) found that using similar models led to higher self-efficacy scores compared to dissimilar models. However, Lirgg and Feltz (1991) showed that model competence had more of an effect on self-efficacy beliefs compared to model similarity. George et al. (1992) found that the model's ability level was more important than the model's gender for enhancing self-efficacy. In all of these studies, the samples used were college-level undergraduate students.

There are a number of types of models, and their effectiveness on self-efficacy varies. Mastery models immediately demonstrate exemplary or error-free performance. Coping or learning models do not. They show a progression from low ability to cope with the demands of the task to exemplary performance. Included in the progression is a change from negative cognitions, affect and behaviours to more positive thoughts, affect, and correct performance. Coping models are generally thought to be most useful in threatening situations, in pain management and injury recovery, or when the task to be learned is difficult (Feltz et al., 2008). Self-modelling involves the repeated observation of oneself on videotape showing only desired target behaviours (McCullagh and Weiss, 2001). Recently, Clark et al. (2006) used the label "self-as-a-model" for interventions when athletes view themselves performing sport skills on video as a means of performance improvement. They distinguished these types of interventions from self-observation, which is the process of viewing oneself performing a skill at one's current skill level. In general, it is assumed that the elimination of one's performance errors enhances self-efficacy. There are two forms of self-modelling: positive self-review and feed-forward. Positive self-review involves using video of successful performances that are considered to be examples of the best the individual has been able to produce thus far. In sport, these may be highlight videos (McCullagh and Weiss, 2001). Feed-forward videos are used to construct behaviours that are possible but have not yet been successfully performed in a particular order or in a certain context. Finally, Rushall (1988) used the term "covert modelling" for when a participant first imagines a fictional model performing successfully and then imagines him- or herself performing the desired behaviour. Using a case study design, he found this to be an effective strategy in raising the self-efficacy level of a wrestler. Recall from the section on past performance accomplishments that another type of modelling is participant modelling, and that it has been shown to be effective in enhancing self-efficacy beliefs (e.g. Brody et al., 1988; Carnahan et al., 1990; Feltz et al., 1979; McAuley, 1985).

The most popular area of sport research relative to modelling has been on self-models. This focus is likely because Bandura (1986, 1997) contends that the more similarity between the model and the observer, the greater the influence on the self-efficacy of the observer. The model–observer similarity is clearly maximised when the individual serves as his or her own model (Bandura, 1986, 1997).

Our review focuses on the effectiveness of self-modelling on self-efficacy beliefs. Early case-study research by Franks and Maile (1991) showed that a self-modelling intervention was effective for training a competitive power lifter. Winfrey and Weeks (1993), however, did not find positive results for the self-modelling intervention they designed for female intermediate-level gymnasts (n = 11). Despite viewing a 60–90-second videotape of themselves three times a week for six weeks prior to practice, the self-modelling group did not differ from the control group on self-efficacy scores or balance-beam performance. As pointed out by Feltz et al. (2007), their study was limited by their small sample size, and they did not use Bandura's recommended procedures for assessing self-efficacy beliefs. Starek and McCullagh (1999) compared self- and other-modelling on the learning of beginning swimming skills and self-efficacy beliefs across two instructional sessions. Their results showed performance differences between modelling groups, with self-modelling producing greater improvements. Both groups improved in their swimming efficacy from baseline, but not significantly so. This study was also limited by the small sample size (n = 10) and the low number of training sessions. Despite using a multiple-baseline single-subject design for five intermediate volleyball players, Ram and McCullagh (2003) failed to find consistent changes in self-efficacy scores across an eight-session self-modelling intervention. They attributed the lack of significant findings to the variability in the baseline measures. More recently, Clark and Ste-Marie (2007) compared self-modelling to self-observation and a control group. Results showed that the children who received the self-modelling intervention had a tendency towards higher self-efficacy beliefs as compared to both the self-observation and the control groups, although these results were not statistically significant. Finally, Law and Ste-Marie (2005) and Feltz et al. (2007) examined whether self-modelling plus physical practice would improve athletes' performances and raise self-efficacy in figure skating and ice hockey, respectively. In the Law and Ste-Marie study, 12 female figure skaters who received a self-modelling intervention were compared to a separate control group of seven skaters. Their results showed no differences between the two groups on any of the dependent variables, although there were slight changes favouring the self-modelling group. Their results were hampered by the presence of ceiling effects. Feltz et al. (2007) assessed the effectiveness of self-modelling videotapes as a tool for improving self-efficacy and the performance of shooting skills in ice hockey. Participants consisted of 22 members of a NCAA Division I ice-hockey team. A pre-test–post-test, control group design with repeated measures was used, such that half of the athletes viewed self-modelling tapes for ten weeks, and the other half acted as controls. Measurements took place prior to the intervention, after five weeks and after ten weeks. Results indicated that the experimental group showed greater shooting accuracy and reported higher shooting efficacy than the control group, with the largest difference occurring after five weeks.

When the effectiveness of modelling-based interventions has been compared to other interventions, most of the results have favoured modelling interventions (Feltz et al., 2008). For example, Hall and Erffmeyer (1983) randomly assigned ten female basketball players to either a videotaped modelling condition or a progressive muscle relaxation and visual imagery (no modelling) condition. The modelling group improved foul-shooting accuracy, but self-efficacy was not assessed. Soohoo et al. (2004) showed that a modelling condition resulted in better performances (on free-weight squat lifts) compared to an imagery con-dition, but there were no differences in self-efficacy scores between the two groups (both groups had increased in self-efficacy scores).

In summary, despite Bandura's (1997) contentions that modelling is one of the most powerful means of transmitting values, attitudes and patterns of thoughts and behaviours, within sport research, the effects of modelling inter-ventions on self-efficacy beliefs have not been as consistent or strong compared to the performance effects. However, given the methodological weaknesses inherent in several of the modelling studies, researchers are encouraged to continue to explore this area.

Strategies for enhancing self-efficacy based on the vicarious experiences source

Feltz (1994) summarised the potential effect of vicarious experiences on self-efficacy beliefs with the statement: "If he or she can do it, so can I." To explain, most interventions based on this source involve people viewing a model (someone much like themselves, or themselves) experience success and coming to believe that they can do the same thing (Maddux and Lewis, 1995). The four conditions that are necessary for effective modelling are attention, retention, production and motivation (Bandura, 1997), and have been described in detail by others (Cumming et al., 2005; McCullagh and Weiss, 2001). Simplified, first, the observer must pay attention to the model. The extent to which this happens will depend on the specific characteristics of the model (e.g. similarity, status, etc.), as well as the person's characteristics (e.g. cognitive ability, arousal level and expectations). Second, the observer must be able to remember the behavi-our that has been observed. There are several methods that can be used to help retain the observed information (e.g. imagery, analogies and verbal cues). Third, the observer must have the ability to replicate the behaviour that the model has demonstrated (which involves including time to practise). Fourth, the observer must have the motivation to want to learn/perform what they have observed.

In terms of application, a considerable amount of research has shown varying levels of support for the effectiveness of different types of modelling on self-efficacy beliefs (e.g. Brody *et al.*, 1988; D'Arripe-Longueville *et al.*, 2002; Feltz *et al.*, 1979, 2007; George *et al.*, 1992; Gould and Weiss, 1981; Hall and Erffmeyer, 1983; Legrain *et al.*, 2003; McAuley, 1985; Ram and McCullagh, 2003; Rushall, 1988; Soohoo *et al.*, 2004; Starek and McCullagh, 1999; Weiss *et al.*, 1998; Winfrey and Weeks, 1993). The key factor identified from the research seems to be model similarity. It is easier for people to believe that they can accomplish a task if they see someone who is similar to themselves perform it. For example, women with little athletic experience have been shown to increase their self-efficacy and improve their performance after watching a non-athletic female model compared to a non-athletic male, or athletic female or male (George *et al.*, 1992; Gould and Weiss, 1981). The research is very clear that upward comparisons can be detrimental (e.g. Schultz and Short, 2006).

Feltz *et al.* (2008) suggested that the type of model used should vary according to what one is trying to achieve. We already noted that participant modelling is one technique that could be used when building self-efficacy (while skill-building). Novice athletes may learn how to execute a particular technique better from observing a proficient model than from observing a non-skilled peer, and this can provide more self-efficacy in learning the skill (Lirgg and Feltz, 1991). However, similar models and coping models provide more self-efficacy information about one's ability to persist at a task and to overcome fear in threatening tasks (George *et al.*, 1992; Weiss *et al.*, 1998). According to Bandura:

> coping modelling is more likely to contribute to resilience in personal efficacy under difficult circumstances where the road to success is long and full of impediments, hardships, and setbacks, and where evidence of progress may be a long time coming.
>
> (1979: 100)

From an applied perspective, Bandura (1997) suggests that coping models do the following: (1) voice hopeful determination and the conviction that problems are surmountable and valued goals are achievable, (2) display decreasing distress as they struggle with difficulties or threats and (3) demonstrate strategies for managing difficult situations. He believes that models who express confidence in the face of difficulties instil a higher sense of self-efficacy and perseverance in others than do models who doubt themselves as they encounter problems. Feltz (1980) provides an example of how modelling techniques were used to help a person overcome a sport-specific fear of water. As noted by Feltz *et al.* (2008), one particularly effective technique may be for the models to describe, and even show, how they had previously suffered from similar problems but overcame them by determined effort. In this format, progressive mastery of problems is described historically rather than enacted presently. This type of strategy may be most useful for athletes during injury rehabilitation. A recuperated athlete model could be used to describe problems, explain how he or she overcame them, and also show that the next stage of the recovery can be reached to a currently injured athlete.

Of all the types of modelling, self-modelling has been shown to be particularly effective (e.g. Feltz *et al.*, 2007; Starek and McCullagh, 1999). For applied purposes, Feltz *et al.* (2008) recommended that these videos be focused and short (typically only two-to-five minutes in length) so they can be watched multiple times. Furthermore, when creating the videos, there are a few additional key points that should be considered. Only those skills that the athlete believes are critical to success should be recorded, and generally no more than three skills should be recorded in one video. If previously taped footage is not being used, then athletes should be encouraged to "go for it" to capture their best performances (mistakes may happen, but these will be edited). Slow motion and freeze-frame technology can be used to emphasise the key components of the behaviour. The video may be set to music which may increase its motivational value for the athlete. Halliwell (1990) showed that such videos were successful in enhancing the confidence levels of professional ice-hockey players.

Interestingly, most readers would agree that, when introducing psychological skills to athletes and teams, a common strategy for sport psychologists is to highlight exceptional athletes who use these skills, perhaps even those who credit their successful performances to such skills (e.g. quotes by Wayne Gretzky and Jack Nicklaus are frequently used to support imagery use). An example that we have used is from Zach Parise, a professional ice-hockey player currently with the New Jersey Devils organisation in the National Hockey League. As he described, Parise images skills, strategies and outcomes related to scoring goals. Sometimes, the image is of a previous goal he has scored against a particular team. For example, if he had scored a goal against the Senators in Ottawa he would go back to the same play and image it happening again. On game day, in the time between warm-ups and stretching in the locker room, he sits on the bench and images himself scoring 50 goals in each net (ten from each corner and ten through the five hole). In addition, he also images three different goals from other players (e.g. Wayne Gretzky) that he considers to be exemplary. In these images, he puts himself in their positions and replicates their exact moves. After this on-ice imagery, he returns to the locker room and images other skills (like making breakout passes). For Parise, imagery is a large part of his pre-game routine, and a key to his mental preparation.

We consider using examples such as this to be an offshoot of modelling. In essence, sport psychologists are using these stories to foster other athletes' sense of "if they use it and this is what they have accomplished, then the same could happen to me if I use it". Thus, this strategy fits into the category of vicarious experience techniques. Whether athletes and teams would be more positively swayed by peer stories or anecdotes compared to those coming from superstar athletes, such as Zach Parise, would be an interesting research study.

Imagery

Although Bandura (1986, 1997) originally considered imaginal experiences as part of vicarious experiences (i.e. cognitive self-modelling), other researchers have included these types of experiences as a separate source (Maddux, 1995). Imagery is one of the most popular psychological interventions used by athletes for performance enhancement:

> Mental imagery refers to all those quasi-sensory or quasi-perceptual experiences of which we are self-consciously aware, and which exist for us in the absence of those stimulus conditions that are known to produce their genuine sensory or perceptual counterparts, and which may be expected to have different consequences from their sensory or perceptual counterparts.
>
> (Richardson, 1969: 2–3)

Imagery experiences have been described as "an experience that mimics real experience. We can be aware of 'seeing' an image, feeling movements as an image, or experiencing an image of smell, tastes or sounds without actually experiencing the real thing" (White and Hardy, 1998: 389). Imagery is not the same as dreaming; people are awake and conscious when using imagery (Richardson, 1969; White and Hardy, 1998).

There is a large amount of research that supports the positive effects of imagery on various sport-related outcomes (for reviews see Martin *et al.*, 1999; Morris *et al.*, 2005). In their meta-analysis of the experimental studies that investigated the effect of mental practice on performance, Feltz and Landers (1983) found an overall effect size of 0.48. This effect size was large enough to conclude that mental practice does, in fact, enhance performance more than just using physical practice on its own.

Recent imagery research has been enhanced by the development of an imagery framework proposed by Paivio (1985). He suggested that imagery could have both cognitive and motivational roles when influencing behaviour, and could be used on both specific and general levels. Using this framework as their basis, Hall and colleagues (Hall *et al.*, 1998, 2005) developed the Sport Imagery Questionnaire (SIQ). The SIQ consists of five imagery sub-scales corresponding to the functions of imagery proposed by Paivio (1985). The scales are defined by their item content: cognitive specific (CS: imaging-specific perceptual motor skills), cognitive-general (CG: imaging strategies), motivation-specific (MS: imaging goal-oriented responses), motivation-general-arousal (MG-A: imaging arousal) and motivation-general-mastery (MG-M: imaging mastering-challenging situations).

The development of the SIQ is primarily responsible for the flourish of recent imagery research (Short *et al.*, 2006). The effect of imagery on different psychological constructs, including self-efficacy, has been an area of interest for many sport-psychology researchers and practitioners. Although the imagery–confidence–performance relationships have been studied extensively (results have generally shown that the most successful athletes were the most confident and used imagery), we review only those studies that examined the relationship between imagery and self-efficacy. These studies vary in methodology from intervention research (e.g. when participants were involved in imagery interventions and their self-efficacy scores were compared pre- and post intervention in an ANOVA-type model) to survey research (e.g. when participants completed imagery and self-efficacy questionnaires and the data was analysed using correlation or regression techniques, or differences between high- and low-confident groups were examined).

The imagery research that has employed interventions has found fairly consistent results (i.e. Callow and Waters, 2005; Callow et al., 2001; Cumming et al., 2006; Evans et al., 2004; Feltz and Riessinger, 1990; Garza and Feltz, 1998; Hanton and Jones, 1999; Jones et al., 2002; Kitsantas and Zimmerman, 1998; McKenzie and Howe, 1997; Mamassis and Doganis, 2004; Martin and Hall, 1995; Nordin and Cumming, 2005; Short et al., 2002; Soohoo et al., 2004; Taylor and Shaw, 2002; Thelwell and Greenlees, 2003; Wilkes and Summers, 1984; Woolfolk et al., 1985). That is, imagery interventions do seem to enhance self-efficacy/confidence levels. Of the studies listed above, only eight of them assessed the effect of an imagery intervention on self-efficacy using a sample of athletes, and of those, only four (Callow and Waters, 2005; Callow et al., 2001; Evans et al., 2004; Garza and Feltz, 1998) had an "imagery only" experimental group. The other interventions were multimodal and included imagery as just one of the components (Hanton and Jones, 1999; McKenzie and Howe, 1997; Mamassis and Doganis, 2004; Thelwell and Greenlees, 2003). The studies by Garza and Feltz (1998), Evans et al. (2004) and Callow and Waters (2005) all found that the imagery interventions increased self-efficacy scores in athletes. However, the results from Callow et al. (2001) were less consistent. Of the four participants in their study, only two showed an immediate increase in self-efficacy scores at post-intervention, while one showed a delayed increase, and the other's score decreased from baseline.

Research assessing the relationship between imagery and self-efficacy in sport does not always utilise athletes as participants. Often, non-athletes participate on sport-related tasks. The intervention studies that have used non-athletes tend to have larger sample sizes (ranging from 22–120), and have a specific imagery condition. The results of these experiments have been mixed, with four studies finding facilitative/positive imagery to positively affect self-efficacy (Feltz and Riessinger, 1990; Jones et al., 2002; Short et al., 2002; Taylor and Shaw, 2002), and five of the studies finding facilitative/positive imagery interventions to not significantly affect self-efficacy (Cumming et al., 2006; Kitsantas and Zimmerman, 1998; Nordin and Cumming, 2005; Soohoo et al., 2004; Woolfolk et al., 1985). Short et al. (2002) and Taylor and Shaw (2002) also found that debilitative/negative imagery had a negative effect on self-efficacy; however, Short et al. found that MG-M debilitative imagery interventions did not decrease self-efficacy in females.

The results from imagery-intervention research have been bolstered by findings from other studies that assessed the relationship between imagery and self-efficacy using non-intervention techniques (e.g. Abma et al., 2002; Beauchamp et al., 2002; Callow and Hardy, 2001; Cumming et al., 2006; Mills et al., 2000; Milne et al., 2005; Moritz et al., 1996; Short and Short, 2005; Short et al., 2005; Vadocz *et al.*, 1997). Because this type of research is typically less time-consuming to complete (i.e. usually only requires meeting participants once for data collection) compared to conducting intervention studies, all of these studies have used athletes as participants. The results of these studies have generally found imagery and self-efficacy to be positively correlated, but there has been some inconsistency in the specific results when the different SIQ sub-scales have been considered.

The first study to investigate the relationship between imagery and self-efficacy using non-intervention methods came from Moritz and colleagues in the mid-1990s. Moritz *et al.* (1996) had international elite-level roller skaters complete the SIQ and the State Sport Confidence Inventory (SSCI: Vealey, 1986). Results showed that only the MG-M and MG-A SIQ sub-scales had significant positive correlations with SSCI scores, and the MG-M and CS sub-scales were the only significant predictors in a regression analysis predicting SSCI scores. In a related study (using the same sample), Vadocz *et al.* (1997) also reported a significant positive correlation between the MG-M sub-scale and the self-confidence sub-scale of the CSAI-2, and showed that MG-M was the only significant predictor in a subsequent regression analysis. In the next study, Callow and Hardy (2001) found that all of the SIQ sub-scales (except for MG-A) were significantly positively correlated with SSCI scores, and that MG-M, CG and MG-A (negative beta weight) were significant predictors in a regression analysis for a sample of lower-skilled netball players. For the higher-skilled netball players, MS was the only sub-scale that was correlated with SSCI scores, and it was also the only significant predictor (CS was not included in the regression analysis because of multicollinearity). In their study with track and field athletes, Abma *et al.* (2002) showed that all of the SIQ sub-scales were positively correlated with TSCI scores. Similar results were obtained by Beauchamp *et al.* (2002) who reported positive correlations between self-efficacy scores and all of the SIQ sub-scales (except MG-A), and also found that MG-M predicted self-efficacy for male golfers, and was a mediator between self-efficacy and performance.

Additional non-intervention research examining the relationship between imagery and self-efficacy has used various "split" techniques (e.g. mean split, median split, tertile splits) to understand how high- and low-confident athletes differ in their imagery use. Six studies (Abma *et al.*, 2002; Callow and Hardy, 2001; Mills *et al.*, 2000; Moritz *et al.*, 1996; Short and Short, 2005; Vadocz *et al.*, 1997) divided participants into "high" and "low" self-efficacy/confidence groups and used these groups as the independent variable, and imagery scores as the dependent variable. All of these studies showed group differences for the MG-M sub-scales. In addition, in some cases group differences were evident for MG-A (e.g. Abma *et al.*, 2002; Mills *et al.*, 2000; Moritz *et al.*, 1996), MS (e.g. Abma *et al.*, 2002; Callow and Hardy, 2001; Mills *et al.*, 2000) and CG (e.g. Abma *et al.*, 2002; Callow and Hardy, 2001). Abma *et al.* (2002) showed that highly confident athletes, when compared to their less-confident counterparts, had higher frequency of use scores on all five SIQ sub-scales. Possible explanations given for these discrepant findings included the type of confidence measure (i.e. state vs trait sport confidence vs self-efficacy), type of sport (i.e. individual vs team) and skill level (i.e. elite vs non-elite). In the most recent study, Short and Short (2005) examined the differences in imagery use between high- and low-confident football players using both the original and a modified version of the SIQ. The modified version took into account that different athletes could use the same image for different functions (the authors computed the SIQ sub-scale scores according to the athletes' perceptions). Results showed that the relationship between imagery and confidence differed according to how the SIQ sub-scale scores were computed. More specifically, when the original SIQ was used, the high-confident group had higher scores on all of the SIQ sub-scales compared to the low-confident group; statistically significant differences were found for CG, CS and MG-A. When the modified SIQ was used, the high-confident group had higher scores for the CG, CS and MG-M sub-scales compared to the low-confident group, whereas the low-confident group had higher scores on the MG-A and MS sub-scales. Statistically significant differences were found only for CS and MG-M.

Overall, these findings from non-intervention studies with athletes have consistently shown that the MG-M sub-scale is positively related to self-efficacy; it is the relationships with the other sub-scales of the SIQ that are less clear. In fact, all the sub-scales, with the exception of CG imagery, have been found to be significantly related to self-efficacy, and MG-A imagery has been found to be both positively and negatively related to self-efficacy depending on the study. Due to these inconsistent results, more non-intervention research should be encouraged to understand the relationship between imagery and self-efficacy (see Short et al., 2006).

In summary, the research examining the relationship between imagery and self-efficacy is far from conclusive. However, compared to some of the other intervention strategies based on the sources of self-efficacy, this research benefits from the use of both intervention and questionnaire (non-intervention) research designs. It is clear that there is a relationship between imagery and self-efficacy, but it is unknown which types of imagery are best used, with the exception being that MG-M imagery has consistently been shown to positively affect self-efficacy/confidence in sporting situations. For the area to grow, more research needs to focus on athlete interventions in the field that isolate imagery.

Another area of future research that would contribute greatly to our understanding of the relationship between imagery and self-efficacy is to assess how PETTLEP-based imagery affects self-efficacy. PETTLEP is an acronym, with each letter standing for a practical consideration to be made when devising an imagery intervention that maximises function equivalence (i.e. Physical, Environment, Task, Timing, Learning, Emotion and Perspective; see Holmes and Collins, 2001). Recent research investigating the effect of PETTLEP imagery interventions has found it to enhance performance more than traditional imagery interventions (Smith et al., 2007, 2008; Wright and Smith, 2007, in press); however, the effect of PETTLEP imagery on self-efficacy has yet to be examined.

Strategies for enhancing self-efficacy based on the imagery source

Imagery is a technique that can be used to *build*, *maintain* and *regain* self-efficacy (Feltz *et al.*, 2008; Ross-Stewart and Short, in press). We think that it is important to differentiate among these sub-functions because, as Feltz *et al.* (2008) noted, athletes' use of imagery may differ depending on whether athletes are building, maintaining or regaining confidence. They defined "building confidence" as when athletes are trying to establish, increase or strengthen confidence levels, "maintaining confidence" as when athletes have a strong sense of confidence and are focused on keeping it at that level and "regaining confidence" as those times when athletes are trying to recover, or get their confidence back again. According to Maddux and Lewis (1995), when situations present difficult challenges, people often produce imagery congruent with their perceptions of low self-efficacy. They cited research showing that maladaptive, distorted imagery was an important component in depression and anxiety. Thus, in addition to building and maintaining confidence, modifying images already used by athletes may be the key to regaining self-efficacy.

To date, only one research study (Ross-Stewart and Short, in press) has differentiated among these confidence sub-functions. In this descriptive study, the authors examined how athletes used imagery to build, maintain and regain their confidence, and looked at the athletes' perceptions of the effectiveness of images for the confidence sub-functions. Participants (142 college-aged student athletes) completed a modified version of the SIQ (Hall *et al.*, 2005). The data were analysed using a repeated-measures design at the sub-scale level, and using descriptive statistics at the item level. For imagery use, there was a significant main effect for imagery sub-scales, confidence sub-functions and a significant interaction between the imagery sub-scales and confidence sub-functions. These results indicated that the MG-M imagery sub-scale was used the most, compared to the other sub-scales, and the MS imagery sub-scale was used the least. The results also showed that athletes used the images differently depending on the confidence sub-functions. The CS, MS and MG-M imagery sub-scales were used more for building confidence than for maintaining confidence, and more for maintaining confidence than regaining confidence. The CG imagery sub-scale was used the same amount for building and regaining confidence, but less for maintaining confidence. The MG-A imagery sub-scale was used the most for maintaining confidence, and the least for building and regaining confidence.

For imagery effectiveness, there were significant main effects for both imagery sub-scales and confidence sub-functions. Results indicated that MG-M imagery was perceived to be more effective than the other four sub-scales, CS was perceived to be significantly more effective than the CG and the MG-A sub-scales and the CG sub-scale was significantly more effective than the MG-A sub-scale. Results also indicated that imagery was perceived to be more effective for building confidence then it was for regaining confidence.

At the individual item level, the analyses revealed that athletes used different images depending on whether they were building, maintaining or regaining confidence. For example, the images "I image the excitement associated with performing" (MG-A) and "I image myself appearing self-confident in front of my opponents" (MG-M) were considered to be two of the most used items for maintaining confidence but not for building confidence. The image "I image myself being interviewed as a champion" (MS) was considered one of the least used for building and regaining confidence, but not for maintaining confidence. Individual item differences based on the confidence sub-functions were also found for effectiveness. For example, "I image the atmosphere of winning a championship" (MS) was considered one of the most effective images for building confidence but not for maintaining or regaining confidence. Another example is the image "I image myself appearing self-confident in front of my opponents" (MG-M) which was considered one of the most effective images for maintaining and regaining confidence but not building confidence.

Interestingly, it was also found that the images that were the most used were not always perceived to be the most effective. For example, "I image myself being mentally tough" (MG-M) was considered to be one of the most used images for building confidence but not one of the most effective images. In general, these results provide sport-psychology researchers and practitioners with a better understanding of the imagery–confidence relationship. The item/image level results are particularly meaningful for sport-psychology practitioners because they revealed the images athletes used and perceived to be the most effective for the confidence sub-functions.

Before implementing any imagery intervention, it is important for the practitioner to assess whether it is the right approach for the specific athlete. Although imagery interventions have been shown to be effective, both in research and in applied settings, they are not for everyone. A practitioner should assess athletes' imagery abilities, ensure that athletes have confidence in their ability to use imagery (Short et al., 2005) and believe in its effectiveness. Although everyone has the ability to use imagery, some people are better at it, more confident in their ability to use it, and more convinced of its effectiveness compared to other people. It is also important to assess whether the athlete has the ability to control his/her images to ensure they are able to use facilitative images and to image events, experiences and/or feelings in the prescribed way. For some athletes, the ability to control one's images is extremely difficult and therefore a practitioner may need to do some initial training before starting a full-fledged sport imagery intervention.

With these checks in place, we offer other guidelines that practitioners can follow when implementing an imagery intervention. First, ensure that the images the athlete is using are serving the desired function (Feltz et al., 2008; Short and Short, 2005). Although researchers have separated images into five different functions (i.e. CS, CG, MS, MG-A, MG-M) according to the SIQ sub-scales, it has been found that athletes do not make these differentiations (Short et al., 2004). For example, an image of a specific skill may be considered CS by researchers, but an athlete may use this same image to maintain his confidence level (an MG-M function). Short et al. (2004) found that athletes use images for multiple functions, and that different athletes use the same image for different functions. Similarly, they showed that some of the images on the SIQ were debilitative to athletes (Short *et al.*, in press). Thus, there must be clear communication between the athlete and the person developing the imagery intervention as to what the goal of the imagery intervention is and how the images affect the athlete. Second, determine which images are most appropriate. Practitioners could provide athletes with a list of images and have them indicate what function each of the images serves for them. For self-efficacy enhancement purposes, images related to the sources of self-efficacy should be selected. Third, encourage athletes to use all of the senses. In other words, athletes should not just see the event, instead they should also try to image the smells, sounds, tastes and feelings associated with their sport. Most imagery interventions, however, focus on the visual and kinaesthetic modalities.

We recommend using imagery approximately three to five times a week for 15 to 20 minutes each time (Feltz *et al.*, 2008). At one point in time we would have made the recommendation that athletes image in a relaxing, quiet setting. However, researchers have recently questioned this idea and instead encourage athletes to image in ways that are as functionally equivalent to the real situation as possible (e.g. Holmes and Collins, 2001). The effectiveness of this PETTLEP approach to imagery interventions on psychological outcome variables like self-efficacy has not been tested.

We conclude this section with one caveat about using imagery-based intervention strategies for building, maintaining and regaining self-efficacy. That is, one needs to consider the expertise of the athlete. There is little value to using imagery in the early phase of learning (Bandura, 1997). According to Bandura, the reason is that the learner may not have formed an adequate conception of the skill to be learned. He believes that skill-learning is best promoted by first structuring the behaviour cognitively and then perfecting it by physical practice and imagery. This finding does not mean that novice athletes cannot benefit from imagery, just not in the early phase of learning.

Verbal persuasion

The importance of the verbal persuasion source of self-efficacy beliefs can be summed up with this quotation: "All effective psychological interventions begin and end with communication, regardless of the techniques employed in between" (Maddux and Lewis, 1995: 55). Although there is considerably less research on this source of self-efficacy, it is important to consider because of its potential impact on all self-efficacy-based interventions. On its own, verbal persuasion is a less potent source of self-efficacy beliefs compared to the other sources presented thus far. Furthermore, the debilitating effects of persuasory information are considered to be more powerful than the enabling/facilitative effects (Bandura, 1997).

The techniques within the category of verbal persuasion include feedback, expectations on the part of others, self-talk, pre-game, halftime or post-game speeches, and other cognitive strategies (Feltz et al., 2008). They predominantly come from other people, although they could also come from oneself in the form of self-talk. Bandura (1986, 1997) hypothesised that the extent of the persuasive influence on self-efficacy would depend on the prestige, credibility, expertise or knowledge, and trustworthiness of the persuader. As pointed out by Feltz et al. (2008), coaches and sport psychologists are usually believed to be credible information sources of their athletes' capabilities and should therefore be able to influence their athletes' self-efficacy beliefs.

The most popular research area within the source of verbal persuasion relates to feedback (Feltz et al., 2008). The feedback given to an athlete can undermine self-efficacy beliefs or boost them (Bandura, 1997). Recall from the section on past performance accomplishments the research studies that used success/failure manipulations. In these studies, the researchers manipulated self-efficacy beliefs by providing feedback to participants. In general, the results showed that success and failure feedback increase and decrease self-efficacy scores, respectively. Furthermore, Escarti and Guzman (1999) showed that self-efficacy mediated the feedback–performance relationship. More specifically, in their study, feedback had direct positive effects on self-efficacy, performance and task choice. The participants who received positive (or success) feedback had higher self-efficacy scores, performed the hurdling task better and chose more difficult tasks compared to those who received negative (or failure) feedback. However, among those athletes who received negative feedback, those who were self-efficacious performed better than those who were less so. Thus, a strong sense of self-efficacy may act as a shield against negative feedback in some cases.

Other types of feedback that have been studied relative to self-efficacy beliefs include bogus feedback (e.g. Fitzsimmons et al., 1991; Weinberg, 1985; Wells et al., 1993; Wilkes and Summers, 1984; Yan Lan and Gill, 1984). Overall, the results of these studies have been equivocal. Feltz (1994) suggested that the different results may have to do with differences in the degree of persuasive influence (were the participants actually persuaded?), the believability of the information (did the participants believe the feedback? Was there a manipulation check?) and the presence of potential confounds (if multiple trials were used, the effect of past performance accomplishments as a source of self-efficacy beliefs may have negated the effects of the bogus feedback). Given Bandura's (1997) recommendation against using bogus feedback to build self-efficacy beliefs, this line of inquiry is not as popular as it once was. Effort should be expended convincing people that they have what it takes to succeed rather than minimising or exaggerating accomplishments.

Attributions are also considered to be a source of self-persuasive information (Feltz et al., 2008). Actually, the relationship between self-efficacy beliefs and attributions is reciprocal as self-efficacy beliefs also influence the attributions people make (e.g. Bond et al., 2001; Chase, 2001; Cleary and Zimmerman, 2001; Gernigon and Delloye, 2003; Kitsantas and Zimmerman, 1998, 2002; Shaw et al., 1992; Zimmerman and Kitsantas, 1997). According to Bandura (1997), those who regard themselves as highly efficacious tend to attribute their failures to insufficient effort and/or situational impediments, whereas those with a low sense of self-efficacy view their failures as stemming from a lack of ability. These attributions then influence one's subsequent self-efficacy beliefs relative to future performance. In general, attributions of success to ability result in increased levels of self-efficacy. For this reason, researchers (Kitsantas and Zimmerman, 1998; Orbach *et al.*, 1999; Rudisill, 1988; Zimmerman and Kitsantas, 1997) have designed intervention studies in which participants have been taught how to make particular attributions and noted their effects on self-efficacy beliefs.

One particular attribution that has received considerable attention by researchers has to do with one's conception of ability as an acquirable skill versus an inherent aptitude. To test the effects of this particular attribution, researchers typically use a manipulation where participants are told that completing certain tasks depend either on natural ability or can be learned with practice (e.g. Jourden *et al.*, 1991; Lirgg *et al.*, 1996; Solmon *et al.*, 2003). In general, those who are led to believe that the skills needed to complete the task can be acquired are shown to be more self-efficacious. There is also some evidence (e.g. Lirgg *et al.*, 1996) showing that females are more affected by the conception of ability manipulations (and that these results interact with the "sex type" of the task). In their study, participants either learned baton twirling (female sex-typed task) or kung fu (male sex-typed task). For females, both the gender appropriateness of the task and the conception of ability affected efficacy beliefs where females were more efficacious than males on the "feminine" task, and when the task was gender appropriate. There were no differences in self-efficacy scores between the innate conception and acquired-conception condition. On the "masculine" task, however, females had lower self-efficacy scores than males, and those who were in the innate-conception group had lower scores than those in the acquired-conception condition. The males, on the other hand, had similar self-efficacy scores for both the feminine and masculine tasks, and they were not affected by the conception of ability manipulation. For more information on gender differences relative to efficacy beliefs, readers are directed to Feltz *et al.* (2008).

Goal setting has also been linked with self-efficacy. To review, goals have been broken into process/performance goals and outcome goals. Process/performance goals are those goals that focus on form, technique, improvement and attainment of a specific performance level, while outcome goals are those that focus on the product of an action such as winning a competition. These types of goals have typically been used as independent variables in experimental research that has examined the effects of goal setting on self-efficacy beliefs (Boyce and Bingham, 1997; Elston and Martin-Ginis, 2004; Kingston and Hardy, 1997; Kitsantas and Zimmerman, 1998; Locke *et al.*, 1984; Miller and McAuley, 1987; Theodorakis, 1995, 1996; Zimmerman and Kitsantas, 1996, 1997).

The relationship between self-efficacy and goal setting is not simply one where goal setting is a source of self-efficacy. Rather, the relationship is reciprocal. Bandura (1997) believes that assigned goals affect self-efficacy and self-efficacy affects the goals a person sets for themselves. This reciprocal relationship has been supported by the research. Studies that have assigned participants to different types of goals (i.e. process/performance and outcome), as well as studies that have assigned participants to either goal or no goal conditions, have consistently shown that being assigned goals, particularly process goals, increases self-efficacy (e.g. Elston and Martin-Ginis, 2004; Kingston and Hardy, 1997; Kitsantas and Zimmerman, 1998; Miller and McAuley, 1987; Zimmerman and Kitsantas, 1996, 1997). Similarly, other studies that assessed the relationship between goals and self-efficacy have shown that those with higher self-efficacy were more likely to set harder goals for themselves (Boyce and Bingham, 1997; Locke et al., 1984). Researchers have also shown that goals serve to mediate the relationship between self-efficacy and performance (i.e. Kane et al., 1996; Lee, 1988; Theodorakis, 1995, 1996). Future research in the area should focus on how goals and self-efficacy are related across time and seasons as both self-efficacy and goals fluctuate depending on the situations the athlete has encountered.

Although the particulars of the self-efficacy–goal-setting relationship are interesting, for applied purposes it is the people who assign the goals that may be most critical. When people assign goals to others, they are engaging in a form of verbal persuasion (Feltz et al., 2008). For example, by assigning a novice challenging goals, coaches, teachers and parents convey their belief that the athlete is capable of attaining that level of performance. Support for this assertion comes from Elston and Martin-Ginis (2004), who conducted an acute controlled experiment examining the effect of self-set versus assigned goals on exercisers' self-efficacy for an unfamiliar task (i.e. grip strength). Participants were randomly assigned to a self-set or assigned-goal group. In the assigned-goal condition, participants were assigned a moderately difficult goal by a fitness expert. Elston and Martin-Ginis reasoned that when the fitness expert conveyed the goal to the exerciser, it would instil goal acceptance and confidence in the exerciser by creating the belief "if an expert thinks I can do it, then I must be able to do it" (2004: 503). The results showed that participants in the assigned-goal condition reported significantly higher task efficacy than those in the self-set condition.

Another way goals are used as a source of self-efficacy beliefs has to do with the feedback they provide (Bandura, 1986). The evaluation of the goals is critical because it is during this time that the motivational and self-efficacy benefits of goal setting become evident (Locke and Latham, 1990). For this reason, Bandura (1986) considers short-term goals to be the most effective because they provide the most frequent evaluation of success.

Another form of verbal persuasion is self-talk. In their book, Feltz et al. (2008) noted that they were surprised by the lack of research in this area given the number of times that self-talk has been mentioned as a way to build self-efficacy. Hardy et al. (2001) found that "building self-confidence" was one of the 17 different functions of self-talk. Our research review shows that when included in multimodal interventions, self-talk led to increases in self-efficacy in studies conducted by Hanton and Jones (1999), Lohasz and Leith (1997) and Thelwell and Greenlees (2003). In experimental research, however, Weinberg

(1985) did not find an interaction between self-efficacy and positive self-talk on endurance performance, although Hardy *et al.* (2005) showed a moderate and positive relationship using a sit-up task. We think that the content of the self-talk is important to consider. Many athletes engage in negative self-talk, convincing themselves that they can't do it or that the task is too hard. The result is that they talk themselves out of the possibility of success. The key to creating successful self-efficacy boosting self-talk interventions is for the person to recognise that they are engaging in a form of self-persuasion which should be designed to help perform or cope with certain tasks. In other words, the function of the self-talk is for athletes to convince themselves that they can accomplish their goals ("I can..." statements). The words and phrases used can vary.

The last form of verbal persuasion we consider here are coaches' speeches. It seems to be that the best part of any sports movie is the pre-game pep talk. In fact, most of the greatest quotes in movie history come from such moments. Who can forget the speech Herb Brooks gave to the 1980 US Olympic hockey team before playing the Soviets in the movie *Miracle*?

> Great moments ... are born from great opportunity. And that's what you have here, tonight, boys. That's what you've earned here tonight. One game. If we played 'em ten times, they might win nine. But not this game. Not tonight. Tonight, we skate with them. Tonight, we stay with them. And we shut them down because we can! Tonight, *we* are the greatest hockey team in the world. You were born to be hockey players. Every one of you. And you were meant to be here tonight. This is your time. Their time is done. It's over. I'm sick and tired of hearing about what a great hockey team the Soviets have. Screw 'em. This is your time. Now go out there and take it.

Although coaches can deliver speeches pre-game, during half-times and time-outs, and post-game, most of the empirical research in this area has examined pre-game speeches. This programme of research has been led by Vargas-Tonsing and her colleagues. In their first study on the effects of pre-game speeches on self-efficacy beliefs, Vargas-Tonsing and Bartholomew (2006) instructed male and female football players to imagine themselves taking part in a championship match. They were then exposed to one of three speeches: informational, emotional or control. The results showed that self-efficacy ratings were higher for the emotional speech group compared to the control and informative speech groups. However, when youth competitive football players were studied, Vargas-Tonsing (2005) found that changes in self-efficacy were related to the amount of perceived information present in pre-game speeches, as opposed to the perceived amount of emotion. The two studies, however, differed in that the 2006 study focused on a championship situation while the 2005 study focused on a regular season game. Vargas-Tonsing and Guan (2007) attempted to reconcile this inconsistency through an exploration of athletes' preferences for pre-game speech content according to various sporting situations. They found that athletes preferred more emotional speeches before a championship game, when competing against an opponent that was higher ranked, and when they were considered an "underdog". More informational speeches were desired when competing against an unknown opponent and when competing against an opponent to whom the athletes had narrowly lost previously. In the most recent study in this area, Vargas-Tonsing and Short (2008) conducted an exploratory examination into athletes' perceptions of their coaches' pre-game speeches. Participants were 151 football players representing ten elite teams (five male and five female teams). They completed a questionnaire at the conclusion of a game that asked them to elaborate on their perceptions of the coaches' pre-game speech. The athletes' responses were analysed qualitatively. Analyses showed that the majority of the athletes reported liking the speech and indicated that the speech impacted their performance, and met their emotional and psychological needs.

Feltz *et al.* (2008) pointed out that research is needed to further examine the salient aspects of verbal persuasion on athletes' efficacy beliefs by athlete type, level and sport. In their book, they list approximately 20 research questions specific to this area. We think that examining the longevity of verbal persuasion efficacy-boosting strategies should also be addressed.

Strategies for enhancing self-efficacy based on the verbal persuasion source

Whether one is teaching novice athletes new skills or refining already learned skills in more experienced athletes, all types of communication (inter-, intra- and body language) are important (Feltz *et al.*, 2008). Many of the intervention studies and intervention techniques already included in this chapter rely strongly on verbal persuasion, although they may not be specifically recognised as such. Interestingly, given the importance of communication, the fact is that with the exception of a few of the forms of verbal persuasion (e.g. goal setting), there is considerably less research in this area when compared to the other sources of self-efficacy. This fact is more surprising because many of the verbal persuasion techniques are widely used by coaches, managers, sport psychologists, friends and peers. In this section, then, we offer research-based suggestions on how to use verbal persuasion to enhance self-efficacy beliefs, but want to emphasise that research in these areas are lacking.

Overall, the key to a successful efficacy-enhancing intervention involves presenting believable information to an athlete in a persuasory manner: "*You can do it.*" The objective is to influence the person's thoughts or actions. It follows that direct appeal messages should be more effective compared to simple inspirational encouragement messages, although this research question has not been specifically tested.

From the research reviewed, we can offer several suggestions for enhancing self-efficacy based on verbal persuasion sources. First, frame feedback by highlighting personal capabilities rather than deficiencies. Doing so also provides success feedback. Athletes should take some time after every practice and competition to identify their successes, because even the small accomplishments add up and help to foster a resilient sense of efficacy (Feltz *et al.*, 2008). Second, advise athletes to measure success in terms of progress made (i.e. self-improvement) rather than using outcome feedback or making upward comparisons. This type of feedback is especially important during the early stages of skill acquisition. On a related note, process goals should also be used at this time. However, product or outcome goals can be emphasised when skills are mastered (Kitsantas and Zimmerman, 1998; Zimmerman and Kitsantas, 1996; 1997). Third, provide contingent positive feedback. Feltz and Weiss (1982) suggest using a positive approach to mistakes that involves a compliment, instructions and encouragement (e.g. "Your approach was timed right; on your last step, though, bring both feet together to prepare to jump; keep up the good work, you'll get it with more practice"). Fourth, provide proper attributional feedback and train athletes to make proper attributions. For example, emphasise success as a result of ability rather than luck, an easy task or lack of effort, and emphasise that ability is an acquirable skill (i.e. a skill can be learned with practice) rather than an inherent ability ("natural talent"). In general, athletes should be taught to make attributions to internal, stable and controllable factors (e.g. strategy). However, in some cases, when maintaining or regaining confidence is key, the occasional attribution to external sources, luck or insufficient effort may be appropriate (Feltz *et al.*, 2008). According to Bandura (1997), if athletes view performance difficulties as simply "unlucky aberrations", then their efficacy beliefs can serve as a protective factor against slumps. The underlying rationale is that these attributions, in these circumstances, can help foster a more resilient sense of self-efficacy because a lack of effort can be rectified more easily than a lack of ability. Fifth, identify and encourage the use of positive self- and task-related statements. It may be necessary to consider the use of cognitive thought-control strategies (i.e. cognitive restructuring) where athletes are taught to make "I can..." statements (Feltz *et al.*, 2008). Sixth, convey positive appraisal information when assigning task (or practice) goals and provide appropriate self-comparative feedback for evaluation. Seventh, design and deliver pre-game speeches with the appropriate content depending on the situation.

It is vital to remember that the debilitating effects of verbal persuasion are more powerful than the enabling effects (Bandura, 1997; Feltz *et al.*, 2008). Feltz *et al.* noted that it is harder for a coach to instil strong beliefs of self-efficacy by persuasion alone than it is to undo those beliefs.

Physiological states

Physiological states are another source of efficacy information. People cognitively appraise their physiological state or condition to form self-efficacy judgements in deciding whether they can successfully meet task demands (Feltz *et al.*, 2008). In his writings, Bandura (1997) combines physiological and affective states because they both have a physiological basis. In sport, however, they relate to different aspects of performance and are therefore often separated (Feltz et al., 2008). According to Maddux:

> physiological states influence self-efficacy beliefs when people associate aversive physiological arousal with poor behavioural performance, perceived incompetence, and perceived failure. When people become aware of unpleasant physiological arousal, they are more likely to doubt their behavioural competence than if the physiological state were pleasant or neutral. Likewise, comfortable physiological sensations are likely to lead one to feel confident in one's ability in the situation at hand.
>
> (1995: 11)

The most important physiological states for athletes are arousal, strength, fitness, fatigue and pain. Their impact on efficacy beliefs is dependent on the situational factors and the meanings given to them. To use Bandura's (1997) example, speakers who ascribe their sweating to intense heat in a room read their physiology quite differently from those who view it as distress reflecting their personal incompetence. Using a sport example, some athletes may play through *normal* discomfort and muscle soreness, while others perceive the same feelings as a lack of personal physical fitness and quit.

Sport research examining physiological states has shown that a person's perception of their physiological state appears to be more important then their actual physiological state (Feltz et al., 2008). Feltz and colleagues (Feltz and Albrecht, 1986; Feltz and Mungo, 1983) found that for participants attempting their first dive, perceived physiological arousal was the most salient source of efficacy information in comparison to actual heart rate and past performance on a similar task. However, there has been relatively little research on the effect of physiological states on self-efficacy beliefs in sport (there is more research in the exercise psychology literature: e.g. Rudolph and Butki, 1998; Rudolph and McAuley, 1986).

Strategies for enhancing self-efficacy based on physiological states

There is very little sport research on physiological states as a source of self-efficacy beliefs. However, the key seems to be teaching athletes to appraise their physiological states in an appropriate manner, which involves the ability to identify serious pain signals. Athletes may interpret the same physiological states differently. Consider, for example, the line of research examining the effects of abstaining from sexual activity before athletic competitions. Interviews from Mohammed Ali report that he would not have sex for six weeks before a fight, and his daughter, Laila Ali, also reports not having sex for at least two weeks before her boxing competitions. Mohammed Ali said that abstention was helpful in that "when you don't get sex for a while, you get mean and angry and it makes you a great warrior" (as cited in Thornton, 1990). Linford Christie, a British sprinter, said that sex the night before a race made his legs feel like lead. Other athletes (e.g. David Wottle and Karin Lee Gardner) attributed their Olympic gold medals in part to their pre-race preparation plans which included sex the night before. However, there are also reports of athletes who have not fared too well with abstinence. Apparently, before the Minnesota Vikings' four Super Bowl games, the coaches separated the players from their wives. Their Super Bowl record to date is 0–4. In their review of the literature, McGlone and Shrier (2000) concluded that sex the night before competition does not alter physiological testing results and suggested that it could alter performance through psychological effects. Marty Liquori, one of the world's top-ranked 5,000-metre runners, stated that "sex makes you happy, and happy people don't run a 3:47 mile".

Using other examples, a novice skater could read fatigue and muscle soreness as a lack of physical fitness, while another could see it as part of normal exertion. Similarly, less-experienced runners could misinterpret an increased heart rate and breathing rate early in a race as lack of stamina rather than as competitive excitement. In these cases, those athletes with the more negative perceptions would be hypothesised to reduce their efforts, rather than trusting in their physical conditioning (although research is needed to test this assertion).

These situations imply that one's coping efficacy (i.e. a person's belief regarding their ability to cope with diverse threats like pain and injury) is important. Athletes with high levels of coping efficacy are more likely to believe that pain and fatigue are manageable and are therefore more likely to control these feelings and play through the discomfort (Feltz *et al.*, 2008). Athletes with lower levels of coping efficacy are more likely to become distracted by their physical discomfort. Bandura (1997) suggests that coping efficacy can be altered through the use of coping models (previously described in the vicarious experiences section).

Emotional states

Although physiological states are important components of emotions (Maddux, 1995), emotional states (i.e. subjective states of feelings and moods) are not simply the product of physiological arousal (Feltz *et al.*, 2008). It is for this reason that physiological states and emotional states are often considered separate sources (although they are certainly related). The same emotional state, just like physiological states, can also be appraised differently by different athletes. According to Maddux (1995), people are more likely to have self-efficacious beliefs about performance when their emotional experience is positive (characterised by happiness, exhilaration and tranquillity) than when it is negative (characterised by sadness, anxiety and depression). Furthermore, people feel more self-efficacious when emotionally calm than when aroused or distressed (Maddux and Lewis, 1995). The more intense the emotional experience is, the greater its impact on self-efficacy beliefs (Bandura, 1997).

Theoretically, emotional states affect behaviour through the cognitive appraisal of the information conveyed by the emotional state (Bandura, 1997). There are a number of factors that can influence this cognitive processing, including the sources of the emotional states, perceptions of control and one's past experiences (Feltz et al., 2008). Thus, the influence of emotional states on self-efficacy beliefs is at least partially mediated by selective recall of past successes and failures (Bandura, 1997; Feltz et al., 2008). For example, successes achieved under positive moods are thought to be associated with a higher level of self-efficacy than failures under negative moods. This potential efficacy-biasing impact of emotional states is more pronounced when mood mismatches performance attainments. That is, people who fail under a happy mood overestimate their capabilities, whereas those who succeed under a sad mood underestimate their capabilities. People also tend to recall more successes from events that occurred in happy moods than in sad moods.

So far in sport, there is limited research on the emotional states source. Furthermore, of the research that has been done, the results have been inconsistent. Kavanagh and Bower (1985) observed changes in self-efficacy scores across a wide range of task domains in response to happy and sad mood inductions, and found that efficacy beliefs were higher in a positive affective state and lower in a negative affective state. On the other hand, when more sport-specific tasks were used (i.e. hand-grip strength and push-ups), they found that mood had no effect on self-efficacy for the hand-grip strength task but did for push-ups (happy participants thought they could perform more push-ups than sad participants; Kavanagh and Hausfeld, 1986). They attributed the difference in results to the type of task: mood altered efficacy beliefs for the familiar task (i.e. push-ups) but not for the unfamiliar task (i.e. hand-grip strength). However, as pointed out by Feltz et al. (2008), push-ups may also have more of an effort component than hand-grip strength, which is not easily influenced by effort. The relationship between emotional states and self-efficacy was supported by Prapavessis and Grove (1994), who found that rifle shooters with high trait sport confidence had different scores on the Profile of Mood States (POMS: McNair et al., 1971) compared to a lower trait sport confidence group. In particular, the more confident group had higher vigour and esteem-related affect, less pre-competitive mood disturbances, and less tension and confusion. Using the Positive and Negative Affective Schedule (PANAS: Watson et al., 1988), Treasure et al. (1996) found a negative relationship between negative affect and self-efficacy, but a positive one between positive affect and self-efficacy in wrestlers prior to a competition. These results have been replicated using participants from different sports (Martin, 2002) and by using measures other then the PANAS (Mack and Stephens, 2000).

One particularly popular cognitive appraisal of arousal is anxiety. In social-cognitive theory, anxiety is considered a co-effect of a low sense of efficacy to meet competitive demands as well as a source of efficacy information (Bandura, 1997). As far as research goes, correlational studies have shown that self-efficacy is negatively associated with anxiety (e.g. Cartoni et al., 2005; Haney and Long, 1995), regression analyses have shown that self-efficacy is a stronger predictor of performance than anxiety (e.g. LaGuardia and Labbe, 1993; Weiss et al., 1989) and path analyses (e.g. Feltz, 1982; Haney and Long, 1995; McAuley, 1985) have consistently shown that anxiety has a direct relationship to self-efficacy, rather than to performance.

Research on the self-efficacy–anxiety relationship has shifted over time. The most recent research has examined athletes' perceptions of arousal or the symptoms of anxiety using a facilitative/debilitative conceptualisation. Given that this research was previously covered in a comprehensive review (see Mellalieu *et al.*, 2006), we highlight only the most robust findings. First, consistent with self-efficacy theory, research has shown that athletes who interpret their anxiety (arousal) as facilitative (often called facilitators) report greater levels of self-confidence than those who view their anxiety as debilitative (debilitators). Second, compared to all other individual difference variables, self-confidence may be the most significant factor in discriminating how athletes manage and interpret stressful situations. Third, a strong, resilient sense of self-efficacy can help one withstand the effects of competitive pressures by protecting one against the debilitating effects of anxiety (e.g. Hanton *et al.*, 2004; Mellalieu *et al.*, 2006) and losses (Brown *et al.*, 2005).

Strategies for enhancing self-efficacy based on emotional states

Strategies for enhancing self-efficacy based on the emotional states source are focused on regulating and controlling emotional arousal; "training the butterflies to fly in formation" (Hanton and Jones, 1999). Doing so should lead to increases in self-efficacy and increase the likelihood of successful performances. Thus, some of the more common strategies for regulating and controlling emotional or physiological arousal and the association between the arousal and low self-efficacy are hypnosis, biofeedback, relaxation training, meditation and medication (Maddux and Lewis, 1995). In their book, Feltz *et al.* (2008) suggested that athletes could also enhance self-efficacy by resting and being more patient.

According to Bandura (1997), researchers in sport psychology should focus on assessing how people interpret arousal, how much attention they pay to it, and their perceived coping efficacy and ameliorative efficacy (which reflects belief in one's ability to alleviate arousal through various cognitive strategies). He argues that if people believe that they cannot cope with a potential threat, they experience disruptive arousal, which may further lower their beliefs that they can perform successfully. Thus, in his view, it is not fear-evoking cognitions in themselves that account for anxiety, but rather the perceived self-efficacy to control them. Within sport, Treasure and colleagues (1996) showed that athletes with higher self-efficacy perceived competitive wrestling situations as less threatening than athletes with low levels of self-efficacy.

Final thoughts about the sources of self-efficacy

From a theoretical perspective, Bandura (1977, 1986, 1997) stated that the categories of efficacy information are not mutually exclusive in terms of the information they provide, although some are more influential than others. Personal performance accomplishments are likely to be the most influential, while vicarious experience, verbal persuasion, and physiological and emotional states are generally seen as less reliable but still important sources of efficacy.

There has been a programme of research established that has inquired about the sources of efficacy information that people use in sport. The first study was conducted by Feltz and Riessinger (1990). As part of their experiment examining the effect of imagery and performance feedback on self-efficacy beliefs and performance in a muscular-endurance task, they asked participants to state the basis for their efficacy judgement in an open-ended format. Results showed that most participants (86 per cent) used a form of past performance accomplishments as the basis for their beliefs. The second most popular category was physiological states (e.g. "I'm in poor shape right now"), which was followed by persuasion (e.g. "I told myself I could do it") and vicarious experiences (i.e. "My comparison to the other guys"). For comparative efficacy (i.e. the participants' certainty about whether they could beat their opponent), participants used past performance accomplishments the most, followed by vicarious experiences and physical states.

Follow-up research was completed by Chase et al. (2003). The purpose of their study was to see if Bandura's (1986) four sources of efficacy information were selected by athletes for self-efficacy (and collective efficacy), whether the athletes used more than one of these sources, and if there were patterns of sources among individual players or teams. Female basketball players from three teams were questioned about the sources they used prior to 12 games spread over the course of a season. The responses were coded as either past performance, persuasion, social comparison or physiological/emotional states using a deductive method of analysis. A fifth category was created to account for "outside sources". The order the sources were used for self-efficacy was past performance, physiological/emotional states, outside sources, social comparison and persuasion. Other interesting findings from the study were that the athletes used practice situations as a source of efficacy information more often than game situations, that negative past performances affected athletes who had high self-efficacy more than their low-self-efficacy counterparts, and that players listed multiple sources.

The only study we found that examined the influence of the different sources of efficacy information on self-efficacy beliefs in an experimental research design was completed by Wise and Trunnell (2001). In their study, each experimental group received three sources of bench-press efficacy information (performance accomplishment, model, verbal message) presented in a different sequence. Bench-press efficacy was measured after each source of efficacy information was presented. Results indicated that performance accomplishment information led to significantly stronger bench-press efficacy than did observation of a model, which in turn was more effective than hearing a verbal message. Performance accomplishment information also enhanced efficacy ratings even when it followed one or both of the other sources (i.e. showing an additive effect). The verbal persuasion message was the most effective in increasing efficacy scores when it followed performance accomplishment information. Taken together, these results show that past performance accomplishments are what athletes rely on most.

With respect to interventions, most readers would agree that successful interventions are likely to involve combinations of more than one source of self-efficacy information (Maddux and Lewis, 1995). In our opinion, it makes little sense to continue testing the effectiveness of a particular source or pitting one source against another. Multimodal interventions (i.e. the combination of several performance-enhancement techniques) should be encouraged. Our suggestion does not mean that researchers should abandon the study of the sources of self-efficacy, however! What is missing from the research is how people weigh and process the various sources to make judgements on different tasks, in different situations and with respect to their individual skills (Feltz et al., 2008). For example, are the performance accomplishments obtained during a competitive season in college sport still a salient source of efficacy information for an athlete now competing in professional sport? How do athletes reconcile their thoughts and feelings when transitioning from one level of sport to the next? What sources of efficacy information are impacted when an athlete shifts from being the best on one team to being a rookie who rarely plays on another team? On a similar note, the majority of research on the sources of self-efficacy has been conducted in a cross-sectional way (measured at one point in time), and therefore longitudinal research designs should be encouraged. Efficacy beliefs fluctuate over the course of a competitive season.

Sport-specific sources of self-efficacy/confidence

In this section, we present the results from two other programmes of research that have investigated the sources of sport confidence. The first programme is Vealey's model of sport confidence which was originally developed over 20 years ago, but was refined ten years ago to include sources of sport confidence. The second programme is Hay et al.'s (2007) recently published qualitative study on the sources and types of confidence in sport. As we will point out, the sources revealed in these programmes have similarities with those in Bandura's theory of self-efficacy. In addition, they also contain unique sources that are specific to athlete populations.

Vealey's model of sport confidence

Responding to the call to construct theories specific to sport, Vealey (1986) developed and modified a sport-specific model of confidence – called "sport confidence". She defined sport confidence as "the belief or degree of certainty individuals possess about their ability to be successful in sport" (Vealey, 1986: 222). The original model consisted of three constructs: competitive orientation (i.e. how individuals define success – winning or performing well), trait sport-confidence (i.e. the belief or degree of certainty individuals usually possess about their ability to be successful in sport) and state sport-confidence (i.e. the belief or degree of certainty individuals possess at one particular moment about their ability to be successful in sport). The underlying theoretical premise was that individual differences in trait sport-confidence and competitive orientation would influence how athletes perceive factors within an objective sport situation and predispose them to respond to sport situations with certain levels of state sport-confidence which would affect behaviour. All of the constructs were operationalised by valid and reliable measurement tools (i.e. Trait Sport-Confidence Inventory, State Sport-Confidence Inventory, Competitive Orientation Inventory: Vealey, 1986, 1988).

In their review, Feltz and Chase (1998) noted the commonalities between sport confidence and self-efficacy. In particular, both are conceptualised as cognitive mediators of people's motivation and behaviour within a goal context, and both are conceptualised as what one can do with one's skills. However, the goal in sport confidence was more broadly defined (e.g. perform successfully in one's sport) than is typical of self-efficacy.

Approximately ten years after the original conceptualisation of sport confidence, Vealey and colleagues (Vealey et al., 1998) revised the model based on a social-cognitive perspective (Feltz et al., 2008). The new model included a single sport-confidence construct, organisational culture, athlete characteristics and sources of sport confidence. This revised model predicts that the organisational culture of a programme and the characteristics of an athlete influence the sources of sport confidence, which then predict sport-confidence levels. Sport confidence, in turn, is hypothesised to predict athletes' affect, behaviour and cognitions. The organisational culture variable includes factors such as competitive level, motivational climate, type of sport and goals of particular sport programmes (e.g. an elite athletic programme has different organisational culture than a high-school programme). Athlete characteristics encompass all of the personality characteristics, attitudes and values of athletes, plus demographic factors such as age, gender and ethnicity.

With respect to the sources of sport confidence, Vealey et al. (1998) sought to identify the most salient sources of sport confidence for athletes, given the unique sociocultural aspects of sport competition. Based on data from multiple samples of high school and intercollegiate athletes, they identified nine sources. These sources are described below.

1   Mastery is confidence derived from mastering or improving one's skills.
2   Demonstration of ability is confidence derived from athletes demonstrating more ability than one's opponent or showing off skills to others.
3   Physical and mental preparation is confidence derived from feeling physically and mentally prepared with an optimal focus for performance.
4   Physical self-presentation is confidence derived from perceptions of one's physical self, or how one perceives one looks to others.
5   Social support is confidence derived from perceiving support and encouragement from significant others in sport, such as coaches, family and team-mates.
6   Vicarious experience is confidence derived from watching others, such as team-mates or friends, perform successfully.

7   Coaches' leadership is confidence derived from believing that the coach is skilled in decision-making and leadership.
8   Environmental comfort is confidence derived from feeling comfortable in a competitive environment, such as the particular field, gym or pool where the competition will be held.
9   Situational favourableness is confidence derived from feeling that the breaks of the situation are going in one's favour.

These nine sources formed the sub-scale structure of the Sources of Sport Confidence Questionnaire (SSCQ; Vealey et al., 1998). The stem for the SSCQ is, "I gain self-confidence in my sport when I…", and ratings for each item are made on a seven-point Likert scale ranging from 1 (not at all important) to 7 (of highest importance). To date, the SSCQ is the only available questionnaire that assesses sources.

The SSCQ has been used to investigate which sources are most important for athletes (Vealey et al., 1998). Results have shown that high-school athletes value mastery, social support, physical and mental preparation, coaches' leadership, and demonstration of ability the most. College-aged athletes from individual sports had highest ratings for physical and mental preparation, social support, mastery, demonstration of ability, and physical self-presentation. In addition, Vealey et al. showed that certain athlete characteristics and organisational contexts influenced some of these sources. For example, at the college level, female athletes relied on physical self-presentation and social support as more important sources of sport confidence than males.

Since its preliminary validation, one other study has investigated the validity of the SSCQ. Wilson et al. (2004) had 216 master athletes (aged from 50 to 96 years) from various sports complete the SSCQ (Vealey et al., 1998) and the Trait Sport Confidence Inventory (Vealey, 1986). Exploratory factor analyses resulted in a model that aligned with Vealey's (1998) SSCQ, excluding, however, the situational favourableness sub-scale. Thus, their modified version consisted of only eight factors. The results from the Wilson et al. study showed that physical/mental preparation and mastery were judged as the most important sources of sport confidence for master athletes.

To date, two other studies have been conducted on the sources of sport confidence. Magyar and Feltz (2003) examined the influence of dispositional and situational tendencies on the sources of confidence using a sample of 180 adolescent female volleyball players from various teams. Participants completed the SSCQ, the Task and Ego Orientation in Sport Questionnaire (TEOSQ; Duda and Nicholls, 1992), and the Perceived Motivational Climate in Sport Questionnaire-2 (PMCSQ-2; Newton et al., 2000). Results from the study showed that the sources that were most significant in building sport confidence were mastery, physical and mental preparation, and social support.

Demaine and Short (2007) examined differences in the sources of sport confidence according to sport involvement factors (i.e. age, total years playing, athletic eligibility, starting status, playing time and athletic scholarship status).

Division II NCAA female college basketball players (n = 265) completed the Sources of Sport-Confidence Questionnaire (SSCQ), the Trait Sport-Confidence Inventory (TSCI) and the Sport Confidence Inventory (SCI: Vealey and Knight, as cited in Vealey, 2005). The SCI is the new multidimensional measure of sport confidence. The questionnaire contains 14 items with three sub-scales: Physical Skills and Training, Cognitive Efficiency, and Resilience. Physical Skills and Training refers to one's confidence in his/her ability to execute the physical skills necessary to perform successfully. Cognitive Efficiency refers to one's confidence that he/she can mentally focus, maintain concentration and make effective decisions to perform successfully. Resilience refers to one's confidence that he/she can regain focus after performance errors, bounce back from performing poorly, and overcome doubts, problems and setbacks to perform successfully. Participants are instructed to rate how certain they are "right now" about their abilities on a seven-point Likert scale ranging from 1 ("can't do it at all – absolutely not at all") to 7 ("totally certain – absolutely sure I can without a doubt").

The results from Demaine and Short's (2007) study showed that the most popular sources were (in order): social support, coaches' leadership, physical and mental preparation, mastery, demonstration of ability, vicarious experience, environmental comfort, situational favourableness and physical self-presentation. Regression analyses showed that the sources accounted for only 7 per cent of the variance in TSCI scores, with physical and mental preparation being the only significant predictor. When the sport-involvement factors were included, the percentage of variance accounted for increased to 14 per cent, adding eligibility and years playing experience as significant predictors. For the SCI, mastery and age were the only significant predictors for the physical-skills training factor (10 per cent of the variance accounted for); physical and mental preparation, situational favourableness, age and years playing were significant predictors for cognitive efficiency (17 per cent), and physical and mental preparation, social support, years playing and eligibility were the significant predictors for resilience (11 per cent). Overall, the sources of sport confidence did not differ according to the sport-involvement factors, but taken together these variables predicted sport confidence.

Hay et al.'s study of the sources and types of confidence

More recently, Hays *et al.* (2007) conducted a qualitative study to identify the sources of confidence salient to successful World-Class athletes (i.e. all participants had medalled in either the Olympic Games, World Championship or World Cup). The participants were asked about the sources of their confidence with the following question: "Where do you think your confidence in yourself comes from?" The raw data themes provided by the athletes were categorised into several sub-themes and higher-order themes, resulting in nine global dimensions. These global dimensions, or sources, are listed below in the order of mention by the athletes.

1   Preparation was defined as good physical, mental and holistic preparation. This dimension included sub-themes reflective of effort, good physical training programme, good physical condition, skill repetition, identifying and rectifying weaknesses, structured goal setting and mental skills.
2   Performance accomplishments were defined as performing successfully either as defined by outcome of the event (i.e. winning) or by achieving one's performance goal.
3   Coaching refers to confidence derived from a coach's ability to train the athlete successfully, and to encourage, give positive feedback/reinforcement and compliments to the athlete. It includes the higher-order themes of the belief in the coach to establish appropriate training programmes, athlete handling, support staff, social support and advice.
4   Social support refers to confidence derived from the social support of family, partners and friends during training and competition.
5   Innate factors refer to confidence derived from an athlete's belief that he/she was born with some innate ability that facilitated his/her success (i.e. "natural talent").
6   Experience refers to confidence generated from past athletic experiences, and includes themes related to coming back from career lows and injuries.
7   Perceived competitive advantage is confidence derived by athletes seeing their competitors perform badly or crack under pressure.
8   Trust was a source of confidence identified by only two male athletes. The raw data themes bolstering this source were "trust in team-mates", and "trust within the support team". This source appears to be related to collective efficacy beliefs.
9   Self-awareness was a source identified by only two female athletes. It refers to confidence derived from personal trust, security and goals (i.e. "Knowing what one is doing, what one wants, and where one is going").

Comparisons to self-efficacy theory

Both research programmes led by Vealey and Hays were conducted to identify the most salient sources of confidence used by athletes within the sport context. Table 7.1 compares these sources to those in Bandura's (1977, 1986, 1997) theory of self-efficacy. Unfortunately, in some cases, the authors have used different terms to characterise the same sources. For that reason, the first column in Table 7.1 gives a description or operationalisation of the source. Subsequent columns indicate whether the source was identified by Bandura, Vealey et al. (1998) and Hays et al. (2007), and also includes the particular name given to the source by the researchers. In our opinion, the programmes of research by Vealey et al. (1998) and Hays et al. (2007) provide additional support for Bandura's sources. Coupled with the values for the most often mentioned sources (Hays et al., 2007), and the results from the SSCQ showing the frequency that athletes use the sources (e.g. Demaine and Short, 2007; Magyar and Feltz, 2003; Vealey et al., 1998; Wilson et al., 2004), it would be reasonable

Table 7.1 Comparison of sources of self-efficacy and sport confidence

Description of source	Bandura	Vealey et al. (1998)	Hays et al. (2007)
Past performances, past skill development, etc.	✓ Performance accomplishments	✓ Mastery Demonstration of ability	✓ Performance accomplishments Experience
Comparing one's skill level to others	✓ Vicarious experiences	✓ Vicarious experiences	✓ Competitive advantage
Feedback from coaches, friends and parents, that lends support to the athlete	✓ Verbal persuasion	✓ Social support	✓ Coaching Social support
Feeling physically fit due to how they look or due to physiological information	✓ Physiological States	✓ Physical and mental preparation	✓ Preparation
Psychologically (emotionally or mentally) being prepared	✓ Emotional states	✓ Physical and mental preparation	✓ Preparation Self-Awareness
Seeing one's self succeeding in one's mind	✓ Imaginal states	✓ Physical and mental preparation	✓ Preparation
Belief in one's coach to put them in the best situation	✓ Verbal persuasion	✓ Coach's leadership	✓ Coaching
Feeling like the breaks are going your way		✓ Situational favourableness	
Perception of how one looks		✓ Physical self-presentation	
Feeling comfortable in the situation		✓ Environmental comfort	
Feeling as though they were born with an innate ability to be successful in their sport			✓ Innate factors
Feeling secure with one's team-mates and/or coaches	✓ Verbal persuasion		✓ Trust

to conclude that the sources from self-efficacy theory are the most important and most used. However, as pointed out by Feltz *et al.* (2008), the distinct social nature of sport suggests that social support, beyond verbal persuasion, may be a salient source for athletes. In addition, the unique sources may have important practical applications for enhancing efficacy beliefs with athletes from various age, gender and ability groups (Feltz *et al.*, 2008).

Coaches' and athletes' perceptions of efficacy-enhancing techniques

Thus far, we have reviewed the theory and research related to the sources of self-efficacy beliefs (and sport confidence), as well as the related research that has tested the effectiveness of various efficacy-enhancing techniques that have been based on these sources. When appropriate, we have also suggested specific techniques and/or guidelines that can be used to build, maintain and regain self-efficacy. Overall, the application of self-efficacy theory provides practitioners with a variety of techniques or strategies that can assist them with building, maintaining and regaining self-efficacy in sport. In this last section, we review a programme of research (Gould *et al.*, 1989; Vargas-Tonsing *et al.*, 2004; Weinberg and Jackson, 1990; Weinberg *et al.*, 1992) that examined how often coaches used certain efficacy-enhancing techniques, and their perceptions of the effectiveness of the techniques. The same 13 efficacy-enhancing techniques were used in all of these studies. They were originally identified by Gould *et al.* (1989) through a content analysis of the self-efficacy and sport research published at that time. The techniques, written from the coaches' perspective, are:

1   ensure performance improvements through instruction and drilling,
2   acting or modelling confidence themselves,
3   encouraging positive as opposed to negative self-talk from athlete,
4   employing hard physical conditioning drills,
5   verbally persuade the athlete that he or she can do it,
6   liberally using rewarding statements,
7   emphasising improvements in technique while downplaying outcome,
8   ensure performance improvements by setting specific performance goals,
9   point out players who are similar and have also achieved success,
10   emphasise that feelings of anxiety are not fear, but a sign of readiness,
11   emphasise that failure results from lack of effort and not innate ability,
12   have the athlete image being successful, and
13   reduce feelings of anxiety by employing relaxation techniques.

Ratings for usage were completed on a five-point Likert type scale anchored by 1 = *never*, 3 = *sometimes* and 5 = *often*. Effectiveness ratings were made on a similar scale (1 = *not effective*, 3 = *somewhat effective* and 5 = *very effective*). The results from the four studies are summarised in Table 7.2.

Table 7.2 Rankings of efficacy-enhancing techniques

Efficacy-enhancing techniques	Gould et al. (1989) Wrestling coaches		Gould et al. (1989) Olympic, Pan-American, national level coaches		Weinberg and Jackson (1990) American coaches		Weinberg et al. (1992) Australian coaches		Vargas-Tonsing et al. (2004) American coaches		Vargas-Tonsing et al. (2004) Athletes males/females/team	
	Freq.	Effect	Freq.	Effect	Freq.	Effect	Freq.	Effect	Freq.	Effect	Freq.	Effect
Enhance performance through instruction-drilling	1	1	1	1	2	3	1	1	1	1	2/2/2	3/3/3
Act confident yourself	2	2	2	3	3	5	3	4	2	3	1/1/1	1/2/2
Encourage positive talk	3	3	3	2	1	1	2	3	3	2	4/4/4	2/1/1
Employ hard physical conditioning	4	5	8	5	7	6	10	10	8	6	8/6/6	6/7/6
Verbally persuade	5	8	6	7	3	3	6	5	4	4	5/8/6	4/4/4
Liberal use of reward statements	6	3	7	4	5	7	4	2	5	5	10/9/9	7/5/7
Emphasise technique improvement, downplay outcome	7	6	4	8	5	7	5	7	6	8	7/7/8	10/8/8
Set specific goals	8	7	5	6	8	8	7	6	7	7	3/3/3	5/6/5
Identify similar athletes who have achieved	9	11	11	13	10	11	12	12	10	12	9/11/10	12/12/12
Emphasise that anxiety is not fear but readiness	10	8	10	11	11	10	13	13	11	11	12/12/12	11/11/11
Emphasise lack of effort, not lack of ability, for failure	11	13	12	12	9	9	8	11	9	9	6/5/5	9/9/9
Imagine success	12	10	9	9	12	12	9	9	12	10	11/10/11	8/10/10
Reduce anxiety by utilising relaxation techniques	13	12	13	10	13	13	11	8	13	13	13/13/13	13/13/13

The first study in this line of inquiry was completed by Gould *et al.* (1989). Their purpose was to examine the degree to which elite coaches used the efficacy-enhancing techniques and to assess the effectiveness of them. In their first study, 126 collegiate wrestling coaches purposely selected from the most and least successful teams in the United States participated. Results showed that the coaches reported using all the techniques, and they were perceived to be at least moderately effective. The specific results for the rankings of usage and effectiveness are in Table 7.2. Further analyses showed no differences in ratings according to coaching success, experience, certification status and division. In their second study, 124 Olympic, Pan American and/or national team coaches from 30 different Olympic sports completed the same questionnaires. Similar results were reported for frequency of use and effectiveness ratings (see Table 7.2). From the other variables considered (i.e. gender, sport skill type – open vs closed, college degree emphasis, coaching experience, sport type – individual vs team), only individual and team-sport coaches differed in their frequency of efficacy-enhancing technique ratings. Team-sport coaches used more instruction and drilling, and modelling confidence themselves compared to individual sport coaches.

The next study in this programme of research was completed by Weinberg and Jackson (1990). They replicated Gould *et al.*'s (1989) study with a sample of high-school age-group male ($n = 136$) and female ($n = 86$) tennis coaches. Even though the coaches were from a different sport and a different level, the results were similar (see Table 7.2). Weinberg and Jackson noted that the coaches tended to use the techniques they found most effective more often compared to the techniques that were given lower effectiveness ratings. Additional analyses were conducted for several variables (i.e. gender, college degree emphasis, highest degree, coaching minor specialisation, experience, win/loss record), and differences were found between masters degree versus bachelor degree coaches, and having a coaching minor or not. Weinberg and Jackson concluded that their sample of high-school tennis coaches were very similar to the college and elite coaches studied by Gould *et al.* (1989), and interpreted this finding to mean that the ability level of the athletes does not significantly alter the types of efficacy-enhancing strategies used by coaches.

In the next study, Weinberg *et al.* (1992) compared their previous findings with tennis coaches from the United States to a similar group of tennis coaches from Australia. Participants were 38 male and 22 female junior-programme level tennis coaches working at the State or club level. Results showed that all of the techniques received ratings over 3.0 (on the five-point scale), again showing that the techniques were used and considered to be at least moderately effective. The rankings from the Australian and American coaches for frequency and effectiveness were very similar (see Table 7.2), although there were some differences between the coaches (these differences were mostly for techniques that were not used very often and were considered to be the least effective). Weinberg *et al.* (1992) noted that the efficacy-enhancing strategies employed most often were those that were under the coaches' control (e.g. encouraging positive self-talk, using verbal persuasion, using instruction and drills, acting confident, and liberally using reward statements). Those that were used less often were generally less under the direct control of the coaches (e.g. relaxation training to reduce anxiety, an emphasis that anxiety is not fear, and identification of similar players who have had success).

In 2004, Vargas-Tonsing et al. extended this programme of research by investigating both coaches' and athletes' perceptions of the 13 efficacy-enhancing techniques. They reasoned that actual coaches' behaviour may not be as important as the athletes' perceptions of coaches' behaviour (see also Horn, 2002; Kenow and Williams, 1999; Smoll and Smith, 1989). Athletes (n = 1,233) and their coaches (n = 78) from various university-level sport teams rated the frequency of use and effectiveness of the efficacy-enhancing techniques using the same five-point Likert-type scale. The results are shown in Table 7.2. Athletes perceived the coaches to use all of the 13 efficacy-enhancing techniques at least on occasion, and indicated that 12 of the 13 techniques were at least moderately effective (the exception being reducing anxiety through relaxation training). More specifically, the athletes gave the highest ratings for use for the techniques of the coach acting confident, instruction and drilling, and setting specific performance goals. The techniques with the lowest ratings were pointing out athletes who were similar, emphasising that anxiety is a sign of readiness, and reducing anxiety through relaxation techniques. For effectiveness, the highest ratings were given to encouraging positive self-talk, the coach acting confident, and instruction and drilling. The least-effective techniques were emphasising that anxiety is a sign of readiness, pointing out athletes who were similar, and reducing anxiety through relaxation techniques. Similar to the other studies, coaches' ratings for use and effectiveness were the same, and were given to the techniques of instruction and drilling, acting confident themselves, and encouraging positive self-talk. The lowest ratings for use and effectiveness were given to pointing out athletes who were similar, emphasising that anxiety is a sign of readiness not fear, having the athlete imagine success and reducing anxiety through relaxation techniques.

Athlete ratings were subsequently aggregated so that each team had one rating (i.e. the sample sizes for the number of coaches and teams were equal at 78). The results from using the team as the unit of analysis showed that the teams perceived the coaches to use the techniques of the coach acting confident, instruction and drilling, setting specific performance goals, and encouraging positive self-talk the most. The teams agreed with their coaches that the techniques of imagining success, emphasising that anxiety is a sign of readiness not fear, and reducing anxiety through relaxation techniques were the least used. For effectiveness, teams indicated that encouraging positive self-talk, the coach acting confident, and instruction and drilling were the most effective. The least-effective techniques were emphasising that anxiety is a sign of readiness not fear, pointing out similar athletes and reducing anxiety through relaxation techniques. Results from the congruency analysis showed that there were many differences between the magnitude of the coaches' and teams' ratings.

Table 7.3 Chapter summary

Source	Research reviewed	Strategies to effect self-efficacy beliefs related to source
Past performance accomplishments	• Relationship between past performance and self-efficacy. • Effects of success and failure manipulations on self-efficacy (including confederates, feedback, bogus feedback, win/loss). • Successful performances (participant modelling).	"Success builds confidence" • Instructional strategies (progressions, performance aids, physical guidance, simulations, equipment modifications). • "Seeing is believing" (goal setting). • Changing attributions.
Vicarious Experiences	• Comparisons. • Impression formation. • Modelling.	"If he/she can do it, so can I" • Thinking, acting, and looking confident. • Modelling. • Videos.
Imagery	• Intervention research. • Questionnaire research (correlation based). • Differences between high- and low-confident athletes.	"What your mind can conceive and your heart can believe, you can achieve" • Differentiation among building, maintaining and regaining self-efficacy. • Modifying images (desired function). • Imagery ability. • Confidence in imagery use. • Belief in imagery effectiveness.
Verbal Persuasion	• Facilitative/debilitative effects. • Success and failure feedback. • Bogus feedback. • Attributions (including acquirable skills versus natural ability). • Assigned goals. • Self-talk. • Coaches' speeches.	*"You can* do it." • Feedback framing. • Self-improvement. • Attribution training. • Positive approach (avoid bogus feedback). • Self-talk. • Positive appraisal information. • Content and delivery of coaches' speeches.
Physiological states	• Association with perceptions of performance and competence. • Dependent on situation and meaning. • Importance of perceptions.	"How you feel is more important than what you feel" • Proper appraisal. • Coping techniques.
Emotional states	• Differential appraisals. • Mood (intensity). • Arousal/anxiety.	"Training the butterflies to fly in formation" • Regulation and control (hypnosis, biofeedback, relaxation, meditation, medication). • Patience and rest.

Unique to the Vargas-Tonsing *et al.* study were the examination of gender differences for the athletes and the consideration of the gender of the coaches. Although these exploratory analyses revealed that male and female athletes differed statistically in their perceptions of frequency and effectiveness, Vargas-Tonsing *et al.* (2004) attributed these findings to the large sample size (because the effect sizes were small). More importantly, they concluded that male and female athletes shared similar perceptions regarding the use and effectiveness of the efficacy-enhancing techniques. Larger differences were found, however, when the gender of the coach was taken into consideration. Female athletes of female coaches found rewarding statements, verbal persuasion and the coach acting confident to be more effective than did female athletes of male coaches. Conversely, female athletes of male coaches found the technique of pointing out similar successful athletes to be more effective.

Taken together, the results from these four research studies show that the efficacy-enhancing techniques that were consistently given the highest ratings for use and effectiveness fall within the sources suggested by Bandura (1977, 1986, 1997; Vargas-Tonsing *et al.*, 2004).

Conclusion

As noted by Feltz (2007), sport psychologists find self-efficacy appealing clinically because efficacy beliefs are modifiable and have great functional value. They can target intervention strategies for athletes, teams and coaches (see Feltz *et al.*, 2008), rather than merely predict behaviour based on personality traits. Self-efficacy theory can provide sport psychologists with some general principles for designing and structuring interventions for a variety of problems (Maddux and Lewis, 1995). We have created Table 7.3 to summarise the content contained in this chapter.

References

Abma, C., Fry, M., Li, Y. and Relyea, G. (2002). Differences in imagery content and imagery ability between high and low confident track and field athletes. *Journal of Applied Sport Psychology*, 14, 67–75.

Bandura, A. (1977). Self-efficacy: toward a unifying theory of behavioural change. *Psychological Review*, 84, 191–215.

Bandura, A. (1986). *Social foundations of thought and action: a social cognitive theory.* Englewood Cliffs, NJ: Prentice Hall.

Bandura, A. (1997). *Self-efficacy: the exercise of control.* New York: Freeman.

Bandura, A. (2001). Social cognitive theory: an agentic perspective. *Annual Review of Psychology*, 52, 1–26.

Bandura, A. (2006). Autobiography. In M. G. Lindzey and W. M. Runyan (eds), *A history of psychology in autobiography* (Vol. IX). Washington, DC: American Psychological Association.

Barling, J. and Abel, M. (1983). Self-efficacy beliefs and tennis performance. *Cognitive Therapy and Research*, 7, 265–272.

Beauchamp, M. R., Bray, S. R. and Albinson, J. G. (2002). Pre-competition imagery, self-efficacy and performance in collegiate golfers. *Journal of Sports Sciences*, 20, 697–705.

Bond, K. A., Biddle, S. J. H. and Ntoumanis, N. (2001). Self-efficacy and causal attributions in female golfers. *International Journal of Sport Psychology*, 31, 243–256.

Boyce, B. A. and Bingham, S. M. (1997). The effects of self-efficacy and goal-setting on bowling performance. *Journal of Teaching in Physical Education*, 16, 312–323.

Brody, E. B., Hatfield, B. D. and Spalding, T. W. (1988). Generalization of self-efficacy to a continuum of stressors upon mastery of a high-risk sport skill. *Journal of Sport and Exercise Psychology*, 10, 32–44.

Brown, L. J., Malouff, M. J. and Schutte, N. S. (2005). The effectiveness of a self-efficacy intervention for helping adolescents cope with sport-competition loss. *Journal of Sport Behaviour*, 28, 136–151.

Burton, D. (1989). Winning isn't everything: examining the impact of performance goals on collegiate swimmers' cognitions and performance. *The Sport Psychologist*, 3, 105–132.

Buscombe, R., Greenlees, I. A., Holder, T., Thelwell, R. C. and Rimmer, M. (2006). Expectancy effects in tennis: the impact of opponents' pre-match non-verbal behaviour on male tennis players. *Journal of Sports Sciences*, 24, 1265–1272.

Callow, N. and Hardy, L. (2001). Types of imagery associated with sport confidence in netball players of varying skill levels. *Journal of Applied Sport Psychology*, 13, 1–17.

Callow, N. and Waters, A. (2005). The effect of kinaesthetic imagery on the sport confidence of flat-race horse jockeys. *Psychology of Sport and Exercise*, 6, 443–459.

Callow, N., Hardy, L. and Hall, C. (2001). The effects of a motivational general-mastery imagery intervention on the sport confidence of high-level badminton players. *Research Quarterly for Exercise and Sport*, 72, 389–400.

Carnahan, B. J., Shea, J. B. and Davis, G. S. (1990). Motivational cue effects on bench-press performance and self-efficacy. *Journal of Sport Behaviour*, 13, 240–254.

Cartoni, A. C., Minganti, C. and Zelli, A. (2005). Gender, age, and professional-level differences in the psychological correlates of fear of injury in Italian gymnasts. *Journal of Sport Behaviour*, 28, 3–17.

Chase, M. A. (2001). Children's self-efficacy, motivational intentions, and attributions in physical education and sport. *Research Quarterly for Exercise and Sport*, 72, 47–54.

Chase, M. A., Feltz, D. L. and Lirgg, C. D. (2003). Sources of collective and individual efficacy of collegiate athletes. *International Journal of Exercise and Sport Psychology*, 1, 180–191.

Chase, M. A., Ewing, M. E., Lirgg, C. D. and George, T. R. (1994). The effects of equipment modification on children's self-efficacy and basketball shooting performance. *Research Quarterly for Exercise and Sport*, 65, 159–168.

Clark, S. E. and Ste-Marie, D. M. (2007). Investigating the impact of self-as-a-model interventions on children's self-regulation of learning and swimming performance. *Journal of Sports Sciences*, 25, 577–586.

Clark, S. E., Ste-Marie, D. M. and Martini, R. (2006). The thought processes underlying self-as-a-model interventions: an exploratory study. *Psychology of Sport and Exercise*, 7, 381–386.

Cleary, T. J. and Zimmerman, B. J. (2001). Self-regulation differences during athletic practice by experts, non-experts and novices. *Journal of Applied Sport Psychology*, 13, 185–206.

Cumming, J., Clark, S. E., McCullagh, P., Ste-Marie, D. M. and Hall, C. (2005). The functions of observational learning questionnaire (FOLQ). *Psychology of Sport and Exercise*, 6, 517–537.

Cumming, J., Nordin, S. M., Horton, R. and Reynolds, S. (2006). Examining the direction of imagery and self-talk on dart-throwing performance and self-efficacy. *The Sport Psychologist*, 20, 257–274.

D'Arripe-Longueville, F., Gernigon, C., Huet, M. L., Cadopi, M. and Winnykamen, F. (2002). Peer tutoring in a physical education setting: influence of tutor skill level on novice learners' motivation and performance. *Journal of Teaching in Physical Education*, 22, 105–123.

Demaine, C. J. and Short, S. E. (2007). Sources of sport confidence and their relationship with sport confidence in college basketball players. *Journal of Sport and Exercise Psychology*, 29, S157.

Duda, J. L. and Nicholls, J. G. (1992). Dimensions of achievement motivation in schoolwork and sport. *Journal of Educational Psychology*, 84, 290–299.

Edmonds, W. A. (2003). *The role of collective efficacy in adventure racing teams*. Unpublished doctoral dissertation, Florida State University, Tallahassee.

Elston, T. L. and Martin-Ginis, K. A. (2004). The effects of self-set versus assigned goals on exercisers' self-efficacy for an unfamiliar task. *Journal of Sport and Exercise Psychology*, 26, 500–504.

Escarti, A. and Guzman, J. F. (1999). Effects of feedback on self-efficacy, performance, and choice on an athletic task. *Journal of Applied Sport Psychology*, 11, 83–96.

Evans, L., Jones, L. and Mullen, R. (2004). An imagery intervention during the competitive season with an elite rugby union player. *The Sport Psychologist*, 18, 252–271.

Eyal, N., Bar-Eli, M., Tenenbaum, G. and Pie, J. S. (1995). Manipulated outcome expectations and competitive performance in motor tasks with gradually increasing difficulty. *The Sport Psychologist*, 9, 188–200.

Feltz, D. L. (1980). Teaching a high-avoidance motor task to a retarded child through participant modelling. *Education and Training of the Mentally Retarded*, 15, 152–155.

Feltz, D. L. (1982). A path analysis of the causal elements in Bandura's theory of self-efficacy and an anxiety-based model of avoidance behaviour. *Journal of Personality and Social Psychology*, 42, 764–781.

Feltz, D. L. (1988a). Self-confidence and sports performance. In K. B. Pandolf (ed.), *Exercise and sport sciences reviews* (pp. 423–456). New York: Macmillan.

Feltz, D. L. (1988b). Gender differences in the causal elements of self-efficacy on a high-avoidance motor task. *Journal of Sport and Exercise Psychology*, 10, 151–166.

Feltz, D. L. (1994). Self-confidence and performance. In D. Druckman and R. A. Bjork (eds), *Learning, remembering, believing: enhancing human performance* (pp. 173–206). Washington, DC: National Academy Press.

Feltz, D. L. (2007). Efficacy belief in sport: research on athletes, teams, and coaches. *Research Quarterly for Exercise and Sport*, 78, A2–3.

Feltz, D. L. and Albrecht, R. R. (1986). The influence of self-efficacy on the approach/avoidance of a high-avoidance motor task. In J. H. Humphrey and L. Vander-Velden (eds), *Psychology and sociology of sport* (pp. 3–25). New York: AMS Press.

Feltz, D. L. and Chase, M. A. (1998). The measurement of self-efficacy and confidence in sport. In J. Duda (ed.), *Advancements in sport and exercise psychology measurement* (pp. 63–78). Morgantown, WV: Fitness Information Technology.

Feltz, D. L. and Landers, D. M. (1983). The effects of mental practice on motor skill learning and performance: a meta-analysis. *Journal of Sport Psychology*, 5, 25–57.

Feltz, D. L. and Lirgg, C. D. (1998). Perceived team and player efficacy in hockey. *Journal of Applied Psychology*, 83, 557–564.

Feltz, D. L. and Mugno, D. A. (1983). A replication of the path analysis of the causal elements in Bandura's theory of self-efficacy and the influence of autonomic perception. *Journal of Sport Psychology*, 5, 263–277.

Feltz, D. L. and Riessinger, C. A. (1990). Effects on in vivo emotive imagery and performance feedback on self-efficacy and muscular endurance. *Journal of Sport and Exercise Psychology*, 12, 132–143.

Feltz, D. L. and Weiss, M. R. (1982). Developing self-efficacy through sport. *Journal of Physical Education, Recreation, and Dance*, 24–26.

Feltz, D. L., Landers, D. M. and Raeder, U. (1979). Enhancing self-efficacy in high-avoidance motor tasks: a comparison of modelling techniques. *Journal of Sport Psychology*, 1, 112–122.

Feltz, D. L., Short, S. E. and Singleton, D. A. (2007). The effect of self-modelling on shooting performance and self-efficacy with intercollegiate hockey players. *Manuscript under review*.

Feltz, D. L., Short, S. E. and Sullivan, P. J. (2008). *Self-efficacy in sport*. Champaign, IL: Human Kinetics.

Fitzsimmons, P. A., Landers, D. M., Thomas, J. R. and Van der Mars, H. (1991). Does self-efficacy predict performance in experienced weightlifters? *Research Quarterly for Exercise and Sport*, 62, 424–431.

Frank, M. G. and Gilovich, T. (1988). The dark side of self- and social perception: black uniforms and aggression in professional sports. *Journal of Personality and Social Psychology*, 54, 74–85.

Franks, I. M. and Maile, L. J. (1991). The use of video in sport skill acquisition. In P. W. Dowrick (ed.), *Practical guide to using video in the behavioural sciences* (pp. 231–243). New York: Wiley.

Galloway, S. (2003). Motivation theory for elite karate athletes: a psycho-physiological approach. *Physical Training Fitness for Combatives*, 1–17. Retrieved 20 August 2005, from www.ejmas.com/pt/ptart_galloway_0703.html.

Garza, D. L. and Feltz, D. L. (1998). Effects of selected mental practice techniques on performance ratings, self-efficacy, and competition confidence of competitive figure skaters. *The Sport Psychologist*, 12, 1–15.

George, T. R. (1994). Self-confidence and baseball performance: a causal examination of self-efficacy theory. *Journal of Sport and Exercise Psychology*, 16, 381–399.

George, T. R., Feltz, D. L. and Chase, M. A. (1992). The effects of model similarity on self-efficacy and muscular endurance: a second look. *Journal of Sport and Exercise Psychology*, 14, 237–248.

Gernigon, C. and Delloye, J. B. (2003). Self-efficacy, causal attribution, and track athletic performance following unexpected success or failure among elite sprinters. *The Sport Psychologist*, 17, 55–76.

Gernigon, C., Fleurance, P. and Reine, B. (2000). Effects of uncontrollability and failure on the development of learned helplessness in perceptual-motor tasks. *Research Quarterly for Exercise and Sport*, 71, 44–54.

Gould, D. and Weiss, M. R. (1981). Effect of model similarity and model self-talk on self-efficacy in muscular endurance. *Journal of Sport Psychology*, 3, 17–29.

Gould, D., Hodge, K., Peterson, K. and Giannini, J. (1989). An exploratory examination of strategies used by elite coaches to enhance self-efficacy in athletes. *Journal of Sport and Exercise Psychology*, 11, 128–140.

Greenlees, I. A. and Crosbie, D. (2005). *The influence of opponents' clothing and competitive history on the valuation of their performance by observers*. Paper presented at the ISSP 11th World Congress of Sport Psychology, Sydney, Australia, 15–19 August 2005.

Greenlees, I. A., Bradley, A., Holder, T. and Thelwell, R. C. (2005a). The impact of opponents' non-verbal behaviour on the first impressions and outcome expectations of table tennis players. *Psychology of Sport and Exercise*, 6, 103–115.

Greenlees, I. A., Buscombe, R., Thelwell, R. C., Holder, T. and Rimmer, M. (2005b). Perception of opponents in tennis: the impact of opponents' clothing and body language on impression formation and outcome expectations. *Journal of Sport and Exercise Psychology*, 27, 39–52.

Grieve, F. G., Whelan, J. P., Kottke, R. and Meyers, A. W. (1994). Manipulating adults' achievement goals in a sport task: effects on cognitive, affective, and behavioural variables. *Journal of Sport Behaviour*, 17, 227–245.

Haggbloom, S. J., Warnick, R., Warnick, J. E., Jones, V. K., Yarbrough, G. L., *et al.* (2002). The 100 most eminent psychologists of the 20th century. *Review of General Psychology*, 6, 139–152.

Hall, C. R., Mack, D., Paivio, A. and Hausenblas, H. A. (1998). Imagery use by athletes: development of the Sport Imagery Questionnaire. *International Journal of Sport Psychology*, 29, 73–89.

Hall, C., Stevens, D. and Paivio, A. (2005). *The Sport Imagery Questionnaire: test manual*. Morgantown, WV: Fitness Information Technology.

Hall, E. G. and Erffmeyer, E. S. (1983). The effect of visuomotor behaviour rehearsal with videotaped modelling on free throw accuracy of intercollegiate basketball players. *Journal of Sport Psychology*, 5, 343–346.

Halliwell, W. (1990). Providing sport psychology consulting services in professional hockey. *The Sport Psychologist*, 4, 369–377.

Haney, C. J. and Long, B. C. (1995). Coping effectiveness: a path analysis of self-efficacy, control, coping, and performance in sport competitions. *Journal of Applied Social Psychology*, 25, 1726–1746.

Hanton, S. and Jones, G. (1999). The effects of a multimodal intervention programme on performers: II. Training the butterflies to fly in formation. *The Sport Psychologist*, 13, 22–41.

Hanton, S., Mellalieu, S. D. and Hall, R. (2004). Self-confidence and anxiety interpretation: a qualitative investigation. *Psychology of Sport and Exercise*, 5, 477–495.

Hardy, J., Gammage, K. and Hall, C. (2001). A descriptive study of athlete self-talk. *The Sport Psychologist*, 15, 306–318.

Hardy, J., Hall, C. R., Gibbs, C. and Greenslade, C. (2005). Self-talk and gross motor skill performance: an experimental approach? *Athletic Insight*. Retrieved 1 September 2005, from www.athleticinsight.com/Vol7Iss2/SelfTalkPerformance.htm.

Harrison, J. M., Blakemore, C. L., Buck, M. M. and Pellett, T. L. (1996). *Instructional strategies for secondary physical education* (4th edn). St Louis: Times/Mirror/Mosby.

Hays, K., Maynard, I., Thomas, O. and Bawden, M. (2007). Sources and types of confidence identified by world class sport performers. *Journal of Applied Sport Psychology*, 19, 434–456.

Holmes, P. S. and Collins, D. J. (2001). The PETTLEP approach to motor imagery: a functional equivalence model for sport psychologists. *Journal of Applied Sport Psychology*, 13, 60–83.

Horn, T. S. (2002). Coaching effectiveness in the sports domain. In T. S. Horn (ed.), *Advances in sport psychology* (pp. 309–354). Champaign, IL: Human Kinetics.

Jones, M. V., Mace, R. D., Bray, S. R., MacRae, A. W. and Stockbride, C. (2002). The impact of motivational imagery on the emotional state and self-efficacy levels of novice climbers. *Journal of Sport Behaviour, 25*, 57–73.

Jourden, F. J., Bandura, A. and Banfield, J. T. (1991). The impact of conceptions of ability on self regulatory factors and motor skill acquisition. *Journal of Sport and Exercise Psychology, 8*, 213–226.

Kane, T. D., Marks, M. A., Zaccaro, S. J. and Blair, V. (1996). Self-efficacy, personal goals, and wrestlers' self-regulation. *Journal of Sport and Exercise Psychology, 18*, 36–48.

Kanfer, F. H. (1984). Introduction. In R. P. McGlynn, J. E. Maddux, C. D. Stoltenberg and J. H. Harvey (eds), *Social perception in clinical and counselling psychology* (pp. 1–6). Lubbock, TX: Texas Tech Press.

Kavanagh, D. J. and Bower, G. H. (1985). Mood and self-efficacy: impact of joy and sadness on perceived capabilities. *Cognitive Therapy and Research, 9*, 507–525.

Kavanagh, D. and Hausfeld, S. (1986). Physical performance and self-efficacy under happy and sad moods. *Journal of Sport Psychology, 8*, 112–123.

Kenow, L. and Williams, J. M. (1999). Coach–athlete compatibility and athlete's perception of coaching behaviours. *Journal of Sport Behaviour, 22*, 251–260.

Kingston, K. and Hardy, L. (1997). Effects of different types of goals on processes that support performance. *The Sport Psychologist, 11*, 277–293.

Kitsantis, A. and Zimmerman, B. J. (1998). Self-regulation of motoric learning: a strategic cycle view. *Journal of Applied Sport Psychology, 10*, 220–239.

Kitsantis, A. and Zimmerman, B. J. (2002). Comparing self-regulatory processes among novice, non-expert, and expert volleyball players: a microanalytic study. *Journal of Applied Sport Psychology, 14*, 91–105.

LaGuardia, R. and Labbe, E. E. (1993). Self-efficacy and anxiety and their relationship to training and race performance. *Perceptual and Motor Skills, 77*, 27–34.

Landers, D. M. (1983). Whatever happened to theory testing in sport psychology? *Journal of Sport and Exercise Psychology, 5*, 135–151.

Landers, D. M. and Landers, D. M. (1973). Teacher versus peer models: effects of model's presence and performance level on motor behaviour. *Journal of Motor Behaviour, 5*, 129–139.

Lane, A. M., Jones, L. and Stevens, M. J. (2002). Coping with failure: the effects of self-esteem and coping on changes in self-efficacy. *Journal of Sport Behaviour, 25*, 331–345.

Law, B. and Ste-Marie, D. M. (2005). Self-modelling and figure skating performance. *European Journal of Sport Sciences, 5*, 143–153.

Lee, C. (1988). The relationship between goal setting, self-efficacy, and female field hockey team performance. *International Journal of Sport Psychology, 20*, 147–161.

Legrain, P., d'Arripe-Longueville, F. and Gernigon, C. (2003). The influence of trained peer tutoring on tutors' motivation and performance in a French boxing setting. *Journal of Sports Sciences, 21*, 539–550.

LeMaire, J., Short, S. E., Ross-Stewart, L. and Short, M. W. (2007). The effect of uniform colour on athletes' readiness for competition and perceptions of opponents' attributes. *Journal of Sport and Exercise Psychology, 29*, S180.

Lirgg, C. D. and Feltz, D. L. (1991). Teacher versus peer models revisited: effects on motor performance and self-efficacy. *Research Quarterly for Exercise and Sport, 62*, 217–224.

Lirgg, C. D., George, T. R., Chase, M. A. and Ferguson, R. H. (1996). Impact of conception of ability and sex-type of task on male and female self-efficacy. *Journal of Sport and Exercise Psychology, 18*, 426–433.

Locke, E. A. and Latham, G. P. (1990). A theory of goal setting and task performance. Englewood Cliffs, NJ: Prentice Hall.

Locke, E. A., Frederick, E., Lee, C. and Bobko, P. (1984). Effect of self-efficacy, goals, and task strategies on task performance. Journal of Applied Psychology, 69, 241–251.

Lohasz, P. G. and Leith, L. M. (1997). The effect of three mental preparation strategies on the performance of a complex response time task. International Journal of Sport Psychology, 28, 25–34.

McAuley, E. (1985). Modelling and self-efficacy: a test of Bandura's model. Journal of Sport Psychology, 7, 283–295.

McCullagh, P. and Weiss, M. R. (2001). Modelling: considerations for motor skill performance and psychological responses. In R. N. Singer, H. A. Hausenblas and C. M. Janelle (eds), Handbook of sport psychology (pp. 205–238). New York: Wiley.

McGlone, S. and Shrier, I. (2000). Does sex the night before competition decrease performance? Clinical Journal of Sport Medicine, 10, 233–234.

Mack, M. G. and Stephens, D. E. (2000). An empirical test of Taylor and Demick's multidimensional model of momentum in sport. Journal of Sport Behaviour, 23, 349–363.

McKenzie, A. D. and Howe, B. (1997). The effect of imagery on self-efficacy for a motor skill. International Journal of Sport Psychology, 28, 196–210.

McNair, D. M., Lorr, M. and Droppleman, L. F. (1971). Manual for the profile of mood states. San Diego, CA: Educational and Industrial Testing Services.

Maddux, J. E. (1995). Self-efficacy theory: an introduction. In J. E. Maddux (ed.), Self-efficacy, adaptation, and adjustment: theory, research, and application (pp. 3–33). New York: Plenum Press.

Maddux, J. E. and Lewis, J. (1995). Self-efficacy and adjustment: basic principles and issues. In J. E. Maddux (ed.), Self-efficacy, adaptation, and adjustment: theory, research, and application (pp. 37–68). New York: Plenum Press.

Magyar, T. M. and Feltz, D. L. (2003). The influence of dispositional and situational tendencies on adolescent girls' selection of sport confidence sources. Psychology of Sport and Exercise, 4, 175–190.

Mamassis, G. and Doganis, G. (2004). The effects of a mental training programme on juniors' pre-competitive anxiety, self-confidence, and tennis performance. Journal of Applied Sport Psychology, 16, 118–137.

Martens, R. (1979). About smocks and jocks. Journal of Sport Psychology, 1, 94–99.

Martin, J. J. (2002). Training and performance self-efficacy, affect, and performance in wheelchair road racers. The Sport Psychologist, 16, 384–395.

Martin, K. A. and Hall, C. R. (1995). Using mental imagery to enhance intrinsic motivation. Journal of Sport and Exercise Psychology, 17, 54–69.

Martin, K. A., Moritz, S. E. and Hall, C. R. (1999). Imagery use in sport: a literature review and applied model. The Sport Psychologist, 13, 245–268.

Mellalieu, S. D., Hanton, S. and Fletcher, D. (2006). A competitive anxiety review: recent directions in sport psychology research. In S. Hanton and S. D. Mellalieu (eds), Literature reviews in sport psychology. Hauppauge, NY: Nova Science.

Mellalieu, S. D., Neil, R. and Hanton, S. (2006). Self-confidence as a mediator of the relationship between competitive anxiety intensity and interpretation. Research Quarterly for Exercise and Sport, 77, 263–270.

Miller, J. T. and McAuley, E. (1987). Effects of a goal-setting training programme on basketball free-throw self-efficacy and performance. The Sport Psychologist, 1, 103–113.

Miller, M. (1993). Efficacy strength and performance in competitive swimmers of different skill levels. International Journal of Sport Psychology, 24, 284–296.

Mills, K. D., Munroe, K. J. and Hall, C. R. (2000). The relationship between imagery and self efficacy in competitive athletics. *Imagination, Cognition, and Personality*, 20, 33–39.

Milne, M., Hall, C. and Forwell, L. (2005). Self-efficacy, imagery use, and adherence to rehabilitation by injured athletes. *Journal of Sport Rehabilitation*, 14, 150–167.

Moritz, S. E., Feltz, D. L., Fahrbach, K. R. and Mack, D. E. (2000). The relation of self-efficacy measures to sport performance: a meta-analytic review. *Research Quarterly for Exercise and Sport*, 71, 280–294.

Moritz, S. E., Hall, C. R., Martin, K. A. and Vadocz, E. (1996). What are confident athletes imaging? An examination of image content. *The Sport Psychologist*, 10, 171–179.

Morris, T., Spittle, M. and Watt, A. (2005). *Imagery in sport*. Champaign, IL: Human Kinetics.

Myers, N. D., Feltz, D. L. and Short, S. E. (2004a). Collective efficacy and team performance: a longitudinal study of collegiate football teams. *Group Dynamics: Theory, Research, and Practice*, 8, 126–138.

Myers, N. D., Payment, C. A. and Feltz, D. L. (2004b). Reciprocal relationships between collective efficacy and team performance in women's ice hockey. *Group Dynamics: Theory, Research, and Practice*, 8, 182–195.

Myers, N. D., Payment, C. A. and Feltz, D. L. (2007). Regressing team performance on collective efficacy: considerations of temporal proximity and concordance. *Measurement in Physical Education and Exercise Science*, 11, 1–24.

Newton, M., Duda, J. L. and Yin, Z. (2000). Examination of the psychometric properties of the Perceived Motivational Climate in Sport Questionnaire-2 in a sample of female athletes. *Journal of Sports Sciences*, 18, 275–290.

Nordin, S. M. and Cumming, J. (2005). More than meets the eye: investigating imagery type, direction, and outcome. *The Sport Psychologist*, 19, 1–17.

Orbach, I., Singer, R. N. and Price, S. (1999). An attribution training programme and achievement in sport. *The Sport Psychologist*, 13, 69–82.

Orlick, T. (2000). *In pursuit of excellence* (3rd edn). Champaign, IL: Human Kinetics.

Paivio, A. (1985). Cognitive and motivational functions of imagery in human performance. *Canadian Journal of Applied Sport Sciences*, 10, 22S–28S.

Pellett, T. L. and Lox, C. L. (1998). Tennis racket head-size comparisons and their effect on beginning college players' achievement and self-efficacy. *Journal of Teaching in Physical Education*, 17, 453–467.

Prapavessis, H. and Grove, J. R. (1994). Personality variables as antecedents of precompetitive mood state temporal patterning. *International Journal of Sport Psychology*, 22, 347–365.

Ram, N. and McCullagh, P. (2003). Self-modelling: influence on psychological responses and physical performance. *The Sport Psychologist*, 17, 220–241.

Richardson, A. (1969). *Mental imagery*. New York: Springer Publishing Company, Inc.

Rink, J. (1992). *Teaching physical education for learning* (2nd edn). St Louis: Times/Mirror/Mosby.

Ross-Stewart, L. and Short, S. E. (in press). The frequency and perceived effectiveness of imagery used to build, maintain, and regain confidence. *Journal of Applied Sport Psychology*.

Rudisill, M. E. (1988). The influence of causal dimension orientations and perceived competence on adult's expectations, persistence, performance and the selection of causal dimensions. *International Journal of Sport Psychology*, 19, 184–198.

Rudolph, D. L. and Butki, B. D. (1998). Self-efficacy and affective responses to short bouts of exercise. *Journal of Applied Sport Psychology*, 10, 268–280.

Rudolph, D. L. and McAuley, E. (1986). Self-efficacy and perceptions of effort: a reciprocal relationship. *Journal of Sport and Exercise Psychology*, 18, 216–223.

Rushall, B. S. (1988). Covert modelling as a procedure for altering an elite athlete's psychological state. *The Sport Psychologist*, 2, 131–140.

Schultz, R. and Short, S. E. (2006). Who do athletes compare to? How the standard of comparison affects confidence ratings. *Association for the Advancement of Applied Sport Psychology – 2006 Conference Proceedings*, pp. 82–83. Madison, WI: AAASP.

Schunk, D. H. (1995). Self-efficacy, motivation, and performance. *Journal of Applied Sport Psychology*, 7, 112–137.

Shaw, J. M., Dzewaltowski, D. A. and McElroy, M. (1992). Self-efficacy and causal attributions as mediators of perceptions of psychological momentum. *Journal of Sport and Exercise Psychology*, 14, 134–147.

Short, S. E. and Short, M. W. (2005). Differences between high- and low-confident football players on imagery functions: a consideration of the athletes' perceptions. *Journal of Applied Sport Psychology*, 17, 197–208.

Short, S. E., Bruggeman, J. M., Engel, S. G., Marback, T. L., Wang, L. J., Willadsen, A., et al. (2002). The effect of imagery function and imagery direction on self-efficacy and performance on a golf-putting task. *The Sport Psychologist*, 16, 48–67.

Short, S. E., Monsma, E. V. and Short, M. W. (2004). Is what you see really what you get? Athletes' perceptions of imagery functions. *The Sport Psychologist*, 18, 341–349.

Short, S. E., Monsma, E. V. and Short, M. W. (in press). Athletes' perceptions of imagery direction on the Sport Imagery Questionnaire. *Journal of Mental Imagery*.

Short, S. E., Ross-Stewart, L. and Monsma, E. (2006). Onwards with the evolution of imagery research in sport psychology. *Athletic Insight*. Retrieved 12 October 2006, from www.athleticinsight.com/Vol8Iss3/ImageryResearch.htm.

Short, S. E., Tenute, A. and Feltz, D. L. (2005). Imagery use in sport: mediational effects for efficacy. *Journal of Sports Sciences*, 23, 951–960.

Slobounov, S., Yukelson, D. and O'Brien, R. (1997). Self-efficacy and movement variability of Olympic-level springboard divers. *Journal of Applied Sport Psychology*, 9, 171–190.

Smith, D., Wright, C. J., Allsopp, A. and Westhead, H. (2007). It's all in the mind: PETTLEP-based imagery and sports performance. *Journal of Applied Sport Psychology*, 19, 80–92.

Smith, D., Wright, C. J. and Cantwell, C. (2008). Beating the bunker: the effect of PETTLEP imagery on golf bunker shot performance. *Research Quarterly for Exercise and Sport*, 79, 385–392.

Smoll, F. L. and Smith, R. E. (1989). Leadership behaviours in sport: a theoretical model and research paradigm. *Journal of Applied Social Psychology*, 19, 1522–1551.

Solmon, M. A., Lee, A. M., Belcher, D., Harrison, L. and Wells, L. (2003). Beliefs about gender appropriateness, ability, and competence in physical activity. *Journal of Teaching in Physical Education*, 22, 261–279.

Soohoo, S., Takemoto, K. Y. and McCullagh, P. (2004). A comparison of modelling and imagery on the performance of a motor skill. *Journal of Sport Behaviour*, 27, 349–365.

Starek, J. and McCullagh, P. (1999). The effect of self-modelling on the performance of beginning swimmers. *The Sport Psychologist*, 13, 269–287.

Taylor, J. and Shaw, D. F. (2002). The effects of outcome imagery on golf-putting performance. *Journal of Sports Sciences*, 20, 607–613.

Thelwell, R. C. and Greenlees, I. A. (2003). Developing competitive endurance performance using mental skills training. *The Sport Psychologist*, 17, 318–337.

Theodorakis, Y. (1995). Effects of self-efficacy, satisfaction, and personal goals on swimming performance. *The Sport Psychologist*, 9, 245–253.

Theodorakis, Y. (1996). The influence of goals, commitment, self-efficacy and self-satisfaction on motor performance. *Journal of Applied Sport Psychology*, 8, 171–182.

Thornton, J. S. (1990). Sexual activity and athletic performance: is there a relationship? *Physician and Sports Medicine*, 18, 148–151.

Treasure, D. C., Monson, J. and Lox, C. L. (1996). Relationship between self-efficacy, wrestling performance, and affect prior to competition. *The Sport Psychologist*, 10, 73–83.

Vadocz, E. A., Hall, C. R. and Moritz, S. E. (1997). The relationship between competitive anxiety and imagery use. *Journal of Applied Sport Psychology*, 9, 241–253.

Vargas-Tonsing, T. M. (2005). An examination of pre-game speeches and their effectiveness in increasing athletes' levels of self-efficacy and emotion. Unpublished manuscript, Michigan State University.

Vargas-Tonsing, T. M. and Bartholomew, J. B. (2006). An exploratory study of the effects of pre-game speeches on team-efficacy beliefs. *Journal of Applied Sport Psychology*, 36, 918–933.

Vargas-Tonsing, T. M. and Guan, J. (2007). Athletes' preferences for informational and emotional pre-game speech content. *International Journal of Sport Science and Coaching*, 2, 171–180.

Vargas-Tonsing, T. M. and Short, S. E. (2005). Athletes' perceptions of their coaches' pre-game speeches. *Association for the Advancement of Applied Sport Psychology – 2005 Conference Proceedings*, p. 45. Madison, WI: AAASP.

Vargas-Tonsing, T. M. and Short, S. E. (2008). Athletes' perceptions of coaches' pre-game speeches. Manuscript under review.

Vargas-Tonsing, T. M., Myers, N. D. and Feltz, D. L. (2004). Coaches' and athletes' perceptions of efficacy enhancing techniques. *The Sport Psychologist*, 18, 397–414.

Vealey, R. S. (1986). Conceptualization of sport-confidence and competitive orientation: preliminary investigation and instrument development. *Journal of Sport Psychology*, 8, 221–246.

Vealey, R. S. (1988). Sport-confidence and competitive orientation: an addendum on scoring procedures and gender differences. *Journal of Sport Psychology*, 10, 471–488.

Vealey, R. S. (2005). *Coaching for the inner edge*. Morgantown, WV: Fitness Information Technology.

Vealey, R. S. (2006). Smocks and jocks outside the box: the paradigmatic evolution of sport and exercise psychology. *Quest*, 58, 128–160.

Vealey, R. S., Hayashi, S. W., Garner-Holman, M. and Giacobbi, P. (1998). Sources of sport-confidence: conceptualization and instrument development. *Journal of Sport and Exercise Psychology*, 20, 54–80.

Watson, D., Clark, L. A. and Tellegen, A. (1988). Development and validation of brief measures of positive and negative affect: the PANAS scales. *Journal of Personality and Social Psychology*, 54, 1063–1070.

Weinberg, R. S. (1985). Relationship between self-efficacy and cognitive strategies in enhancing endurance performance. *International Journal of Sport Psychology*, 17, 280–292.

Weinberg, R. S. and Gould, D. (2003). *Foundations of sport and exercise psychology* (3rd edn). Champaign, IL: Human Kinetics.

Weinberg, R. S. and Jackson, A. (1990). Building self-efficacy in tennis players: a coach's perspective. *Journal of Applied Sport Psychology*, 2, 164–174.

Weinberg, R. S., Gould, D. and Jackson, A. (1979). Expectations and performance: an empirical test of Bandura's self-efficacy theory. *Journal of Sport Psychology*, 1, 320–331.

Weinberg, R. S., Gould, D., Yukelson, D. and Jackson, A. (1981). The effects of pre-existing and manipulated self-efficacy on a competitive muscular endurance task. *Journal of Sport Psychology*, 3, 345–354.

Weinberg, R., Grove, R. and Jackson, A. (1992). Strategies for building self-efficacy in tennis players: a comparative analysis of Australian and American coaches. *The Sport Psychologist*, 6, 3–13.

Weinberg, R. S., Yukelson, D. and Jackson, A. (1980). Effect of public and private efficacy expectations on competitive performance. *Journal of Sport Psychology*, 2, 340–349.

Weiner, B. (1985). An attributional theory of achievement motivation and emotion. *Psychological Review*, 92, 548–573.

Weiss, M. R., McCullagh, P., Smith, A. L. and Berlant, A. R. (1998). Observational learning and the fearful child: influence of peer models on swimming skill performance and psychological responses. *Research Quarterly for Exercise and Sport*, 69, 380–394.

Weiss, M. R., Wiese, D. M. and Klint, K. A. (1989). Head over heels with success: the relationship between self-efficacy and performance in competitive youth gymnastics. *Journal of Sport and Exercise Psychology*, 11, 444–451.

Wells, C. M., Collins, D. and Hale, B. D. (1993). The self-efficacy–performance link in maximum strength performance. *Journal of Sports Sciences*, 11, 167–175.

White, A. and Hardy, L. (1998). An in-depth analysis of the uses of imagery by high-level slalom canoeists and artistic gymnasts. *The Sport Psychologist*, 12, 387–403.

Wilkes, R. L. and Summers, J. J. (1984). Cognitions, mediating variables, and strength performance. *Journal of Sport Psychology*, 6, 351–359.

Wilson, R. C., Sullivan, P. J., Myers, N. D. and Feltz, D. L. (2004). Sources of sport confidence of master athletes. *Journal of Sport and Exercise Psychology*, 26, 369–384.

Winfrey, M. L. and Weeks, D. L. (1993). Effects of self-modelling on self-efficacy and balance beam performance. *Perceptual and Motor Skills*, 77, 907–913.

Wise, J. B. and Trunnell, E. P. (2001). The influence of sources of self-efficacy upon efficacy strength. *Journal of Sport and Exercise Psychology*, 23, 268–280.

Woolfolk, R. L., Murphy, S. M., Gottesfeld, D. and Aitken, D. (1985). Effects of mental rehearsal of task motor activity and mental depiction of task outcome on motor skill performance. *Journal of Sport Psychology*, 7, 191–197.

Wright, C. J. and Smith, D. (2007). The effect of a short-term PETTLEP imagery intervention on a cognitive task. *Journal of Imagery Research in Sport and Physical Activity*, 2. Available from www.bepress.com/jirspa/vol2/iss1/art1.

Wright, C. J. and Smith, D. (in press). The effect of PETTLEP imagery on strength performance. *International Journal of Sport and Exercise Psychology*.

Yan Lan, L. and Gill, D. L. (1984). The relationships among self-efficacy, stress responses, and a cognitive feedback manipulation. *Journal of Sport Psychology*, 6, 227–238.

Zimmerman, B. J. and Kitsantas, A. (1996). Self-regulated learning of a motoric skill: the role of goal setting and self-monitoring. *Journal of Applied Sport Psychology*, 8, 60–75.

Zimmerman, B. J. and Kitsantas, A. (1997). Developmental phases in self-regulation: shifting from process goals to outcome goals. *Journal of Educational Psychology*, 89, 29–36.

8 Letting the social and cognitive merge

New concepts for an understanding of group functioning in sport

David W. Eccles and Michael B. Johnson

Introduction

In recent years, researchers have been re-examining how extant concepts in sport psychology can account adequately for the functioning of groups in sport (e.g. Eccles and Tenenbaum, 2004, 2007; see also the 2006, Volume 4, special issue of the *International Journal of Sport and Exercise Psychology*). A particular concern has been that the existing research on sport groups such as teams and organisations has predominantly involved only social concepts. Furthermore, when it has involved cognitive concepts, the focus has been on understanding the cognitive processes mediating the performance of an individual performer within a group, but seldom those mediating the performance of the group. While each of these perspectives has provided important insights into group functioning in sport, the proposal in this chapter is that the current understanding of this topic could be enhanced substantially by a perspective that involves an integration of both social and cognitive concepts.

Thus, this chapter is concerned with a social-cognitive perspective on group functioning in sport. This perspective, as it is explicated in the chapter, is based on concepts that originate in disciplines other than sport psychology. These concepts have been concerned with understanding how humans, animals, or humans and technological agents function effectively in collaborative, goal-directed groups. These disciplines include biology, cognitive science, human factors and ergonomics, industrial and organisational (I/O) psychology, philosophy, social-cognitive psychology and sociology. It is proposed that a consideration of the social-cognitive concepts presented in these disciplines has relevance for the study of group functioning in sport.

The chapter begins with a discussion of the contributions and limitations of the extant research on group functioning in sport. Following this, there is an overview of key concepts relating to a social-cognitive perspective on group functioning that have the potential to enhance the current understanding of group functioning in sport. Next, these concepts are used to interpret the functioning of a real-world sport organisation, which involves a national orienteering squad's preparation for major competitions. Finally, implications of a social-cognitive perspective on group functioning for best practice in sport are proffered, and future research directions related to this perspective are suggested.

Contributions and limitations of the extant research on group functioning in sport

This section involves a discussion of how group functioning in sport has been considered predominantly from a social perspective, and how researchers interested in cognitive aspects of sports performance have been concerned predominantly with the individual performer. Following this discussion, there is an attempt to articulate some specific limitations of these perspectives with regard to accounting for group functioning in sport.

The predominance of a social perspective on group functioning in sport

To date, when the individual has been the unit of analysis in sport psychology, researchers have considered both cognitive and social processes. For example, there is an extensive literature within sport psychology on cognitive processes underlying individual performance, especially skilled performance (Starkes and Ericsson, 2003; Williams and Hodges, 2004). Furthermore, there has been much concern with how social processes, such as social support, influence individual performance (e.g. Rees et al., 1999). However, there has been less consideration for how an individual's cognitive processes might be affected by the social processes inherent to the social group in which the individual is almost always embedded (Collins, 1996). As will be argued in more detail later, this embeddedness exists even if the individual's sport is individual in nature. Furthermore, a cursory analysis of current introductory texts on sport psychology is enough to reveal that, for the most part, when the unit of study involves more than one individual, an interest in cognitive processes disappears, leaving only an interest in social processes. For example, the text by Weinberg and Gould (2003) includes four chapters related to the topic of group processes, which are respectively entitled group and team dynamics, cohesion, leadership and communication. The chapter on group and team dynamics covers concepts such as group development, group norms, team climate and social loafing within groups. With regard to creating an effective team climate, the authors describe how the existing research has provided some support for how social support, team-members' perceptions of their team's distinctiveness and the extent to which coaches treat players fairly affect team climate. Thus, these concepts are predominantly social in nature, and this perspective is reflected throughout the current research literature on group functioning in sport.

The predominance of the individual as the unit-of-analysis in studies of cognition in sport

Current studies of the cognitive processes mediating sport performance have focused predominantly on individual performance. Key texts (e.g. Starkes and Ericsson, 2003; Williams and Hodges, 2004) and reviews (Hodges et al., 2007;

Williams and Ward, 2007) relating to this topic provide evidence of this individual focus. These works have considered how perception, attention and memory processes operate to mediate an individual's performance, and how these processes change as a result of practice and experience so that a higher level of performance is achieved. For example, the review by Williams and Ward (2007) provided evidence that, as athletes develop in sport-team settings, they are better able to search for and identify contextual information in their environment, which, in turn, allows them to better anticipate the upcoming actions of team-mates and opponents and thus prepare earlier and more appropriate responses to those actions.

Limitations of traditional perspectives on group functioning in sport

The following anecdote is useful in illustrating the limitations of the traditional perspectives on group functioning in sport (Eccles and Tenenbaum, 2007). In the Rugby Union World Cup final in 2003, England and tournament host Australia were tied at 17–17 in the final 25 seconds of the game. In a breathtaking finale, Matt Dawson spun the ball out of the England's line-out to Jonny Wilkinson. While under great pressure, Wilkinson dropped the ball to his feet and executed a stunning drop-goal to clinch the game and seal England's name in the history books as the first northern-hemisphere side to win the World Cup. After the game, Wilkinson was asked to reflect on his drop-goal. His response was, "We had a clear routine of how we'd get a drop-goal. It just went absolutely like clockwork. That's why you win these big games" (British Broadcasting Corporation, 2003).

From a research standpoint, there are various questions that might be asked in an attempt to understand how the "routine" Wilkinson described is achieved. Who created the routine? What was the process by which it was created? How many people on the team needed to learn the routine? Did they need to understand the entire routine or just that pertaining to how they contributed to it? If they didn't really contribute to it, how much about it, if anything, did they need to understand? If all the players who needed to know the routine did not help create it, how was the created routine communicated to those players who were not part of its creation? Was the timing of the routine within the game planned prior to the game or did it emerge in a more self-organised way? Alternatively, was it initiated by one or more than one member during the game and, if so, how? Was it through communication? If so, from whom and in what form? How was it decided which person should undertake the communication? Was it through conventional authority (e.g. was the communicator the captain) or by planning prior to the game? For Eccles and Tenenbaum (2007), and for the authors of this chapter, answers to most if not all of these questions seem to require the consideration of both social and cognitive concepts and, more specifically, the allowance that these concepts merge (Eccles, 2007; Giere and Moffat, 2003).

However, there have been few attempts to consider such a perspective. To elaborate, concepts from cognitive psychology are infrequently applied at the group level. For example, Levine *et al.* proposed that cognitive psychology "has traditionally been a psychology of the individual" and "little attention has been paid to … cognitive functioning in interaction with others" (1993: 586). The limitations of the traditional individual perspective on cognition are made clearer when it is considered that the human is a social animal that exhibits a propensity for interpersonal interaction that is rarely paralleled in other species. Hutchins (1991) suggested a test to exemplify such interaction. From where you sit, try to identify an object that is not the product of human collaboration. The present authors suggest a similar test: identify the number of different types of groups, teams and larger organisations (e.g. family, work and social) within which you are a member. It is usually harder to identify activities undertaken solely as an individual. Thus, as the poet John Donne asserted (Carey, 2000), few of us are "islands". Consequently, we rarely think in a "social vacuum" (Levine *et al.*, 1993: 586). By contrast, we are firmly embedded in a society and culture that constrains and shapes our thought-processes. Despite this, social and cultural factors have essentially been "set aside as problems to be addressed after a good understanding of individual cognition has been achieved" (Gardner, 1985; Hutchins, 1995a: 353).

However, researchers in various disciplines have called for an acknowledge-ment of the impact of social structures and processes on human cognition. In the cognitive sciences, researchers have argued that even when an individual is engaged in a solely individual activity, that individual's cognition is still affected by the social network and cultural context within which he or she operates (D'Andrade, 1981; Resnick *et al.*, 1996). Collins asserted that the "neglect of the social embeddedness of both humans and computers" is what limits the capabilities of intelligent machines (1996: 103). In sociology, a major topic is human agency, which describes the extent to which humans can think and act in ways independent of the social structures in the environment (Lukes, 1977). In biology, it is understood that "processes such as thought, perception, emotion, and even memory, are usually shared events within tribal, family, and community groups. Exceptions are rare and sometimes celebrated, but do not represent the customary basic mode of human experience" (Goerner and Combs, 1998: 126). Given that social and cognitive factors seem to interact to affect group performance, and that sport psychologists have proffered that organisational, social, and cultural perspectives might enhance the understand-ing of the psychology of sports performance (Woodman and Hardy, 2001), the next section involves an overview of key concepts relating to a social-cognitive perspective on group functioning.

A merging of social and cognitive concepts

This section comprises a discussion about how social and cognitive concepts might be merged to create a social-cognitive perspective on group functioning that has the potential to enhance the current understanding of such function-ing in sport. While social cognition is a broad area, the key social-cognitive concepts that could relate to group functioning in sport can be parsed into two sub-areas (Eccles and Tenenbaum, 2007). The first sub-area concerns the effects of social processes inherent within groups on an individual group member's cognition. For example, evidence has been provided that an individual's cognitions can be influenced by expectations associated with the role that the individual is allocated within a group or team (for reviews, see Eccles and Tenenbaum, 2007; Kerr and Tindale, 2004; Levine *et al.*, 1993). The second sub-area concerns group- and team-level cognition, which relates to cognition arising specifically in the context of group and team interaction. The section that follows is focused on this second sub-area, as we believe it offers the most opportunities to advance the current understanding of group functioning in sport.

The division of labour

A central concept related to an understanding of how collaborating living systems function is the division of labour. As anyone who has ever watched a group of ants carrying a large object will know, "many hands make light work" (or legs, in the case of the ants). There are two key aspects to the concept of the division of labour. First, it is possible to divide labour so that similarly skilled group members (e.g. members with similar muscular endurance) are each allocated labour of a similar quality (e.g. shovelling sand) so that the group can undertake and accomplish a task involving labour demands greater than any one individual group member can supply. Second, it is possible to divide labour so that differently skilled group members (e.g. a quarterback and running back in American football) are each allocated labour of a different quality (e.g. the quarterback is allocated throwing, and the running back carrying the football).

It is this second aspect of divided labour that can dramatically enhance a group's capabilities. A central theme in economics, sociology and biology is the notion that a group's productivity is greater when the different types of labour the group must undertake are allocated so that each type is undertaken by an individual (or individuals) specialised in those types than when all group members partake in all types of labour equally. In biology, the division of labour among specialised organisms is thought to increase reproductive fitness. Biologist Tschinkel asserted that, for humans, "it is the division of labour within groups that makes us so scary – we call these groups corporations, armies, teams, hunting parties, posses, agencies, assembly lines, or factories" (2006: 273). Human societies increasingly cultivate specialisation of their members as means of increasing their fitness. Consider, as did sociologist Durkheim (Jones, 1988), that our education systems constrain us to specialise. Our governments attempt to predict and redress shortfalls in specialist areas to retain national fitness. For example, recent predictions that current decreases in US science, technology, mathematics and engineering expertise will reduce US competitiveness in the global economy have prompted the United States Congress to attempt to address this shortfall (National Academy Press, 2007).

The division of cognitive labour

Theorists have introduced the notion of the division of labour into the cognitive realm to explain how the cognitive labour involved in mediating some tasks is divided among group members (Cannon-Bowers et al., 1993; Hutchins, 1995a; Rouse et al., 1992). Consider, for example, how the control of a rally car is cognitively mediated during the race by two collaborating group members: the driver and co-driver. The driver is allocated the task of driving the car. The co-driver is allocated the task of interpreting and reading aloud to the driver pace notes, which contain information about the nature of the upcoming road (e.g. a sharp left turn is approaching). Considering only the attentional demands associated with the control of the car, neither the driver nor co-driver alone could attend to driving and to the pace notes as carefully as when both driver and co-driver work together, as anyone who has tried to drive a car and attend to a map in an unfamiliar town knows. Indeed, the attentional demands associated with map-reading while driving or piloting are the rationale for much research on electronic "head-up" navigational displays (Eccles et al., 2006; Tufano, 1997).

However, the control of the rally car is not only explained by the division of attentional demands between driver and co-driver but by the differential division of the cognitive labour involved in the control. To elaborate, the cognitions involved specifically with driving are allocated to the driver and with the reading of pace notes to the co-driver, each a relative specialist in his or her own task. Given that driver and co-driver are often quite skilled at each other's tasks, performance is likely to be better when the driver reads the pace notes and the co-driver drives (equal labour division) than when driver or co-driver alone tries to drive and read pace notes (no labour division). However, performance in either scenario is likely to be far inferior to a scenario in which the driver drives and co-driver reads the pace notes, given their respective specialities (differential labour division).

While this is a hypothetical scenario, the division of cognitive labour among group members has been studied in a variety of real-world tasks. An early example of some advantages of the equal division of cognitive labour was offered by Shaw (1932). Individuals or groups of four students at New York's Columbia University were asked to undertake a range of now-classic problems including the "cannibals and missionaries" and "Tower-of-Hanoi" problems. An attempt was made to trace the groups' solution protocols by listening to the intra-group communication and by observing and recording the groups' manipulations of the problem stimuli. A key finding was that groups solved many more problems than individuals. The protocol data indicated that the groups' superior performance was in large part due to the effect of incorrect ideas proposed by one group member being rejected by another group member. By contrast, external checks of this kind were unavailable to the individual working alone.

More recently, Hutchins, a recipient of the coveted MacArthur "genius" grant, offered several real-world examples of the advantages of the differential division of cognitive labour. Hutchins studied the division of cognitive labour in maritime ship navigation (1995a) and aircraft cockpit teams (1995b). The study of maritime ship navigation teams revealed that a fundamental task required for ship navigation is to record the spatial relations between the ship and the world. One such relation is the angular position of the ship at sea relative to a landmark. Hutchins (1995a) described how several personnel are responsible for the processing of navigational information from its initial encoding using the ship's alidade (a type of compass), to its plotting on the ship's navigational chart, and to its final use in actually controlling the ship.

Cognitive affects of social organisation and communication in groups

Researchers studying the division of cognitive labour in groups have asserted that the cognitive properties (or capabilities) of groups are determined by a range of social factors that extend beyond the division of cognitive labour among group members to include the group's social organisation (e.g. whether it has a hierarchy) and its communication (e.g. who can communicate with whom) (Hinsz et al., 1997; Hutchins, 1991, 1995a). Thus, while the group members in two groups might be identical in terms of the knowledge they possess and their capacity for information processing (i.e. for perceiving, attending to, encoding and retrieving information), the cognitive properties of the two groups will be different if the groups differ on any of these dimensions.

Roberts (1964), a cultural anthropologist, provided an example of these concepts. He studied four Native American tribes to identify, for each tribe, how information was retrieved from the tribe when it was needed for problem-solving. The tribes were pre-industrial and non-literate and so information was not stored within the tribes via artefacts (e.g. books). Thus, information important to problem-solving was located only within the memories of the tribal members. Roberts concluded that some tribes were more efficient than others at storing, retrieving and utilising such information for decision-making and that the determinants of a tribe's efficiency were organisational and communicational in nature. These included tribe size, the distribution of information between tribal members, and the patterns and time course of the interactions between members.

Closely related to the notions proposed by Roberts is Wegner's (1986) transactive memory theory. Stated succinctly, transactive memory is concerned with knowledge about "who knows what" (Moreland and Argote, 2003: 135). More formally, it is "a set of individual memory systems in combination with the communication that takes place between individuals" (Wegner, 1986: 186). Central to transactive memory theory is the notion that an individual does not need to know a target piece of information to be able to access it if he or she knows of, and is able to easily access, the location of that piece of information in the external environment. The external environment includes objects such as books and other individuals.

Within established social networks, individual members not only develop a sophisticated awareness about what knowledge is held by other individuals (i.e. the locations) but also have well-established channels of communication with those members so that access to that information is efficient, rapid and reliable. This produces a knowledge "holding" and access system that is larger and more complex than any of the memory systems of the individual members of the social network (Wegner, 1986: 189). Retrieval of information within an established transactive memory system may be a complex process. Wegner (1986) provided an example of this complexity. A boss is asked for information about which she has no idea but thinks her secretary might and so asks the secretary. The secretary might know where the information is located and can access it and provide it to the boss. However, even if the secretary does not know the location, he may know that he provided it to the boss when she asked for it a week earlier and may remind the boss of this episode. This reminder may function as a retrieval cue that allows the boss to access the item either internally from memory or externally, perhaps from a file cabinet. Thus, transactive memory systems provide an example of how an individual's membership within a social organisation, and the social structure of that organisation, can affect the individual's cognitive (specifically memory) capabilities.

Hutchins (1991) used connectionist models of group cognition to explore how confirmation biases in decision-making in a group could be affected by the social organisation of the group. Confirmation bias is defined as the tendency to stick with prior interpretations of a situation and discount any disconfirming evidence. The motivation for the creation of the models arose from an actual shipping accident. The accident occurred after members of the ship's crew appeared to have reinforced beliefs amongst themselves that a nearby ship was sailing away from the crew's ship. By contrast, the nearby ship was actually being sailed towards the crew's ship. Even while holding the cognitive properties of the individuals comprising the two teams constant, the models showed that teams can possess different cognitive properties depending on the nature of the communication within the team. They also showed that, in some circumstances, confirmation bias can be exacerbated at the group level compared to the individual level.

Another area of research that has provided evidence of the effects of social processes within a group on that group's cognitive properties involves the distribution of decision-relevant knowledge among group members. Stasser and Titus (1985) showed that two members of a group must hold the same piece of information for it to be discussed by the group. If the information is only available to one member of the group, it tends to be treated as mere opinion and is therefore less likely to be discussed. However, when more members hold that information, those members tend to provide social support for each other regarding the value of the information. This process appears to be accentuated by time pressure, such that shared information receives attention early during discussion, but unshared information is mentioned relatively late in discussion. The problems arising from time pressure are suggested to play a role in information-processing biases in groups.

Adler and Rodman (2002) proposed a solution to this problem. They suggested that there would be more discussion of information held by only one group member if groups adopted a simple rule that allowed each group member a certain amount of uninterrupted time to introduce and discuss his or her ideas. This provides an example of how a change in the structure of the social processes of a group can potentially affect that group's cognitive capabilities.

The challenges of coordinating the division of cognitive labour

A particular problem for groups in which members have at least partial autonomy is coordination (Eccles and Groth, 2006a, b, 2007; Eccles and Tenenbaum, 2004, 2007). A dictionary definition of "coordination" is "the regulation of diverse elements into an integrated and harmonious operation" (Dictionary.com). Furthermore, the term "coordination" is etymologically distinct from the terms "collaboration" and "cooperation", which are often used erroneously as synonyms with coordination within and beyond the I/O literature on teamwork (Fiore and Salas, 2006). Coordination is derived from three separate concepts – arrange, order and together – which, when applied to the domain of teamwork, can be conceptualised as "the appropriate sequencing and integration of team inputs" (Fiore and Salas, 2006: 371). When this definition is applied to groups, it is each member's labour and, more specifically, the operations each member undertakes, that represent these "elements" or "inputs". Members' operations must be sequenced or integrated in a timely way to form a composite of the operations that achieves satisfactory performance.

The importance of coordination is made clearer following a consideration of the evidence that individual performance within groups actually decreases as group size increases. Steiner's (1972) conceptual framework of group productivity proposed that the potential for group productivity increases with group size, owing to the extra resources provided by the extra group members. However, the increase in group productivity decreases with each additional member, until productivity reaches a plateau so that any increase in membership has no additive effect on productivity. Steiner (1972) called the loss of per-person productivity *process loss*, and the loss of productivity resulting from poor coordination specifically has become known as a *coordination decrement* (Fiore et al., 2003). Clearly, the full potential of the human resources available within a team are wasted when process losses occur. Following Steiner's work, Hackman and Morris have proposed that attempts to increase coordination in groups are actually less concerned with increasing the group's productivity than with "minimizing inevitable process losses" (1975: 64).

An unpublished but classic study by Ringelmann (cited in Kravitz and Martin, 1986) provides an example of Steiner's predictions. Ringelmann studied group tug-of-war performance wherein the addition of group members increased group productivity but decreased individual efficiency. Steiner (1972) proposed that one reason for the loss of efficiency was decreases in personal accountability, which are known to accompany increases in group size. Such decreases cause a reduction in individual motivation and an increase in social loafing. The social loafing account of Ringelmann's findings is now often considered as the only one proposed by Steiner. However, Steiner also proposed that increases in group size present challenges to achieving coordination within the group.

The relationship between group size and coordination is exponential if every group member's operations must be coordinated with every other member's operations. If the coordination of operations between two group members is considered a coordination link (Carron and Hausenblas, 1998), the number of coordination links for a given group size is determined by the following formula:

coordination links = $N (N - 1)/2$ (1)

where N equals the number of group members. If two people crew a sailboat, there is only one coordination link between group members, but if eight people crew the same sailboat, providing four times the resources, there is the potential for 28 coordination links.

Consider a hypothetical model in which (a) each member of a group must coordinate his or her operations (i.e. form a coordination link) with all remaining group members; (b) the control of the coordination involved in one coordination link involves an equivalent of 10 per cent of one individual's cognitive resources; and (c) the relationship between the resource "cost" of each cognitive resource link and the number of links in a group is linear. Within this model, a sailboat operator who attempts to double the cognitive resources available to crew his boat by recruiting a second crew member will only achieve a 90 per cent increase in available cognitive resources. This is because the formation of the coordination link between the members will impose 10 per cent coordination "overhead" on one member or 5 per cent on both members if the labour is equally divided. Furthermore, an attempt to double cognitive resources in even slightly larger groups will impose a much higher coordination overhead. Doubling the cognitive resources of a four-member crew by recruiting four more members imposes a 280 per cent overhead, equating to 35 per cent per person. This is why even small groups find it useful to appoint a manager (or "skipper" in sailing parlance), a crew member with a specialisation in dealing with coordination and other team-based work, termed *teamwork* in the I/O literature (Eccles and Tenenbaum, 2004, 2007; McIntyre and Salas, 1995). Most of the labour associated with the coordination overhead can be allocated to the manager, leaving the remaining crew members to undertake more of the task-based work, termed *taskwork* in the I/O literature.

In addition to group size, a key factor affecting the requirement of a group to achieve coordination is the type of task being undertaken. While researchers have proposed different classification systems for the types of task that groups typically undertake, such as McGrath's (1984) task circumplex, Steiner (1972) has provided the most explicit descriptions of how the requirement for coordination of a group's activities could depend on the type of task being undertaken. Steiner proposed four types of task in this regard: disjunctive, conjunctive, additive and discretionary (Steiner, 1972). *Disjunctive tasks* are those that only need one group member to be capable of achieving the task. For example, if one group member can solve a mathematical equation provided as a task to the group, then the group can solve it. Thus, this type of task requires little coordination within the group as group members can work independently to undertake the task. *Conjunctive tasks* lie at the opposite end of a continuum to disjunctive tasks. Thus, conjunctive tasks are those requiring all group members to contribute if the group is to be successful and thus require the group to coordinate its efforts. Conjunctive tasks can be found in team sports. For example, within a rugby union defence that is spread out in a line over the field in defence of its territory, each player must be active in his or her own defending role to avoid penetration of the line by an opponent. An interesting feature of the disjunctive–conjunctive task continuum is that performance is often limited in disjunctive tasks by the competence of the strongest group member – the member that solves the equation fastest – and in conjunctive tasks by the competence of the weakest member – the least-skilled player in the rugby team's defence.

Additive tasks involve group members' contributions being combined by summation to yield a group outcome such as the total annual volume of sales achieved by a sales team where each team member works independently in their own sales territory. Additive tasks can require the coordination of the group's activities but not to the extent required for conjunctive tasks. The coordination demand imposed by *discretionary tasks* can vary because, for this task type, the group has discretion in terms of how to divide labour among its members. For example, project-management teams in business are often self-governing and, thus, when presented with a project, are able to decide how to organise their team structure and allocate tasks across or between team members. As McGrath (1984) noted, many domains, including sports, involve multiple tasks that must be undertaken simultaneously and that differ in terms of the task types proposed by Steiner.

Studies have provided evidence of the challenges associated with such coordination. An early example in the cognitive arena was provided by Thorndike (1938). Thorndike asked individuals and groups of students to undertake various tasks such as completing sentences and limericks, and solving and creating crossword puzzles. Groups outperformed individuals on all tasks with the exception of crossword-puzzle creation. The reason proffered for the groups' relative inferiority on this task was that the creating process was of such a high cognitive demand that sharing a "line" of creative thought within the group required cognitive resources that could be used more productively for developing that line in one's own mind. Consequently, "the group product frequently amounted to nothing but the best individual performance of a member of the group, turned in for the group" (1938: 413).

An early example of the problems associated with group coordination in the motor domain was provided in a study by Comrey (1953), which involved a pegboard assembly task. In an "individual condition", two men sat across from one another at a table. Each man undertook his own pegboard assembly task. Both men were given the same amount of time to complete the task. Immediately following this, and with the men still seated in their original positions, a "group condition" was created by positioning a board between the two men and asking that they complete overlapping operations as if working on a production line, so that the coordination of their activities was required. Similar to the finding of the tug-of-war study presented earlier, the key finding of the study by Comrey was that, while the absolute performance of a group was superior to that of an individual, it was always less than the sum of the group members' individual performances.

Evidence of the challenge presented by group coordination has also been found in the sports domain. In order to investigate the effects of group size on group cohesion and performance, Widmeyer et al. (1990) assigned college students to basketball teams of three, six or nine members who played three-on-three games in a weekly basketball league for a ten-week period. The teams comprised of six members outperformed teams of three and nine. It was asserted that the performance of the teams of three was negatively affected by physical fatigue, whereas the teams of other sizes were able to avoid this problem because they had enough players to rotate in and out of play. The explanation of the relative inferiority of performance by the teams of nine was less clear. However, Widmeyer et al. surmised that poor motivation was unlikely. Instead, these authors argued that poor coordination was the most likely explanation, although coordination was not measured.

Control mechanisms mediating the organisation and coordination of the division of cognitive labour

Returning to the example of the drop-kick routine, it is clear that the challenge of achieving effective coordination in groups can be met. What is less clear, however, is how. Few studies have provided insight into the mechanisms that might mediate the control of a group's operations so that coordination can be achieved. A starting point, then, might be to consider the mechanisms that are purported to mediate the performance of *individuals* within group settings. The current research literature on this topic indicates that, as the performer acquires experience and engages in practice, there are gradual increases in the amount of and improvements in the organisation of domain-specific knowledge, as well as rapid and flexible memorisation of, and access to, that knowledge during performance (Ericsson and Kintsch, 1995). These adaptations drive the performer's search of the environment for task-relevant sources of information and afford him or her rapid integration of that information with his or her existing knowledge, the product of which is considered a model (Kintsch, 1988) or profile (McPherson, 1999) of the current situation or event. In team sports that require rapid responses to continually changing, dynamic and open environments (such as football), a key benefit of a performer's ability to construct an elaborate situation model is an improvement in his or her ability to anticipate environmental changes. With regard to coordination, elaborate situation model construction in team sports allows the performer to anticipate changes in the actions of team-mates and, in turn, more time to select, prepare and execute appropriate responses to those actions (i.e. coordinate their operations; McPherson, 1999; Ward and Eccles, 2006; Ward and Williams, 2003).

The role of planning in the construction of situation models

In group settings, a key source of information used in the construction of group-members' situation models is plans. Several studies (e.g. Comrey, 1953; Kidd, 1961; Naylor and Briggs, 1965) have provided evidence that sources of inefficiency in group settings are not only the result of instances of poor coordination, such as when the individuals in the study by Comrey (1953) simultaneously attempted to place pegs in the same pegboard hole, but also from attempts by group members to rectify problems with coordination. To elaborate, group members in these studies occasionally ceased their operations following coordination problems in order to communicate so that a plan could be constructed about how to avoid these problems and thus enhance coordination on future trials.

Thus, group-level planning seems important for coordination. The dictionary definition of a plan is "a scheme or method of acting, doing, proceeding, making, etc., developed in advance" (Dictionary.com). As labour in groups is often divided according to group-member specialisation, planning involves "developing in advance" of the intended labour a "scheme of proceeding" that specifies the group's goal and who (i.e. which group member) will do what (i.e. which operations) and when, as a means to achieving that goal. Thus, a plan allows each group member to obtain and integrate information into his or her situation model about the nature and timing of the operations he or she is to perform. This facilitates coordination and, in turn, performance (Cannon-Bowers *et al.*, 1993; Rouse *et al.*, 1992; Stout *et al.*, 1999).

However, some scholars have questioned the utility of plans as a resource for structuring behaviour, be it at the individual or group level, in at least some types of tasks (Ward and Eccles, 2006). For example, in open and dynamic task environments that involve multiple degrees-of-freedom, football being the exemplar, plans would seem to be only a very loose resource for group members to use to structure the group's activities. By contrast, performance in these environments would seem to require more online, or so-called "on-the-fly", moment-to-moment adaptations than a plan would permit (Ward and Eccles, 2006). This concern is related to a much larger debate in the cognitive sciences about the utility of plans. For example, Suchman wrote that "the circumstances of our actions are never fully anticipated and are continuously changing around us. As a consequence our actions, while systematic, are never planned in the strong sense that cognitive science would have it" (1987: viii). In Suchman's view, preformulated mental representations of operations such as plans (cf. Miller *et al.*, 1960) are "best viewed as a weak resource for what is primarily ad hoc activity" (Suchman, 1987: ix).

However, implicit in Suchman's view of plans is that they function to structure operations at a relatively specific level. This overlooks the possibility that plans can structure operations at different levels of abstraction, ranging from general to specific (Eccles and Tenenbaum, 2004, 2007; Hayes-Roth and Hayes-Roth, 1979; Ward and Eccles, 2006). When the function of plans is considered in terms of providing constraints on behaviour (Newell, 1986), plans at the general end of the abstraction continuum provide only a few "loose" constraints on behaviour, but these constraints still function to help achieve coordination in groups. For example, a team plan for a football game may include only a specification of group members' roles: "You two play in defence, you on the right wing, you on the left ..." etc. When Player A is assigned the role of "defender", she is provided with only a few specific constraints on her moment-to-moment selection of operations, which means that she can remain relatively flexible and adapt to the dynamic game situation. Nonetheless, the constraints function to restrict her from selecting most operations related to offensive tactics. Furthermore, if the plan was known to the entire team (i.e. was integrated into each player's situation model), then Player A's team-mates would know that her role was that of a defender, which would place constraints on whether and when they should pass to her in a given situation. Thus, the plan's specification of roles helps the group achieve the desired coordination of divided labour.

General strategies constitute another example of how plans at the general end of the abstraction continuum can provide only a few "loose" constraints on behaviour but nonetheless help achieve coordination. For example, the strategy of attacking down the wings in the first half of a football game provides few specific constraints on team-members' moment-to-moment selections of operations during the game. This means that players can be flexible and adaptive in the specific nature and timing of their attacks. However, the few constraints that are specified by this strategy still function to limit players' attacks down the middle of the field in the first half of the game. Thus, general plans can be used to achieve group coordination in open sports because they specify constraints only at a macro-level of operations, which allows for flexibility and adaptation at a micro-level.

By contrast, plans at the specific end of the abstraction continuum provide many more constraints on the nature and timing of team-members' operations. Thus, specific plans are useful in the coordination of team sports characterised by discrete sequences of operations. American football is an excellent example of a team sport in which a range of plans or "plays" involving relatively "tight" constraints on group-members' operations are devised prior to the game. These are selected by the coach for each phase or "down" of the game in order to coordinate the team's operations during that down. As Wikipedia's entry on "American football" suggests: "Before each down, each team chooses a play, or coordinated movements and actions, that the players should follow on a down" (Wikipedia, http://en.wikipedia.org/wiki/American_football).

However, while American football might operate nearer the specific end of a plan abstraction continuum, this does not mean that team operations in American football are highly constrained; simply that there are tighter constraints on members' operations than in, say, football. There remains the potential for flexibility even within the relatively tight constraints imposed on a receiver by a receiver-route specified as part of a "play" planned by an offensive coach. This is because the receiver and quarterback do not memorise specific receiver routes to be run. By contrast, they memorise spatial constraints that form the outer boundaries of a spatial "corridor" on the field within which the receiver can adapt in order to evade defensive opponent players or when faced with other similar perturbations.

The shared requirement

Researchers interested in group functioning in I/O psychology have asserted that coordination is more likely to be attainable if information about plans designed to achieve coordination is integrated into each group member's situation model so that the plan is *shared* by all group members (Cannon-Bowers *et al.*, 1993; Marks *et al.*, 2000; Mathieu *et al.*, 2000; Smith-Jentsch *et al.*, 2001; for a review, see Salas and Fiore, 2004). The term "shared" in this instance means to be "held in common" (Dictionary.com). The process of setting up a meeting provides a simple example of the social-cognitive concept of knowledge sharing. Two critical pieces of information that must be not only obtained but also shared by those intending to meet are the timing (i.e. date and time) and the location of the meeting. This is evident in the following text, which represents a typical telephone exchange between the first author and one of his colleagues:

AUTHOR: "Hey, fancy a coffee?"
COLLEAGUE: "Ok, how about, say, half three at [a coffee company] on Tennessee Street?"
AUTHOR: "Um, how about 3:45, I've got a student coming in beforehand?"
COLLEAGUE: "Ok, 3:45's fine, see you then."
AUTHOR: "Will do, see you mate."

Furthermore, some analysis of this exchange also indicates that group members involved in arranging a meeting must reach a second shared state that is meta-cognitive in nature; that is, it involves knowing about what is known (Flavell, 1979). To elaborate, the first shared state relates to knowledge of the plan: each member knows he must meet the other member at the coffee shop on Tennessee Street at 3:45. The second shared state relates to knowledge that the first shared state has been achieved: each member knows that both members are aware that the plan has been successfully shared. The utterance "see you then" by the colleague functions to communicate to the author that the colleague currently understands that the pair are intending to meet at 3:45. Furthermore, the utterance implicitly requests, via social convention in language, that the author confirms (or corrects) this understanding (see Smith, 1977, for similar conjectures). When one individual knows that another possesses some particular knowledge, this is a meta-cognitive state not in a traditional individualistic sense, wherein one knows what one does (or does not) know, but in a social sense, in that it involves knowledge of another's knowledge. Meta-cognition in this instance is akin to the concept of transactive memory proposed by Wegner (1986) and described earlier.

In the process of attempting to reach the shared states described, it is possible for group members to achieve the second state without achieving the first. For example, the author could "know" that both he and his colleague know they are meeting for coffee at 3:45, while the colleague could "know" that both he and the author know they are meeting at 3:30. There is little doubt that the reader has at one time or another experienced this situation and, in relation to it, has uttered a statement such as: "I thought we agreed to meet at…" A documented example of this problem occurs in the sport of mountaineering. Mountaineering teams often split up during an expedition, owing to various factors such as team members developing mountain sickness, but arrange to meet at some later time and location. The different subgroups often achieve the second shared state in that each subgroup knows that all subgroups share the arranged meeting time and location, but in reality the arrangements are not shared and thus the first shared state is not achieved. Consequently, the subgroups fail to meet and, believing that the other subgroups have failed to get off the mountain safely, contact a mountain rescue team. Only later is it discovered that all subgroups got off the mountain safely and are worrying about one another from, for example, different cafes. In the words of the rescue services of the Alpine Club of Canada, "A high number of searches result simply from parties splitting up while not coming to reasonable understanding about who is going to do what" (Alpine Club of Canada, n.d.). Thus, it appears that effective communication within groups facilitates the control of coordination via the establishment and maintenance of shared situation models (Cooke et al., 2001; Endsley, 1995; Orasanu and Fisher, 1992).

Communication

One of the strongest sources of evidence for the role of communication in the control of group coordination is provided by a finding in the life sciences that all species depending for survival on membership of a collaborative social group are characterised by an effective system of intra-group communication (e.g. Boinski and Garber, 2000; Pastor and Seeley, 2005; Tschinkel, 2006). For example, research on animal groups has revealed that coordination depends on effective inter-animal communication (P. Feltovich, personal communication; Smith, 1977). Animals exhibit behaviours that, like those of humans, allow or disallow other animals to collaborate. For example, animals have ways of displaying a readiness to interact, which includes kinds of chirping, various forms of bowing, "tidbitting", in which a morsel of food is offered, and touching. By contrast, absence of an opportunity to interact is indicated by various forms of sticking-out-the-tongue, displaying the tongue, chattering barks and vocalisations at special and unusual frequencies (Feltovich et al., 2004).

In addition, a long-prevalent paradigm in animal studies is that communication, in the form of various signals, increases "the predictability of the individual signaller's current and future behaviour", which, in turn, facilitates coordination within groups (Boinski, 2000: 422). For example, a challenge for species that depend on coordinated locomotion is reaching a group-level "plan" about when and where to travel. Research has shown that locomotion displays by certain members of the group provide this information in advance of the movement so that group members can anticipate and thus prepare for movement. For example, geese, which fly as a coordinated group, toss their heads before taking flight in order to indicate imminent flight (Smith, 1977). Furthermore, lead members of groups of primates that move in troops provide loud calls, such as "deep, hoarse, clucks", to indicate the imminence and intended direction of the movement (Boinski, 2000: 422). Similarly, honey bees engage in "buzz-runs", which involve runs through the most clustered part of the colony, as a signal to the colony that whole-colony travel is imminent (Dyer, 2000).

Other research on insects has provided examples of signalling used to coordinate the division of labour. Worker bees within honey bee colonies utilise at least four signals for coordinating food foraging and collection activities. These include the waggle dance, tremble dance, shaking signal and brief piping signal (Dyer, 2002; Pastor and Seeley, 2005; Schneider and Lewis, 2004). When a colony needs to gather nectar, forager bees that are successful in finding nectar use waggle dances to direct other, less-successful foragers to nectar sources. When a colony's rate of nectar collection exceeds its rate of nectar processing, successful foragers use tremble dances to signal to other bees that they should begin working to process nectar and to inhibit foragers from producing waggle dances. When a colony needs to activate foragers after a period of low foraging activity (e.g. due to bad weather), successful foragers shake to signal to other foragers that they should follow waggle dances. The use of the piping signal is less clear, but studies have provided evidence that it is used as a "stop signal" to stop other bees from waggle dancing (e.g. Pastor and Seeley, 2005).

With regard to human groups, I/O psychologists have asserted that members of effective groups use two key types of communication to exchange information allowing the creation and maintenance of a model of the current situation: intentional and unintentional communication (MacMillan *et al.*, 2004; see also Fisher and Hawes, 1971; Gouran and Hirokawa, 1983; Poole *et al.*, 1986). Intentional verbal communication involves speech between group members (e.g. "I'll be finished in five minutes"). Intentional non-verbal communication involves non-verbal signals between group members (e.g. holding up five fingers to indicate that a task will be finished in five minutes). Unintentional communication is communication that is unintentionally sent by one party to another. In group settings, unintentional communication is usually in a non-verbal form. One such form involves sensations of other group members' operations (e.g. I can see or hear what this group member is doing) or of the environmental affects of other group members' operations (e.g. the boxes are stacked and thus the group member responsible for packing them must have finished packing them; Eccles and Tenenbaum, 2004, 2007).

Direction

A final mechanism underlying the control of divided labour in groups is direction. As Hutchins asserted, "Mass labor must be coordinated and led" (1995a: 177). Such direction is usually provided by an individual or a few individuals within the group. These individuals are often deemed by the remainder of the group members as being in exclusive possession of some specific assets relevant to the directorial role that warrants these individuals being allocated this role. Typical examples of such assets include intellectual capabilities, as in the example of coaches in sport or a board of directors of a company, and specific skills in managing, leading and coordinating groups. One key function of such directors, even in highly democratic groups, is to use their authority to end debate about, and then make final decisions regarding, how labour will be divided and controlled within the group so that coordination can be achieved.

Summary of concepts

This section began with a description of how labour, and cognitive labour in particular, can be divided among group members so that groups can maximise the efficiency with which they undertake tasks involving demands that would overwhelm an individual. Following this, there was a discussion of how the social organisation of, and communication within, groups can affect the group's cognitive properties. Next, the challenges of achieving coordination amongst multiple group members and their operations were introduced. Lastly, the control mechanisms that can enable such coordination to be achieved, such as planning, communication and direction, were described.

A social-cognitive understanding of a sport organisation's preparation for competition

In this section, there is an attempt to illustrate the utility of a social-cognitive perspective by adopting this perspective within a case study of the functioning of a sport organisation. There is also an attempt to show how such a perspective provides insights that are complementary to, but that would not have been provided by, more traditional perspectives on group functioning. To our knowledge, such an interpretation in the field of sport psychology is without precedent and should promote further research in this area.

The organisation studied here is a national orienteering squad. This squad has been observed during studies of elite-level orienteering that have been undertaken by the first author and his colleagues over the last decade (Eccles, 2006, forthcoming; Eccles et al., 2002a, 2002b, 2006, 2008). These observations were made during and following interviews, communications, and laboratory- and field-testing sessions with the squad's members, coaches and sport psychologist, and in particular during the first author's attendance at one squad training camp in 1998 that involved eating, sleeping, travelling and training alongside the squad.

Competition preparation in orienteering

Orienteering is an individual sport in which winning is achieved by being the fastest to navigate on foot through a set of points, known as controls, in a specific order over wild terrain. The distance from one control to the next is known as a leg. An orienteering course typically comprises 25 legs over 15 kilometres. Controls are symbolised by circles printed on a map. The map is presented only seconds before the race begins and is carried with a compass during the race. Given the time constraint inherent in the sport, orienteers will typically run during the race as fast as possible given the distance.

Typically, elite orienteers attempt to peak at only a small number of major competitions each year, such as the World Championships. Eccles *et al.* (forthcoming) identified that elite orienteers prepare in different ways for each major competition because the task constraints (Newell, 1986; Vicente, 2000) inherent within a competition change between competitions. While Eccles *et al.* (forthcoming) described changes to various sets of task constraints across competitions, for brevity the focus here is on only one such set, which is that relating to the competition's terrain. To elaborate, as each major orienteering competition is held in a different country each year, the terrain can vary dramatically between competitions. The terrain can be considered to constitute a set of task constraints because it determines, in large part, the navigation and running-related demands of the competition (Eccles *et al.*, 2002a). For a simplified example, orienteering in hilly compared to flat terrain places different physical demands on the orienteer. Additionally, navigating in forest-covered sand dunes versus on treeless moors places very different navigational demands on the orienteer.

Because the constraints associated with the terrain change with each competition, at least at a specific level, it is imperative that orienteering squads identify the constraints unique to an upcoming competition, termed *competition constraints*, and subsequently use them to identify and design practice environments that represent those constraints as closely as possible (Araujo *et al.*, 2004). Consequently, prior to competition, squad members may better achieve "maximal adaptation to task constraints" (Ericsson and Lehman, 1996: 273; Vicente, 2000). The identification of the constraints unique to an upcoming competition becomes a task in itself, and one that must be undertaken before the competition and with enough time that representative practice environments can be identified, designed and utilised. However, the identification task has its own constraints. The competition organisers prohibit access to the actual site of the competition for up to two years prior to the competition to prevent orienteers living local to the competition site gaining an unfair advantage. Thus, direct identification of the competition constraints is made impossible.

However, the national orienteering squad observed by the first author used various strategies to help identify competition constraints without violating the access rule. The primary strategies are described as follows. To provide some context within which to interpret the strategies, the organisation of the squad involved a head coach, two assistant coaches, a doctor, a sport psychologist, a variety of volunteer organisers who were often parents of squad members, and approximately ten male and ten female squad members. One raw representative quotation from studies by Eccles *et al.* (2002a, forthcoming) is used to describe each strategy.

Sharing of existing knowledge of terrain

When the location for a major upcoming competition is first announced by the competition organisers, squad coaches ask all members of the squad to share with the remaining members any knowledge they may have about the terrain at the competition location and about other similar terrain from which inferences about the competition terrain can be made. Squad members usually have experience orienteering in a wide variety of terrain in many different countries. Consequently, they may have acquired knowledge about the terrain at the competition location having previously orienteered within similar terrain located in the region or country of the upcoming competition. Also, squad members have often acquired knowledge during their orienteering careers about the terrain at the competition location from various narrative sources (see Bal, 1997) such as stories, anecdotes and accounts of orienteering from other orienteers and coaches (e.g. "The terrain is always very technical in Sweden"). Consider the following example of an orienteer's acquired knowledge of terrain in southern Norway:

> Most of my orienteering abroad last year was done in southern Norway .... You [are] moving through the terrain so slowly ... it seems to make you want to ... need more detail as you're going along the leg .... It's just fairly low visibility and there's very little in the way of man-made line features so you're always having to read the ... detail and having to stay in contact with the map a lot more of the time .... You're looking at it all the time .... It becomes much more than simply checking off the big features because all the features look the same ... you need to be checking for shapes, getting down to much more detail.
>
> (Male orienteer)

Utilising externally located information

Squad coaches also ask squad members to make use of *locations* (Wegner, 1986) external to the squad known to contain or have the potential to contain information about the competition terrain or terrain similar to the competition terrain. One key type of location involves materials such as topographical maps, specialist orienteering maps and aerial photographs. Orienteers often assemble collections of such materials over their orienteering careers for a variety of purposes. The squad members search any collections they may have for these materials and share their findings with the remainder of the squad.

Another key type of location concerns *contacts* external to the squad, such as coaches and other orienteers. Often, squad members have acquired many such contacts over their orienteering careers and inquire of these contacts whether they have experience of, and thus knowledge about, terrain similar to the competition terrain. Squad members then share any obtained information with the remainder of the squad.

Squad members also utilise higher-order locations, which are locations that contain or have the potential to contain information about other locations. For example, members will ask their contacts whether they have any relevant materials that could be provided to the squad or know any other contacts with relevant knowledge. Members will also use the Internet to search for websites that might contain relevant materials. An example is a land survey company website containing aerial photographs from a recent survey of relevant terrain. The following orienteer provides evidence of such processes: "I knew a few people from other countries going who I'd met up with in competitions in Sweden ... and they told me about what they expected ... [and] about maps that were relevant [to the competition terrain]" (male orienteer).

Travelling scout groups

A third strategy involves small subsets of the squad, termed here *scout groups*, travelling to the host country at various times throughout the year preceding the competition. Each scout group's task is to gather information about the competition terrain. This is undertaken by first identifying areas of terrain similar to the competition terrain and then, where possible, orienteering within these areas to better understand the competition constraints. The groups also take video recordings and photographs of the terrain. While there, the groups often also meet with local orienteers who function as information locations by imparting to the squad members relevant knowledge they possess about areas of similar terrain and lending the members materials, such as maps. Upon their return home, the scout groups share their gathered information with the remainder of the squad. This process is described in the following quote:

> The orienteers [acting as scouts] came back from Japan and said, "The ground coverage is mostly bamboo grass and it tramples very easily and makes paths, and the ground is steep and quite sandy, which is good for 'contouring in' and, you know, all of that information is passed on [to the remainder of the squad]."
>
> (Male coach)

Identifying representative local terrain

Once some of the uncertainty about the competition constraints has been reduced, squad coaches ask squad members to consider areas of terrain that are representative of the competition terrain but located nearer to the squad's region or country. Because these areas involve constraints representative of those at the competition, they constitute "ready-made" practice environments.

The same processes involved in identifying the competition constraints are used in identifying representative local terrain.

First, individual squad members are asked to share any existing knowledge they may possess about such areas. Squad members come from different regions within the squad's own country, and each member possesses a good knowledge of the terrain in his or her home region that can be used to identify representative terrain. Second, the squad makes use of external locations (i.e. materials and contacts) to help identify areas of representative local terrain. Third, when potential areas have been identified, coaches ask squad members with homes in the regions containing those areas or who are involved in upcoming competitions in those regions to visit the areas and evaluate their potential as practice venues. When areas of terrain have been identified as useful for practice, the squad coaches organise training camps for the squad within those areas. This process is described in the following quote:

> And we'll obviously look at everything when we're over there [in Japan] and spend lots of hours in the terrain over there. But then, once we get back here, well, we have been trying to find similar areas in Europe .... And there's not many but you can find a few that are technically [i.e. navigationally] similar or physically similar. On the physical side, Japan is very hilly and extremely steep and there's lots of ups and downs. We've been looking for areas like that. On the technical side, it's quite tricky finding the best route. It's quite difficult – we can't find areas with compact valley systems which Japan has and where the routes are almost the same. We just pool our memories together and ... there was an area in Scotland someone came up with. Someone else also said, "Oh, there's tons of terrain like that in Lithuania." So we're having a team selection right now in Lithuania.
>
> (Male orienteer)

Division of information-gathering labour

While the labour involved in gathering information about the competition constraints and, subsequently, identifying representative local terrain was divided among the group's members, it is typical that this division is not equal in quantitative or qualitative terms. The cause of this inequality involves differences on a variety of dimensions among the individual squad members. These dimensions include available resources such as time and finances, specialist knowledge of information about the competition constraints and the locations of areas of representative local terrain, and motivation. Thus, some squad members are allocated tasks requiring considerable time and money, such as travelling to the host country, because they have the fewest constraints on these resources (e.g. some members were university students with long holidays). In addition, some squad members undertake exclusive tasks owing, for example, to their unique knowledge. To elaborate, some members possess unique knowledge of contacts and thus contact them for relevant information. By contrast, other members with no such knowledge possess exclusive knowledge of representative local terrain and visit them to evaluate their potential as practice venues.

Communication of information

Group members share existing knowledge and, as they become available, share information and materials relating to the competition constraints with other squad members using a variety of communication mechanisms including: (a) face-to-face interaction at squad training camps and, for subsets of the squad, at local orienteering club meetings; (b) telephone calls; (c) email; and (d) various other electronic media such as web forums. Given the number of squad members and communication mechanisms, the communication flow among the group members is complex and frequent. Two communication mechanisms in particular appear noteworthy for their utility. The first is face-to-face inter-action at the squad training camps. Coaches set up a series of these camps for all squad members at various locations around the squad's own country in the months preceding a major competition. There are several advantages of face-to-face interaction at these camps compared to the other communication mechanisms used by the squad. First, the camps allow squad members to easily share information via a variety of media including verbal accounts, photographs, maps and video. Additionally, squad members juxtapose these media and thus easily compare and contrast the information they provide. Second, communication at the camps is synchronous rather than asynchronous, which means that members receiving information are able to quickly and easily seek clarification or ask for elaboration about some item of information from the member providing that information and receive a response with no delay (Fiore *et al.*, 2003). Finally, many squad members are involved simultaneously in the discussion of a given item of information, which is useful given the diversity of knowledge afforded by a large group (as discussed above, pp. 302–303).

The second communication mechanism noteworthy for its utility is email. Squad members use email to send messages and materials such as photographs and maps to all the members and thus new information, almost regardless of the sender's location, is disseminated easily. For example, the scout groups, while travelling, send reports by email about the terrain they are exploring back to the squad members in the squad's home country.

Control and direction

The control of the division of labour within the squad is achieved in part by direction. Direction is provided by the coaches and its effectiveness is facilitated by their possession of authority. Authority is assigned to the coaches through a variety of mechanisms including: (a) the social convention that "appointed coaches are the squad leaders"; (b) respect of the coaches' experience and knowledge, and for their effort and motivation towards enhancing the squad's performance; and (c) an understanding of their power to select the squad members who will represent their country at major competitions. The coaches play a key role in allocating the labour required to gather information about the competition constraints and allocating deadlines, or at least preferred deadlines, for the delivery of that information. Deadlines are often the dates of the squad training camps so that squad members can disseminate their gathered information to those attending the camps. In addition, the control of the division of labour is achieved in part through the group's self-organisation. When labour is being allocated, squad members often volunteer to undertake some specific form of labour, usually because they are aware of their possession of a specialisation or resources relating to undertaking that labour (as discussed above, pp. 302–303).

Extent of plan sharedness

A plan specifying the operations that are to be undertaken by each squad member is formulated predominantly by the squad coaches. Each squad member is only required to know what operations he or she should undertake and that the other operations important for the squad as a whole, such as travelling to the country hosting the competition, are going to be undertaken by other members of the squad. Thus, the only individuals with full knowledge of the plan are the coaches. The remaining squad members possess only part of this plan. This is because there are few instances in which group members must coordinate their operations while they are being undertaken.

By contrast, there is a need to coordinate the outcomes of these operations, in that certain operations have deadlines for their completion (as discussed above, this page). Thus, the requirement for, and extent of, plan sharedness in this instance does not extend fully to the nature of the operations but just to one temporal component of those operations, which is their completion date.

Interpretations from a social-cognitive perspective

From a social-cognitive perspective, a key finding relating to the functioning of the squad in preparation for major competitions is that, while orienteering is essentially an individual sport, there are clear advantages for the individual squad member and his or her preparation with regard to being a member of the squad described. The first advantage relates to the process of sharing existing knowledge about the competition terrain. The individual squad member has rapid access to information about the competition constraints that would otherwise require considerable time and effort to gather, and, perhaps for some information, be impossible to gather. Quantitatively, the individual squad member has the potential for access to over 20-times the knowledge relating to the competition constraints that he or she possesses individually due to the number of members comprising the squad. Qualitatively, the individual squad member has the potential for access to rich, elaborate and relatively exclusive knowledge relating to these constraints owing to the extensive experience of other squad members such as the coaches. Viewed in terms of transactive memory theory, the goal of the squad in sharing the existing knowledge of each member is to move from a set of differentiated memories, in which each squad member holds different knowledge about the terrain, to a fully integrated memory system, in which each squad member holds the knowledge about the terrain derived from all of the remaining squad members (Wegner, 1986).

The second advantage relates to the division of labour in gathering information about the competition constraints. With each squad member actively gathering information, each individual member is potentially able to benefit from over 20-times the gathering labour compared to him or her working alone. If each squad member is able, on average, to obtain information from one external contact and access one material item such as a map, an individual squad member has potential access to over 40 sources of information about the competition constraints. The travelling scout groups exemplify the advantages of the division of labour. Those squad members who have fewest constraints on travel will tend to volunteer to travel to the country hosting the competition, gathering information that would otherwise be unavailable to the individual orienteer who was unable to undertake this travel.

Finally, the labour associated with controlling the division and coordination of the labour associated with gathering information about the competition constraints and identifying representative local terrain is undertaken largely by the coaches. The coaches also undertake most of the labour associated with organising squad meetings to help facilitate the sharing of gathered information, training within representative local terrain and travel arrangements for the scout groups. Thus, individual squad members are burdened minimally with the labour required to control the division of labour that affords them the cognitive advantages discussed above.

Thus, at least in this instance, membership of a social group that has a shared goal, in which labour is allocated on the basis of member expertise and resource availability, and in which this labour is directed and controlled so that its coordination is achieved, can convey clear cognitive advantages for the individual group member. Specifically, when compared to operating alone, an individual operating in a group of this nature can access task-relevant information of superior quantity and quality, more rapidly and with less effort.

Limitations of the presented case study

During an excellent review of this chapter, an anonymous reviewer proposed two related limitations of this case study. The first concern was that there is a noteworthy difference between the type of coordination featured within the case study – that is, the coordination of the orienteering squad's efforts to prepare for competition – and the type of coordination required for effective team performance in sports such as football and rugby union. We do not disagree. One important difference is temporal. Because the environment in which a sports team such as a football team operates is often unpredictable, externally paced and changes rapidly, sports teams must coordinate their actions very rapidly, which, among other things, restricts use of intentional verbal communication as a means to achieve coordination (Eccles and Tenenbaum, 2004). By contrast, within the case study, there were few time constraints on the orienteering squad as it prepared for competition and thus intentional forms of communication were used extensively to coordinate the squad's work. However, while both the orienteering squad and dynamic sports teams differ in terms of the specific means by which coordination is achieved, both scenarios (a) involve a division of labour; (b) require coordination of that labour; and (c) use planning, sharedness, communication and direction to achieve such coordination. Thus, describing differences between the two scenarios in terms of the means by which coordination is achieved usefully captures more of the variance in the concept of coordination in sport but does not invalidate the collection of higher-order concepts proposed here as each concept within the collection generalises to, and hence is useful in understanding, both scenarios.

The second limitation raised concerned the use of the case study in demonstrating the potential of a social-cognitive perspective for enhancing understanding in the area of group functioning in sport. Specifically, it was proposed that the squad's preparation for competition is an activity that offers not nearly as interesting insights into coordination as a competition requiring dynamic coordination. Our concern with this argument is that it is "competition-centric". To elaborate, this argument largely ignores the extensive period of practice and preparation that precedes, and is the only means to achieving, competitive performance. In general, sport psychologists are as interested in practice and preparation for competition, given its importance, as with actual competitive performance. Furthermore, there have been recent calls for research on, and an increased interest in the impact of, organisational factors on a sport performer's psychological preparation for competition (Eccles and Tenenbaum, 2007; Hanton et al., 2005; Pain and Harwood, 2007; Woodman and Hardy, 2001). Thus, we believe that introducing well-established concepts from social-cognitive psychology (e.g. transactive memory theory) to help explain how an organisation provides a cognitive advantage to its individual members prior to competition is unprecedented, timely and of utility to the sport psychology community.

Implications of a social-cognitive perspective on group functioning for athletes, sport psychologists and other practitioners

In this section, various implications of the social-cognitive concepts described in the present chapter for athletes, sport psychologists and other practitioners are proposed.

Unlock the group's cognitive potential

Coaches, managers and heads of sport organisations sometimes bring together the group members they train or oversee in an attempt to "tap their heads". For example, they might ask leaders in the sport organisation to brainstorm about how to turn a period of low morale around in the organisation, ask coaches for their opinions about why there is poor cohesion in the team, or ask players to identify what strategies they think will work best against a difficult upcoming opponent. Given that research has shown that, in a group setting, information only available to one group member tends to be treated as mere opinion and thus is less likely to be discussed (Stasser and Titus, 1985), it is recommended that each group member is allowed a certain amount of uninterrupted time to present his or her ideas to the group (Adler and Rodman, 2002). This way, a key social process that would otherwise stifle the cognitive potential of the group will be ameliorated and the potential for otherwise hidden expertise and creative thinking within the group more effectively "unlocked".

Enhance plan communication

In situations where the group leader, such as a coach, constructs plans independently of all or even some of his or her group members, a key challenge becomes effectively communicating those plans to members of the group. Poor communication may mean that some members fail to comprehend plans and thus the desired shared state is not reached. Based on a review of research addressing coordination in living systems, Eccles and Groth (2006a) proposed three principles of communication for enhancing group communication. These are adapted here so that they pertain specifically to the communication of plans to group members.

First, messages about plans are more likely to be comprehended correctly if they are presented in *multiple sensory modes*. For example, in American football, the coach may demonstrate a play to an offensive team by asking the team to attend visually to a poster-sized schematic of the field layout and the intended player movements, while explaining the play verbally. Second, messages are more likely to be received if there are *redundant* communication mechanisms. With regard to a presentation of a schematic and a verbal explanation, the American-football coach may also show a video of the play being run by another team and provide a page-sized version of the play in the team's playbook. Multiple, redundant sources of information about a group's plans will make the group more robust in the face of perturbations. If a group member fails to listen correctly, shows up late when plans are explained or, in the case of the American football player, loses his or her playbook, additional sources of information about the plan are available (Hutchins, 1995a). Finally, plans are more likely to be understood if plan information is *enduring* rather than transient such that these sources of information are made as *continually available* as possible. This way relevant information can be accessed on demand, such as when certain aspects of the plan may become hard to recall owing to retroactive interference, say, from learning about other plans, or simply due to forgetting. The playbook is an example of an enduring source of information. By contrast, the coach's verbal explanation of the plan is a transient source of information. However, in the same a way that business employees might use a mini-tape-recorder to document the proceedings of an important meeting with their co-workers, an athlete could use a recorder to document the coach's verbal explanation of a plan to provide a more enduring source of plan information.

Use "check-backs"

Since it is possible for group members to erroneously believe that each member shares the group's plans, such as game plans, it might be beneficial to develop methods of checking whether group members understand the group's plans and their role in these plans. In team sports, coaches might (a) encourage team members to come forward with queries about plans while they are being developed; (b) provide structured "IDU" opportunities for team members to say "I don't understand" privately to a coach in order to avoid social pressures "not to look foolish" in front of the team; and (c) develop a routine of checking back with each team member that the member fully understands the plans. A coach can operationalise this last strategy by asking a team member to provide a verbal report of his or her understanding of the team's plan. Check-backs are used in the military where it is critical that plans are correctly shared, and have been referred to in the I/O literature as a form of closed-loop communication (McIntyre and Salas, 1995; McIntyre et al., 1988; Porter et al., 2003).

In addition, check-backs also increase members' accountability because once a player has shown the coach that he or she understands the plan through the use of a check-back, the player knows that a failure to undertake his or her part in the plan cannot be blamed on a failure to understand the plan. Within sport psychology, research has highlighted the importance of role clarity and acceptance by members of groups, albeit for social rather than cognitive reasons (e.g. Bray et al., 2005). Nonetheless, as Eccles and Tenenbaum (2005) asserted, in football the strategies outlined above might be beneficial in helping players better understand their role on the team.

Enhance group member communication

As group communication appears to be a key mechanism by which group members' situation models can be created and maintained, enhancing communication among group members should facilitate coordination. There is some existing research indicating that members of expert teams develop shared knowledge of a highly specific code used for communication. Such development is reflected by succinct, domain-specific and standardised messages (Bastien and Hostager, 1988; Kanki et al., 1989; Smith-Jentsch et al., 1998). This reduces communication costs in various ways, such as by increasing the quality and quantity of information transferred in a discrete communication and increasing the accuracy and reliability of message interpretation. For example, Bastien and Hostager reported that what appeared to be spontaneous jamming in jazz bands was actually concurrently coordinated through band members' communication in the form of intentional verbal and non-verbal codes that "have become a tradition in the profession" (1988: 588). These codes could be interpreted by other band members owing to the band having achieved a shared knowledge of them. An example of the non-verbal codes included turning to an individual, making eye contact at particular points in the performance, and changing the volume of one's playing. These codes allowed the musicians to communicate so that in-process coordination could be achieved but remained relatively undetectable by the viewing and listening audience.

Kanki *et al.* (1991), through the use of aircraft simulators, studied the communication patterns of 18 aircrews that had different error-rates during landings. Crew communications were coded into categories such as commands, questions, observations, replies and acknowledgements. The frequencies of utterance dyads, defined as an initiating utterance followed by a response utterance, were then computed. One variable of interest in the study was communications variation, defined as the degree to which a given crew varied from the overall expected frequencies generated from an analysis of all crews' communications. The communication variations of low-error crews were low when compared to those of high-error crews, suggesting that a standard and specific communication code had been adopted by the low-error crews resulting in higher group performance. Kanki *et al.* (1991) proposed that, by adopting such a code, the within-crew communications became more efficient, which aided coordination and, in turn, performance.

Thus, one method of enhancing group-members' ability to maintain their situation models is to establish a shared language within the group. The language should contain code words that are short, not easily confused with other code words and convey specific information so that group members understand exactly what message is being transferred. The code words can be in both verbal (shouts) and non-verbal (gestures) forms, and can also be encrypted. Message senders can also better signal which group member is the intended recipient by having the team develop succinct nicknames. These can also be encrypted in an effort to minimise the opposing team's ability to intercept the message and to know to whom the message is being sent.

Use cross-training

Industrial and organisational researchers have advocated cross-training as a means of enhancing group coordination and overall productivity (e.g. Ebeling and Lee, 1994; Hopp and van Oyen, 2004). This involves an individual group member spending time performing the role usually occupied by another member with whom there is a coordination link. One function of cross-training is that group members gain a better appreciation of the nature of the operations, both cognitively and behaviourally, undertaken by those with whom they interact, which, in turn, allows them to adapt their own operations so that coordination among the interacting group members can be enhanced. Another function is that group members can more flexibly take up other members' work when they are overloaded. For example, if a quarterback in American football has received good training in blocking and tackling, he or she is better able to make crucial blocks or tackles that might be missed by overloaded offensive-line members and thus allow a thrown-to receiver to gain more territory.

Future research

Future research in this area might benefit initially from adopting a "work-backward" approach. To elaborate, studies might be focused first on identifying groups that can demonstrate reliably superior performance. The group-level mechanisms responsible for the division and coordination of labour within these groups could then be examined (Ericsson and Smith, 1991). For example, studies might be focused on the communication profiles of high- versus low-performing groups in sport. Following the method utilised by Kanki *et al.*, group-member communications in groups exhibiting different levels of performance could be captured by videotape during a game and coded into categories such as commands, questions, observations, replies and acknowledgements (see also Bowers *et al.*, 1998; Lausie *et al.*, forthcoming). The frequencies of the various combinations of utterance dyads could then be computed and the communication characteristics of the teams compared. When insights into the mechanisms responsible for the division and coordination of labour within superior-performing groups have been obtained, a work-forward research approach could then be adopted. To elaborate, interventions that are based on these insights could be designed and their efficacy for enhancing coordination, and ultimately performance in groups, tested via traditional experimental protocols.

Summary and conclusion

In this chapter, it was proposed that an understanding of group functioning in sport will be enhanced if the topic is studied from a social-cognitive perspective. Furthermore, it was suggested that sport psychologists might begin to move beyond examining (a) group functioning in sport from a social perspective; and (b) cognitive aspects of sport performance from an individual perspective, to considering a perspective that involves both social and cognitive concepts and in particular their interaction. The chapter began with a discussion of the contributions and limitations of the extant research on group functioning in sport. It was followed by an overview of key concepts relating to a social-cognitive perspective on group functioning that have the potential to enhance the current understanding of group functioning in sport. Next, there was an attempt to interpret the functioning of a real-world sport organisation, which involved an orienteering squad preparing for major competition using the described concepts. Finally, implications of a social-cognitive perspective for best practice were proposed and future research directions related to this perspective suggested.

To conclude, if sport psychologists are prepared to let the social and cognitive merge, there is the potential for a substantial extension of what is currently known about group functioning in sport. To return to the example of the England rugby union team's winning drop goal in the 2003 World Cup final, adopting this new perspective may enhance our understanding of how a team of 15 players handling a small, oddly shaped leather ball can operate "like clockwork".

Acknowledgements

This work was made possible in part by generous grant awards to the first author from the Financial Industry Regulation Authority Investor Education Foundation, grant number 2007–06–015, Florida Department of Education, grant number 07A224 and US Office of Naval Research, grant numbers N00014–05–1-0785 and N00014–07–1-0189. The authors would like to thank Melanie Hinkle, Lauren Tashman and an anonymous reviewer for their comments on an earlier version of this chapter.

References

Adler, R. B. and Rodman, G. (2002). *Understanding human communication* (8th edn). Oxford: Oxford University Press.

Alpine Club of Canada. (n.d.). Alpine accidents in Canada. Retrieved 3 August 2007, from www.alpineclub-edm.org/accidents/accident.asp?id=391.

Araujo, D., Davids, K., Bennett, S. J., Button, C. and Chapman, G. (2004). Emergence of sports skills under constraints. In A. M. Williams and N. J. Hodges (eds), *Skill acquisition in sport: research, theory, and practice* (pp. 409–433). London: Routledge.

Bal, M. (1997). *Narratology: introduction to the theory of narrative.* Toronto: University of Toronto Press.

Bastien, D. T. and Hostager, T. J. (1988). Jazz as a process of organisational innovation. *Communication Research,* 15, 582–602.

Boinski, S. (2000). Social manipulation within and between troops mediates primate group movement. In S. Boinski and P. A. Garber (eds), *On the move: how and why animals travel in groups* (pp. 421–469). Chicago, IL: University of Chicago Press.

Boinski, S. and Garber, P. A. (eds). (2000). *On the move: how and why animals travel in groups.* Chicago, IL: University of Chicago Press.

Bowers, C. A., Jentsch, F., Salas, E. and Braun, C. C. (1998). Analyzing communication sequences for team training needs assessment. *Human Factors,* 40, 672–679.

Bray, S. R., Beauchamp, M. R., Eys, M. A. and Carron, A. V. (2005). Does need for role clarity moderate the relationship between role ambiguity and athlete satisfaction? *Journal of Applied Sport Psychology,* 17, 306–318.

British Broadcasting Corporation. Wilkinson: Team spirit won the World Cup. Retrieved 6 June 2006, from http://news.bbc.co.uk/sport2/hi/rugby_union/rugby_world_cup/3230650.stm.

Cannon-Bowers, J. A., Salas, E. and Converse, S. A. (1993). Shared mental models in expert decision making teams. In N. J. Castellan, Jr. (ed.), *Current issues in individual and group decision making* (pp. 221–246). Hillsdale, NJ: Erlbaum.

Carey, J. (ed.). (2000). *John Donne: the major works.* Oxford: Oxford University Press.

Carron, A. V. and Hausenblas, H. A. (1998). *Group dynamics in sport* (2nd edn). Morgantown, WV: Fitness Information Technology.

Collins, H. M. (1996). Embedded or embodied? A review of Hubert Dreyfus' "What computers still can't do". *Artificial Intelligence*, 80, 99–117.

Comrey, A. (1953). Group performance in a manual dexterity task. *Journal of Applied Psychology*, 37, 85–97.

Cooke, N. J., Stout, R. and Salas, E. (2001). A knowledge elicitation approach to the measurement of team situation awareness. In M. McNeese, E. Salas and M. R. Endsley (eds), *New trends in cooperative activities: understanding system dynamics in complex environments* (pp. 114–139). Santa Monica, CA: Human Factors and Ergonomics Society Press.

D'Andrade, R. G. (1981). The cultural part of cognition. *Cognitive Science*, 5, 179–195.

Dictionary.com. (n.d.). http://dictionary.reference.com.

Dyer, F. C. (2000). Group movement and individual cognition: lessons from social insects. In S. Boinski and P. A. Garber (eds), *On the move: how and why animals travel in groups* (pp. 127–164). Chicago, IL: University of Chicago Press.

Dyer, F. C. (2002). The biology of the dance language. *Annual Review of Entomology*, 47, 917–949.

Ebeling, A. C. and Lee, C. Y. (1994). Cross-training effectiveness and profitability. *International Journal of Production Research*, 32, 2843–2859.

Eccles, D. W. (2006). Thinking outside of the box: the role of environmental adaptation in the acquisition of skilled and expert performance. *Journal of Sports Sciences*, 24, 1103–1114.

Eccles, D. W. (2007). What are we missing when we take an individual approach to the study of cognition in expert sports performers? *Proceedings of the Association for Applied Sport Psychology Annual Conference*, Louisville, KY, October 2007, 46. Madison, WI: AASP.

Eccles, D. W. (2008). The expert's circumvention of natural human resource limitations: an example from sport. *Military Psychology*, 20, 5103–5121.

Eccles, D. W. and Groth, P. (2006a). Problem solving systems theory: implications for the design of socio-technological systems. *Technology, Instruction, Cognition, and Learning*, 3, 323–343.

Eccles, D. W. and Groth, P. (2006b). Agent coordination and communication in sociotechnological systems: design and measurement issues. *Interacting with Computers*, 18, 1170–1185.

Eccles, D. W. and Groth, P. (2007). Wolves, bees, and football: enhancing coordination in sociotechnological problem solving systems through the study of human and animal groups. *Computers in Human Behaviour*, 23, 2778–2790.

Eccles, D. W. and Tenenbaum, G. (2004). Why an expert team is more than a team of experts: a cognitive conceptualization of team coordination and communication in sport. *Journal of Sport and Exercise Psychology*, 26, 542–560.

Eccles, D. W. and Tenenbaum, G. (2005). Ten top tips for team building in the pre-season. *Insight: The Football Coaches Association Online Journal*. August Edition.

Eccles, D. W. and Tenenbaum, G. (2007). A social cognitive perspective on team functioning in sport. In G. Tenenbaum and R. C. Eklund (eds), *Handbook of sport psychology* (3rd edn, 264–283). New York: Wiley.

Eccles, D. W., Walsh, S. E. and Ingledew, D. K. (2002a). A grounded theory of expert cognition in orienteering. *Journal of Sport and Exercise Psychology*, 24, 68–88.

Eccles, D. W., Walsh, S. E. and Ingledew, D. K. (2002b). The use of heuristics during route planning by expert and novice orienteers. *Journal of Sports Sciences*, 20, 327–337.

Eccles, D. W., Walsh, S. E. and Ingledew, D. K. (2006). Visual attention in orienteers with different levels of experience. *Journal of Sports Sciences*, 24, 77–87.

Eccles, D. W., Ward, P. and Woodman, T. (forthcoming). The role of competition-specific preparation in expert sport performance. *Psychology of Sport and Exercise.*

Endsley, M. R. (1995). Toward a theory of situation awareness in dynamic systems. *Human Factors*, 37, 32–64.

Ericsson, K. A. and Kintsch, W. (1995). Long-term working memory. *Psychological Review*, 102, 211–245.

Ericsson, K. A. and Lehmann, A. C. (1996). Expert and exceptional performance: Evidence of maximal adaptations to task constraints. *Annual Review of Psychology*, 47, 273–305.

Ericcson, K. A. and Smith, J. (1991). *Toward a general theory of expertise: prospects and limits.* Cambridge: Cambridge University Press.

Feltovich, P. J., Bradshaw, J. M., Jeffers, R., Suri, N. and Uszok, A. (2004). Social order and adaptability in animal and human cultures as analogues for agent communities: toward a policy-based approach. In A. Omacini, P. Petta and J. Pitt (eds), *Engineering societies for agents world IV* (pp. 21–48). Heidelberg: Springer-Verlag.

Fiore, S. M. and Salas, E. (2006). Team cognition and expert teams: developing insights from cross-disciplinary analysis of exceptional teams. *International Journal of Sports and Exercise Psychology*, 4, 369–375.

Fiore, S. M., Salas, E., Cuevas, H. M. and Bowers, C. A. (2003). Distributed coordination space: toward a theory of distributed team process and performance. *Theoretical Issues in Ergonomic Science*, 4, 340–364.

Fisher, B. A. and Hawes, L. C. (1971). An interact system model: generating a grounded theory of small groups. *Quarterly Journal of Speech*, 42, 444–453.

Flavell, J. H. (1979). Metacognition and cognitive monitoring: a new area of cognitive-developmental inquiry. *American Psychologist*, 34, 906–911.

Gardner, H. (1985). *The mind's new science.* New York: Basic Books.

Giere, R. N. and Moffat, B. (2003). Distributed cognition: where the cognitive and social merge. *Social Studies of Science*, 33, 1–10.

Goerner, S. and Combs, A. (1998). Consciousness as a self-organizing process: an ecological perspective. *BioSystems*, 46, 123–127.

Gouran, D. and Hirokawa, R. (1983). The role of communication in decision-making groups: a functional perspective. In M. Mander (ed.), *Communications in transition* (pp. 168–185). New York: Praeger.

Hackman, J. R. and Morris, C. G. (1975). Group tasks, group interaction process, and group performance effectiveness: a review and proposed integration. In L. Berkowitz (ed.), *Advances in experimental social psychology* (Vol. 8, pp. 47–99). New York: Academic Press.

Hanton, S., Fletcher, D. and Coughlan, G. (2005). Stress in elite sport performers: a comparative study of competitive and organisational stressors. *Journal of Sports Sciences*, 23, 1129–1141.

Hayes-Roth, B. and Hayes-Roth, F. (1979). A cognitive model of planning. *Cognitive Science*, 3, 275–310.

Hinsz, V. B., Tindale, R. S. and Vollrath, D. A. (1997). The emerging conceptualization of groups as information processors. *Psychological Bulletin*, 121, 43–64.

Hodges, N. J., Huys, R. and Starkes, J. L. (2007). A methodological review and evaluation of research of expert performance in sport. In G. Tenenbaum and R. C. Eklund (eds), *Handbook of sport psychology* (3rd edn, pp. 161–183). New York: Wiley.

Hopp, W. J. and van Oyen, M. P. (2004). Agile workforce evaluation: a framework for cross-training and coordination. *IIE Transactions*, 36, 919–940.

Hutchins, E. (1991). The social organisation of distributed cognition. In L. B. Resnick, J. M. Levine and S. D. Teasley (eds), *Perspectives on socially shared cognition* (pp. 283–307). Washington, DC: American Psychological Association.

Hutchins, E. (1995a). *Cognition in the wild*. Cambridge, MA: MIT Press.

Hutchins, E. (1995b). How a cockpit remembers its speeds. *Cognitive Science*, 19, 265–288.

Jones, R. A. (1988). *Emile Durkheim: an introduction to four major works*. Beverly Hills, CA: Sage.

Kanki, B. G., Folk, V. G. and Irwin, C. M. (1991). Communication variations and aircrew performance. *The International Journal of Aviation Psychology*, 11, 409–419.

Kanki, B., Lozito, S. and Foushee, H. (1989). Communication indexes of crew coordination. *Aviation, Space, and Environmental Medicine*, 60, 56–60.

Kerr, N. L. and Tindale, R. S. (2004). Group performance and decision making. *Annual Review of Psychology*, 55, 623–655.

Kidd, J. S. (1961). A comparison of one-, two-, and three-man work units under various conditions of workload. *Journal of Applied Psychology*, 45, 195–200.

Kintsch, W. (1988). The use of knowledge in discourse processing: a construction-integration model. *Psychological Review*, 95, 163–182.

Kravitz, D. A. and Martin, B. (1986). Ringelmann rediscovered: the original article. *Journal of Personality and Social Psychology*, 50, 936–941.

Lausie, D., Eccles, D. W., Jeong, A., Johnson, T., and Tenenbaum, G. (forthcoming) Intra-team communication and performance in doubles tennis. *Research Quarterly for Exercise and Sport*.

Levine, J. L., Resnick, L. B. and Higgins, E. T. (1993). Social foundations of cognition. *Annual Review of Psychology*, 44, 585–612.

Lukes, S. (1977). *Essays in social theory*. New York: Columbia University Press.

McGrath, J. E. (1984). *Groups: interaction and performance*. Englewood Cliffs, NJ: Prentice-Hall.

MacMillan, J., Entin, E. E. and Serfaty, D. (2004). Communication overhead: the hidden cost of team cognition. In E. Salas and S. M. Fiore (eds), *Team cognition: understanding the factors that drive process and performance* (pp. 61–82). Washington, DC: American Psychological Association.

McIntyre, R. M. and Salas, E. (1995). Measuring and managing for team performance: emerging principles from complex environments. In R. Guzzo and E. Salas (eds), *Team effectiveness and decision making in organisations* (pp. 9–45). San Francisco: Jossey Bass.

McIntyre, R. M., Morgan, B. B., Salas, E. and Glickman, A. S. (1988). Teamwork from team training: new evidence for the development of teamwork skills during operational training. *Proceedings of the 10th Annual Interservice/Industry Training Systems Conference* (pp. 21–27). Washington, DC.

McPherson, S. L. (1999). Tactical differences in problem representations and solutions in collegiate varsity and beginner female players. *Research Quarterly for Exercise and Sport*, 70, 369–384.

Marks, M. A., Zaccaro, S. J. and Mathieu, J. E. (2000). Performance implications of leader briefings and team-interaction training for team adaptation to novel environments. *Journal of Applied Psychology*, 85, 971–986.

Mathieu, J. E., Heffner, T. S., Goodwin, G. F., Salas, E. and Cannon-Bowers, J. A. (2000). The influence of shared mental models on team process and performance. *Journal of Applied Psychology*, 85, 273–283.

Miller, G. A., Galanter, E. and Pribram, K. H. (1960). *Plans and the structure of behaviour*. New York: Holt, Reinhart, and Winston.

Moreland, R. and Argote, L. (2003). Transactive memory in dynamic organisations. In R. Peterson and E. Mannix (eds), *Understanding the dynamic organisation* (pp. 135–162). Mahwah, NJ: Lawrence Erlbaum Associates.

National Academy Press (2007). *Rising above the gathering storm: energizing and employing America for a brighter future*. Washington, DC: National Academy Press.

Naylor, J. C. and Briggs, G. E. (1965). Team training effectiveness under various conditions. *Journal of Applied Psychology*, 49, 223–229.

Newell, K. M. (1986). Constraints on the development of coordination. In M. Wade and H. T. A. Whiting (eds), *Motor development in children: aspects of coordination and control* (pp. 341–360). Dordrecht: Martinus Nijhoff.

Orasanu, J. M. and Fisher, U. (1992). Team cognition in the cockpit: linguistic control of shared problem solving. *Proceedings of the 14th Annual Conference of the Cognitive Science Society*. Hillsdale, NJ: Erlbaum.

Pain, M. A. and Harwood, C. (2007). The performance environment of the England youth soccer teams. *Journal of Sports Sciences*, 25, 1307–1324.

Pastor, K. A. and Seeley, T. D. (2005). The brief piping signal of the honey bee: begging call or stop signal? *Ethology*, 111, 775–784.

Poole, M. S., Seibold, D. R. and McPhee, R. D. (1986). A structurational approach to theory-building in group decision-making research. In R. Y. Hirokawa and M. S. Poole (eds), *Communication and group decision making* (pp. 237–264). Beverly Hills, CA: Sage.

Porter, C. O., Hollenbeck, J. R., Ilgen, D. R., Ellis, A. P., West, B. J. and Moon, H. (2003). Backing up behaviours in teams: the role of personality and legitimacy of need. *Journal of Applied Psychology*, 88, 391–403.

Rees, T., Ingledew, D. K. and Hardy, L. (1999). Social support dimensions and components of performance in tennis. *Journal of Sports Sciences*, 17, 421–429.

Resnick, L. B., Levine, J. M. and Teasley, S. D. (eds). (1996). *Perspectives on socially shared cognition*. Washington, DC: American Psychological Association.

Roberts, J. M. (1964). The self-management of cultures. In W. Goodenough (ed.), *Explorations in cultural anthropology: essays in honour of George Peter Murdock*. New York: McGraw-Hill.

Rouse, W. B., Cannon-Bowers, J. A. and Salas, E. (1992). The role of mental models in team performance in complex systems. *IEEE Transactions on Systems, Man, and Cybernetics*, 22, 1296–1308.

Salas, E. and Fiore, S. M. (eds). (2004). *Team cognition: understanding the factors that drive process and performance*. Washington, DC: American Psychological Association.

Schneider, S. S. and Lewis, L. A. (2004). The vibration signal, modulatory communication, and the organisation of labour in honey bees, *Apis mellifera*. *Apidologie*, 35, 117–131.

Shaw, M. E. (1932). A comparison of individuals and small groups in the rational solution of complex problems. *American Journal of Psychology*, 44, 491–504.

Smith, W. J. (1977). *The behaviour of communicating*. Cambridge, MA: Harvard University Press.

Smith-Jentsch, K. A., Campbell, G. E., Milanovich, D. M. and Reynolds, A. M. (2001). Measuring teamwork: mental models to support training needs assessment, development, and evaluation. *Journal of Organizational Behavior*, 22, 179–194.

Smith-Jentsch, K. A., Johnston, J. H. and Payne, S. C. (1998). Measuring team-related expertise in complex environments. In J. A. Cannon-Bowers and E. Salas (eds),

Making decisions under stress: implications for individual and team training (pp. 61–87). Washington, DC: American Psychological Association.

Starkes, J. L. and Ericsson, K. A. (eds). (2003). *Expert performance in sport: advances in research on sport expertise*. Champaign, IL: Human Kinetics.

Stasser, G. and Titus, W. (1985). Pooling of unshared information in group decision making: biased information sampling during discussion. *Journal of Personality and Social Psychology*, 48, 1467–1478.

Steiner, I. D. (1972). *Group process and productivity*. New York: Academic Press.

Stout, R. J., Cannon-Bowers, J. A., Salas, E. and Milanovich, D. M. (1999). Planning, shared mental models, and coordinated performance: an empirical link is established. *Human Factors*, 41, 61–71.

Suchman, L. (1987). *Plans and situated actions: the problem of human–machine communication*. New York: Cambridge University Press.

Thorndike, R. L. (1938). On what type of task will a group do well? *Journal of Abnormal Psychology*, 33, 408–412.

Tschinkel, W. R. (2006). *The fire ants*. Cambridge, MA: Harvard University Press.

Tufano, D. R. (1997). Automotive HUDS: the overlooked safety issues. *Human Factors*, 39, 303–311.

Vicente, K. J. (2000). Revisiting the constraint attunement hypothesis: reply to Ericsson, Patel, and Kintsch (2000) and Simon and Gobet (2000). *Psychological Review*, 107, 601–608.

Ward, P. and Eccles, D. W. (2006). A commentary on "Team cognition and expert teams: Emerging insights into learning and performance for exceptional teams." *International Journal of Sport and Exercise Psychology*, 4, 463–483.

Ward, P. and Williams, A. M. (2003). Perceptual and cognitive skill development in soccer: the multidimensional nature of expert performance. *Journal of Sport and Exercise Psychology*, 25, 93–111.

Wegner, D. M. (1986). Transactive memory: a contemporary analysis of the group mind. In B. Mullen and G. R. Goethals (eds), *Theories of group behaviour* (pp. 185–208). New York: Springer-Verlag.

Weinberg, R. S. and Gould, D. (2003). *Foundations of sport and exercise psychology* (3rd edn). Champaign, IL: Human Kinetics.

Widmeyer, W. N., Brawley, L. R. and Carron, A. V. (1990). The effects of group size in sport. *Journal of Sport and Exercise Psychology*, 12, 177–190.

Williams, A. M. and Hodges, N. J. (eds). (2004). *Skill acquisition in sport: research, theory, and practice*. London: Routledge.

Williams, A. M. and Ward, P. (2007). Anticipation and decision-making: exploring new horizons. In G. Tenenbaum and R. C. Eklund (eds), *Handbook of sport psychology* (3rd edn, pp. 203–223). New York: Wiley.

Woodman, T. and Hardy, L. (2001). A case study of organisational stress in elite sport. *Journal of Applied Sport Psychology*, 13, 207–238.

9 Mental toughness in sport
Conceptual and practical issues

Declan Connaughton and Sheldon Hanton

Introduction

Psychological characteristics are now commonly accepted as being major contributors to success within the area of sporting performance – in particular, motivational factors, self-confidence levels, and the ability to cope with and interpret anxiety-related symptoms as facilitative under pressure (cf. Hanton *et al.*, 2008; Hardy *et al.*, 1996; Mellalieu *et al.*, 2006). Another characteristic that is frequently used to describe why certain individuals have become "the best in the world" in their respective sports is that of "mental toughness" (Loehr, 1986; Williams, 1988). Indeed, athletes themselves, coaches, members of the press and sports commentators have cited mental toughness as core to the execution of successful performance, while certain psychologists working in the field of sport suggest mental toughness as key to the advancement of knowledge regarding successful athletes (e.g. Bull *et al.*, 1996; Goldberg, 1998; Gould *et al.*, 2002; Loehr, 1982, 1986, 1995). Since the 1950s, mental toughness has been associated with winning performances and linked to the characteristics of sporting champions. Examples included descriptions such as mental toughness having "more to do with winning than do such obvious physical attributes as speed and power" (Williams, 1988: 60), the most important asset for an athlete (Goldberg, 1998), and critical to possess if the long hours of strenuous training associated with top-level performance are to be endured (Bull *et al.*, 1996).

A cursory glance through Internet search results reveals many commentaries that testify to the importance of mental toughness in elite sport. In an article surrounding Tiger Woods (*USA Today*), Blauvelt (2004, para. 1) declared that, "for all the physical skills the golf gods gave Tiger Woods, the mental toughness he brings to his sport might be just as important in setting him apart". The specific example Blauvelt used to illustrate Woods' mental toughness was during the Bay Hill Invitational tournament in Orlando, 2003. Woods was suffering from severe food poisoning on the Saturday night of the competition and this continued into the final round on Sunday. However, despite the debilitating physical symptoms associated with the condition, he continued to play and won the tournament, by 11 strokes, for the fourth consecutive year. The 2004 Ladies tennis final at Wimbledon also resulted in sports commentators bearing witness to the importance of what they perceived to be mental toughness as a contributor to the outcome of the match. Tracy Austin of NBC Sports commented on the final between Maria Sharapova, the eventual champion, and Serena Williams, remarking:

> Maria Sharapova's mental toughness and her physical power led her to win the Wimbledon Ladies' singles title.... I wrote in my preview of the match that the 17-year-old Russian is so mentally tough and she's not awed by anyone – two things she proved in defeating Serena in straight sets.
>
> (Austin, 2004: para. 1)

Observing the same match, Linda Pearce wrote an article entitled "Sharapova's arrival a victory for mental toughness" (Pearce, 2004).

The explanation for unsuccessful performances has also been linked with mental toughness, this time the absence of it. For example, England cricket team captain Michael Vaughan was quoted as "slamming England's domestic structure for failing to produce players 'mentally tough enough' for international cricket" (Wisden Cricinfo Staff, 2003). Also, in the *Daily Mail* newspaper, Geoff Boycott (described as a former England opening batsman and Yorkshire legend) suggested that Duncan Fletcher's English team had been "murdered" by Australia in the defence of the 2006 Ashes. Boycott accused the team of "a lack of mental toughness after they completed the five-Test series ... becoming the first England side to lose all five matches in an Ashes contest since 1920–21" (*Daily Mail*, 2007). An initial inspection reveals that while many of these comments link mental toughness with qualities such as persistence and emotional control, none of them specifically define their interpretation of mental toughness based on the type of empirical research commonly adopted within the literature. Therefore, while many performers, coaches and commentators are highlighting mental toughness as a valuable asset or attribute to possess, this seems to be based on their own personal experiences from the world of sport – a central issue discussed throughout this chapter.

In the field of sport psychology, for example, mental-toughness research appears to be comprehensive in nature, replete with definitions, measurement tools, developmental perspectives and intervention strategies designed to enhance mental-toughness levels. Even so, a closer inspection of the available literature reveals two important factors: first, a precise and widely accepted definition of mental toughness has, until recently, not existed; and, second, the majority of studies in this area have been based on anecdotal evidence rather than specific investigations into defining and understanding mental toughness. While the previous point may suggest the absence of a definition of mental toughness, this is not the case; indeed, mental toughness has been defined in a multitude of ways by various investigators since the 1950s, and examples of these are presented in Table 9.1. The various mental-toughness definitions and explanations have been diverse and associated with, by and large, positive psychological characteristics such as resilience or insensitivity to criticism, an ability to rebound from adversity and failures, and the use of mental skills. With so many contradictory explanations of mental toughness, no clear or broadly accepted definition formerly emerged from the literature. The conceptual confusion created from this lack of consistency and understanding resulted in numerous positive psychological characteristics being incorrectly labelled as mental toughness (see Jones *et al.*, 2002).

The aim of this review chapter is to uncover and critically discuss the central issues surrounding the area of mental toughness. To encourage the pursuit of quality research, we have presented the review in two parts: part 1 appraises and critiques the multitude of definitions and explanations that were based on anecdotal accounts and psychometrically questionable measures, and how this research has created ambiguity within the mental-toughness literature in sport psychology; part 2 provides a rationale for, and findings of, recent empirical studies which have attempted to address the central issues raised in part 1. Specifically, in relation to establishing a conceptually accurate and consistent definition of mental toughness,

Table 9.1 Mental toughness definitions

"The ability of an athlete to withstand strong criticism and to avoid becoming upset when losing or performing poorly" (Tutko and Richards 1971: 46).

"The degree of insensitivity the individual has to criticism playing badly or losing" (Alderman 1974: 149).

"Mental toughness is a learned skill ... and concerns freedom from stress and pressure in high-level championship matches" (Jones 1982: 31).

"A constellation of mental skills all of which are learned that are characteristic of mentally tough competitors" (Loehr 1982: 11).

"You may have the determination to stay at something to keep trying to never give up but mental toughness means you also have the self-control and focus to limit your efforts to only the ones that are effective" (Tunney 1987: 49).

"Mental toughness is really another name for desire. Given talent and luck desire overcomes just about everything" (Williams 1988: 60).

"Achieving consistency is the ultimate measure of MT" (Graham and Yocom 1990: 47).

"Mental toughness is the outward manifestation of an inner commitment. It's a refusal to quit on that dream no matter what" (Goldberg 1998: 219).

"Mental toughness is the ability to stand tall in the face of adversity. It's a psychic resilience that allows you to rebound from setbacks and failures time and time again" (Goldberg 1998: 219).

"Mental toughness is the ability to sustain high levels of motivation activity and confidence in the face of anything that life throws at you" (Teitelbaum 1998: 2).

"Mental toughness is the ability to keep picking yourself up no matter what life hits you with – to keep marching steadily forward to achieve the specific victories you have made up your mind you *are* going to make happen" (Teitelbaum 1998: 7).

---

identifying the essential underlying characteristics, proposing a working framework of mental toughness, and the exploration of the perceived mechanisms by which mental toughness may be developed and maintained in athletes. The review concludes by highlighting the practical implications of these recent investigations, and provides directions for researchers to pursue the development of psychometrically sound measures of mental toughness along with potential intervention programmes to enhance levels of mental toughness.

Part 1: examining mental toughness from different perspectives

There are numerous articles (e.g. Goldberg, 1992; Hodge, 1994; Jones, 1982; Williams, 1988) and books (e.g. Bull *et al.*, 1996; Gibson, 1998; Goldberg, 1998; Loehr, 1982, 1986, 1995; Luszki, 1982) which refer to mental toughness, either within the title or inherent within the text itself. From reviewing these sources, it appears that most of the commentary on mental toughness appears to be based on anecdotal evidence and personal opinions rather than scientific research, and often the studies investigated mental skills rather than mental toughness per se. This section of the chapter discusses, in detail, the six source areas recently highlighted by Connaughton *et al.* (in press) and includes: (a) citations which have included mental toughness in the title only; (b) studies that have defined mental toughness as a personality trait; (c) references that have identified mental toughness as a decisive factor accounting for successful performance; (d) articles that have suggested mental toughness as a defence mechanism against adversity; (e) mental skills programmes which are purported to enhance performance through the development of mental toughness; and, finally, (f) research that has attempted to address mental toughness based on previous studies and psychometrically problematic measures.

Mental toughness as a title heading

There has been frequent citing of mental toughness within the title of articles and books with little explanation, or even mention, of mental toughness contained within the text (e.g. Bull *et al.*, 1996; Favret and Benzel, 1997; Gibson, 1998; Hodge, 1994; Loehr, 1982, 1986, 1995; Williams, 1998). For example, in an article titled, "Mental toughness in sport: lessons for life. The pursuit of personal excellence", Hodge suggested that athletes should develop mental toughness when pursuing personal excellence as this was vital to be able to handle the stressful and publicly evaluated situations that occur in sport. Hodge proposed that "champions are just ordinary people who do extraordinary things and emotional experiences need to be harnessed to develop mental toughness" (1994: 12). Indeed, the building blocks of mental toughness, according to Hodge, are achieved by practising at being mentally strong enough to endure the pressure, while remaining focused on mastery goals, hard work, determination and commitment. However, Hodge based these building blocks on his experience and personal observations throughout his career as a sport psychologist/coach, and no explanation of mental toughness within the article was offered.

Similarly, Bull *et al.* (1996) devoted a full chapter to mental toughness within their applied text, "The Mental Game Plan". They endorsed toughness as important in assisting athletes to cope with injuries and setbacks, as well as the pressures of intensive training workloads. Bull *et al.* suggested developing mental skills to improve what they felt were the six specific attributes of mental toughness: a strong desire to succeed, staying positive in the face of challenge and pressure, being able to control the "controllables", demonstrating high commitment with a balanced attitude, having a high level of self-belief, and lastly, displaying positive body language. While providing many useful practical examples to support these attributes, Bull and colleagues did not provide a working definition or details of a programme of research which resulted in the six attributes. In fact, their suggestions were based on the authors' experiences of working with many world-class performers, rather than grounded in theoretical and scientific research. These two examples represent a common approach that researchers have employed when investigating this construct, and despite the clear value of working with such elite performers, and the intuitive appeal of the observations, the lack of empirical research is problematic. The following sections discuss how the understanding of mental toughness, beginning within the personality literature, has evolved since the mid-1950s.

Mental toughness as a personality trait

As early as 1955, Cattell *et al.* described mental toughness as one of the most important personality traits for success, and that it tended to be culturally or environmentally determined. Supporting this, Tutko and Richards (1971, 1972) and then Tapp (1991) identified mental toughness as one of a number of personality traits that were related to high athletic achievement and success. It was suggested that "the athlete who is mentally tough is somewhat insensitive to the feelings and problems of others" (Tutko and Richards, 1971: 46), and that "being able to handle pressure off the field can help you be mentally tough on it" (Tapp, 1991: 45). Further, developing mental toughness in "sensitive" athletes could be achieved "by informing the individual ahead of time that, he will often be required to take a chewing out to get across a message with strong emphasis" (Tutko and Richards, 1972: 46). Tutko and Richards (1972) also proposed a measure of mental toughness, the Motivation Rating Scale (MRS); however, no clear explanation of mental toughness was offered (by Tutko and Richards, or Tapp), and no details on how a scale assessing "motivation", lacking any reliability and validity data, was alleged to measure mental toughness was provided. In fact, Dennis concluded that, "there is still some question as to whether mental toughness is a valid personality construct" (1981: 386). It was clear at this time that researchers regarded mental toughness as an important component in sport, and pursued its investigation as one of the influential qualities necessary for successful performance.

The importance of mental toughness in sporting success

In 1974, Alderman suggested that top-level sport was a ruthless, cold and hard business, and no place for the tender-spirited, with successful athletes being not only physically tough, but mentally tough as well. Luszki (1982) viewed mental toughness as an important factor to successful performance and one of the four principles required to win at the highest levels of competition. Luszki also suggested that, when the best athletes are competing, these four factors (i.e. physical well-being, skill, experience and mental toughness) were working together. Importantly, though, mental toughness was proposed as being ultimately responsible for the acquisition of the other three principles. Similarly, Tunney (1987) identified four factors that winning teams were built on: self-discipline, self-sacrifice, mental toughness and teamwork, and proposed that the individuals who were mentally tough possessed the self-control and focus to limit their efforts to only the effective ones. Jim Loehr has written extensively on the subject of mental toughness, and in his three books (1982, 1986, 1995), suggested that the world's greatest athletes give testimony to the existence of mental toughness each time they perform. Mental toughness, according to Loehr, separates the few who achieve ultimate accomplishment from the thousands who are unsuccessful in sport, proposing that mentally tough performers consistently responded to problems, pressure, making mistakes and competition with the right attitude. In a similar manner, Goldberg suggested that most coaches readily believe mental toughness is necessary for success and that "the ability to handle competitive pressures is a cornerstone skill of mental toughness" (1992: 60).

While this approach of linking mental toughness with the qualities of successful performers was popular and intuitively appealing, other investigators tried to adopt the perspective that a lack of mental toughness was the reason for unsuccessful performances. Williams (1988), for example, proposed that fear and insecurity were the main causes for performance failures, and individuals who were mentally weak latched on to these reasons for losing. Goldberg (1992) linked non-mentally tough performers with lack of control by suggesting that the opposite of mental toughness was being out of control and powerless. Likewise, Pankey (1993) suggested that the absence of toughness interferes with the ability to cope with challenge, and negatively affects a person's self-image as an effective master of adversity. Additionally, those who are not "tough" react to stressors in a more disorganised manner, resulting in ineffective coping, helplessness and, ultimately, depression.

Similar to the personality research discussed in the previous section, these studies were a result of personal belief and coaching experience rather than empirical research. Additionally, many of the studies did not set out primarily to investigate mental toughness, but addressed other psychological factors related to successful and unsuccessful performances, such as coping skills. As a result, no definition of mental toughness or explanation with regards to its make-up was provided. The variability and haziness in the literature has resulted in confusion surrounding the exact make-up of mental toughness, and led many investigators to approach the understanding of mental toughness from the perspective that, somehow, it provided protection from adversity.

Mental toughness as a defensive mechanism against adversity

Certain authors have suggested that possessing mental toughness allows a performer to overcome adversity and provide a degree of insensitivity to criticism (Alderman, 1974; Bull *et al.*, 1996; Favret and Benzel, 1997; Goldberg, 1992, 1998; Graham and Yocom, 1990; Loehr, 1982, 1986, 1995; Pankey, 1993; Tapp, 1991; Taylor, 1989; Williams, 1988; Woods *et al.*, 1995). For example, Pankey reported that mental toughness helps individuals to grasp the coping skills needed to overcome adversity, while Goldberg (1992, 1998) equated mental toughness to numerous mental skills, including the ability to bounce back quickly from setbacks or when faced with misfortune. Loehr (1982) claimed that mentally tough individuals can consistently sustain their ideal performance state during the heat of competitive battle and increase their flow of positive energy in crisis and adversity. As is becoming a consistent theme within this review, these studies were either based on personal beliefs acquired from consulting with elite performers and not grounded in empirical research or, once more, did not overtly address mental toughness. To illustrate this point, Pankey's text identified the qualities necessary for successful performance and not the qualities of mental toughness. Similarly, other authors proposed specific mental techniques and skills professed to sustain a performer's ideal performance state (Loehr, 1982, 1986, 1995), and overcome slumps in the achievement of peak performance in sport (Goldberg, 1998). These mental skills and techniques were then suggested to be components of mental toughness, without the provision of any underlying rationale or supporting data. Therefore, the association with mental skills and specific positive psychological characteristics has been unjustified and responsible for the misinterpretation of mental toughness with more or less every positive psychological characteristic (Jones *et al.*, 2002). Despite this, researchers have continued to propose mental skills training to develop mental toughness, rather than specific mental-toughness programmes, in an attempt to enhance athletic performance.

Developing mental toughness

As it was believed that mental toughness was not an inherited gift, but the fruits of learning which were acquired through hard work, understanding and practice, many specific mental-skills and physical-training programmes have been designed to develop mental toughness in performers (e.g. Jones, 1982; Loehr, 1982, 1986, 1995; Tapp, 1991; Watts, 1978). Watts, for example, devised various techniques to develop mental toughness, which consisted of extreme physical workouts with minimal rest. He believed that this taught performers to accept adversity and pain as a natural part of training, thereby allowing athletes to rise above such pain and dull their awareness of it in competition. Loehr

(1982, 1986, 1995) suggested that the acquisition of nine specific characteristics were required to be a mentally tough competitor. These were: being self-motivated and self-directed, positive but realistic, in control of emotions, calm and relaxed under fire, highly energetic and ready for action, determined, mentally alert and focused, doggedly self-confident, fully responsible. Furthermore, Loehr (1986) suggested the ultimate measure of mental toughness was consistency, and devised the Psychological Performance Inventory (PPI) to profile a performer's mental strengths and weaknesses. Loehr regarded this profile as the individual's mental toughness score, which was subdivided into seven sub-scales (i.e. self-confidence, negative energy, attention control, visual and imagery control, motivational level, positive energy and attitude control). Each sub-scale contained six items with scores ranging from six to 30. Strategies were proposed to overcome any sub-scale deficiencies via a sixth stage, "Athletic Excellence Training Program" (AET). The AET claimed to be able to educate an athlete on how to create a greater self-awareness and better understanding of their "Ideal Performance State" (IPS), which contributes to enhanced emotional control during competition. The proposed impact of the AET was to increase performance consistency, which Loehr viewed as the most important aspect of mental toughness.

In a similar vein, Goldberg (1998) provided guidance on specific mental techniques and skills he believed necessary to become mentally tough within a text that was designed to be a practical approach to achieving peak performance. The techniques and skills entailed seven characteristics that performers possessed when "they are at their best ... but are conspicuously absent when you're caught in the clutches of a slump" (Goldberg, 1998: 4). These included: passion and fun, high self-confidence, concentration on the process of the performance, resilience, a sense of challenge, a non-thinking automatic quality and a sense of relaxation during the performance. Goldberg then proposed ten "slump busting steps" to develop a positive attitude in order to achieve peak performance and mental toughness. These were: ruling out non-mental causes, establishing self-control, developing a championship focus, dealing with your fears, expecting success, developing positive images, setting slump-busting goals, building self-confidence, becoming mentally tough and insuring against future slumps.

Despite the practical appeal of such approaches, the work of Watts, Loehr and Goldberg omitted to reveal any underlying systematic research, or indeed, provide an evidence base to describe the methods involved in defining and measuring what they suggested mental toughness to be. No research appears to have been carried out to determine the effectiveness of Goldberg's slump-busting steps and Loehr's AET, or whether Watts' methods actually developed mental toughness or contributed to the team's success. Equally, no psychometric support for the PPI (Loehr, 1986) was presented or has since been made available, and it has been criticised for lacking predictive validity (Middleton et al., 2004). The mental techniques Goldberg proposed were based on personal experience of dealing with elite athletes, and no other published research has supported any of this author's assertions. Finally, the combined list of psychological skills necessary to achieve Loehr's and Goldberg's states of mental toughness appear to be endless, creating further confusion for researchers trying to understand the complexity of mental toughness. Despite these issues, certain investigators have applied Loehr's (1982, 1986) explanation and measurement of mental toughness to their investigations. This has resulted in researchers proposing inventories and methods of developing and enhancing mental toughness based on questionable conceptualisations and potentially invalid measures (e.g. Clough *et al.*, 2002; Golby *et al.*, 2003; Goldberg, 1998; Hodge, 1994; Lee *et al.*, 1994; Shin and Lee, 1994). These issues are afforded additional discussion in the following section.

Research purporting to investigate mental toughness

Using Loehr's (1986) Psychological Performance Inventory (PPI), Shin and Lee (1994), and Lee *et al.* (1994), investigated mental toughness in elite and non-elite female performers, and Korean table-tennis players, respectively. Based on their findings, Shin and Lee (1994) proposed mental toughness as one of the best indicators in identifying membership to skill-level groups, while Lee *et al.* (1994) suggested that athletes who participated in volleyball, archery and shooting displayed higher levels of mental toughness in comparison to athletes who participated in table tennis and badminton. Not surprisingly, because the PPI was purported to be a measure of mental toughness (Loehr, 1986), neither study made any attempt to define or identify the characteristics of mental toughness. More recently, Golby *et al.* (2003) examined the relationship between demographic characteristics of rugby league players and selected aspects of psychological performance in rugby league football. Once again, the PPI (Loehr, 1986) was used to measure mental toughness, and findings suggested no significant differences in mental toughness across the groups under investigation. Golby *et al.* then concluded that the PPI contained insufficient discriminative power and only measured distinct attributes of mental skills and not mental toughness. As already mentioned, to use the PPI (Loehr, 1986) as a central measure of mental toughness in these studies appears to be deceptive inasmuch as the originator failed to define or justify the inventory as a specific measure of mental toughness.

Coming from a different perspective, Clough *et al.* (2002) proposed that mental toughness was "hardiness" transposed into a more sport-specific setting with an additional inclusion of confidence. Confidence was justified as an element of mental toughness as Clough and colleagues felt it was an important factor relating to sports performance. They defined mental toughness in terms of characteristics that individuals possess, suggesting that:

> Mentally tough individuals tend to be sociable and outgoing; as they are able to remain calm and relaxed, they are competitive in many situations and have lower anxiety levels than others. With a high sense of self-belief and an unshakeable faith that they can control their own destiny, these individuals can remain relatively unaffected by competition or adversity.
>
> (Clough *et al.*, 2002: 38)

Clough et al. also devised a 48-item questionnaire (MT48; and an abridged version titled the MT18) based on Loehr's (1982, 1986, 1995) explanation of mental toughness (i.e. a constellation of mental skills), anecdotal evidence gathered from athletes, coaches and sport psychologists, and the hardiness literature. The construction of the MT48 was based on what Clough et al. (2002) proposed as the four Cs of mental toughness, which consisted of the three elements of the dispositional construct of hardiness (commitment, control and challenge: Kobasa, 1979), and confidence. The MT48 has been reported by Clough et al. (2002) to have an overall test–re-test coefficient of 0.90, with internal consistency of 0.73 (Control), 0.71 (Commitment), 0.71 (Challenge) and 0.80 (Confidence), and participants who scored high on the MT48 reported lower ratings of exertion during a 30-minute cycle ride compared with participants who achieved a low score. Further, Crust and Clough (2005) found significant correlations between MT48 scores and the time a relative-weight dumbbell (1.5 per cent of body weight) could be suspended directly in front of the body. However, Clough et al. did not provide details regarding the participants, data-collection procedures, or a rationale for their conceptualisation of mental toughness (i.e. hardiness and confidence). Theorists would argue that hardiness (Kobasa, 1979) may be a distinct conceptual construct, and no research has thus far, to the current authors' knowledge, investigated any direct association between hardiness and mental toughness. Therefore, it would appear that the findings of the MT48 are conceptually and theoretically based on elements of hardiness theory, and not mental toughness; as such, the MT48 cannot be considered a valid measure of mental toughness. This is problematic, considering that studies (i.e. Clough and Earle, 2002; Crust and Clough, 2005; Levy et al., 2006) have used the MT48 in an attempt to measure mental toughness. Other measures of mental toughness have also been proposed (e.g. Middleton et al., 2004); however, to date, no research supporting the psychometric properties or rationale for the construction of such a measure has been published.

Critically, it appears that Lee, Clough and Golby (and colleagues) have based their research on personal opinion, or previous research that did not directly investigate mental toughness (e.g. Loehr, 1982, 1986). The PPI appears to measure a collection of mental skills which Loehr (1986) linked with a performer's IPS rather than mental toughness. The psychometric properties lack norms, or any reliability or validity data, and provide no clear rationale for the construction or selection of inventory items (cf. Murphy and Tammen, 1998). Equally, the MT48 lacks any sound psychometric properties that specifically relate to mental toughness, and theorists would argue that hardiness (Kobasa, 1979) is a distinct conceptual construct. Finally, Clough and colleagues have omitted to offer any satisfactory rationale as to why mental toughness is a sport-specific form of hardiness. Therefore, we would warn against the use of the PPI and MT48 (and MT18) in future mental-toughness investigations. With no comprehensively sound measure of mental toughness in existence (Middleton et al., 2004), a quantitative approach can only create more confusion in the understanding of mental toughness, and this conclusion led certain researchers to begin to examine this construct through qualitative means.

In 2001, Fourie and Potgieter published a qualitative study in a South African national journal which was purported to investigate the components of mental toughness using expert coaches and elite athletes from a variety of different sports. Coaches and athletes provided written statements regarding their interpretation of the characteristics of mental toughness resulting in the identification of 12 components: motivation level, coping skills, confidence maintenance, cognitive skill, discipline and goal-directedness, competitiveness, possession of prerequisite physical and mental requirements, team unity, preparation skills, psychological hardiness, religious convictions and ethics. Additional findings suggested that the coaches regarded concentration as the most important characteristic of mental toughness, while the athletes rated perseverance the highest. However, upon closer inspection, many of the same conceptual issues found in previous studies were evident here. Specifically, less than a quarter of participants competed or coached at international level, questioning the validity of this being as an elite and expert a sample as had been suggested. In addition, no definition of mental toughness was investigated or proposed, and there appeared to be some confusion with the wording and meanings of the 12 components. For example, Fourie and Potgieter defined "psychological hardiness" as "the ability of the athlete to reveal a strong personality, emotional and psychological well-being, to take charge and show autonomy" (2001: 68), which is in contrast to Kobasa's (1979) established and accepted definition of hardiness. Another component, "cognitive skill", was defined as "the ability to concentrate, focus, think, make decisions and analyse" (2001: 67). There is, of course, the strong possibility that many performers can demonstrate this quality (i.e. cognitive skill) but may not necessarily be regarded as mentally tough.

A recent review of the mental-toughness literature by Crust (2007) typifies the misunderstanding and lack of conceptual clarity with regard to the concept of mental toughness. The review fails to distinguish between empirical research that has specifically addressed mental toughness (e.g. Bull *et al.*, 2005; Jones *et al.*, 2002; Thelwell *et al.*, 2005) and anecdotal evidence, such as book chapters (e.g. Bull *et al.*, 1996; Clough *et al.*, 2002) and populist texts based primarily on personal accounts (e.g. Gibson, 1998; Goldberg, 1998; Loehr, 1982, 1986, 1995), and as a result, there is much contradiction and conceptual confusion evident. For example, Crust proposes the need to derive a definition of mental toughness from relevant theories of personality and development. The suggestion to uncover a theory and attempt to align mental toughness with it, almost in a post hoc fashion, resulted in the identification of the 4Cs of mental toughness and the development of the MT48 (Clough *et al.*, 2002). However, as previously explained, Clough *et al.* did not provide a rationale as to why mental toughness is a sport-specific form of hardiness, or justification for the conceptualisation of the 4Cs as sub-scales of a measure of mental toughness (i.e. the MT48). Furthermore, Crust highlights the inadequacies of the development of Clough *et al.*'s MT48 by suggesting that the authors did not justify the transposition of hardiness to mental toughness.

Therefore, using hardiness as the conceptual and theoretical basis for the majority of the MT48 sub-scales, and applying it as a specific measure of mental toughness was unjustified. Despite this questionable rationale, Crust (2007) devoted much of the review to supporting the MT48 as measure of, and means to further enhance, the understanding of mental toughness.

Précis of conceptual misinterpretation

To sum up the conceptual misinterpretation and previous commentary, mental toughness has been a popular topic and subjected to repeated investigations over the years. It has been defined by authors in a multitude of ways that have suggested it as a constellation of learned mental skills (Goldberg, 1998; Jones, 1982; Loehr, 1982, 1986). With no clear, accepted or consistent definition, the majority of explanations only served to confound the precise nature and make-up of mental toughness. Indeed, many studies failed to investigate mental toughness, but linked the characteristics of mental toughness with successful performance and coping with adversity. The findings from non-empirical studies appear to be based on anecdote, acquired more from consulting and working with elite performers rather than from any systematic programme of research. Additionally, they have incorrectly associated the possession of psychological skills as an indicator of mental toughness. Certain studies have tried to investigate mental toughness via quantitative means using problematic measures such as the PPI and MT48, despite researchers' agreement that no comprehensively sound measure of mental toughness exists. Therefore, after reviewing the literature, it was evident that: (a) a widely accepted definition of mental toughness did not exist; (b) the component attributes, and methods for development, were highly inconsistent across investigations, and included numerous positive psychological attributes and mental skills; and (c) although certain psychometric inventories were purported to be available for examining mental toughness, these lacked sound psychometric properties and focused primarily on hardiness and mental skills.

The following sections of this review detail how researchers have attempted to address some of the conceptual issues highlighted in the first part of the chapter. Specifically, part 2 discusses the findings of six recent studies that have implemented a more rigorous and systematic approach to researching and understanding mental toughness (i.e. Bull *et al.*, 2005; Connaughton *et al.*, 2008; Gucciardi *et al.*, 2008; Jones *et al.*, 2002, 2007; Thelwell *et al.*, 2005).

Part 2: conceptualising mental toughness: an empirical approach

Consistent with a number of studies that have established detailed information regarding challenging subject areas (e.g. Gould *et al.*, 1993; Hanton and Connaughton, 2002; Hanton and Jones, 1999) and the issues highlighted in part 1 of this review, qualitative research programmes were implemented in order to empirically investigate and conceptualise mental toughness. Enabling "data-rich" individuals' responses regarding mental toughness to be probed in detail, studies incorporated: purposive sampling techniques (cf. Patton, 2002), the development of semi-structured interview guides, a combination of focus-group sessions and individual interviews, and adopting Personal Construct Theory (Kelly, 1955) and performance profiling as guiding frameworks. These procedures were deemed the most appropriate means of gathering information to start to generate an accurate definition of mental toughness and its essential component characteristics (Bull *et al.*, 2005; Gucciardi *et al.*, 2008; Jones *et al.*, 2002, 2007; Thelwell *et al.*, 2005), and factors that influence both the development and maintenance of mental toughness in sports performers (Bull *et al.*, 2005; Connaughton *et al.*, 2008). The following sections discuss these issues in more detail.

Mental toughness: definition and characteristics

Jones *et al.* (2002) was the first study to address the limitations of the mental-toughness literature highlighted in part 1 of this review. The purpose of the study was to present a definition and identify the attributes of mental toughness in a sample that would reflect the beliefs and perceptions of a diverse sport population (e.g. sex, sporting discipline, task demands). The investigation adopted a three-stage approach, consisting of a focus group, individual interviews and the completion of individual rating and ranking procedures for the definition and attributes. As a result of inductive analysis, a definition of mental toughness was generated, as well as 12 distinct attributes that were considered fundamental to the make-up of a mentally tough performer.

Definition

Jones *et al.* defined mental toughness as:

> Having the natural or developed psychological edge that enables you to: generally, cope better than your opponents with the many demands (competition, training, lifestyle) that sport places on a performer; specifically, be more consistent and better than your opponents in remaining determined, focused, confident, and in control under pressure.
>
> (2002: 209)

Inherent within the definition was the notion that athletes can possess a "natural" mental toughness that they bring with them to the sport environment, as well as the possibility that mental toughness can be developed over time. The definition also made the distinction between general and specific dimensions, emphasising both competition and other factors required to attain high levels of performance (e.g. training and general lifestyle aspects). Adopting similar procedures to Jones *et al.* (2002), Bull *et al.* (2005) and Thelwell *et al.*

(2005) examined mental toughness in the singular sports of cricket and football, respectively. Bull et al. (2005) did not specifically investigate or propose a definition; however, they suggested Jones et al.'s definition as a positive development in mental-toughness research. The definition revealed by Thelwell et al. also closely matched Jones et al.'s. In fact, with regard to rhetoric, participants in both studies only differed on one word, with Thelwell et al. claiming that mentally tough performers "*always* cope better" than their opponents, rather than "*generally* cope better" from Jones et al.'s findings. With differences so minimal, and to provide a consistent approach to how mental toughness should be defined, Thelwell et al. forwarded Jones et al.'s definition to a group of professional football players in the second part of their study. Responses provided strong support for the definition within the sport of football.

In a more recent study, Gucciardi et al. (2008) defined mental toughness in Australian-rules football as: "a collection of values, attitudes, behaviours, and emotions that enable you to persevere and overcome any obstacle, adversity, or pressure experienced, but also to maintain concentration and motivation when things are going well to consistently achieve your goals." Although this description was described as specific to Australian-rules football, it does provide support for Jones et al.'s definition. Specifically, both refer to a collection of interrelated protective and enabling factors that allow mentally tough performers to cope with the demands and pressures of sport in order to consistently produce superior performances. Overall, therefore, this suggests that mental toughness can be defined in a similar manner, irrespective of sport (cf. Thelwell et al., 2005).

The definition proposed by Jones et al. has also received some criticism. In a review on mental toughness, Crust (2007) purported that it defined mental toughness in terms of what it enables athletes to do, rather than what exactly mental toughness is. The review further suggested that Jones et al. gave little attention to background theory, calling for a definition that is derived from relevant theories of personality and development. Jones et al.'s definition, however, reflects the desired end state of being mentally tough, and support for its accuracy has been provided in a number of studies (e.g. Bull et al., 2005; Connaughton et al., 2008; Gucciardi et al., 2008; Jones et al., 2007; Thelwell et al., 2005). Additionally, as is evident from part 1 of this review, the background theory regarding mental toughness was based on opinion and anecdotal evidence, and was, therefore, suffering from many limitations. To attempt to find a theory, as Crust suggested, and then fit mental toughness into it (e.g. hardiness), without any justification or rationale, would only exacerbate the confusion and misunderstanding surrounding mental toughness.

Finally, the definition of mental toughness contained a continual reference to an outcome component (e.g. a psychological edge, being able to cope better than opponents, be more consistent and better than opponents); indeed, the specific wording of the definition involves a comparison with opponents that ultimately results in a successful outcome (cf. Jones et al., 2002; Thelwell et al., 2005). This suggested the need to investigate mental toughness in those performers who have achieved the ultimate outcome within their sporting discipline (i.e. Olympic and World Champions). Interestingly, all of the attributes proposed by Jones *et al.* (2002) and many of those proposed by Bull *et al.* (2005), Thelwell *et al.* (2005) and Gucciardi *et al.* (2008), also contain an outcome dimension, and these characteristics are now discussed.

Characteristics

Jones *et al.* (2002) identified 12 attributes that were considered essential to the ideal mentally tough performer. Presented in Table 9.2, the attributes were compiled in order of importance, and are accompanied by a quotation from the interview transcripts as an illustration.

Table 9.2 Mental toughness attributes (source: Jones *et al.*, 2002)

	Attribute	Ranking	Quotation
1	Having an unshakable self-belief in your ability to achieve your competition goals.	1st	"If you want to be the best in the world you have to be strong enough to believe you are capable of that."
2	Bouncing back from performance set-backs as a result of increased determination to succeed.	2nd	"Yea, we all have them [setbacks], the mentally tough performer doesn't let them affect him, he uses them."
3	Having an unshakable self-belief that you possess unique qualities and abilities that make you better than your opponents.	3rd	"He made the right decisions about how he was going to train, but he had the self-belief in his ability to know that he was making the right decisions."
4	Having an insatiable desire and internalised motives to succeed.	Equal 4th	"Will do almost anything (within the rules) to succeed, whatever the cost (e.g. win)."
5	Remaining fully-focused on the task at hand in the face of competition-specific distractions.	Equal 4th	"If you want to be the best, you have got to be totally focused on what you are doing."
6	Regaining psychological control following unexpected, uncontrollable events (competition-specific).	6th	"Even when you think things are against you, like abandoned matches, the weather ... the mentally tough performer is able to compose himself and come back and still win."
7	Pushing back the boundaries of physical and emotional pain, while still maintaining technique and effort under distress (in training and competition).	7th	"It is a question of pushing yourself ... it's mind over matter, just trying to hold your technique and perform while under this distress and go beyond your limits."

(continued over leaf)

Table 9.2 Continued

	Attribute	Ranking	Quotation
8	Accepting that competition anxiety is inevitable and knowing that you can cope with it.	8th	"I accept that I'm going to get nervous, particularly when the pressure's on, but keeping the lid on it and being in control is crucial."
9	Thriving on the pressure of competition.	Equal 9th	"Mental toughness is being resilient to and using the competition pressure to get the best out of yourself."
10	Not being adversely affected by others' good and bad performances.	Equal 9th	"The mentally tough performer uses others good performances as a spur rather than say 'I can't go that fast'. They say 'well, he is no better than me, so I'm going to go out there and beat that."
11	Remaining fully-focused in the face of personal life distractions.	11th	"Once you're in the competition, you cannot let you mind wander to other things … it doesn't matter what has happened to you, you can't bring the problem into the performance arena."
12	Switching a sport focus on and off as required.	12th	"You need to be able to switch it (i.e. focus) on and off, especially between games during a tournament. The mentally tough performer succeeds by having control of the on/off switch."

The attributes highlighted can be placed into a number of general categories: self-belief, desire and motivation, focus (performance-related), focus (lifestyle-related), dealing with competition-related pressure (external) and anxiety (internal), and dealing with physical and emotional pain. Self-belief revealed two dimensions, belief in the ability to achieve one's goals, and believing that you are different to, and therefore better than, your opponents. Motivation became importance when using setbacks as a source of desire and determination to "bounce back". Self-discipline was also seen as an important aspect of mental toughness when used alongside finely tuned focusing skills. Five attributes related to focus in some form, three related to remaining focused despite distractions in competition, while the remaining two enabled the performer to stay focused in the face of personal life distractions (both positive and negative), and to be able to switch a sport focus "on" and "off" when required. Not surprisingly, factors associated with competition stress were evident in the list of mental-toughness attributes. The mentally tough performer thrived on the external pressure of competition and was able to cope with the internal anxiety response. Finally, one attribute facilitated the maintenance of technique and effort while experiencing both physical pain (e.g. fatigue) and emotional pain resulting from failure. Overall, the specific wording of attributes emerged as being crucial and fundamental to how each characteristic contributed to a performer's state of mental toughness. Specifically, the distinguishing factors for self-belief and desire in the mental toughness process was the magnitude of these factors (i.e. unshakable and insatiable), while the description of the 12 attributes revealed further evidence of an outcome component. For example, attributes referred to the achievement or successful completion of an action rather than possessing the ability to achieve, or the potential to successfully complete an action. Interestingly, similar attributes have been identified in the single-sport population studies of cricket (Bull *et al.*, 2005), football (Thelwell *et al.*, 2005) and Australian-rules football (Gucciardi *et al.*, 2008).

Bull *et al.* (2005) set out to gain a greater insight into how mental toughness might be more systematically developed within young English cricketers, and to provide strategies and practical recommendations for coaches with the ultimate goal of improving performance at international level. Bull and colleagues presented 20 global themes that were suggested as the characteristics of a mentally tough cricketer, as well as highlighting factors to aid its development. The global themes were organised under five general dimensions to help clarify their meaning: developmental factors, personal responsibility, dedication and commitment, belief, and coping with pressure. Bull *et al.* compared many of the global themes to Jones *et al.*'s attributes (e.g. thriving on competition), and provided further support for highlighting specific distinguishing factors within the mental-toughness process. For example, they identified "resilient confidence" as a characteristic suggesting that confidence alone was not sufficient to ensure mental toughness. However, much of the supportive quotation and descriptions of themes referred to success or a winning mind, rather than mental toughness. This reference to success throughout the study created some confusion, as the attributes of mental toughness are not purported to be exactly the same as the characteristics of successful performances (cf. Jones *et al.*, 2002). In other words, while mental toughness may contain a component that leads to successful outcomes, this does not necessarily mean that all successful performers are mentally tough. Finally, it is unclear which themes specifically related to characteristics of mental toughness in cricket, and which ones assisted in the development of mental toughness. As a result of this overlap, the work of Bull *et al.* is discussed in relation to development later in this review.

Thelwell *et al.* sought to identify variations in Jones *et al.*'s (2002) attributes held by footballers and proposed ten attributes: (a) having total self-belief at all times that you will achieve success; (b) having the ability to react to situations positively; (c) having the ability to hang on and be calm under pressure; (d) having the ability to ignore distractions and remain focused; (e) wanting the ball/wanting to be involved at all times; (f) knowing what it takes to grind yourself out of trouble; (g) controlling emotions throughout performance; (h) having a presence that affects opponents; (i) having everything outside of the game in control; (j) enjoying the pressure associated with performance. Self-belief and dealing with competition pressure were proposed as being most important to mental toughness, while having everything in control outside of the game and enjoying the pressure associated with performance were ranked as least important. Additionally, those players who demonstrate high levels of self-belief, and an ability to cope with the internal and external pressure of elite-level competition, tended to be perceived by Thelwell *et al.* as mentally tough. While Thelwell *et al.*'s attributes were specific to football, and many resembled those forwarded by Jones *et al.* (2002), certain attributes appear to be characteristics that mentally tough performers display rather that specific attributes of mental toughness. For example, mentally tough footballers may display the characteristic of "wanting the ball/wanting to be involved at all times"; however, there are many performers who may want the ball and to be involved at all times but are not necessarily perceived as mentally tough.

Gucciardi *et al.* (2008) also investigated mental toughness in the team sport of football, this time Australian-rules football, and identified 32 characteristics that were categorised under 11 key components: (a) self-belief; (b) motivation; (c) tough attitude; (d) concentration and focus; (e) resilience; (f) handling pressure; (g) personal values; (h) emotional intelligence; (i) sport intelligence; (j) physical toughness; and (k) work-ethic. Interestingly, Gucciardi *et al.* also revealed 11 factors perceived to contrast mental toughness: (a) self-doubt; (b) being lazy; (c) having poor integrity and personal philosophy; (d) being unmotivated and/or extrinsically motivated; (e) having a weak attitude; (f) being easily distracted; (g) having a fragile mindset; (h) choking under pressure; (i) having a weak emotional make-up; (j) lacking sport knowledge and understanding of the game; and (k) avoiding physically demanding situations. This study proposed similar findings to Bull *et al.* (2005), Jones *et al.* (2002) and Thelwell *et al.* (2005) in relation to the characteristics of mental toughness, and the notion that certain characteristics may be more important than others. They also suggested that some characteristics may be specific to particular sport types, citing team unity as more relevant to team-orientated sports (e.g. rugby union) when compared to individual sports (e.g. tennis).

Summary of definition and characteristics

In summary, these four studies provided a much-needed clarity and consistency with regard to the conceptualisation of mental toughness. Jones *et al.* (2002) represented a starting point for the empirical investigation of mental toughness, distinguishing between what mental toughness is, and the attributes required to be mentally tough. Their definition reflects the desired end-state of mental toughness, and highlighted a distinction between general and specific dimensions. Recent studies have provided support for the contention that, irrespective of sport, mental toughness can be defined in a similar manner. Mentally tough performers were perceived as being able to deal with general lifestyle and training demands as well as aspects of competition. Therefore, structuring a performer's lifestyle around all of these factors in order to perform optimally appears to be a vital component to being mentally tough, and suggests an important role for coaches and sport psychologists trying to develop the characteristics of mental toughness.

The plethora of attributes within the four studies discussed above may, at first glance, appear to confuse the overall understanding of mental toughness. However, several characteristics were consistently identified within all four studies, and were comparable under the following categories: self-belief, focus, motivation, handling pressure, dealing with physical and emotional pain, anxiety and attention control. This suggests that, although mental toughness might vary slightly in specific sports, a general template or framework of mental toughness can be developed irrespective of sport. Importantly, from a research perspective, these initial studies highlighted a number of avenues that had the potential to expand the mental-toughness knowledge base further, and included: (a) the development of a user-friendly framework of mental toughness which can be disseminated by coaches and performers; (b) the examination of mental toughness in performers who have achieved ultimate success in their respective sports (i.e. Olympic or World Champions); and (c) eliciting the opinions of sport psychologists and coaches who have worked closely with world-beating athletes.

Developing a framework of mental toughness

The findings of Jones *et al.* (2002), as well as the recent studies by Bull *et al.* (2005), Gucciardi *et al.* (2008) and Thelwell *et al.* (2005), were based on the assumption that the person being interviewed had an in-depth knowledge of mental toughness. However, the outcome dimension contained within the definition and attributes of Jones *et al.* suggested that the inclusion of Olympic/World Champions, and coaches and sport psychologists who have worked closely alongside these athletes, would be valuable with regard to defining mental toughness and developing a framework of mental toughness via its underpinning attributes. Therefore, Jones *et al.* (2007) replicated the procedures adopted by Jones *et al.* (2002) in a broad-range sample of sports performers, coaches and sport psychologists who had achieved the highest levels in their disciplines.

Participants within Jones *et al.*'s (2007) study proposed a definition of mental toughness that contained no discernable difference to Jones *et al.* (2002), confirming the definition as an accurate description of mental toughness. The identification of the attributes of mental toughness revealed some interesting differences between Jones *et al.* (2002) and Jones *et al.* (2007). Specifically, the super-elite participants in Jones *et al.* (2007) identified 30 attributes, compared to the 12 attributes in Jones *et al.* (2002), thereby displaying a greater insight and understanding into the precise make-up of mental toughness. To create an overall framework of mental toughness, the 30 attributes were categorised into four dimensions, and then further divided under sub-components within each dimension. The development of the framework of mental toughness, presented in Figure 9.1, supported the distinction of general and specific elements within the definition. The framework contained a general dimension (attitude/mindset) and three time-specific dimensions (training, competition, post-competition), providing not only a clear description of its make-up, but the precise settings in which each separate attribute is necessary.

Framework

Seven of the attributes identified related to the general dimension, "attitude/mindset", and could be further divided in two sub-components, "belief" and "focus". The dimension highlighted the characteristics that enabled mentally tough performers to remain on course, regardless of obstacles and circumstances, in achieving their ultimate goal. Belief comprised of four attributes and described the performer's unshakable self-belief, through their awareness and inner arrogance, in reaching their true potential despite obstacles and barriers that people or organisations put in their path. Focus contained three attributes which prioritised the long-term goal over any short-term gains that could hinder achievement of this goal. The sub-components within the three time-specific dimensions contained six (Training), 13 (Competition), and four (Post-competition) attributes, and identified the psychological characteristics that mentally tough performers possessed, and the strategies they used to achieve and maintain mental-toughness levels in training, competition and post-competition. Specifically, the training dimension contained three sub-components – using long-term goals as the source of motivation, controlling the environment and pushing yourself to the limit – that portrayed how mentally tough performers kept motivation levels high when dealing with the years of patience, discipline and work required to reach the top. Every aspect of the training environment and challenging situation was used to their advantage, and they were not swayed by extraneous factors, that they could not control (e.g. weather conditions). The six sub-components of the competition dimension – belief, staying focused, regulating performance, handling pressure, awareness and control of thoughts and feelings, and controlling the environment – explained how the ideal mentally tough performer behaved under the extreme pressure of high-level competitions. The mentally tough performer possessed total commitment to goal achievement, was not fazed by mistakes occurring, remained totally focused "on the job in hand", made the correct decisions, controlled their thoughts and feelings, channelled their anxiety, and was able to adapt and cope regardless of distractions, in the achievement of optimal performance. The final dimension, post-competition, contained two subcomponents, handling failure and handling success. These four attributes depicted how mentally tough performers rationalised and learned from failure to drive them to further success, and how they dealt with the extra pressures that resulted from competition successes.

The categorisation of the 30 attributes into sub-components highlighted specific aspects that must be achieved in order to reach a state of mental toughness

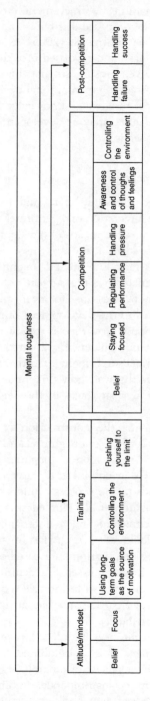

Figure 9.1 Mental toughness framework: dimensions and subcomponents.

within each dimension. The development of the framework could contribute to the exploration of the mechanisms by which mental toughness is developed and maintained. Interestingly, the proposed attributes and characteristics identified in Jones *et al.* (2002), and by Bull *et al.* (2005), Gucciardi *et al.* (2008) and Thelwell *et al.* (2005), can also be categorised into the sub-components of the framework. Although tentative, this suggests that this framework may be used as a general template for understanding mental toughness, irrespective of sport and skill level. However, in order to advance knowledge further, it is necessary to understand how mental toughness may be developed, and this research avenue is discussed in the following section.

Mental toughness development

Bull *et al.* (2005) initiated the study of mental toughness development in cricket and highlighted the interaction of a performer's environment, character, attitudes and thinking as a possible means of developing mental toughness and "a winning mind".While the identification of this interaction is recognised as a positive step, several issues regarding mental-toughness development were in need of future attention, including: the subjective meaning for each of the themes may not necessarily be the same for every player; it is unclear which specific global themes related to the development of mental toughness; and no supportive data or explanation is forwarded as to how mental toughness actually develops. For example, "parental influence" was cited as an important influence at various stages in a performer's upbringing. However, there is no clarification as to what kind of influence this was, how this influence impacted on mental-toughness development, or at what stages in the performer's career this influence actually took place.

Concurrent to investigating the construction of a framework of mental toughness (i.e. Jones *et al.*, 2007), Connaughton *et al.* (2008) began the process of addressing the development of mental toughness. Based on Jones *et al.*'s (2002) recommendations, Connaughton *et al.* investigated the perceptions of elite performers with regards to the process of mental-toughness development and maintenance. Connaughton *et al.* adopted the procedures from previous empirical studies in developmental and maintenance research (e.g. Durand-Bush and Salmela, 2002; Gould *et al.*, 2002; Hanton and Jones, 1999), integrating an involvement-progression questionnaire based on Bloom's (1985) careers phases, and questions based on Jones *et al.*'s definition and 12 attributes of mental toughness. These authors also re-interviewed the original participants from Jones *et al.* as the former participants had an intimate knowledge of the specific meanings of each attribute.

The findings of Connaughton *et al.* (2008) revealed that a multitude of underlying mechanisms operated in a combined, rather than independent, manner to facilitate the development of mental toughness over three distinct career phases. With regard to maintenance, findings suggested that, once acquired, mental toughness was a psychological construct that needed to be maintained with effort or diminish. The developmental phases aligned with Bloom's (1985) early, middle and later years of elite-performer development, and the experiences of perceived critical incidents (e.g. disruptions at school, loss of a peer, parental divorce) were identified as having a crucial role in cultivating mental-toughness development. Specifically, during the *early years*, advice from significant others (e.g. parents, coaches), and observing older, elite performers in a training and competitive environment provided a source of knowledge, inspiration and encouragement that imparted a powerful influence in enabling the efficient mastery of relevant skills. This, along with effective leadership from coaches, assisted in nurturing the correct motivational climate that was challenging, rewarding and enjoyable in the development of three of the 12 attributes (Table 9.1, attributes 1, 3, 4). These three attributes were considered the foundations for mental-toughness development, and related to acquiring an unshakable self-belief, and influencing an insatiable desire and internalised motives to successfully achieve specific outcome goals. Whilst these three attributes were further enhanced during the *middle years*, the development of five additional attributes were affected by competitive rivalry in training and competition, rationalisation of successes and failures, and receiving guidance from an understanding social-support network. The five attributes (Table 9.1, attributes 2, 6, 7, 8, 9) related to bouncing back from setbacks, regaining psychological control, pushing back the boundaries of pain, accepting and coping with competitive anxiety, and thriving on pressure. The remaining four of Jones *et al.*'s (2002) attributes were reported to develop in the *later-years* phase (Table 9.1, attributes 5, 10, 11, 12); specifically, switching a sport focus on and off as required, remaining fully focused on the task at hand in the face of competition-specific distractions, not being adversely affected by other athletes' good and bad performances, and remaining fully focused in the face of personal-life distractions. The experience of elite-level competition, simulation training and the extraction of positive experiences and rationalisation of setbacks, via reflective practice, contributed to development. Finally, once acquired, mental toughness needed to be maintained through the use of a variety of mental skills and strategies, including goal-setting, mental imagery, self-talk, cognitive reconstruction, pre-performance and pre-race routines, simulation training and the establishment of a social support network.

While the initial results of this study can facilitate performers, coaches and sport psychologists to implement training programmes, the findings were based on elite performers' perceptions of mental toughness and its development. However, the clearer insight achieved by the super-elite sample and the construction of the mental-toughness framework (Jones *et al.*, 2007) would suggest that a greater knowledge of mental-toughness development could be achieved by integrating these factors with the procedures adopted by Connaughton *et al.* (2008). Therefore, this investigation was viewed by Connaughton *et al.* as a starting point to understanding the development and maintenance of mental toughness. The final section discusses the practical implications that have emerged from these recent research programmes and the future directions for mental toughness investigations, and concludes with a summary of the recent research findings.

Practical implications

Mental-toughness research, we feel, is still best described as a research area in its relative infancy, and the recent findings offer more in terms of avenues for further investigation than practical implications. However, the consistent findings from recent research (i.e. Bull et al., 2005; Connaughton et al., 2008; Gucciardi et al., 2008; Jones et al., 2002, 2007; Thelwell et al., 2005) propose some general practical assistance for coaches and performers trying to understand and develop this construct. They relate to the definition, the attributes and framework, and the development and maintenance of mental toughness.

Definition

Jones et al.'s (2002) definition contained the suggestion that athletes possess a "natural" mental toughness that performers bring to the sport environment. The identification of this "natural" element in young talented performers may assist youth development and athlete-talent identification initiatives with regards to mental toughness. Research proposes that the possession of mental toughness leads to success (cf. Jones et al., 2002, 2007; Thelwell et al., 2005) and can be defined in a similar manner irrespective of sport (cf. Bull et al., 2005; Gucciardi et al., 2008; Thelwell et al., 2005); this may help coaches to identify mentally tough athletes from a variety of different sports. Additionally, the established definition suggests that mental toughness can be developed, highlighting an important role for sport psychologists and their involvement with athletes and coaches at the different career stages. Specifically, teaching mental skills and strategies to enhance and optimise focus, confidence and control in pressure situations is consistent with mentally tough behaviours and characteristics (Bull et al., 2005; Connaughton et al., 2008; Gucciardi et al., 2008; Jones et al., 2002, 2007; Thelwell et al., 2005). The distinction between general and specific dimensions within Jones et al.'s (2002) definition emphasises the need to deal with training and general lifestyle demands as well as aspects of competition. Therefore, viewing the athlete in a holistic manner, and not just dealing with the specific sport issues, may be of greater benefit to athletes at all levels. This may include balancing the demands of training and competition with every aspect of performers' social and personal lives. Although speculative, mental-toughness development may assist with this balance by enabling the performer to acknowledge and focus attention on the correct priorities for any given situation. The definition also suggests mentally tough individuals produce consistently high-level performances via the use of superior mental skills and psychological strategies. Therefore, simulation training, via mental imagery or in actual simulated conditions, could be used to mimic the circumstances where performers can practise harnessing specific mental-toughness characteristics, and encourage consistent and successful responses in competitions (e.g. the experience of performing under pressure).

Attributes and framework

The outcome dimension of Jones *et al.*'s (2002) definition and many of the attributes identified within recent studies (e.g. Bull *et al.*, 2005; Gucciardi *et al.*, 2008; Jones *et al.*, 2002, 2007; Thelwell *et al.*, 2005) implies that mental toughness may be determined on the successful completion of an action rather than having the ability or potential to do so. Although subjective, performance successes (and failures) that result from mental-toughness training programmes may assist coaches trying to determine the efficacy of the approaches that they have implemented. The lack of a measure of mental toughness prevents the development of precise interventions; however, mental-skills training most likely to benefit performers developing mental toughness should include the characteristics that were common to all five recent studies investigating its make-up. These include developing or enhancing the control of desire/motivation, focus, confidence/self-belief and handling pressure/stress. The additional development of a framework of mental toughness (Jones *et al.*, 2007) provides sport psychologists, coaches and performers with the potential to further facilitate understanding regarding the precise mechanisms required to achieve a state of mental toughness. Not only does the framework categorise attributes under general characteristics or sub-components, but it provides coaches and performers with details regarding the precise settings where development of these sub-components is required (e.g. training, competition). This knowledge, in conjunction with the process of performance profiling (cf. Butler and Hardy, 1992; Kelly, 1955), may assist in the identification of strengths and weaknesses that performers possess in relation to mental toughness (e.g. how mentally tough performers achieve their goals, and how they handle the pressures, successes and failures associated with competing). Although tentative, this could assist in providing direction for career planning and mental-skills training programmes to counteract any identified weaknesses and to further enhance any strengths within the appropriate dimensions and sub-components. Finally, the results of the ranking procedure in each dimension suggests, with caution, that some attributes might be more important than others, and this may be particularly relevant to differing variables, such as sex and sport type (cf. Bull *et al.*, 2005; Gucciardi *et al.*, 2008; Thelwell *et al.*, 2005).

Development and maintenance

Given that mental toughness was perceived to develop over a performer's career (Connaughton *et al.*, 2008), it would be advisable for performers to received support and mental-toughness training from an early age rather than in the later stages of their sporting careers. (cf. Connaughton *et al.*, 2008). Coaches and sport psychologists should also be aware of the developmental requirements that are perceived to operate within each specific career stage (e.g. early, middle and later years: Bloom, 1985). Specifically, in the early stages, young performers should be encouraged to engage in sporting activities as a means of skill accomplishment, socialisation, enjoyment, and to develop a sense of discipline and work ethic, while parents and coaches could assist in creating the correct motivational environment for these attributes to be acquired (cf. Connaughton et al., 2008; Durand-Bush and Salmela, 2002; Gould et al., 2002). In the middle years, performers may benefit most from observing and learning from knowledgeable role models (e.g. expert coaches and older, elite performers). Indeed, gaining knowledge from more-experienced individuals has been documented in the development of a number of positive psychological qualities (Bloom, 1985; Durand-Bush and Salmela, 2002; Gould et al., 2002; Hanton and Jones, 1999; Hanton et al., 2007). In the final developmental phase (i.e. later years) and during the maintenance years, sources such as experience of international competitions, the use of psychological skills and strategies, and a wide-ranging social support network, are alleged to assist in the enhancement and maintenance of mental toughness to what was described as their highest perceived levels. Overall, educating and providing exposure to a variety of situations and environments would assist performers in acquiring the experience necessary to develop mental toughness (Connaughton et al., 2008). Finally, the experience of critical incidents appears to help cultivate mental toughness throughout all developmental stages. While these incidents may be outside the control of the coach and sport psychologist, being able to recognise how and when these experiences occur would be of great use to coaches and psychologists trying to facilitate the enhancement of mental toughness; this along with other relevant issues that require attention are now discussed.

Future directions

With regard to understanding mental toughness, there is a need to investigate possible differences between individual and team mental toughness (cf. Gucciardi et al., 2008), which has been found to be evident in research examining individual and collective efficacy (Bandura, 1997). Connaughton et al. (2008) was the first study to specifically investigate the development of mental toughness; however, their sample spanned across a number of sports. Bull et al. (2005), Gucciardi et al. (2008) and Thelwell et al. (2005) suggested that mental toughness may possess slight variants in specific sports, and it may be that subtle differences also exist to how it is developed. Therefore, research should address how mental toughness is developed within a specific sport context. Connaughton et al.'s findings were based on Jones et al.'s (2002) 12 attributes of mental toughness, and with the proposed framework of mental toughness (Jones et al., 2007) containing 30 attributes, using this framework as a base, coupled with a super-elite sample of performer, coaches and sport psychologists, could provide a more comprehensive insight into the development of mental toughness, its maintenance and the conditions under which it fluctuates. Further, the area of perceived critical incidents also requires investigation to determine what constitutes a critical incident, the different types of critical incidents (positive and negative), their influence within career phases and how critical incidents assist in creating the psychological environments that are necessary for mental toughness to develop. Without doubt, the most important avenue for future research is the development of a conceptually accurate and psychometrically valid and reliable measure of mental toughness. The development of the framework of mental toughness (Jones *et al.*, 2007) may form the basis for the development of such a measure, allowing for perceived levels of mental toughness to be assessed. Once developed, a measure would facilitate cross-sectional comparisons of groups, as well as the predictive validity of the scale and athletes' performances. Talented but mentally weak performers could be identified to see what sub-components or attributes require attention, and interventions could then be designed and implemented to facilitate the development of enhanced levels of mental toughness.

Conclusion

In this review, mental toughness has been identified as an important psychological factor and worthy of investigation. Part 1 appraised the vast literature purporting a multitude of varying explanations and definitions which were found to be based on opinion, coaching and counselling experience, and anecdotal evidence, rather than empirical research. Additionally, inventories reported to measure mental-toughness levels lacked sound psychometric properties and focused primarily on hardiness and mental skills. Consequently, the construct has been misunderstood and confounded with an array of mental skills. In response to this confusion, part 2 of the review addressed the recent empirical investigations that have sought to conceptualise mental toughness. These studies have resulted collectively in a greater understanding of mental toughness, regarding its definition, the identification of its component parts, the development of a working framework of mental toughness, and an explanation of the processes and mechanisms involved in the development and maintenance of this construct. Although this is a positive step, and some practical applications for performers, coaches, and sport psychologists have emerged from these studies, several issues still require attention, most notably relating to measurement and intervention. Finally, and most importantly, there is the need for researchers to move away from the anecdotally based investigations and focus exclusively on empirically based mental-toughness research.

References

Alderman, R. B. (1974). *Psychological behaviour in sport*. Toronto: W.B. Saunders Company.

Austin, T. (2004). Sharapova's finishing touch. Retrieved 6 July 2004, from www.msnbc.msn.com/id/5359133.

Bandura, A. (1997). *Self-efficacy: the exercise of control*. New York: Freeman.

Blauvelt, H. (2004). Tiger's biggest club is his mental strength. *USA Today*, 10 February. Retrieved 26 April 2004, from www.usatoday.com/sports/golf/2004–02–10-tiger-toughest_x.htm.

Bloom, B. (1985). *Developing talent in young people*. New York: Ballantine.

Bull, S. J., Albinson, J. G. and Shambrook, C. J. (1996). *The mental game plan: getting psyched for sport*. Eastboune: Sports Dynamics.

Bull, S. J., Shambrook, C. J., James, W. and Brooks, J. E. (2005). Towards an understanding of mental toughness in elite English cricketers. *Journal of Applied Sport Psychology*, 17, 209–227.

Cattell, R. B., Blewett, D. B. and Beloff, J. R. (1955). The inheritance of personality: a multiple variance analysis determination of approximate nature–nurture ratios for primary personality factors in Q data. *American Journal of Human Genetics*, 7, 122–146.

Connaughton, D., Hanton, S., Jones, G. and Wadey, R. (in press). Mental toughness research: key issues in this area. *International Journal of Sport Psychology*.

Connaughton, D., Wadey, R., Hanton, S. and Jones, G. (2008). The development and maintenance of mental toughness: perceptions of elite performers. *Journal of Sports Sciences*, 26, 83–95.

Clough, P. J. and Earle, K. (2002). When the going gets tough: a study of the impact of mental toughness on perceived demands. *Journal of Sports Sciences*, 20, 61.

Clough, P. J., Earle, K. and Sewell, D. (2002). Mental toughness: the concept and its measurement. In I. Cockerill (ed.), *Solutions in sport psychology* (pp. 32–43). London: Thomson.

Crust, L. (2007). Mental toughness in sport: a review. *International Journal of Sport and Exercise Psychology*, 5, 270–290.

Crust, L. and Clough, P. J. (2005). Relationship between mental toughness and physical endurance. *Perceptual and Motor Skills*, 100, 192–194.

Daily Mail (2007). Boycott blasts England's "bottlers" while Gatting blames poor preparation. *Daily Mail*. Retrieved 25 June 2007, from www.dailymail.co.uk/pages/live/articles/sport/cricket.html?in_article_id= 426608&in_page_id=1849.

Dennis, P. W. (1981). Mental toughness and the athlete. *Ontario Physical and Health Education Association*, 7, 37–40.

Durand-Bush, N. and Salmela, J. (2002). The development and maintenance of expert athletic performance: perceptions of world and Olympic champions. *Journal of Applied Sport Psychology*, 14, 154–171.

Favret, B. and Benzel, D. (1997). *Complete guide to water skiing*. Champaign, IL: Human Kinetics.

Fourie, S. and Potgieter, J. R. (2001). The nature of mental toughness in sport. *South African Journal for Research in Sport, Physical Education and Recreation*, 23, 63–72.

Gibson, A. (1998). *Mental toughness*. New York: Vantage Press.

Golby, J., Sheard, M. and Lavallee, D. (2003). A cognitive-behavioural analysis of mental toughness in national rugby league football teams. *Perceptual and Motor skills*, 96, 455–462.

Goldberg, A. S. (1992). Training the psychological dimension. *Soccer Journal*, 37, 58–60.

Goldberg, A. S. (1998). *Sports slump busting: 10 steps to mental toughness and peak performance*. Champaign, IL: Human Kinetics.

Gould, D., Dieffenbach, K. and Moffett, A. (2002). Psychological characteristics and their development of Olympic champions. *Journal of Applied Sport Psychology*, 14, 172–204.

Gould, D., Eklund, R. C. and Jackson, S. A. (1993). Coping strategies used by U.S. Olympic wrestlers. *Research Quarterly for Exercise and Sport*, 64, 83–93.

Graham, D. and Yocom, G. (1990). *Mental toughness training for golf.* Lexington, MA: The Stephen Greene Press/Pelham Books.

Gucciardi, D. F., Gordon, S. and Dimmock, J. A. (2008). Towards an understanding of mental toughness in Australian Football. *Journal of Applied Sport Psychology,* 20, 261–281.

Hanton, S. and Connaughton, D. (2002). Perceived control of anxiety symptoms and its relationship to self-confidence and performance: a qualitative inquiry. *Research Quarterly for Exercise and Sport,* 73, 87–97.

Hanton, S. and Jones, G. (1999). The acquisition and development of cognitive skills and strategies. I. Making the butterflies fly in formation. *The Sport Psychologist,* 13, 1–21.

Hanton, S., Cropley, B., Miles, A., Mellalieu, S. D. and Neil, R. (2007). An in-depth examination of experience in sport: competitive experience and the relationship with competitive anxiety. *International Journal of Sport and Exercise Psychology,* 5, 28–53.

Hanton, S., Neil, R. and Mellalieu, S. D. (2008). Recent developments in competitive anxiety direction and competition stress research. *International Review of Sport and Exercise Psychology,* 1, 45–57.

Hardy, L., Jones, G. and Gould, D. (1996). *Understanding psychological preparation for sport: theory and practice of elite performers.* Chichester: Wiley.

Hodge, K. (1994). Mental toughness in sport: lessons for life. The pursuit of personal excellence. *Journal of Physical Education New Zealand,* 27, 12–16.

Jones, C. M. (1982). Mental toughness. *World Bowls,* November, 30–31.

Jones, G., Hanton, S. and Connaughton, D. (2002). What is this thing called Mental Toughness? An investigation with elite performers. *Journal of Applied Sport Psychology,* 14, 211–224.

Jones, G., Hanton, S. and Connaughton, D. (2007). A framework of mental toughness in the world's best performers. *The Sport Psychologist,* 21, 243–264.

Kelly, G. A. (1955). *The psychology of personal constructs.* New York: Norton.

Kobasa, S. C. (1979). Stressful life events, personality, and health: an inquiry into hardiness. *Journal of Personality and Social Psychology,* 37, 1–11.

Lee, K. H., Shin, D. S., Han, M. W. and Lee, E. (1994). Developing the norm of Korean table tennis players' mental toughness. *Korean Journal of Sport Science,* 6, 103–120.

Levy, A. R., Polman, R. C. J., Clough, P. J., Marchant, D. C. and Earle, K. (2006). Mental toughness as a determinant of beliefs, pain, and adherence in sport injury rehabilitation. *Journal of Sport Rehabilitation,* 15, 246–254.

Loehr, J. E. (1982). *Athletic excellence: mental toughness training for sports.* New York: Plume.

Loehr, J. E. (1986). *Mental toughness training for sports: achieving athletic excellence.* Lexington, MA: Stephen Greene Press.

Loehr, J. E. (1995). *The new toughness training for sports.* New York: Plume.

Luszki, W. A. (1982). *Winning tennis through mental toughness.* New York: Everest House.

Mellalieu, S. D., Hanton, S. and Fletcher, D. (2006). A competitive anxiety review: recent directions in sport psychology research. In S. Hanton and S. D. Mellalieu (eds), *Literature reviews in sport psychology* (pp. 1–45). Hauppauge, NY: Nova Science.

Middleton, S. C., Marsh, H. W., Martin, A. J., Richards, G. E. and Perry, C. (2004). Developing the mental toughness inventory (MTI). *Self Research Centre Biannual Conference, Berlin.* Available from http://self.uws.edu.au/Conferences/2004_Middleton_Marsh_Martin_Richards_Perrya.pdf.

Middleton, S. C., Marsh, H. W., Martin, A. J., Richards, G. E., Savis, J., Perry, C. *et al.* (2004). The Psychological Performance Inventory: Is the mental toughness test tough enough? *International Journal of Sport Psychology,* 35, 91–108.

Murphy, S. and Tammen, V. (1998). In search of psychological skills. In J. Duda (ed.), *Advances in sport and exercise psychology measurement* (pp. 195–209). Morgantown, WV: Fitness Information Technology.

Pankey, B. (1993). Presence of mind: five ways to lower your class drop-out rate with mental toughness. *American Fitness*, 11, 18–19.

Patton, M. (2002). *Qualitative research and evaluation methods*. Newbury Park, CA: Sage.

Pearce, L. (2004). Sharapova's arrival a victory for mental toughness. [Electronic version]. Retrieved 6 July 2006, from www.theage.com.au/articles/2004/07/04/1088879371559.html?oneclick=true.

Shin, D. S. and Lee, K. H. (1994). A comparative study of mental toughness between elite and non-elite female athletes. *Korean Journal of Sport Science*, 6, 85–102.

Tapp, J. (1991). Mental toughness. *Referee*, 16, 44–48.

Taylor, J. (1989). Mental toughness (part 2): a simple reminder may be all you need. *Sport Talk*, 18, 2–3.

Teitelbaum, D. (1998). *The ultimate guide to mental toughness: how to raise your motivation, focus, and confidence like pushing a button*. Kensington, MD: Demblin Communications, Inc.

Thelwell, R., Weston, N. and Greenlees, I. (2005). Defining and understanding mental toughness in soccer. *Journal of Applied Sport Psychology*, 17, 326–332.

Tunney, J. (1987). Thoughts on the line. Mental toughness: biceps for the mind. *Soccer Journal*, 32, 49–50.

Tutko, T. A. and Richards, J. W. (1971). *Psychology of coaching*. Boston, MA: Allyn and Bacon, Inc.

Tutko, T. A. and Richards, J. W. (1972). *Coach's practical guide to athletic motivation*. Boston, MA: Allyn and Bacon, Inc.

Watts, G. (1978). Mental toughness for disadvantaged track teams. *Scholastic Coach*, 47, 100–102.

Williams, M. H. (1998). *The ergogenics edge: pushing the limits of sports performance*. Champaign, IL: Human Kinetics.

Williams, R. M. (1988). The U.S. open character test: good strokes help. But the most individualistic of sports is ultimately a mental game. *Psychology Today*, 22, 60–62.

Wisden Cricinfo Staff. (2003). Vaughan hits out at lack of "mental toughness" in domestic game. Retrieved 6 July 2005, from www.cricinfo.com/link_to_database/ARCHIVE/CRICKET_NEWS/2003/AUG/241629_CI_25AUG2003.html.

Woods, R., Hocton, M. and Desmond, R. (1995). *Coaching tennis successfully*. Champaign, IL: Human Kinetics.

Index

Tasha
the Tap Dance
Fairy

For Megan, Ella, and Asha Delderfield
with lots of love.

Special thanks to Sue Mongredien

No part of this work may be reproduced, stored in a retrieval system,
or transmitted in any form or by any means, electronic, mechanical,
photocopying, recording, or otherwise, without written permission
of the publisher. For information regarding permission, write to
Rainbow Magic Limited c/o HIT Entertainment,
830 South Greenville Avenue, Allen, TX 75002-3320.

ISBN-10: 0-545-10620-6
ISBN-13: 978-0-545-10620-7

12 11 10 9 8 7 6 5 4 3   10 11 12 13/0

Printed in the U.S.A.

First Scholastic Printing, May 2009